THE HORIZON BOOK OF THE AGE OF NAPOLEON

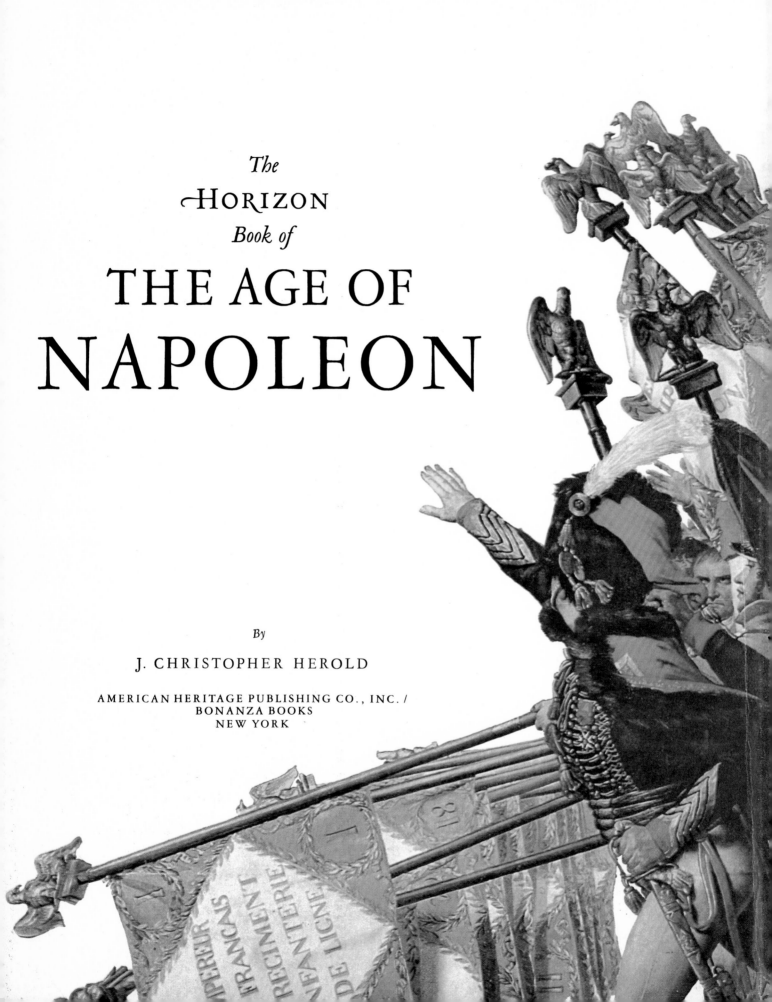

The
HORIZON
Book of
THE AGE OF
NAPOLEON

By

J. CHRISTOPHER HEROLD

AMERICAN HERITAGE PUBLISHING CO., INC. /
BONANZA BOOKS
NEW YORK

Staff for this Book

EDITOR

Marshall B. Davidson

ASSISTANT EDITORS

Norman Kotker
Dale Haven

PICTURE EDITORS

Mary Sherman Parsons
Phyllis Tremaine Iselin

COPY EDITORS

Jane Ferguson Hoover
Miriam R. Koren

DESIGNER

Joel Szasz

This 1983 edition is published by Bonanza
Books, distributed by Crown Publishers, Inc.
by arrangement with American Heritage
Publishing Co., Inc.

Manufactured in Hong Kong

**Library of Congress Cataloging in
Publication Data**

Harold, J. Christopher.
    The Horizon book of the age of Napoleon.
    Includes index.
    1. France—History—Consulate and
Empire, 1799–1815.   2. Napoleon I,
Emperor of the French, 1769–1821.
I. Davidson, Marshall B.   II. Horizon (New
York, N.Y.)   III. Title   IV. Title: Age of
Napoleon.
DC201.H45   1983   944.04   83-7129

ISBN: 0-517-415240

h g f e d c b a

Title page, a detail of David's Distribution of the Eagles; *right,
ceremonial swords belonging to Napoleon and two of his brothers*

Dictator of Circumstance

The currents of history run fitfully. At some points they turn sluggish, spreading out into what seem like stagnant pools of time, as in Europe's "Dark Ages." At other points they appear to rush on, cutting new channels toward the future, as they did, for instance, in the early years of the sixteenth century. In 1789, with the storming of the Bastille, the flow of human events suddenly broke into a rapids which in its swirling, turbulent course had no precedents. Madame de Pompadour's cynical prophecy, *après nous le déluge,* had barely hinted at the floods that were in fact released by the fall of the old regime in France. For a quarter of a century, ending with the maelstrom at Waterloo, people and principalities were tossed about by forces that shattered the peace of Europe and disrupted its established structure—forces that, before they were spent, reached to far corners of the world with revolutionary consequences.

It has been argued that the changes ultimately wrought in such distant parts, as a result of the shock of the Revolution and the Napoleonic wars, were of greater significance than anything determined in the courts or on the battlegrounds of Europe. While the Continent struggled to contain its internal disturbances, in the Americas and in the Indies old empires disintegrated and new ones took shape, new nations were conceived and others were born to larger destinies. But during those crucial years Europe remained the center of the world stage, and for most of them Napoleon Bonaparte played such a dominant role that, as has been said, the man quickly became the epoch. It was probably Metternich who first called this brief phase of history the "age of Napoleon." Few men were in a better position than the Austrian statesman to characterize the contemporary scene. In any case, a century and a half after Waterloo the label is still valid.

It seems almost impossible to consider Napoleon dispassionately. In his own day he was variously regarded by his enemies and adherents with fear, hatred, awe, respect, admiration, devotion, and even veneration—but rarely with love, even by members of his own family, and never with indifference by any who fell within the range of his influence. Ever since, he has remained the subject of continuous interest and controversy—sometimes cast as a demigod, sometimes as a demon, practically always seen as a figure considerably larger than life. Probably no other mortal has received so much attention from historians and biographers, critics and enthusiasts.

Yet in spite of the prodigious amount of study that has

been devoted to the man and his times, there is still little general agreement as to whether Napoleon is more important as a product and a symbol—a victim, perhaps—of circumstances that were not of his making, or as a man who, pursuing his own destiny, shaped circumstances that governed the course of history. Like all great men, Napoleon was both, of course; but to a degree uncommon in other great men, he was also an opportunist who took circumstances as he found them and used them to his own ends. He did not count on luck, but by studied calculation of the risks and by swift decision he counted on mastering luck. By his own confession his ultimate objectives were often not clear. In the final analysis it was his own destiny that mattered, and this he identified or confused with the destiny of civilization itself. As Madame de Staël observed, "he wanted to put his gigantic self in the place of mankind."

At the moment Napoleon appeared on the world scene the destiny of Western civilization seemed to hang on the outcome of the French Revolution—that transcendental phenomenon, as Thomas Carlyle viewed it, "overstepping all rules and experience . . . 'the Death-Birth of a World!'" Chaotic forces had been loosed that quickly brought France to a state of terror and charged much of the surrounding world with excitement and apprehension. But with these convulsive beginnings Napoleon had had little to do. The megalomania that seized France in the years immediately following the Terror was not induced by Napoleon either, but by the impetus of the Revolution and the ideas it projected. Nevertheless, when as First Consul he acquired supreme control of the nation, Napoleon appeared to many as the true child of the Revolution—the embodiment of its spirit and the saviour of it principles. Beyond the boundaries of France he appeared no less "the Revolution incarnate," as Metternich termed him. Napoleon himself fancied the role of liberator, by whose agency the revolutionary doctrines would reach other, less favored lands. And before the high price he put on "liberation" became apparent, there were those—Beethoven among others—who applauded his performance.

Neither the Revolution nor the Napoleonic wars completely broke the stream of French tradition. Napoleon's most constructive accomplishments followed historic trends that had deep roots in the policies of his royal precursors. His Civil Code, his centralization of the administration of France, and the monuments he had raised were but refinements and enlargements of the intentions of Richelieu and Louis XIII, Colbert and Louis XIV more than a century earlier. Even his Egyptian campaign was a long-deferred enactment of schemes hatched by royal ministers of the past to secure the "master key to world commerce" and unlock convenient channels to the fabulous wealth of the Indies.

The success with which Napoleon rapidly reorganized the administration of his own country, unified its laws, and reduced its economic confusion was the envy of such other rulers as Alexander of Russia. In achieving those positive ends he was giving reality to ideals of system, order, and efficiency that had stirred the imagination of philosophers as well as that of "enlightened despots" throughout the eighteenth century. That his reforms were to be buttressed, both against internal strains and external threats, by effective military force added stability to a structure of widely approved design. Such a highly organized, powerful system of bureaucratic control had not been seen in the Western world since the decline of imperial Rome; and France bears its imprint to this day. The impact of these reforms was felt—is still felt—far beyond the confines of France. The Civil Code by which the new government was administered (and which Stendhal claims to have read to improve and clarify his own writing) has been termed one of the few books that have influenced the whole world. It was, Napoleon himself claimed, "the code of the age. It not only ordains tolerance but systematizes it, and tolerance is the greatest blessing of mankind."

That Napoleon assumed dictatorial authority in bringing the Revolution so sharply to order at first caused little enough concern, save in French royalist circles. The men whose writings had done so much to undermine the foundations of the old regime—Montesquieu, Diderot, Turgot, Rousseau, and the *philosophes* in general—had made no great claims for republicanism as such, no more than they did for democracy; but to a man they had aimed at a more rational order of society. They sought a formula to express those "natural" principles which, once discovered and applied to government, would assure human liberty and social harmony. It should matter little under what auspices the principles were put to practice, but likely enough it would take a strong man to dictate such enlightenment to a land so long in the shadows of outworn tradition.

So far Napoleon indeed appears as the child of his age, an offspring of the ambiguities that so distinctively characterized the eighteenth century. Beyond this, however, he becomes an anachronism, at once a throwback to a vanished past and a herald of times yet to come. The epoch

FINLAND

BERGEN
NORWAY
CHRISTIANIA

SWEDEN
UPPSALA
STOCKHOLM
Åland Islands

ÅBO
HELSINGFORS
FREDRI

NORRKOPING
GOTEBORG
JONKOPING

BALTIC SEA

REVAL

DOR

RIGA
DUNABU

ABERDEEN
DUNDEE
LONDONDERRY
GLASGOW
EDINBURGH
BELFAST
NEWCASTLE

Ireland
UNITED KINGDOM

DUBLIN
MANCHESTER
YORK
CORK
WEXFORD
LIVERPOOL
HULL
BIRMINGHAM
NORWICH

NORTH SEA

DENMARK

LIBAU

MEMEL

KIEL
COPENHAGEN
MALMO

PLYMOUTH
BRISTOL
LONDON
SOUTHAMPTON
PORTSMOUTH
BRIGHTON
DOVER
CALAIS
BOULOGNE

THE HAGUE
AMSTERDAM
Holland
GHENT
ANTWERP
BRUSSELS
WATERLOO
Belgium

HAMBURG
BREMEN
HANOVER
MUNSTER
BRUNSWICK
DUSSELDORF
Berg
CASSEL
ERFURT

Rhine

LUBECK
Pomerania
KINGDOM OF PRUSSIA
STETTIN
BERLIN
Westphalia
Saxony
LEIPZIG
DRESDEN

Elbe
Oder

DANZIG
KONIGSBERG
EYLAU
FRIEDLAND

Vistula

TILSIT
Niemen

GRODN
BIALYSTO

POZNAN
Vistula
WARSAW
GRAND DUCHY OF WARSAW

Niem

CHERBOURG
BREST
ROUEN
AMIENS
REIMS

Seine

FRANKFURT
JENA
AUERSTADT

CONFEDERATION
OF THE RHINE

PRAGUE
Bohemia
Silesia
BRESLAU

Oder

KRAKOW
Galicia

LUBLIN
LVOV

RENNES
VERSAILLES
ST. CLOUD
FONTAINEBLEAU
PARIS
VERDUN
VALMY

STRASBOURG
Baden
Wurttemberg

Rhine

BRUNN
AUSTERLITZ

NANTES
TOURS

Loire

DIJON
ULM
AUGSBURG
MUNICH
LINZ
WAGRAM
AUSTRIAN EMPIRE

VIENNA
PRESSBURG
DEBRECEN

ATLANTIC OCEAN

LA ROCHELLE
ROCHEFORT
FRENCH EMPIRE

Loire

BERN
ZURICH
SWITZERLAND
INNSBRUCK
Bavaria
LEOBEN
GRAZ
Hungary
BUDAPEST
KLAUSENBURG
SZEGED

BORDEAUX

LYONS
GENEVA
LAUSANNE
Savoy
Piedmont
GRENOBLE

Rhone

MILAN
TURIN
MARENGO
KINGDOM OF ITALY
MANTUA
Po
VENICE
TRIESTE
Illyrian Provinces
ZAGREB

CORUNNA
OVIEDO
BILBAO
BURGOS
BAYONNE
VITORIA

GENOA
PARMA
BOLOGNA

Po

Bosnia

BELGRADE
Walac

OPORTO
PORTUGAL

TOULOUSE

NICE
LUCCA
FLORENCE

ZARA
RAGUSA

Serbia

Bulgar

SALAMANCA
CIUDAD RODRIGO
Guadarrama Mountains
SAN ILDEFONSO
SARAGOSSA
Catalonia
Ebro

MARSEILLES
TOULON

Tuscany
Corsica
BASTIA
AJACCIO
ELBA

ROME
PONTE CORVO
BENEVENTO

ADRIATIC SEA

SOFIA

NTRA
SBON

Tagus
TALAVERA
MADRID
Tagus
BADAJOZ
TOLEDO
ARANJUEZ

BARCELONA

Minorca

SKOPLJE

Albania

SALONIKA

KINGDOM OF SPAIN

NAPLES
BARI
KINGDOM OF NAPLES
BRINDISI
OTRANTO

YANNINA

Corfu
Greece

SEVILLE
BAILEN

CADIZ
MALAGA
Cape Trafalgar
GIBRALTAR
CEUTA

Majorca

KINGDOM OF SARDINIA

CAGLIARI

LARISSA
MESOLONGION
PATRAS
NAUPLIA
NAVARINO

CORINT
ATH

AEG

PALERMO
MESSINA
REGGIO

Morocco
ALGIERS
ORAN
BONE

KINGDOM OF SICILY
SYRACUSE

Algeria

TUNIS
Tunisia

Malta

MEDITERRANEAN SEA

Cre

SFAX

GABES

TRIPOLI

DERNA

Tripolitania

BENGASI

Cyrenaica

that so heavily felt his influence begins to resemble an aberration of history, a deviation explicable only in terms of the temperament and genius of one man. Over the previous centuries Europe had been partitioned into kingdoms that were in effect private estates of their ruling dynasties, estates conveyed by one generation to another by royal marriages, or, should dynastic schemes become hopelessly snarled, by royal wars of succession—relatively "civilized" wars compared to those that would follow. Tradition and circumstance had long established among these diverse states a fluctuating balance of power. That relatively comfortable stability was shattered by the marching French armies which under Napoleon became a war machine such as the world had not seen.

As the citizen soldiers of revolutionary France—mobilized in great masses to serve their *patrie*—swarmed across national boundaries, the professional armies of tradition were quickly proved obsolete. In self-defense against this new military pattern the rest of the world would have little choice but to follow suit. Warfare was converted from "the sport of kings," as it was once called, to the total effort of a people struggling either for prestige or for survival, as the world has had continued reason to remember.

In retrospect the imbalance of power created by the sudden rise of French might proved to be an anomaly. The separate traditions of the nations of Europe were so deeply rooted that even the withering blasts of Napoleon's armies could not long stunt their growth. On the contrary, as it happened, they found new vigor during the passing storms; in the century that followed, nationalism flowered as it never had before. Yet for a decade or more all Europe, from the Urals to the Atlantic and from Archangel to Cape Matapan, was subject to strife and conquest; the fate of all nations lay within the reach of a single individual. Beyond its Channel fortress even England was threatened with invasion. (As a reminder that it had been done before and a suggestion that it could be done again, Napoleon had the famous Bayeux tapestry brought to Paris for special exhibition.) And before this abnormal state of affairs was corrected, the dead would have to be counted and institutional debris would have to be cleared away.

Goethe recalled from the days of his childhood that the walls of Frankfort's Roman Hall had been hung with portraits of the ancient line of Holy Roman Emperors until there was space for but one left—a space filled with the accession of Francis II in 1792. No more space was needed. More than a thousand years after Pope Leo had crowned the Frankish king in St. Peter's, almost two thousand years after Caesar conquered at Pharsalia, Napoleon overcame the emperors of Austria and Russia, who claimed to represent the old and the new Rome respectively. Francis abdicated his imperial title and Europe's most venerable institution came to its end, and with it an era of world history. The self-styled "Emperor of the French" could hope to rule all Europe from Paris as Caesar had ruled it from Rome. And this, as the accompanying map indicates, he came remarkably close to doing. At the peak of his influence, Napoleon's international domain included a greater area than the European holdings of the entire empire of the Caesars or Charlemagne.

For Frenchmen who survived them, those were unforgettable days. Even under Louis XIV, the Grand Monarch, France had not known such glory and grandeur, or such power. To the parades of victorious armies Napoleon added the pageant of imperial ceremony on a continental scale. Within a year and a half he created more kings than the Holy Emperors had in a millennium. (His mother philosophically reflected, "one of these days I shall have seven or eight sovereigns on my hands.") Abandoning the barren Josephine for a Hapsburg princess, he married into one of Europe's oldest and proudest families. Thanks to the interrelationships of European royalty, he could now with elaborate casualness refer to "my uncle, Louis XVI." The saga of the little Corsican was, up to the turning point of his fortune, the greatest success story ever told.

When his success ran out and a new European balance sheet was drawn up, the results were contrary to almost everything Napoleon had envisioned. England stood firmly at the crossroads of world commerce, supreme mistress of the seas. Russia had emerged as an important power in the West for the first time in history. The way was prepared for a federation of German states under the domination of Prussia. The people of Italy were reminded of their own ancient unity. And France remained, somewhat shrunken on the map, at the crucial center of aroused nationalism and international rivalries.

Along with the divisive tendencies that kept Europe so effectively split into competing national camps went an old, recurrent dream of continental unity—a dream that has not yet lost its power to stir the minds of men. Under the single law and language of ancient Rome, proudly shared by diverse peoples, Europe had known such unity over a period of centuries, a period that was recalled with nostalgia long after the dissolution of the Roman Empire. Again under Charlemagne and during the early Middle Ages most of Europe was united, by a common religion and a common social structure, into a single church-empire that only slowly broke apart and faded away. At other times and in other ways the dream has been revived. The cosmopolitanism of the eighteenth century led toward a cultural unity that was charged with creative energies. As Sir Harold Nicolson has pointed out, the writers, artists, and thinkers of that century thought of themselves, not as natives of any particular country, but as citizens of a single Republic of Letters.

With the Napoleonic age the dream became something of a nightmare. The kind of political unification Napoleon hoped to impose upon the Continent—if not upon the world—proved to be premature, if not simply specious. His pragmatism in applying what he chose to consider the principles of the French Revolution betrayed the weakness of eighteenth-century philosophy. Goethe stated with more enthusiasm than accuracy that "Napoleon was the expression of all that was reasonable, legitimate, and European in the revolutionary movement." But, even had Goethe been right, there are loyalties and habits which men will not forsake in the name of reason. Napoleon's failure to consolidate the Continent in a unified system was in a sense the failure of the eighteenth century to redeem itself in the name of reason.

In one of his moods Napoleon contended that the causes of his ultimate defeat remained beyond the reach of either man or reason. "The obstacles before which I failed did not proceed from men but from the elements," he rationalized at St. Helena. "In the south it was the sea that destroyed me; and in the north it was the fire of Moscow and the ice of winter; so there it is, water, air, fire, all nature and nothing but nature; these were the opponents of a universal regeneration commanded by Nature herself! The problems of Nature are insoluble!"

As Napoleon faded from the scene, what followed seemed an anticlimax, and Europe suffered the *mal du siècle* which spread in epidemic fashion among the romantics of the century. To such heirs of the age of Napoleon he became a symbol of human genius struggling with Fate—a Prometheus reborn to fire the insatiable yearnings of the human spirit. Few heroes—or villains—of the past have put such a firm claim on the imagination of posterity.

The Editors

THE FRENCH REVOLUTION

Before Thomas Carlyle had completed his history of the French Revolution, the sole manuscript of the work was inadvertently burned as rubbish. Carlyle immediately set about rewriting the impassioned narrative, which was published in 1837. He was too close to the cataclysmic event—in his words "a cup of trembling which all nations shall drink"—to record the progress of the Revolution with total objectivity; his sympathy for the lofty egalitarian goals of the revolutionary leaders, as well as his bitter scorn of the brutish methods and misdirection that soon became apparent, strongly colored his interpretation. But for these reasons the history contains the most stirring and vivid record of the French upheaval ever written.

Carlyle's narrative, selections from which have been adapted to describe the events that are pictured on the following pages, deals first with the dying Louis XV and the conditions in eighteenth-century France on which the revolutionary spirit fed: "Alas, much more lies sick than poor Louis: not the French King only, but the French Kingship; the Church, which in its palmy season, seven hundred years ago, could make an Emperor wait barefoot in the snow, has for centuries seen itself decaying; these two will henceforth stand and fall together. Such are the shepherds of the people: and now how fares it with the flock? They are not tended, they are only regularly shorn. They are sent for, to do statute-labour, to pay statute-taxes; to fatten battlefields (named 'bed of honour') with their bodies, in quarrels which are not theirs. Untaught, uncomforted, unfed: this is the lot of the millions. In such a France, as in a Powder-tower, where fire unquenched and now unquenchable is smoking and smouldering all round, has Louis XV lain down to die."

For the old regime and its effete leader, Louis XVI (opposite), all princely pleasures, like the evening fete at the Petit Trianon above, ceased when revolution ravaged France.

THE DECLINE OF THE OLD REGIME

"It is singular how long the rotten will hold together," wrote Carlyle, "provided you do not handle it roughly. The grand events are but charitable Feasts of Morals, with their Prizes and Speeches. There are Snow-statues raised by the poor in hard winter to a Queen who has given them fuel. There are masquerades, theatricals; beautifyings of little Trianon, purchase and repair of St. Cloud; journeyings from the summer Court-Elysium to the winter one. There are poutings and grudgings; little jealousies, which Court-Etiquette can moderate. Wholly the lightest-hearted frivolous foam of Existence; pleasant were it not so costly. Her Majesty appearing at the Opera is applauded; she returns all radiant with joy. Anon the applauses wax fainter, or threaten to cease; she is heavy of heart, the light of her face has fled."

[Addressing the Estates General in May, 1789] "The King, gorgeous as Solomon in all his glory, runs his eye over that majestic Hall. He rises and speaks, with sonorous tone, a conceivable speech. Satisfaction plays over his broad simple face: Let Liberalism and a New Era, if such is the wish, be introduced; only no curtailment of the royal moneys! Which latter condition, alas, is precisely the impossible one. Happy were a young 'Louis the Desired' to make France happy; if it did not prove too troublesome, and he only knew the way. But there is endless discrepancy round him; so many claims and clamours; a mere confusion of tongues. Not reconcilable by man; not manageable, suppressible, save by some strongest and wisest man; for France at large, hitherto mute, is now beginning to speak also."

[July] "Paris is in the streets;—rushing, foaming like some Venice wine-glass into which you had dropped poison. Poor Lackalls, all betoiled, besoiled, encrusted into dim defacement; to them it is clear only that eleutheromaniac Philosophism has yet baked no bread. At every street-barricade, there whirls simmering a minor whirlpool, and all minor whirlpools play distractedly into that grand Fire-Maelstrom which is lashing round the Bastille. Let that rock-fortress, Tyranny's stronghold, look to its guns! And so it roars, confusion as of Babel; noise as of the Crack of Doom! Sinks the drawbridge, rushes-in the living deluge: the Bastille is fallen! The Versailles Ball and lemonade is done; the Orangerie is silent except for nightbirds. In the Court, all is mystery, not without whisperings of terror; His Majesty, kept in happy ignorance, perhaps dreams of double-barrels and the Woods of Meudon. Late at night, the Duke de Liancourt unfolds the Job's-news. Said poor Louis, 'Why, that is a revolt!'—'Sire,' answered Liancourt, 'it is not a revolt,—it is a revolution.' "

OVERLEAF: The Storming of the Bastille, *July 14, 1789*

POLITICAL FACTIONS

Comte de Mirabeau, royalist revolutionary

Madame Roland, a leader of the Girondins

[March, 1791] "The spirit of France waxes ever more acrid, fever-sick: towards the final outburst of dissolution and delirium. Suspicion rules all minds: contending parties cannot now commingle; stand separated sheer asunder, eyeing one another, in most anguish mood, of cold terror or hot rage. Mark, again, how the extreme tip of the Left is mounting in favour, if not in its own National Hall, yet with the Nation, especially with Paris. For in such universal panic of doubt, the opinion that is sure of itself, as the meagrest opinion may the soonest be, is the one to which all men will rally.

"Incorruptible Robespierre has been elected Public Accuser in our new Courts of Judicature; virtuous Pétion, it is thought, may rise to be Mayor. Danton sits at the Departmental Council-table; colleague there of Mirabeau. Of Robespierre it was long ago predicted that he might go far, mean meagre mortal though he was; for Doubt dwelt not in him. As for the King, he as usual will go wavering chameleon-like. Suppose Mirabeau, with whom Royalty takes deep counsel, as with a Prime Minister that cannot yet legally avow himself as such, had got his arrangements *completed?* They say he was ambitious, that he wanted to be Minister. It is most true. And was he not simply the one man in France who could have done any good as Minister? It was he who shook old France from its basis; and, as if with his single hand, held it toppling there, still unfallen. One can say that, had Mirabeau lived, the History of France and of the World had been different. But Mirabeau could not live another year. From amid the press of ruddy busy Life, the Pale Messenger beckons silently: wide-spreading interests, projects, salvation of French Monarchies,—he must suddenly quit it all, and go. 'When I am gone, they will know what the value of me was. The miseries I have held back will burst from all sides on France. I carry in my heart the death-dirge of the French Monarchy; the dead remains of it will now be the spoil of the factious.' What things depended on that one man! King Mirabeau is now the lost King; and one may say with little exaggeration, all the People mourns for him."

[October, 1791] "First of the two-year Parliaments of France—it had to vanish dolefully within *one* year; and there came no second like it. The poor Seven Hundred and Forty-five, sent together by the active citizens of France, are what they could be. That they are of Patriot temper we can well understand. Aristocrat Noblesse had fled over the marches, or sat brooding silent in their unburnt Châteaus; small prospect had they in Primary Electoral Assemblies. What with Flights to Varennes, with plot after plot, the People are left to themselves; [they] must needs choose Defenders of the People, such as can be had; our only Mirabeau now is Danton, whom some call 'Mirabeau of the Sansculottes.' An eloquent Vergniaud we have, from the region named Gironde; sharp-bustling Guadet; considerate grave Gensonné; kind-sparkling mirthful young Ducos; Valazé doomed to a sad end: all these likewise are of that Gironde or Bordeaux region: men of fervid Constitutional principles; who will have the Reign of Liberty establish itself, but only by respectable methods. Round whom others of like temper will gather; known by and by as *Girondins,* of which sort note Condorcet, Marquis and Philosopher; [and] the highest faculty of them all, Hippolyte Carnot. Nor is *Côté Droit,* and band of King's friends, wanting: who love Liberty, yet with Monarchy over it; and speechless nameless individuals sit plentiful, as Moderates, in the middle. Still less is a *Côté Gauche* wanting: extreme Left; sitting on the topmost benches, as if aloft on its speculatory Height or *Mountain,* which will become a practical culminatory Height, and make the name of Mountain famous-infamous to all times and lands."

[1793] "Gironde and Mountain are now in full quarrel; the weapons of the Girondins are Political Philosophy, Respectability, and Eloquence, or call it rhetoric. The weapons of the Mountain are those of mere Nature: Audacity and Impetuosity which may become Ferocity. We discern two sore-places, where the Mountain often suffers: Marat, and Orléans Egalité. Squalid Marat, for his own sake and for the Mountain's, is assaulted ever and anon; held up to France, as a bloodthirsty Portent. The Mountain murmurs, ill at ease: this 'Maximum of Patriotism,' how shall they either own him or disown him? As for Marat personally, he, with his fixed-idea, remains invulnerable to such things; nay, the People's-friend is evidently rising in importance, as his befriended People rises. And poor Orléans Egalité, the disowned of all parties, sheltered, if shelter it be, in the clefts of the Mountain, will wait.

"Nor are Peace-makers wanting; one fast on the crown of the Mountain, broad Danton is loved by all the Mountain; but they think him too easy-tempered, deficient in suspicion: in the shrill tumult Danton's strong voice reverberates, for union and pacification. But the Girondins are haughty and respectable: this Titan Danton is not a man of formulas, and there rests on him a shadow of [the] September [massacres]. What a pang is it to the heart of a Girondin, this first withering probability that the despicable unphilosophic anarchic Mountain, after all, may triumph! Wroth is young Barbaroux; silent, like a Queen, sits the wife of Roland.

"[On] Sunday the second of June 1793, the Mountain has a clear unanimity; the denounced are voted to be under 'Arrestment in their own houses.' Already yesterday, Central Insurrection Committee had arrested Madame Roland; imprisoned her in the Abbaye. Thus fell the Girondins; and became extinct as a party."

Danton, spokesman of the radicals

Marat, a radical Jacobin

THE FALL
OF MONARCHY

When the insurgent mob, unmindful of the Swiss Guard's fire, sacked the Tuileries in August, 1792, the royal family fled to the Assembly Hall. The Gérard drawing (left) shows them in their refuge —a small barred room that served as a press box.

"The King has left the Tuileries—for ever. Patriotism reckons its slain by the thousand, so deadly was the Swiss fire from these windows; deluges of frantic Sansculottism roared through all passages of this Tuileries, ruthless in vengeance. Thus is the Tenth of August won and lost.

"King Louis [has] gone over to the Assembly. The Constitution not permitting debate while the King is present, finally he settles himself with his Family in the *'Loge* of the *Logographe,'* in the Reporter's-Box of a Journalist; which is beyond the enchanted Constitutional Circuit. To such Lodge, measuring some ten feet square, is the King of broad France now limited: here can he and his sit pent, under the eyes of the world, or retire into their closet. Such a peculiar moment has the Legislative lived to see.

"Before four o'clock much has come and gone. The New Municipals have come and gone; with three Flags, *Liberté, Egalité, Patrie.* Vergniaud, he who as President few hours ago talked of dying for Constituted Authorities, has moved that the Hereditary Representative *be suspended;* that a NATIONAL CONVENTION do forthwith assemble to say what further! King Louis listens to all; ye hapless discrowned heads! Swift dispatches rush off to all corners of France; full of triumph, blended with indignant wail, for Twelve-hundred have fallen. France sends up its blended shout responsive; the Tenth of August shall be as the Fourteenth of July, only bloodier and greater. The Court has conspired? Poor Court: the Court has been vanquished."

The jailor Simon beating the dauphin in prison

The head of Louis XVI displayed to the populace, January, 1793

Marie Antoinette, on her way to the executioner

THE FATE
OF THE
ROYAL FAMILY

[Louis XVI] "Kinghood in his person is to expire here. He mounts the scaffold. The Axe clanks down; a King's Life is shorn away. Pastry-cooks, coffee-sellers, milk-men sing out their trivial quotidian cries: the world wags on, as if this were a common day. Not till some days after did public men see what a grave thing it was. At home this Killing of a King has divided all friends; and abroad it has united all enemies. It is even as Danton said: 'The coalised Kings threaten us; we hurl at their feet, as gage of battle, the Head of a King.'"

[October, 1793] "Marie Antoinette—a worn discrowned Widow of Thirty-eight, grey before her time—was brought out. She had on an undress of *piqué blanc:* she was led to the place of execution, in the same manner as an ordinary crim-

inal; bound, on a Cart. At a quarter past Twelve, her head fell; amid universal long-continued cries of *Vive la République.*"

"The Royal Family is now reduced to two: a girl and a little boy. The boy, once named Dauphin, was taken from his Mother while she yet lived; and given to one Simon, by trade a Cordwainer, on service then about the Temple-Prison, to bring him up in principles of Sansculottism. Simon is now gone to the Municipality: and the poor boy, hidden in a tower of the Temple, from which in his fright and bewilderment and early decrepitude he wishes not to stir out, lies perishing, 'his shirt not changed for six months'; amid squalor and darkness, lamentably,—so as none but poor Factory Children and the like are wont to perish, and *not* be lamented!"

A NEW FAITH

In 1794 Robespierre proclaimed that France was to have a new religion; emanating from his own deistic convictions, the short-lived cult centered about a "supreme being" and was intended to add spiritual content to the otherwise godless principles of the Revolution. David designed a fantastic inaugural ceremony, in which a statue symbolizing atheism was set afire and a second statue, Wisdom, rose out of the smoke and ashes. The crowd laughed at the spectacle, for Wisdom's face appeared blackened by the smoke. The drawing shown at right depicts part of the proceedings.

"What thing is this going forward in the Jardin National, whilom Tuileries Garden? All the world is there, in holiday clothes: this day, in the brightness of leafy June, we are to have a New Religion. Catholicism being burned out, and Reason-worship guillotined, was there not need of one? Incorruptible Robespierre, not unlike the Ancients, as Legislator of a free people, will now also be Priest and Prophet. He is President of the Convention; he has made the Convention *decree* the 'Existence of the Supreme Being,' and 'the Immortality of the Soul,' the basis of rational Republican Religion.

"This *is* our Feast of the *Etre Suprême;* our new Religion, better or worse, is come! The seagreen Pontiff takes a torch; strides resolutely forward, in sight of expectant France; set his torch to Atheism and Company, which are but made of pasteboard steeped in turpentine. They burn up rapidly; and, from within, there rises 'by machinery,' an incombustible Statue of Wisdom. Mumbo-Jumbo of the African woods to me seems venerable beside this new Deity of Robespierre; for this is a *conscious* Mumbo-Jumbo, and *knows* that he is machinery. O seagreen Prophet, unhappiest of windbags blown nigh to bursting, what distracted Chimera among realities art thou growing to! This then, this common artificial fireworks of turpentine and pasteboard; *this* is the miraculous Aaron's Rod thou wilt stretch over a hag-ridden hell-ridden France, and bid her plagues cease? Vanish, thou and it! The grand question and hope, however, is: Will not this Feast of the Tuileries Mumbo-Jumbo be a sign perhaps that the Guillotine is to abate? Far enough from that!"

Above, an artist's version of the Loiserolles incident; at right, Robespierre, having executed all others, guillotines the executioner.

ROBESPIERRE AND THE REIGN OF TERROR

"Plots still abound, the Law of the Suspect shall have extension, and Arrestment new vigour and facility. Death then, and always Death! New Catacombs, some say, are digging for a huge simultaneous butchery. Convention to be butchered, down to the right pitch: Jacobin House of Lords made dominant; and Robespierre Dictator.

"And still the Prisons fill fuller, and still the Guillotine goes faster. In the Prison of Saint-Lazare, Lieutenant-General Loiserolles, a nobleman by birth and by nature, hurrying to the Grate to hear the Death-list read, caught the name of his son. The son was asleep at the moment. 'I am Loiserolles,' cried the old man: at [executioner] Tinville's bar, an error in the Christian name is little; small objection was made.

"On 26th July 1794, Robespierre reappears in Convention; mounts to the Tribune! The biliary face seems clouded with new gloom. Longwinded, unmelodious as the screech-owl's, sounds that prophetic voice: Degenerate condition of Republican spirit; corrupt Moderatism; backsliding on this hand and on that; I, Maximilien, alone left incorruptible, ready to die at a moment's warning. For all which what remedy is there? The Guillotine; death to traitors of every hue!

"The old song this: but today, O Heavens, Robespierre, greener than ever before, has to retire, foiled; discerning that it is mutiny, that evil is nigh! [The next day] accusation passes; the incorruptible Maximilien is decreed Accused. Thither again go the Tumbrils. All eyes are on Robespierre's Tumbril. This is the end of the Reign of Terror. How little did any one suppose that here was the end not of Robespierre only, but of the Revolution System itself!"

"[His] death was a signal at which great multitudes of men, struck dumb with terror heretofore, rose out of their hiding-places; in [the] National Convention broken, bewildered by long terror, perturbations and guillotinement, there is no Pilot. Grim generals of the Republic are there; among which latter do we not recognize, once more, that little bronze-complexioned Artillery-Officer of Toulon, home from the Italian Wars!

"It remains to be seen how the quellers of Sansculottism were themselves quelled, and sacred right of Insurrection was blown away by gunpowder; wherewith this singular eventful History called *French Revolution* ends."

HERO FOR AN AGE

*There is nothing modern in you; you are
entirely out of Plutarch. (Paoli to young Bonaparte)*

Shortly after midnight on December 19, 1793, there began in the port and along the water front of Toulon a magnificent fireworks which lasted several hours. Ten ships of the line were going up in flames, the arsenal was ablaze, the sky was filled with masses of smoke, the masts and riggings of the burning ships were outlined in clear fire, and explosions shook the ground for miles along the coast. Toward the horizon, British and Spanish squadrons could be seen sailing away in a long silent procession, their signal lights vanishing in the distant gloom. Toulon was about to be recaptured by the forces of the French revolutionary government from the allies—Englishmen, Spaniards, Sardinians, Neapolitans, and French royalists— who had occupied it in the name of Louis XVII since August. Whatever ships the English could not take with them, they had set on fire before pulling out.

With the fireworks of the early hours of that December day began the rise of Captain Napoleone Buonaparte (as he then still spelled his name), a young artillery officer of twenty-four. It was the kind of spectacle he enjoyed, and it seemed fitting that his career should have entered its decline nineteen years later with an even more brilliant display: " . . . mountains of red, rolling flames," as he recalled it, "like immense waves of the sea, alternately bursting forth and lifting themselves to skies of fire, and then sinking into the ocean of flame below. Oh, it was the most grand, the most sublime, and the

most terrifying sight the world ever beheld!" The sublime sight he was thus to describe to his Irish physician at St. Helena was the fire of Moscow.

When dawn revealed the smoking wrecks of the burned ships, the republican troops prepared to enter the city. It was at the height of the Reign of Terror; only two months earlier, carrying out the orders of the Committee of Public Safety, the People's Representatives Jean Marie Collot and Joseph Fouché, a former cleric, had supervised the destruction of the rebellious city of Lyons and the execution of thousands of its citizens. Marseilles, which had also resisted the central revolutionary authority, had suffered terrible reprisals even more recently. On the day the French troops entered Toulon, the People's Representative Antoine Christophe Saliceti, a Corsican and the protector of Captain Bonaparte, wrote to the National Convention at Paris in the typical style of the time: "Almost all the inhabitants have fled. Those who have stayed behind will serve to appease the shades of our brave brothers in arms who have died in valiant combat."

The republican troops were welcomed at the city gate by the naval troops of Toulon, who had only reluctantly obeyed the allies during the occupation and done their

The rugged landscape of Napoleon's Corsican homeland, with its rock-walled southern coast (shown opposite), served as a natural fortress for the island's proud, embattled patriots.

26

An English version of the blazing holocaust in Toulon harbor

best to prevent the burning of the arsenal. Accompanied by part of the population, with their band playing revolutionary hymns, they hoped to convince their liberators of their loyalty to the Republic; the republicans, however, were not impressed by the tricolored flags and the laurel wreaths held out to them by naval troops, two hundred of whom were lined up against a wall and shot without any formalities. This was only a beginning. The looting, the raping, the mass executions went on for several days.

Then legality, in the shape of a revolutionary tribunal and the guillotine, took over. "There is a high incidence of mortality among the subjects of Louis XVII," wrote the People's Representative Fréron in a humorous vein. After one of the mass executions by musket fire, someone cried: "Let all the wounded stand up, the Republic will pardon them!" A number of wounded managed to rise and were shot down. A man ninety-four years old was carried to the guillotine in a chair. "All goes well here," Fréron reported to Paris. "We have requisitioned 1,200 masons to demolish and raze the city. Every day since our entry we have had two hundred heads cut off." One day, in twenty minutes, nineteen heads fell under the guillotine. After witnessing these horrors for a week, unable to stop them, the general in command of the republican troops requested his recall (which was refused).

Although in later days Napoleon minimized the massacres at Toulon—he spoke of only about a hundred victims—there can be no doubt that he witnessed them as an onlooker. The spectacle can only have confirmed him in the sentiment he had expressed in a letter to his younger brother Lucien half a year earlier: "Among so many conflicting ideas and so many different perspectives, the honest man is confused and distressed and the skeptic becomes wicked. . . . Since one must take sides, one might as well choose the side that is victorious, the side which devastates, loots, and burns. Considering the alternative, it is better to eat than to be eaten." Twenty-eight years

later, on his deathbed, he said, "In my youth I had illusions; I got rid of them fast." Undoubtedly he had got rid of them by the time he directed the artillery in the capture of Toulon and with the hero's cold, impassive eyes observed the results of his victory. Indeed, rightly or wrongly, the fall of Toulon was credited to his plan of attack, and after years of frustration, false starts, and failures he saw a career opening up before him. To see and to seize an opportunity was instinctive with him. At the same time, not caring for life, he was utterly fearless and, having lost his illusions, utterly unscrupulous. Given a little luck, a man with such qualities is irresistible.

The arsenal of ideas with which Napoleon emerged from his formative years was deceptively similar to a number of ideas then very much in fashion. According to Talleyrand (the ex-bishop who was to be Napoleon's foreign minister), a person who had not lived in France during the last years of the old regime could not know "the sweetness of being alive." This may have been true of a great many people whose fortunes or temperaments enabled them to savor the sweetness of life, but young Napoleon was decidedly not one of them, and enough others shared his contempt for their times to create the necessary climate for a social regeneration—or, as it turned out, a revolution. To them, all seemed puny, petty, corrupt, immoral, and insincere. Women ruled everything. For getting ahead, merit, genius, and character were positive obstacles; flattery, intrigue, elegant clothes, social grace, and a talent for sleeping with the right people were the keys to success. Virtue was nonexistent, genuine feeling was ridiculed, manliness, energy, greatness, and enthusiasm were stifled in the bud.

It is irrelevant to point out that this kind of criticism, whether justified or not, can be made of any complex society in any age. What matters is that there are phases in history when more than the usual number of intelligent and gifted people feel excluded from the possibility of self-fulfillment in the society they live in and are dissatisfied with the complexities of their civilization. Such a phase began in the second half of the eighteenth century.

It is possible to see forerunners of these malcontents in Molière's *Misanthrope* or even in Cervantes' *Don Quixote*. These however were creatures of fiction, and caricatures to boot. Nobody in the seventeenth century would have dreamed of adopting their opinions. Jean Jacques Rousseau was something else; his writings offered not only the most eloquent criticism of modern civilization but also—or so it seemed—vistas of regeneration on every plane of human activity. Cervantes and Molière, by making their public laugh at their lovable but eccentric heroes, had upheld conformism. With Rousseau the laughter ceased (excepting the sardonic variety) and nonconformism was consecrated. It *was* possible to create a new society, a new man, a new relationship between man and woman, a new bond between mankind and nature—this, at least, is what

Rousseau's most ardent disciples thought, but whether Rousseau himself believed it is not at all certain.

Against what was thought to be a decadent, effeminate society, the examples of a more virile and virtuous past were held up. Spartan ideals seduced the inhabitants of modern Babylon. The Roman Republic and its great men—Cincinnatus, Cato, Brutus, and the rest—became fashionable. Rousseau saw the ancient virtues in his native Republic of Geneva until the Genevans burned his books and stripped him of his citizenship, just as Napoleon was to see them in Corsica until the Corsicans sent him packing. Goethe's Werther, an outsiders' outsider, blew out his brains because society was against him; all Europe was still weeping with him (and a few literal-minded lads were imitating his example) when young Schiller began to work on his *Robbers,* under the motto *"Contra tyrannos,"* in which the moral superiority of the bandit's vigorous outdoor life over the scheming pettiness of the puling age is clearly demonstrated.

Where were the ancient heroes—men who placed love of fatherland and liberty above all else, whose lives were simple and pure, who served their country without seeking power or riches, who led the oppressed against tyranny? Where could one find men comparable to a Leonidas, an Aristides, a Cincinnatus, the Horatii, a Mucius Scaevola, the Gracchi, or a Brutus? Glumly and with knitted brow the young enthusiast would survey the scene and conclude that their number was few. Who would have thought that a few decades later heroes would march across Europe by the millions and let themselves be killed by the hundreds of thousands?

Fortunately for the lovers of virtue, their demand for great men did not go entirely unappeased even in the 1760's and '70's. Almost simultaneously two great patriots appeared on the scene who answered all the specifications. George Washington, though second in order of appearance, was probably the greater of the two—or, at any rate, the more successful. He was the modern Cincinnatus; his army of embattled farmers, unspoiled by the corrupting influence of urban civilization, had left their plows and were giving their lives to found a free republic in which the proudest title would be that of Citizen, and he himself, like Cincinnatus, would return to his farm once his task was done. (When Chateaubriand saw Washington in Philadelphia in 1791, he was disappointed to see him riding in a coach; he had expected to find him behind a plow.) Patrick Henry's "Give me liberty or give me death!" rang around the world, and two decades later every French politician would utter this sentiment at the drop of a hat. Even Americans, who should have known better, saw themselves as successors to the early Roman Republic—witness the rash of classical names inflicted on defenseless babes and towns.

The other hero sprang up in a place closer to home but even less expected. Pasquale Paoli (1725–1807) had led the people of Corsica in their rebellion against their Genoese masters and won them a precarious independence under his rule. From his mountain stronghold at Corte he governed as a dictator, having united the feuding clans in the struggle for liberty. Paoli was by all accounts a man of remarkable presence, ability, and strength of character. Dr. Johnson, who was to know him well, asserted that he had "the loftiest port of any man he had ever seen." For twelve years Paoli succeeded in beating back the repeated attempts of the Genoese and their mercenaries to reconquer the island; at the same time he tried to transform a people of shepherds, goatherds, and brigands into a unified nation; he built schools, founded a university, and even sought (not too successfully) to substitute legal procedure for the traditional *vendetta* as the means of settling the personal differences of the islanders.

Although Rousseau wrote, on the request of the Corsicans, a constitution for their island (which needless to say was not adopted), Paoli's struggle went relatively unnoticed until James Boswell happened to visit Corsica and upon his return to London—still wearing the Corsican costume, pistols and all—enlisted English public opinion in support of the brave islanders. The British cabinet was not infected by his enthusiasm. "Foolish as we are," declared Lord Holland, "we are not so foolish as to go to war because Mr. Boswell has been to Corsica."

In May, 1768, just about the time when Boswell published his *Journal of a Tour to Corsica,* the Republic of Genoa, having grown weary of the struggle, sold its rights to the island to the king of France. The French forces dispatched to take possession of Corsica were something quite different from the Genoese. For a year the Corsicans held out in the unequal contest; but although the eyes of Europe were upon them, nobody was so rash as to come to their aid. In May, 1769, at Ponte Nuovo, Paoli's brave army was annihilated by the French, and Paoli's twenty years of exile began. Letizia Bonaparte was six months pregnant when the rout of the Corsicans forced her to hide out in the mountains for several weeks before she could return to Ajaccio and give birth, on August 15, quite painlessly, to her second son, Napoleon.

Technically, Napoleon was born a subject of the king of France. However, although the French took over control of the island with the help of a rather large military establishment, the Corsicans remained intensely Corsican. The regime of the French governor, the comte de Marbeuf, was benign and conciliatory, but this did not prevent the more ardent among the patriots from declaiming against their conquerors' ferocity. "The chief satisfaction of the islanders," Boswell had noted, "when not engaged in war or hunting seemed to be that of lying at their ease in the open air, recounting tales of bravery of their countrymen, and singing songs in honor of the Corsicans, and against the Genoese."

Napoleon, in his earliest years, heard these tales from

David's The Oath of the Horatii *(1785), which celebrates classical heroism, was interpreted by some as an anti-royalist allegory.*

his father, who had been one of Paoli's chief lieutenants, and from his mother, whom Paoli had compared to Cornelia, mother of the Gracchi. At the age of seventeen, after seven years of separation from his island and a French education at the king's expense, Napoleon wrote in his notebook, on the occasion of Paoli's sixty-first birthday and in praise of Corsica's heroes: "Modern effeminates, almost all of whom are languishing in comfortable slavery, those heroes were far above your craven souls!" "What shall I see when I return home?" he wrote a few days later. "My compatriots, loaded with chains and trembling as they kiss the hand of their oppressor. They no longer are the same brave Corsicans whom a hero could inspire with his virtues, who were the enemies of tyranny, of luxury, of vile courtiers. Proud, filled with the noble consciousness of his importance as an individual, a Corsican used to regard himself as happy if he had spent his day in public business. His night was spent between the tender arms of a cherished wife . . . Tenderness and nature made his nights comparable to those of the gods. But, along with liberty, those happy days have vanished like a dream. Frenchmen, not content to take from us everything we cherished, you have also corrupted our morals! . . . If in order to free my countrymen it were enough to destroy one man, I should set out this instant and plunge into the tyrant's breast the avenging sword of the fatherland and the violated laws."

Strange language for a lad but recently commissioned a lieutenant by the king of France! Stranger still for a man who in the last years of his life could say: "I am more at home in Champagne than in Corsica, for I have been brought up at Brienne from the age of nine . . . Of all the insults that have been heaped on me in so many pamphlets, the one to which I was the most sensitive was that of being called 'the Corsican'." But in 1817 Napoleon was addressing the gallery of posterity. He might say this or that, depending on what effect he wished to achieve. What he wrote in his notebook in 1786—the clichés, the banalities, the untalented imitation of Rousseau's incandescent rhetoric, and the sincere conviction behind it— all this he addressed to himself only. Undoubtedly he stood under the influence of Rousseau, but his patriotism, his rootedness in the values of antiquity were not the products of his readings—they were his heritage by birth.

The Corsica in which he spent his first nine years was quite unlike any other country. What was literature on the Continent was reality there. For twenty centuries its proud passionate people had defended their individuality against all intruders—Romans, Goths, Moors, Pisans, Genoese, and finally, French. Their history was an epic of strong, heroic deeds, of violence and feuds, sometimes of treachery, never of pettiness or decadence. In their harsh Italian dialect, they spoke with the terse simplicity of Homer's or Corneille's heroes. When, during the fighting of 1769, a French officer, astonished to find that the Corsicans had no military hospitals, asked a prisoner what became of their wounded, the prisoner replied simply, "We die." In 1799 when Napoleon stopped at Corsica on his return from Egypt, his wet nurse presented him with a bottle of milk, saying, "My son, I have given you the milk of my heart; all I can offer you now is that of my goat."

Corsica seemed to confirm Rousseau's thesis that the progress of civilization had corrupted virtue. Living conditions in Corsica were simple and primitive. Even the few noble families (among them the Bonapartes) were poor; almost kings in their island because of the loyalties they commanded and the prestige they carried, they would nevertheless have been snubbed as peasants by the courtiers of Versailles. Roads were virtually nonexistent until Paoli built some. A higher education could be obtained only on the mainland until Paoli founded the University of Corte. The arts, the sciences, the superfluous ornaments of life were neglected. But virtue—in the old, virile, Latin sense of the word—had remained uncorrupted. War, vendetta, and stories of loyal love were the themes of the mountaineers' songs. Love was violent; the punishment for infidelity, even more so. Politics was conducted with the same passion as war, vendetta, and love; so were civil lawsuits. As for criminal offenses or injuries to a person's or family's honor, the vendetta took care of that. (It was only in the present century that the French police stamped out its last traces.)

A family's wealth and power were measured not only in goods, land, and chattels but also in the number of children and of cousins. Carlo and Letizia Bonaparte had twelve children (four of them died in infancy, one became emperor, three became kings, one a queen, another a grand duchess), and they had several hundred cousins. As Napoleon recalled in St. Helena, his maternal grandmother, Angela Maria di Pietra Santa, whenever she needed help in a dispute, could count on between two and three hundred relatives to descend from their mountains in order to support her side of it. When Madame de Staël asked Napoleon what woman, dead or alive, he thought was the greatest, he replied, "The one that has borne the most children." The answer was not as malicious or antifeminist as it sounds; it was simply Corsican.

The passionate attachment of Corsicans to their soil, their liberty, their way of life was both stimulated and facilitated by the physical nature of their land. Not only is it an island but it is also a mountain stronghold, cut by deep gorges and grown over with what was then an almost impenetrable cover of fragrant shrubs—the famous *macchia* or *maquis*. Here outlaws and patriots could hide and fight forever. Only the goatherds knew the paths. Apart from being rugged and easily defensible, the country was, and is, intensely beautiful in a strong, sensual, and unforgettable way. "Everything was better there," Napoleon reminisced in St. Helena. " . . . The very smell of its soil is so present to my senses that with my eyes closed I could recognize the earth I trod as a small child!" He also recalled the wine of the family vineyard at Sposenta, regretting its

bouquet, for it alone could freshen his mouth. He gave the vineyard, while emperor, to the wet nurse who had given him the milk of her heart and of her goat.

Here was no figment of Rousseauan nostalgia, here was a reality that could be seen, touched, tasted, and smelled. Napoleon's parents had been the friends of a hero; he had heard the thunder of battle while in his mother's womb; and after the disaster of Ponte Nuovo, Letizia had carried her unborn child through the mountain fastnesses near Corte, hiding in the granite caverns of Monte Rotondo, fed by the gifts of goatherds, and as night fell, listening to the women who improvised songs on the deeds and deaths of heroes. The first talk he heard was of politics—not politics as it is practiced in Washington or Paris or Westminster, but politics as the main occupation of a free, full-blooded man, politics as it was practiced in ancient Athens and early Rome or in the Florence of Dante. Talk of liberty or death, of chains

Paoli inspired revolutionary leaders.

and of daggers, all the phrases that were to sound so hollow in the mouths of the French revolutionists, had a very genuine ring on the island where Napoleon spent his youth. Still, the French were in control, peace was enforced, and the very gentle chains had to be borne. The daggers were kept for possible future use, but as the years passed they became more and more rusty and rhetorical.

Napoleon and his brother Joseph, who was one year older, grew up in Ajaccio under the firm hand of their mother, an exceptionally beautiful, austere, and untalkative woman—though when she spoke, she spoke forcefully. (Their father, an easy-going and more modern soul than Letizia, left the discipline of his children entirely to his wife.) Madame Bonaparte managed to combine strictness with permissiveness in judicious doses. Thus she set aside a large room, bare of all furniture, in which the boys were let loose on rainy days to do what they liked, even paint on the walls. Napoleon, it seems, painted rows upon rows of soldiers in order of battle.

At the age of five, according to his and his mother's testimony, he was placed in a kind of nursery school for girls (the same thing happened to Hercules at a more dangerous age), where he fell passionately in love with a small beauty named Giacominetta. Since his stockings always fell down to his heels, his love was not reciprocated and the girls sang an annoying song about him. He did not remain in the girls' school for long but learned to read and write from a priest named Recco, whom he never saw again but to whom he left twenty thousand francs in his will. To encourage competition among his pupils, the abbé Recco placed half of them under the Roman standard, with the letters S.P.Q.R. upon it, and the other half under the standard of Carthage. Napoleon resented being a Carthaginian and bullied his brother, who was on the Roman side, into switching places. He hated to lose. "To die is nothing," he said when his career was done, "but to live defeated and without glory is to die every day."

Napoleon did not learn much at his Corsican school (nor at any other school, for that matter), but he soon developed a taste for study and solitude, and particularly for numbers. When he was eight, he escaped his noisy brothers and sisters (Lucien was two years old, Elisa was just born) to study mathematics in a wooden shack especially constructed for him on the terrace of the Casa Bonaparte. This, at least, is what his mother recalled long after his death—but it is notorious that mothers cannot be trusted in such matters.

Not all of Napoleon's early childhood was spent at Ajaccio. He went on frequent trips to the inland country, where his family had their vineyards and orchards and chestnut groves and goats and cousins. In all his reminiscences, written or spoken, his first nine years in Corsica stand out as a happy period—the only happy period in his life—and he always equated happiness with rootedness in the land of one's birth. Whatever humanity and virtue there were in him had been implanted in him in Corsica, in his childhood. This childhood ended abruptly in his tenth year. Toward the end of 1778 his father took him and his elder brother to France, to be educated there. He would not see Corsica again for eight years.

Though a patriot, Carlo Bonaparte was also a realistic man and a lawyer; though careless with his money and pleasure-loving, he was concerned about his children's future. Lacking the singleness of purpose of a Paoli, he did not refuse to compromise with the inevitable. France, he realized, would never let go of Corsica; the most sensible thing to do, then, was to be on good terms with the victors while trying to protect the local liberties so far as this was possible. He had solicited from the king a scholarship for one of his two sons in one of the royal military schools for children of noble birth. The scholarship was awarded to Napoleon since Joseph, for some reason, seemed more suited for the Church than for the army. (He was decidedly unsuited for either.) Early in January, 1779, Carlo left the two boys at the College of Autun.

Joseph was to remain there; Napoleon was to stay only long enough to learn French before going on to the military school at Brienne, an institution run by a religious order. In May the two brothers separated. Joseph wept copiously; Napoleon shed one single tear. Years passed before either saw any member of his family again. In 1784, Carlo Bonaparte stopped briefly at Brienne to leave Lucien, his third son, there; on the same trip, he took his eldest daughter to the aristocratic school of St. Cyr, also on a royal scholarship, and brought Joseph back to Corsica. Carlo was a very ill man by then. Less than a year later he died at Montpellier of a stomach cancer.

It would be difficult to imagine a more complete separation of a child from everything familiar than that experienced by Napoleon when he went to Brienne, nor could there be a greater contrast than between Corsica and the bleak, chilly plains of Champagne, or between the freedom he had enjoyed at home and the prisonlike atmosphere of the school. From the moment of his arrival at Brienne, though not yet ten years old, Napoleon was on his own; also, from that day, he was conscious of his complete loneliness.

Very little is known of Napoleon's years at Brienne. Almost everything that has been reported on them belongs to legend or fiction. The frequently made assertion that he felt at a disadvantage because he received no pocket money from home is probably a fabrication. The regime of the military school was democratic and Spartan: the pupils were rarely, if ever, allowed to leave the school grounds, and there were no vacations; all scholarship pupils received the same modest pocket money from the king, were issued two uniforms per year, changed their linen twice a week, occupied identical rooms (each pupil by himself), and were forbidden to receive any gifts—even books—from outside. None of Napoleon's classmates belonged to the higher nobility, and Napoleon was as noble as any of them.

Nevertheless it is true that he felt isolated and different from the rest. To his comrades, his accent and appearance seemed as bizarre as his name and origin. He insisted on pronouncing "Napoleone" in the Italian manner, which made his classmates call him *la paille au nez*—"Straw-in-the-nose." He was smaller than average, skinny, of rather yellow complexion (his skin became marble-white only many years later), uncouth, and in constant warfare with his clothes and his hair. To the French boys, he was a Corsican savage. Though by no means unsocial, he liked to be by himself to study and to dream. Above all, he was preternaturally serious; there was nothing childlike or boyish about him.

At fifteen—a year before his father's death—he wrote letters that reveal his extraordinary sense of responsibility. Already he regarded himself as the head of the family, for his elder brother Joseph appeared to him too frivolous to shoulder the burden. The mediocre aspirations of his fellow students struck him as contemptible. The future that they took for granted—the idle and pleasurable life of an officer in garrison—was not for him. His separation from family and home had made him only more intensely Corsican. The son of the vanquished, he lived surrounded by the victors and their mockery, and in his humbled pride he saw himself more as a princely hostage than as a French provincial brought up at the king's expense. He felt no obligation to the conquerors of his country; instead he wished for the day when he could lead his countrymen in recovering their freedom. Undoubtedly he read his Plutarch and dreamed of greatness—but, at that time, Brutus seemed to be a greater man than Alexander.

Apart from mathematics, for which he had a marked aptitude, Napoleon was a mediocre student. His handwriting was and always remained appalling; his spelling was hair-raising; his French, barbarous; his syntax and rhetoric, a shapeless tangle; his vocabulary, full of malapropisms. He had no ear for poetry and showed a monumental lack of talent in his attempts at verse. Most of the knowledge he acquired later was self-taught, and it was always very spotty. It is true that nobody learned much at Brienne, for the simple reason that the good fathers who taught there did not know much, but there can be no doubt that Napoleon showed little aptitude for learning in the ordinary sense. Whatever information he felt that he needed, he absorbed with astonishing facility, but this for the most part, was not the kind of information that one was likely to acquire in schools.

Having chosen the artillery in preference to the navy as his branch of service, Napoleon succeeded in securing, in October, 1784, an appointment to the Ecole

Militaire in Paris, where, at the end of a year's study, he was commissioned a second lieutenant and assigned to his regiment, at Valence in southern France. On the roster of graduates, he ranked forty-second among fifty-eight; however, he had completed in one year a course which took most others two or three. There was more comfort at the Ecole Militaire than at Brienne; the food was Lucullan by comparison; and a large part of the curriculum was devoted to the acquisition of social graces. To young Bonaparte, such an un-Spartan state of affairs was profoundly shocking. However, the discipline was as strict as at Brienne, and it was only in his garrison days, at Valence, that Napoleon found for the first time in his life the leisure and the freedom to follow his own inclinations and to seek himself. He was sixteen.

The character that emerges from the pages of Napoleon's early writings is that of an uncommonly *farouche* young man. Even if he had had enough money to indulge himself in the usual amusements of a lieutenant in garrison, his puritanical self-discipline, his almost physical revulsion from pleasure would have kept him in the path of virtue. What time he did not devote to his duties and to his correspondence with his family he spent in self-

---

In the autumn of 1793, when revolutionary ardor was at a peak, the National Convention decreed a new calendar whose chronology and nomenclature would more closely correspond to the spirit and ideas of the time than the old Gregorian calendar. In line with other dechristianizing developments (such as the conversion of many churches into Temples of Reason), the names of days, months, and other intervals of time would be divorced from all religious associations and would be replaced by symbols denoting the "natural" order of things so dear to republican principles. Thus, days of the week were given such rural names as lamb's lettuce, plow, billy goat, and spinach; the holidays were known as Opinion, Labor, and so on; the intercalary day (the day that served the same purpose as February 29th of our Leap Year) was called "the day of the Revolution." The new system was started retroactively from September 22, 1792, which by a happy coincidence celebrated both the true autumnal equinox and the creation of the French Republic. A summary of the seasons and months of the Revolutionary calendar (all corresponding with the climate of Paris) with their traditional equivalents follows:

AUTUMN

VENDEMIAIRE	*(month of vintage)*	22 SEPT.–21 OCT.
BRUMAIRE	*(month of fog)*	22 OCT.–20 NOV.
FRIMAIRE	*(month of frost)*	21 NOV.–20 DEC.

WINTER

NIVOSE	*(month of snow)*	21 DEC.–19 JAN.
PLUVIOSE	*(month of rain)*	20 JAN.–18 FEB.
VENTOSE	*(month of wind)*	19 FEB.–20 MAR.

SPRING

GERMINAL	*(month of budding)*	21 MAR.–19 APRIL
FLOREAL	*(month of flowers)*	20 APRIL–19 MAY
PRAIRIAL	*(month of meadows)*	20 MAY–18 JUNE

SUMMER

MESSIDOR	*(month of harvest)*	19 JUNE–18 JULY
THERMIDOR	*(month of heat)*	19 JULY–17 AUG.
FRUCTIDOR	*(month of fruit)*	18 AUG.–16 SEPT.

Sans-culottides: 17–21 SEPT., inclusive, plus extra day in leap years.

On January 1, 1806, Napoleon restored the Gregorian calendar as one gesture of conciliation towards the Church.

improvement. He subscribed to a lending library, and he discovered, first of all, Rousseau.

Judging from appearances, Jean Jacques' impact on Napoleon was explosive. At St. Helena the emperor remarked that, in his youth, he would have fought to the death for Rousseau. This, however, is only a figure of speech. In his first writings, the young man certainly tried to imitate Rousseau's style, with slightly ludicrous results. Yet even in his most romantic days, his mind worked along eminently practical lines. Whether it was politics, the arts, the sciences, religion, or history—whatever the subject of his inquiries—he never approached it with a desire to gain knowledge but as an arsenal he could ransack for whatever weapons he required for his purpose. "History," he once told Madame de Rémusat, "I conquered rather than studied: that is to say, I wanted from it and retained of it only what I could add to my ideas, I spurned what was of no use, and I seized upon certain conclusions that pleased me." It was the same with all his other studies. He raided knowledge as a starving army raids the countryside. The method may seem practical, but ultimately it leads to a parting of ways with reality.

When Napoleon first came upon Rousseau, his only real interest lay in Corsica. His first known manuscript seems, on the surface, inspired by *The Social Contract,* but in fact Napoleon treated *The Social Contract* as if it had been specially devised to justify his thesis that Corsica had a unilateral right to secede from France. It may be said with complete conviction that Napoleon was never inspired by an idea; he was inspired only by action, and he used ideas the way an express courier uses a horse: he did not care if they died under him, so long as they got him where he wanted to go.

It is not surprising that one of Napoleon's greatest admirers should have been Goethe. In one of the early scenes of *Faust,* Goethe has the doctor translate the opening of the Gospel according to Saint John: "In the beginning was the Word." The word—*logos*—is the idea. Faust balks at this; he ends by translating the passage, "In the beginning was the Deed." Napoleon never read *Faust,* but he read *The Sorrows of Young Werther* during his garrison days and probably reread it several times later. As was true in the case of Rousseau the impact seems—but only seems—to have been deep.

Read nowadays, *Werther* may strike one as merely an extreme example of what used to be called sensibility, distinguished from similar outpourings by the superior genius of its author. But *Werther* introduced something new and poisonous into the emotional climate of the times. Rousseau had rejected society and civilization as he found them, and he felt rejected by them like Werther; his one great love affair proved a monumental fiasco like Werther's; he reveled in the sweet pleasures of melancholy like Werther; but he never expressed despair. On the contrary, to live, to live truly, rather than merely pretend to live, this was the object to which he clung with heroic tenacity, even through crises of insanity. Young Werther yielded to despair, rejected life, and killed himself.

Napoleon was not yet seventeen when he wrote this Wertherian soliloquy: "Always alone in the midst of men, I come to my room to dream by myself, to abandon myself to my melancholy in all its sharpness. In which direction does it lead today? Toward death. . . . What fury drives me to my own destruction? Indeed, what am I to do in this world? Since die I must, is it not just as well to kill myself? . . . Since nothing is pleasure to me, why should I bear days that nothing turns to profit? How far men have got away from nature! How cowardly they are, how vile and rampant! . . . Life is a burden to me because I taste no pleasure and all is pain to me . . . because the men with whom I live, and probably always shall live, have ways as different from mine as the moon from the sun. Thus I cannot pursue the only way of life that could make life tolerable—hence distaste for everything."

This effusion *à la* Werther, with a dash of Hamlet ("How weary, stale, flat, and unprofitable/Seem to me all the uses of this world") was not, as in the case of so many other distraught youths, a literary mimicry. However declamatory the statement of despair may sound, each phrase has a concrete meaning. He was not made for pleasure: but what *was* he made for? Many a teenager asks himself this question, and we smile with the knowledge that life will take care of the answer—or, rather, of his curiosity. But this particular teenager happened to be Napoleon Bonaparte, and it is difficult to smile at him with the same condescension that experienced failure so readily extends to naive aspiration.

Five years later, in 1791, Napoleon competed for a prize offered by the Academy of Lyons for the best essay on the question of happiness. None of the entries earned a prize, but Napoleon's did not even win an honorable mention, and in fact it hardly deserved one: only a clairvoyant could have realized its interest, which was in the author rather than in the writing. Napoleon's conception of happiness in the essay was identical with that which he had always held, would always hold, and was incapable of even approximating. Happiness was love—love of the native soil, of one's people, friends, family, and wife, a simple, loyal, courageous, and sensual kind of love. Love between man and woman, he declared one day to his Council of State, was "an exchange of perspirations."

It was as simple as that: to melt in the intimacy of an embrace, to make the soil produce, to see the continuity of life in one's children, to give one's life for the preservation of all these things, this was patriotism, this was happiness. Strife must be taken for granted, but poverty and oppression, no. Such happiness, Napoleon observed in St. Helena, no longer existed. The French Revolution had destroyed it. "A person who has lost the room in which he was born, the garden where he played as a child, the house of his forebears—such a person has no fatherland." At seventeen, despite all his suicidal musings, Napoleon still had the prospect of returning to his room, his garden, his fatherland. But seven years later, at Toulon, he had lost his fatherland along with his room and his garden. In the course of his career, he was to order several thousand houses and gardens to be burned and razed.

Napoleon's conception of happiness, though Rousseauan in its expression, was rooted in his love of fatherland. His incapacity for pleasure, his suicidal thoughts, his consciousness of being different from other men, his despair of finding his place in the world, his all-pervading sadness, all these tendencies seem to belong to the time in which he lived and can be found in the *Weltschmerz* of young Werther and in the *mal du siècle* of Chateaubriand's and Byron's heroes. But there was a great difference. Unlike theirs, Napoleon's despair did not spring from introspection or boredom. The mainspring of his being was his urge to act, and his despair would be forgotten the instant he found a field of action.

His prospects in the French service were mediocre. He briefly entertained the notion of serving with the British army in India, and he may have had other dreams, but fundamentally his ambition was concentrated on Corsica. To be somebody in his own country seemed the only worthy aim. Since the French army under the old regime was exceedingly generous in granting leaves, Napoleon had ample opportunity to reacquaint himself with his native land. In September, 1786, after one year's duty with his regiment, he left for Corsica on a six-month leave, which he prolonged by another six months; then, late in 1787, he went to Paris, obtained yet another prolongation—all this with full pay—and returned to Corsica for half a year before resuming his garrison duty. Although such extended vacations were not unusual, few officers excelled Napoleon in his ability to solicit them.

What did the young man accomplish during these eighteen months of absence from his regiment? Judging from the evidence available, nothing of note. His chief activity seems to have been to put his family's affairs in order. Carlo had left his heirs no cash whatever, and Napoleon's great-uncle Lucciano Bonaparte, archdeacon of Ajaccio, who was in charge of the family's finances, was content to keep all the revenues hidden under his mattress, where they remained until his death.

Apart from inspecting vineyards, mulberry bushes, and goats, Napoleon was absorbed in his studies. He had arrived at Ajaccio with a small suitcase containing his clothes and a large trunk containing his books—Plutarch, Plato, Cicero, Cornelius Nepos, Livy, Tacitus (all in translations, to be sure; he was no linguist), Montaigne, Montesquieu, the abbé Raynal's *Philosophical History of the Two Indies,* and Macpherson's spurious Ossianic poems, which he loved, "but only for the same reason that I like to hear the whisper of the wind and the waves of the sea." He read and took

Letizia Bonaparte

Carlo Bonaparte

The house in Ajaccio where Napoleon was born August 15, 1769

notes; he relearned Italian, which he had half forgotten; he collected an impressive set of documents relative to the history of Corsica since 1700; he planned to write a history of Corsica. Indeed, it was a time when the pen was mightier than the sword (he was to change this), and the most effective way to serve his fatherland and to make a name for himself was to write in its defense and for its glory. His youth seemed to him an advantage: "I still have the enthusiasm which a better knowledge of men often destroys in our hearts. The venality of mature age shall not soil my pen."

The drawing above may be the earliest likeness of Napoleon; it is dated 1785.

During his three months in Paris (October–December, 1787) he had little to do save solicit another leave, collect his pay in arrears, and petition the government on behalf of his mother, who desired a state subsidy for her mulberry bush nursery. With more time, freedom, and money than ever before, he became almost dissipated. He went to the theatres, to the Opera. He walked about Paris, gaping and idling like any raw provincial youth. "There is nothing that surpasses Paris, with its public parks and libraries," he observed thirty years later. "With just five francs, you can get into any theatre. . . . In Paris you don't notice the weather: rain or snow, it's always fine." It may have seemed thus in retrospect, but in 1787 the contrast between the glittering world of wealth and fashion, the unapproachable and all-powerful great ladies, and his own unprepossessing shabbiness did not strike him as amusing. Still, he was young, and poverty is more bearable in Paris than in most large cities.

It was in the frail arms of a very young and very pale streetwalker, whom he picked up one chilly November evening in the garden of the Palais-Royal, that the future emperor must have lost his innocence. The experience seems to have disturbed him. All his fellow officers were in love, or thought nothing of offering themselves a good time with a chance encounter. But he, Napoleon, brooded on love. He did not feel suited for love as he observed it—be it a romantic courtship or a half-hour affair—nor was this what he thought love should be. "It takes time to make oneself be loved," he remarked after he had become First Consul, "and even when I had nothing to do I always vaguely felt that I had no time to waste." He never had patience with the devious and complicated preliminaries on which women seemed to insist. Moreover, even if he should find happiness in the simple conjugal love which he never ceased to seek, would such happiness not make him unfit for greatness?

In 1794 he wrote a novel whose hero, Clisson, is quite obviously the author as he saw himself. "Clisson," he wrote, "could not accustom himself to those little formalities. His ardent imagination, his fiery heart, his severe reason, his cold intelligence could not help but be bored with the simpering of coquettes." Nevertheless, Clisson falls in love (at that time, Napoleon hoped to marry Désirée Clary, whose dowry seemed desirable); he sacrifices his future glory as a warrior; he marries, has innumerable children, and does not live happily ever after. His sudden recall to the army is not an unwelcome interruption. In war his merit finds its reward: "His name became the signal of victory. . . . He succeeded in everything." However, Clisson discovers that his wife no longer loves him. Why live? He decides to sacrifice his life in battle. "At the age of twenty-six," he writes in his farewell letter to his wife, "I have exhausted all the ephemeral pleasures of fame, but in your love I tasted the sweet sensation of human life." Needless to say, he dies gloriously on the morrow.

It is easy to smile at this; yet it was prophetic both of the author's own career and of his disenchantment with his wife Josephine. He had just won the victory at the pyramids and learned of his wife's infidelity when he wrote to his brother Joseph from Cairo: "Greatness bores me; all my feelings are dried up. Glory is stale when one is twenty-nine; I have exhausted everything." His conclusion, however, was different in 1798 from what it had been in 1794: "There is nothing left for me," he informed Joseph, "but to become really and completely selfish." The Wertherian longing for death had given way to the Napoleonic craving for power, with a supreme indifference to the risk of death, be it his own or that of others.

This, however, was in 1798; in 1787, all his feelings had not yet dried up, and he had many illusions left. Back in Corsica during the first six months of 1788, Napoleon continued his private studies and reasserted his Spartan conception of love in a curious essay entitled "Parallel Between Love of Fatherland and Love of Glory," which is addressed to an unnamed and possibly fictitious young lady. "If I had to compare the eras of Sparta and of Rome with our modern times," he declares, "I would say: 'Now men are ruled by love; then, love of the fatherland ruled them.' Considering the opposite effects produced by these two passions, it is surely permissible to believe that they are mutually incompatible."

Having made this forthright if ungallant assertion, Napoleon observes that a people entirely absorbed by eroticism (as, in his opinion, the French were) had lost even the energy needed to conceive that there could be such a thing as a patriot. Fortunately, the heroes of modern Corsica proved that there could be, even in the effeminate eighteenth century. He also shows that love of fatherland must not be confused with love of glory. The latter, which characterizes monarchic societies, often causes great men to turn against their own people, whereas love of fatherland subordinates all private ambitions to the common good, and it is characteristic of republican societies.

The distinction is identical with that drawn by Montesquieu between the principles of honor and of virtue, and the style of the composition echoes the most declamatory features of Rousseau, Diderot, and Raynal. However, whereas these writers had merely analyzed or criticized the various political systems (they regarded themselves as philosophers, not as politicians), Napoleon's essay, despite all its "philosophical" trappings, is nothing but a special plea for a special cause—his fixed idea, the independence of Corsica. The marked preference he expresses for the republican form of government should not be mistaken for an early rumble of the imminent French Revolution; as he himself was to say, he never anticipated events, he followed them. It took some rather earth-shaking events to pry him loose from his fixation on Corsica.

An eighteen-month leave with pay being about the limit of what a lieutenant could reasonably expect, Napoleon left Corsica on June 1, 1788, to return to his regiment, then stationed at Auxonne. He was to remain there for the next year and a half and thus did not witness the early phase of the Revolution in Paris. His studious tastes, sartorial neglect, patriotic zeal, and lack of cash once again saved him from the pitfalls of youth. For the first time in his life he showed some interest in purely military matters, as his several exercise books filled with notes on gunnery would seem to indicate. Indeed, excellent courses in artillery and higher mathematics were offered at Auxonne.

It was at this time that he began to write fiction. *The Earl of Essex, an English Novel* did not go beyond the first few pages, which was just as well. The most characteristic sentence in the fragment is this description of its hero: "The Earl of Essex was known for his stern morals, his austere way of life, and his strict justice. He could have said, like Cato, that since he had never forgiven himself any fault, he forgave no one." Napoleon's Corsican studies were interrupted during those eighteen months; on the other hand, his awareness of the many gaps in his general education manifested itself in several hundred pages of notes extracted from his extraordinarily varied readings. They reveal little beyond an overriding, greedy absorption of facts and ideas with scarcely a comment or personal opinion. There are notes on Plato's *Republic,* on the history of ancient Assyria, Egypt, Persia, Greece, and Carthage, on the campaigns of Frederick the Great (his first sign of interest in modern warfare), on geography (one of the notebooks ends with the words, "St. Helena, a small island"), on baron de Tott's *Memoirs of the Turks and Tartars,* on the history of the Arabs, on the government of Venice, on the liquidation of the French India Company, and on many similar subjects.

The catholicity of his note-taking is astonishing. Thus, among the bits of information extracted from a work entitled "The English Spy, or Secret Correspondence Between Lord All-Eye and Lord All-Ear," one gleans some intriguing items on the fashionable brothel which a Madame Gourdan kept for what must have been a jaded clientele, side by side with such information as "Lord North headed the English cabinet in 1775," "Boston is more than ten degrees colder than London," "Monsieur de Boulainvilliers, Provost of Paris, distilled liquor in his basement," "The rabbi Hillel maintains that a husband cannot repudiate his wife without cause, but that the least cause is sufficient, for instance if she overcooks his dinner," "After three years of war America was recognized [as an independent nation] by France in 1777."

If "The English Spy" contained interesting though not always accurate information, Buffon's *Natural History* seems a more authoritative guide to its subject; nevertheless some of the alleged facts Napoleon culled from it in his notes (thirty-seven printed pages) are quaint. Since it was not customary to tell children the facts of life, Napoleon's interest in that discipline seems only natural, even if some of the information he noted down in his scholarly zeal appears questionable: "Many African tribes have their daughters circumcised one or two weeks after birth, so large is the clitoris in those climes. . . . The Hottentots cut off

Brienne, 1780, sketched while Napoleon was enrolled there.

one of their testicles to be swifter runners." There is no end to these marvels. But with his curiosity about the facts of life Napoleon combined an interest in vital statistics: he copied the life expectancy tables which Count George Louis Leclerc de Buffon reproduced in his work.

If it had not been for the sequence of upheavals that became known as the French Revolution, Napoleon might well have remained an ambitious but frustrated artillery officer or, worse, might have turned into a mediocre author and politician. It was the Revolution that made his career possible, and it was his career that, for a long time and perhaps even now, lent some plausibility to any ambitious young man's dream of becoming a Napoleon.

In conventional historiography, the Revolution is said to have started on July 14, 1789, with the storming by the populace of the virtually undefended and untenanted prison fortress, the Bastille. Possibly the origin of this convention should be credited to the duc de La Rochefoucauld-Liancourt. When the duke apprised the king that the people had taken the Bastille, Louis XVI remarked, "Why, that is a revolt!" "Sire," replied the duke, "it is not a revolt,—it is a revolution." Actually, it was not even a revolt; it was only a big riot. The French Revolution might easily have remained the mere readjustment—a little violent, to be sure, but not cataclysmic—of an antiquated set of social conditions to modern requirements if it had not been for two closely related factors, both of which were extremely favorable to such climbers as Bonaparte.

The first of these factors was the emigration of a large part of the nobility, which began in July, 1789, and gathered momentum with every week; this emigration depleted the officers' corps of all the armed services and opened up unhoped-for prospects of rapid promotion to those officers, and even enlisted men, who remained in France. To appreciate the importance of the emigration in this respect, it is sufficient to imagine what would happen if more than half of the officers of the United States army, navy, and air force suddenly departed for the Soviet Union, or vice versa. The emigration, in turn, set off another event—the outbreak of war in the spring of 1792 between revolutionary France (by then a constitutional monarchy) and a coalition of European monarchies. With two very brief interruptions in 1802–3 and 1814–15, the war was to last for twenty-three years, seventeen of which were dominated by the figure of Napoleon. Apart from this, the outbreak of war led within a few months to the downfall of the French monarchy, to the Reign of Terror, to the complete disruption of the social fabric. It was the war which forced the revolutionists to face the stark alternative of victory against an overwhelming alliance or the annihilation of their positive accomplishments as well as their persons. It was the war which enabled Napoleon to prove his military genius, to lead the Revolution to victory, to end the Revolution, and to substitute himself for it.

Napoleon instinctively welcomed the Revolution from the beginning. Though technically a nobleman, he belonged in fact to the middle class and shared all its aspirations. He despised the society that was about to be overthrown. The language of the more radical among the leaders of the Revolution, their Rousseauan phraseology, their constant references to Sparta and to Rome, to Anacharsis and to Brutus, to virtue and to patriotism—all this could not help but strike a responsive chord in him. Yet it would be untrue to say that he embraced the French Revolution in the same sense as did the majority of Frenchmen. In his own eyes, he was not a Frenchman, and the events of the first

Louis XVI, in a liberty cap, drank with the revolutionists.

four years of the revolutionary period were reflected in his life in a peculiarly distorted way. Indeed, he persisted in viewing the tremendous upheavals taking place in France through the inverted spectacles of a Corsican nationalist: the French Revolution gave new life to the hope for Corsican independence—or, at least, self-government—and this prospect opened up unexpected opportunities for the ambitious Bonaparte family.

The details of Napoleon's political activities in Corsica from 1789 to June, 1793, are both complex and obscure, although their end result was clear and simple. Except for the period from February to September, 1791 (which he spent on duty at Auxonne and at Valence), and the period from May to September, 1792 (which he spent in Paris), he was in Corsica throughout those four fateful years. When he first arrived, the island was still untouched by the Revolution. With his brothers Joseph and Lucien (an unusually brash firebrand of fifteen) he threw himself into politics with almost reckless abandon, helped to found revolutionary clubs, and in all probability played a leading role in the uprising which forced the French governor to recognize the reforms passed by the National Assembly, which was then meeting in Paris.

As a result, the Assembly, which was in a generous mood, terminated the special military regime under which Corsica had been governed since its acquisition by France and declared the island an integral part of French territory; at the same time, on Mirabeau's motion, all Corsican exiles, including Paoli, were permitted to return. After a triumphal tour through France, where he was hailed as another Washington, General Paoli landed on Corsican soil on July 14, 1790. Louis XVI and the National Assembly had invested him with virtually dictatorial powers, both military and civil, over the island. This state of affairs was satisfactory to the sixty-five-year-old Paoli as a temporary solution, but he clung uncompromisingly to his hope of making Corsica into an independent state under the protectorate of the French or of the British crown—he did not care which.

Despite their youth, Joseph and Napoleon Bonaparte took it for granted that they would play a brilliant part in the new scheme of things—Joseph in the provincial government, Napoleon in the National Guard. Paoli, however, notwithstanding his high regard for their mother, had no use for the young men and kept them at arm's length. He did not share their revolutionary enthusiasm. They struck him as forward and ambitious, devoted to their own cause rather than to his or to Corsica's. Above all, he regarded them as too French—and, indeed, no matter how Corsican Napoleon may have felt while in France, there can be no doubt that in Corsica he was French. At the same time, Paoli was too good a politician to make outright enemies of the Bonapartes. Joseph eventually received a seat in the departmental governing council, and Napoleon managed to get himself elected a lieutenant colonel in the Corsican National Guard.

During his stay at Auxonne and Valence in 1791, Napoleon reverted to his studies and literary ambitions, no doubt for lack of something better to do. With his unfortunate essay on happiness, which he submitted to the Academy of Lyons, he seems to have got Rousseau out of his system. At any rate, all his subsequent remarks on Rousseau were hostile and derisive. He also ceased to brood over the purpose of existence. His most significant words on happiness are to be found not in the Lyons essay but in a fragment written about the same time: " . . . when a man asks himself 'Why do I exist?'—then, in my opinion, he is the most wretched of all. His machine breaks down, his heart loses the energy that is proper to man." Action, even if it does not lead to happiness, is better than introspection, which inevitably leads to wretchedness: Napoleon reached this conclusion just as he was about to throw himself into action for the next twenty-five years of his life.

The first results of action were exceedingly disappointing. Elected to his lieutenant-colonelcy after his return to Corsica, Napoleon found no employment for his talents even after war broke out in April, 1792; on the other hand, his absence from France had cost him his commission in the artillery. He left precipitately for Paris in May, to seek his reinstatement in the regular army. Despite the hostility of several of the Corsican deputies in Paris, Napoleon succeeded in straightening out his military status, was reinstated in the artillery with the rank of captain, and

received leave to serve in the Corsican National Guard. The issue of that trivial affair was regarded by the Bonaparte clan as a great victory over their enemies and rivals.

Napoleon's stay in Paris coincided with the dramatic events that led to the abolition of the monarchy and the birth of the First French Republic. On June 20 he and his former schoolmate Bourrienne were about to enter a restaurant near the Palais-Royal when they saw a mob of several thousand people armed with pikes, axes, swords, muskets, roasting spits, and sticks marching in the direction of the Tuileries Palace. The two friends decided to forego their dinner and to follow the mob to see what would happen.

The mob threw down the gates of the Tuileries gardens and with thirteen thousand National Guards standing by broke into the palace. They presented the king with two cockades—the white one of the old regime and of the army of émigrés forming in Germany, and the blue, white, and red of the Revolution—and told him to choose between them. Louis XVI, without losing his calm or dignity, chose the tricolor and placed the red bonnet of liberty on his head. This satisfied his visitors, who offered him a drink and remained in the palace for four hours. Napoleon was appalled. He had welcomed the Revolution, but he hated and despised the rabble—the *canaille,* as he called it. "The Jacobins are madmen," he wrote to Joseph. What impressed him most in the scene he had witnessed was the king's weakness. If he had been in Louis XVI's place, he would have ordered the troops to fire at the *canaille,* who would certainly have dispersed with the first volley.

The lesson was not lost on him. At the same time, foreseeing the bloody chaos that would come of this, he adopted a guarded tone in his letters to his family. Already he was aware that the political world was a jungle where a man had to eat or be eaten, and that to avoid being eaten one had to dissemble. His caution displeased his brother Lucien, then seventeen years old, who in a letter to Joseph made this remarkable comment on Napoleon's character: "I believe that a man should place himself above circumstances and commit himself to a definite choice if he wants to be something and to make a name for himself. The most hated men in history are those who sail according to the wind. . . . I have always been aware of a completely selfish ambition in Napoleone. . . . He seems to me to have the potentialities of a tyrant and I believe that he would be one if he were a king, and that his name would be held in horror by posterity." The incompatibility between the two brothers, which flared into open hostility a decade later, is clearly prefigured in Lucien's letter. Lucien, the theorist, believed that a man must have convictions and follow them regardless of circumstances. Napoleon, the opportunist, believed that "the greater a man is, the less will he must have. He depends on events and circumstances."

On August 10, 1792, Napoleon witnessed the overthrow of the monarchy. Again a mob, led by the National Guard freshly arrived from Marseilles, invaded the Tuileries. The king had fled with his family to seek asylum in the Legislative Assembly; when the Swiss Guards opened fire to defend the palace, he sent orders to cease firing. The Swiss were massacred. Napoleon, after watching the fighting from a window, entered the Tuileries gardens along with a crowd of other curiosity seekers, while the massacre was still in progress. "Never since," he reminisced at the end of his career, "has any battlefield given me the same impression of so many corpses as did the sight of the masses of dead Swiss. . . . I saw some very well-dressed ladies committing the worst indecencies on their cadavers." He wrote Joseph at the time: "If Louis XVI had shown himself on horseback, he would have won the day."

After fetching his sister from the school of St. Cyr, which the government had closed, Napoleon left for Corsica in early September, while 1,368 political prisoners, including forty-three children, were massacred by the patriots in Paris. A collective insanity seemed to have seized the nation and turned them into something worse than beasts. The princesse de Lamballe, Marie Antoinette's intimate friend, was literally torn to pieces; her head, breasts, and pudenda were paraded on pikes before the windows of the Temple, where the royal family was imprisoned, while a man boasted drunkenly at a cafe that he had eaten the princess' heart, which he probably had.

Whatever thoughts may have passed through Napoleon's mind in those days, he kept them to himself. He still regarded the social and political changes brought about by the Revolution as necessary and worth defending, hoping at the same time for the establishment of an authority strong enough to restore order and stability. He probably did not in the least suspect that he would be that authority. At St. Helena, he summed up his views on the subject in a striking manner: "General rule: No social revolution without terror. Every revolution is, by its nature, a revolt which success and the passage of time legitimize but in which terror is one of the inevitable phases. . . . The French Revolution was a nation-wide convulsion as irresistible in its effects as a volcanic eruption. . . . A revolution can be neither made nor stopped."

Upon his return to Ajaccio, Napoleon discovered that the gap between his family and the Paolists had widened. Paoli, while still paying lip service to the Revolution, secretly looked toward England, under whose protectorate he hoped to place Corsica; the Bonapartes, on the other hand, were definitely committed to the Revolution and hence to France. Napoleon expected to win his first laurels in an expedition against a group of islands off Sardinia, whose king had declared war on the French Republic—a rather futile operation which, however, had been vociferously promoted by the patriots, including Napoleon, for political rather than military reasons. The troops—the larger part of them Corsican volunteers—had been landed and Napoleon had set up his batteries, when the

commander of the expedition, Colonna Cesari, inexplicably ordered the troops to re-embark and the ships to return to Corsica. (Cesari was following Paoli's secret orders to do his utmost to prevent the force he commanded from obtaining any results.) Napoleon was outraged. He was cautious enough, however, not to accuse Paoli of outright treason. Not so Lucien who, without the knowledge of his brother, denounced Paoli to the revolutionary club at Toulon as a traitor and had the club address a resolution to that effect to the National Convention in Paris. The Convention ordered Paoli to be put on trial. The die was cast, and an eighteen-year-old hothead had cast it. It was war now between the Paolists and the partisans of the Revolution. The Paolists were decidedly in a majority, and they held all the key positions. After a desperate attempt to seize the citadel of Ajaccio by force, Napoleon had to go into hiding. However, no matter what a Corsican's political allegiance might be, he still was a Corsican and personal loyalties prevailed over political ones. The Bonapartes' goatherds guided Napoleon through the *maquis,* saved him from capture, and gave him asylum. He remembered their names in his will, in which he bequeathed considerable sums to them or their descendants.

Fleeing from place to place, Napoleon reached the seaport of Calvi, where he found refuge aboard a French warship. Meanwhile the Bonapartes' house at Ajaccio had been pillaged, and his family was in hiding. An attempt of the French squadron to bomb the citadel of Ajaccio into submission having utterly failed, the squadron sailed to Bastia, whence Napoleon rode on horseback to Calvi. There he found his family assembled—his mother, his brothers Joseph, Louis, and Jerome (who was only nine years old), and his sisters Elisa, Pauline, and Caroline. (Lucien, the unwitting cause of the family disaster, was in France.) On June 11, 1793, the family of refugees, with only such belongings as they could carry, left Calvi aboard a small coaster for Toulon, which they reached two days later.

Napoleon's expulsion from Corsica was undoubtedly the turning point in his history. Proscribed in his fatherland, stranded in a country where men had turned on each other like ferocious beasts, penniless except for his captain's pay, with a family including six minors, he faced a rather grim prospect. To suppose that in such circumstances he had the least inkling that his flight from Corsica was the first step in a career of world conquest is patently absurd. All he was concerned with was survival, and he would grasp at every opportunity to survive. It so happened that he had an unrivaled genius for seeing opportunities where others did not and for seizing them unhesitatingly, boldly, calculating the risks and taking them. In the jungle world created by the Revolution, a man could go far that way; three years after his landing at Toulon, it seemed to Napoleon that there was no limit how far. His next fourteen years were spent in seeking the limit—but he never looked farther than one step ahead.

Peering through a spyglass, Napoleon surveys the accuracy of his shore fire, aimed at the British fleet in the harbor at Toulon.

The first step after landing and finding shelter for his family was to look for employment in the artillery. Since many artillery officers had emigrated and the whole south of France was in a state of civil war, this was not difficult. He was lucky in finding General du Teil, the brother of his former commander, at Nice. Du Teil, it seems—this part of Napoleon's career is very obscure—sent him to Avignon to bring some supplies back to Nice, but Napoleon was unable to reach Avignon, which was in the hands of the insurgents. However, he came across a force commanded by General Carteaux, which had been dispatched

Napoleon asks Carteaux for fresh troops.

by the Convention to help quell the royalist insurrection in the south. He joined Carteaux, took a creditable part in the capture of Avignon, and found time to write a pro-Jacobin pamphlet, *Le Souper de Beaucaire,* his first published work. It so happened that the commander of Carteaux's artillery, Dommartin, was wounded in combat shortly before Carteaux began the siege of Toulon, which since August had been in the hands of the royalists and the Allies; it also happened that Saliceti, the Corsican representative sent by the Convention, with several colleagues, to supervise the operations in the south, had returned from Corsica and proposed that his friend and countryman, Captain Bonaparte, replace General Dommartin. There followed several months of frustration for the captain, however, during which Carteaux obstinately refused to follow Bonaparte's plan of attack. At last General Carteaux was replaced by Dugommier, Bonaparte's plan (which any other good artillery officer would also have thought of) was adopted, and Toulon fell. General du Teil recommended the young captain to the minister of war in the highest terms; so, presumably, did Saliceti in his report to the Committee of Public Safety. A couple of months later, Napoleon Bonaparte was a brigadier general. He had lost his fatherland and got rid of his illusions.

THE RISE
TO POWER

*Is it because they are lucky that
{great men} become great? No, but being great,
they have been able to master luck.*

When General Bonaparte appeared on the world stage in the spring of 1796, France was entering the fifth year of her war against the First Coalition. Like all wars, it had broken out because enough factions on both sides wanted it, each for its own purpose. In France the royalist right wanted war in the hope that Louis XVI would be restored to full authority by the Austrian and Prussian armies; the constitutional monarchists wanted it in the expectation that a victorious French army would consolidate the new regime and keep the republican left in check; the republican left (with such exceptions as Robespierre and Marat) also wanted war, which they thought, quite correctly, would afford them an opportunity to overthrow Louis XVI and establish a republic. Abroad, the French émigrés pushed for war and succeeded in convincing a number of monarchs that unless Louis XVI were restored to absolute authority, the Revolution would spread to their own territories.

What everybody wants usually comes to pass, to be regretted later. By the beginning of 1792, the majority of the French Legislative Assembly had convinced themselves that the newly formed Austro-Prussian alliance represented an aggressive interference with French internal affairs, and on April 20 Louis XVI reluctantly read out his declaration of war against his wife's nephew, Emperor Francis II. Prussia stood by its alliance with Austria, and the duke of Brunswick was given supreme command over the Allied armies—Prussian, Austrian, and French émigré. Spain, the United Netherlands, Sardinia, Naples and Sicily, England, and Portugal also acceded to the Coalition, in 1793, after the execution of Louis XVI.

The Allies opened hostilities with a self-confidence bordering on madness. France was in chaos, her army disorganized; within a few weeks the Prussians and Austrians would enter Paris and restore order. The battalions of volunteers—clerks, shopkeepers, workingmen—who had rallied to the colors in defense of the endangered fatherland would run away at the first whiff of gunsmoke; the regular army would join its émigré brothers-in-arms. Such were the Allies' delusions as they entered France, proceeding at the stately pace of eighteenth-century warfare. The results of the first border engagements seemed to justify their optimism, and the duke of Brunswick issued his famous manifesto, threatening to raze Paris if any harm befell the royal family before the Allies reached the capital.

In Paris the response to the French defeats and to Brunswick's manifesto was immediate and violent. The defeats were blamed on treason. With the help of the freshly arrived volunteers from Marseilles, whose marching

A winged lion, symbol of Venice's patron, Saint Mark, and bronze horses atop the saint's basilica, recall the glorious history of the Venetian Republic, destroyed by Napoleon in 1797.

song was to become the hymn of the Revolution, and later of France, the mob invaded the Tuileries on August 10, massacred the Swiss Guards, and toppled the monarchy. The royal family was imprisoned, along with thousands of suspected traitors (to be a traitor it was enough to be an aristocrat), many of whom were massacred on September 2. The Republic was proclaimed on September 22. Two days earlier an artillery duel at Valmy had turned the tide of the war. The cannonade of Valmy, of which Goethe, an eyewitness, remarked that it began a new epoch in world history, was not in itself a decisive engagement. What made it decisive was the duke of Brunswick's inexplicable decision to order a general retreat and the gloom it spread over the Allied camp. Perhaps the duke's order was prompted by rain, mud, and dysentery. Whatever his reasons, his action demoralized the Allies and restored the confidence of the republicans, who passed to the offensive. General Custine took Mainz and Frankfort; General Dumouriez, the victor of Valmy, routed the Austrians at Jemappes and marched to Brussels; the National Convention, which had succeeded the Legislative Assembly, proclaimed its intent to carry the Revolution to all oppressed nations.

Up to the French Revolution, the armies of Europe were small. They were officered almost exclusively by men of noble birth, and the ranks consisted of professionals serving for pay or of peasant recruits. The respectable middle classes footed the bill for the fighting but did not fight. As late as 1806 the idea of taking up arms was inconceivable to the average German burgher. The lesson of the American War of Independence had not yet been absorbed outside France. To be sure, the French volunteers would have been defeated if they had fought by themselves; but they were not fighting by themselves. The regular army, despite the emigration, was still close to the level of excellence it had reached during the 1770's and 1780's, and the volunteer units, which were eventually merged with it, soon rose to its standards of efficiency. Nevertheless, the setbacks suffered in the first half of 1793 convinced the revolutionary government that a more thorough mobilization of national resources was needed to achieve victory. On August 23 a decree of the Convention ordered a *levée en masse,* the total mobilization of France. "Young men will go to the front," it said; "married men will forge arms and transport foodstuffs; women will make tents and uniforms and serve in the hospitals; children will tear rags into lint."

If in its rhetoric the decree harks back to the war hymns of ancient Sparta, its content announces modern total war. France became an armed camp and a vast munitions factory. The economy was subordinated to the war effort by the strict enforcement of maximum price laws; forges and munitions plants sprang up everywhere under the administration of the eminent mathematician Gaspard Monge, who also invented a new method of extracting saltpeter (desperately needed for gunpowder) from the soil; and no less

than fourteen armies (about 1,500,000 men) were raised and equipped within two years. By the end of 1793 the Allies had been driven from France; in 1794 French armies occupied the Low Countries and drove across the Rhine into Germany; in 1795 Prussia, Spain, and Holland made peace with France, and the royalist insurgents in the Vendée agreed to a truce. Holland, transformed into the Batavian Republic, and Spain became allies of the French. Only England, Austria, and Sardinia remained in the field.

The republican armies won their victories—against the foreign enemy and against the counterrevolutionists at home—without paying much heed to politics. The Reign of Terror ran its course; after 9 Thermidor, when Robespierre fell, the "white terror" or "Thermidorian reaction" succeeded the red. Still, the same man—Lazare Carnot, the "organizer of victory"—continued to direct military planning in the Committee of Public Safety. The Allied commanders, on the other hand, were handicapped by the mutual distrust of their respective governments.

Among the consecrated clichés of history there is this: that the French republican armies were imbued with the spirit of patriotism and self-sacrifice, while the Allied troops were mere mercenaries of the tyrants; hence the invincibility of the French. Like most such clichés, this one contains more truth than falsehood. Needless to say, there never was any army in which those who would prefer being at home in bed did not outnumber those who found satisfaction in glorious death or discomfort. But judging from thousands of citations for individual bravery, the proportion of the latter among the French revolutionary troops was

Invading French forces plant a liberty tree in a German town.

astoundingly large. They were the first European soldiers in more than a century who could regard the cause for which they were fighting as their own, the first commoners permitted to distinguish themselves individually by such acts of personal initiative and heroism as until then had been tolerated only in the noble-born.

Unlike the stolid automata opposing them, the French citizen-soldiers were individualists. The French soldier, Napoleon remarked once, "is not a machine to be put in motion but a reasonable being that must be directed. . . . [He] loves to argue, because he is intelligent. . . . When he approves of the operations and respects his superiors, there is nothing he cannot do. But it is equally true that in the contrary case, one cannot count on victory." Shortly after his first victories in Italy, Bonaparte reported to his government: "Nothing equals the soldiers' courage unless it is the cheerfulness with which they bear up under the most exhausting marches. They sing in turn of fatherland and of love. You would think at least that on reaching the bivouacs they would want to sleep. Nothing of the sort. Everybody tells of what he has done, or else he talks about the next day's plan of operations, and often I find that they grasp things very clearly." Whatever caused the high morale among the French soldiers of the Revolution, their dash and their *élan* were at best rare among their opponents. Historians may point to many reasons, some of them far-fetched, why the French were victorious in 1794; the inescapable fact remains that the French made heroic sacrifices for their cause whereas the Allies did not.

There was, however, a significant paradox in the spirit of the French army: the longer the army fought for the preservation of the Republic, the farther it drew apart from its government. During the Reign of Terror, even those who deplored the regime preferred it to seeing France defeated by foreigners; at any rate, they could drown their doubts in the intoxication of battle and victory. After Thermidor the disunity, instability, and corruption of the civilian authorities at home led to a growing sense of detachment and independence in the armies at the fronts. More and more their allegiance went to their victorious commanders, less and less to their government, which they regarded as a gang of timeservers and shysters. The troops were the nation; they preserved the spirit of the Revolution in its purity; their hands alone were clean, for they had nothing to do with politics. Now, an army that takes a conscious stand against politicians becomes *ipso facto* a formidable political power in the hands of a leader whose chief political asset is his claim to be above politics.

While revolutionary France was struggling for survival, what was Napoleon Bonaparte doing? As has already been seen, he spent most of 1792 and half of 1793 on a partly unauthorized leave of absence, politicking in Corsica. His expulsion forced him to take notice of the fact that there was a war going on. He stumbled into the siege of Toulon,

Wounded soldiers were often billeted in the homes of the rich.

was promoted, and was given command over the artillery of the Army of Italy, which had been languishing for some time in the mountains above Nice, busying itself mainly with scrounging food. As at Toulon, he elaborated a plan of attack that won the approval of the revolutionary commissioners attached to headquarters, notably of Robespierre's younger brother Augustin. Thanks to Bonaparte's plan, it seems—there is little evidence to go by—the Army of Italy established contact with the Army of the Alps, but he reaped no rewards for this accomplishment. He had howled with the wolves and obtained Augustin Robespierre's protection, but on 9 Thermidor—July 27, 1794— another pack of wolves took over. General Bonaparte was suspended, arrested, and indicted, rather unfairly, as a terrorist. His indignant letter of protest to the Convention probably did less to secure his release than did the intervention of his patron Saliceti.

Released, he returned to the Army of Italy, which continued to starve and freeze in the mountains, but he made frequent trips to Marseilles, where his family was settled in rather straitened circumstances. His brother Joseph had married Julie Clary, the daughter of a prosperous merchant; Napoleon courted her sister Désirée—in vain, however, for Citizen Clary *père* declared that one Bonaparte in the family was enough. In May, 1795, Napoleon appeared in Paris, was assigned a command in the army fighting the Vendéan insurrection, refused it on the pretext of ill health, applied (unsuccessfully) to be attached to a military mission to Turkey, and in August found employment in the Topographical Bureau—the planning section—of the Committee of Public Safety. Judging from his letters to Joseph, he was enjoying life to the degree he was able, frequenting theatres, libraries, salons, admiring the women, and making useful connections in the gaudy, immoral society of the time, among them the influential politician

Napoleon's troops fire on the Paris mob on the steps of the Church of St. Roch to suppress a revolt against the Directory.

Paul François Barras and Barras' slightly faded mistress, the widow Josephine Beauharnais.

By this time, a new constitution had been approved by a plebiscite, from which about 90 per cent of the voters abstained. It provided for an executive consisting of five directors, elected by the two legislative chambers—the Council of Elders and the Council of Five Hundred. The members of the two chambers were elected by an indirect vote in two stages, from which the non-propertied classes were carefully excluded. The obvious purpose of the Constitution of the Year III was to keep the power in the hands of those who had it and to prevent both royalists and democrats from upsetting the *status quo.* To make sure that the royalists would not gain a majority in the impending elections, the outgoing Convention decreed that two-thirds of the candidates to the new legislature must be chosen from among the members of the old. This trick struck the royalists as a little too bald. On 12 Vendémiaire—October 4— several royalist-controlled "sections" of the Commune of Paris appeared in the streets under arms. General Jacques François Menou, the commander of the government troops in Paris, ordered them to disperse; they refused. Menou

withdrew and was promptly dismissed by the government.

In the evening of October 4, General Bonaparte was in a box of the Feydeau Theatre, watching a play, when— according to his account—friends informed him of what was happening. He instantly went to the Convention—out of sheer curiosity, he says—and took a seat in the spectators' gallery. The Convention was "extremely agitated": the Republic was in danger. Several representatives (Napoleon's account does not name them) proposed Bonaparte as the man most capable of saving the Republic, and sent for him. He affected to search his soul for half an hour, at the end of which he consented to save "the great truths of our Revolution," even if this meant shedding blood. Accordingly, the Committee of Public Safety named Barras commander in chief of the armed forces in Paris and put Barras' protégé Bonaparte in charge of the operations.

The next day, 13 Vendémiaire, shortly after four o'clock in the afternoon, two insurgent columns moved toward the Tuileries—then the seat of the government—one from the Left Bank, by way of the Quai Voltaire, the other through the Rue St. Honoré. General Bonaparte took no chances. He used his artillery, which was fired point-blank into the rebel columns; about five or six hundred people were killed or wounded, most of them on the steps of the Church of St. Roch. The Republic was saved; the new constitution went into effect; and General Bonaparte received command of the Army of the Interior. A few months later he was appointed commander in chief of the Army of Italy. The promotion seems astonishing, for little was known of him at the time except that he was a capable artillery commander, a man with a quick eye to size up a situation, and an opportunist to his finger tips. It is true that he could hardly have been less capable than General Barthélemy Schérer, whom he was to replace, but surely more positive qualifications were required. The most likely explanation is that on the eve of the 13 Vendémiaire, Bonaparte had obtained a promise from Barras that he would be given the command of an army as a reward for putting down the royalist insurrection; the Army of the Interior had given the ambitious young man too much political power, and it was more convenient for Barras to send him to Italy. Since Bonaparte's marriage with Josephine Beauharnais took place about that time, the suggestion has been made that he obtained his command as a favor for having taken her off

Gros' portrait of Josephine hung in Napoleon's bedchamber.

Barras' hands; but a man like Barras did not need a Bonaparte to help him get rid of a mistress.

At St. Helena, Napoleon once confided to General Henri Bertrand that he had married Josephine because he thought she had money. If so, this was a pity, because Josephine Beauharnais married General Bonaparte in the belief that he could pay her debts. It is true that she made him believe she was rich, but there can be no question that he was thoroughly infatuated with her. Though she was six years older than he, her body had preserved a lithe, youthful beauty that haunted his senses; that she was an ex-vicomtesse flattered him; she represented everything that was feminine and elegant. She had been married as a young girl to General Alexandre de Beauharnais, whom she bore a son, Eugene, when she was eighteen, and a daughter, Hortense, when she was twenty. The couple soon separated and was reunited in prison during the Reign of Terror. The general was guillotined; his widow was spared for a dramatic future.

Freed after Robespierre's downfall, Josephine rejoined her children (Eugene, future viceroy of Italy, had been apprenticed to a carpenter; Hortense, future queen of Holland, to a seamstress) and emerged as one of the three queens of Thermidorian society. The other two were the ever-virginal Juliette Récamier and the not so virginal Theresa Tallien, whose husband had played a decisive role in the overthrow of Robespierre. Madame Tallien shared honors with Josephine Beauharnais in being mistress to Barras, an ex-nobleman and ex-terrorist whose appetite for beautiful women, beautiful young men, and money was the only wholesome trait in his character.

General Bonaparte waged his courtship with Corsican impetuosity. Josephine was terrified of him. She was equally terrified of her creditors. What to do? She asked Barras for advice. Barras thought General Bonaparte had a future. The general was already her lover; she resigned herself to being his wife. They were married in a civil ceremony (the only kind allowed at the time) on March 9, 1796; on the certificate of marriage they made themselves respectively two years older and four years younger than they were.

Not only was the new Madame Bonaparte very seductive, but she was also very expensive. This would not have been too tragic if the general had not had a mother, four brothers, and three sisters, most of them also expensive, in addition to a wife and two stepchildren—a rather large family to maintain for a young man of twenty-six whose only income was the not too generous pay of a divisional commander. The post of commander of the Army of the Interior promised little glory and even less wealth. On the other hand, a victorious campaign abroad promised a great deal of both. Providentially, General Schérer had proved himself incompetent and was about to be recalled. Toward the end of March, 1796, the young general arrived at Nice to take over Schérer's command. Less than half a year later all Europe was astonished by the victories he had won; possibly the man who was most astonished was Barras.

The operations on the Italian front were to be part of a three-pronged offensive planned by Carnot, then one of the five Directors. General Jean Baptiste Jourdan was to strike southeast into Germany from the Low Countries; General Jean Victor Moreau, to take the offensive in southern Germany; Bonaparte, to drive the Austrians from Piedmont and Lombardy. The operations in Germany, to be commanded by two generals far more experienced than Bonaparte, held the more important places in the over-all plan. Indeed, the Army of Italy was considerably smaller than either of the others, and it was the Cinderella among the armies of the Republic. It so chanced that the new Austrian commander in Germany, Archduke Charles, although even younger than Bonaparte and subject to epileptic fits, was one of the most brilliant generals of his time. By September, 1796, he had driven both Moreau and Jourdan back to the Rhine, while Bonaparte, opposed by more plodding men, had conquered most of Italy. If Charles had won the campaign, his fame would have eclipsed Bonaparte's; but he lost the last battle.

The army Bonaparte took over from Schérer had been stagnating at the foot of the Alps for three years; its morale and its physical condition were at a nadir. One might expect that the arrival of a general twenty-six years old, 5 feet 2 inches tall, whose most decisive feat of arms had been the massacre of a few hundred civilians in the Rue St. Honoré, would do little to stir the enthusiasm of either the troops or the staff officers. But Napoleon was the kind of man who could make himself obeyed with one glance of his cold, gray eyes. He also was a man who knew how to speak to soldiers. With his electrifying proclamation to the army, made at the start of the campaign, the great adventure began: "Soldiers! You are ill-fed and almost naked. The government owes you a great deal, but it can do nothing for you. Your patience and courage do you honor but give you neither worldly goods nor glory. I shall lead you into the most fertile plains on earth. There you shall find great cities and rich provinces. There you shall find honor, glory, riches. Soldiers of the Army of Italy! Could courage and constancy possibly fail you?"

It was thus that Alexander of Macedon, or Cortez, might have addressed his men. Bonaparte's plan was to avoid the strongly fortified Alpine passes leading into Piedmont and to skirt the Alps, marching across Genoese territory. This perilous operation he carried out with extraordinary speed, beating the Austro-Sardinian forces under General Jean Pierre de Beaulieu in four successive engagements— at Montenotte, Millesimo, Dego, and Mondovi. With the French army virtually at the gates of his capital, Turin, the king of Sardinia agreed to an armistice, signed at Cherasco on April 28, while the Austrian forces fell back to protect Milan. "You have won battles without artillery," Bonaparte told his soldiers, "crossed rivers without bridges, made forced marches without shoes, and bivouacked without

liquor and often without bread. . . . only the soldiers of liberty could have endured what you endured." He also addressed the Italian nation: "Peoples of Italy! The French army comes to break your chains. The French nation is the friend of all nations; receive us with trust! Your property, your religion, your customs will be respected. We shall wage war like generous enemies, for our only quarrel is with the tyrants who have enslaved you." Two years later, he would tell the same thing to the Egyptian population, with equal lack of candor.

His next objective was Milan, the seat of the Austrian governor of Lombardy. Beaulieu, a man in his seventies, prepared its defense according to the rules of eighteenth-century warfare. But General Bonaparte did not play the game according to the rules. His formula for victory was simple: other things being more or less equal, victory belongs to the general who has numerical superiority at a place and time of his choosing. Throughout his Italian campaign Bonaparte's forces were inferior to the combined forces of the Austrians. However, the Austrians kept their forces divided, whereas Bonaparte kept his together, out-marched the enemy, and defeated him piecemeal. His capacity for action knew no limits, and he was able to obtain from his men such records of endurance as no one else thought possible. By May 10, 1796, his army had turned Beaulieu's defensive line, bypassed Milan to the south, and without pausing for rest, defeated Beaulieu at Lodi, on the Adda. Five days later the French entered Milan amidst the acclaim of the jubilant population.

"My life here is inconceivable," Bonaparte wrote to the Directors shortly after the start of the campaign. "I arrive tired, I must stay up all night for administrative work, and I must go everywhere in person to restore order. The ill-fed soldiers let themselves go to excesses of cruelty that make one blush for being a man. . . . I shall make some terrifying examples of the looters. Either I shall restore order or I shall cease to command these bandits." Looters were shot by the dozens, but even more effective in restoring discipline and morale were the victories and their material rewards. Unlike the troops opposing them, the French had a personal stake in victory. Defeat to them meant starvation, rags, and misery; victory meant food, cash, clothes, women, and wine.

When the French entered Milan, they were still in rags. Stendhal, in his *Memoirs of Napoleon,* cites the example of three officers who owned among them but one pair of presentable shoes, taken from a dead Austrian officer, and two other officers who shared one pair of breeches and three shirts between them; the one who happened to be without breeches disguised his want by buttoning up his riding coat. In such attire the French presented themselves at La Scala, on the Corso, in the cafes, in the drawing rooms; and the ladies, who were beautiful, adored them. The French were young and flushed with victory; they were, says Stendhal, "amiable, gay, and very enterprising. If the Milanese were mad with enthusiasm, the French officers were mad with happiness . . . " It must be said that the capture of Milan marked the high point of the Italian campaign. After that, the happiness of the soldiers diminished somewhat, and the enthusiasm of the Italians cooled even more.

Napoleon was never a man to give himself or his troops much rest. A few days at Milan were enough for him to set up—without his government's authorization—a provisional republican government for Lombardy and to levy war contributions staggering enough to sober up the liberated Italians. He promised the cash-starved Directory twenty million gold francs, to be levied in Italy. (This was far less than he actually raised.) Soon the troops were paid in hard cash, and their appearance became more prosperous. The army's treasury was bursting with gold, and fabulous fortunes were amassed by some of the subordinate generals as well as by the civilian contractors in charge of the army's supplies, hospitals, and other services. The assertion that Bonaparte himself had no share in the profiteering is essentially but not entirely true. Although he sent his whole pay to his wife, he was quite well-to-do at the end of a campaign that he had begun virtually without a penny in his pocket. General Louis Desaix, who saw him in Italy in 1797, noted in his diary: "He is very rich, as well he might be, since he draws on a whole country's revenues. . . . He believes neither in probity nor in decency. He says all this is foolishness."

It had been Bonaparte's plan to pursue the Austrians into the Tyrol; the Directory, however, insisted on his swerving south to threaten on various pretexts the Grand Duchy of Tuscany, the Duchies of Modena and Parma, the Papal States, and Naples. The purpose of this operation was only partly military and political; the main objective was simply loot. Bonaparte's southern excursion (it can hardly be called a campaign) took less than a month. In July he was back in Milan, before the Austrian army under Field Marshal Dagobert von Wurmser, dispatched to drive him back, had had time to reach Lombardy. Naples, though the most distant of Bonaparte's objectives, was the first to request an armistice, according to the terms of which it had to withdraw its fleet from the Coalition. The duke of Parma bought neutrality for two million francs in cash; the duke of Modena, for seven hundred fifty thousand, and several millions' worth of art treasures. The Papal Legations of Bologna and Ferrara came next. Pope Pius VI paid twenty-one million francs to dissuade the French from advancing to Rome. The horses, equipment, arms, ships, foodstuffs, and munitions obtained under the armistice agreements amounted to several more millions. Most spectacular, however, was the looting of cultural treasures, supervised by a six-man "Governmental Commission for the Research of Artistic and Scientific Objects in Conquered Countries." (Its two most eminent members were the chemist Claude Berthollet and the mathematician and physicist Monge.) The cash value in terms of mid-twentieth-century prices of the treasures carried off to Paris would be in the order of nine or ten digits; even in the 1790's, it must be evaluated at several tens of millions of dollars. To keep one single Correggio, the duke of Modena offered a million francs, without success.

Although Bonaparte had announced to the Directory as early as May, 1796, that Italy was in French hands, the Austrians thought otherwise and sent fresh armies into the Lombard plain, while Bonaparte received no appreciable reinforcements. Despite his brilliant victories at Castiglione in August and at Arcole in November, he was unable to obtain the capitulation of the key fortress of Mantua, where Wurmser had locked himself up, until his decisive victory in the three-day Battle of Rivoli in January, 1797. Bonaparte did not wait to accept the aged field marshal's surrender in person but dashed south with part of his forces to invade the Papal States once again, this time on the pretext that the pope had violated the armistice of June, 1796. On February 15 the emissaries of Pius VI, whose troops had done more running than fighting, signed the Treaty of Tolentino, by which the pope surrendered his claims to Bologna, Ferrara, and the Romagna and agreed to pay an indemnity of thirty million francs, in addition to a treasure worth seven million captured by the French during the fighting.

Having accomplished this exploit in three weeks' time, Bonaparte began his march north through the Alps, while Archduke Charles, with his somewhat inferior army, advanced south to head him off. The French victory at the Tagliamento, though indecisive, forced Charles to fall back. On March 30 Bonaparte was at Klagenfurt, virtually at the gates of Vienna. The advocates of continued resistance in the Austrian capital had to give in to the peace party, and on April 18, at Leoben, Bonaparte —who had no authority to do so—signed a preliminary peace treaty with the Austrian plenipotentiaries. The terms granted to Austria, which in their main features were incorporated into the final treaty, were very generous. Indeed, both Napoleon and the Austrian negotiators were fully aware of the precarious position in which he had placed his army: he might take Vienna, but the Austrians' resources were far from being exhausted whereas the French were in danger of being cut off from their bases. Nevertheless, the terms granted to France were equally generous; and such mutual generosity was made possible by the understanding that the peace would be made at the expense of a third party, the Republic of Venice.

Bonaparte's Italian policy has been called statesmanlike by some and cynical by others; it is a quarrel over synonyms. He encouraged hopes for Italian independence by creating the provisional Cispadane and Transpadane Republics, but

While traveling to join Napoleon's army, Josephine and her retinue are attacked by Austrian cannon on the shores of Lake Garda.

at the same time he avoided giving them any guarantees and kept a free hand to deal with them as he pleased when peace was negotiated. "The Italian people . . . is ill-suited for freedom," he confided to a correspondent.

Up to the spring of 1797, Bonaparte had found it convenient to maintain the fiction of the neutrality of the Venetian Republic, despite the fact that the campaign was fought in part on Venetian territory. As early as June, 1796, however, he wrote to the Directory: "If it is your intention to extract five or six millions from Venice, I have provided just the rupture you need for the purpose . . . If your intentions go beyond this, I think we ought to keep this opportunity for dissension alive." In the Preliminary Peace of Leoben, he hid not scruple to award the larger part of Venetian territory to Austria, in exchange for the Austrian Netherlands (modern Belgium). A few days later, the news of the massacre of several hundred French soldiers and civilians by a mob in Verona offered a greedily seized pretext for making war on Venice. "We want blood," he wrote to the Directors. On May 16 French troops occupied Venice. The terms of surrender provided for the usual indemnities in cash and art treasures;

the Titians, the Tintorettos, and the bronze horses of St. Mark's were carted off to Paris; the battleships, cannon, and stores in the Arsenal were confiscated; the tree of liberty was erected in St. Mark's Square; and the aristocratic government fell, after centuries of Byzantine pomp and splendor, with a dull thud.

The Franco-Austrian peace negotiations dragged on from month to month. The Austrians' delaying tactics were motivated by their knowledge that a royalist conspiracy to unseat the French government was afoot. On the other hand, Bonaparte was loath to break off negotiations, despite —or rather, because of—the fact that Moreau's army had begun to advance victoriously in Germany: a break would deprive him of the opportunity to negotiate *his* peace. However, he played a decisive part in foiling the royalist plot. A royalist agent had been arrested by the French at Trieste in June; among his papers were documents implicating in the conspiracy General Charles Pichegru, one of the most distinguished French commanders. Bonaparte sent the evidence on to Barras, who welcomed it as an instrument for getting rid of his fellow Directors Carnot and François Barthélemy, both of them sympathetic to the rightist groups. Not only did he furnish Barras with the pretext for the coup d'état of 18 Fructidor (September 4), which crushed the rightist opposition; he also guaranteed the support of his army and dispatched one of his subordinates, General Pierre Augereau, to Paris to command the troops that carried it out. Carnot and Pichegru escaped abroad; Barthélemy, some fifty rightist deputies, and several newspaper editors were deported to Guiana, where most of them died. There was no more reason for the Austrians to hope for a royalist take-over in France, and negotiations were speedily concluded.

The Treaty of Campoformio, signed on October 17 by Bonaparte for France and by Count Ludwig von Cobenzl for Austria, yielded the entire left bank of the Rhine to France; since some of that territory did not belong to Austria, a congress was to be called at Rastatt to discuss a general peace with the states of the Holy Roman Empire. France also yielded what was not hers; the entire Venetian Republic east of the Adige, including the Dalmatian coast (except Corfu and the other Ionian Islands) went to Austria. The islands—already occupied by Bonaparte's forces—went to France. The Cisalpine Republic, which Bonaparte had patched together out of the provisional Transpadane and Cispadane Republics and the Romagna, was recognized by Austria. Both France and Austria had reasons to be satisfied. Feelings among the Italian patriots were divided. The creation of the Cisalpine Republic gave them a state of sorts, and most of the liberals in the government, Count Melzi at their head, threw in their lot with French interests; others, especially in Venetia, felt not without cause that their liberator had sold them out.

It was only after his victory at Lodi, Napoleon declared at St. Helena, that he conceived the first ideas of high ambition. "From that moment, I foresaw what I might be. Already I felt the earth flee from beneath me, as if I were being carried into the sky." When he returned to Paris in December, 1797, he was much more than a victorious general. He had created a new state, opened the gates to the Levant, changed the map of Europe from Belgium to Greece, and from a distance of several hundred miles played a decisive part in a coup d'état that brought him several steps closer to supreme power. Already he acted by instinct as if he owned the world. Already he viewed mankind with contempt; already mankind looked up to him as the hero of centuries.

It would be an exaggeration to say that General Bonaparte was universally acclaimed. Men who, like Count Cobenzl, had come into close contact with him had observed with a sense of shock that the courteous general could be a brutal fellow; nor had his unscrupulous ambition escaped the observation of many of his associates and superiors. But to the liberal public, not only in France but throughout Europe, Bonaparte was the youthful hero, a pure and bright promise after the horrors and disillusionments of the Revolution and its sequels. As a general, he was invincible; as a victor, he was generous. His sword brought liberty with peace and order. His ascent seemed to symbolize the advent of youth, which would sweep away the cobwebs and decay of Europe. His victories and statesmanship had made the Revolution respectable again; or as he put it in St. Helena: "We have drowned its earlier shame in floods of glory." In the public imagination of Europe, the picture of the bestial sans-culotte dripping with blood was gradually replaced by that of the lean, eagle-faced young Corsican.

In Paris, upon his return, the general was given a triumphal reception. The National Institute (which had replaced the French Academy) elected him a member of its Mathematical Section, where he would sit side by side with such colleagues as Pierre Laplace, Joseph Lagrange, and Monge, even though his studies in mathematics appear to have stopped at trigonometry. The Directors, in full regalia, welcomed him solemnly in the court of the Luxembourg Palace, where an altar to the fatherland, decorated with captured flags, had been erected. Bonaparte appeared in simple uniform. Talleyrand, the foreign minister, made the welcoming speech. "Ah! far from fearing what some would call his ambition," he said of Bonaparte, "I feel that the time will come perhaps when we must tear him away from his studious retreat." Indeed, since his election to the National Institute, Bonaparte had been speaking of withdrawing to a country retreat and devoting himself to a life of studies. Modesty seemed the proper attitude to take at the time.

Actually, even before leaving Italy, Bonaparte had accepted his appointment as commander in chief of the Army of England—that is, the forces then being concentrated along the Channel coast for the purpose of invading the British Isles. Whether he ever seriously believed that the project could be realized is doubtful; in any event, after a brief inspection tour early in 1798, he reported to the Directory that the means at his disposition were utterly inadequate (which was true) and proposed several alternative courses of action, among them the possibility of seizing Egypt in order to strike at Britain's possessions in India.

The project of seizing Egypt for France was not new. Louis XV's foreign minister, the duc de Choiseul, had proposed it as early as 1769. Egypt, Choiseul thought, would compensate France for the loss of her American colonies. French settlers would diversify Egypt's crops by introducing indigo, cotton, and sugar cane; a canal would be cut through the Isthmus of Suez, bring about a revolution in world trade, and give France a stranglehold over the India route. Choiseul's successor, the comte de Vergennes, shelved the plan, since he opposed on principle any curtailment of the territorial integrity of the Ottoman Empire, France's oldest ally, of which Egypt was a part.

Nevertheless, a number of Foreign Office and consular officials continued to study the project in the following decades, and their memoranda were filed away for possible future use. The Ottoman Empire, they pointed out, was breaking up; if France did not secure her share in time, Russia and Austria would swallow up the whole. Egypt really belonged to nobody, since the sultan's authority over it was virtually nil. The beys who governed it were subjecting the French merchants to all manner of vexations; armed intervention to protect French rights and interests would be justified. Militarily, the operation was easy; a few thousand troops would suffice.

In April, 1797, a few days before signing the Preliminary Peace of Leoben, General Bonaparte had an interview with Raymond Verninac, the French envoy to Constantinople, who was on his way to Paris. Verninac carried in his baggage two detailed reports on the advantages of seizing Egypt and on the best methods of going about it. In the months following, Bonaparte's preoccupation with Venetian affairs directed his imagination toward the East. France must hang on to the Ionian Islands at all costs, he wrote to the Directory and to Talleyrand; France should also seize Malta; and "the day is not far off when we shall appreciate the necessity to seize Egypt, in order really to destroy England."

It was Talleyrand, however, rather than Bonaparte, who persuaded the Directory to adopt the Egyptian scheme. The moment seemed opportune: England had withdrawn her fleet from the Mediterranean in 1796, and the Continent was at peace. (At any rate, France had been able, in the early months of 1798, to overrun with impunity the Swiss Confederation and the Papal States and to transform them into the puppet Helvetic and Roman Republics, without any power coming to the aid of either.) No time was lost. On March 5 Bonaparte submitted his plan for the conquest of Malta and Egypt to the Directory; on May 19 the expedition began. The main convoy left from Toulon, to be joined by three other convoys, from Genoa, Ajaccio, and Civitavecchia. Together the armada consisted of almost four hundred ships, including thirteen ships of the line, and covered from two to four square miles when on the open sea. Aboard were about 34,000 land troops (for the most part veterans of the Army of Italy), 16,000 sailors and marines, and at least 1,000 civilian personnel, including administrative officials and the 167 members of the Scientific and Artistic Commission. Also aboard was a treasury of 4,608,908 francs—just about enough to meet the army's payroll for four months. (Of this fund, 3,000,000 francs had been confiscated from the treasury of Berne.) Obviously, the Directory expected Egypt to pay for the expense of being conquered, just as Italy had.

In sending this armada to Egypt, the Directory was undoubtedly pleased to have found distant employment for a politically ambitious general and his obstreperously Jacobin troops. Bonaparte, on the other hand, saw in the Orient a field of activity worthy of his genius. "Europe is a molehill," his secretary Bourrienne quotes him as saying. " . . . Everything here wears out; my glory is already past. This tiny Europe does not offer enough of it. We must go to the Orient; all great glory has always been acquired there." Did he really think of conquering India as well as Egypt, as Bourrienne asserts? He may well have dreamed of that possibility—but he knew for a certainty that a few victories in Egypt would prove useful to his ambitions after his return to France.

The preparations for the campaign were completed with the utmost haste and secrecy. The fact that a huge fleet was being fitted out at Toulon could not escape the British government; however, the French government, by leaking contradictory information to the press, managed very adroitly to confuse the British. Twelve days after the French fleet had left Toulon, William Pitt, the British prime minister, still believed that its destination was Ireland; many others thought it was England, and an invasion hysteria swept the country. To be on the safe side, the British Admiralty dispatched a squadron to the Mediterranean, with the mission of finding and destroying the French fleet. Its commander was Admiral Sir Horatio Nelson.

Bonaparte's first objective was Malta, held since 1530 by the Knights of St. John of Jerusalem, or Knights Hospitalers, a military and religious order consecrated to the profitable task of raiding Moslem shipping. Its great days were past, and in 1798 only some three hundred knights (most of them French) were left on the island. On June 12, after a day's token fighting, the knights surrendered the island to the French Republic in exchange for lifetime pensions. Bonaparte set up a provisional government, established a garrison, liberated the Turkish and Moorish galley slaves, ransacked the Arsenal, and removed from the Church of St. John about six million francs' worth of treasures. This done, the armada sailed on June 19 for its next destination, Alexandria.

Two days before Bonaparte's fleet left Malta, Admiral Nelson's fourteen ships of the line anchored in the Bay of Naples. The British minister, Sir William Hamilton, suggested that the French might be off Malta. Nelson set off in hot pursuit, guessing the destination of the French to be Egypt. Sailing at twice the speed of the slow French convoy, he unwittingly passed it at a few miles' distance during the foggy night of June 22-23. From then on, the unsuspecting quarry trailed the impetuous pursuer. On June 29, in the morning, Nelson was off Alexandria and found no sign of the French; he left the same day, in the direction of Crete; the same evening, the French frigate *La Junon,* sent ahead of the main fleet by Bonaparte, anchored off Alexandria and took aboard the French consul. Two days later—July 1—the entire French armada arrived in sight of the city. The people ashore, says an

A medal struck to commemorate Napoleon's command in Italy

Arabic chronicler, "when they looked at the horizon, could no longer see water but only sky and ships; they were seized by unimaginable terror."

The weather had been fairly rough during most of the six-week crossing. The troops were almost all seasick, squeezed together like cattle, and reduced during the last lap of the journey to eating rotten salt meat and wormy biscuit, and drinking fetid water. Most of them could not swim; none had been trained in landing operations; nobody had thought of equipping them with such elementary necessities as water flasks. Bonaparte, informed by the French consul at Alexandria that Nelson's fleet had just left, ordered an immediate disembarkment, before Nelson had a chance to return, on the treacherous coast west of Alexandria. Sick, starving, exhausted, the troops spent more than twelve hours landing during a stiff gale. Shortly after midnight, without artillery, they began their march on the city. By 11 A.M. they had taken Alexandria. Had they not done so, they would have died of thirst. Two days later, with most of the equipment not yet unloaded, the army began its march to Cairo.

The troops had been told that they would find villages, food, and water; instead, they found only desert, ruined hovels, mirages, sandstorms, and cisterns filled in by the Bedouins. At one well thirty men were trampled to death in a stampede for a few drops of brackish water. Stragglers were mutilated and killed by the ever-present Bedouins. Scores of men lost their wits and shot themselves. In vain did Generals Desaix and Jean Louis Reynier, who commanded the vanguard divisions, plead with Bonaparte for rations, medicine, and draft animals; all he sent them was reams of his proclamation to the Egyptians. The entire army was seized by a sense of despair and abandonment

that never quite left it throughout its stay in Egypt.

By July 11 all the French forces save the garrisons left at Alexandria and Rosetta were assembled at El Rahmaniya, on the Nile. The sight of the river drove the men mad with joy. Some stayed in it for hours; some died from a surfeit of water. After two days' rest the army resumed its march to meet the enemy at the village of Shubra Khit.

Who was the enemy? The Mamelukes, the troops had been told, but they hardly knew who the Mamelukes were. The Mamelukes (the word means "bought men" in Arabic) were a warrior caste that had ruled, or rather misruled, Egypt since the middle of the thirteenth century. Originally imported from the Caucasus as young slaves by the Ayubite sultans of Egypt to serve them as soldiers, they soon overthrew the dynasty and set up their own. When the Ottoman sultan Selim I conquered Cairo in 1517, Egypt became nominally a Turkish province governed by a pasha, but the actual government remained in the hands of twenty-four Mameluke beys, or princes, and their *kachefs,* or subgovernors. It was they who held virtually the entire cultivated land in military fee and collected the rent from the fellahin, or peasants. Out of their huge revenues they paid a fraction to the pasha of Cairo, who sent it on to Constantinople as tribute. At times they ceased paying tribute altogether until the sultan sent an army to reason with them.

All in all, there were about ten thousand Mamelukes in Egypt. Although they imported wives, mainly from Georgia and Circassia, and had innumerable concubines of every race and color, they rarely produced offspring and down to the last man practiced homosexuality. To replenish themselves they bought boys nine to ten years old—mostly from Georgia and Armenia, though there was a sprinkling of Russians, Germans, Greeks, and Negroes among them— and brought them up as warriors. Each Mameluke was a

Entering the town of Bassano, French troops routed an Austrian army. OVERLEAF: *A pontoon bridge thrown across the Adige allowed Napoleon to battle the Austrian army at Arcole, on ground of his own choosing.*

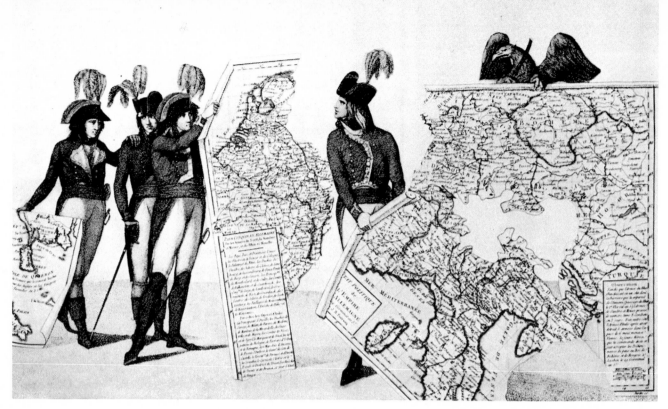

France's victorious generals, Hoche, Moreau, Pichegru, and Bonaparte, display maps of lands conquered by the revolutionary armies.

mounted one-man arsenal and had at least two servants-at-arms on foot. His usual equipment consisted of a musket, a brace of pistols, several javelins, a scimitar of damascene steel, and an assortment of battle-axes, maces, and daggers. Nothing exceeded his courage except his arrogance, ignorance, cruelty, and greed. For a long time the only enemy the Mamelukes had fought was their Turkish overlords, but they kept themselves in practice by fighting each other, the beys being chronically engaged in a struggle for supreme power. At the time of the French invasion that power was held jointly by Ibrahim Bey, who governed Cairo, and by Murad Bey, who controlled the customs receipts and resided at Giza.

Even before landing, Bonaparte had caused to be printed aboard his flagship *L'Orient* a proclamation to the Egyptian people, in Arabic. The French, he declared in flowery language, came as friends and liberators and as allies of His Majesty the Sultan (may God perpetuate his rule!) to punish the Mameluke tyrants. "Henceforth, with God's help, no Egyptian shall be excluded from high office. . . . Those who are the most intelligent, educated, and virtuous shall govern, and thus the people shall be happy." Religion and property, he promised, would be protected.

Bonaparte's assertion that the French came with the blessings of the sultan was not a deliberate lie. It had been agreed before Bonaparte left Paris that Talleyrand would go in person to Constantinople in order to explain to the Sublime Porte why the French occupation of its richest province should be regarded as a friendly and helpful action. Perhaps Talleyrand could have persuaded

the sultan to accept his point of view if he had gone; but he never went, and when another ambassador was appointed in September, Turkey had already declared war on France. These developments Bonaparte could not foresee. At the time he was marching to Cairo, he had no reason to expect that he would have to fight any enemies other than the Mamelukes.

At daybreak of July 13 there burst upon the weary French army simultaneously the sound of the *Marseillaise* and the sight of the Mameluke cavalry—some three or four thousand of them—supported by about ten thousand men on foot. The French drew in their breath with astonishment. General Nicolas Desvernois, who was at that time a mere lieutenant, recalled the moment in his *Memoirs:* "In the background, the desert under the blue sky; before us, the beautiful Arabian horses, richly harnessed, snorting, neighing, prancing gracefully and lightly under their martial riders, who are covered with dazzling arms, inlaid with gold and precious stones. Their costumes are brilliantly colorful; their turbans are surmounted by aigret feathers, and some wear gilded helmets. . . . This spectacle produced a vivid impression on our soldiers by its novelty and richness. From that moment on, their thoughts were set on booty."

With all its dash and glitter, the Mameluke cavalry was devoid of discipline or method; as for the foot soldiers, they could be discounted altogether. The combat at Shubra Khit set the pattern for all future encounters. The French divisions formed in squares several ranks deep and waited for the attack. The Mameluke cavalry charged with incredible speed and fearlessness, trying now this, now that side of the squares, only to be repulsed by a murderous point-blank fire of musketry, grapeshot, and cannon balls, and eventually sped off, leaving the foot soldiers to fend for themselves. Thus, though invariably defeated when they gave battle, they were never caught.

The painful march was resumed immediately. On July 21, at 2 P.M., during the worst heat of the day, the French reached Embaba, on the left bank of the Nile opposite Cairo and ten miles north of the pyramids of Giza, which loomed in the haze. Here Murad Bey's army was awaiting them, supported by some Turkish regulars (mostly Albanians) who had entrenched themselves in a strong position at Embaba. Another army, under Ibrahim Bey, was waiting on the right bank but never had a chance to join in the battle. After only one hour's rest, Bonaparte ordered his divisions to advance, hoping to cut off Murad's retreat. As at Shubra Khit, the Mamelukes charged swiftly and wildly for about one hour, then fled south. Several hundred of them, cut off from the rest, withdrew to the fortified position but were thrown into the Nile, where most of them drowned. The Albanian infantry and artillery was cut down in a frightful carnage. That night Bonaparte slept at Murad Bey's country house in Giza, while his army sorted out the fabulous loot left on the battlefield. Murad retreated south; Ibrahim Bey, taking the Turkish pasha with him, fled with his army toward Syria.

To dramatize the event, Bonaparte chose to call the battle at Embaba the Battle of the Pyramids. According to him, the enemy's strength was seventy-eight thousand men, or three times his; actually, it must have been equal or inferior to the French. Before the battle, he says, he addressed to his troops the famous words, as he pointed to the pyramids, "Soldiers, forty centuries look down upon you." There was no occasion when he could have addressed his entire army, but he may have said something of the sort to some officers standing near him. The victory was not decisive, since the larger part of the enemy forces escaped intact, with their leaders; but the report of it in Europe and America, coupling Bonaparte's name with the magic of the pyramids, produced an impression worth several great victories. Almost overnight in Europe, and ultimately in America, all things Egyptian became the rage and Bonaparte's prestige rose to new heights.

Bonaparte entered Cairo on July 24. One week later, in the early afternoon of August 1, Admiral Nelson and his squadron discovered the French fleet at anchor in Abukir Bay. Despite the late hour, he ordered an immediate attack, thus catching the French commander, Admiral François Brueys, with one-third of his crew on shore. Nevertheless, Brueys' position was very strong—thirteen battleships extending in a mile-long line and presenting more than five hundred guns toward the sea. It would have been stronger still had Brueys anchored his ships closer to shore. Defying the shoals, several of the British ships bearing down on the French managed to turn the head of the French line and to attack it from the shoreside; others maneuvered into positions between the French ships. Within a couple of hours the ships of the French van and center, with the British guns blazing at them within pistol range, were so many floating shambles, while the rear, under Admiral Pierre Villeneuve, stood by inactive. Brueys was wounded early in the battle but refused to leave the bridge; soon after, a cannon ball carried away his thigh and killed him. About the same time, Nelson received a severe head wound.

The battle reached its climax about ten at night, when Brueys' flagship, the huge L'Orient, caught fire and blew up with an explosion that shook the shore within a fifteen-mile radius. For ten minutes the thousand guns of the two belligerents fell silent; then the battle recommenced and did not cease until two o'clock the following afternoon. Eleven French battleships had been captured or destroyed; two others, and two frigates, managed to escape. About seventeen hundred French sailors, including one admiral and three captains, had been killed. What happened in the inferno of the explosion to Captain Louis Casabianca of L'Orient and his ten-year-old son—the boy who stood on the burning deck—nobody could tell for sure; not a shred was found of either, and the official reports are no more explicit than Mrs. Hemans' slightly confused poem. But there could be no doubt that the Battle of the Nile—as Nelson chose to call it rather fancifully—had cut off Bonaparte's army from the homeland.

On August 19 Nelson departed from Abukir Bay, leaving behind a small cruising squadron to blockade the Egyptian coast. Bonaparte's first reaction to the disaster was, in essence, to shrug it off and to blame it—quite unfairly—on Brueys. True, the army was now cut off, but it was intact; it would double its efforts and establish itself permanently in Africa and perhaps even in Asia.

To Nelson it seemed that with the destruction of its fleet the position of the French army in Egypt was hopeless in the long run. The larger part of the French army shared this belief, and so, especially, did the highest ranking officer after Bonaparte, General Kléber. In retrospect historians must adopt the same position, but in the circumstances such as he knew them in 1798 Bonaparte had good reasons for refusing to regard himself as doomed. The British blockade was not completely effective. With a little good will the Directory could maintain regular communications with Bonaparte and even send occasional reinforcements and supplies. Another fleet might be fitted out. He still believed that Talleyrand had gone to Constantinople and that Turkey would remain neutral. In fact, anything might happen and change the situation for the better—and at worst his presence in Egypt would have considerable nuisance value when a peace with England was eventually negotiated. All these hopes, though reasonable, turned out to be illusory. With the destruction of its fleet, the French army in Egypt was doomed.

The Battle of the Nile had wide repercussions. In September, yielding to English and Russian pressure, Sultan Selim III declared war on France. Czar Paul of Russia, who had declared war after the French seizure of Malta, now was able to send his Black Sea fleet into the Mediterranean and to seize, after a long naval siege, Corfu and the other French-held Ionian Islands. King Ferdinand of Naples, emboldened by Nelson's victory and encouraged by Nelson personally, attacked the French forces in Italy; it was only a matter of time before Austria joined the new anti-French coalition. In Ireland the uprising of the United Irishmen, inadequately supported by French units, was crushed; this defeat, combined with the loss of its Mediterranean fleet, determined the Directory to abandon the idea of invading the British Isles and to employ the Army of England to fight the Vendéan royalists, who had risen once more. In fact, the entire plan of which the expedition to Egypt was a vital part had gone awry. Bonaparte was not informed of all this until several months later; even then, for some time, he pretended not to know it.

Bonaparte received the news of the destruction of his fleet on August 13, 1798; he left Egypt to return to France one year and one week later. The intervening period, despite all its dramatic happenings and heroic accomplishments, may be characterized as a year of make-believe. He made believe that he controlled Egypt, when in fact he never controlled more than Cairo and a few other key cities. In the rest of the country his troops, unless operating in large numbers, were constantly exposed to ambushes and massacres by Bedouin tribes and by embattled peasants. He made believe that he was in Egypt with the approval of the sultan for three months after the sultan had declared war and vowed his destruction. He set up divans, or local governing councils, in Cairo and in the provincial capitals, but the function of the divans was to serve as buffers between the French administration and the population rather than to govern. He encouraged the sheiks of the Divan of Cairo to believe that he and his army were about to embrace Islam and that his coming had been predicted in the Koran; the sheiks did not believe a word of it, but they dutifully passed on the good word in their proclamations to the populace, which did not believe it either. In October, 1798, when the people of Cairo, led by some fanatics, rose in rebellion, he magnanimously forgave the sheiks of the Divan, who had had no part in it, and at the same time wrote to one of his generals: "Every night we have about thirty heads chopped off, many of them belonging to the ringleaders. This I believe will serve them as a good lesson."

In his financial make-believe General Bonaparte displayed true virtuosity. The treasury was chronically empty, the soldiers were not always paid, but he somehow made

do by forced loans, pledging anticipated customs receipts, pawning the revenues of crops not yet sown, farming out tax collection, exacting special contributions from the merchant communities, levying fines, and confiscating property on an infinite variety of pretexts. All the same, when he departed in 1799 he left his successor, Jean Baptiste Kléber, in the red by twelve millions. His army, almost to a man, was seized by an epidemic of homesickness and despair; almost one-third of his forces was afflicted with the Egyptian eye disease; a goodly proportion contracted syphilis and gonorrhea; all were bored and short of wine and liquor; and in December bubonic plague made its appearance. Yet to the Directory he wrote: "We lack nothing here. We are bursting with strength, good health,

and high spirits." And when the plague struck in earnest, he made believe that it was just "a fever with buboes" and would go away if manfully ignored. He was cut off, abandoned by his government, losing strength every day, faced with a hostile population, and ringed by enemies. To maintain such fictions in the teeth of such realities borders either on true heroism or on sheer madness.

By January, 1799, Bonaparte could no longer blink the fact that the sultan had declared war, since a Turkish army was preparing to invade Egypt through Syria. He resolved to head off the Turks, conquer Syria—that is, modern Israel, Jordan, Syria, and Lebanon—perhaps even to recruit an army composed of Christian Arabs and Druses and then march on to Constantinople. Later in his life, in his conversations and memoirs, he suggested that he might have marched as far as India and founded an Asiatic empire; it is quite likely that he had such dreams even in 1799, but he must have realized the inadequacy of his means, and his objectives for the time being were probably more limited.

The Syrian expedition was hastily prepared and ill supplied. At first all went well. Jaffa fell after a brief one-day siege, some two thousand soldiers of the Turkish garrison were put to the sword, and the town was sacked in an orgy of rape and murder. Two or three thousand Turks who held out in the citadel surrendered the next day on the promise that their lives would be spared; in the course of the three days following, they were taken to the beach and shot, bayoneted, or drowned. "Among the victims," says a French eyewitness, "we found many children, who in the act of death had clung to their fathers." The nauseating massacre had been ordered by Bonaparte personally: there was not enough food to feed the prisoners. (It is true that only a few days before the capture of Jaffa, the French had been reduced to eating their horses and camels, and that what food they found in Syria was just enough for themselves.)

The massacre was still in progress when Bonaparte summoned the pasha of Acre, a ferocious old man who called himself Djezzar ("the Butcher"), to surrender to the French and trust their mercy. "Since God gives me victory," Bonaparte wrote, "I wish to follow his example and be merciful and compassionate, not only toward the people but also toward the rulers." No sooner had this blasphemy been uttered than the plague in the French army struck with redoubled violence.

The fortress of Acre was an indefensible medieval stronghold, held during the Crusades by the Knights Hospitalers after it had been captured from Saladin by Richard Coeur de Lion. There was no reason to expect that it could withstand Bonaparte's army of thirteen thousand. But Djezzar Pasha was as obstinate as he was cruel. Among his garrison there was a contingent of European-trained Turkish gunners; the walls of Acre, however old, were thick; and two rather remarkable men helped Djezzar to organize the defense. One was Captain Sir William Sidney Smith of the English navy, a somewhat histrionic firebrand who had crossed Bonaparte's path once before, at Toulon in 1793, when he volunteered to set fire to the ships the Allies had to leave behind in the harbor. He now was accredited to the Porte as an envoy plenipotentiary and was also in command of the squadron cruising off Egypt and Syria. The other man was Colonel Louis de

Phélippeaux, a former classmate of Bonaparte's at the Ecole Militaire in Paris, who had emigrated during the French Revolution, helped Sidney Smith to escape from a French prison in 1798, and been commissioned in the British Army. Even before the siege of Acre began, Sidney Smith had intercepted the French siege artillery, which came by sea. The captured siege guns were installed in the fortress and Phélippeaux, an expert artilleryman, took charge of the preparations for the defense. (He exerted himself so unstintingly that he died of exhaustion toward the end of the siege.)

Without waiting for a new shipment of siege guns to arrive, Bonaparte ordered one assault after another, each murderous and futile. The trenches were filling up with rotting corpses, which could not be removed, and each new wave of assailants had to step over their decomposing brothers. Meanwhile the plague continued to rage. On May 20, after a two-month siege, Bonaparte gave it up and began his retreat to Egypt. Of his 13,000 men, at least 2,200 had been killed in action and by the plague, and about 2,300 were ill or crippled. Bonaparte, Kléber once remarked, was the kind of general who needed a monthly income of ten thousand men.

The retreat was a nightmare lit up by flaming fields and villages—for Bonaparte wanted to lay waste the land to slow down the pursuing Turks. In Jaffa he ordered about fifty incurable plague patients to be poisoned, an order only imperfectly carried out if carried out at all. At the

Above, a portrait of General Kléber. Gros' drawing below shows Napoleon at Jaffa, visiting soldiers stricken by the plague.

same time he saw to it that his return to Egypt should look like a triumph. When they marched through a town, the troops were preceded by their bands playing and by the captured flags waving. Prisoners of war and trophies were sent ahead to Cairo, along with bulletins of victory. All this Bonaparte topped off with his proclamation to his own men: they had accomplished their mission gloriously, he told them; Acre had been razed, except for the citadel, which was not worth taking; now they must return to Egypt to defend it against a possible hostile landing. On June 14 Bonaparte and the more presentable part of his army entered Cairo in triumph, with palm fronds in their hats; at this point, make-believe bordered on the sublime. A civilian member of the expedition, describing its horrors in a letter to his mother, concluded his gruesome report with the words: "The report of the commander in chief, which I enclose, will prove to you how much a man must lie to be in politics."

On July 15 Bonaparte received word from Alexandria that the Turkish army that he had destroyed in his bulletins had just landed at Abukir. He wasted no time; ten days later, with a force of about ten thousand men, he attacked the Turks, who were still entrenched near the beach, and drove the larger part of them into the sea, where they drowned—a sight he described as terrible and beautiful. The Turkish landing, with an inadequate force, was an ill-advised operation, undertaken in all likelihood on the rash promptings of Sidney Smith, whose squadron stood by during the battle. Bonaparte, by doubling the number of the Turks in his report to the Directory, transformed a foregone conclusion into a spectacular victory. A man must indeed lie to be in politics, and Bonaparte's projects at the time were decidedly political.

Shortly after the battle, two French officers had gone aboard Smith's flagship to arrange for an exchange of prisoners. Smith obligingly presented them with a set of European newspapers that brought Napoleon up to date on recent events. Although some of the bad news must have been familiar to him, he affected great surprise and indignation as he read it. Austria had declared war in March. Her armies, under Archduke Charles, were driving the French out of Germany, while the Russians and Austrians under Field Marshal Alexander Suvorov were routing the French in Italy. France herself was in a political and financial crisis. Delightful tidings! The fruit was ripe for the hero to come and pick. Taking only half a dozen men into his confidence, Bonaparte prepared to leave for France. About three in the morning on August 18, 1799, he slipped out of Cairo with a handful of chosen men; on August 23 he sailed from Alexandria with two frigates and a couple of smaller craft, the coast being temporarily clear of English ships. After a stop at Ajaccio—the last time he ever saw his native city—he landed at Fréjus on October 9, preceded by the report of his latest victory.

Bonaparte's administration of Egypt has been much praised by his admirers. The objective mind will find difficulty seeing in it anything but a succession of ineffectual makeshifts, but the overall conception was impressive, and equally impressive was the energy, the quick decisiveness with which Bonaparte addressed himself to every practical problem, be it political, administrative, fiscal, religious, legal, or military. Undoubtedly he was the artist, and his critics mere critics. Many of his projects—dams, an improved and expanded irrigation system, the Suez Canal, the introduction of new crops and industries—were carried out in the following century by Mohammed Ali and his successors. Bonaparte could not realize them, partly because he lacked the time and the means; partly because he never enjoyed the confidence of the uneducated population and of the skeptical, conservative elite; partly because the imperious needs of the day forced him to adopt measures directly contrary to his long-term aims. In two respects, however, he was the originator of very positive achievements: he attached to his expeditionary force a large scientific commission, and he ordered General Desaix to undertake the conquest of Upper Egypt as far south as Aswan.

The inclusion of a scientific commission seems to have been Bonaparte's own idea. The commission—about 170 men strong—consisted for the most part of technical personnel: engineers, mechanics, surveyors, cartographers, interpreters, printers, architects, surgeons, pharmacists. However, there were also a number of physicists, chemists, mathematicians, astronomers, geologists, zoologists, archaeologists, economists, artists, musicians, and poets. Some of them were, or later became, men of the first rank in their field: the mathematicians Monge and Fourier, the chemist Berthollet, the economist Say, the zoologist Geoffroy Saint-Hilaire, the geologist Dolomieu, the physicist Malus, the artist Vivant Denon.

Shortly after capturing Cairo, Bonaparte established, on the model of the French National Institute, the Institute of Egypt, which included the more distinguished members of the Scientific Commission, several generals (among them Bonaparte, elected vice president), and a few civilian administrative officials—all French. Both the Commission and the Institute had their headquarters in a group of fine houses in a garden district at the edge of Cairo. Here were their library (to which the local population was welcome), their laboratories, their workshops, their observatory, their museum, their zoological and botanical collections, their aviary, their agricultural-experiment station, their artists' studios, their printing plant, their living quarters, and their meeting hall. Freed from the social distractions of Paris, the scholars gave themselves over with adventurous zeal to their various pursuits, which ranged from simple practical questions submitted to them by Bonaparte (could the army's baking ovens be improved? could beer be brewed without hops?) to the study of the

fish of the Nile, of mummified cats and birds, of desert insects, of Oriental music. Field teams were assigned to such tasks as surveying the Isthmus of Suez, compiling detailed topographical maps of Egypt, and exploring the ruins and antiquities. The result of their labors was a monumental and possibly unique work, the *Description de l'Egypte,* in ten volumes of text and fourteen magnificent volumes of plates, published between 1809 and 1828.

As might be expected, it was in the domain of archaeology that the savants' labors bore the most fruit. Until the arrival of the French in 1798, Egypt was known only through the unreliable accounts of travelers, from Herodotus to Savary. The hieroglyphs were as yet undeciphered. The key to an understanding of ancient Egypt was found in 1799, when a French captain of engineers stumbled on the Rosetta Stone, inscribed with an identical text in Greek and in hieroglyphic and in demotic characters. It was only thirty-two years later that Jean François Champollion fully deciphered the Egyptian text, but the impetus that brought the new science of Egyptology into existence was given by Bonaparte, when he ordered General Desaix to pursue Murad Bey in Upper Egypt and to bring the provinces from Beni Suef to Aswan under French control.

Desaix's campaign is one of the great epics of modern times. For eleven months, with only three thousand infantry, one thousand horse, and a few guns, the thirty-year-old general pursued the elusive Murad and his Mamelukes in a succession of forced marches and countermarches that totaled well over three thousand miles. Desaix never caught Murad, though he defeated him several times and at one point forced him to retreat deep into the Sudan. His division was chronically out of shoes, medicine, and ammunition, and one-third of his men was suffering from purulent ophthalmia. Yet despite their hardships, Desaix's men experienced an exhilarating sense of adventure and discovery. Their marches took them, repeatedly, through the monumental ruins of Dendera, Luxor, Karnak, the Valley of the Kings, Hermonthis, Edfu, and Philae, and they could inscribe their names beside those of Roman legionaries. When, one day at sunrise, they were confronted by the breath-taking sight of Thebes spread out before them, the entire division halted spontaneously to applaud and to present arms, while the bands struck up.

With the vanguard of the division there rode a civilian in his fifties whose chief baggage consisted of a vast portfolio and a supply of pencils. Denon, known until then only as an amiable courtier at the Versailles of Marie Antoinette and as a gifted illustrator and pornographer, was discovering a new world. It is difficult to say which sentiment prevailed in him—enthusiasm over the glories of ancient

A Sèvres dinner service made for Napoleon shows Egyptian landmarks circled by a border of characteristic Egyptian motifs. The designs are taken from Denon's drawings of the sites.

Egyptian art and architecture or frustration at having to pass by the ruins at the speed of an army in hot pursuit. On his first visit to Thebes he barely had time to make a few sketches; fortunately, he returned several times at greater leisure. Soon his portfolio was bursting with sketches of sights and of details; it was through his eyes, from his drawings, that the world became acquainted with Egyptian art. Later, another expedition of experts was dispatched to Upper Egypt for a systematic exploration of its treasures, whose grandeur has fascinated men's minds ever since. "The true conquests," Bonaparte had written shortly before going to Egypt, "the only ones that leave no regret, are those that have been wrested from ignorance." The sentence might stand as an epitaph for the entire Egyptian campaign.

As for the ephemeral conquest—Egypt—it was retained for two years after Bonaparte's return to France. Kléber, whom he had appointed to be his successor without even consulting him, was anxious to bring the army back to France before disease and more Pyrrhic victories had annihilated it. By the Convention of El Arish reached with the grand vizier and Sir Sidney Smith, he agreed to evacuate Egypt aboard Turkish transports. The Convention, however, was disavowed by the British government, and Kléber, who had already evacuated most of Lower Egypt, was obliged to reconquer it. On June 14, 1800—less than three months after his brilliant victory at Heliopolis—he was assassinated by a Moslem fanatic. His successor, General Menou, a convert to Islam, boasted that he would defend Egypt to the last man. As incompetent and foolish as Kléber had been able and realistic, Menou was obliged to capitulate, on August 30, 1801, to a British expeditionary force of some seventeen thousand men, which had invaded Egypt simultaneously with a large Turkish army under the grand vizier. Under the terms of the capitulation, the British navy repatriated all the French forces in Egypt—about half of their original strength—with all their arms and baggage. On October 1, shortly before their return, a preliminary peace between England and France was signed at London. This anti-climactic conclusion of the Egyptian adventure took place two years after General Bonaparte had seized the power in France. Futile as it was, the campaign had served the general's personal advancement.

Having landed at Fréjus on October 9, 1799, General Bonaparte arrived in Paris a week later—almost too late. Since his departure for Egypt, the Directory had been shaken by several minor convulsions; of the original five Directors, Barras was the only one left; among the new Directors, the most influential was the ex-abbé Emmanuel Sieyès. Three out of the five Directors were plotting to overthrow their own government: Barras was negotiating with the exiled Bourbon court for a monarchist restoration (his price was twelve million francs); Sieyès, supported by his colleague Pierre Roger Ducos, was planning a coup d'état to unseat the Directory and establish a stronger executive, republican but oriented to the right. Since the existing government lacked the support of any large segment of public opinion, almost any change of regime seemed desirable to the majority of Frenchmen.

The news of Bonaparte's landing had caused a brief flurry among the Directors. Was he authorized to leave his army? Should he be put on trial? It was agreed that it would be impolitic to shoot him, but his official reception was cool. His declaration that he had braved the British fleet to rush to the succor of the fatherland was somewhat weakened by the fact that by October the fatherland was no longer in danger; General André Masséna had just routed an Austro-Russian army at Zurich, and an Anglo-Russian expeditionary force in Holland had just surrendered to General Guillaume Brune. Masséna's and Brune's new glory made Bonaparte's pale a little. Nevertheless, however cool his official reception, Bonaparte soon noticed that both Sieyès and Barras approached him unofficially and separately with considerable warmth. Both needed what was called a "sword"—that is, a general willing to back up their respective coups d'état by force—and the man who had acted so decisively and unsentimentally on 13 Vendémiaire seemed an ideal choice. Each sounded him out; he turned a deaf ear. In his opinion, he was past the point where he had to act as someone else's sword; the victor of Rivoli, the Pyramids, and Abukir, strong with his glory and above factional strife, could command a majority of both houses and be offered, like another George Washington, the presidency of the Republic. After a few days' sulking he realized his error; nobody came to intrude on his proud seclusion. It was clear that within a month he would be forgotten.

On November 1 he agreed to talk business with Sieyès, at the house of his brother Lucien. A member of the Council

During the coup d'état of 19 Brumaire, members of the Council of Five Hundred assaulted Napoleon and tried to outlaw him.

of Five Hundred, Lucien had just been elected its president; also, he was Sieyès' chief ally in the lower house. Bonaparte declared himself ready to support Sieyès' scheme, on the condition that the new government would be provisional only, pending the elaboration of a new constitution. The maneuver stunned Sieyès, but he had to accept the condition. The following week was spent in preparations for the coup d'état, with Talleyrand, then Bonaparte's chief adviser, acting as liaison between the plotters. On the appointed day, the Council of Elders, on whose leading members Sieyès could count, would declare an emergency, give Bonaparte the command of the troops in the Paris region, and transfer the seat of both houses to St. Cloud. There, protected from undue influences by the bayonets of Bonaparte's men, the legislators would be encouraged to vote the new government into existence.

Everything went well on 18 Brumaire (November 9); the Elders voted as bidden, Bonaparte took his oath as commander, Barras was persuaded by Talleyrand to resign as he emerged, unsuspecting, from his bathtub, and the two recalcitrant Directors, Gohier and Moulins, were placed under guard. The next day, at St. Cloud, almost ended in disaster. Some of the Elders had second thoughts about the action of the preceding day; the Five Hundred was decidedly hostile. Bonaparte lost his head. Escorted by a squad of grenadiers, he stalked into the Elders' meeting hall and made an incoherent speech that might have impressed the Divan of Cairo but not an assembly of French politicians. He then proceeded to the Five Hundred, where bedlam broke loose. The deputies leaped onto their benches; some shouted "Outlaw the dictator!" while others grabbed and manhandled the general, who had to be dragged to safety by his grenadiers. The uproar continued, and about half an hour later another squad of grenadiers went back into the hall to rescue the president, Lucien.

The two brothers seemed at the end of their wits when Sieyès calmly suggested that they should simply put the deputies out of their hall. Napoleon and Lucien dashed into the courtyard of the château of St. Cloud, where the Legislative Guards were assembled, leaped on horseback, and addressed the troops: a minority of raving madmen, said Lucien, was terrorizing the majority of the Five Hundred with their daggers; Napoleon, in his speech, even declared that they had tried to kill him. With drums rolling and bayonets fixed, the grenadiers charged the meeting hall in the Orangerie, while the deputies leaped out of the windows and ran, leaving their togas in the shrubbery. A few hours later, in a chastened mood, both houses were reconvened and voted to establish a provisional government; Sieyès, Ducos, and Bonaparte were named provisional consuls—that is, the chief executives of the new regime.

Things had gone less smoothly than Bonaparte would have wished, but no blood had been shed and the essential objective was accomplished: he was in power. Indeed, there was little doubt either in his or in Sieyès' mind that the real winner of the day was not Sieyès but the "sword," General Bonaparte. This also became plain to the general public as they read the broadsheets and proclamations which Bonaparte had taken care to have printed in advance (without Sieyès' knowledge) and which gave him billing as the hero of the day. The Revolution was over, they announced. Now its benefits would be consolidated. All Frenchmen must unite, regardless of their political opinions and past, in support of their government, which would lead France back to victory, prosperity, law, and order.

The coup d'état of 18–19 Brumaire was greeted with almost universal satisfaction in France. It is probably true that the Directory had not been nearly as inefficient and incompetent as Bonaparte claimed; but the mass of the people was weary of ten years of upheavals, wars, corruption, politics, and financial sacrifices. To them, Bonaparte held out the hope of peace and stability. He also had the support of the political leaders and of the elite. Those who had helped him into power—the conservative republicans—though they distrusted his ambitions, regarded him as the "necessary man," the "man of the hour," who would establish a firm and stable government under which they could continue to enjoy the wealth and influence they had acquired in the Revolution. (Once he had accomplished this, they hoped to get rid of him.) The Jacobin left saw in him the man who would prevent a royalist restoration. The royalists, including the exiled Louis XVIII, hoped that he would ease the way to a restored monarchy.

Abroad his advent was generally welcomed. To the conservatives, he had written *finis* to the Revolution; to the liberals, he had consolidated it. Although he was a soldier, he was a man of peace. Because he was a soldier, he was not associated with the highway robberies practiced by the Directory. Public opinion everywhere leaned over backward to see only the best in him. In England the Whig opposition took heart. In Russia the eccentric Czar Paul withdrew from the Coalition and became a passionate admirer of General Bonaparte. Even Madame de Staël, who soon afterward would declare war on him, was beside herself with joy when he took power. Her father, old Jacques Necker, was more sober. "Your nerves are overwrought," he wrote to her. "Unfortunately, everything rests on the life of one man." He had put his finger on the weak spot, of which Bonaparte himself was only too aware. The "man of the hour" had no desire to be merely that; yet to be more he could not rest until he had made sure that what he had wrought would outlive him. Surely he had no idea at that time that this necessity would lead him to found a dynasty, but just as he had shied from nothing to attain power, so he would seize every opportunity to increase and perpetuate it.

WAR AND PLUNDER

"The sovereignty of all the arts should pass to France," the Directors solemnly announced, "in order to affirm and embellish the reign of liberty." Inspired by high-minded pronouncements such as this, French art commissioners followed the revolutionary armies, systematically looting the art treasures of Italy, Germany, and the Low Countries. They felt few pangs of conscience; since France was the homeland of liberty, it was obvious that all the noblest works of the human spirit naturally belonged there. "All men of genius . . . are French," Napoleon proclaimed, "no matter in what country they may have been born." French agents assiduously studied foreign guidebooks to find the richest troves of art, selecting the choicest pictures from palaces and churches so that the French public might enjoy those aesthetic pleasures once reserved for the aristocracy and the clergy. The artist Denon was placed in charge of the looting; above he is shown kneeling to inspect pictures in the gallery at Cassel.

Carrying away his paintings, the duke of Modena flees the French.

ITALY'S TREASURES

The French were not alone in appropriating the art treasures of less powerful nations. The age that witnessed their plundering of Italy also saw the shipment to England of the Elgin marbles, and Sir William Hamilton's collection of the antiquities from Pompeii and Herculaneum. The Austrians transferred paintings from scores of Flemish churches and monasteries to the royal galleries at Vienna. But France was far more covetous than other nations. The Treaty of Tolentino required the pope not only to hand over a hundred paintings, statues, and vases, and five hundred precious manuscripts, but also to pay for their transportation to Paris. Jewels from the Vatican went to adorn the Directors, and three of the pope's tiaras were melted down for gold. Florence was forced to surrender the *Medici Venus,* and from the shrine at Loreto a miraculous image of the Virgin, attributed to Saint Luke, was taken away. More modern artists were equally prized. Venice lost most of its Titians and Tintorettos, and at Parma frescoes by Correggio were stripped from the walls. In order to keep their paintings, Italian princes attempted to bribe the French, and in Rome French commissioners were mobbed by the angry populace, but these efforts were in vain. Along with the list of provinces liberated, prisoners taken, and guns and ships captured, the victory banner that Napoleon ordered for the Army of Italy proclaimed: "Sent to Paris all the masterpieces of Michelangelo, Guercino, Titian, Paolo Veronese, Correggio, Albano, the Caracci, Raphael, and Leonardo da Vinci."

Four ancient bronze horses, which had once stood in the hippodrome at Constantinople, adorned the façade of St. Mark's Basilica in Venice. The Venetians had stolen them from the Byzantines in 1204; in 1797, when French armies marched in to put an end to the Venetian Republic, they were stolen again and sent to Paris. The engraving above shows one of the horses being pulled down from the façade. At right, French commissioners ransack the duke of Parma's picture gallery.

THE TROPHIES OF VICTORY

A fanciful design intended for a Sèvres vase shows the ceremonial entrance of Italian art treasures into the Louvre. The Apollo Belvedere *(below left), divested of the fig leaf that it had been required to wear in the Vatican Museum, is followed by chariots bearing the* Laocoön *(above) and a later acquisition, the* Medici Venus *(above left).*

The horses from St. Mark's were placed atop a victory arch (above) that Napoleon built in the Place du Carrousel in Paris. An imaginative drawing (right) shows Denon in the Musée Napoléon amidst projects for monuments and relics of the Italian and Egyptian campaigns.

FOUNDING OF THE LOUVRE

Bands played and flags flew, and a company of singers chanted patriotic hymns as the Italian art treasures were conducted into the new national museum at the Louvre in 1798. The museum had been established in 1793, in quarters that had been used before as the residences of artists under royal patronage. Now it was hung with hundreds of paintings, many of them trophies of Napoleon's victories. In later years, after renaming the entire collection the Musée Napoléon, the emperor held his state receptions amidst these plundered treasures. Vivant Denon, who was to make the Louvre the finest museum in the world, was placed in charge of it in 1804. He accompanied the emperor on campaigns, collecting art so greedily that Napoleon made him promise to "ask only for pictures by those artists we do not already have in the museum." (At one time the Louvre held seventy-five Rubens.) Still, Denon requisitioned many more paintings than even the vast galleries of the Louvre could accommodate, and hundreds of pictures were handed over to provincial museums. These were overlooked when, after Waterloo, the victorious Allies returned most of the looted art to its rightful owners despite the impassioned protests of the French, who failed to understand why the spoils of war were being taken away from them.

IDEAS IN
CONFLICT

The true conquests, the only ones that leave no regret,
are those that have been wrested from ignorance.

It may be stated as a sound historical hypothesis that events of a crude and violent nature—the outbreak of wars and revolutions, the issue of battles, the rise (but not the fall) of despots—are usually affected or even determined by chance combinations of circumstances, whereas the broad and gradual transformations in men's ideas, beliefs, knowledge, and techniques are essentially independent of trivial accidents. At every stage of its progress, the French Revolution could easily have taken a different direction from that which it took—a direction that might have made the ascent of a Bonaparte quite unlikely. Or, to choose a more specific example, if the night of June 22, 1798, when Nelson overtook Bonaparte's armada off Sicily without spying it, had not been dark and foggy, there might never have been an Emperor Napoleon, an Arc de Triomphe, or a Trafalgar Square. "All great events hang by a single thread. The clever man takes advantage of everything, neglects nothing that may give him some added opportunity." Thus wrote General Bonaparte to Talleyrand in September, 1797.

If by great events he meant winning battles, snatching a province from the Ottoman Empire, staging an 18 Brumaire and pointing a bayonet at a deputy's rear, he was unquestionably right, and no man was more adept than he at taking advantage of everything and neglecting nothing. On the other hand if, among great events, one includes the advent of Euclidian geometry, Italian Renaissance painting, the steam engine, Mozart concertos, the germ theory of disease, or nuclear fission, it can hardly be said that they hung by a single thread. Ideas, unlike emperors, do not emerge out of nowhere, ride the crest of opportunity, and end in a Waterloo. Thus, against the background of cataclysmic events—the French Revolution, the Napoleonic wars—the flow of ideas continued, somewhat disturbed by guillotines and guns but never interrupted.

Historians of ideas have found it convenient to view the French Revolution as the dividing line between eighteenth-century rationalism and the romantic reaction of the nineteenth century. This oversimplification not only ignores the real complexities of intellectual development but also creates artificial new ones. (For instance, it forces one to classify people who were neither rationalists nor romantics as either romantics or rationalists—a dreary game.) No one would deny that the Revolution affected, to a varying degree, almost all schools of thought in all fields, and that in its wake there came a rash of seemingly new ideological systems—the "isms" under whose influence the world has lived ever since. Yet these systems were derived directly

The desk at which Beethoven worked still displays the composer's writing stand, spectacles, and ear trumpet, and a bust of Brutus, whose example inspired all the opponents of tyranny.

from eighteenth-century thought, which was considerably more diverse than is usually realized.

The French Revolution, whatever its "causes," could not have taken place except in a favorable intellectual climate. It was not the work of a single political party or ideological group, with a definite program of action and a clearly defined set of goals. Yet however much the early leaders and supporters of the Revolution might disagree with each other on the exact shape of the new society that they hoped to create, they shared the belief that the old society, with its abuses and iniquities, was contrary to the natural order of things, and that society could be regenerated only by restoring the natural order. To them freedom was to obey the laws of nature.

The revolutionists of 1789 made certain assumptions, derived from a great variety of sources—such as Rousseau's Social Contract theory, the "self-evident" truths set forth in the American Declaration of Independence and elaborated in the French Declaration of the Rights of Man, Montesquieu's theory of the division of powers, and the liberal economics set forth by the French physiocrats and by Adam Smith. Above all they accepted the notion, which has never been really disproved, that human society is subject to natural laws much as the physical world is—a notion based not only on an analogy with Newton's laws of motion but perhaps even more on the pioneer work done by Beccaria, Condorcet, and others in the application of mathematical methods to political problems.

It was only after the "unnatural" old order had been destroyed that some perplexity arose as to just what that natural order was. It should have materialized spontaneously, but it did not. As the Revolution took its ever more violent course, the reformers were replaced by theorists, and the arch-theorist, Robespierre, gradually eliminated the others. His aim was to remake society in the image of Rousseau's *Social Contract*. Since men had become corrupted under the old order, the new order had to be imposed on them by a handful of incorruptible leaders who represented the "general will"—that is, the will that the majority of the people should have had but had not. Robespierre's interpretation of Rousseau would no doubt have been abhorrent to his master; it also was obnoxious to the mass of the politicians, who regarded the reign of uncompromising virtue as the most unnatural order of all and who rallied to overthrow it on 9 Thermidor.

By 1795, when the Directors took office, political and social thought had crystallized around the three basic attitudes that came to be known as conservatism, liberalism, and radicalism. According to the liberal school of thought, the Revolution, despite its deplorable excesses, had accomplished its historic purpose: it had abolished class privilege, established the people as the source of sovereignty, given equality of opportunity to all, and extended political rights to the responsible part of the citizenry—that is, the property

owners. The constitution could be improved, and so could the caliber of the politicians, but this was a matter of time; within its framework, there was room for both the rightist and the leftist opposition to make themselves heard.

This view was first set forth by Madame de Staël in a pamphlet calling on all Frenchmen to make peace with one another and on the Allies to make peace with France, and it was elaborated later by her lover Benjamin Constant, who was able to refine it thanks to his profound understanding of the English political system. In its main features the substance of the pamphlet has remained the creed of political liberals to this day. Tocqueville summed it up when he stated that "the gradual and progressive development of equality is both the past and the future of human history."

There were those, however, who thought that the Revolution had not gone far enough. Wealth and power had changed hands, but they were still held by the few, and the masses were, if anything, worse off than before. During the Reign of Terror the followers of Hébert had attempted to level fortunes and sought to protect wage earners by introducing maximum price laws. Their ideas threatened the sanctity of private property, which the Social Contract guaranteed; accordingly, Robespierre had the Hébertists guillotined. The maximum price laws, however, remained in effect until the Thermidorian Reaction. It was then that the proletarian was put in his place—to fill his stomach with bullets was more convenient than to fill it with bread. The Jacobin leaders, propertied or professional men for the most part, were not disconsolate at this trend. They were not socialists, and a discontented proletariat was their political capital. Some of the rank and file, however, felt that this was not the way to practice equality and fraternity.

Among them was François Noël Babeuf, the editor of a radical newspaper, who had changed his first name to Gracchus. With several like-minded men he formed a small secret coterie, the Society of Equals, whose doctrine recalled some of the apocalyptic visions of earlier religious leveling sects and foreshadowed communism. In their opinion the Revolution had failed. The rich had grown richer, the poor, poorer. If the people were to share equally in the natural wealth of the nation and in the fruits of their labors, another, final, revolution was needed. In the new society all land would belong to the state, all men would have a right to work, and the products of labor would be distributed to all. But it was not only economic inequality that the Equals wished to destroy: they were against every sort of distinction and they were more Spartan than the Spartans. Frivolous pursuits such as literature, art, and religion would be outlawed, cities would be razed, children would be brought up by the community, and all would wear the same clothes.

Babeuf hoped to bring about his millennium by recruiting a secret army among the proletariat and the ranks of the armed forces, but his conspiracy was nipped in the bud and he was executed in the spring of 1797. Communism,

At her estate a literary gathering surrounds Madame de Staël.

society. (It would be pointless to object that in Rousseau's thought "natural man" was as dead as the Dodo bird; since both his followers and his enemies chose to distort his thought in the same direction, it must be accepted here at its distorted face value.) It was easy for Burke to point at Jacobin maniacs, their arms dripping with blood, and to affirm with conviction that when a society was destroyed, the liberated natural man who emerged from it was not a model of goodness.

In Burke's view, a human society could not be created on the basis of abstract principles, however rational and just. Every society was a living, organic whole, a bond of past, present, and future generations, functioning by habit and tradition, a single fabric, in which each class had its assigned place and whose very strength lies in its complexity. It might be improved and renewed, but never at the sacrifice of its continuity, for once that is broken, all restraint on human passions is removed and man turns into a beast. Men have reason, but they do not act rationally; they act from habit. Tradition, however irrational it may seem, is wiser than rational but rash reform; society is wiser than man. Society is a manifestation of the divine order; consequently all reforms other than the correction of abuses must be viewed with suspicion, and even the abuses are to be borne patiently if their correction threatens the existence of the whole fabric.

By placing his argument on a theological basis, Burke and his followers have obscured its most original aspect. Indeed, his political thought can be separated from its theological prop and from its antirationalist bias, for it is essentially psychological. The error of the more radical French revolutionists was that, in their inexperience, they sought to abolish brutally all past habits and traditions. It was Burke's merit to point out that human nature was not only a set of qualities with which men were born but also a set of traditions which they inherited. The persistence of traditional social patterns under totally changed conditions and in defiance of the most despotic attempts at extirpating them has fascinated modern sociologists and must be taken into account by those who would manipulate societies.

Burke appealed to tradition, which is history, but his view of history was still theological and, therefore, static. Man, tainted by Original Sin, remains unchanged through the ages; left to his own devices, he is evil. Only society can make him obey God's laws (more or less); and since his passions and needs remain unchanged, societies, whatever form they take, also remain essentially the same. This doctrine was carried to extreme conclusions by Joseph de Maistre, a diplomat in the Sardinian service, who regarded the French Revolution as a divine punishment and Napoleon as God's unwitting instrument in bringing about a universal society which was to be ruled by monarchs under the supreme authority of the pope.

This theological view of history and the belief in the un-

except in its more fanciful utopian forms, went underground and remained there throughout the Napoleonic era. Still, though it did not yet have an articulated formal doctrine, its supporters did not disappear from the earth; in fact, as workingmen's conditions grew steadily worse, its potential following increased. It is not without reason that Marxist socialists regard Babeuf as their John the Baptist.

Those who took a radical stand against the entire Revolution fell into two categories—the articulate and the sputtering. The latter, almost all émigrés who expected to be restored to their former rights and privileges simply because they were they, need not detain us here. The articulate found their first and greatest spokesman in an Irish-born member of the House of Commons, Edmund Burke. As early as 1790, in his *Reflections on the French Revolution,* Burke sounded the warning signal and predicted quite accurately the course the Revolution would take: it would end in military dictatorship. His position, stated with brilliance and passion, remains the basis of all conservative thought. It has been repeated *ad nauseam* that his basic assumption was the exact opposite of the rationalistic assumption which had led to the Revolution. The revolutionists believed in a natural order; Burke, in a God-given order. The difference is not very great, and both assumptions are not rationalistic but metaphysical.

The real difference lies in Burke's rejection of the Rousseauan belief, vaguely held by all supporters of the Revolution, that man is born good but has been corrupted by changeableness of human nature had been challenged ever since the beginning of the eighteenth century. History, it seemed, was following certain patterns and perhaps was moving in a definite direction. The Italian philosopher Giovanni Battista Vico saw history as a cyclical process—theocracy, aristocracy, democracy—in an ever-recurring repetition, and his philosophy did not imply indefinite progress. During his lifetime, however, the French literary scene was shaken by the quarrel between the partisans of the Ancients and those who held that the Moderns were at least the equals of the Greeks and Romans. The argument involved only works of art but its application to all things social was manifest.

Each generation inherits the experience of the past, the Modernists argued; consequently the Ancients were children, the Moderns mature. Applied to artistic creation, the argument is debatable at best and has been generally abandoned by even the most fervent believers in human progress. But the progress of scientific knowledge since Galileo and the refinement of civilization, thanks to the discovery of a new continent and to the expansion of trade, were undeniable facts. Knowledge was cumulative; so was wealth; so was technology: the average man of 1750 knew more, lived better, was more enlightened, less brutish than the average man of the year 1000. The more men knew, the more they were able to master nature and to exploit the wealth of the earth, the better were their chances of liberating themselves from superstition, despotism, poverty, disease, and war. A better age was at hand, an age of reason and sensibility.

The earliest systematic presentation of the history of scientific progress can be found in D'Alembert's preliminary discourse to the *Encyclopédie*. In D'Alembert's scheme the human mind had entered a new phase of development inaugurated by Francis Bacon's empirical method. D'Alembert's friend Turgot, who retired to a life of studies after serving briefly as finance minister to Louis XVI, formulated a more comprehensive theory of progress. Perhaps the most interesting and revolutionary feature in Turgot's thought was his insistence that change was a good thing in itself and that all permanence was evil. In this, of course, he stood at the opposite pole from Burke. Turgot did not live to see the French Revolution, but his friend and collaborator, the marquis de Condorcet, lived long enough to be killed by it.

A brilliant mathematician—his contributions to the theory of probability were particularly valuable—Condorcet believed passionately in reason, and reason to him meant mathematics. The history of man according to him was the history of his mental habits, and he divided it into nine epochs of intellectual development. (How far we are from dynasties, empires, and battles, which used to form the subject of history!) He embraced the Revolution with enthusiasm, for it promised to usher in the tenth and final epoch, in which human society would reach its perfection—supervised, of course, by mathematicians and statisticians.

An eighteenth-century portrait depicts Rousseau as a herbalist.

He threw himself into politics and, as one of the leaders of the Convention, drifted to a position that was quite incompatible with his benign and peaceful temperament. His former title of marquis and his disapproval of terror as a political means earned him a warrant of arrest. He hid out for months in a Paris garret; then when this became too dangerous, roamed the countryside, a tragic, hunted figure, bearded and in rags, turned away by his closest friends. Eventually arrested, he either killed himself in his cell or died of a stroke. He left behind him a manuscript, composed during the nightmarish months of his persecution, in which he reasserted his faith in human progress and reason. Parts of his *Sketch of a Historic Table of the Progress of the Human Spirit* were circulated before its publication in 1801–4. By that time the idea of human perfectibility had become an intellectual commonplace that annoyed the First Consul as much as it had annoyed Burke.

The first intellectual to draw Bonaparte's ire was Madame de Staël, who in 1800 published her book *On Literature Considered in Its Relationship to Social Institutions*. The earliest attempt to consider thought and artistic creation in their social context, her book also expounded a theory of progress influenced by Condorcet but leaving out his utopianism. Progress to her was the gradual growth and diffusion of civilization, partly by the accumulation of knowledge, partly by its extension to new countries (for example, to America) and to the lower segments of society. It can be set back by external events, but can never be stopped. The book, which has its weak spots but bristles with fruitful ideas, is six hundred pages long; Bonaparte studied it for a quarter of an hour and instructed his literary executioner, Louis de Fontanes, to damn it.

"The masses," wrote Fontanes in the *Mercure de France,* "must be led by a well-informed government. But if the masses themselves marched forward, as our innovators would have them, we would relapse into anarchy and ignorance in the name of the progress of the human mind." In another article, probably dictated by Bonaparte himself, the point is made even clearer: "He [Bonaparte] does not lose himself in futile theories. He knows that men have always been the same, that nothing can change their nature, and it is from the past that he will draw his lessons in order to regulate the present." His aversion for Madame de Staël extended to *idéologues* in general, a term he applied to all those who believed in the perfectibility of man. "They have a craze for interfering with my policies," he complained to Lucien. "They talk, talk, talk."

For all practical purposes, Napoleon's conservatism was undistinguishable from that of his enemies Burke and Maistre. Like them he derided the rationalist assumptions of those who believed in human perfectibility; like them he was convinced that legislation must be adapted to "human psychology and historic lessons"; like them he believed that no social order was possible without religion. Their opposition was largely theoretical: to Burke and Maistre, the social order was a divine necessity, and to Napoleon God was a social necessity.

Despite his contempt for *idéologues* Napoleon had an ideology of his own. He did not search for final causes, since he tacitly assumed that the final cause was power; compared to the ideas thus far discussed and to be discussed presently, Napoleon's stand out in stark and lucid simplicity. The art of government is to keep the people reasonably happy by giving them what they want and to obtain from them all one can get. To do this one must know men. In Napoleon's view, men were either good or bad—they were what circumstances made them. The good could be corrupted; as for the bad, "a legislator must know how to take advantage of even the defects of those he wants to govern." "Men are like ciphers: they acquire their value merely from their position." "Men are moved by two levers only: fear and self-interest." To make them behave, one must play on both levers. The ruler must teach them respect ("Nothing is more salutary than a terrible example given at the right time"), but the lesson must be given sparingly ("Great men are never cruel without necessity"). The ruler must also satisfy the people's basic wants. Liberty is not among these. Few men really care about it: "consequently it can be repressed with impunity. . . . Liberty means a good civil code. The only thing modern nations care for is property." The masses desire equality, but "they would gladly renounce it if everyone could entertain the hope of rising to the top. . . . What must be done then is to give everybody the hope of being able to rise."

Napoleon's own rise, of course, symbolized that hope. Thanks to the French Revolution it was possible to reconcile the two basic but conflicting needs of human vanity—love of equality and love of distinction—in equality of opportunity. "My motto has always been: A career open to all talents." In fact, equality of opportunity had become limited severely the moment that the First Consul put an end to the Revolution, but this did not matter so long as Napoleon could make people believe that it still existed for all Frenchmen.

Such was Napoleon's philosophy of government. Men were there to be used. The best in them could be exploited by appealing to their vanity; the worst could be put to equally good use. "Men would have to be exceptional rascals to be as bad as I assume them to be," he once remarked, but this did not prevent him from making the rascals kings, ministers, and generals. This philosophy owes little to the intellectual trends of his time: it is timeless. Machiavelli and La Rochefoucauld gave it expression and have been called cynics, but Burke's pessimistic assumptions are no less cynical, though his doctrine sounds more high-minded. The purpose for which Napoleon put men to use, and whether it was noble or not, are questions to be looked into elsewhere. What matters here is that he regarded those who believed in human progress as dangerous fools, and that they regarded him as a despotic cynic.

The designation *idéologue,* which Napoleon used very broadly, actually should be applied only to a small group of thinkers who, ironically, had been very influential in bringing General Bonaparte to power and whose help he had not disdained at the time of 18 Brumaire. (Even *idéologues* can be put to use.) Although Madame de Staël was close to the *idéologues,* she was not one of them. They were strongly influenced by Condorcet as well as by the subtle and fruitful ideas of Etienne Bonnot de Condillac, one of the founders of modern psychology.

From Condorcet they took their belief in human perfectibility and in the primary role to be played in the future society by men of science. Their knowledge of psychology did not carry over into practical affairs; indeed, they thought that because General Bonaparte had made high-minded statements on science and belonged to the Institute, he would be their man. Their foremost spokesman was the Comte Destutt de Tracy, whose Condillacian theory of sensations was to have its echoes in the psychology of William James. The others were almost all medical men: Dr. Georges Cabanis, whose emphasis on the reciprocal influence of the moral and the physical foreshadowed modern psychosomatic medicine; Dr. Philippe Pinel, one of the first physicians to treat mental patients as medical cases; and Dr. François Bichat, an anatomist and physiologist who pioneered in the study of tissues. Each is acknowledged

For his utopian city, New Harmony, Robert Owen proposed a quadrangular plan, with houses and public buildings around a garden.

as one of the great men in modern medicine; Napoleon regarded them as a pack of babbling fools.

Among Dr. Pinel's patients in 1813, at the insane asylum of Charenton, were two remarkable people—the marquis de Sade and the comte de Saint-Simon, both progenitors of "isms." The latter in more prosperous days had played host to the *idéologues;* after a riotous and checkered life, he had settled down to work out the improvement of mankind. At the time Dr. Pinel was nursing him back to reason, Saint-Simon had only begun to formulate his theories. Like Condorcet and the *idéologues,* he wished to see scientists at the top of the political structure, but he went a bit further in that he proposed the establishment of a scientific priesthood of the Religion of Newton, a notion that might have impressed Newton unfavorably. In the Utopia expounded in his later works (published only a decade after the Napoleonic era) he added industrialists and artists to the scientists and, stressing that emotions must be satisfied as well as reason, proclaimed in his *Le Nouveau Christianisme* (1825) that the scientifically organized society must be balanced by the religion of the Brotherhood of Man. Summed up thus cavalierly, Saint-Simon's doctrine (which his disciples changed into a religion) must sound quite unrealistic. Yet his writings contain brilliant flashes of insight; several of his most improbable prophecies have come true or been surpassed; and he influenced some of the most distinguished and sanest minds of the nineteenth century. The same can be said of another utopian eccentric, François Marie Charles Fourier.

A clerk employed by an American wholesale house in Paris, Fourier published the first version of his philosophy in 1808. Though he was influenced by the same intellectual trends as Saint-Simon, his Utopia was radically different

from the count's, for he had no use for either scientists or businessmen or progress. The Saint-Simonians and *idéologues* wanted to change human nature; Fourier wanted to liberate it. What makes men happy? Their passions. What makes them miserable? The inhibition of their passions. The conclusion to be drawn is obvious: far from imposing reason on passions, the legislator must create a society in which men and women can indulge their passions to the full, yet safely and harmoniously. What about destructive passions? Like Napoleon, Fourier found use even for them: in his ideal community, lads who showed homicidal tendencies would be employed as butchers.

Cities would be abolished, and society would be organized into autonomous rural units called phalansteries, whose ideal population Fourier calculated to be one thousand six hundred twenty, a figure he based on his classification of the twelve passions into eight hundred ten types, each of them to be represented by a male and a female, and all to be merged in harmony through diversity. In the phalanstery all would work together, but there was to be no economic equality (which would have inhibited the legitimate passion of acquisitiveness); they would also satisfy their passions together. Fourier's infinitely detailed descriptions of life in his phalansteries make them sound like the combination of an Israeli kibbutz and an ideal brothel.

Although Fourier had let it be known that he would be home every day at an appointed hour just in case a millionaire should call on him to supply the funds necessary for establishing a phalanstery, the millionaire never appeared. In the United States, however, toned-down versions of Fourierist phalansteries were established, the best-known being Brook Farm. Today many of Fourier's ideas, once regarded as eccentric, have become almost respectable—for instance, the idea that the liberation of the sexual impulse, whatever the form it takes, is basic to human happiness.

Fourierism made its appearance in the United States only long after the Napoleonic era, at a time when America had ceased to export ideas. During Napoleon's life span, the transatlantic trade in ideas was perhaps more active in the opposite direction. Benjamin Franklin had been an intimate of Condorcet's circle before the French Revolution, and in a way he symbolized the ideal of the statesman-scientist, just as George Washington symbolized the ancient civic virtues. The marquis de Lafayette and Thomas Paine had gone to America to help make the American Revolution and came back to Europe to help make the French one.

The most impressive intellect, however, among the transatlantic carriers of ideas belonged to Thomas Jefferson, who was born twenty-six years before Napoleon and died five years after him. Jefferson was the eighteenth century incarnate; in him, all the hopes, all the ideals, all the immensely vital and universal intellectual curiosity of his time were embodied harmoniously. His mind was cosmopolitan in the best sense. It would be difficult to be more American than Thomas Jefferson, and yet his thought was the product of the English empiricist philosophers and of the French Enlightenment. Whatever he had received from Europe he paid back with interest when he drafted the Declaration of Independence.

It would be difficult to think of another statement that had repercussions as universal as these few succinct words were to have: "We hold these truths to be self-evident, that all men are created equal, that they are endowed by their Creator with certain unalienable Rights, that among these are Life, Liberty and the pursuit of Happiness.—That to secure these rights, Governments are instituted among Men, deriving their just powers from the consent of the governed.—That whenever any Form of Government becomes destructive of these ends, it is the Right of the People to abolish it, and to institute new Government. . . ." A more compact and polished synthesis of the many diverse and often conflicting strands of eighteenth-century rationalist thought could not be formulated.

As American minister to the French court in 1789, Jefferson witnessed the beginning of the Revolution that owed so much to his words. His emphasis on the intrinsic value of change and renewal ("A little rebellion now and then is a good thing," he wrote) echoes the thought of Turgot. His linking the growth of democracy with the expansion of education is paralleled in the writings of Condorcet and Madame de Staël (his personal acquaintances). His preference for a rural over an urban civilization no doubt is Rousseauan, but his economic views, which reflect that preference, are strongly influenced by the teachings of the French physiocrats, whose most articulate spokesman was Jefferson's friend Pierre Samuel du Pont de Nemours. The Jeffersonian version of physiocracy—a predominantly rural

When built, New Harmony failed to fulfill Owen's ideal.

America with a maximum of local self-government—though it bears little resemblance to Fourier's Utopia, nevertheless appealed to the same kind of temperament (Horace Greeley's, for instance) that was attracted to Fourierism. All in all Jefferson typifies, perhaps better than any other man, not only his nation and his age but also the transition of ideas from continent to continent and from one century to the next.

Whoever embarks on a sightseeing tour of ideas must be a nimble traveler; their tangle is as intricate as that on a map of the networks of the world's airlines. In the year 1800 Jefferson was elected President, Bonaparte became First Consul, Madame de Staël published her book *On Literature,* Madame de Condorcet was preparing the publication of her husband's great posthumous work, Saint-Simon and Fourier were meditating the imminent establishment of the Golden Age, and Robert Owen took over a textile factory at New Lanark, Scotland.

Owen was a new kind of man, such as the eighteenth century had not known. A saddler's son, he began to work in a cotton mill at the age of ten. In those times a working day of fourteen hours was standard. Young Owen not only worked but also managed to read practically everything written in the past hundred years; he not only read but also managed to rise from the ranks, and at the age of twenty-three he owned one of the most profitable cotton mills in Manchester. The facts suggest that Robert Owen was a remarkable lad. Among prosperous cotton manufacturers he was particularly remarkable in that he did not regard the wretched lot of his workers as the necessary reward of their sinful and brutish ways. Around his mills at New Lanark, Owen built a model industrial community, with decent housing for the workers, schools, sanitation, and non-profit-making stores. In the factories working conditions were, measured against the prevailing standards, almost humane. To the consternation of his fellow manufacturers, far from being ruined by such extravagances, Owen made bigger profits than ever. Owen may be regarded as the founder of co-operative socialism, which he propounded in his writings and sought to put into practice in 1825, when he established the socialist community of New Harmony in Indiana. Like the Fourierist Brook Farm, so the Owenite New Harmony was a high-minded experiment. Both foundered—Brook Farm because of financial troubles, New Harmony in dissension.

While Owen tried to improve the workers' lot (the passing of the Factory Act of 1819 was due largely to him), Jeremy Bentham proved mathematically that the working-man's happiness was best promoted by the industrialist's self-interest; Thomas Malthus argued that any attempt to feed the starving masses only increased the masses and their misery; and David Ricardo demonstrated that it was no use to increase the workers' wages. Like Jacobin radicalism, these doctrines rested on eighteenth-century rationalist assumptions, but the conclusions derived from them were more pleasing to the wealthy and well-born.

The true progenitor of Benthamism, or utilitarianism, probably was not Bentham but the great Italian reformer Cesare di Beccaria. Beccaria's *Essay on Crime and Punishment* (1767) is not only the basis of modern penology but one of the few books that deserve the gratitude of all mankind. Written a decade after Damiens was drawn and quartered for having scratched Louis XV with a pen knife, the *Essay* argued that a more rational relationship between the gravity of a crime and its punishment was desirable. Following the general secular trend of his time, Beccaria substituted social usefulness for theologically derived notions of punishment in his scheme for the treatment of criminals. Beccaria was also a pioneer, with Condorcet, in the application of mathematics to the social sciences. His ideas found their place in Jeremy Bentham's *Principles of Morals and Politics* (1789).

Bentham was one of England's great eccentrics—not only because (among many other things) he promoted his cat in an ecclesiastic career culminating in the dignity of bishop, but chiefly because, like so many English eccentrics, he gave up a lucrative profession for the sake of devoting his life to improving the lot of humanity. He was a lawyer by training; he had read Beccaria on penal reform and on the applied uses of statistics; he had also read the French psychologists. His readings made him decide to renounce the practice of law so he might help its victims. His great book was the result of fifteen years of exertions for prison reform, but it went far beyond that subject, for his studies had convinced him that happiness could be measured mathematically by the intensity, duration, certainty, propinquity, fecundity, purity, and extent of pleasures.

The premise of his theory, that the greatest good is the greatest happiness of the greatest number, by no means originated with him. The novelty of his system lies in his proposition that moral value is a function of the quality and quantity of pleasure. Usefulness and goodness thus are identical: what gives the most pleasure to the most people is the most useful and hence the best. In its cruder interpretations and applications, Benthamite utilitarianism can justify almost anything, even the average television program offered to American viewers.

Bentham's disciple James Mill sought to translate it into action and was one of the leaders of the English reform movement in the early nineteenth century. Mill's son, John Stuart, who became a Greek scholar in 1809 at the age of three, eventually rebelled against utilitarianism without rejecting it: in his hands it became more refined and less mathematical. The cruder aspects of the calculus of happiness, which J. S. Mill dreaded, have recently emerged from oblivion in barely disguised form: the increasing use made of psychologists by industries to measure the happiness of their employees and customers makes Bentham look like something of a prophet.

The greatest pleasure for the greatest number was not what the Reverend Dr. Malthus had in mind when, in 1798, he published his *Essay on the Principle of Population*. Malthus, too, divine though he was, believed that mathematical laws presided over human affairs. He applied them to the procreative process, and the results were glum. In his opinion the gap between the supply of food and the number of people to be fed was fatally bound to increase at an accelerating pace, for population increased at a geometrical ratio and food at an arithmetical ratio. There were some bright spots in the picture, he noted with relief— wars, famines, epidemics; by 1803, however, when he published a revised edition of his work, he had reached the conclusion that those beneficial correctives were not sufficient. The problem could never be solved, seeing the carnal and lustful disposition of mankind, but at least it could be kept within bounds in two ways, both negative.

Since the poor invariably tend to produce a couple of children more than they can afford, their subsistence must be kept at a minimum. Increase their wages or lower the food prices, and they will procreate more beggars. Coddle the beggars in poorhouses, and you will only encourage their irresponsible fertility. Charity, said Saint Paul, is the greatest virtue, but charity to the poor is misplaced, said Malthus. Instead of charity, preach them continence. Malthus' solution—to deny the greatest pleasure to the greatest number— was impractical and hardly humane. The problem to which he addressed himself was, however, very real and as every one knows is becoming acute. Methods of birth control were by no means unknown in Malthus' day, and they provide the utilitarian answer to it. Yet Malthus did not think of advocating such methods, either because he judged

Freemasonry and other mystical rites and doctrines attracted many who were dissatisfied with society and the established churches.

them immoral or perhaps because nobody had told him about them. He himself had fourteen children.

Among those influenced by Malthus was David Ricardo, an English Jew who retired in 1797 from his brokerage business, in which he had made a fortune, at the ripe age of twenty-five. Thenceforth he devoted his life to the study of economic theory. His contributions to that science were manifold and great; both classic and Marxist economics rest on the foundations he provided. Among laymen he is best remembered for the formulation of a "law" no less gloomy than Malthus' predictions—the "Iron Law of Wages," according to which wages cannot rise above the minimum required for subsistence. Ricardo's influence made itself felt only later in the century; during his lifetime, the liberal economics of Adam Smith, still generally accepted in England, gained wide currency on the Continent.

All the thinkers sampled thus far believed in the necessity of regulating society to some extent. Their main concern was to discover the laws—God-given or natural—under which society would function best. Some of them, however—Rousseau being the most notable among them—shared in an entirely different tradition of thought, a tradition concerned with individual happiness and salvation. To them, the values of society were fundamentally false; life can be truly lived only through direct experience. The tradition was a very ancient one. Diogenes found salvation in complete self-sufficiency, the mystics in direct communion with God. The eighteenth century was not only an age of reason and science but also an age of spiritual anxiety, of uneasiness and dissatisfaction with the increasing complexities of civilization.

While institutionalized religion fell into disrepute, mysticism suddenly gained a large following both in Catholic and in Protestant countries. Quietism in France, Pietism in Germany, Quakerism and Methodism in England and America all stressed the primacy of the individual's inner light or conscience over the standards of organized society and religion. To those who were more worldly and less pious, Rousseau offered an equivalent comfort: man was born good, with an infallible conscience; civilization had corrupted him; yet, while civilization could not be undone, man as an individual was free to detach himself from it and to live in harmony with nature.

Despite the stress they laid on individual experience, neither the mystics nor Rousseau were indifferent to the society surrounding them. Rousseau theorized on the Social Contract; the Quakers, more practical people, exerted themselves to abolish slavery and to humanize conditions in prisons and insane asylums. However critical they were of social conditions, however active in their efforts to improve them, none of them advocated violent rebellion. Yet as the century drew to its close, all its conflicting intellectual, religious, and emotional trends combined to create an explosive and destructive spirit of humanitarian fanaticism. Science and material progress seemed to promise a new and golden age for mankind; so did the belief in the innate goodness of man, which needed only to be freed from the corrupting chains of civilization to reassert itself; so did the religious or pseudo-religious enthusiasm of the numerous philanthropic and occult societies that had thrown a network over all Europe—Freemasons, Illuminati, Rosicrucians, and the like.

With the outbreak of the French Revolution, the new era was dawning. To the extremists among the enthusiasts it seemed that Paradise on earth had to be created with fire and sword. The manifesto of a Swedish secret society (whose adherents plotted the murder of King Gustavus III) may give an idea of the mystico-rationalist hodgepodge current at the time: "The edifice of the universal republic to be established has, as its ultimate aim, the

Kaspar David Friedrich's painting of Gothic ruins utilizes a number of the stock motifs of Romantic art—nature, religion, and death.

happiness of mankind. . . . Those who excel by their intelligence must govern the world. . . . We must set fire to the cities and destroy them, for they are the schools of tyranny, corruption, and misery. . . . By a spontaneous return to nature, free societies will then form on the model of the Golden Age. . . . It is the French Revolution that will accomplish all these marvels; the Revolution is the divine deed *par excellence,* the most solemn deed ever witnessed on earth since the Deluge." The men who spoke thus were not down-trodden proletarians; they were noblemen and intellectuals. Their aims were undoubtedly noble and humanitarian, but their fundamental motives were destructive and anarchic. While they raved of reason and light, their darkest unconscious instincts were rebelling against the restraints of civilization.

Fourier, it may be recalled, believed that vice, crime, and unhappiness in general are caused not by the passions but by their inhibition. His cure-all was a kind of institutionalized anarchy—the phalanstery. The Englishman William Godwin, though sharing Fourier's anarchist assumptions, did not believe in organized license. According to his *Political Justice,* published in the midst of the Reign of Terror, Paradise could be created on earth simply by the removal of all constraints and inhibitions, including gov-

ernment, church, family, marriage, and schools. Godwin had been a nonconformist minister and was influenced by the mystic tendencies of the religious revival as much as by Rousseau's teachings of the innate goodness of man; though he defended the French Revolution, he neither advocated violence nor approved of people who took his theories too literally. When in 1814 young Percy Bysshe Shelley—by then already the author of "The Necessity of Atheism" and of "Queen Mab"—put some of Godwin's principles in practice and went to live in sin with Godwin's seventeen-year-old daughter Mary (the future author of *Frankenstein*), Godwin was not pleased.

Godwin's and Shelley's anarchism was idealistic and poetic; the destructive instinct was balanced by love of justice and beauty. The most logical anarchist of the Napoleonic or any other era died in the insane asylum of Charenton in the year that Shelley eloped with Mary Godwin. He too believed in the maximum satisfaction of the individual's impulses, but he had no illusion that men were born good, or that their impulses were virtuous, or that all men had an equal right to satisfy them. In his philosophy the good were the weak, and they existed only for the gratification of the strong. The strong alone were free, and they formed a kind of society of equals in evil. In the last analysis, there was no reality except the self, and that reality was enhanced by the destruction of all else. The philosopher who expounded this doctrine in both his life and writings was the count and self-styled marquis de Sade.

Sade reached the ultimate limit of rebellious self-assertion. Yet the individual's rebellion against social constraint, which characterized the latter part of the eighteenth century, did not necessarily take on anarchic and destructive forms. Perhaps one of the most revolutionary innovations of the Napoleonic era was the work of a saintly if slightly eccentric Swiss school teacher, Johann Heinrich Pestalozzi, who sought to liberate the child's individuality and at the same time make him a well-adjusted member of society. The experimental school that Pestalozzi established at Yverdon in 1805 was the cradle of modern progressive education. In Rousseau's pedagogical theory the child was to develop freely, according to its own nature, learning through experience and immediate perception; the teacher's role was not to instruct but to guide and above all to protect his pupil from the corrupting influence of society. Pestalozzi adapted this theory to practical conditions and made it his aim to educate his pupils for life rather than cram them with knowledge. His experiment tended to show that the removal of pressure and constraint, far from encouraging children's rebellious and anarchic urges, produced good citizens.

The German Romantic movement, which began as a rebellious and somewhat anarchic assertion of the individual, tended in its later stages not to good citizenship but to the immersion of individuality in the community. Its most productive period coincided almost exactly with the Napoleonic era, and the impact it made on the nineteenth and twentieth centuries was at least as great as that made by Napoleon. Strictly considered, German Romanticism was not a unified movement but a number of trends, some of which were in conflict with others. They manifested themselves in every field of intellectual and artistic activity and revolutionized all of them except the exact sciences. However diverse, they had in common at least this one characteristic: to the German Romantic, reason touched merely the surface of things, while feeling, instinct, and intuition plumbed their depths. When Henry Crabb Robinson, a young English disciple of the Romantics, told Madame de Staël that she would never understand Goethe's poetry, she replied haughtily: "Sir, I understand everything that deserves to be understood; what I don't understand is nothing." To a true Romantic this was sheer philistinism: only the things that could not be understood deserved understanding, and whatever was clear was shallow.

The conviction that truth must be experienced by the soul rather than apprehended by reason is not particularly German; it has its roots in the age-old philosophy of mystical experience. What is peculiar to the German Romantic movement is that it systematically applied that conviction to areas other than religious experience. Furthermore, the movement created not only a new literature, philosophy, and aesthetics but also a conscious sense of national identity. Germany in the eighteenth century, a loose confederation of some three hundred and sixty sovereign states and free cities, lacked political unity and had no great cultural centers such as London and Paris. Culturally, the country had been completely dominated by French classicism for at least a century, and the ruling class was entirely French-oriented. Frederick the Great regarded German as a language fit for stable boys.

The intellectuals, on the other hand, originated for the most part in a modest middle-class milieu that was decidedly un-French, and their rebellion against the cultural tyranny of France was the origin of German nationalism. Since Germany had no political unity, this nationalism was from the start not political but cultural. The first thing to do was to create a national literature, and for that purpose French literature had to be discredited. This was done with considerable effect by Gotthold Ephraim Lessing, who proved that French classicism was an effete caricature of the Greek model and that Shakespeare honored the spirit of Aristotelian poetics more than did Corneille and Racine. With Lessing's own plays modern German literature came into existence. Lessing, however, was not a Romantic. He regarded himself as the restorer of classicism in its purity; his humanitarian philosophy and theology were rationalistic, and they left the younger generation cold. It was Rousseau, and particularly the antirationalist aspects of Rousseau's teachings, that fired their enthusiasm. Lessing had liberated Germany from the yoke of French taste; Rousseau freed her from the frigid shackles of mere common sense. Yet if Rousseau was the emotional catalyst that set off the first phase of German Romanticism, it was a German pastor who gave the eighteenth-century movement its content and direction.

Johann Gottfried Herder was born at Riga, a stronghold of Protestant Pietism, in 1744. His childhood was spent in poverty. Both the Pietism and the poverty left marks on all his subsequent thought: the former found expression in his stress on the instinctive and the naive, the latter in his radical and somewhat aggressive social ideas. In his mind the Rousseauan postulate of the goodness of primitive man set off a completely original and very fruitful reaction. He was the first to investigate the anonymous, unconscious, collective creations of the unsophisticated people—the *Volk* or folk. He collected and translated thousands of folk songs and romances from virtually every nation, including Greenland; he formulated theories on the origin of language; he studied Gothic architecture, which he considered the collective expression of a national spirit (the German spirit, he thought); he probed the Romance, Hebrew, and German poetry of the Middle Ages.

In Herder's theory, every national group had its own

genius, spontaneously expressed in its collective art, and the many voices of the nations joined in the chorus of humanity. In his conception of nationalism, each voice had equal worth, yet each nation must follow its own particular characteristics lest it lose its national soul. Questionable as Herder's premises and conclusions may be, they proved immensely stimulating. Anthropology and some of its branches—ethnology, philology, folklore—all stand in debt to him, and the appreciation of "primitive" art forms, which have revolutionized twentieth-century aesthetics, is but another phase of the process started by Herder. At the same time, and rather ironically, the same Herder who saw humanity united in diversity also unwittingly gave impetus to racist philosophies that fastened upon and distorted his conception of the "folk-soul"—particularly his ideas about the German folk-soul.

Herder's immediate influence made itself felt in 1770 when in Strasbourg he met young Goethe, then a student there, and a group of other talented and enthusiastic youths. To them, who were already imbued with Rousseauan sensibility and boiling over with youthful ferment, he revealed Gothic architecture, the German Middle Ages, and Shakespeare as the founts from which the northern, Germanic soul should draw its inspiration. The result was an explosion of poetic creativity which on the literary plane prefigured the French Revolution in its violence. Aptly named *Sturm und Drang* (Storm and Stress) after a drama by one of Herder's disciples, the new movement threw all restraining rules to the winds and unleashed the strong, restless, rebellious, yearning, heaven-storming, Promethean, and chaotic emotions of its protagonists, each of whom regarded himself as an "original genius," subject to no rules save those of his own nature. Coupled with this was a morbid, neurotic sensibility that contrasted rather sharply with the naive and folklike qualities preached by Herder.

Among the productions of this period are Goethe's *Werther* and some of his finest lyrics; Gottfried August Bürger's marvelously paced and immensely popular ballads, especially *Lenore,* which soon also swept England in translation; and Schiller's dramas, *The Robbers, Fiesco,* and *Cabal and Love,* which contained a note of revolutionary social protest less clearly audible in his fellow writers. Although *Sturm und Drang* as a literary movement petered out in the 1780's, when its representatives had become either respectable or mad, its prolonged influence can be felt clearly in the music of Beethoven. Perhaps the noblest and most mature legacy of its spirit can be found in Schiller's *Ode to Joy,* written in 1785 and set to music by Beethoven in 1823.

Sturm und Drang as a movement may be said to have ended in 1786–87 when Goethe, by then a minister of state to the duke of Weimar, found his classical self in Italy, and when Schiller, having completed *Don Carlos,* perhaps his finest play, decided to give up the theatre to devote himself to historical and philosophical studies. The philosopher under whose influence Schiller had fallen was one of the towering minds of modern times, Immanuel Kant. Born in 1724 at Königsberg, from which he never strayed more than a few miles, Kant had his roots in the same Pietist middle-class milieu as Herder. Barely five feet tall, hollow-chested, slightly deformed, a lifelong bachelor with habits so regular that the people of Königsberg set their watches by him, he was a man all mind. It was only in 1781 in his fifty-eighth year that he published his first great work, the *Critique of Pure Reason.* His later writings were largely elaborations of the first. The main problem Kant set himself was to break out of the dead-end of Hume's skepticism. This he accomplished to his satisfaction by two devices: in the realm of ethics he accepted the necessity of an inner and universal moral law (actually not very different from that of his Pietist forebears or from Rousseau's conscience); in his theory of knowledge he distinguished between things of our experience, or phenomena, which may be known, and things-in-themselves, or noumena, which cannot be known.

This basic distinction in Kant's philosophy, which left the world of phenomena within the exclusive area of rational and scientific inquiry, did not satisfy his Romantic successors, who continued to build on, to expand, and to transform the Kantian edifice in blissful indifference to the fact that in doing so they were knocking its main prop from under it. What they seized upon was Kantian ethics and especially Kantian aesthetics and theology. In Kant's system the noumenal world though closed to rational investigation could be apprehended in some transcendental, nonrational manner in ethical, aesthetic, or religious experience. This is a thought that needs must appeal to poetic, emotional, and mystical temperaments; yet to the same kind of temperament the notion that the phenomenal world of scientific knowledge and the noumenal world of subjective experience must remain forever separate is acutely painful.

Friedrich Schiller's admirable writings on aesthetics still were very close to Kantian teachings. However, in the late 1790's there gathered around him at Jena, where he held a professorship of history, a group of men whose views soon diverged very radically from his. They were a brilliant, gifted, and highly neurotic lot: the poets Novalis and Ludwig Tieck; the philosophers Johann Gottlieb Fichte and Friedrich Schelling; the critic and translator August Wilhelm Schlegel and his brother, Friedrich Schlegel, a versatile man who formulated the aesthetic creed of Romanticism, championed woman's right to orgasm in a barely disguised autobiographical novel, ran away with and married a Jewess, became a Catholic convert, and introduced Hindu philosophy to Europe. What the members of the group had in common was their mystical bent, their enthusiasm for art, their love of the fantastic, and—at least in the cases of the Schlegels and of Schelling—their wives. They all were deeply influenced by the pantheism of Spinoza—"a man drunk with God," in Novalis' words; they all were steeped in the mystical literature of the seventeenth and eighteenth centuries. They all were determined to make a completely new beginning in virtually every field of intellectual and creative activity, and they succeeded in fulfilling this ambition.

What they admired most was their own emotions; what they despised most was other people's opinions. They were extremely erudite, exceptionally intelligent, and brilliantly imaginative. With these qualities, whatever they touched was transformed as if by magic. In the hands of Fichte and Schelling, Kantian philosophy was transmuted, by successive amputation, grafting, and rarefaction, into a mixture of Platonist idealism and Spinozist pantheism, which in turn produced Hegel's dialectical idealism, in which the Absolute Being unfolds itself in Becoming. Since Karl Marx, who was decidedly anti-Romantic, adapted Hegel's dialectics to his materialist philosophy, it may be said that the entire nineteenth and twentieth centuries were deeply affected by the German Romantic philosophers.

The pantheistic outlook of the Romantics was reflected in the theology of Friedrich Schleiermacher, a member of the circle, who sought to bridge what Kant had separated— the worlds of phenomena and of noumena—and whose influence is still felt in present-day attempts to reconcile science and religion. Aptly enough, Schleiermacher means in German "maker of veils." Ten years after Friedrich Schlegel published his great work on Hindu philosophy, Arthur Schopenhauer published his *The World as Will and Idea* (1818), the Western version of Buddhist pessimism, whose influence on modern thought has been immeasurable. In aesthetics the Romantics' impact was equally decisive: they were the first to view all art as a symbolic language addressed to a deeper, unconscious awareness in the human soul. Even Freudian psychology, in its stress on what is most unrational in man and in its dependence on symbols, is largely indebted to the German Romantics of the early 1800's.

No matter how high a place the Romantics assigned to originality and individual self-expression, they tended to cultivate those emotions and yearnings that obliterate individual identity in a sense of belonging to something greater and more lasting than the ephemeral self: mystic union with God or the Infinite; pantheistic self-identification with Nature; the ecstasy of sexual love; and an urge for death. They rejected and loathed the prosy, philistine, common-sense world in which they lived; they looked back to the Catholic Middle Ages as an era of cultural universality and of German greatness, in which the basic aspirations of the human soul found satisfaction in a harmonious synthesis. Gothic architecture, which they regarded as peculiarly akin to the spirit of the German people, sym-

Chateaubriand's writings introduced Romanticism to France.

bolized both the upward striving of the mind and the humble subordination of the self to collective endeavor.

The Gothic revival, which had begun in England half a century earlier as an architectural fad, became for them a matter of *Weltanschauung,* a way of viewing the universe. German nationalism might have remained on this rarefied metaphysical plane for a long time if Napoleon's defeat in Russia had not channeled it in a more warlike direction. The general uprising of Germany against Napoleon in 1813 had little to do with the theories of the Romantics and a great deal with the intolerable tyranny of the Napoleonic regime. Yet those who constituted themselves the voice of their nation were for the most part ardent Romantic intellectuals, and their yearning for self-identification with the people and for self-destruction found an ideal outlet in the glorification of war. Paunchy university professors turned into soldiers and felt happiness for the first time in their lives, while promising young poets such as Theodor Körner likened their sword to their bride (a curious inversion of sexual symbolism) and looked forward to death on the battlefield with a lover's impatience for the bridal bed. (Körner's wish was granted: he fell in 1813 at the age of twenty-two.)

It was in literature and to a lesser degree in art that the Romantics' nostalgia for the Middle Ages found its most fruitful expression. The utter remoteness of the idealized image from historical reality was a positive asset. The medieval world such as we find it, for example, in Novalis'

Condorcet

Bentham

Jefferson

A. W. Schlegel

Humboldt

Goethe

The astonishing ferment of the German romantic movement was paralleled, if not equalled in other countries. England could boast geniuses as diverse as Burke and the romantic poets; political theorists gained control of the intellectual life of America and France. Some of the era's great thinkers are shown on this page.

Herder

Schiller

Burke

Fulton

Schopenhauer

unfinished novel *Heinrich von Ofterdingen* is a pure poetic creation, marvelous and mysterious yet fresh and bright, like the fairy tale forests that became so popular in German literature. In less gifted hands the romance of chivalry soon bogged down in somewhat cloying clichés, and eventually under Sir Walter Scott's influence the fantastic medieval world of the early Romantics, which had been all poetry and image and symbol, degenerated into pseudohistorical pseudorealism.

The folk tale and lyrical poetry fared better: Tieck invented some lovely folk stories; Brentano and Achim von Arnim collected the marvelous and incomparable volumes of folk songs known as *Des Knaben Wunderhorn,* and the brothers Grimm, besides siring modern philology, published their famous collection of German fairy tales. The quest for the naive and the simple, for *das Volkstümliche* (the folklike) in art probably found its supreme expression in the German *Lied,* which in Schubert's hands combined simplicity with the highest sophistication. Indeed, since Romanticism aimed at expressing the inexpressible and in giving form to the elusive, music was its most appropriate medium. In architecture it produced nothing of value; in painting the German school of the "Nazarenes," centered in Rome, produced interesting theories anticipating the Pre-Raphaelites but not many good pictures. Romanticism in painting, quite distinct from the theories of the German Romantics, began in Napoleonic France with the work of Gros and Géricault.

The systems and theories of the German Romantics were extremely stimulating in their novelty and opened up not only a new psychology of art but a systematic approach to the unplumbed depths of man's irrational soul. Yet their originality should not overshadow the fact that some of the greatest and most original minds of early nineteenth-century Germany stood outside the Romantic movement, no matter how much they may have been influenced by it. Schiller, Kantian though he was, had no patience with the medievalizing and mystical tendencies of the Romantics; Beethoven in his outlook belonged to the Enlightenment and in his aesthetics was entirely independent; Kleist, whose *Novellen* and plays are profoundly original, shared little with the Romantics apart from his nationalism and neuroses; the beauty and power of Hölderlin's poems are the product of his genius (too soon beclouded by insanity) and of the Greek ideal.

As for the towering figure in literature, Goethe, he flirted with the Romantics for a while and accepted incense from whatever source, but it was he who made the remark, "I call classical that which is healthy and Romantic that which is sick." His aversion for Newtonian mechanics and mathematics in general combined with his interest in the sciences enticed him into espousing Schelling's *Naturphilosophie,* with questionable results, but in the main it may be said of him that everything was grist for his poetic mill.

He simply appropriated what he found poetically useful—paganism, Catholicism, mysticism, medievalism, classicism, Orientalism, and all the rest. Protean, he delighted in mystifying the public; Olympian, he was a rule to himself.

Romanticism as a state of mind was not confined to a particular school of thought or country. In England, Samuel Taylor Coleridge and Walter Scott stood definitely under the influence of German Romantic philosophy, and William Wordsworth's nostalgia for the lost awareness, the "vision splendid" of childhood, harked back to Rousseau. On the whole, however, English Romanticism developed gradually and independently in the eighteenth century and did not make a sharp break with tradition. The four most original English poets of the early Romantic period were not associated with any literary movement: Blake's mysticism was unsullied by sophisticated literary theory; Keats and Shelley, like Hölderlin in Germany, yearned for pagan Greece; as for Byron, he was completely a child of the eighteenth century; his models were Dryden and Pope, and there was nothing Romantic in him except his Byronism.

Byronism was essentially the same phenomenon as the *mal du siècle* that Chateaubriand made fashionable with his novel *René*—a compound of disabused boredom, weariness, restless striving after new sensations, and constant agonizing awareness of the transience and vanity of all things. That it was not a mere romantic pose must be clear to anyone who looks into the diaries of Benjamin Constant, by no means a Romantic but decidedly a sufferer from the disease. Chateaubriand's attempt to rehabilitate Christianity by showing in caressing prose how aesthetically satisfying and pleasurable it was bears superficial resemblance to the German Romantics' nostalgia for the Catholic Middle Ages; yet Chateaubriand had nothing mystical about him, and in his politics he had a thoroughly realistic grasp of modern trends and conditions. In France Romanticism did not come into bloom until later in the nineteenth century, when the schoolboys of the Napoleonic era had grown into manhood.

The philistine drabness that succeeded the imperial glory created a favorable climate for the cultivation of the *mal du siècle,* and the influence of German Romanticism was making itself felt, thanks largely to Madame de Staël's book *De l'Allemagne,* which was first published in London in 1813. Madame de Staël had traveled in Germany in 1803–4 and in 1808 and had seen almost everybody worth seeing. She had absorbed the new ideas (sometimes a little superficially), and although she was not always in sympathy with them she had found them stimulating. Intellectual life in France had become anemic under Napoleon's heavy hand and, she thought, needed a blood transfusion. In 1810 her great work on Germany was ready and printed; on Napoleon's specific order the entire edition was confiscated and destroyed. The suggestion that *la Grande Nation* could learn anything from another nation displeased

the master. As his minister of police, Savary, wrote to Madame de Staël: "We have not yet reached the point where we have to model ourselves on the nations you admire. Your last work is un-French."

To be French, in Napoleon's view, was to belong to *la Grande Nation.* Richelieu and Louis XIV had made the French nation great but it was he, Napoleon, who was making it supreme and therefore embodied France. To attack French supremacy in any way whatever, as Madame de Staël had done, was to attack his own supremcy. Literature, architecture, sculpture, painting, music—all must be monumental, patriotic, and martial in inspiration. If the empire style is impressive at its worst and admirably graceful at its best, this is because the men into whose hands Bonaparte entrusted the arts had taste, wit, and tradition. Late Roman and early Egyptian monumentality were happily adapted to the intimacy and lightness of the Louis XVI and Directoire styles.

Apart from the decorative arts, the official classicism produced little of great value. David's heroic paintings (unlike his admirable portraits and sketches) are lifeless rather than classical, especially when compared to the great French classical painters of the seventeenth century—Poussin and Claude Lorrain. For strength, originality, and innovation in painting one must look to Gros, who rebelled against David's academism, and especially to Turner in England and to Goya in Spain. The official French musical and literary life was equally academic. On the stage, Talma triumphed as a tragic actor, but not a single French play of any worth survives from the Napoleonic period—the time when Schiller, Goethe, and Kleist produced their greatest works in Germany. It would be unfair to blame this blight entirely on Napoleon. Undoubtedly French arts and letters would have gone through a relatively sterile period even without his heavy hand. Still, it cannot be denied that he disliked and suppressed any kind of intellectual and artistic ferment. Glorious and colorful as his pageantry may have been, it was hardly art.

What of technology and science? Both made tremendous strides during Napoleon's reign, but apart from establishing cash prizes and setting up specialized schools, he did little to encourage them. Jean Antoine Chaptal, who served under Napoleon as minister of the interior from 1801 to 1809, modernized and expanded the networks of roads and canals in France, promoted improved agricultural methods, and, being a chemist himself, took a special interest in the application of chemistry to industry. Nicolas Appert invented the first method of canning food in response to a prize offered by the government for a way of preserving food in army and navy depots. Joseph Jacquard invented a loom that revolutionized the textile industry. The state bought the patent for it from him in 1806, but inventions of less immediate usefulness impressed Napoleon less favorably. "Bah!" he said of Robert Fulton, whose submarine *Nautilus* had just been demonstrated in the Seine. "All these inventors, all these project mongers are either schemers or visionaries. Don't mention him again."

Although Napoleon's appreciation of the technological and scientific progress in his time was only sporadic, the progress was steady, continuous, and on the whole unaffected by either the noise of Napoleon's armies or the siren song of German *Naturphilosophie*. The so-called Industrial Revolution, then already well in progress, owed little or nothing to scientific discovery. Ingenious though they may be, such inventions as Richard Arkwright's power loom or Eli Whitney's cotton gin are the works of mechanics, not of scientists. William Murdock, who produced the first gas light in London in 1803, merely exploited commercially what the Persians had known since the time of Zoroaster. The same cannot be said of Humphrey Davy's invention of the arc lamp (1801), for although electricity as a phenomenon had been known since ancient times, its nature was only beginning to be understood and its practical uses were in the future.

Since Cavendish, Galvani, Volta, Lavoisier, Davy, Coulomb, Gay-Lussac, and Dalton were contemporaries of Napoleon, his era might well be called that of the Physical Revolution, for it fundamentally changed man's conception of the physical universe. In mathematics Lagrange, Laplace, and Gauss were opening up new horizons. In astronomy Sir William Herschel counted some twenty-five hundred nebulae and reached the conclusion that the solar system was moving through space, while Laplace gave scientific formulation to the nebular hypothesis of the universe. In the biological sciences Karl Ernst von Baer made a systematic comparative study of embryonic development, Georges Cuvier laid the foundations of paleontology, and the zoologist Geoffroy Saint-Hilaire formulated the theory (which greatly appealed to Goethe) that all animals conformed to a single plan of structure.

Goethe himself contributed to the evolutionary theory first proposed by Buffon when he discovered the rudiment of the intermaxillary bone in man. Of greater interest, however, was the work of Jean Baptiste de Lamarck, who in 1801 made public his evolutionary system of the origin of species. Lamarck's hypothesis, which implied the inheritance of acquired characteristics, was later displaced by Charles Darwin's theory of natural selection. Although Bernard Shaw tried to revive it (one wonders how seriously), its importance is more historic than scientific. The Austrians Friedrich Anton Mesmer and Franz Joseph Gall, whose ideas were tremendously popular in their day, although they were at least 60 per cent charlatans, stimulated the advance of psychology and psychiatry—Mesmer by introducing hypnosis into medical treatment, Gall by inventing phrenology, which assigned the several faculties of the mind to specific localities of the brain. Among more orthodox physicians, the Englishman Sir William Jenner introduced vaccination against smallpox and the Frenchman René Laënnec invented the stethoscope—which he used for the first time in 1817 in Paris to listen to the last heartbeats of Madame de Staël.

Man's knowledge (or what he thought to be knowledge) of himself and of the physical universe was expanding. Although the heroic era of discoveries was long past, the earth was now beginning to be explored systematically. Captain Cook's last expedition, with its carefully selected personnel and equipment, had set an example to later explorers. Alexander von Humboldt's exploration of the South American continent was entirely scientific in character; the observations made by him and by his French companion Bompland were equally valuable to meteorology, geology, botany, and zoology. Even Bonaparte's Egyptian campaign, as has been seen, yielded important scientific, ethnological, and archaeological information. Mungo Park explored the totally unknown interior of central Africa; the Lewis and Clark expedition, due to Jefferson's initiative, opened up the North American continent to United States expansionism and at the same time made contributions to physical geography and ethnology. It was by no means accidental that the first systematic hypothesis of the origin of the earth, James Hutton's *Theory of the Earth,* should appear about that time, in 1795.

An attempt, however sketchy, has been made in the foregoing pages to pursue the strands of ideas, intellectual attitudes, and scientific studies both backward into the eighteenth century and forward into our own time. If intellectual historians have found it convenient to stop the eighteenth century in 1789 and to begin the nineteenth century in 1815, they have undoubtedly spared themselves many difficulties, but they have not served the cause of truth. For it was precisely in this interval from 1789 to 1815 that the old ideas came together and in the shock and friction of a violent age of transition generated new ones. Ideas had been fairly set before 1789; they again became fairly set after 1815. In the interval they were in marvelous disorder, in a veritable orgy of cross-fertilization. Neither the armies nor the police nor the marblelike gaze of Napoleon could discipline them. Just as in the Paris dance halls under the Directory ex-dukes would disport themselves shoulder-to-shoulder with ex-Terrorists, and ex-monks cavort with ex-harlots, so the things of the mind mixed freely for a brief moment, heedless of former labels and classifications, dressed up in a riot of fantastic new fashions. Meanwhile, the scholar continued to read as if nothing were happening, the physicist made new experiments suggested by the old, and the astronomer observed the stars and counted nebulae.

A TIME OF CHANGE

"It is impossible to appreciate the state of public depravity," the Paris police announced a few years after the Revolution. Men no longer raised their hats to ladies, and the young freely *tutoyered* their elders, obscene graffiti appeared everywhere on the walls, and the number of illegitimate births increased alarmingly. In Paris the populace affected absurd costumes, and the peasants in the fields looked more brutish than ever, for with the reform of the calendar they now shaved every ten days instead of every Sunday. But after the fall of Robespierre society quickly resumed a more orderly course. "Luxury, pleasure, and the arts are reviving astonishingly," Napoleon wrote to his brother from Paris in 1795. Although the new society incorporated a sizable share of parvenus and criminals, Paris could still boast its brilliant and cultivated circles, and hostesses as charming as the beautiful young Juliette Récamier, who is shown above in a portrait by Gérard.

Above, left to right: gowns of the old regime, the early Revolution, and the Directory; the women below are wearing a crossed belt commemorating a guillotined victim, a Grecian gown and shawl, and a turban, made stylish by Napoleon's Egyptian campaign.

FASHIONS

The Revolution forced Louis XVI to exchange his crown for a red cap of liberty. His subjects varied their costumes as radically; after the Revolution fashions changed at so dizzying a pace that even the editors of fashion journals, published every five days, confessed themselves unable to keep up with the innovations. Before 1789 the ornate costumes of the old regime (seen at left, in the top row of fashion plates reproduced on the facing page) were giving way to garments of revolutionary simplicity (top row center). Soon this style was superseded by a craze for "antique" gowns made of the flimsiest muslin, which clung to the wearer's body and revealed the extent of her charms. This daring fashion was too conservative for some, however; they bared their bosoms entirely or appeared in gowns of transparent gauze, with nothing on beneath. Doctors remonstrated in vain against these bold innovations, reminding the ladies that the climate of France was far harsher than that of Greece, but the French-woman's only concession to the elements was to don a voluminous shawl.

After the Reign of Terror women whose relatives had been guillotined commemorated them by wearing a crossed belt on their backs and sometimes—a more macabre fashion—a thin red ribbon tied about their necks. Both sexes cropped their hair close or pushed it away from the nape of the neck in imitation of the victims. Most bizarre of all were the *Incroyables,* Parisian dandies who affected a look of untidy old age. With their spectacles, unkempt hair, and baggy trousers, and their necks swaddled in high collars and flowing cravats, they strongly influenced men's fashions for a few years during the period of the Directory.

A caricature of a Parisian beau (right) shows him in the Incroyable's *high collar and ill-fitting trousers.*

OVERLEAF: *The fashionable world of Paris gathered at establishments such as Frascati's to dance, gamble, and enjoy ices. Frascati's grand ballroom was decorated in the classical manner, like most of the women assembled there. The ladies shown here are wearing the high-waisted "classical" gowns typical of the Empire period.*

PARIS AT PLAY

The age's great tragedian, Talma, was a friend of the emperor.

At the height of the Reign of Terror, even the prostitutes of Paris had feared to walk the streets at night, preferring to sacrifice their livelihoods rather than risk their lives. The children of the city played with toy guillotines, but their elders hardly dared to play at all. They were forced to rely for amusement on a theatre devoted to propaganda plays, or on those joyless public festivals of dedication which dictators even today favor for the entertainment of their subjects. But with the fall of Robespierre Paris once more became a city of pleasure. Courtesans resumed their customary promenades. Speculators, enriched by the sudden inflation, crowded the gambling houses and pleasure gardens. Bourgeois families patronized the city's many new restaurants, which were opened by chefs whose aristocratic employers had been killed or had been forced to flee the country. (Among other innovations, the Revolution had inaugurated the great French tradition of fine public restaurants.) But most of all, the populace danced.

A mania for dancing swept over Paris. Wherever there was an empty space large enough, a dance hall was opened, in gardens, in the palaces of exiled aristocrats, in disused convents. The Church of St. Sulpice, on the left bank, was painted yellow and a dance hall opened in its cemetery, where the customers pranced about on a board floor laid above the gravestones. Under the Directory the city had hundreds of dance halls, some the cheap resorts of servants, but many more, pretentious establishments, where ambitious mothers might bring their daughters to seek out

suitable mates. After 1797 suitors were better enabled to assess these maidens' charms by the introduction of the waltz, described by an early practitioner as "a dance of familiarity demanding the amalgamation of two dancers." The female partner was invariably clad in an exceedingly scanty fashion.

The theatre, too, attracted its devotees. Tickets were cheap and performances changed often; it was customary for citizens of every class to attend a play once or twice a week. The enthusiasm which in dictatorships today is often devoted to football teams, in lieu of political activity, was then given to supporting rival performers. Each of the great actors had a claque, which greeted his performances with noisy appreciation, gratifying the actor, perhaps, but annoying the rest of the audience.

Under Napoleon, censorship was severe. "Freedom of thought is the main conquest of the century," a government spokesman proclaimed, "and the emperor wishes it to be respected." Nevertheless, Corneille and Racine were expurgated of any lines that might seem to reflect on Napoleon's usurpation of the throne. The censors' task was not solely negative, however. Some verses were added to Corneille's *Héraclius* which seemed to make that playwright justify Napoleon's seizure of power. If the censors, as is their custom, were ridiculously conscientious, the audience on the other hand compensated for it. It was extremely quick to respond, with laughter or cheers, to any lines in the classics that might conceivably have topical application.

The sport of chariot racing evoked the spirit if not the splendor of classical Rome. The water color is by Carle Vernet.

The Luxembourg Gardens were crowded, as they are today, with lovers, elderly and loquacious men, and children at play.

The gambling salons of Paris were frequented by royalist intriguers as well as by those who were addicted to roulette.

Fashionable ladies, like those shown above, took ices daily at a favorite cafe. A craze for dancing reached all strata of society; in the satirical engraving below, even household pets and the pictures on the wall reflect the current mania.

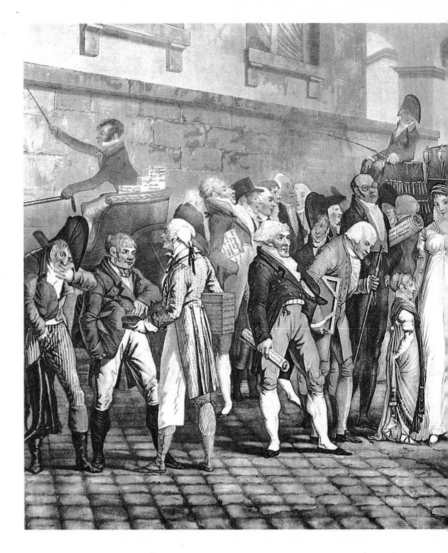

"If you want . . . a good deal, you should come and buy [the estate of M. de Montigny]," Napoleon wrote to his brother Joseph in 1795. *"... I am sure you can get this place for 80,000 francs in silver; before the Revolution, it was worth 250,000."* For people on the way up socially, like the Bonapartes, the years after the Revolution were prosperous ones, but for others, like the impoverished aristocrat shown below fishing in the Seine for his dinner (with disappointing results), they were less pleasant. As it had before the Revolution, Paris displayed astonishing contrasts of poverty and wealth, with many near starvation and others spending money prodigally. Sharing in the prosperity of the rich were hundreds of artisans, dressmakers, and tradesmen in luxury goods, like those seen at right, waiting outside the house of a patron.

THE NEW SOCIETY

When the Catholic religion was re-established in France, speculators were quick to take advantage of the nation's spiritual revival. They cornered the market in prayer books and sold them to the public at exorbitant prices. An age of revolution offered the astute entrepreneur unlimited opportunities for enrichment. Millions were made selling sugar that had been smuggled past the British blockade. Purveyors of military supplies and successful generals acquired great fortunes. Speculation in the value of *assignats,* the paper money that the government issued feverishly in an attempt to overcome the scarcity of specie, was also lucrative. Between 1793 and 1796 inflation was widespread, and the holders of paper money, which seemed to depreciate in value day by day, were eager to exchange it for real property. The best bargains were the former estates of the nobles and the Church, which had been confiscated by the state and which were being sold to the public. Eventually a large influential class arose, with wealth based on this property; it had a vested interest in keeping the old order

A former washerwoman who became a duchess, the wife of Marshal Lefebvre was nicknamed "Madame Sans-Gêne" (roughly,"Lady Free-and-Easy") because she never lost the manners of her youth.

from returning to power. The ranks of the *nouveaux riches* were joined by the industrialists who amassed great fortunes from their country's control of European markets during the Napoleonic wars. These people, the prototypes of the powerful upper bourgeoisie who were to rule France throughout the nineteenth century, were the real beneficiaries of the French Revolution.

As they had acquired the property, so they acquired the tastes, if not the flavor of the old aristocracy. Ruinous sums were spent on gowns and parties, and on the decoration of apartments. (Certain hostesses even changed the furniture in their drawing rooms to match their new dresses.) But despite the expense, the results were often less than distinguished. The vulgar pretensions of the *nouveaux riches* were parodied on the stage in 1796 in a popular play entitled *Mme. Angot, or the Parvenu Fishwife.* Thanks to the destruction of the old nobility, its heroine had attained a high place in society, but she still retained her awe of the aristocracy and a secret desire for a title. Unlike most of the plays of the period, this literature was remarkably true to life; within a few years Napoleon was to create a new nobility for his imperial pageant and gratify many of the parvenus with titles of their own.

Above, escorted by a troop of Mamelukes, Napoleon rides along the banks of the Seine in his carriage. Across the river are the Invalides dome and the Chamber of Deputies. The Concorde Bridge leading to them was built in part of stones from the Bastille. Soldiers (or men with a military bearing) achieved success with the ladies, as the engraving (left) shows.

THE
MARTIAL
SPIRIT

French schoolboys marched to school wearing military uniforms. Their classes started and ended with the sound of drums. For throughout the Napoleonic era military influence was in evidence everywhere in France. At the Paris opera, dragoons with drawn swords stood guard over the audience. Furniture was often decorated with eagles and trophies, symbolizing victory, and the loyal wives and mistresses of Napoleon's officers might sleep in beds with curtains draped in the shape of a military tent. "A martial air reigns through the town," an English visitor to Paris wrote in 1802. "Soldiers parade most of the principal streets and keep the peace; the utmost respect is paid to everything military." France worshiped its defenders unreservedly, and they in turn took full and often unethical advantage of the fact. They elbowed civilians aside and monopolized the ladies, both in the fashionable salons and on the streets. Some cudgeled civilians who failed to make way for them, and joyously engaged in duels with each other in the public thoroughfares, to the peril of innocent passersby.

OVERLEAF: *An 1810 painting shows the fountain and column in the Place du Châtelet, built to honor the soldiers who had fought in Egypt.*

FROM CONSUL
TO CAESAR

It is for the sake of a remote, indeterminate goal,
which they themselves do not fully apprehend,
that men became heroes and that the inspired
minority triumphs over the inert masses.

During a meeting with Goethe in 1808, Napoleon impressed that great man with some "very significant" remarks on the subject of tragedy. As Goethe recalled the interview, "he was also led to criticize the tragedies of fate. 'What do they want from fate in our age?' he said. 'Politics is fate.'" This was an idea Napoleon had uttered several times before. For example, during the night preceding the Battle of Austerlitz, he philosophized: "The principle of political necessity is a rich source of strong emotions, a fertile germ of the most dramatic situations, a modern fate no less imperious, no less ineluctable than that of the ancients. . . . Thus everything that is called a coup d'état or political crime could become a fit subject for a tragedy: horror being mitigated by necessity, a new and sustained kind of pathos would result." To Fouché, his minister of police, he wrote a year later: "It is politics which leads to catastrophe without there being a real crime." Ironically enough, it was Fouché who had remarked, after Napoleon's murder of the duc d'Enghien, "It's worse than a crime—it's a mistake." If, in the Napoleonic conception of politics, crimes may be justified by necessity, surely errors cannot.

When Bonaparte came to power late in 1799, blood was already on his hands; the man who had ordered some two to three thousand Turkish prisoners of war to be shot and bayoneted had a very elastic notion of what constituted necessity. But the crimes—or mistakes—he had perpetrated

in Egypt and Syria were not yet known in Europe, and the plague-ridden, half-blind army he had left behind would return only two years later. English propagandists, it is true, spread rumors of his deeds, but the truth in their stories was embedded in such masses of crude lies that only the prejudiced believed them. Those close to him—among them his mother, his brothers, his wife—feared him instinctively, not so much for any specific reason as because of the terrifying and ruthless strength that emanated from him. "The terror he inspires is inconceivable," Madame de Staël wrote to her father after spending a weekend at Joseph Bonaparte's estate. "One has the impression of an impetuous wind blowing about one's ears when one is near that man." Those not near him, although they were astonished by his energy and activity, admired them at first without sensing their fearsome implications.

The achievements of the first two years of Napoleon's rule seemed stupendous indeed; in the eyes of the general public he appeared a second Augustus, a demigod, who not only restored the world to order and peace but also was proof incarnate that greatness had finally come back to dwell on earth. Then, with seeming suddenness, came

Napoleon made Malmaison his country residence during the
period he served France as First Consul; the château library,
shown at right, today contains some of his campaign maps.

As First Consul, Napoleon installs the Council of State in 1799; with him are the Second and Third Consuls, Cambacérès and Lebrun.

the flagrant crime and usurpation—the murder, in 1804, of the duc d'Enghien and Napoleon's coronation as emperor. Some thought the murder a trifle or an unfortunate mistake, and experienced no shock at usurpation—and tyranny. Thus Goethe could write of him, as late as 1811:

> *What centuries have dimly meditated*
> *His mind surveys in brightest clarity;*
> *All that is petty has evaporated,*
> *Here nothing is of weight save earth and sea.*

And Heinrich Heine, still a small boy, seeing the emperor lead his cavalcade across the municipal lawn at Düsseldorf, despite the signs saying that stepping on the grass was *streng verboten,* conceived a lifelong worship for the hero. "His countenance," Heine could write long after Napoleon's career had run its course, "was of the complexion we find on the marble heads of Greeks and Romans. The features were

as nobly proportioned as those of ancient statues, and on his face was written: Thou shalt have no other god but me."

Professor Georg Wilhelm Hegel was scarcely less impressed when he saw Napoleon ride through Jena after his great victory in 1806; the emperor seemed the embodiment of the Absolute Ideal. Others reacted differently. After Enghien's murder, Chateaubriand resigned from government service (later, he would ignore the emperor's threat to have him sabered down on the steps of the Institute), and when Beethoven learned of Bonaparte's decision to have himself crowned emperor, he angrily crossed out his dedication to him of the *Eroica Symphony.* To most it seemed that between 1800 and 1804 the First Consul underwent a metamorphosis both spiritual and physical. While his features were filling in and his complexion changing to marble whiteness, he transformed himself, by successive steps, from a republican general into a Roman *imperator:* the hero at the bridge of Arcole, as painted by Gros, and the despot in his coronation robes, as painted by Ingres, could not be the same person.

Napoleon's remarks on political necessity having the strength of fate were undoubtedly intended to create the impression that his progress toward Caesarism was ineluctable. He hoped thus to gain the sympathies of the liberals. To Benjamin Constant he made this astonishing confession shortly before Waterloo: "I wanted to rule the world, and in order to do this I needed unlimited power. . . . I wanted to rule the world—who wouldn't have in my place? The world begged me to govern it . . ." Anybody would have done what he did, not excluding Washington, he told Las Cases at St. Helena. "If Washington had been a Frenchman at a time when France was crumbling inside and invaded from outside, I would have dared him to be himself; or, if he had persisted in being himself, he would merely have been a fool. . . . As for me, I could only be a crowned Washington. And I could become that only at a congress of kings, surrounded by sovereigns whom I had either persuaded or mastered. Then, and then only, could I have profitably displayed Washington's moderation, disinterestedness, and wisdom. In all reasonableness, I could not attain this goal except by means of world dictatorship. I tried it. Can it be held against me?"

The thought that Napoleon's quest for world dictatorship was imposed on him by fatal necessity just as the cross was imposed on Christ (with whom he occasionally deigned to compare himself) taxes one's credulity. The necessity arose only out of his character, not out of the circumstances, which merely presented him with the opportunities. And although some of his characteristics became more pronounced as he came closer to his goal and more millions had given their lives for it, it cannot be said that any real metamorphosis took place in him despite the seeming change during his years as First Consul.

The first to feel Bonaparte's "impetuous wind" blowing about his ears, recalling the phrase of Madame de Staël, was Sieyès. Of the three consuls, he enjoyed the greatest reputation as a politician and an oracle on constitutional theory. Ducos, too, had seniority over Bonaparte, having been a member of the Convention and of the Directory. But Citizen Bonaparte, who was young enough to be their son and had never held political office, was dissatisfied with the constitution proposed by Sieyès, and so his two colleagues had to call on him every night in order to revise the draft. After a few days, Bonaparte became impatient; there was too much talk, and the prospect of having to submit the instrument, once it was completed, to two legislative commissions appointed for that purpose was positively intolerable. On the night of December 13—only five weeks after 18 Brumaire—he cut short the palaver by summoning the members of the commissions to his apartment and bidding them sign the articles as revised; they complied. There remained the formality of submitting the

constitution to the nation in a plebiscite, a time-consuming procedure in those days. Napoleon's impatience could not brook such a delay. On December 25, 1799, long before the plebiscite was completed, the new constitution was declared to be in force.

The Constitution of the Year VIII was a compromise between appearance and substance. Certain of its provisions were concessions to Sieyès' ideas, but they barely disguised its essential feature, which was the concentration of authority in the hands of one man. At the basis of the constitution was the electorate. The electorate, however, did not elect anybody; it merely drew up lists of candidates, who in turn drew up lists of candidates from among themselves, who in turn drew up a "national list," from which the Senate was to select the members of the legislative bodies and of the executive. This masterpiece of democratic procedure had been devised by Sieyès. Even if it had ever functioned, it would have made a mockery of suffrage; as it happened, at the start all important officials were selected without the help of the lists, which were used later only when vacancies occurred.

Among the four assemblies established by the constitution, the most bizarre was perhaps the Conservative Senate. It was to appoint the members of the three other assemblies as well as the chief executive; senators were to hold office for life and to fill vacancies in their body by co-option. The question of who was to appoint the senators was solved neatly on the night of December 13, when Bonaparte appointed Sieyès and Ducos senators while they appointed him First Consul. Sieyès and Ducos along with Lebrun and Cambacérès then named the rest of the senators. If these club rules seem humorous, so do the rules under which the two legislative chambers were to function. There was a Tribunate, in which proposed legislation was discussed but not voted upon, and there was a Legislative Body, in which legislation was voted upon but not discussed. Neither body could initiate laws. As may be imagined, the Tribunate was soon muzzled, and the Legislative Body became a mere rubber stamp. As for the fourth assembly, the Council of State, its functions and composition were not defined in the constitution proper but in an executive ordinance issued on December 26. The Council of State became the administrative organ of France.

If certain constitutional clauses were devised to nullify or to by-pass suffrage and representative government, the provisions concerning the executive branch were calculated to strengthen its head. General Bonaparte was made First Consul, a title roughly equivalent to that of *princeps,* given by the Roman Senate to Augustus. The two other consuls served only in an advisory capacity, although authority might be delegated to one or both of them in the First Consul's absence. Needless to say, they were appointed by Bonaparte; his choice fell on Jean Jacques Cambacérès, a distinguished jurist and notorious pederast, for Second Consul, and on Charles François Lebrun, a political nonentity with royalist leanings and some literary ambitions, for Third Consul. The Council of Ministers was organized in such a manner as to create a maximum of duplication of duties: besides the Ministry of Finance, there was a Ministry of the Public Treasury; besides the Ministry of War, a Ministry of Military Administration; besides the Ministry of the Interior, a Ministry of General Police. No doubt this division of administrative tasks increased the efficiency of some departments but it also weakened the authority of the ministers and reduced them to the status of civil servants. Only two of them—Talleyrand and Fouché, respectively ministers of foreign affairs and of general police—retained a degree of independence, and that was due partly to the nature of their offices, partly to their formidable personalities.

As for local government, it was defined by an organic law issued on February 17, 1800, and was characterized by complete centralization, with all officials at all levels—prefects, sub-prefects, and mayors—appointed by and responsible to the central government. This feature outlasted the Napoleonic regime and has remained essentially unchanged. On the day following the promulgation of the law, the result of the plebiscite was announced: 3,011,007 votes for the new constitution and 1,526 votes against. The ratio might have been somewhat different if the voting had been secret; nevertheless, there can be little doubt that any constitution promising stability and order would have received overwhelming popular approval. No sooner was the result announced than, on February 19, the First Consul took residence in the former royal palace of the Tuileries.

Napoleon's repeated recourse to plebiscites was a significant feature of his regime. The device had been used as early as 1792 to ratify the annexation of the papal possessions of Avignon and the Comtat Venaissin to France, but it was Napoleon who first used it to legitimize dictatorship. In principle, the plebiscite acknowledged the fundamental assumption of the French Revolution, that all sovereignty resided in the people; in practice, it was the instrument by which the people abdicated its sovereignty. Even more important from the practical point of view, it identified Napoleon with the virtually unanimous consensus of the nation and enabled him to silence his critics on the ground that they were "anti-national." Finally, it was a convenient device that could always be resorted to when it seemed desirable to bypass the regular organs of government or to consecrate any fundamental constitutional change. The parallel of Napoleon's use of plebiscites with the use made of them in the Fifth French Republic is inescapable, but so are the differences. Plebiscites can be manipulated to sanction dictatorship and they can also be used to give democratic expression to the popular will. In either case, their function is to stress national unity at the expense of representative parliamentary government.

It must have been obvious to the knowledgeable that France was headed for a regime at least as autocratic as and even more centralized than that of Louis XIV. A few critics raised their voices; the fact that they were quickly silenced only emphasized their point. On the whole, however, the dictatorial nature of Bonaparte's government was both disguised and mitigated by his genuine determination to make use of the ablest men available, regardless of their political past, to create a strong, united, and prosperous France. Jacobins, royalists, all were to put aside sterile ideology and become simply Frenchmen. A "loyal opposition," he thought, might have a useful function in England, but in France it was impossible, and he argued this point rather convincingly during a session of the Council of State. In England, he said, the political parties were not in disagreement on matters of principle. "With us, it is quite different. Here the opposition consists of the Jacobins and of the ex-privileged classes. . . . The former want their clubs back, the latter the old regime. There is a great deal of difference between free discussion in a country whose institutions are long established and the opposition in a country that is still unsettled." The argument was cogent and it led inevitably to the point where the First Consul could write to one of his ambassadors: "In France there is but a single party and a single will."

The word *positive* constantly recurred in Napoleon's utterances. Everybody had to be positive—that is, to abstain from negative criticism. However, especially during the first half of his rule, Napoleon was by no means intolerant of criticism expressed within the limits of his councils, so long as only his means but not his aims were questioned. Nowhere does he appear in a more favorable light than in the transcripts of the meetings of the Council of State held under his chairmanship. The Council of State was Napoleon's own creation, and its very organization testifies to an extraordinary grasp of the essentials of modern statesmanship. Its members, whose number fluctuated between forty and forty-five, were chosen on the sole basis of their ability, experience, and efficiency; they included former revolutionists, returned émigrés, civil servants who had held office under the old regime, as well as military and naval men, lawyers, and financial experts.

After 1802 cabinet ministers and certain other high functionaries also were given seats in the Council, which had from the beginning been divided into five sections—finance, law, war, naval affairs, and domestic affairs. Each section met daily to consider the business before it, and joint sessions were held frequently, sometimes every night, at the Tuileries under Napoleon's presidency. As it developed, the Council of State became the supreme legislative, judiciary, and administrative organ of the government of France, usurping the functions of all the other bodies as well as of most of the ministries. The meetings, which often lasted late into the night, were informal and free-wheeling, even after Napoleon became emperor. In the year 1804 no less than 3,365 subjects were discussed in the general meetings—almost four times as many as in 1800. While each councilor was free to state his opinion, Napoleon displayed an astounding ability to direct discussion away from either generalities or petty detail and toward the core of each point at issue.

There can be no question but that the Council of State raised havoc with the principle of the separation of powers —executive, legislative, and judiciary; yet on the other hand it anticipated certain devices adopted in the twentieth century by several American presidents, to break away from the legislative paralysis inherent in the principle of separation—the so-called "brain trusts" and presidential advisory boards. Napoleon's novel practice of working with each cabinet minister separately rather than jointly in a Council of Ministers was another device for increasing administrative efficiency at the same time as consolidating all executive functions in his own person; so was his creation of various administrative boards, some permanent, some temporary, within the ministries but actually independent of them and headed by councilors of state. These tendencies, too, can be found in the contemporary United States, both on the Federal and on the state level, where a number of administrative boards and commissions are operating quite independently and often are endowed even with judicial powers. In Napoleonic France, however, these proliferating bodies were not counterbalanced by a vigorous legislature; they simply were extensions of Napoleon.

Apart from setting up an administrative machinery, Bonaparte faced three formidable tasks at the outset of his rule: to pacify the insurrection in the Vendée; to avoid the bankruptcy of the state; to defeat the Coalition. The first two of these were the most pressing.

The Vendéan uprising, which had flared again for the third time in 1799, was decidedly Catholic, royalist, and popular in character. Well supplied with weapons (partly from England), the Vendéans in the west and the *Chouans* in Normandy waged a stubborn guerrilla warfare against the republican government and virtually controlled several provinces. Late in 1799 General Hédouville, in command of the Army of England, a man of tact and diplomatic ability, succeeded in negotiating an armistice with their leaders as a preliminary to peace. There is reason to believe that Louis XVIII's government in exile, then in England, regarded the coup d'état of 18 Brumaire as a step toward a monarchist restoration, with Bonaparte playing the part that General George Monck had played in the restoration of Charles II. However, the terms for peace in the Vendée presented to Bonaparte by the chief royalist agent, Hyde de Neuville, displeased the First Consul. Although he found it politic to keep the royalists' hopes alive for several more months, he was determined not to negotiate with the Vendée, for unless the uprising were put down by force,

The minister of foreign affairs, Talleyrand

A portrait of Joseph Fouché, Napoleon's efficient minister of police

he would seem to owe the pacification of the west to the royalists rather than to his own strength.

In his proclamation of December 28, 1799, he ordered all Vendéans and *Chouans* to lay down their arms within ten days, failing which they would be treated as rebels. On January 5, 1800, he instructed Hédouville in these unmistakable terms: "The First Consul believes that it would serve as a salutary example to burn down two or three large communes chosen among those whose conduct is worst. Experience has taught him that a spectacularly severe act is, in the conditions you are facing, the most humane method. Only weakness is inhuman." Since Hédouville seemed temperamentally unsuited for this kind of humaneness, he was replaced on January 8 by General Brune, who carried out the First Consul's exhortations to burn and punish with great strength and kindliness. By February, organized resistance was at an end; the Vendée was as quiet as Egypt had been at that time a year before.

David's glorification of Napoleon's mule ride over the St. Bernard Pass

The next step was to give the peasants of the western provinces what they wanted—the restoration of the Catholic Church, which Bonaparte was even then beginning to meditate. (In 1790 the National Assembly had remodeled the Church to make it responsible to the French government rather than to the pope, and had confiscated most of its property.) "My policy," he said, "is to govern men the way the great majority wants to be governed. . . . By making myself Catholic, I brought the war in the Vendée to an end. By becoming a Moslem, I established myself in Egypt."

In truth, the war in the Vendée came to an end only with Napoleon's downfall. Despite the gruesome reprisals inflicted on the peasantry by the army and later by the gendarmerie, the "brigands," as the guerrillas were called, continued sporadically to harass the regime. If Hédouville's conciliatory policy had been followed, this would probably not have happened. It is not amiss to ask the question: was Napoleon's Vendéan policy dictated by necessity or was it that thing worse than a crime—a mistake?

Simultaneously with his efforts to pacify the Vendée, Bonaparte addressed himself to the problem of replenishing the public treasury, which was virtually empty. In this, he was ably assisted by his minister of finance, Martin Gaudin. However, his initial success was owed not so much to his or to Gaudin's financial genius as to the vote of confidence given him by the Paris bankers in the form of an advance.

These resources were supplemented by a special drawing of the national lottery. Meanwhile, direct taxation could be reorganized on more efficient lines (and at a moderate rate). In February, 1800, Bonaparte transformed the former Bank of Current Accounts into the Bank of France, with a capital of thirty million francs. The bank remained a private corporation, controlled by its shareholders (among them Bonaparte and his family), but acquired an official character, with the exclusive privilege to issue bank notes.

Although the national debt rose by several millions under Napoleon's rule, this rise was due to the fulfillment of previous obligations, which the government discharged scrupulously. The confidence of the financial world in the new regime was perhaps most unequivocally manifested in the Paris Bourse, where the government life annuities at five per cent rose from seven francs in 1799 to forty-four francs in 1800. The bankers' and brokers' honeymoon with Napoleon was of short duration, however: they had counted on him to establish a stable regime, make peace, and revive French foreign trade, which had come to a virtual standstill; they had not counted on his ambitions to set up a dynasty and to conquer the world, and they were reluctant to stake their capital on such dreams.

With the first five months of his rule, Bonaparte had proved himself a modern Augustus: he had transformed a triumvirate into a dictatorship veiled by constitutional forms; brought a long civil war to an end; created an administrative system that in its essential features still survives in France; and preserved and saved the state from bankruptcy and chaos. Still, everything continued to hang in the balance: a single major victory would confirm him in his power; a single major defeat would mean his ruin. To win a quick and decisive victory, he had to emulate not Augustus but Hannibal and Caesar.

Actually, hardly anybody in France was particularly eager for a decisive victory. A peace on honorable terms, even if it meant the sacrifice of some of the territories gained since 1792, would have been far more welcome. Aware of this, Bonaparte, before opening his campaign against the Allies, made overtures of peace to England and to Austria; these overtures, however, contained no concrete proposals for a basis of negotiations, and since the Allies believed France to be far weaker than she was, they were rejected. This suited Bonaparte, who was convinced that only a triumphant peace could give him lasting power.

Though in charge of military planning and operations, the First Consul was deemed under the new constitution to be a civilian magistrate; officially, therefore, he was not in command of either of the two armies that were to take the field against Austria. By far the larger of these two forces was the one stationed along the Rhine between Strasbourg and Constance, about 110,000 strong, under the command of General Moreau. The other was the Army of Italy, reduced to less than forty thousand, under General Masséna,

The French army, having managed the crossing of the Great St. Bernard Pass, begins the descent to Aosta and the Italian plains.

stationed in the vicinity of Genoa. In addition, there was an Army of Reserve, some forty thousand strong and including units no longer needed in the Vendée.

The original plan was to reinforce Moreau's army and to concentrate on the German theatre of war. This, however, would have meant that Bonaparte would play no personal part in the campaign, since a man of Moreau's reputation was unlikely to take direct orders from him. Indeed, by May, 1800, Moreau had outmaneuvered his Austrian opponent, General Kray, and driven him to Ulm, and this despite the fact that he had ignored Bonaparte's instructions. On the other hand, Masséna had been bottled up in Genoa by Field Marshal Melas; the necessity to relieve him offered Bonaparte the opportunity to direct the reserve army, nominally under the command of General Berthier, to Italy. Instead of reinforcing Moreau, Bonaparte detached eighteen thousand men from Moreau's forces and had them march into Lombardy by way of the St. Gotthard Pass. His plan, revealed only at the last moment, was spectacular: the reserve army would cross the Great St. Bernard Pass, join the units detached from Germany, pounce upon Melas before he knew it was there, and cut his communications at the very start of the campaign. This bold strategy required Bonaparte's personal leadership; consequently, the First Consul left Paris on May 5 for Switzerland to join the Army of Reserve in the

canton of Valais. The crossing of the Great St. Bernard Pass began on May 15, and was completed five days later.

The Great St. Bernard road was completed only in 1905; to cross the pass in 1800, with an army of forty thousand, including field artillery and baggage trains, was an achievement comparable to Hannibal's crossing of the Alps. Bonaparte's share in the achievement was to order it; the balance of the credit should go to the soldiers who carried out the order, to the horses and mules, and to General Berthier, who had organized the expedition. This is not the impression conveyed by David's celebrated painting of Bonaparte crossing the Alps on his white charger, which suggests that in order to make an army get over a mountain pass it is enough to point one's arm in the right direction in an *Excelsior!* sort of spirit and to make one's horse rear in a monumental pose; the truth is that Napoleon crossed the St. Bernard on a mule.

On June 2 Bonaparte entered Milan, lost to the French since 1799, while Melas marched to the defense of Turin. Eight days later, at Montebello, in Piedmont, he was joined at his headquarters by General Desaix, who had just returned from Egypt on Bonaparte's request. Desaix was given the command of a corps of six thousand men. A decisive battle was imminent, and in Paris the entire opposition—Jacobins, constitutionalist republicans, and royalists—was waiting eagerly for news from Italy and

OVERLEAF: *A detail from Lejuene's* Battle of Marengo *shows Napoleon (center) looking over his shoulder as Desaix (top center) falls. Napoleon did not actually witness Desaix's death.*

was ready to overthrow the consular regime should the First Consul be defeated.

Field Marshal Melas seemed unfindable. Thinking that he had retreated south or west, Bonaparte detached several of his units, among them Desaix's corps, to look for him. Ironically, the reason why Melas seemed so elusive was simply that he had spent several days sitting quiet and doing nothing. In the forenoon of June 14, near the village of Marengo, he suddenly pounced on Bonaparte's army with superior forces; by 3 P.M. he had defeated the French and gone to rest at nearby Alessandria.

About the same time, Desaix and his corps appeared on the battlefield. "Well, General Desaix," said Bonaparte, "we've had quite a brawl." Desaix glanced at his watch. "It is three o'clock," he remarked. "The battle has been lost; there is time to win another." He offered to lead the attack. A few minutes later, the French opened up with their entire artillery on the unsuspecting Austrians. This was followed by a charge of Desaix's fresh troops, combined with a flanking attack by the cavalry under General Kellermann the younger. Before the sun went down, the Austrian victory had turned into a rout. After nightfall, by the light of a lantern, Desaix's body was found among a heap of others, his heart torn to pieces by a bullet. It was almost at the very instant of Desaix's death at Marengo that General Kléber was assassinated in Cairo.

The Battle of Marengo cost the French about six thousand and the Austrians about nine thousand men. Five days later Moreau won a greater but less publicized victory over the Austrians at Höchstädt. If the strategy of the Marengo campaign was brilliantly planned and executed, the battle itself was by no means one of Napoleon's masterpieces. Although it did clear northwest Italy, it was decisive only in the sense that if Bonaparte had not won it, his subsequent career would in all likelihood have been far less impressive.

Bonaparte's victory bulletin was typical in every respect of the many hundreds that were to follow in the course of the next thirteen years—the eagerly awaited bulletins, from Germany, from Austria, from Poland, from Russia, from Spain; the bulletins that set the imagination of young boys on fire and whose memory made the postwar years seem so drab and dull to them; the bulletins that old couples and young wives and mistresses and sisters would pore over, wondering whether the digits and the ciphers representing the crippled and the dead, the brave who were immortalized in an anonymous glory, included those they loved; the bulletins to which there seemed to be no end, as if henceforth the purpose of men's lives would be forever the gain of honor at the price of death; the bulletins that spoke, in lapidary yet incandescent prose, of the beauty of battlefields, the splendor of cities aflame; the glorious, hateful bulletins, with their exhilarating statistics· of captured flags and guns, of enemies killed and wounded, of individual acts of bravery, that form the stanzas of the epic of Napoleon.

Like all the rest, it was a tissue of lies and distortions. It made the Battle of Marengo appear like the fulfillment of a plan. "The grenadiers of the Guard were placed like a granite redoubt in the midst of this immense plain; nothing could breach it." How artistically the words *granite, immense,* and *nothing* are placed! "The battle *appeared* to be lost." But, of course, it was not. "The enemy was *allowed* to advance within musket range of the village of San Giuliano, where General Desaix's division was drawn up in line of battle." General Desaix's division, in truth, had just come upon the scene, to Bonaparte's surprise, barely in time to draw up a line of battle. According to the bulletin, however, it was not Desaix's intervention that saved the day: "The presence of the First Consul revived the morale of the troops. 'My children,' he addressed them, 'remember it is my custom to camp on the field of battle.'" The sleeping habits of the First Consul must not be upset, and so, "to cries of 'Long live the Republic! Long live the First Consul!' Desaix attacked the center at the double."

This, of course, was what the First Consul had planned all along, and the rout of the enemy was complete: "We have taken fifteen flags, forty guns, and six to eight thousand prisoners. More than six thousand of the enemy were killed." The figure is exaggerated, but Bonaparte makes up for it by patriotically minimizing the number of French casualties: "Our losses have also been heavy"— there is always a fly in the ointment—"we have lost six hundred men killed, fifteen hundred wounded, and nine hundred prisoners." Doubled, the figures would be almost correct. Some credit had to be given to Desaix, and so he was supplied with the appropriate dying words: "Go tell the First Consul that I die regretting not having done enough to live in posterity." Since Desaix was shot straight through the heart, his death must have been instantaneous, and he cannot have said anything. However, the invented statement, linking the title *First Consul* with the phrase *live in posterity,* is a happy literary achievement. The composition would not have been complete if the First Consul had not been shown to be a man of feeling: "When, in the midst of the hottest fire, the news of [Desaix's] death was brought to the First Consul, there escaped him but these words: 'Why am I not allowed to weep?'" Bonaparte heard of Desaix's death only after the battle was over, and nobody would have held it against him if he had wept. If he did not weep, this was because he was very pleased at having escaped disaster.

On the same day as he dictated this bulletin, Bonaparte also signed an armistice with Melas, who agreed to evacuate the larger part of Lombardy. The next day he wrote to Emperor Francis, "from the battlefield of Marengo, in the midst of suffering and surrounded by fifteen thousand corpses," imploring him to make peace on the basis of the Treaty of Campoformio. The Austrian government, however, did not regard Marengo as a crushing defeat; it agreed to an armistice and stalled for time until the end of November, when peace negotiations were broken off and the war was resumed both in Italy and in Germany. On December 3 Moreau routed the Austrian army under Archduke John at Hohenlinden in a battle that cost the Austrians about seventeen thousand casualties. This victory, coupled with the successes of the French forces under Generals Brune and Macdonald in Italy, forced the Austrians to accept Bonaparte's terms in the peace treaty signed at Lunéville on February 9, 1801, by Count Cobenzl for the emperor and by Joseph Bonaparte for France.

It was Hohenlinden, not Marengo, which made Bonaparte the master of Europe. However, although Marengo was a narrow escape rather than a triumph, Bonaparte exploited the victory in every conceivable way. On June 18, four days after the battle, in the Cathedral of Milan, he was present at a solemn *Te Deum* sung to give thanks for the French victory.

About the same time he made speeches assuring the Italians of his devotion to the Catholic Church and opened negotiations with the pope for the restoration of the Church in France. It was clear enough why he wanted to pose as a good Catholic in Italy; if he had the good will of the Church, the main obstacle to French rule in Italy was removed. It was less clear to his collaborators why he wished to restore the Church in France, and his project met with considerable opposition in his own councils. His talk about religion being a sort of vaccine sounded unconvincing to the anti-clerical minds that made up virtually his entire entourage. The concordat that was being negotiated, it seemed to them, would pave the way to a restoration of the monarchy, with either himself or a Bourbon at its head. They were not mistaken; on the other hand, it seems clear in retrospect that Bonaparte's decision to come to terms with the papacy, to heal the split within the French Church, and to regulate religious worship was in itself wise and statesmanlike.

Among other things, the restoration of the Church knocked out the main prop from under the royalist opposition to his regime. The terms of the Concordat, which Bonaparte ratified in July, 1801, were very favorable to the secular authorities. The Church property confiscated during the Revolution was not restored; bishops were to be nominated by the First Consul; the clergy would be paid by the government. These terms were supplemented by the so-called Organic Articles, knowledge of which was withheld from Pope Pius VII until after he had issued the bull ratifying the Concordat.

The articles, which regulated public worship for both the Catholic and the Protestant churches, clearly asserted the supremacy of state over Church and reaffirmed Louis XIV's four Gallican Articles of 1682, which maintained among other things that the temporal ruler was not subject to the pope and that general Church councils superseded the pope. Thus, while restoring Christendom with one hand, he revived the age-old conflict between Church and state with the other. In a note dictated at St. Helena on the subject of the Concordat, Napoleon asserted that he "wanted to make use of [religion] as a social means in order to repress anarchy, consolidate his domination over Europe, and enhance the prestige of France and the influence of Paris." The Concordat, which was repealed in 1905, accomplished none of these objectives and did not deter Napoleon from making the pope a prisoner in 1809. He might have done better in simply restoring freedom of worship.

Almost two years had been spent in negotiations with the Papal See when, on Easter Sunday, April 18, 1802, the recently published Concordat was celebrated with a *Te Deum* in the Cathedral of Notre Dame, in the First Consul's presence. The thanksgiving service symbolized a great deal more than the conclusion of the Concordat. Only three weeks earlier, on March 25, a treaty had been signed at Amiens between England and France; for the first time in ten years all Europe was at peace. On April 26 Bonaparte proclaimed a general amnesty for virtually all categories of émigrés (a large number of whom had already returned under the terms of previous partial amnesties); on May 8 the Senate extended his term as First Consul by ten years; on May 19 he created the Legion of Honor; in August, after another plebiscite (3,568,885 for, 8,374 against), the constitution was amended and Bonaparte was named First Consul for life. He was king in all but name by the time he celebrated his thirty-third birthday.

It was not only in France that his will was law. In 1801 he had rammed a new constitution down the throats of the Dutch, making the Batavian Republic a virtual French protectorate; in the same year, he annexed Piedmont to France, made the Ligurian Republic (Genoa) into a French puppet state which eventually was also annexed, and gave a new constitution, patterned on the French, to the Cisalpine Republic.

In the case of Italy, his remark to Benjamin Constant, that the world had "begged" him to govern it, surely had some justification. During Bonaparte's first Italian campaign (1796–97), it may be recalled, the French were received at first as liberators but made themselves hated by their looting and extortions. These disagreeable impressions were wiped out, however, when the Austrians reconquered northern Italy in 1799. Their reprisals against all those who had sympathized with France and the Revolution were as brutal as they were stupid, and they caused the French to be remembered with nostalgia.

When Bonaparte re-entered Italy in 1800, he managed to gain the favor of a large part of the public by his professed

OVERLEAF: *Monsiau's canvas shows the assembly at Lyons, during which delegates from the Cisalpine Republic proclaimed Napoleon (seated upon the dais) president of their nation.*

respect for the Church and by his promises, addressed to the liberal patriots and the educated classes, of a free and united Italy. In 1801 he drew up the constitution for the reorganized Cisalpine Republic, adopted without change by the *consulta* at Milan. This done, he arranged for a deputation of leading Italian citizens to come to Paris and beg him to appoint the chief officials of the Republic. He graciously consented and agreed to meet a commission of some four hundred fifty members early in 1802, at Lyons. There, under his guidance, they distributed the various offices, leaving the presidency of the Republic to the last. A committee nominated Count Melzi, in the belief that the choice would please the First Consul, and were mystified when he raised objections. A hint dropped by Talleyrand cleared up the mystery, and the assembly begged Bonaparte himself to accept the presidency. This he did, and he changed the name of the state from Cisalpine to Italian Republic. To be sure, the Republic comprised only a portion of Italy, but the name raised the hope in the breasts of optimistic patriots that this was but the first step toward national unity.

A united Italy may have been a remote goal in Napoleon's mind, but it had to be united under French domination. He held the Italian people to be incapable of self-government, and his many contemptuous utterances on the subject are crude and blind to a point where the historian feels embarrassed to quote them. Meanwhile, pending a final solution of the Italian problem, he regarded the various regions of Italy as so many horses to be traded.

The secret Treaty of San Ildefonso, negotiated between France and Spain in 1800, is known chiefly for the terms by which Spain retroceded what came to be called the Louisiana Territory to France; however, it also provided for territorial compensation of Spain in Italy. The pawn in question was the Grand Duchy of Tuscany, ruled by an Austrian archduke: by the Peace of Lunéville, the Grand Duchy was united with the Duchy of Parma, whose ruler, a virtually imbecilic young man who had married a daughter of the king of Spain, was created king of Etruria. The Kingdom of Etruria lasted until 1807, when Napoleon annexed it to the French Empire. The same fate, as will be seen, awaited the Papal States; and as for the Republic (later Kingdom) of Italy and the Kingdom of Naples, they were to become mere tributaries of imperial France.

Napoleon's Italian policy showed his opportunism in its worst light. His measures may have seemed expedient, but they were not dictated by either political necessity or statesmanlike foresight. If, instead of missing no chance to display his contempt for the Italian nation and its aspirations, he had created a strong and independent Italy, as it lay within his power to do, the history of Franco-Italian relations ever since would have been quite different, and far more beneficial to both countries, than they turned out to be. If he had wished, Italian unification could have been an accomplished fact by 1814.

The same planlessness and cynical opportunism is manifest in all of Napoleon's foreign policy. His German policy, of which more will have to be said, may be justified to at least this extent, that it sought to create a few medium-sized German states, all but Prussia beholden to France, at the expense of the petty princes. But this policy aroused the antagonism of the normally docile Germans; and it was dangerous for Napoleon to do this—as he did—without at the same time pursuing a firm and unwavering policy with regard to Poland and to Russia. With its third and final partition, in 1795, Poland had ceased to exist. Thousands of Polish patriots who had fought under Thaddeus Kosciusko when he made his last stand volunteered to serve in the French revolutionary army against Austria. Many fought under Bonaparte in Italy in 1796–97 and a few followed him to Egypt.

When Russia joined the anti-French Coalition in 1798, it was not unreasonable for the Poles to suppose that in the event of a French victory, at least the Russian and Austrian parts of Poland would be restored to independence. (Prussia, being a neutral friendly to France, could not be expected to give up her share.) However, in 1799, Czar Paul of Russia chose to leave the Coalition, and in 1800 he formed, together with Sweden, Denmark, and Prussia, the League of Armed Neutrality, in defense against British interference with neutral shipping. This amounted to a virtual alliance with France (as indeed the Danes found out when in 1801 Admiral Nelson destroyed their fleet). In those circumstances, Bonaparte judged it inexpedient to press the issue of Polish independence. As a consequence, he ordered Fouché in that year to suppress all pro-Polish propaganda. In 1806 Napoleon was at war with Paul's successor, Alexander. "It is in the interest of Europe," declared Napoleon that year, "it is in the interest of France that Poland should exist."

In 1807 Alexander suddenly became Napoleon's ally. "Do not mention Polish independence and suppress everything tending to show the emperor as the liberator of Poland, seeing that he has never explained himself on that subject," Napoleon wrote in May, 1807. And in 1810: "Poland exists only in the imagination of those who want to use it as a pretext for spinning dreams." But in 1812, he was preparing war against Russia. "It has always seemed to me," he told his ministers, "that the restoration of Poland is desirable for all the Western Powers." Napoleon's correspondingly fluctuating policy toward Russia will be examined in another chapter; the passages just quoted are sufficient to exemplify his utter lack of principle in foreign policy as well as his disregard for the most potent political factor of his age—national aspirations towards unity and independence. Abraham Lincoln's dictum that some of the people could be fooled some of the time, etc., probably came closer to real *Realpolitik* than did Napoleon's assumption that the proper mixture of terror, bribes, and flattery could fool all the people all the time.

After Napoleon's downfall he and his apologists maintained that the seeming lack of principle in his foreign policy was merely the result of temporary circumstances; that if he had attained his ultimate objective, Europe would have become a federation of free and sovereign states—under French hegemony, it is true, but benefiting at the same time from the liberal principles of the French Revolution. The real obstacle was England, whose reactionary and greedy government never ceased to stir up war against France by means of bribery and intrigue; as long as France was obliged to defend herself against the attacks of now this, now that hireling of Whitehall, her foreign policy necessarily had to fluctuate according to the requirements of any particular moment.

Undoubtedly there is some truth in this assertion, but the terms of the short-lived Peace of Amiens make it quite clear that both Bonaparte and the British government regarded the peace as a mere truce. England could never accept the realization of Napoleon's ultimate objective—supremacy over Europe and, perhaps, even Asia—and Napoleon could never accept the existence of an undefeated England. Here indeed is the key to Napoleon's erratic foreign policy: foreign policy presupposes the permanent existence of rival powers, whereas Napoleon presupposed permanent war until France had gained unchallenged supremacy. He could score diplomatic triumphs, but these triumphs were merely part of the military struggle. It was an obsession with Napoleon's example that induced the Prussian military writer Clausewitz to state the monstrous axiom that war is a continuation of politics by different means; the same confusion of politics and war made the untenable concept of a "cold war" widely accepted in our own day. War is not the continuation but the breakdown of politics, and foreign policy is distinct from diplomacy in that the former must rest on stable principles whereas the latter may vary according to the need of the moment. Napoleon was a superb diplomat, but since his ultimate aim was world conquest, he lacked the most rudimentary notion of what constitutes foreign policy.

The main terms of the Peace of Amiens seem fair and unexceptionable: England undertook to restore to France and her Dutch and Spanish allies all conquests made since 1793, excepting the former Spanish possession of Trinidad and the former Dutch possession of Ceylon; the integrity of the Ottoman Empire was to be guaranteed; England was to evacuate Malta and restore it to the Knights of St. John of Jerusalem; and France was to evacuate the Papal States and her bases in the Kingdom of Naples.

The treaty was decidedly favorable to France—but then, despite her loss of Egypt and of Malta, France had won the war. What made the treaty unacceptable to England on a permanent basis was what had been left out—a trade agreement. It was hard enough for English commercial interests to swallow the fact that Belgium remained French, and Holland a French protectorate; but that all the trade restrictions imposed on English goods during wartime should be maintained in time of peace—and Bonaparte insisted on maintaining them—made the whole treaty illusory. If the House of Commons ratified it, this was only because the government had thrown out a barely veiled hint to the effect that the arrangement was merely a matter of temporary expediency. If Napoleon had wanted genuine

The English patronizing a Paris café following the Peace of Amiens

peace, he could have had it easily enough by supplementing the treaty with a liberal trade agreement. To revive French trade, a few years of peace were essential, and there could be no hope of such a peace if Britain's vital commercial interests were not recognized.

The "peace" lasted for thirteen months and three weeks —from March 27, 1802, to May 18, 1803. Its immediate and most tangible result was the sudden influx of tens of thousands of English tourists to the Continent and, particularly, France. For ten years, the English upper classes had been penned up on their island; possibly they had made peace only to break out of it for a few months. By September, 1803, there were about ten thousand Englishmen in Paris alone. The social scene was more brilliant than it had been during the last years of the old regime. The great salons, including the celebrated one of Madame Récamier, were open to the more distinguished of the English visitors, and such new and dazzling places of entertainment as the Tivoli and Frascati's were open to all who wanted to see them.

Women were no longer addressed as "Citizeness" but as "Madame." The consular court at the Tuileries presented a fascinating mixture of military dash and dazzle with the old forms borrowed from the court of Versailles. The most popular landmark for sightseers was, of course, the First Consul himself, and many a bribe was paid for admission to one of his receptions. It was an impressive spectacle to see him in his gold-embroidered uniform of state walk briskly through the two ranks of guests, stopping here and there to ask a few brusque questions, as if the visitors were so many grenadiers. Madame Bonaparte was universally adjudged a model of charm and grace. Monsieur Talleyrand, on the other hand, according to the duke of Argyll, was "the most disgusting individual I ever saw. His complexion is that of a corpse considerably advanced in corruption." The other ministers and generals were inspected with no less curiosity. On the whole, the mood seemed to be one of reconciliation, and the cosmopolitan spirit of the eighteenth century reasserted itself after ten years of repression.

While the European continent enjoyed its year of precarious peace, the larger part of a French expeditionary force of thirty thousand men was perishing from yellow fever in Haiti, whence the forces under the negro general Jean Jacques Dessalines expelled them in 1803. This ill-advised adventure hastened the conclusion, in 1803, of the treaty by which France sold her territories on the North American continent to the United States. The Louisiana Purchase was signed less than three weeks before the resumption of warfare between England and France.

Both these events—the disastrous expedition to Santo Domingo and the Louisiana Purchase—will be examined in the context of the world-wide colonial developments during the Napoleonic Age. It is not amiss at this point, however, to draw a parallel between Napoleon's foreign policy and his stand with regard to slavery. His opportunism and lack of principle are equally manifest in both respects. On Christmas Day of 1799 he announced, in a proclamation to the people of Santo Domingo, "Remember, brave Negroes, that France alone recognizes your liberty and your equal rights."

In April, 1802, after the Peace of Amiens had restored Martinique and Guadeloupe to France and General Victor Leclerc's forces in Santo Domingo had established their short-lived control over that island, he modified his promise considerably. The decree which he drafted then to regulate the status of Negroes divided the colonies into two classes —"those where the laws emancipating the blacks have been published and more or less carried out and those where the old order has been preserved." In the latter (for example, Martinique), slavery was to be maintained exactly as it had existed in 1789.

In colonies where slavery had been abolished, all Negroes liberated before February 14, 1794, and "those black individuals who have helped defend the territory of the Republic against its enemies or who have rendered service to the state in any other way" were to be declared free.

As if this provision were not sufficiently hedged in, it was further qualified by four additional clauses: (1) Negroes owning no property or having no skilled trade "will be subjected to police regulations which will assign them to landed proprietors as agricultural laborers; the regulations shall fix their wages and prescribe what measures are to be taken to prevent vagrancy and insubordination." In other words, they were to be held in peonage. (2) "Insubordinate individuals and inveterate vagrants" could be struck from the lists of freemen. (3) All the Negroes not specifically declared free were subject to the Black Code as it existed in 1789—that is, they were slaves. (4) The importation of black slaves was authorized.

These were the regulations for the brave Negroes whose liberty and equal rights France alone recognized. Possibly, in drafting them Napoleon was influenced by the prejudices of his wife, who had grown up on her father's plantation in Martinique; more important, however, was the pressure brought on him by the families and commercial establishments whose interests depended on the continuation of slavery in the islands. At any rate, the regulations could not be justified under the principles of the Civil Code which Bonaparte and his advisers were even then in the process of drawing up.

The Civil Code, or Code Napoléon, is generally regarded as Napoleon's most solid and lasting accomplishment. While the usefulness of codifying law may be questioned in principle, there can be no doubt that in the specific case of post-revolutionary France codification was imperative. Law had varied from province to province under the old regime, and revolutionary legislation only added to the confusion. To reconcile revolutionary law with what remained of the old customary law and to create a uniform legal system was a necessity apparent even during the Reign of Terror, when the Convention entrusted the drafting of a code to a commission headed by Cambacérès. A new commission was appointed after the coup d'état of 18 Brumaire; by January 1, 1801, its four members— Tronchet, Portalis, Bigot de Préameneu, and Maleville— had completed the draft, which made extensive use of Cambacérès' previous work and, of course, of Roman law. The printed text was then sent to the various sections of the legislature, in the light of whose comments and criticism it was further revised by the Council of State. In this revised form it was submitted, article by article, to the Council of State as a whole: it was only at this point that Napoleon began to take part in its formulation.

The minutes of the discussions have been published, in a rather edited and digested form, and they testify, as indeed they were intended to do, to the important share that Bonaparte took in the final version of the code named after him. To be sure, he did not originate the code, he lacked all technical knowledge of the law, and he did not participate in all the discussions; entire portions of the code were worked out without his presence. Nevertheless, his extraordinary grasp of the social and political implications of civil law, his strong convictions in these matters, and his ability to illuminate, with a few striking words, the human and social aspects of an abstract legal concept left a deep imprint on the code and, hence, on modern civil law throughout the world.

The Code Napoléon has been criticized for many valid reasons. Some of its most questionable features can be traced to Napoleon's personal influence. They are, without exception, illiberal, not to say reactionary, and they profoundly affected the social structure of France ever after. The father was assigned almost despotic power over the family, including the right to imprison his child for one month; natural children were barred from inheritance or, in case they were legitimized, were entitled to only a reduced share; the highly permissive divorce laws of the revolutionary period were tightened considerably in an attempt to restore the family rather than the individual as the basic unit of society.

As for the civil status of women, the code marked a large stride backward. A bride, Bonaparte remarked to the Council of State, "must be made to realize that on leaving the tutelage of her family she passes under that of her husband." This principle was applied in the code to the fullest degree: wives were subject to their husbands, had no rights in the administration of common property, were forbidden to give, sell, or mortgage property, and could acquire property only with their husbands' written consent. Under the old regime, married women had enjoyed wide freedom, separate property rights, and an influential place in society. The Revolution had widened their rights. Napoleon imposed on French society his view that women must be treated as irresponsible minors throughout their lives. "Women should stick to knitting," he once told the son of Madame de Staël, who is not known to have knitted much. To the Council of State he declared: "The husband must possess the absolute power and right to say to his wife: 'Madam, you shall not go out, you shall not go to the theatre, you shall not receive such and such a person; for the children you will bear shall be mine.'" A French husband under the old regime would not have got very far with such a speech. Napoleon, who had an aversion to the moral laxity of the eighteenth century, which he blamed on the domination of society by women, was determined to reform family life on Roman, or perhaps rather Corsican, principles. It was with him, not with Queen Victoria, that Victorian morality originated. Just as Napoleon was the sole authority in the state, so the husband and father was to exercise authority over his

New discoveries as well as tourists crossed the Channel during the peace; vaccination was introduced to Parisians at the time.

Brigandage flourished until the First Consul restored order.

family. Unfortunately the only possible result of despotism on either level is hypocrisy.

The Civil Code became law in 1804 and was followed by the Code of Civil Procedure, the Code of Commercial Law, the Penal Code, and the Code of Criminal Procedure. All these, but most particularly the first, despite their many defects and authoritarian features, embodied for the first time in the history of modern nations a system of unified law, applicable without distinction to all classes of citizens. In this respect it might be claimed for them, as Napoleon did claim, that they gave permanence to the essential accomplishments of the French Revolution—national unity and civic equality. Modified and amended, the Code Napoléon remains the basis of most civil law in the modern world, and even in those polities where common law prevails—the British Commonwealth and the United States—the Code persists in certain areas, such as the province of Quebec and the state of Louisiana. Although it represented a step backward in France, it had a generally liberalizing influence in the rest of the world.

The codes, the creation of an administrative system, the reorganization of finances, the regularization of the relationship between Church and state, the pacification of the Vendée, and the conclusion of a general peace were not the only achievements of Napoleon during the first years of his rule. He also created a system of public education; began a program of public works, planned on a vast scale and with considerable foresight; and by means of cash prizes and industrial and agricultural exhibits, stimulated the languishing economy of France. It is true that Bonapartist historians have somewhat exaggerated the state of disruption into which France had fallen as a consequence of the French Revolution and of the Directory's

mismanagement. In fact there were symptoms of economic recovery even before Bonaparte seized the power, and the new prosperity cannot be credited solely to him and to his very able ministers. Yet it was Bonaparte who had created the essential conditions without which a normal development of economic and cultural life would have been impossible—peace, order, and stability.

Like the Concordat, the codes, and the administrative system he created, Bonaparte's educational system is subject to criticism. It placed all schools under the direct supervision of the state, yet it allocated state funds only to the higher specialized schools and to the *lycées*—secondary schools providing a thorough education for especially promising pupils and for sons of officers. The other secondary schools and the primary schools depended for their funds on the local authorities or on private enterprise. Since the communes and municipalities disposed of very limited revenues only (and these also had to satisfy the needs of public charity, which was left entirely to the local authorities), the education of the mass of the people was generally neglected. The principle of equality of opportunity was honored by the possibility of obtaining scholarships to the *lycées;* but as late as 1814 there were in all France only thirty-six *lycées* with nine thousand pupils, most of them drawn from the middle and upper classes. For a population of almost thirty million this was clearly insufficient. The curriculum of studies prescribed for the communal schools was rudimentary, with religious and political indoctrination receiving priority. It was Bonaparte's conviction that too much instruction for the lower classes was dangerous to the social order.

The program of public works was impressive. When Bonaparte came to power, the road system was in disrepair and the roads were infested with bandits and highwaymen. At the end of his rule, he had built a magnificent network of roads, and banditry had disappeared. To be sure, his drastic legislation against vagrancy, and a penal code which prescribed enforced labor for an amazing number of offenses provided for an ample and cheap labor supply, which was further increased by prisoners of war. The list of roads, harbor installations, and canals built under Napoleon is often cited as proof of his positive accomplishments; yet the methods by which they were built prefigure—on a small scale, it is true—those employed by Hitler in our time. In one respect only did Napoleon show more concern for the laboring class than did most governments of his time: he exercised a strict control over the prices of food staples. "I fear insurrections when they are caused by hunger," he remarked to his minister Chaptal. "I would be less afraid of a battle against an army of two hundred thousand."

At the beginning of 1803, in his thirty-fourth year, Napoleon Bonaparte had reached the point beyond which no man could go without either stepping down or raising himself to blasphemous heights of power. He had placed himself beside Alexander, Hannibal, Caesar, and Augustus; in the redaction of the Civil Code, he played the figure of a new Justinian. He was the head and dictator of two countries. He had made France larger than she had ever been, adding several million Belgian, German, and Italian subjects to her population. He succeeded where Louis XIV had failed, in making the French Church virtually independent of the papacy. The Treaty of Lunéville, which provided for the territorial reorganization of the Holy Roman Empire, had made him the arbiter of the Germanies.

For two years after the signature of the treaty, the German Diet deliberated at Ratisbon under the First Consul's shadow, suppressing nearly all the ecclesiastic fiefs and forty-two out of forty-eight Free Imperial Cities, and dividing the spoils among the temporal princes, mainly those of Bavaria, Württemberg, and Baden. In the scramble for territory, the princes' ambassadors to the First Consul had vied with each other in currying his favor and lavished millions in bribes on his foreign minister, Talleyrand. The Batavian Republic had become a mere appendage to France; the Helvetic Republic, as Switzerland had been called since its occupation by France in 1798, had appealed to Bonaparte to end the civil strife that was tearing it, and by his Act of Mediation of 1803 he restored its former confederate structure and at the same time made it a French dependency. Austria and Prussia stood in fear of him; all Italy was at his mercy; and Spain had been reduced to a satellite. No man since Charlemagne, and perhaps not even Charlemagne, had held such power—and all this power rested on the flimsiest of planks.

The precariousness of his power at home was ever-present to Napoleon's mind. His authority rested not on the loyalty but on the fear he inspired. At the beginning of his rule, he enjoyed the qualified support of both republicans and royalists; yet it was not to his taste to fulfill the expectations of either faction. He would neither step down from power like General Washington, whose bust adorned his study, nor hand it over to a king, as General Monck had done. Apart from considerations of personal ambition, he reasoned, maybe correctly, that either course would plunge France once more into discord and perhaps civil strife. That this risk might be a lesser evil than the course he chose to follow may be true; the question, however, is academic, since it was entirely contrary to Napoleon's nature to contemplate the possibility of relinquishing his power. Thus, because of what he described as fateful political necessity, he had no alternative but to silence all opposition. His goal, no doubt genuine, was to submerge party politics in a quest for national glory and to unite republicans and royalists behind himself; he succeeded only in uniting them against himself.

While the royalists remained hopeful for several months,

A plot to kill Napoleon failed in the Rue St. Nicaise, 1800.

the republican opposition made itself heard almost as soon as the consular regime was established. On January 5, 1800, the tribune Benjamin Constant warned that if the government imposed its wishes on the Tribunate, "there would be nothing left but servitude and silence—a silence that all Europe would hear." Bonaparte's reaction to the speech was threatening: "There are, in the Tribunate, twelve or fifteen metaphysicians fit to be drowned. They are a vermin I carry on my clothes, but I'll shake them off." Twelve days later he suppressed sixty out of the seventy-three existing newspapers and forbade the publication of any new ones; shortly afterward the Ministry of General Police was entrusted with the censorship of the press and the Ministry of the Interior with the censorship of the theatre.

These measures were directed primarily at the republican critics; the royalists, in the meantime, were treated with kid gloves, except for the bloody reprisals in the Vendée. Louis XVIII had written to the First Consul as early as February 20 to sound him out about his stand on a monarchist restoration. By September 7, 1800, Bonaparte felt strong enough to reply with a categorical No; Louis' return, he wrote, could be effected only over one hundred thousand corpses. This reply should not be mistaken for a victory of the republicans. When he made it, Bonaparte had already begun negotiations with the pope for the restoration of the Church and had allowed thousands of émigrés to return to France, thus winning over a substantial part of Louis' supporters.

Convinced that the leftist opposition was a greater danger to his plans that was that of the right, he deliberately turned a blind eye to the royalist conspiracies against him and occasionally exploited them to chastise the republicans. On Christmas Eve of the year 1800 the First Consul was driving to the Opera to hear the first performance of

Haydn's oratorio *The Creation,* when an infernal machine concealed in a water wagon exploded, barely missing his carriage and killing several members of his escort. Without hesitation Bonaparte blamed the crime on the Jacobins.

When Fouché brought him proof that, on the contrary, it was the work of royalist *Chouans,* the First Consul angrily pointed out that the Jacobins were criminals by definition and that such a fine opportunity for punishing them must not be wasted. Fouché, an ex-Jacobin himself, took the hint, drew up a list of subversives, and had fifty of them deported to the colonies. Of the real authors of the crime, one, Limoëlan, escaped to the United States (where he became a Catholic priest) and the other two were quietly executed in April. Early in 1802 Bonaparte expelled from the Tribunate twenty of its most obnoxious metaphysicians and vermin, among them Constant. "I do not think," he explained to his fellow consuls, "that it is possible to carry on if the constituent authorities are made up of enemies." Only a few weeks before, he had purged the armed forces by sending to Santo Domingo thirty thousand troops known for their obstreperous republicanism or lack of discipline.

If the First Consul's severity concentrated on the republicans, the reason was obvious: the ratification of the Concordat was hanging in the balance, and in their opposition to it the republicans were making their last stand. As for the royalists, their attitude toward the Concordat was divided. Louis XVIII's government in exile opposed it bitterly; on the other hand, Bonaparte had the support of most returned émigrés. Among them was the vicomte de Chateaubriand, an unknown and penniless young man just back from exile in England, whose principal baggage consisted of the original draft of his *Le Génie du Christianisme.* Its publication made Chateaubriand famous overnight, and it became suddenly fashionable to believe in Christianity. The revival of this fashion, which had died with Louis XIV, suited Bonaparte's purposes. Chateaubriand was rewarded first with a secretaryship at the French embassy in Rome, later with the post of minister to the tiny puppet Republic of the Simplon—the canton of Valais, which had been detached from Switzerland. (It was this later post which Chateaubriand refused to take in protest over the murder of the duc d'Enghien.)

Madame de Staël also loved Christianity, but as a Protestant she distrusted the Roman Church and as a liberal she distrusted Bonaparte. In her salon, which she called a "hospital for defeated parties," she united all shades of the opposition to the consular regime as well as some of the most prominent members of Bonaparte's administration, including his brother Joseph. "At the time of the Concordat," Napoleon reminisced at St. Helena, "she suddenly united the aristocrats and the republicans against me. 'You have not a moment to waste,' she cried to them. 'Tomorrow the tyrant will have 40,000 priests at his command.'"

Among her closest political associates at the time was General Bernadotte, Joseph Bonaparte's brother-in-law, who made no secret of his republican convictions and who had watched Napoleon's rise with ill-concealed jealousy. Beginning in April, 1802, he held secret meetings with about a dozen other generals—among them Augereau, Brune, Jourdan, Lannes, Masséna, and Moreau—to discuss the overthrow of "the sultan," as they called Bonaparte. Sieyès and Madame de Staël were certainly, and Fouché was possibly, connected with the plot. Toward the end of May, Bernadotte's chief of staff, General Simon, began to dispatch pamphlets to various units in France. "Soldiers, you no longer have a fatherland," they declared. "The Republic has ceased to exist. A tyrant has seized the power, and that tyrant is Bonaparte."

Meanwhile Fouché's police did what they could to throw suspicion on every quarter save the actual plotters. Simon's arrest late in June could leave no doubt as to the focus of the conspiracy. The First Consul displayed astonishing leniency: Simon was merely dismissed from the service; the other generals received a stern warning not to try any such nonsense again; Bernadotte was advised to take the waters at Plombières; Madame de Staël was forbidden to return to Paris; Fouché was made a senator; and the police was placed under the Ministry of Justice. To take sterner measures would merely have advertised to what high places disaffection had spread. With the collapse of the generals' plot, republican opposition was effectively ended, and the plebiscite which made Bonaparte consul for life opened a wide and straight road to the throne.

As amended in 1802, the constitution gave Napoleon every attribute of royal power save the crown. This had been enough for Octavian Augustus, but Augustus' situation had been quite different from Napoleon's. With the suicide of Mark Antony, he was rid of all rivals, and there was no power, nor any possible combination of powers, outside the Roman Empire that could threaten him. Thus Augustus could afford to respect the forms of republican government and to begin that long and unique era known as the Roman Peace. Napoleon lacked these advantages. His power rested on a coup d'état; Louis XVIII, who had shifted his court to Warsaw, still claimed to be the legitimate king of France; the First Consul's generals still regarded themselves as his equals and were growing restive after a year of peace; and a powerful coalition of England, Russia, and Austria could form against him at any moment.

His authority was challenged even within his own family. Lucien, in defiance of Napoleon's wishes, married a divorcée in 1803 and retired to Italy, where his mother took his side against her second son; as for the eldest son, Joseph, he felt slighted in his rights as head of the family, flirted with the opposition, and feared that his brother's ambition would wreck the pleasant and luxurious life he was leading at his estate at Mortefontaine. Even Josephine felt apprehensive of her husband's ambition for the throne,

The First Consul by Gros (right) is one of the few portraits for which Napoleon posed; he ordered it as a gift for Cambacérès.

sensing that, once crowned, he would divorce her and marry a wife who could bear him a son.

An implacable logic forced Bonaparte to imperil all he had gained. Louis XVIII's claims, he believed, would be nullified if his own authority were consecrated by God's vicar on earth, Pius VII. He would be crowned like Charlemagne and force Charlemagne's ward, Emperor Francis II, to abdicate his title of Holy Roman Emperor. He could be certain that his enemies would reopen war, and he would welcome it, for war was the only way to keep his generals loyal and the French nation submissive. He would make marshals, dukes, princes, and kings out of his generals and his brothers; he would amuse the nation with an ever-changing pageantry of victory and conquest; he would keep on taking more and more only so he could give more and more, for the instant he ceased to give, his beneficiaries would cut his throat. That he must serve the greed of those who served him was always clear to him, and he was dimly aware that the process would stop only with his rule; yet at the same time he hoped, not too rationally, that his heir would reign over the empire he had built and consolidate in peace what he had wrested from war.

While it is plain that Bonaparte wanted war, it is also true that the English government most obligingly presented him with a convenient excuse for it—in fact, forced war on him some time sooner than he had intended. Contrary to the provisions of the Treaty of Amiens, England had not evacuated Malta and restored it to the Knights. It was the contention of the British government that the continued French occupation of Holland, Switzerland, Piedmont, and Genoa was contrary to the spirit of Amiens, proved Bonaparte's aggressive intentions, and justified England in delaying the evacuation of Malta.

On March 13, 1803, in the presence of the entire diplomatic corps, Bonaparte performed a scene of "calculated rage" that none of those present could ever forget. Planting himself in front of the British ambassador, Lord Whitworth, he delivered a violent tirade, accompanied by menacing gestures. "It is you who are determined to make war on us," he screamed. "You want to drive me to it. You will be the first to draw the sword; I shall be the last to sheathe it. Woe to those who show no respect for treaties!" Having finished, he stalked out of the room, astonishing those outside by his perfect composure; the scene had been put on in the expectation that England would back down under the threat of war. Yet if the purpose of the outburst was to delay rather than precipitate war, its effect was the opposite. Britain now made conditions that were patently unacceptable: France should evacuate Holland and Switzerland and consent to a ten-year occupation of Malta by English forces. Negotiations continued until May, with Talleyrand and Joseph Bonaparte exerting themselves in favor of peace. Since neither Bonaparte nor the British cabinet yielded an inch, the talks collapsed. Lord Whitworth brusquely left for

England, and on May 18 George III declared war on France.

Whether or not the formidable armaments built up by Napoleon at Boulogne were seriously intended for an invasion of England is a question to be examined in another chapter. Certain it is that by 1805, when he definitely gave up the invasion project, he had created at Boulogne the Grand Army with which he was about to overrun Europe. In the meantime, the state of war between France and England worked to his disadvantage. To invade England proved impossible; the war was a mere resumption of piracy on the high seas; it offered no diversion to the French public and no activity for Bonaparte's generals. On the other hand, it offered the agents of Louis XVIII an opportunity to intensify their activities in France.

Fouché, ex-cleric, ex-Terrorist, ex-minister of general police, was an uncommonly subtle man. He had, says Madame de Staël, "a transcendental intelligence in matters revolutionary." "Always in everybody's shoes," Napoleon said of him. Although dismissed from his ministerial post, he kept a private network of agents. A certain Méhée de la Touche, who arrived in London in February, 1803, was almost certainly one of them. Méhée brought the happy news to the royalist leaders in London that the republican opposition in France was ready to make common cause with them to overthrow Bonaparte. A plan of operations was worked out: insurrections would be organized, with the help of English subsidies, in Paris, the Vendée, and Provence, and a prince of the royal blood would land, when the time was ripe, to lead the uprising. Late in August a group of royalist agents, headed by Georges Cadoudal, one of the chief commanders in the Vendéan uprising, were smuggled into France aboard a British cutter. Cadoudal carried drafts for a million francs, provided by the English government. He was followed in January, 1804, by General Pichegru, who had escaped to England in 1798 at the time of the coup d'état of 18 Fructidor.

In Paris, the conspirators established contact with General Moreau, whom they regarded as the leader of the republican faction. Moreau agreed to an interview with his old friend Pichegru, but when Pichegru appeared in the company of Cadoudal, he left abruptly. He was a republican, and he refused to associate himself with a royalist plot. Moreau's integrity did not fit into Fouché's plans: if Fouché's agents had assured the royalists of Moreau's willingness to co-operate, this was in order to implicate him in the affair. Meanwhile the police had arrested some of the conspirators but were unable to get at the bottom of the mystery or to identify the leaders of the plot. Bonaparte, of course, had by then been informed by Fouché, but he kept quiet, hoping that if given time Moreau would compromise himself. Moreau, however, sat tight, and on February 15, Bonaparte decided to act. Moreau was arrested, despite the lack of serious evidence against him; the arrests of Pichegru, Cadoudal, and the other conspirators followed

A drawing depicts the imperial couple at their religious wedding ceremony, without which Pius VII refused to bless them.

in the next few days. Pichegru strangled himself in his cell—or so it was said; the others were put on trial.

The plotters, for almost a year, had been the unwitting puppets of Fouché, who manipulated the strings. But there was one thing Fouché did not know: who was the mysterious prince whose arrival had been promised? Cadoudal, who perhaps knew, could not be brought to name him. At first suspicions centered on the comte d'Artois, Louis XVIII's brother. It soon became obvious that he was not the man. However, on March 8, intelligence arrived from Strasbourg that the duc d'Enghien, the only son of the prince de Condé, was living at Ettenheim, in the Duchy of Baden, just across the Rhine from France, and occasionally made secret visits to Strasbourg. The House of Condé was a collateral branch of the House of Bourbon; this, and his proximity to France, was the only evidence against him. At a meeting of his Privy Council on March 10, Bonaparte decided that the duke was the promised prince and ordered a small detachment to cross into Baden territory, arrest the duke, seize his papers, and bring him back to Paris for trial.

In truth, the unfortunate young man did not even know that a conspiracy existed. His mysterious presence at Ettenheim had a simple explanation: he was spinning a discreet love idyll with his mistress. On March 14 the French detachment, in violation of Baden's sovereignty, kidnapped the duke. They did not even give him time to change from his hunting clothes before they hustled him off; the duke's dog refused to leave him and had to be taken along. On March 20 the duke arrived at the fortress of Vincennes,

just outside Paris, still in hunting clothes, still with his dog, still ignorant of the charges against him. At one in the morning he was taken before a court martial, consisting of seven members and headed by Napoleon's brother-in-law Joachim Murat.

Meanwhile, the duc d'Enghien's papers had been scrutinized; to anyone not determined to find him guilty, it was evident that he was a victim of mistaken identity. But Bonaparte was determined to find him guilty, and he had instructed the judges accordingly. The court martial was very brief. The duke assured his judges of his innocence and requested a confrontation with the First Consul. The judges found him guilty. The number of the article under which he was sentenced to death was left blank, to be filled in later. It was never filled in, for it did not exist. The duke, still in his hunting clothes, was taken to the moat; a lantern was placed beside him, to enable the firing squad to aim; his dog pressed against his leg; he managed to leave a message for his mistress; then, at 2:30 A.M., ninety minutes after his trial had begun, he was shot.

The twelve shots of the firing squad at Vincennes rang around the world. In France, where the mass of the people depended for their news on what the government press fed them, the accusations against the duke were generally believed; besides, since public opinion was leaning toward republicanism, the execution of a Bourbon tended to reassure the people of the First Consul's anti-aristocratic sentiments. Abroad, the news was received with horror and indignation. (Perhaps if the victim had not been of royal blood, it would have been taken more philosophically.) Czar Alexander decreed solemn mourning for his court and sent a fiery protest to Paris; the French Foreign Office replied that France had not meddled with Russian internal affairs when Alexander's friends had assassinated his father, and the exchange was followed by a rupture of diplomatic relations. Though the immediate political effects of Napoleon's action were favorable to him on the whole—after all, it secured him the imperial crown—the moral effect was incalculably damaging, and the murdered duke's ghost was to haunt him for the rest of his life.

It was very well for Fouché to say that the execution was worse than a crime: the whole affair was the result of his own devious plot, which earned him his reinstatement as minister of general police. But neither Fouché nor anyone else ever satisfactorily explained what made Napoleon commit the mistake of murdering Enghien. Was it his purpose to win republican support for his impending bid for the crown? Was it to serve notice on the royalists that if they wanted a monarchy, it had to be his, not the Bourbons'? Was it to link his associates more firmly to his person by making them accomplices in a crime? Was it a symbolic execution of Louis XVIII himself? Or was it merely a way of prodding the constituted authorities into offering him the crown? Whatever it was—and it may have been a combination of several of these things—it was a miscalculation. There probably was not a single action in his life that did him more harm when the hour of reckoning came, nor was there any other occasion in his life when he let down his mask more cynically. Many a lesser man committed more and worse crimes and was forgiven them; it was the very greatness of Napoleon and the gratuitousness of his act that made it so shocking. On those exquisitely shaped hands, white and translucent like marble, there was the blood of an innocent man of thirty-two. It was worse than a mistake—it was unaesthetic.

Contrary to the First Consul's expectations, the legislative bodies needed a good deal of prodding before they offered him the crown. What also grieved him was that Moreau's public trial seemed to be turning into a public display of anti-Bonapartist sentiment. The courtroom was filled every day with Moreau's well-wishers, headed by the resplendently beautiful Madame Récamier. Only Bonaparte's pressure prevented the judges from acquitting the victor of Hohenlinden; they finally passed a two-year sentence on him, thus enabling Bonaparte to pardon him magnanimously for a crime he had not committed and to allow him to go into exile in the United States. He returned to Europe in 1814 to serve against Napoleon with the Russian army and was killed that year in the Battle of Dresden. Cadoudal and nineteen others were sentenced to death.

It was in the tense atmosphere of these trials that one of Bonaparte's tools, the tribune Curée, proposed that Bonaparte be declared emperor and that his office be made hereditary in his family. On May 3 the Tribunate voted in favor of the proposal, with Lazare Carnot casting the only vote against. On May 18 the Senate passed the measure. There remained the formality of a plebiscite, whose outcome was made public only on November 26, six days before the coronation: 3,572,329 votes in favor and 2,569 against. One admires the courage of the 2,569. Meanwhile Napoleon's uncle Fesch, who by then had risen to be a cardinal of the Church and French ambassador to the pope, had persuaded the reluctant Pius VII to journey to Paris in order to place the imperial crown on the head of the murderer of the duc d'Enghien. The emperor's mother showed more firmness than did the supreme pontiff. She delayed her arrival in Paris from Italy until two weeks after her son's coronation, in the hope of bringing about a reconciliation between Napoleon and Lucien.

In Paris, Pius VII was treated with cool courtesy; the man who was to crown the emperor was made to feel that he was pope but by the emperor's grace. The ceremony, which was held at Notre Dame, was set for December 2, 1804. At the last minute the pope demurred: the imperial couple had not been married in church. On the evening of December 1, in a private ceremony, Cardinal Fesch joined Napoleon and Josephine in holy wedlock.

The coronation ceremony was a theatrical triumph. So, in fact, was the extravagant imperial mummery that followed: Napoleon knew, and everybody else knew, that his power rested on power and nothing else. Yet the world accepted the anachronistic revival of Roman imperial pageantry and Carolingian pretensions with relatively little mockery. After all, within barely a decade, it had witnessed in quick succession a revival of Roman republicanism, of Spartan virtue, of Grecian robes, and of Egyptian architecture: why not Augustus *cum* Charlemagne? In private, some began to talk of Tiberius and Nero.

Napoleon's attempt to found an imperial dynasty was illusory. His time was the nineteenth century, a bourgeois age of businessmen and factories, when even legitimate monarchs had to yield to demands for suffrage, parliamentary reform, and workers' rights. The monarchies lasted through it, simply because they had been there for a long time. What place was there for a new Caesar? By the sheer power of his will and his personality, Napoleon imposed his imperial make-believe on a prosaic world for ten years. But if he was Caesar, he was the last of the Caesars. At the same time his methods of gaining power, his nationalist version of absolutism, his use of pageantry and propaganda, of intimidation and deceit, of cajolery and brute force, of plebiscites and honors, and of every conceivable device to subordinate all human activity to the demands of the state —all these were far from anachronistic. There is nothing the dictators of the twentieth century could have taught him, except perhaps the lesson that a dictator must never try to be emperor or king.

THE CORONATION

To portray Napoleon at his coronation, Jacques Louis David first sketched the emperor with his back turned rudely to the pope; in this haughty stance, Napoleon simultaneously crowns himself emperor of the French and holds a sword against his heart (above). The artist explained: "This grand gesture recalls to the admiring onlookers the truth so widely acknowledged—that he who has known how to win the crown will also know well how to defend it." Napoleon in fact held no sword at the moment he placed the crown upon his head, and David eventually portrayed him crowning Josephine (although he did so for reasons of aesthetics rather than for historical accuracy). To some observers, however, the weapon symbolically dominated the coronation ceremony. One of the emperor's chief ecclesiastical advisors, who later became the archbishop of Malines, Dominique de Pradt, declared that despite the presence of Pope Pius VII Napoleon appeared to have "been consecrated only by his sword."

THE PREPARATIONS

The coronation and consecration ceremonies were calculated to dazzle the world with traditional majesty and splendor. Since few in the emperor's retinue had any first-hand knowledge of royal conventions, Napoleon appointed Louis Phillippe de Ségur, a diplomat who had served in several European courts, to handle the arrangements. The emperor, however, finally settled certain details, designing the pageantry to suit his political purpose as well as his whim.

Shortly after Napoleon's hereditary rule was established, he had decreed that his coronation would take place in the Church of the Invalides, the scene of many Republican celebrations. Ségur repeatedly urged the emperor to follow this plan, but Napoleon changed his mind; he would receive the crown of empire in the Cathedral of Notre Dame. According to historian Frédéric Masson, Napoleon argued that the recently "re-Christianized" Invalides was too small for the grand event. More likely, Notre Dame's long and sacred history appealed to the emperor's newly whetted appetite for tradition—the older church provided a more fitting prologue to his papal consecration. Ironically, when the redecoration of Notre Dame by Percier and Fontaine was complete, one spectator observed: "So much work has been done that God Himself would lose His bearings."

In search of a heritage, the emperor called for all the ornaments of office used at Charlemagne's coronation, but what was accessible could not be thoroughly authenticated. In the end, the Carolingian crown, with which Napoleon had originally hoped to establish his link with the past and future, was nothing more than a skillful reproduction.

In an engraving (left), Napoleon and Josephine arrive for their coronation at Notre Dame. The cathedral is partly encased in a temporary neo-Gothic facing. An entry ticket appears below.

DÉPUTATIONS
MILITAIRES,
Côté droit du Trône,
3me. Étage.

GRAND MAITRE
DES
CÉRÉMONIES

David was enraged when Ségur sent him only two tickets to the coronation for he claimed the emperor had promised him a special stand;
he later took the liberty of painting himself, his family, and his friends in the gallery above Napoleon's mother, who did not attend but

who appears seated in the center of the picture. Standing are other members of the emperor's family, marshals, and political dignitaries. Long after the ceremony, Napoleon instructed David to alter the portrait of the pope, so that his hand is raised as if to bless the event.

Josephine kneels to receive her crown in the David sketch above: below, a sketch of Ségur, Grand Master of Ceremonies.

PARTS AND PLAYERS

Accounts of the coronation report that Napoleon yawned during the proceedings, prodded his uncle Cardinal Fesch with his scepter, and whispered to Joseph, "If only our father could see us now!" Some of the stories may be apocryphal but the morning undoubtedly passed with somewhat less dignity than David's portrayal suggests. To everyone's discomfort, the weather was cold, wet, and windy. Mademoiselle Avrillon, an attendant to Josephine, afterward complained: "We were all dressed as if for a well-heated drawing room, and our only protection, . . . our cashmere shawls, we were obliged to take off as we entered the gallery." Colder still were the spectators, many of whom had waited in the cathedral from daybreak for the ceremony. To their dismay, most of the service was hidden from them by strategically placed dignitaries. The sausages and rolls which were surreptitiously peddled inside the church must have been small consolation to the patient crowd.

Some of the participants were equally disgruntled. Months before the event, Napoleon's sisters had bitterly protested Josephine's imperial rank, which elevated her above them; nor would they suffer their brothers' wives being called "princesses" when they were not. They wept and fainted and finally persuaded Napoleon to make them princesses as well. Their hysterics over the part they were to play in the coronation proved less successful. Napoleon threatened them with exile if they would not carry the train of Josephine's imperial mantle in the procession. Of course they acquiesced, but at the moment in the ceremony when Josephine began to climb the stairs leading to her throne, she staggered. Speculation ran high that the princesses had given the mantle a vicious tug before they let it fall.

Pius VII accepted his humiliating role with more gracious resignation. His participation had been severely limited. Napoleon not only crowned himself; he also refused to receive the holy oils in the traditional manner—he did not wish to prostrate himself before the power of the Church as the anointing rite required—and he would not take communion. The pope's only protest was to withdraw while Napoleon read the constitutional oath, in which he swore to support the Concordat (by which the Church had been largely compromised) and to maintain the freedom of worship in France, an even more direct insult to the papacy.

David worked for three years on his painting of the coronation, developing the major figures in the nineteen-by-thirty-
foot canvas from sensitive individual sketches. Pius VII
(above) was one of his favorite subjects; the artist painted
three portraits of the pope at this time. The sketch at
right is of Madame Soult, wife of one of Napoleon's marshals.
Below is Marshal Kellermann, said to have carried the
copy of Charlemagne's crown in the coronation processional.

THE RETURN
OF ELEGANCE

Commercial Paris welcomed the coronation, for with the age of Empire came a new era of prosperity. According to Bourrienne: "The revival of old customs gave occupation to tradespeople who could get no employment under the Directory or Consulate, such as saddlers, carriagemakers, lacemen, embroiderers, and others. By these positive interests were created more partisans of the Empire than by opinion and reflections." But although business flourished as visitors poured into the capital for the coronation, a notice in the Carrousel announced with caustic humor: "The Imperial Comedians will today present . . . 'The Emperor in spite of all the World,' followed by 'The Forced Consent.' This spectacle is presented on behalf of an indigent family."

The decorative nef, or boat-shaped receptacle, shown on the opposite page, is one of the most impressive pieces from a silver-gilt table service presented to the imperial couple by the city of Paris. This, with the candelabrum at right and the clock (below) were among the furnishings of Malmaison, where they are still to be seen. Under the new emperor, classical modes in form and ornament, displayed by all three pieces, developed into what is known as the empire style.

OVERLEAF: The painting by Boilly commemorates the first public exhibition of David's gigantic painting of the coronation ceremony; it was displayed in 1808.

THE CONQUEST
OF EUROPE

All my life I have sacrificed everything—
comfort, self-interest, happiness—to my destiny.

The so-called Constitution of the Year XII (1804) removed from France the last vestiges of legislative independence, but it maintained the fiction that the nation, though ruled by an emperor, was a republic. This fiction was soon allowed to fall into oblivion. The Tribunate, deprived of what little usefulness it still had, continued to vegetate for three years and then died a quiet death. The emperor's will became law either by the promulgation of decrees or in the form of *senatus consulta.* In the latter case the emperor would send the text of the proposed law to the Senate for its approval; the Senate would pass it unanimously, without change, and thank the emperor for his gracious communication in abjectly servile terms reminiscent of senatorial practice under Tiberius and Nero. As for the Legislative Body, it continued its shadowy existence until New Year's Day, 1814, when, having dared oppose the emperor's will, it was dismissed by him with a violent diatribe.

While it was clear to the emperor that a generation that had passed through the French Revolution and witnessed his climb to power could never, in its innermost heart, accept him as a monarch by divine right, he expected to bring up the future generations in that faith. The school system, as reorganized by him in 1807 and 1808, placed all education, on all levels, under the central authority of the University of France—that is, of the state. "There will be no political stability," he wrote in 1805, "so long as

there is no teaching body based on stable principles. So long as children are not taught whether they must be republicans or monarchists, Catholics or freethinkers, and so on, the state will not constitute a nation but rest on vague and shifting foundations, ever exposed to disorder and change." Contrary to the pope's expectations, education was not restored to the Church, but religion nevertheless became one of its basic features, and the cornerstone of religion was the catechism Napoleon had drawn up for France (without consultation with the Holy See). Here is what all French children were taught under Napoleon's reign: *"Question:* What should one think of those who fail in their duties to our emperor? *Answer:* According to the Apostle Saint Paul, they would resist the order established by God Himself and would make themselves deserving of eternal damnation."

Children might believe such a thing, but Napoleon's ministers, councilors, generals, and family assuredly did not. To have to begin, virtually overnight, to address him as "Your Imperial Majesty" must have caused them some strain. To remedy this strain, it seemed to him, a hierarchic structure had to be created, with a new nobility putting some distance between himself and the people. A

At a high point of power, Napoleon imposed his imperial insignia on the decor of Fontainebleau, ancient residence of French kings. His throne there, shown at right, was designed by Jacob.

Designed for a piece of Sèvres porcelain, the allegorical study above commemorates Napoleon's reformation of French education.

man may experience difficulty in calling another man, who all his life has been his equal, "Your Majesty"; but the difficulty is considerably lessened if that man himself is suddenly addressed as "Your Highness." In recognition of this principle of human vanity, the Constitution of the Year XII raised Napoleon's brothers to the rank of prince (except Lucien, who was excluded from the succession but whom the pope created prince of Canino) and established a number of "grand imperial dignities," both civil and military. Joseph Bonaparte became grand elector; Cambacérès, grand chancellor of the empire; Eugene de Beauharnais, arch-chancellor of state; Lebrun, arch-treasurer; Louis Bonaparte, constable; Murat, grand admiral; Fesch, grand almoner; Duroc, grand marshal of the palace; Talleyrand, grand chamberlain, and in 1807 also vice grand elector; Caulaincourt, grand master of the horse; Berthier, grand master of the hunt; Ségur, grand master of ceremonies; and fourteen generals were raised to the rank of marshal of the empire. The titles suggest an attempt to combine the great honorific offices of the Holy Roman Empire with those of the former French monarchy. Needless to say, the positions brought considerable remuneration.

All this, as will be seen, was only a modest start. In 1806 Napoleon began to make kings; in 1808 he gave the title "prince" to all great dignitaries (a measure that resulted in such grotesque combinations as "Prince Lebrun") and created a new nobility—dukes, counts, and barons of the empire—which he endowed generously with revenue-producing property. The old nobility was not restored to its former titles, but many of its members were eager enough to accept the new ones or to fill various offices at the imperial court—chamberlains, ladies in waiting, and the like. "I offered them commissions in the army," Madame de Staël quotes Napoleon as saying; "they didn't want them. I offered them posts in the administration; they turned them down. But I opened my antechambers to them, and they came running."

The establishment of the imperial nobility, though much ridiculed and criticized, was in fact one of Napoleon's most admirable inspirations. It created an aristocracy of merit. Most titles, to be sure, were made hereditary; but if the system had lasted, the ranks of the new nobility would have remained open to new talents. At the same time, the system bound the elite more closely to the throne, and it provided the most powerful impetus conceivable to emulation within the complicated hierarchy of the emperor's service. This emulation could be felt in all fields of endeavor, for the new counts and barons were not only administrators and soldiers, but also scientists, artists, and professional men. Never before had talent been rewarded more generously by the state or been put more effectively under government control.

If the new aristocracy contributed to the image of France as the great nation and of Paris as the capital of the world, the pomp and splendor of the imperial court and army—with their glittering and exuberant uniforms, their glistening helmets and swords and eagles, their dazzling balls, their clattering of cavalcades, their mixture of feminine grace and military dash, their swanlike beauties and their grizzled grenadiers, their counterpoint of violins and guns—

provided a spectacle and created a mystique that intoxicated a generation and set the style for a century. France was intoxicated with glory, which enhanced life and nullified death. It was a decidedly masculine mystique. Love, as Napoleon put it, was "the warrior's relaxation." Woman's purpose was to bear sons, to be beautiful and gentle, to adorn man's world with simple grace, while men strutted like peacocks in their plumes and gold braid, and their skintight breeches, with a clatter of swords and medals.

It was all very theatrical, tawdry in the merciless light of history, but staged by a dramatic genius. To cap the effect, the director and main actor in the pageant reserved for himself, with unfailing instinct, the most appropriate trick to upstage the rest: surrounded by his generals and marshals, by the kings and princes of his creation, who towered above him respectfully in sartorial and martial splendor, he commanded obedience with his imperious eyes, dressed in his simple uniform, his gray riding coat, his little hat. The contrast between the creator and his creatures could not have been symbolized with greater dramatic impact. He was what he was, and they were what he had made them.

To create all this splendor, and to make the impassive marble features and the sober silhouette of its creator into the symbols they became, required the spending of human lives on a lavish scale. But men and arms were cheap in those days. In 1811 the budget for the entire French Empire showed only a little over 1,300,000,000 francs in expenditures, 51 per cent of which were for military purposes. Empress Josephine spent an average of a million francs a year on dress alone; but a conscripted recruit could buy another man to take his place for fifteen hundred to four thousand francs, if he had them. Conscripts were chosen by lot. During the period 1801–4, 60,000 men were called up each year; in 1805 the figure jumped to 210,000, and the total for the period 1805–13 has been estimated at more than 2,300,000 men. (These figures, it should be added, represent goals rather than the number of conscripts actually embodied in the army, which appears to have been considerably lower.)

The intoxication with glory did not extend to the classes that furnished the bulk of the cannon fodder. With each levy, the number of deserters rose; thousands mutilated themselves to avoid conscription; and squads of gendarmes covered the country to track down deserters and refractories. Since married men were exempted, the number of marriages rose significantly from 203,000 in 1811 to 387,000 in 1813. "I have only one passion, only one mistress," the emperor once said, "and that is France: I sleep with her. She has never failed me, she has lavished her blood and her treasures on me. If I need five hundred thousand men, she gives them to me." She did indeed submit to his murderous embrace, but he was flattering himself if he thought that he gave her much pleasure. The assertion that his

soldiers invariably adored him is a myth. The only troops whose cries of *Vive l'Empereur!* were uttered spontaneously were the Imperial Guard, his elite, whom he never committed in action except as a last resort.

For more than two years after the resumption of warfare between England and France in 1803, the Continent remained at peace. By the close of 1804, however, it was clear that a new coalition against France was in the making. In January, 1805, the English government set aside the sum of five million pounds for subsidies to those monarchs who would undertake to put land armies into the field against France (the price of men's lives, let it be repeated, was cheap) and began to press its negotiations with the sovereigns of Russia, Austria, and Prussia. In April England and Russia signed an offensive alliance. Austria, on the other hand, proved hesitant. Her minister of war, Archduke Charles, aware of the inadequacy of the Austrian army and eager to complete its reform, advocated peace at almost any price as the only salvation. His position was undermined, however, partly by Russian pressure, partly by Napoleon's provocative actions in Italy. Indeed, on May 26, at Milan, Napoleon added the iron crown of Lombardy to his imperial one and was proclaimed king of Italy. While in Milan he appointed his stepson Eugene viceroy of Italy, graciously granted the request of the Ligurian Republic to be annexed to France, and threatened to expel the Bourbons from Naples. Frightened by his aggressive tone and prodded by Czar Alexander, Emperor Francis joined the Coalition two months later and was followed shortly thereafter by Sweden.

British diplomacy was less successful in the Germanies. Prussia clung to neutrality, announcing that she would fight whatever power invaded her territory first, but at the same time kept angling for Hanover, which had been occupied by French troops. Since George III was the elector of Hanover, and since Napoleon had physical possession of it, either of these two sovereigns was in a position to offer Prussia the

The Replacement Merchants *caricatures conscription dodging.*

prize. The British cabinet, however, refused to broach the matter to His Majesty, fearing that the very suggestion of his ceding Hanover would once again unhinge his rather unstable mind. Napoleon, on the other hand, temptingly dangled the prize in front of King Frederick William III's nose. Still, Frederick William hesitated; he was afraid of Russia, and Napoleon might lose the war. He preferred to remain sitting on the fence, meanwhile reaffirming Prussian neutrality. As for the sovereigns of the south German states, the more important among them frankly threw in their lot with France; Bavaria, Württemberg, Baden, and Hesse-Darmstadt became the allies of Napoleon, who rewarded them richly. Strange though it may sound to modern ears, the remark of Madame de Staël (who visited Germany in 1804), that the Germans lacked a national spirit, was largely true at the time. If it ceased to be true but a few years later, Napoleon had only himself to blame for the change.

The burgomaster of Vienna presenting the keys of the city to Napoleon

By late August, 1805, the alignment of the powers had become fairly clear: on the one side, England, Russia, Austria, and their lesser allies Sweden and Naples; on the other side, France, Spain, and Napoleon's tributaries; in the middle, cajoled and threatened by both sides, prudent Prussia. Technically, however, the Continent was still at peace. The Allied plan for a simultaneous attack by some three hundred fifty thousand troops in Italy, Bavaria, and Hanover was completed and agreed upon; in the meantime Napoleon's Grand Army, some one hundred eighty thousand men, stood poised at Boulogne, at Brest, and in Holland, apparently ready to invade England.

Whether at that time Napoleon still clung to his invasion project is a question to which no certain answer can ever be found. What cannot be debated is that two conditions had to be fulfilled if the project was to have the least chance of success. First, the outbreak of war on the Continent had to be delayed by several weeks or months; second, Napoleon needed temporary control of the English Channel. In appearance, at least, Napoleon bent all his energy to the fulfillment of these conditions. Well-informed of the Allies' secret preparations, he sent a stern warning to Emperor Francis II, hoping to restrain him by intimidation. At the same time he urged Admiral Villeneuve, who commanded a large French and Spanish squadron at Cadiz, to proceed to the Channel with the utmost expedition. The invasion troops were embarked, he informed his

minister of marine; if Villeneuve could control the Channel for but twenty-four hours, England would fall. These measures, however, do not constitute conclusive evidence that England was Napoleon's real target; quite possibly they were intended to lead the Allies astray. On August 22 orders went out to Brest by semaphore telegraph that Villeneuve, as soon as he appeared, should be directed to sail up the Channel; on the same day the minister of marine wrote to the emperor, pleading with him to leave Villeneuve at Cadiz and to postpone the invasion project to a more favorable season. A few days later Napoleon abandoned the invasion and ordered the Grand Army to march into Germany. The double result of this decision was the Battles of Trafalgar and Austerlitz.

Napoleon's decision was so sudden, and his Grand Army began its march so incompletely equipped, that it cannot have been altogether premeditated. He still hoped to gain time by negotiation; but the Austrian government had rejected his threatening note and opened hostilities by invading Bavaria, and two Russian armies were on the march. In the Allies' calculations the Grand Army could not reach Bavaria before early November; yet such was the speed of the French advance that the Austrians were taken completely off their guard. On October 20 the Austrian commander, General Karl von Mack, capitulated with twenty-five thousand men at Ulm; on November 13 Napoleon entered Vienna, having encountered no serious resistance, and went to sleep at the palace of Schönbrunn. Emperor Francis, with what troops remained to him, had withdrawn into Moravia, as had the Russian army under Mikhail Kutuzov.

Napoleon's victorious advance had put him in a delicate position. He was more than four hundred miles from France; the corps of his Grand Army reached from Moravia to the Tyrol, from Swabia to Carinthia; winter was approaching; and he had just received the shattering news that on October 21 the Franco-Spanish fleet had been annihilated at Trafalgar. The opposing Russian army, still intact, was about to be joined by another one; Prussia, whose territory Napoleon had violated in his haste to reach Vienna, seemed about to declare war; and Archduke Charles, with some eighty thousand men, was on his way from Venetia. Napoleon's attempt to split the Coalition by separate negotiations with the Russian and the Austrian emperors, though it might have succeeded if pursued long enough, only gave the Allies time to rally their forces. A quick and crushing blow at the Austro-Russian armies was imperative; but the Austro-Russian armies in Moravia, led by Emperors Francis and Alexander, outnumbered the forces Napoleon could spare against them. On November 20 Napoleon arrived at Brünn, the Moravian capital, where he continued to negotiate. One week later the Russian army, based at Olmütz, began to march on Brünn, apparently in an attempt to cut the French off from Vienna. Alexander, who directed the operation personally, was about to commit a colossal blunder. Divining the purpose of Alexander's maneuver, Napoleon correctly predicted his moves and led him into an inextricable trap.

The point where, in Napoleon's estimate, the enemy was most likely to begin the movement designed to out-flank him was located near the village of Austerlitz, a few miles from Brünn, on the Olmütz road. The strongest posi-tion there was the Heights of Pratzen, which Napoleon carefully refrained from occupying; instead he stationed the larger part of his troops behind the heights and osten-sibly made preparations for a rearguard action designed to protect his retreat.

The Battle of Austerlitz was, beyond any doubt, Napo-leon's most brilliant victory, and the bulletin in which he described it, on the morrow of the battle, was the most truthful of his bulletins as to the main facts (though not the figures); also, no poetry could have expressed the exul-tation of victory as did Napoleon's clear and ringing prose. Here is the emperor on the eve of the battle: "On Decem-ber 1 the Emperor, from the height of his bivouac, ob-served with indescribable joy that the Russian army, almost within artillery range of his outposts, was beginning a flanking movement intended to turn his right. He could see then to what extent presumptuousness and ignorance of the art of war had misled the councils of that brave army. He said several times, 'Before tomorrow night this army will be mine.' Meanwhile, the enemy displayed quite a different mood. They exposed themselves at pistol range from our main guard. They strung themselves out over a line four leagues long in a flanking march alongside the French army, which appeared to be afraid of leaving its positions. The enemy's only fear was that the French army might elude them. Everything was done to confirm them in that notion. Prince Murat ordered a small body of cavalry to advance into the plain, but suddenly, as if astonished at seeing the enemy's huge forces, it hastily retreated. Thus everything tended to confirm the Russian commander in the ill-calculated plan he had decided upon."

The night before the battle is described with perhaps more drama than truth: "At nightfall the Emperor wished to visit all the bivouacs, on foot and incognito, but no sooner had he walked a few steps than he was recognized. It would be impossible to describe the soldiers' enthusiasm when they saw him. Instantly, straw torches were tied to thousands of poles, and eighty thousand men turned to the Emperor, greeting him with cheers."

The weather on the day of the battle was glorious: "On December 2 dawn came at last. The sun rose radiant, and that anniversary of the Emperor's coronation, on which one of the most glorious feats of the century was to take place, was one of the finest autumn days." It was the famous sun of Austerlitz, and the sky so poignantly described in Tolstoi's *War and Peace,* into which André Bolkonsky, lying on his back wounded, gazes serenely, at peace with

life and death. "Passing in front of several regiments in battle array," the bulletin continued, "the Emperor said, 'Soldiers! We must end this battle with a thunderclap that will confound the arrogance of our enemies'; and instantly their hats waving at the ends of their bayonets and [their] shouts of *Vive l'Empereur!* gave the actual signal for the battle to begin. . . ."

What Napoleon had expected happened. The Austro-Russian troops descended from the Heights of Pratzen, which Napoleon had allowed them to occupy, to attack the French. As soon as they had cleared the Heights, the French divisions marched to the attack, cut the Austro-Russian forces in two, and took the undefended Heights. "Finding themselves attacked," as Napoleon put it, "when they had thought that they were the attackers, they looked upon themselves as half defeated." After four or five hours' fighting, in the course of which the Austro-Russians lost some twenty-six thousand men and the French nine thousand, the Austro-Russian right and center, with the two emperors, were in headlong retreat, and the rest had been destroyed. But what made the victory truly decisive was its moral and psychological effect on the enemy. The Allied commanders were stunned, and when they ceased to be stunned, they began to quarrel.

Two days after the battle Emperor Francis requested an interview with Napoleon. An armistice was arranged between France and Austria, on the condition that the Russian forces evacuate Austrian territory; if Francis could persuade Alexander to make peace and enter into an alliance against England with France, Napoleon prom-ised to leave Austrian territory intact at the conclusion of peace. Alexander would not let himself be persuaded, but he agreed to evacuate Austria. On December 26, at Pressburg (Bratislava), peace was made between Austria on the one hand and France and Bavaria on the other. It was a crush-ing peace, Talleyrand having exerted himself in vain to convince Napoleon that the continued existence of a strong Austria was in the best interests of Europe. Austria had to cede all Venetia (including Istria and Dalmatia, but not Trieste) to the Kingdom of Italy, Tyrol and the Vorarlberg to Bavaria, and several smaller districts to Württemberg and Baden—in all about three million subjects.

Even before the Treaty of Pressburg was signed, the Prus-sian chief minister, Count von Haugwitz, concluded an offensive alliance with Napoleon; he had come to Vienna in order to present the French emperor with an ultimatum but had correctly judged it wise to await the outcome of the battle before making any move. The reward for this about-face was, of course, Hanover. In the circumstances, it is not difficult to understand the profound contempt for Prussia that characterized Napoleon's German policy.

The Peace of Pressburg made Napoleon the master of western Europe. The Coalition had been broken up, tem-porarily at least; Austria had been made innocuous; the

Resentful Germans take up arms against the French invaders.

Holy Roman Empire had ceased to exist all but in name, and ceased to exist in name also when, on August 6, 1806, Emperor Francis II abdicated as Roman emperor, retaining the title Francis I, emperor of Austria, which he had adopted in 1804. The Franco-Italian empire now extended from the Atlantic to the borders of the Ottoman Empire. On the day the Treaty of Pressburg was signed, Napoleon made the public declaration that the Kingdom of Naples had ceased to exist and that he would "hurl from the throne that criminal woman [Queen Marie Caroline] who has so shamelessly violated everything that is held sacred by men." In mid-January the king and queen of Naples fled to Sicily, where they continued to rule under the protection of British troops, and a French army took possession of their mainland kingdom.

At the same time, Napoleon, returning to Paris, stopped long enough to marry his stepson Eugene, viceroy of Italy, to a daughter of Maximilian of Bavaria, whom he had just made a king, and his stepniece Stephanie de Beauharnais to the crown prince of Baden. Frederick of Württemberg, who had also been raised to the rank of king by the Treaty of Pressburg, promised his daughter in marriage to Napoleon's youngest brother, Jerome; the contract was to be executed as soon as Jerome's ill-considered marriage to Miss Elizabeth Patterson of Baltimore, who had borne him a child, was annulled. Not only did Napoleon connect his family with the legitimate dynasties of Europe; he also began to distribute kingdoms among them: Joseph was made king of Naples; Louis became king of Holland; Murat, who had married Napoleon's sister Caroline, was made grand duke of Berg. The Principality of Neuchâtel (today a Swiss canton), which its ruler, the king of Prussia, had yielded to France, was given to Napoleon's chief of staff, Marshal Louis Berthier, in reward for his services.

Next, Napoleon turned to the reorganization of Germany. By the terms of a treaty ratified at St. Cloud on July 19, 1806, the Confederation of the Rhine came into existence. Headed by the former archbishop of Mainz, Prince Dalberg, now grand duke of Frankfort, the Confederation was to consist of the Kingdoms of Bavaria and Württemberg and the Grand Duchies of Frankfort, Baden, Hesse-Darmstadt, and Berg; its Diet was to meet at Frankfort. Hundreds of formerly sovereign petty princes—counts, barons, and knights of the Holy Roman Empire—were "mediatized": their territories were distributed among the members of the Confederation of the Rhine, but they retained their feudal rights and the ownership (though no longer sovereign) of their domains. Thus, with a stroke of the pen, Napoleon swept away the medieval political structure of Germany and at the same time unwittingly prepared the way for her unification.

The Confederation of the Rhine was tied to France by a defensive-offensive alliance; it undertook to furnish France with sixty-three thousand men in the event of war on the Continent and gave Napoleon the title "protector." Meanwhile, the Grand Army, 170,000 men strong, remained in southern Germany at the expense of the German states, ready to strike in any direction at any moment. To say that Europe was stunned is hardly an exaggeration. Before, it had merely feared Napoleon; now that he held it in his power, it trembled with terror and fascination. It was at this time of all times that Prussia, whose conduct, in Fox's words, had been "a compound of everything that is contemptible in servility with everything that is odious in rapacity," chose to play David to Goliath, with somewhat less success.

It is scarcely surprising that at the beginning of the year 1806, having won almost total victory on land and suffered a crushing defeat on the sea, Napoleon judged the time ripe to negotiate for a general peace. His most inflexible opponent, the architect of the Third Coalition, William Pitt, had died shortly after receiving the news of Austerlitz (it may have hastened his death). The dominant figure in the cabinet that succeeded his was Charles James Fox, who became foreign minister and who was known to be favorably disposed toward peace. In March, 1806, Fox chivalrously sent warning to Talleyrand that he had knowledge of a plot to assassinate Napoleon. Through Talleyrand, the emperor expressed his gratitude and at the same time hinted at the possibility of negotiations. Fox replied that he would negotiate only jointly with Russia. Czar Alexander, though faithfully informed of this by Fox, nevertheless suspected Fox of wishing to make peace at any price and at Russia's expense, and sent a plenipotentiary to Paris to look after his interests.

Thus, in effect, thanks to Alexander's tortuous duplicity, Napoleon obtained what he wanted—separate negotiations with each of the two great powers still confronting him. If he failed to profit from this initial advantage, it was because his own duplicity equaled if it did not surpass Alexander's. When word leaked through to London that the Russian envoy in Paris had signed an agreement by which the Balearic Islands, which belonged to Spain, were promised to the Bourbons of Naples in exchange for Sicily, Fox was disgusted. As it happened, he died soon afterward (on September 13); yet even if he had lived another twenty years, he would never have accepted peace on that basis, for it was under Britain's guarantee that the Bourbons ruled Sicily. By September the mood in St. Petersburg had also changed; Czar Alexander refused to ratify the agreement and stiffened his demands. At the same time, Prussia was preparing to go to war against France in alliance with Russia, England, and Sweden.

The shifty policies of Frederick William III and his minister Haugwitz had long been criticized by an important segment of Prussian public opinion. Not only did the critics chafe under the repeated humiliations borne by Prussia, which under Frederick the Great had defeated France in two wars, but they were also animated by a new spirit of patriotism and reform. The militarist wing of the opposition had its leaders in the royal family itself—Prince Louis Ferdinand of Prussia and Queen Louise, a woman equally remarkable for her beauty and her pluck; the reformers were headed by Baron vom Stein, who was to create the modern Prussian state. (It was the misfortune of Prussia —and of Germany—that the narrow-mindedness of Frederick William III and of his successor should force these

two elements—the militarist-nationalist and the liberal-reformist—to become so closely associated.) In 1806 the war party had its way, but it was only in 1807, when its policy had led Prussia into her most humiliating defeat, that the reformers were given a chance.

If Prussia had joined the Coalition before the thunder-clap of Austerlitz, she might have tipped the scales against France. When, in the summer of 1806, it became known in Berlin that the price of Prussia's dishonor—Hanover—had been blandly offered to England by Napoleon, the reaction was understandably indignant. An additional cause of Prussian resentment was the establishment of the Confederation of the Rhine, which for all practical purposes excluded Prussia from German affairs and nibbled away at Prussian territory. Frederick William's attempt to create a North German Confederation, headed by himself with the title of emperor, was vetoed by Napoleon. Still, no matter how provoking Napoleon's cavalier treatment of Prussia might be, the moment for making war could not have been worse chosen. The Prussian army, it is true, still enjoyed a high reputation, but it had not proved itself since 1763. Its achievements in the campaign of 1792–95 were nothing to boast of, and the insane self-confidence of the Prussian military leaders in 1806 can only be ascribed to their collective delusion.

The wave of warlike feeling that swept Prussia was owed in large part to an incident that brutally illustrated Napoleonic arbitrariness. A bookseller at Nuremberg,

Napoleon, on his horse, surveys the corpse-strewn field at Eylau; scavengers moved in to rob the dead the moment the battle ended.

Emissaries from the shah of Persia meet with Napoleon at Finkenstein to negotiate terms of an anti-British, anti-Russian alliance.

J. P. Palm, had issued an anonymous pamphlet entitled *Germany in Her Deep Humiliation,* which gave offense to Napoleon. Nuremberg having recently been given to Bavaria, the emperor's long arm could reach there. He ordered that Palm be arrested and tried by a French military commission, and on August 25 Palm was shot. The execution sparked such indignation in Berlin that the king, pressed by his own family and by the czar, could no longer remain neutral. Alexander had promised his aid, and by mid-September the elector of Saxony reluctantly joined Prussia in mobilizing his army. The Prussian ultimatum to Napoleon reached the emperor only on October 7, when he was already at Bamberg, in Bavaria, ready to strike at his foolhardy opponents. The supreme command over the Prussian and Saxon forces was entrusted to the aged duke of Brunswick, who accepted it with little enthusiasm.

The Grand Army—about one hundred sixty thousand men—began its march north on October 8. Two days later, in an action at Saalfeld, a Prussian division under Prince Louis Ferdinand was routed, and the prince himself killed. On October 14—one week after he had received the Prussian ultimatum—Napoleon won one of the most complete and most bizarre victories recorded in the annals of warfare. In the morning of that day, at Jena, he came upon a Prus-

sian corps commanded by Prince Hohenlohe, which he mistook for the main Prussian army. Napoleon sent orders to Marshals Bernadotte and Davout to join their corps, which were at some distance, with his forces, and he then began the attack. Neither Bernadotte nor Davout showed up, but even without their presence Hohenlohe's corps had no chance against Napoleon's ninety-five thousand men. It stood its ground through most of the day and then retreated.

Napoleon was still exulting in his victory when he received word that Marshal Davout, at Auerstädt, about twelve miles from Jena, had just destroyed the Prussian army. "Your marshal sees double," he said to Davout's aide-de-camp, who had brought him the news. Davout, however, had not seen double; it was Napoleon who had been blind. Davout's victory was all the more remarkable since he had only twenty-six thousand men against Brunswick's sixty thousand and only one gun for every five of the Prussians'. Brunswick was mortally wounded in the battle. Except for a few battalions, the Prussian army simply evaporated. The king, and the queen, who had ridden into the battle like an Amazon, were in flight; the troops were throwing away their arms. The curious thing about the Battle of Jena is that Napoleon won it over an army that was not there; the curious thing about the Battle of Auerstädt, that Davout won it over an army twice his strength, whose reputation was second to none; the curious thing about both battles, is that Marshal Bernadotte, who happened to be sulking, marched his corps straight between them, hearing gun fire from both sides, without making the least attempt to find out what was going on.

Except for a few pockets of resistance that were soon wiped out, north Germany was at Napoleon's mercy. On October 25 the French entered Berlin, whose population had reverted from its martial temper to complete docility. Although peace negotiations were in progress with the king of Prussia, who had taken refuge in his eastern provinces, Napoleon's stiffening terms made it plain that he was not eager to bring them to a quick conclusion. On the other hand, he dealt swiftly with Prussia's north German allies. Toward the elector of Saxony, whose troops had dissociated themselves from the Prussians immediately after the battles of Jena and Auerstädt, Napoleon was generous; he made him king and allowed him to join the Confederation of the Rhine. The elector of Hesse-Cassel, who had remained a neutral but had mobilized his forces, was summarily deposed, as was the new duke of Brunswick; their territories were to form the core of the new Kingdom of Westphalia, which Napoleon created a year later and gave to his brother Jerome. A war levy of one hundred sixty million francs was imposed on the north German states, and Prussia was to bear the brunt.

Of the remaining adversaries, two—Sweden and Prussia—were negligible, and Napoleon could deal with them at leisure. As for England, Napoleon expected, now that he was master of all Europe, to bring her to her knees by ruining her trade. The Berlin Decree, placing Great Britain under blockade, was the basis of the ill-fated Continental System, which will be dealt with in another chapter.

With Russia, Napoleon hoped to come to an agreement. To put Czar Alexander in a receptive frame of mind, he had instructed his ambassador to the Porte, General Horace Sébastiani, to encourage Sultan Selim III to take an aggressively anti-Russian stand; accordingly, Selim dismissed the pro-Russian governors of Moldavia and Walachia (modern Rumania), a move that Alexander promptly countered by sending an army of eighty thousand men to occupy these principalities. With a large part of his forces tied up in the war with Turkey (which was to end only in 1812), Alexander might well choose to come to terms with Napoleon rather than fight him. To secure his co-operation Napoleon was prepared to offer a partition of the Ottoman Empire—his ally, whom he had just incited into war with Russia—and to propose a joint Russo-French attack on India. Indeed, his old dreams of a French empire in Egypt and Asia and of crushing England by striking at India were again dominating his mind. Moreover, if he could reach an agreement with Alexander, he would then be free to impose whatever terms he wished on Prus-

sia; and it was this Machiavellian consideration that caused him to prefer to keep Prussia as an enemy rather than to make peace with her.

Napoleon's cynical scheme succeeded—but neither as promptly nor as completely as he had hoped. Far from showing any disposition to make peace, Czar Alexander promised to come to the aid of the king of Prussia, provided the king did not make peace; at the same time he tried (unsuccessfully) to draw Austria back into the Coalition. The possibility that Napoleon might reconstitute Poland naturally tended to bring the three despoilers of Poland—Russia, Prussia, and Austria—together in an alliance against him. The combination might well have proved fatal; indeed, as at almost any moment in Napoleon's career, the entire structure of his power hung by the thinnest of threads. Since Russia would not make peace, he would have to fight her in a winter campaign, in the icy climate of Poland and East Prussia, with an army ill-equipped for that kind of warfare. The loss of a single major battle was likely to bring Austria back into the war and almost certain to encourage his enemies at home to stage a coup d'état against him. The Russian army, despite the Turkish war, was still formidable, and it would be supported by the remnants of the Prussian army—about fifteen thousand men—and possibly by Swedish forces.

To make up for his inferiority, Napoleon could count on the support of the Poles; yet, while encouraging their hopes for independence, he carefully refrained from committing himself officially, for to do so would have ended whatever hope there was of an understanding with Alexander, and would have provoked Austria. Napoleon solved this particular dilemma in his usual manner. He told the Poles that if they wanted liberty, they must prove that they deserved it by fighting for it. If they supplied him with thirty thousand men and fought bravely, he might consider the question of independence in due time.

Although a great many unpleasant rumors trickled into France from the frozen plains of Poland and East Prussia, the full horror of the winter campaign of 1806–7 was not known to the general public. The sufferings of the troops were incredible, and the sufferings they inflicted on the population, with official sanction, in order to keep themselves fed and warm, were scarcely less appalling. The first phase of the campaign ended early in January, 1807. A series of inconclusive engagements had brought the larger part of Poland under French control but left the enemy army intact. Napoleon returned to Warsaw—which he had taken on December 18—with the idea of resuming the offensive when the weather improved.

The social scene at Warsaw was shocking in contrast to the grim campaign for it was an unending series of feasts and balls. The most beautiful ladies of Poland—which is to say, the most beautiful women of all Europe—triumphed over the emperor's officers and were not averse to letting the officers triumph over themselves. The emperor too was indulging in the warrior's proper relaxation. His health, he wrote to his brother the king of Naples, had never been better nor his amorous powers more vigorous. The cause of this rejuvenation was Countess Marie Walewska, a modest beauty in her eighteenth year, whose scruples against accepting the conqueror's embraces had been overcome by the united Polish nobility; it was she, they convinced her, who would wrest a guarantee of Polish freedom from the emperor, as Esther had saved the Jews by bewitching King Ahasuerus of Persia.

Napoleon proved an ardent lover to a girl who until then had known only the weak embraces of a decrepit husband; however, he remained a cautious diplomat as far as Poland was concerned. The news of the affair, which resulted in the birth of a son, gave some alarm to Empress Josephine. She was rightly alarmed for the wrong reason; as Napoleon pointed out in a conversation with his brother Lucien, "Yes, I am in love, but subordinately to my policy, which requires me to marry a princess, although I should prefer to have my mistress crowned."

After several weeks of feasts and love at Warsaw, Napoleon saw what he took for an opportunity to crush the Russian army, which had concentrated in East Prussia. On February 8 he found a Russian force of seventy-five thousand at Eylau; his own force was far inferior (fifty thousand at the most), but he expected the corps of Marshals Ney and Davout to join him during the battle and ordered an attack. The carnage was the worst thus far seen in modern history. Davout's corps was prevented from joining the main forces by the Prussian corps that fought alongside the Russians. At the end of the day, the Allies retreated and left Napoleon in possession of the battlefield, thus enabling him to claim a victory, despite the inconclusive nature of the battle. It is true that the Allies lost more than a third of their forces in killed and wounded, but French casualties were even higher; the Allies fought close to their bases, while Napoleon was very far from his, and his chances of recovery therefore were slimmer than theirs.

Napoleon inspected the battlefield. "To visualize the scene," he wrote in his victory bulletin, "one must imagine, within the space of three square miles, nine or ten thousand corpses; four or five thousand dead horses; rows upon rows of Russian field-packs; the remnants of muskets and swords; the ground covered with cannon balls, shells, and other ammunition; and twenty-four artillery pieces, near which could be seen the corpses of the drivers who were killed while trying to move them—all this sharply outlined against a background of snow. A sight such as this should inspire rulers with the love of peace and the hatred of war." It should indeed, but according to one witness, the emperor remarked as he made his way past the frozen corpses that most of them were only simple soldiers. An additional eighty thousand recruits were being conscripted in France, and they would soon replace the "little people" lying dead on the snows of Eylau.

Napoleon's bulletin did not disclose the actual extent of French losses; nevertheless, the leaders of the opposition in Paris were aware that the battle had been dreadful. Another such victory, and they would feel strong enough to overthrow him. Conscious of this, Napoleon made peace overtures to the Russian and Prussian sovereigns. Alexander and Frederick William were not mistaken in interpreting his offers as a sign of weakness, but they were definitely mistaken in rejecting them. Once again, with a single, brilliant victory, Napoleon was to escape destruction and rise to new heights of power.

For several weeks following the Battle of Eylau, the French army, while holding on to its conquests, seemed to be in the process of disintegration. Filthy, in rags, hungry, and cursing their emperor, the troops turned into so many marauders. Nothing edible, combustible, or furry was safe from them. The news that the emperor, at his headquarters at Finkenstein, was negotiating an alliance with the shah of Persia gave them little comfort. The coming of spring and the capture of Danzig (May 26) by Marshal Lefebvre's German and Polish corps were more cheering. Still, the situation had been critical, and Napoleon's new recruits were mostly teen-age boys who normally would have been called to arms only in 1808. The Grand Army was turning into a Moloch. Only a quick victory followed by peace could silence the protest that was mounting in France. On June 14 the opportunity presented itself to Napoleon to do just that.

On the morning of that day, the Russian commander in chief, Count Bennigsen, with a force of sixty thousand, came upon the corps of Marshal Lannes near Friedland, in East Prussia. The temptation to destroy Lannes' corps was irresistible, and Bennigsen ordered his troops to attack. Lannes, however, was favored by the terrain and despite the inferiority of his forces managed to hold out until 5 P.M. when Napoleon brought three additional corps to the field of battle. This gave the French a slight numerical superiority. Leaving eighteen thousand dead and wounded behind, the Russians retreated in headlong flight. Thus, on the seventh anniversary of the Battle of Marengo, Napoleon had won a victory far more complete and decisive than Marengo. Czar Alexander, hoping to gain time to reorganize his forces, requested an armistice to which Napoleon consented. The truce was signed on June 21, and a meeting of the emperors was arranged for June 25. Prussia up to that point was not a party to the armistice.

The interview of the two emperors, which took place on a raft moored in the middle of the Niemen, opposite Tilsit, was one of the most astonishing episodes in all history. The conversation was held without ear witnesses, and it lasted three hours. What was said can never be known, of course, but may be guessed easily enough. While the two

Napoleon and Czar Alexander of Russia greet each other on the raft near Tilsit where they conducted their secret negotiations.

emperors talked, the king of Prussia was obliged to wait on the shore in the rain to hear the verdict.

Czar Alexander was an unpredictable and unstable compound of idealism and shrewdness, liberalism and mysticism, moral rectitude and unscrupulous ambition. Perhaps—though this was not apparent to his contemporaries—he had inherited a strain of his late father's insanity. In any event, he was full of surprises, and his mental processes remain as enigmatic as the circumstances of his death. (His tomb in the Kremlin, when opened in the 1920's, was found to be empty.) His appearance was extremely handsome and noble, and all witnesses agree that he possessed extraordinary charm.

It may be surmised that much of the emperors' three-hour interview was spent in a competition of mutual flattery, at which both were supremely adept. Alexander came away from the interview with the impression (perhaps mistaken) that susceptibility to flattery was Napoleon's weak point; Napoleon (perhaps with equally little reason) thought the same of Alexander. "I am satisfied with Alexander," he later wrote to Josephine, "and he must be satisfied with me. If he were a woman, I think I would make him my mistress." The thought is staggering. Yet even if Alexander was not prepared to become Napoleon's mistress, there can be no doubt that he had quite suddenly developed something close to hero worship for his conqueror and that he was determined to ally himself with France. The terms of the alliance, as will be seen shortly,

were no less sensational than was the sudden passion that the two monarchs conceived for each other.

One of the things decided during that first meeting was that out of regard for the feeling of the Russian emperor, the French emperor would grant an armistice to the king of Prussia and instead of wiping Prussia off the map, as he had planned, would wipe only half of Prussia off the map. A second interview took place the next day, in Frederick William's presence, and in the two weeks following the terms of the two separate peace treaties—one with Prussia, the other with Russia—were worked out.

During the negotiations, the three monarchs were joined by Queen Louise of Prussia, who had been sent for at Memel. The queen, a radiant beauty, neglected no means whatever to soften Napoleon's harsh demands on her country. She had every reason to hate him, for not only had he humbled Prussia but also, in his bulletins, he had publicly and repeatedly insulted her, to the point of casting doubt on her marital fidelity, until Josephine begged him to refrain from such insults to her sex. Yet if Louise hated Napoleon, she possessed enough will power to disguise her feelings. She flattered him in every conceivable way; she bantered with him; she flirted with him; she even hinted—if Napoleon's testimony is to be trusted—that she would give herself to him if he agreed to leave Magdeburg to Prussia. Napoleon remained unmoved. "The queen of Prussia," he wrote to Josephine, "is really charming and full of coquettishness toward me. But don't be jealous; I am made of oilcloth and all this just slides off. It would cost me too dearly to play the gallant."

The terms on which Napoleon insisted were the cession to France of all Prussian territory west of the Elbe; the cession of the district of Cottbus to Saxony; the cession of Danzig, to be made into a free city; and the cession of her Polish provinces, to be made into the Grand Duchy of Warsaw—all in all nearly half the territory and population of Prussia. In addition Prussia was to join France in her war against England in case Alexander's effort to mediate a peace between England and France should fail, and she was to pay an unspecified amount of contributions to France. In a supreme effort to touch Napoleon's heart, Queen Louise resolved on an action that has no parallel in modern history: she requested a private interview and literally threw herself at his feet. The emperor remained inflexible. "I asked her to be seated," he reminisced at St. Helena. "Nothing is better suited for cutting a tragic scene short. Once a person has sat down, it turns into comedy." The queen's husband stumbled into the room soon afterward, thus relieving Napoleon of an embarrassing situation. The terms of the treaty stood as dictated earlier.

The treaties of peace and alliance between France and Russia were signed on July 7, two days before the Prussian treaty. In the peace treaty, which was made public, Alexander recognized the various cessions of territory made by Prussia and the creation of the Grand Duchy of Warsaw, which was to be ruled by the king of Saxony; he also agreed to evacuate the Ionian Islands and the part of Dalmatia held by Russian troops. In addition Alexander undertook to act as mediator between England and France, and Napoleon undertook to act as mediator between Russia and the Ottoman Empire.

The provisions of the Russian treaty were eminently moderate; but the secret treaty of alliance that supplemented them was one of the most brazen documents in the history of power politics. If England should refuse to make peace on certain minimum conditions, Russia would join France against her; furthermore France and Russia would summon Austria, Portugal, Denmark, and Sweden to join the alliance; in the event that Sweden (still at war with France) refused, Denmark would be invited to make war on Sweden. If the sultan of Turkey (whom Napoleon had incited to make war on Russia) should refuse Napoleon's mediation, Napoleon would join Russia in war against him; only Constantinople and a small part of European Turkey would be left to the sultan, the rest of his territories to be disposed of by agreement between Their French and Russian Majesties. Since neither mediation offer was likely to succeed, the secret treaty amounted to the partition of the world between two powers.

Considered as a package, the three treaties of Tilsit were a compound of grandioseness, shabbiness, and error. The

Napoleon receives Queen Louise at Tilsit, in a painting by Goss

treatment of Prussia was an error. If Napoleon had dealt generously with her, and removed his fiscal and military yoke over the German states in general, he would have had the confidence and loyalty of the German people, instead of rousing that peaceful and docile nation to hysterical belligerency and hatred; if he had abolished Prussia entirely and divided her up among the other German states, he could have achieved the same result. By leaving her halved and humbled, he made her the leader in the eventual uprising against him. As for Poland, he treated her shabbily: the Grand Duchy of Warsaw fell far short of what he had led the Poles to hope for. But then his shabbiness toward the Poles, his betrayal of the sultan, and his high-handed treatment of the lesser powers all were part of the grandiose scheme of partitioning the earth. If, on the other hand, that

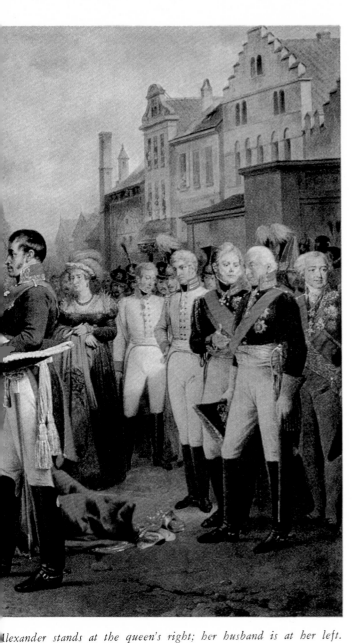

Alexander stands at the queen's right; her husband is at her left.

a year later, when Napoleon stood at his zenith, Talleyrand, whose cheek and pluck bordered on the superhuman, would stealthily begin to dig the emperor's grave.

The British government replied politely to Alexander's offer of mediation; at the same time, divining Napoleon's intentions, it ordered a squadron to seize the Danish fleet before Napoleon had a chance to seize it. On September 2, 1807, the English squadron began its terrible three-day bombardment of Copenhagen; on September 5 the Danes sued for terms, and two days later they surrendered their fleet. This attack against a weak neutral, without a declaration of war, profoundly shocked European opinion; even in retrospect it is difficult to excuse the action on any ground save the necessities of self-defense in a struggle for survival. Anglo-Russian negotiations continued despite the bombardment of Copenhagen but collapsed on November 8, when Alexander broke off relations with England. The quixotic king of Sweden, Gustavus IV Adolphus, proved as intractable as England. His stand, though honorable, was hardly wise; it cost Sweden all of Finland, which Alexander grabbed with Napoleon's blessings, and it ended in 1809 by costing Gustavus his throne.

Napoleon's attempt at mediation met with no more success than did Alexander's—though this failure was partly due to the lack of good intentions of both the French and the Russians. The articles of the public treaty signed at Tilsit stipulated that prior to a final peace settlement between Russia and Turkey, Russia withdraw her troops from Moldavia and Walachia. A preliminary armistice between Russia and Turkey was concluded in August, 1807, with the help of the French diplomat Guilleminot; but Alexander still postponed the evacuation of the Danubian provinces, on the ground that Napoleon was postponing the withdrawal of French troops from Prussia.

This in turn gave Napoleon a pretext for offering to let Alexander keep the Danubian provinces if the Russian emperor agreed to yet another partition of Prussia. This offer Alexander rejected with indignation—but he did not pull his troops out of Moldavia and Walachia. According to the secret articles of the Treaty of Tilsit, France was bound to assist Russia against Turkey in the event that no peace was made; but Alexander was not eager for French help unless France let him have Constantinople, and Napoleon was not eager to help Alexander unless he was sure that the Russians would *not* have Constantinople. The problem had been sufficiently befogged by Alexander's dragging in the Prussian issue; it was befogged even more by the fact that in May, 1807, Sultan Selim was deposed by his Janissaries for the crime of wanting to reform the Turkish army. It was not quite clear just who ruled the Ottoman Empire until a year later, when, in quick succession, Selim was strangled by the Janissaries, Selim's successor was deposed by Selim's supporters, and Mahmud II became sultan. By then, however, the question of Franco-Russian

scheme came to nothing, the reason was that both parties to it turned out to be shabby bargainers.

The conference of Tilsit ended in a glorious and martial display of Franco-Russian brotherliness and solidarity, with the two armies that but a few weeks earlier had been murdering each other paying tribute to each other's bravery under the benevolent eyes of their respective emperors. It was a spectacle such as has never been seen before or since and in the reality of which none of the participants could quite believe. Not long after Tilsit, Talleyrand resigned as foreign minister. His counsels of moderation had long since ceased to carry weight with the emperor; the proceedings at the conference left him no doubt that Napoleon was doomed by his own arrogance and folly. He would not be associated with the emperor's megalomaniac schemes; and co-operation against Turkey had become entirely academic.

The turmoil in Constantinople was paralleled at the other extremity of Europe, in the Iberian Peninsula. Indeed, since the fateful meeting on the raft at Tilsit, Napoleon's preoccupations had become global. On his return from Tilsit he stopped at Dresden, where the king of Saxony showed him his celebrated picture gallery; Napoleon barely glanced at the paintings, racing by them at such a pace that the king almost had a fit of apoplexy trying to keep up with him. He was absorbed in other problems —the division of Turkey, the invasion of India, the Danish fleet, the Portuguese fleet, the grabbing of the Iberian Peninsula, of Tuscany, of the Papal States, of Sicily, and perhaps even of Egypt. Back in Paris, the news of the English seizure of the Danish fleet sent him into an understandable rage. He must, at least, have the Portuguese fleet and, if possible, Spain and Portugal as well. When he summoned Portugal to join France in the struggle against England— Portugal's traditional ally for centuries, populated by the world's most formidable consumers of port wine—the Portuguese government submitted to every one of his demands save one: they refused to confiscate British property in Portugal. This gave Napoleon a welcome opportunity to take sterner measures.

The Treaty of Fontainebleau, signed on October 27, 1807, between France and Spain, provided for a joint Spanish-French campaign against Portugal. Portugal would be divided into three parts, one of them to be given to the grandson of Charles IV of Spain in exchange for Etruria, the other to Charles' chief minister, Manuel Godoy, and the third to France, pending a final disposition. The Spanish government eagerly embraced this dishonorable scheme, which proved to be its undoing. The Treaty of Fontainebleau was not even signed when General Junot with a French corps crossed into Spain and, reinforced by Spanish units, marched on Portugal. Hunger and torrential rains decimated the Franco-Spanish troops on the march. The Spanish forces alone lost some seventeen hundred men from hunger, disease, and drowning. Against these bedraggled divisions of starvelings, the Portuguese made no resistance. Instead, on November 29, the day before the French reached Lisbon, the prince regent embarked with his family (including his mother, the queen, who was mad) and sailed to Brazil with his fleet. He would not have done even this much if the commander of the British fleet off Lisbon had not pressed him to do it; the commander happened to be the same Sir Sidney Smith who had foiled Bonaparte at the siege of Toulon in 1793 and at the Battle of Acre in 1799.

It is difficult to decide whether Napoleon's insatiable rapacity was the necessary consequence of his struggle against England or whether England's persistence in her struggle against Napoleon was caused by Napoleon's insatiable rapacity. At any rate, both causes and effects went hand in hand. The English, in the space of three months, had appropriated the two fleets that Napoleon had counted on appropriating; in addition, they had countered his Berlin Decree with their Orders in Council, designed to intercept all neutral trade with France. Exasperated by England's successes and emboldened by his own, Napoleon on December 17 issued his Milan Decree, which declared that any neutral ship submitting to the British Orders in Council was subject to seizure by France. The far-flung and fatal consequences of these two decisions—the occupation of the Iberian Peninsula and the intensification of economic warfare—will form the main subject matter of some of the chapters to follow. Indeed, they were the decisive causes of Napoleon's downfall. This, however, became apparent only toward the end of 1812. In the meantime, Napoleon's power kept growing until it seemed that there was nothing left in the world except Napoleon. His power reached its height in the year 1808, but it never approached the extent of his ambition, which was frustrated at the moment of his greatest outward glory.

In March, 1808, Napoleon ordered his forces to occupy Spain, and in May he placed his brother Joseph on the Spanish throne. (The throne of Naples, thus vacated, he gave to Murat.) The circumstances in which these events took place and the fierce war that resulted will be examined in greater detail in the chapter to follow. Napoleon, who watched developments in Spain from Bayonne, believed at first that the uprising of the Spanish people could be put down in a few weeks; then he would be free to address himself to more important matters—the division of Asia between France and Russia. Negotiations toward that end were in happy progress in St. Petersburg between the Russian foreign minister, Nikolai Rumiantsev, and Napoleon's special ambassador, Louis de Caulaincourt. They had been triggered by a letter Napoleon wrote to Alexander on February 2, 1808, when he was readying himself to pounce on Spain. The letter is an extraordinary document, and it reveals with astounding frankness the nature of the conversation held by the two emperors on the raft at Tilsit. It also reflects on the character of its recipient, who exclaimed, upon reading it: "There's the man in all his greatness! . . . This is the way he spoke at Tilsit."

The letter begins with the premise that England was in an irreconcilable mood and that, as a consequence, "it is only by means of grand and vast measures that we can attain peace and consolidate our system. Your Majesty must increase and strengthen his army." If Alexander did not mind taking advice, Napoleon would suggest that he make war on Sweden (until recently Russia's faithful ally) and "extend his border in that direction as far as he could." As for Napoleon's ally, Turkey, an army of fifty thousand men—"Russians, Frenchmen, perhaps even a few Austrians"—would be enough to march on Constantinople and "bring England down on her knees before the Continent.

... A month after we have reached an agreement, that army could be on the Bosphorus. The blow would be felt in India, and England would submit." To reach such an agreement (on the division of the spoils), perhaps a conference between the two emperors would be advisable. "Everything could be signed and settled before March 15. By May 1 our troops could be in Asia, while Your Majesty's troops are at Stockholm."

To be sure, like the Walrus and the Carpenter, Napoleon regretted the necessity to eat so many oysters with Alexander: "Your Majesty and I should have preferred the sweetness of peace and to spend our lives in our vast empires, applying ourselves to make our peoples happy by their industry and the benefits of a good administration; but the enemies of mankind do not wish it. We must be even greater, despite ourselves. It is the part of wisdom and of politics to do what destiny ordains and to march in the direction in which the irresistible course of events leads us. Only then will that swarm of pigmies . . . give way and follow the impetus that Your Majesty and I shall have given them, and the Russian peoples will enjoy the glory, the riches, and the happiness that will result from these great events. In these few lines, I am revealing to Your Majesty my entire soul. The policy laid down at Tilsit will determine the destiny of the world. Perhaps both Your Majesty and I, being a trifle pusillanimous, would tend to prefer a certain and present good to something even better and more perfect. But since England will not let us, we must acknowledge that the era of great changes and great events has arrived." That it is possible for a sane man, the head of a modern state, to write such a letter to a colleague, and that the colleague should read it with enthusiastic admiration, is enough to send chills down the spines of mankind, which prefers sweet peace to great events.

Alexander wasted no time in taking advantage of the green light Napoleon had given him in the direction of Sweden and proceeded to conquer Finland. Things proved a little more difficult in the direction of Turkey. Both Napoleon and Alexander drew up plans for the division of the spoils, but the plans did not agree. Alexander insisted that Napoleon accept his plan as a basis for an agreement before any meeting took place; Napoleon pointed out to his envoy, Caulaincourt, that it was "precisely to negotiate these points" that he wanted a meeting. "I told Alexander: 'Let us reconcile the interests of our two empires.' Now, to reconcile the interests of the two empires can hardly mean that one of them should sacrifice its interests to the other and even endanger its independence." If Russia were allowed to seize control of Constantinople and the Dardanelles, "a clash would then become inevitable, for . . . she would be at the gates of Toulon, Naples, and Corfu. Thus you must make it clear," Napoleon concluded, "that Russia wants too much and that France cannot agree to such an arrangement, that this is a difficult problem to solve, which is the

Jubilant Paris welcomed home the heroes of Eylau and Friedland; by 1808 an anxious France was once more engaged in war.

very reason why I tried to come to an understanding at a conference. At bottom, the question is always this: Who shall have Constantinople?"

Napoleon wrote the letter to Caulaincourt quoted above on May 31. By that time, it was obvious that the Spanish insurrection was more than a brief episode. On July 23 an entire French corps of eighteen thousand men, under General Dupont, surrendered to the Spanish insurgents at Bailen; on August 30, by the Convention of Cintra, General Junot agreed with the commander of the British troops landed in Portugal, Sir Hew Dalrymple, to evacuate all of Portugal. News of these two events did not exactly put Alexander in a mood for concessions, especially since early in July Napoleon reluctantly acknowledged that his Eastern scheme had to be postponed until Spain was pacified.

Meanwhile, a new threat had risen. Napoleon's high-handed treatment of the Bourbons of Spain and the Braganzas of Portugal had filled the court of Vienna with indignation; the gallant stand of the Spanish people against the French, which forced Napoleon to commit a large part of his forces in the Iberian Peninsula, gave heart to the entire Austrian people. At last Archduke Charles and Count Philip Stadion, the foreign minister, had their way in their demands for a radical reform of the Austrian military and administrative systems. On June 9 a decree was issued creating a national militia, and the population responded with enthusiasm. The Austrian mobilization was largely defensive, growing out of the fear that Napoleon was about to deal with the Hapsburgs as he had just dealt with the Braganzas and the Bourbons. Nevertheless it disquieted Napoleon, who responded with his customary threats to the Austrian ambassador, Klemens von Metternich, and pleaded with Alexander to threaten Austria with war if she did not disarm. It was in these inauspicious circumstances that the long-delayed meeting between Napoleon and Alexander took place, at the small Thuringian town of Erfurt, from September 27 to October 14.

The Congress of Erfurt dramatized Napoleon's power and weakness as did no other single event in his life. Here, besides the two emperors and their courts, were the kings of Bavaria, Saxony, Westphalia, and Württemberg; princes and dukes swarmed by the hundreds; and Goethe, who represented the empire of the mind, bowed deep before the lord of matter. The entire Comédie Française was present to play before "a pit of kings." One of the plays chosen for the occasion was Voltaire's *Oedipe*. When the celebrated Talma reached the line, "The friendship of a great man is a gift of the gods," the two emperors in their box rose, holding hands, to the applause of the crowned groundlings. The histrionics, however, could barely disguise the fact that the Tilsit honeymoon was over, and the most conspicuous monarch was the absent Emperor Francis of Austria, who had sent a Baron Vincent to represent him.

The only positive thing Napoleon could obtain from Alexander was the avoidance of a break; the alliance of the two empires was reaffirmed in the final proceedings. Agreement on the partition of the Ottoman Empire was postponed indefinitely, but Alexander extracted Napoleon's consent to Russia's acquisition of Moldavia, Walachia, and Finland. As for Napoleon's plea for a joint French and Russian ultimatum to Austria, Alexander avoided it. The roles of Tilsit had been switched; it was no longer Napoleon but Alexander who controlled the situation. It is doubtful whether Alexander would have been as firm as he showed himself at Erfurt if his private conferences had been only with Napoleon. But there was another man with whom he conferred in tête-à-tête, at night, after listening to Napoleon, and that man was Talleyrand.

Although he had resigned as foreign minister in the preceding year, Talleyrand had accompanied Napoleon to Erfurt in his capacities of grand chamberlain and vice grand elector. Exactly what Talleyrand said to the Russian emperor will never be known, but the gist of his thought was clearly revealed in a remark he made to Metternich after his return to Paris: for the good of Europe, for the good of France, for the good of Napoleon himself, Napoleon must be stopped, and only an alliance of Austria and Russia would stop him. That alliance came about only five years later; nevertheless, it was at Erfurt that the basis of Napoleon's plans collapsed.

Talleyrand was a man who, while he had deep convictions, also liked to be paid for acting upon them. It has not been proven, but it is more than likely, that he was in Austrian pay beginning about the time of the Erfurt Congress. The fact that he was a traitor does not invalidate his convictions. The truth is that there were only two powers in all Europe that had a foreign policy: England was one, and Talleyrand the other; the rest merely grabbed when they could and yielded when they had to.

It was Talleyrand's opinion that the French frontiers of 1792 were perfectly satisfactory to the overwhelming majority of Frenchmen, and that neither peace nor stability could be had until these frontiers were restored and a balanced system of power established. His estimate of French public opinion was corroborated by the journalist Joseph Fiévée, whom Napoleon employed as a secret agent. In a confidential report Fiévée summed up the consensus of his informants. "Public opinion is sick with anxiety," he wrote succinctly. "If one were asked to describe the moral condition of France, one would have to say that the only dupes left are those who still base their calculations on popular credulity." Of the anxiety, there could be no doubt; even before Erfurt, Napoleon had ordered that the class of 1809 be conscripted before the end of 1808; no sooner was he back from Erfurt than he prepared to go to Spain and direct military operations there in person. He recaptured Madrid from the insurgent forces on December 13 and shortly afterward returned to Paris, but the war in Spain was by no means ended (patriot armies were still resisting the French in almost every province), and another war—with Austria—was threatened.

The fear that gripped Europe also gripped France. Amidst this atmosphere of apprehension, Talleyrand and Fouché, two men who until then had constantly intrigued against each other, drew together to intrigue against their master. The subject of their conversations seems to have been merely the question who was to succeed the emperor if something happened to him, but the implications were explosive. Napoleon, informed while still in Spain of the Fouché-Talleyrand alliance, dashed back to Paris with considerable haste. Fouché managed to soothe the emperor and was allowed to remain minister of police for another year. Talleyrand bore the brunt of Napoleon's fury at a memorable official reception that took place on January 23, 1809. In front of the entire court, stony-faced, silent, and courteous, he listened to the emperor's tirade—in which he was compared to a silk stocking full of excrement—then limped out on his club-foot. Like all Napoleon's outbursts, this one had been put on for the benefit of the spectators. The silk stocking full of excrement was deprived of his position as grand chamberlain, but retained his dignities as vice grand elector and continued to go to court. Biding his time, he waited for the inevitable catastrophe and then, five years later, when the time was ripe, delivered the final blow to the man who had insulted him.

THE NAPOLEONIC WARS

Eighteenth-century generals maneuvered as much as they fought, for their highly trained armies were too valuable to risk. Against them revolutionary France sent into the field a largely untrained army whose strength lay in its numbers and its spirit. Marching swiftly, attacking furiously, this army astonished Europe with victory after victory. Napoleon forged it into an invincible force, whose men, as confident as the gunner shown above, triumphantly carried a new kind of warfare throughout Europe. But it was not Napoleon's generalship that was the age's greatest contribution to the art of war; it was rather the creation of a citizen army and the mobilization of an entire nation, which established a new pattern of warfare that still prevails.

Boilly's painting, the Departure of the Conscripts, *shows a company of youths bidding farewell to their families at the Porte St. Denis*

in Paris in 1807. Almost three million Frenchmen served in the army during the twenty-five years of war that followed the Revolution.

The splendidly attired drum major holding a baton, at left, and the infantryman at the right were members of Napoleon's Imperial Guard.

The decorated musket above, a fusil d'honneur, *was awarded for bravery. Below, an officer's crested helmet*

THE
SOLDIERS
OF
FRANCE

At the left, a mustachioed hussar, armed with a sabre. The color sergeant shown on the right belonged to a regiment of the line infantry.

Whether or not he subscribed to the popular cult of military glory, every Frenchman called up by the draft was obliged to march off to help Napoleon conquer Europe, unless he chose to become a fugitive or a bridegroom instead, or cut off his fingers or take out an eye, or hire a substitute to do his army duty for him. His military career was supposed to last at least four years, if he were able to survive that long. The unfortunate conscripts of the last campaigns were often inadequately trained. Those who joined the army in the early years, when the emperor was not hard pressed for men, were better off, however. They found themselves placed in the ranks with seasoned soldiers who trained them to maneuver with speed from columns into lines or squares. They were taught how to prime, load, and fire their clumsy flintlock muskets and to keep their powder dry; if it got wet, they would be unable to fire their muskets and would have to rely on bayonets alone. Each man also had to carry a few days' rations of bread, for army supply trains were unable to transport large amounts of food. On campaigns, men often had to live off the countryside—a difficult task in Spain, Poland, and Russia—or else purchase food from *vivandières,* the female provisioners who traditionally followed in the train of the French army and supplied the troops with tobacco, brandy, and wine. Soldiers had to improvise replacements for their clothing, too, for inevitably the colorful uniforms to which they had devoted such meticulous attention in times of peace were torn to shreds on campaigns, and they were forced to dress in uniforms sewn from captured cloth and shoes stripped from the dead on the field of battle.

The painter David predicted that posterity would cry, "What men and what an emperor!", on seeing his painting of the distribution of the eagles. The drawing at right, a study for the painting, shows Napoleon calling on his men to swear loyalty to him while a celestial figure strews them with laurel. Josephine is shown seated next to him; by the time the painting was finished, however, she was no longer empress, and was painted out. The battle flag below belonged to a grenadier regiment of the Guard.

THE QUEST
FOR GLORY

Three days after his coronation, Napoleon presented his soldiers with their new battle standards, imperial eagles that were to be carried on a flagstaff at the head of each regiment to symbolize the emperor's presence. "Soldiers," proclaimed the emperor, "here are your flags! These eagles will always be your rallying point. . . . Do you swear to lay down your lives in their defense . . . ?" "We swear!" shouted the colonels who represented the regiments. They raised their standards high. Bands began to play. The troops presented arms. The Parisians who had braved the rain to witness the ceremony cheered frantically. Despite the histrionic qualities of the scene, the army's expressions of fidelity were real, for Napoleon had labored assiduously to earn its loyalty. He encouraged his troops to present him with their petitions. He promoted the brave to higher rank and handed out pensions and rewards with a liberal hand. Above all, he catered to his soldiers' thirst for glory.

It was an age that believed devoutly in the ethos of military glory. French soldiers wept with rage at missing the chance to participate in a battle, and while they were on bivouac, pored over anthologies of tales of bravery on the battlefield, looking for examples to follow. It was not only the French who were seized by romantic if hazardous dreams of distinguishing themselves in

"*Men are led through baubles. But it is not everyone who can appreciate honors alone,*" *Napoleon once remarked;* "*a little cash doesn't hurt.*" *Members of the Legion of Honor were awarded both a medal and a small pension. The medal shown above is in the form of a star, with a crown above it and a portrait of the emperor at its center. The eagle below was the standard of the Fifth Regiment of Dragoons, led by Louis Bonaparte.*

battle. "Order them to shoot me. I am unworthy to live for I have lost all my guns!" begged a Russian prisoner after Austerlitz. ("Calm yourself, young man," Napoleon replied. "It is no dishonor to be defeated by *my* army.") With his own men, however, Napoleon exploited this craving for fame. Even before he seized power in France he ordered "arms of honor"—specially designed muskets and sabers—to be awarded to the brave. Later he instituted the Legion of Honor, primarily composed of those who had served with distinction on the battlefield.

Within each regiment, the best soldiers were rewarded with transfer to the elite corps, the Imperial Guard. There, the pay was higher, the food was better, and uniforms were more imposing. In some Guard regiments the common soldier enjoyed the rank of corporal and the chance of being stationed in Paris between campaigns. By 1809 there were more than thirty thousand men in the Imperial Guard. In their eyes, the only disadvantage in belonging to the Guard was that it was treasured so highly by the emperor that he was reluctant to risk it in battle.

OVERLEAF: *Napoleon handed out titles lavishly. General Duroc (left) became duke of Friuli; Bernadotte, at right, prince of Ponte Corvo.*

A bronze table, made to commemorate the victory of Austerlitz, is set with Sèvres porcelain miniatures of Napoleon and thirteen of his generals. At the center the emperor is shown seated upon his throne, holding a scepter, and crowned with laurel. Murat is directly beneath him. The others, beginning with Murat and reading clockwise, are Berthier (Napoleon's chief of staff), Bernadotte, Lannes, Ney, Bessières, Duroc, Caulaincourt (whose memoirs of the Russian campaign are a major historical source), Marmont, Davout, Mortier, Soult, and Augereau. Of the thirteen, only Caulaincourt and Duroc were not marshals of the Empire, although Duroc held the civil title of grand marshal of the palace.

THE MARSHALS

His marshals thought they were indispensable, Napoleon complained. "They don't know I have a hundred division commanders who can take their places." As so often happened, the emperor was exaggerating, for he was fortunate in being surrounded by an extraordinary constellation of military talents. Although some of the marshals were given their title (traditional in France, but abolished by the Revolution) merely as a reward for their personal loyalty or to pacify certain army cliques, and others failed to live up to their promise as military leaders, many were great generals. Davout was a brilliant tactician, never defeated in battle. The swaggering cavalry leader Murat was as bold as any Homeric hero. Among contemporary generals Masséna was second only to Bonaparte himself and Berthier was one of the greatest chiefs of staff in all history. The peerless Ney was called "the bravest of the brave," and he had well earned this epithet.

They were fighting for a rejuvenated nation that lived, like all young nations, in a heroic age. In the marshals, France found suitable heroes, young and bold, as impassioned as children or savages. They were notoriously touchy about their reputations, jostling each other fiercely for precedence and for the favor of the emperor. Their fathers had been, for the most part, farmers, millers, or petty bourgeoisie. But they collected vast fortunes, exotic titles and pretensions to match them. Soult, a notary's son, became duke of Dalmatia, and angled for the crown of Portugal. Bernadotte became king of Sweden, and Murat, king of Naples. Most of the marshals became dukes, but those given the names of provinces (Mortier, duke of Treviso, Victor, duke of Belluno) were jealous of those who were given the titles of their victories (Augereau, duke of Castiglione, Lannes, duke of Montebello). Several were jealous of the emperor himself, because they felt that they were equally talented.

They may not have been as talented as Napoleon, but each was as fiercely individualistic. After one battle, Gouvion Saint-Cyr retired to the most secluded chamber he could find and there spent several hours alone playing the violin. Murat devoted a considerable part of his energy to designing flamboyant uniforms for himself and his aides. Masséna, Soult, and Augereau were notoriously avaricious, and plundered wherever they could. "I do not want the money for myself," Masséna unctuously remarked. "But the emperor has given us a position and the title of marshal, and we must maintain them." Ney was far more concerned with glory than with cash. Placed in charge of the rear guard during the last half of the terrible retreat from Moscow, he fought doggedly to salvage whatever he could of Napoleon's forces and was the last soldier in the French army to leave the territory of Russia.

Marshal Ney, shown above in an unfinished portrait by Baron Gros, was given the titles duke of Elchingen and prince of the Moskva. His victory at Elchingen during the Austrian campaign of 1805 blocked the escape of an Austrian army and prepared the way for the French triumphs at Ulm and Austerlitz. Napoleon created Ney prince of the Moskva on the evening after the Battle of Borodino, in which Ney commanded the center of the French army. (The battle took place beside the Moskva River.) Below is a detail of a finely wrought presentation gun, made at Versailles by the master gunsmith Boutet and traditionally supposed to have been given to Ney by Napoleon. Some of Ney's other rewards were even more substantial; under the Empire his annual income was 600,000 francs.

THE GRAND ARMY

It was not its size alone that endowed the Grand Army with its name. The army was an international one; by 1812 less than one-third of its troops was French. German, Italian, Belgian, and Dutch soldiers, whose homelands had been incorporated into Napoleon's empire, were integrated into French regiments. Napoleon's puppet kings sent battalions to fight alongside the French, under their own flags and led by their own officers. In 1812 Austria and Prussia became "allies" of France and were forced to provide the emperor with tributary troops. Naturally, these soldiers were sometimes unreliable in battle, and Napoleon had to take this into account whenever he planned to use them.

Some of the foreign troops, however, were as loyal to the emperor as the most fervent Frenchman could be. Throughout the Napoleonic wars, Polish volunteers fought in the French army, piously hoping to re-establish Poland's independence and to aid in the liberation of other nations. They were joined by a ferocious band of Tatar horsemen, who had never reconciled themselves to serving Russian overlords. A regiment of Dutch youths, most of them under sixteen years old, found a home in the Imperial Guard; they were the orphans of soldiers and had nowhere else to go. Most devoted and most colorful of all were the "Mamelukes," who had been recruited after Napoleon's expedition to Egypt. They were formed into several companies of horsemen, attired in brilliant oriental costume. Despite their costumes and the romantic name of their regiment, most of them were not Mamelukes at all, but Copts and Greeks and native Frenchmen.

Napoleon's domain reached from Spain to Poland, and from the English Channel to
the coast of Dalmatia. Each of its vassal kingdoms was required to provide troops for
the emperor. The engraving above shows Eugene de Beauharnais, Napoleon's viceroy
in Italy, reviewing his cavalry. He is seen in the foreground riding a dapple gray horse.
Both the Mameluke opposite and the Polish general at right served with the French.
OVERLEAF: Austerlitz was Napoleon's masterpiece, the battle of which he was proudest.
A detail of Simeon Fort's painting of the battle shows the French army sweeping down
from the Heights of Pratzen overlooking the village of Austerlitz, where the emperors
of Austria and Russia had established their headquarters. Two French divisions, under
the command of Marshals Soult and Bernadotte, descended from Pratzen to break
the enemy line in two. Part of the enemy forces retreated into the village of Austerlitz; others tried to escape over a frozen pond, but drowned when French artillery
bombardment broke up the ice across which they were fleeing. The French lost only
nine thousand men in the battle; the Austrians and the Russians, twenty-six thousand.

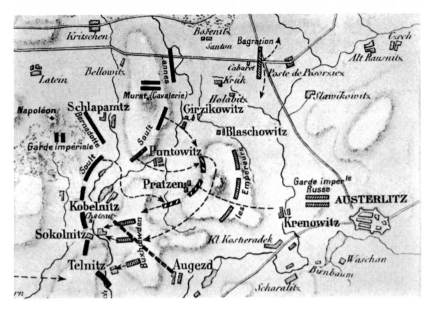

Troop movements during the Battle of Austerlitz are shown on the map above. Opposite, a painting by Taunay shows French troops struggling across the snow-covered Guadarrama Mountains during their pursuit of the English through Spain.

NAPOLEON'S STRATEGY

Napoleon's equation for measuring the power of an army was simple and persuasively scientific: power equaled the mass times the velocity. Moving a great many men swiftly was the key to the emperor's tactical system, and to his strategy, of which his battle tactics were an integral part. The entire campaign was designed to bring the enemy to battle on a field of Napoleon's own choosing, where the French would be at a distinct advantage. By means of swift, secret marches, he placed his own troops athwart the enemy's line of communication, forcing his opponents to fight while they were cut off from contact with their own bases.

Napoleon's main object was not the conquest of enemy cities or the capture of enemy fortresses; it was rather the destruction of the enemy's army. In order to accomplish this he usually kept most of the enemy line occupied with a series of animated attacks, or distracted it by a flanking movement with a small and highly mobile force. Then he opened up a sudden artillery barrage to prepare the way for a hammer blow that would break through the line at the enemy's most vulnerable spot.

"It is with artillery that war is made," Napoleon once remarked. The emperor had begun his military career as an artillery officer, and developed great skill in the utilization of cannon on the battlefield. Even before 1789 French artillery had been the best in Europe; throughout his career Napoleon kept adding to his artillery, making it increasingly mobile and thus an increasingly important factor on the battle-field. (Until his time civilians, who were notoriously reluctant to risk their lives, had been in charge of the gun carriages; he replaced them with soldiers.) In his skillful use of artillery Napoleon set a pattern that is followed in contemporary warfare, where the reliance on massed firepower still continues.

To Napoleon, more than anyone else, is due the credit for the introduction of modern war. Studying the Napoleonic wars led the contemporary Prussian general and military philosopher Karl von Clausewitz to formulate his famous doctrine that the object of war was the destruction of the enemy's ability to fight back. The total mobilization of France during the revolutionary wars inevitably led to another of Clausewitz's theories, one that is increasingly practicable today, that war should be fought against the entire population of the enemy, and not against his army alone.

OVERLEAF: *A detail of Simeon Fort's watercolor of the Battle of Eylau in 1807 shows Murat's cavalry massing in preparation for a charge against the Russian line. French infantry, commanded by Marshal Augereau, had been driven back, after blundering into a concentration of Russian artillery during a blinding snowstorm; they can be seen reforming their ranks on either flank of the cavalry. Following up Augereau's repulse, the Russians had advanced over the snow-covered battlefield almost as far as the ridge at upper left, where the emperor stood surveying the battle. Before the combat, Napoleon had attempted to cut the Russian army off from its base, but for once this maneuver failed, for the enemy had intercepted a messenger carrying his orders.*

A somber procession of wounded soldiers (above) passes through the streets of Paris during the campaign of France in 1814. For this campaign Napoleon was forced to muster a makeshift army of over-age men, and boys normally considered too young to serve, for he had lost two armies in two years, one in Russia and another in Germany. Géricault's drawing (right) shows one of the soldiers wounded in Russia.

THE CASUALTIES OF WAR

Glorious though they may have been, the battles of the Grand Army were inordinately bloody. Musket fire was inaccurate at long range, but at close range it was murderous, and each army customarily held its fire until the enemy was near. Artillery, which was increasingly used in the later battles, also exacted a heavy toll. Although France boasted one of the best army medical services in Europe, and Napoleon's troops were probably the first in history to enjoy the benefits of having medical officers and regimental aid stations move forward along with them, mortality rates were high among the wounded.

Inadequate treatment cost as many lives as enemy guns did. There were many reasons for this. Medical knowledge was far from complete, and although the surgeons themselves were conscientious, their aides, mostly draft dodgers who had finally been apprehended by the service, cared little for the wounded. During a battle, soldiers were forbidden by Napoleon to help their wounded comrades leave the battlefield, since this would take too many men out of his firing line. There was a chronic shortage of medical personnel, of linen for dressing wounds, and of ambulances for transporting the wounded off the battlefield; sometimes they were carried off in wheelbarrows requisitioned from the local populace. Under the Consulate, there were no more than fifteen hundred doctors and pharmacists for the whole French army. Eventually the number increased, but it failed to keep pace with the astonishing growth of the army itself. The shortage of transport sometimes forced the French to abandon wounded men on the battlefield. The shortage of medical personnel often brought about a paradoxical and unfortunate situation, which allowed men with minor wounds who could walk away during a battle in search of medical attention to be treated more quickly than the severely wounded, who were unable to move.

Injured men who did not die of their wounds or of exposure on the battlefield were finally sheltered in improvised hospitals; there they lay on beds of straw, when there was straw to be had, and were nourished with a soup made of horse meat. In these makeshift hospitals sanitation was deplorable. Thousands of the survivors of the Battle of Austerlitz died during a typhus epidemic in the month following the battle. These were the conditions in the good years, when Napoleon's star was in the ascendant. Later, most notably during the retreat from Moscow, they became unspeakably worse.

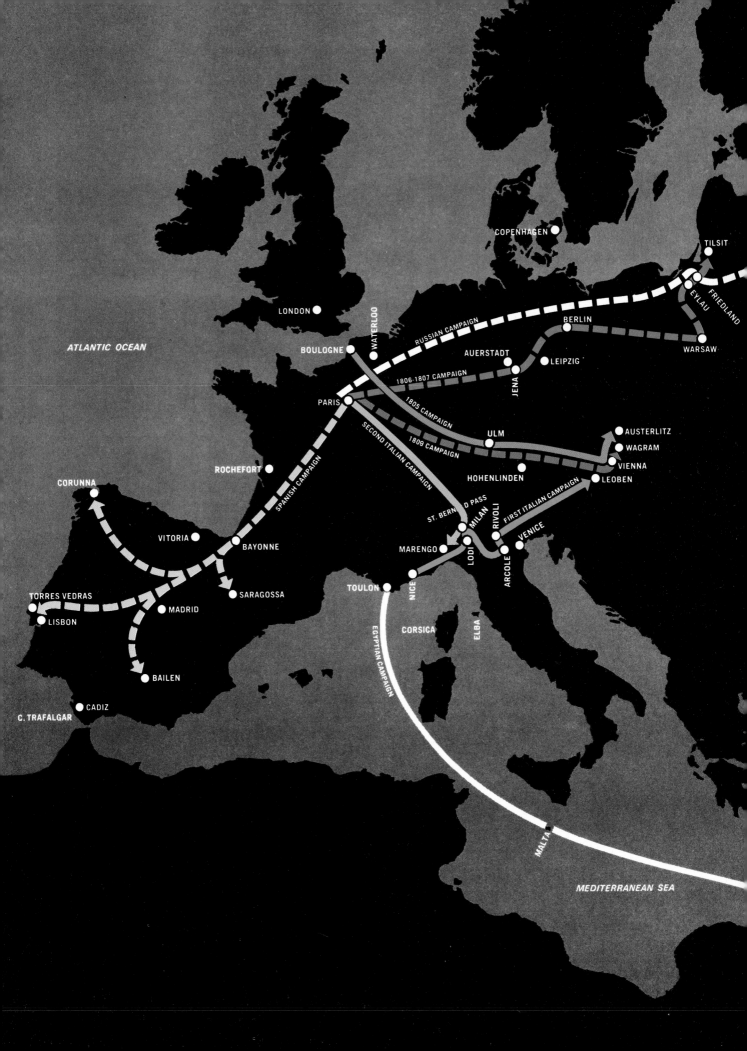

ATLANTIC OCEAN

COPENHAGEN

TILSIT

FRIEDLAND

EYLAU

LONDON

WATERLOO

BERLIN

WARSAW

BOULOGNE

RUSSIAN CAMPAIGN

AUERSTADT

LEIPZIG

1806-1807 CAMPAIGN

JENA

PARIS

1805 CAMPAIGN

SECOND ITALIAN CAMPAIGN

1809 CAMPAIGN

ULM

AUSTERLITZ

WAGRAM

ROCHEFORT

VIENNA

HOHENLINDEN

LEOBEN

CORUNNA

SPANISH CAMPAIGN

ST. BERNARD PASS

MILAN

RIVOLI

FIRST ITALIAN CAMPAIGN

VITORIA

BAYONNE

MARENGO

LODI

ARCOLE

VENICE

SARAGOSSA

TOULON

NICE

TORRES VEDRAS

MADRID

LISBON

EGYPTIAN CAMPAIGN

CORSICA

ELBA

BAILEN

CADIZ

C. TRAFALGAR

MALTA

MEDITERRANEAN SEA

BORODINO ● MOSCOW

SMOLENSK

BLACK SEA

ACRE
JAFFA

ABUKIR

ALEXANDRIA

CAIRO

THE CAMPAIGNS
OF NAPOLEON

On forced marches the soldiers of the French armies traveled both day and night, stopping for five minutes every hour, and occasionally for an hour or two, to take a rest. As they marched along dirt roads in dry weather, they kept a straw clenched between their teeth to avoid swallowing dust, and linked arms to make sure that no one fell down. Drummers played the charge to keep the men awake, but whole ranks still sometimes tumbled fast asleep into ditches along the roadside. The emperor journeyed along with his men in a green military carriage equipped with files and a writing desk. He would work as he traveled, directing his armies' progress and governing his empire. He had not always traveled so elegantly. Mention has already been made of his crossing the Great St. Bernard Pass on muleback. In Spain, during a snowstorm, he crossed the Guadarramas on foot, leaning on one of his marshals.

Whether he traveled in comfort or shared the distress of the common soldiers, Napoleon insisted on forced marches in order to surprise the enemy. Some of the marches were of extraordinary length. In thirty days one French battalion traveled from Boulogne to Danzig, a distance of more than a thousand miles, walking most of the way. (The supply trains had to carry plenty of leather; during a campaign each soldier might wear out half a dozen pairs of shoes.) The element of surprise was especially important in several of the campaigns: the second Italian campaign, in which the French took a short cut over the Alps to swoop down on the Austrians in Lombardy; the Austerlitz campaign, when an army poised to invade England was suddenly diverted to central Europe; and the Egyptian campaign, in which a great French armada embarked for a destination that the enemy thought would be England or Ireland.

The emperor's chief adversary was England, but it was the lands of central Europe that saw war most frequently. Austria was invaded four times, and Italy even more often. On their way to Prussia, Austria, Poland, or Russia, the French marched across western Germany time after time, living off the land. Even in years of peace, the allied German states had to support a large French army. The French themselves were to pay the full price of war only in Spain, Poland, and Russia, where the land was barren and food was scarce, and the population often hostile.

The range of Napoleon's principal armies during his foreign campaigns is shown by means of arrows on the map at left, along with sites of major significance in the Napoleonic wars.

Napoleon himself wrote the newspaper dispatches that informed the populace of his armies' progress. In the army, the phr

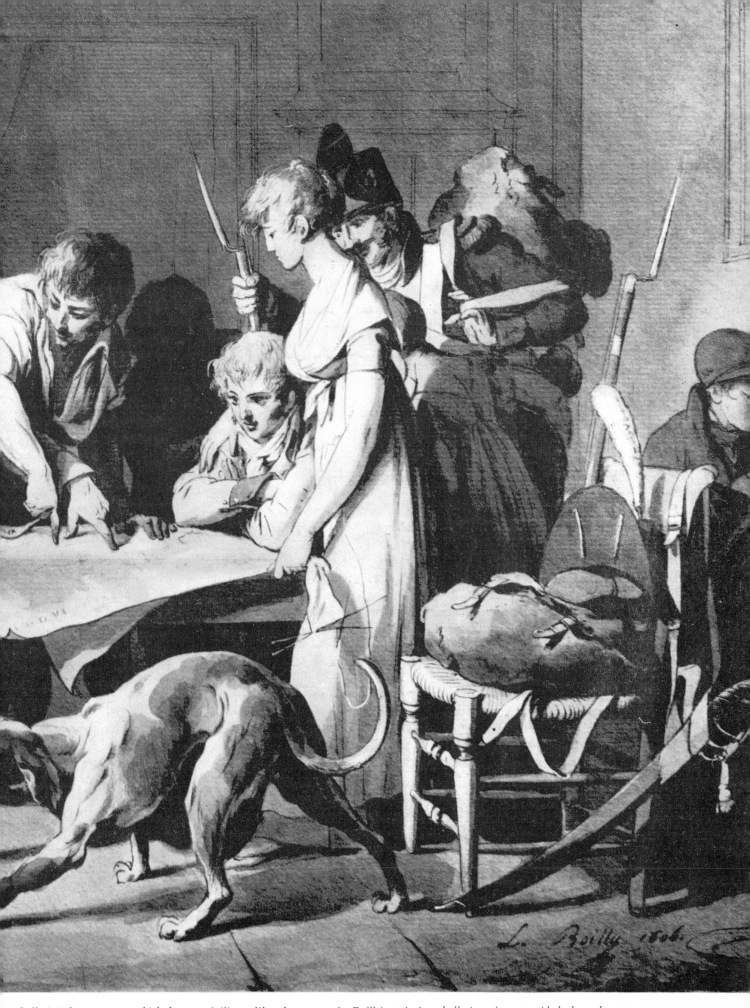

a bulletin" became proverbial, but to civilians, like those seen in Boilly's painting, bulletins often provided the only news.

THE
SPANISH
ORDEAL

*I admit that I started off on the wrong foot
in this whole {Spanish} business. . . . The whole thing
remains ugly, since I lost out. . . . And yet posterity
would have commended my deed if it had succeeded.*

European royalty, which in past centuries had produced a higher percentage of vigorous, intelligent, capable, and responsible men and women than one has a right to expect, had sunk to a sorry level in the Napoleonic era. Czar Paul was insane; his son Alexander, though gifted, was unstable in mind, perhaps because he owed his throne to his father's assassins. King George III was insane on and off; his son, the prince of Wales, whatever his merits, was a bigamist, a drunkard, and a family tyrant. Gustavus IV of Sweden was a noble-minded fool. The kings of Prussia and Sardinia were not precisely heroes. Ferdinand IV of Naples was a man of subnormal intelligence, sometimes debonair, sometimes vicious, and completely dominated by his queen, who slept with his chief minister. The Austrian emperor Francis, though kindly and well-intentioned, was limited in intelligence and more interested in his hobbies—notably raising plants and making children—than in statecraft; his heir was a little weak in the head. The queen of Portugal was mad. The king of Etruria was a moron. The king of Württemberg was shrewd and witty but so monstrously fat that a bay had to be cut out of his dining table to enable him to reach his food. Among this collection of grotesques, the royal family of Spain set a record of viciousness and moral degradation.

In 1808 Charles IV of Spain was sixty years old and had ruled for twenty years. By certain standards he was

a paragon of virtue: he probably was the only gentleman in Spain who never rose from bed later than five in the morning, never touched a woman other than his wife (he gave up even that when told it was bad for his health), never drank anything but water, and completely trusted his wife's fidelity. Though not very bright, he was well-meaning. He started every day by hearing two masses in a row. He then proceeded to his workshops, took off his coat, rolled up his sleeves, and, assisted by his artisans, built cabinets and forged pistols. This done, he would partake of an enormous meal and at 1 P.M. sharp, rain or shine, drive off to go hunting. He shot from a stand, killing prodigious numbers of beasts that were driven by; each hunting expedition required the services of close to five hundred horses and seven hundred men. Back from the hunt, he would devote thirty minutes to government business. After that came a concert (he himself played the violin with royal inaccuracy), cards, supper, and, at eleven, bed. In some ways he showed a democratic turn of mind. He treated his stableboys and his grandees with equal familiarity. It amused him to beat servants and dukes, using his stick with all his strength and roaring with good-natured laughter as he did so.

The Virgin of Pilar, whose image is honored with a state robe (right), inspired the defenders of Saragossa. Besieged, they sang: "The Virgin . . . says she does not want to be French."

Such was the king of Spain and of the Indies. Queen Maria Luisa, his wife, of the House of Bourbon-Parma, did not share his virtues. Her husband's hasty, frequent, and therapeutic embraces left her unsatisfied, and she took as a lover a young guardsman, Manuel Godoy, who served her better and whom she gradually propelled into the post of chief minister. Maria Luisa ruled the king, and Godoy ruled Maria Luisa, whom he treated with coarse and brutal contempt. The relationship was known to everybody in Spain except to her husband, who liked to joke good-naturedly about his cuckold cousin the king of Naples and Sicily. When Godoy tired of the queen, she kept him in her favor but took on other lovers, notably a certain Mallo, major-domo of the palace, on whom she lavished money and jewels, whom she despised, and without whom she could not manage. The only talent she possessed for government was an extreme aptitude at dissembling and brazen lying. As to appearance, witnesses agree that she looked every inch a madam.

The eldest male offspring of this royal couple was Ferdinand, prince of Asturias. In the eyes of his contemporaries, Ferdinand possessed three great virtues: he despised his father, loathed his mother, and detested Godoy. On the strength of these virtues it was supposed that he possessed yet others, an illusion that he dispelled in the minds of his supporters only in 1814, after several hundred thousands of them had shed their blood for his cause.

The real ruler of Spain was the royal favorite, Manuel Godoy, who had been given the title "Prince of the Peace" in 1795, for concluding the Peace of Basel with France. Godoy was by no means an incapable man, but his talents were heavily outweighed by his greed, unscrupulousness, indolence, and dissolute morals. It became his habit, toward the end of his administration, to admit only female petitioners to his evening audiences; the prettier ones among them could be seen leaving his study in a disheveled state. The petitions over, the minister would receive the foreign diplomats and entertain them with the details of the way he had managed his evening's work.

It seems inconceivable that the Spanish Empire should have tolerated the misrule under which it had fallen; nor, indeed, did it tolerate it for long. But the misrule had developed only gradually, and it had been preceded by the most excellent and enlightened administration the Spanish monarchy had ever had. It is a common misconception to view the history of the Spanish Empire from Ferdinand and Isabella to Charles IV as a steady decline. Actually, toward the end of the eighteenth century Spain was still the third-ranking power in the world, after Britain and France, and she was on the way up rather than down. Nor is it true to suppose, as is generally done, that Spain was on the margin of Europe, untouched by the intellectual currents and the material progress of the age; and though it is true that the mass of the population was sunk in medieval superstition and ignorance and com-

pletely dominated by the Church, this cannot be said of the middle and upper classes.

For reasons too complex and too controversial to analyze here, the Spanish monarchy had reached a low point in the late seventeenth century under its last Hapsburg kings. While the symptoms of the decadence were mostly of an economic nature, the causes were manifold. Under the Bourbon kings who succeeded the Hapsburgs—Philip V, Ferdinand VI, and Charles III—a steady process of regeneration took place. This process culminated during the reign (1759–88) of Charles III, the least known and most admirable of the "enlightened despots" of the eighteenth century. Charles and his principal advisers—Floridablanca, Campomanes, Aranda, Patiño, Jovellanos—like most of the Spanish elite, were deeply influenced by the reformist and liberal ideas of the French Enlightenment. Whereas the French government, except during Turgot's brief administration in 1774–76, was generally hostile or indifferent to the ideas of the *philosophes* and the economists, the Spanish government earnestly tried to put these ideas into practice, and succeeded quite remarkably.

One thing that Charles III had in common with the other great "enlightened despots"—his contemporaries, Catherine II of Russia, Frederick II of Prussia, and Joseph II of Austria—was that all four believed that reform must come from above, for the benefit of the people but not by the people. Here, however, the resemblance stops. Leaving the rather special case of the Austrian monarchy outside this discussion, it may be said that Prussia and Russia were aggressive, expanding states, composed mainly of peasants (many of them serfs) and a military aristocracy. Lacking an overseas empire and trade, they were newcomers, have-nots, and greedy, and their rulers' display of enlightened and liberal principles only thinly disguised their ruthless ambitions. The case of Spain was quite different. Spain had all the resources and wealth and territory she could wish. Her territorial ambitions were limited to a jockeying for position in her contest with her only great rival, England.

The population of Spain proper, however poor and ignorant in certain parts of the realm, was not nearly as poor and ignorant as that of many another European country. The Spanish peasant, though oppressed and exploited by feudal absentee landowners, was a free man: there were no serfs in Spain, as there were in Russia, Prussia, and many of the Austrian crown lands. There also was a large, and on the whole prosperous, middle class of petty nobles (*hidalgos*), artisans, merchants, and professionals. The Spaniard might be proud of his noble status, but for the majority of nobles this status implied only honorific privileges: thus all Biscayans, including peasants, were held to be noble by birth, and a number of royal ordinances affirmed that a nobleman who engaged in any honorable trade or labor did not thereby forfeit his noble rank. In this respect, the Spanish conception of nobility differed radically from that in other countries. With the pride in status characteristic of the Spanish people there went an equally characteristic reluctance to let oneself be pushed around and considerable diffidence toward innovations that might threaten traditional rights and privileges.

As Charles III and his reforming ministers saw the problem, the main evils afflicting Spain were stagnation of trade, inadequate exploitation of her natural resources, an inefficient administrative system, the decay of industries and arts, and backward agricultural methods. (An additional evil—absentee landownership—was characteristically ignored, the reformers being also the landowners.) All these conditions improved to a large degree under Charles' rule. The alliance with France relieved Spain of the necessity of keeping up a large land army and allowed her to rebuild her decaying navy, an essential prerequisite for the defense of her colonies. Peace with the Ottoman Empire (made earlier in the century) and improved relations with the Barbary States opened new markets to Spanish trade. The administrative system was overhauled both in Spain and in the colonies. New industries and model factories were set up by the government, and a number of "economic societies" sprang up all over Spain for the promotion of scientific methods of production and agriculture. On the whole, the reformers favored industrial expansion over agriculture—probably rightly so, since there was a vast surplus of agricultural labor. Campomanes, Charles' chief economic adviser, far ahead of his time, advocated public education for the working class, and Spain was probably the first European country to pass labor laws.

Charles III's reforms were carried out in an atmosphere of enthusiasm and effervescence. The mass of the people, to be sure, was indifferent and occasionally even hostile to reform, but the administrative and intellectual elite supported it wholeheartedly. They were in close rapport with the French *philosophes* and Encyclopedists, especially with the circle of Turgot and d'Alembert, and formed the active vanguard of the new ideas. Contrary to what might be assumed, the Spanish Church, which was virtually independent of the papacy, did not oppose reform. Catholicism was so deeply ingrained in the Spanish nation that not even the wildest reformer would have dreamed of challenging its position. Apart from asserting its rights in certain jurisdictional disputes, the government left the Church alone; the suppression of the Jesuits in 1767 created hardly a ripple in Spain and was approved by most of the non-Jesuit clergy.

As for the Inquisition, it was losing its teeth. By the end of the eighteenth century heretics were no longer being burned in Spain, except in the fantasies of anticlerical propagandists. The Inquisition, it is true, still had its tribunals and prisons, but the tendency was toward liberalization and tolerance. Civil disabilities were removed from Catholic descendants of Jews, and considerable latitude was allowed to writers and scientists to express their opinions. The result of the more liberal attitude was a general cultural as well as economic revival.

The Spain that Charles IV inherited from his father in 1788 was not a retarded, medieval country in the backwash of Europe but was moving rapidly with the times. Needless to say, the rosy picture must be qualified. The landowning system, the plight of the agricultural laborers, the continuing abuses of feudalism, the disproportionately large number of priests and monks, the iniquities of the colonial system—all these and other evils continued, and perhaps outweighed the reforms already accomplished. What matters more, however, is the direction in which Spain was moving. Louis XIV's pronouncement, "There are no more Pyrenees," seemed on the point of fulfillment, though not in the sense he meant it. Spain was becoming part of the European mainstream, and there was justifiable hope that

Manuel Godoy, "Prince of the Peace"

in the century to come the Spanish Empire would attain a new era of greatness and prosperity, adjust itself to the exigencies of modern times, and remain united by its own peculiar and deep-rooted traditions. The ineptitude of Charles III's successors, the brutal fist of Napoleon, and the Spanish people's admirable but unprofitable stand against him were to combine in the destruction of these hopes.

At the beginning of his reign, Charles IV retained his father's reforming ministers. As Godoy rose in power, however, these were gradually replaced by Godoy's own creatures, and the exemplary administration of the past three decades was allowed to fall apart from sheer neglect. Fear of the spread of French revolutionary ideas led to a tightening of censorship, and after the execution of Louis XVI in 1793 Spain joined the Allies in the war against France. The temporary partnership between Spain and Britain was an uneasy one, and the French advance across the Pyrenees determined the Spanish government in 1795 to make peace with the French Republic. The Treaty of Basel was supplemented in 1796 by a treaty of alliance between France and Spain. The reversal was a logical return to eighteenth-century Spanish foreign policy: it was thanks to her alliance with France that Spain had obtained Louisiana from France in 1763 and recovered Florida from England in 1783; the ever-expanding sea power and commercial interests of Great Britain, on the other hand, threatened the security of the Spanish Empire.

Yet logical though it may have seemed, the decision to

tie Spain's fate to that of France turned out to be a fatal mistake. Louis XV and XVI had treated their Spanish allies as equal partners, the Directory treated Spain as an inferior, and Napoleon dealt with her even more cavalierly. A series of treaties signed in 1800 transformed the Spanish military forces, and particularly the Spanish navy, into a mere adjunct of the French and obliged Spain to pay subsidies to France. In exchange for the creation of the Kingdom of Etruria, under Charles IV's son-in-law, Spain retroceded all Louisiana to France. The cession was effected under the condition that France would not alienate Louisiana—an area then including all French possessions west of the Mississippi—to any power save Spain. The sale of the Louisiana Territory to the United States in 1803 thus was in direct violation of the Treaty of San Ildefonso; nevertheless, after making a weak protest, Charles IV acquiesced, having no desire to become embroiled in war with the United States. Indeed, there was nothing he could do. The sale of Louisiana was an accomplished fact, and it marked the beginning of the end of Spanish power on the North American continent.

The naval co-operation between France and Spain led to the disaster of Trafalgar; its impact on Spanish public opinion was such that the court contemplated a withdrawal from the French alliance and began secret negotiations with Britain. Somewhat belatedly, Godoy remembered the dignity and interests of Spain and addressed threatening communications to Napoleon. The moment was ill-chosen; Napoleon had just crushed Prussia at Jena and Auerstädt.

Napoleon chose to ignore Godoy's bold language. Instead of replying with counter-threats, he began an interesting cat-and-mouse game. He was resolved to drive the Bourbons from the Spanish throne and have the Bourbons themselves serve as the unwitting instruments of their own destruction. The reasons for his decision to bring all of the Iberian Peninsula under direct French control were manifold. First, there was the danger of a British landing in Portugal, which might bring the entire peninsula into the Allied camp; second, he needed the Spanish and Portuguese naval resources in his struggle with Britain; third, to enforce the Continental System, the whole Atlantic coastline had to be controlled by France; fourth, he could not deal on equal terms with Russia unless he obtained complete domination over the Mediterranean; and fifth, the folly and

Ferdinand VII, a prisoner at Bayonne, sits disconsolately with his uncle and brother.

greed of the Spanish court presented him with an irresistible opportunity to attain his goal without a great effort.

The trap was baited late in 1806 at Fontainebleau, when Napoleon offered the partition of Portugal. The offer was hungrily snapped up. It is extremely doubtful whether Napoleon ever intended to reward Godoy for his duplicity with a principality consisting of one-third of Portugal; it is equally doubtful whether he meant to compensate King Louis of Etruria with another third for the loss of his kingdom, which was annexed to France in January, 1808. The dual purpose of the Franco-Spanish expedition against Portugal was, first, the obvious one of bringing Portugal under French control and, second, the hidden one of bringing French troops into Spain under the cover of an alliance. Lisbon fell in November, 1807, yet more French troops kept pouring into Spain early in 1808, ostensibly to defend Portugal against a British landing but actually to occupy the northern provinces of Spain and even Catalonia.

While obtaining a foothold in Spain by playing on the fear and greed of Charles IV and Godoy, Napoleon had been in secret correspondence with Charles' son, the prince of Asturias. Ferdinand headed a faction of malcontents who had at least one thing in common—hatred of Godoy. To overthrow Godoy (and possibly also his father), he curried Napoleon's favor, requested the emperor's "paternal protection," and asked to marry a daughter of the House of Bonaparte. Napoleon did nothing to discourage him. On October 27, 1807, King Charles arrested his son and put him on trial for high treason. The charges were that Ferdinand had plotted to depose his father and to murder his mother and Godoy. This pretty family quarrel gave Napoleon an opportunity to slip his troops into Spain while assuring each side of his support and protection. On his intercession, Ferdinand was released in January, 1808, a verdict of "not guilty" having been brought in. Far from suspecting that the French troops pouring into Spain were intended to take over the country, each of the two factions regarded them as protectors against its rival. It was only in the latter half of February, when French forces seized the citadels of Pamplona and Barcelona, that both sides became aware that they had been tricked. By mid-March one hundred thousand French troops were in Spain.

The one course of action which the Spanish court does not seem to have considered at this juncture was resistance to the invader. Instead, instant flight to America was decided upon, largely upon Godoy's advice. The court had got no farther than Aranjuez when its flight to Cadiz was halted by a popular uprising. A furious mob of soldiers and peasants invaded the palace with the obvious intention of lynching Godoy. Terrified, the royal couple yielded to the arguments of their son, who promised to protect their favorite from violence if Charles abdicated in his favor. The king signed his abdication, the prince of Asturias was hailed as Ferdinand VII, and Godoy was taken to prison.

It might be supposed that Ferdinand, having satisfied his hatred of Godoy, would realize that the Spanish people expected him to lead them in resistance against the French. Whether he realized this or not, it was not in his nature to keep faith or to act courageously. Instead of organizing his forces in the south, he returned to Madrid, which was already occupied by the French under Marshal Murat, and wrote an abject letter to Napoleon, promising good behavior and renewing his demand for a wife. While Ferdinand begged Napoleon to recognize him as king, his father also wrote to Napoleon, protesting that his abdication had been extorted from him under duress and begging the emperor to restore him to the throne.

This unexpected and somewhat farcical turn of events placed Napoleon before a fateful choice. He could either recognize Ferdinand as king and, in exchange, obtain whatever concessions he wished, or take advantage of the imbroglio and make one of his brothers king of Spain. The former course, which would have accomplished his main objectives, would probably have been the wiser, since Ferdinand, however undeservedly, enjoyed the confidence and support of the Spanish people. Napoleon, however, judged nations by the example of their rulers. The thought that the Spanish people might offer serious resistance never entered his head. The Spanish royal family were corrupt fools, and he would trick them out of their kingdom; the Spanish people was a rabble that could be ignored. He sent word to King Ferdinand that he was minded to take him into his favor and to give him a princess of the House of Bonaparte in marriage; to this end, he proposed a meeting. As trusting as he was treacherous, Ferdinand crossed the French border to meet the emperor at Bayonne. No sooner had he arrived than Napoleon sprang the trap: Ferdinand was put under arrest and summoned to abdicate his throne in favor of his father; if he agreed to do so without fuss, he would be given the Kingdom of Etruria as a consolation prize.

Sullenly and stubbornly, Ferdinand refused to abdicate. He was still in a sulking mood when, a few days later, Napoleon gave him another surprise: he confronted him with his parents, who had been brought to Bayonne for that purpose. Charles IV, Napoleon declared, was still king of Spain, and unless Ferdinand acknowledged that fact, he was guilty of high treason. Ferdinand countered with glum silence and refused to sign the document that was thrust at him, thus provoking his irate father into threatening him with his cane, while his mother screamed at him like a brothel keeper wronged. Napoleon put a stop to the domestic scene by having Ferdinand thrown out of the room. The royal couple's parental wrath at their son's insubordination seems all the more peevish since Charles IV had secretly agreed to hand over to Napoleon the kingdom he claimed so self-righteously from his son. In exchange for a pension and property, Charles IV signed a document on May 5 by which he renounced all his claims to the Spanish throne in favor of the emperor of the French.

On the following day, threatened with a summary trial for high treason, Ferdinand agreed to sign his abdication in favor of his father; only after having signed was he informed that his father had renounced his throne the day before. While Charles, Maria Luisa, and Godoy (who had also been spirited to Bayonne) departed in freedom to spend a comfortable life in exile, Ferdinand was taken under escort to the château of Valençay where he remained a prisoner until Napoleon's downfall in 1814. His reluctant jailer was Talleyrand, the owner of the château, who made his stay as pleasant as he could. Even before Charles IV and Ferdinand VII had signed their abdications, Napoleon had instructed Marshal Murat, his lieutenant in Spain, to have remaining members of the royal family conveyed to France.

On May 2, 1808 (*Dos de Mayo*), rumor spread in Madrid that the last of Charles' sons, the thirteen-year-old Prince Francisco, was about to be conducted to Bayonne. A large crowd gathered in the Plaza de Oriente, where several coaches were waiting in front of the royal palace. The mood was one of anxiety rather than fury. The events of the past weeks—the flight of the royal family, the arrival of French troops, the riots of Aranjuez, the virtual disappearance of government—had stunned the population, which realized instinctively that it was being betrayed and sold. As the crowd waited, word spread that the young prince refused to leave the palace, let alone Madrid, and was having a tantrum. The child's tears set off a revolution. The crowd, with sticks and knives, fell upon the French soldiers who were to form the prince's escort and cut through the thongs of the coaches. The French answered with musketry and dispersed the crowd.

This, however, was only the beginning. The sound of the musketry brought the larger part of the population into the streets. Armed with whatever weapons they could procure or improvise, the infuriated masses threw themselves upon the French, killed and wounded some thirty officers and several hundred men, and for about an hour virtually controlled the capital. Then, however, the French troops stationed outside the city began to pour in, shooting and sabering down all opposition. The Spanish garrison, meanwhile, stood by idly, except for a handful of officers and men who joined the insurgents. By evening all was over, and during the night the mass executions began. Murat believed himself in full control of the situation; it was just another Cairo rebellion.

In the days following the *Dos de Mayo,* Murat organized a Council of Regency, recruited mostly from among Godoy's

OVERLEAF: *Francisco Goya's masterpiece,* The Third of May, *bitterly commemorates the brutal execution of forty-three Spanish insurgents by a French firing squad on a hillside near Madrid.*

creatures. On May 13 he suggested to them that Napoleon would be pleased if they petitioned him to give Spain a new king—preferably his brother Joseph. The council responded with alacrity. Napoleon, still at Bayonne, sent back word that Joseph might consent, provided the Spanish nation really and sincerely desired him. As a token of sincerity, one hundred fifty grandees and notables should form a deputation and present their request to the emperor at Bayonne. Almost two-thirds of the persons listed in Napoleon's reply responded to the call and on June 15 proclaimed Joseph Bonaparte king of Spain.

The Spanish people proved to be less docile than its leaders. Even before Joseph was proclaimed king at Bayonne, insurrections had broken out in every province of Spain. The Spanish uprising has no parallel in European history, for it was completely spontaneous. There was no central leadership, no organization, no preparation. The people rose, not against their masters, but despite their masters. It is true that revolutions are almost never planned; however, in all revolutionary situations save that of Spain in 1808 there is a body of men ready to take leadership and to impose a program on the popular movement. In Spain, in 1808, there could have been neither a leadership nor a program, for the events that precipitated the insurrection had occurred too swiftly and unexpectedly. The Spanish people were not led into rebellion; they rebelled because they were leaderless. For nearly three months they had watched with apprehension as French troops poured into their country; then, suddenly, their worst fears were confirmed and they found themselves betrayed and abandoned. Their first reaction was fear and fury—fear of the unknown fate awaiting them and fury against their betrayers.

Spontaneous movements are never rational, and often there enters into them an element of vengefulness and cruelty whose first victims are the defenseless. During the early phase of the insurrection, hundreds of Spanish officials were murdered by mobs; in Valencia, the rabble, led by a priest, massacred the entire colony of French merchants. It was only gradually that the forces of violence were channeled into the single purpose of combatting the French army, and it took several months before an effective attempt was made at co-ordinating the various regional juntas of defense. Four years elapsed before the leadership of the insurgent forces worked out a political program other than mere resistance to the invader. Even more curious, no dominant personality emerged as a leader throughout the six years that the war lasted. These singular features of the Spanish war deserve at least an attempt at an explanation.

It seems most unlikely that a general, spontaneous uprising would have taken place in Spain merely because a foreigner had been placed on the throne. After all, the Bourbons were a foreign dynasty, too. It was not King Joseph but the presence of a large French army that was intolerable. Not only was occupation by foreign troops humiliating to national pride but it also foreboded the destruction of the institutions and traditions in which the Spanish people was rooted—foremost among them the Catholic faith and the privileges of the various regions.

Indeed, although the Spanish monarchy had been united for three centuries, regionalism remained a powerful force. It was entirely in the Spanish tradition that the juntas should operate independently in the several kingdoms that made up the Spanish monarchy and that regional rather than national leaders should emerge out of the struggle for independence. This was unfortunate, for in the absence of a strong political leadership Ferdinand VII was made the figurehead of the popular uprising, which was thus prevented from turning into a genuine social revolution. It was in the name of Ferdinand that Spain fought Napoleon's army—Ferdinand *el deseado*, the Desired, who was represented to the Spanish people as a hero and martyr while in fact he was writing abjectly flattering letters to Napoleon, still begging him to give him a wife and even congratulating him on his victories in Spain.

Joseph Bonaparte, the king against whom the Spaniards were rebelling in the name of Ferdinand the Desired, came to Madrid with the best of intentions. Like his brother King Louis of Holland he took his royal job quite seriously. The so-called Constitution of Bayonne, approved by the ninety-one Spanish deputies who had assembled there to offer him the crown, promised freedom, reforms, respect for the Catholic religion, and a great many other good things. There is every reason to believe that Joseph intended to keep these promises. He was by no means a paragon of virtue, but his vices were relatively innocuous: he was a compulsive skirt-chaser and, like all Bonapartes, he pushed acquisitiveness to the point of rapacity. However, he was a peace-loving man, had sincere liberal convictions, and felt a deep sense of responsibility toward the people he was to rule. These fine qualities put him in an absolutely untenable position. On the one hand, he had to make war on his subjects before he could make them prosperous and happy; on the other hand he was constantly reminded, in a series of hectoring letters from his younger brother, that his first duty was not to Spain but to Napoleon.

Nevertheless he attempted to rule according to his own convictions. During his two years as king of Naples, he had managed, in rather unpropitious circumstances, to introduce a number of liberalizing reforms, to overhaul the fiscal system, to set up free schools, and to reduce official corruption to a minimum. He proposed to take similar measures in Spain, and in this he had the co-operation of a Council of Ministers that took its duties far more seriously than it had under Godoy. By no means all Spaniards sided against the French; in fact, a substantial part of the elite—nobles, prelates, financiers, officials, and intellectuals—supported King Joseph. Their motives varied. Some simply feared Napoleon; others regarded the rebellion as a dangerous popular movement against the king's legally constituted authority; others yet, particularly the intellectuals, looked

The men of Spain, often armed only with clubs, clashed with the French to protect their families from the cruelty of the invaders.

to France—even to Napoleonic France—as the bearer of the liberal principles of the French Revolution. Under French influence and under the rule of Joseph and his successors, feudalism would be swept away, the power of the religious orders would be broken, and civic equality would be established—in other words, the unfinished work of Charles III would be completed.

In these hopes, they were probably not mistaken, and if Joseph had been allowed to rule in relative peace, the chances are that his reforms would have left a permanent and beneficial imprint on Spain. Moreover, if the Spanish people had not made war on Joseph, Napoleon would have had less opportunity to interfere in the affairs of his brother's kingdom, and the larger part of the French troops would have been withdrawn, since they were badly needed elsewhere. Last but not least, Spain might have kept her American possessions on which her status as a great power depended—not kept them as colonies, perhaps, but as dominions in personal union with the Spanish crown.

The forces opposing the French, and their motives, are difficult to define. Among their early leaders, there was undoubtedly a high percentage of monks and of feudal landowners. The Spanish Church in general had little to fear from French rule; however, there was no question that, as in France, the monastic orders would be either suppressed or reduced to a minimum. In no Catholic country did the religious orders wield more power than in Spain; it was they rather than the secular clergy that controlled the conscience

of the masses and had a vested interest in keeping fanaticism alive. As for the landowners, the majority of them depended for their living on the maintenance of feudal rights. While the large landowners could afford to toy with liberal reform (they also had vast commercial interests, and their income from rents would still have been enormous, even if the feudal dues were abolished), the lesser landed nobility would have been ruined by the suppression of feudal dues and the abolition of entails. To them, the possibility of the Code Napoléon being introduced into Spain must have been an intolerable thought. It is doubtful whether either monks or landowners went through any rational process when they made up their minds to stir the population to resistance: they knew instinctively that the French were their worst enemies.

To stir up the population required no great effort. The behavior of the French troops had created a most favorable climate of resentment. They acted as if in conquered territory, and it was plain that few among them were devout Catholics. The masses only had to be told it was pleasing to God if they killed the enemies of the Faith and the captors of their king. This is not to say that the Spanish people did not take arms out of patriotism and in defense of their soil and their liberty; but this patriotic *élan* gained momentum only after thousands of local spontaneous uprisings had coalesced into one vast national movement, supported by the regular armed forces. It was then that the insurrection ceased to be an emotional and basically reactionary flareup and turned into a truly popular war. The nature of its leadership changed accordingly, becoming increasingly enlightened and liberal. The masses, however, remained conservative, and although the split between the leaders and the masses was concealed as long as the struggle lasted, it became tragically evident in the aftermath.

The warfare was of two kinds. One kind was the conventional warfare of movements and sieges, fought by more or less organized bodies of troops; the other was guerrilla warfare or, to borrow an expression from the Second World War, "underground warfare." Both went on simultaneously, but while conventional warfare came to a standstill whenever the French forces gained temporary control, the guerrilla war continued with unabated violence until the complete expulsion of the French. It was fought with incredible cruelty by both sides. Every day French detachments were ambushed, supply trains raided, individual soldiers sniped at or knifed. Food might be poisoned; a friendly host, giving shelter to some tired courier, might turn out to be a guerrilla leader and murder him in his sleep; churches might be arsenals; priests might carry pistols concealed in their habits; accommodating wenches might turn into Judiths.

The sense of constant danger and hatred created an almost psychotic state of mind among the French. They were not content with the usual methods of reprisal—mass shootings of civilians taken arms in hand, burning of villages, confiscation of cattle, horses, and goods—but found release from their nervous tension in inflicting the most sadistic punishments and mutilations, in rape, in the desecration of churches, convents, and monasteries. Only in the larger cities, garrisoned by the French, was there any degree of security and a more or less normal life for them. Needless to say, the operations of the guerrillas greatly complicated the conduct of regular warfare for the French.

The troops Napoleon had sent into Spain early in 1808 were by no means his best. The generalized nature of the uprising took him completely by surprise. Even so, he had a low opinion of the Spanish army, and an even lower opinion of the Spanish army's auxiliary forces—the peasants and burghers raised by the local juntas, undisciplined, without uniforms, and inadequately armed. As he watched the operations from Bayonne, his surprise changed into fury when General Dupont's capitulation at Bailen caused the French to evacuate Madrid and to withdraw behind the Ebro. As has been seen in the preceding chapter, these developments forced Napoleon to postpone if not to abandon his designs in the Orient and put him into a very unfavorable bargaining position with regard to Russia. Europe was no less astounded than was Napoleon; the Spanish people's stand showed the way to the other nations under his yoke.

There was nothing Napoleon could do until he had brought reinforcements from Germany into Spain. His hope to make sure of the continued neutrality of Austria was punctured at Erfurt in October. This diplomatic defeat made it imperative for him to win a lightning victory in Spain before Austria had a chance to attack him in Germany. There was another reason why speed was essential: on August 30 General Junot had signed a convention with the commander of the British expeditionary corps in Portugal by which the French were to evacuate that country. The British were slow in following up that advantage, but it could be safely assumed that sooner or later they would cross the border and join with the Spanish forces.

Napoleon barely halted in Paris on his way back from Erfurt and proceeded immediately to the Ebro front, where in the meantime close to two hundred thousand French troops had been assembled. The Spaniards, after their initial successes in June and July, had been fully as slow as the British in taking advantage of them to consolidate their position. It was only toward the end of September that the Central Junta was formed; even then, no unified military command was created, but the conduct of operations was left to the individual provincial commanders, under the authority of the Central Junta, which had no experience in military matters. No new troops were brought up to the front, so that when Napoleon began his offensive in late October the Spanish forces were outnumbered almost two to one. The result was a series of crushing defeats inflicted on them by the French. By the end of November the Spanish armies had been annihilated or scattered, and on December 3, 1808, the French re-entered Madrid. In the north, only Saragossa held out.

Two days after Madrid had fallen, General Sir John Moore, who then commanded the British expeditionary force in Portugal, made up his mind to come to the aid of Madrid. Moore was one of the best and certainly one of the most enterprising generals England ever had, and the responsibility for his lateness was not altogether his. However, in view of the fact that British historians of the Peninsular Campaign have tended to speak in somewhat less than gracious terms of the Spanish armies and their commanders, it is not amiss to point out that if the British forces had shown up earlier, there would have been no cause for them to complain of the disintegration of the Spanish forces. According to the most eminent authority on the Peninsular War, Sir Charles Oman, the responsibility for the Spanish defeats in November and December, 1808, must be placed on the Spanish commanders, whose rivalries and quarrels prevented them from drawing up a unified plan and from bringing sufficient reinforcements to the fronts. The charge is justified, but it should not be forgotten that Napoleon in person directed the French operations, and that the Spanish commanders were not the first to be routed by him.

Furthermore, it can hardly be said that the British command in Portugal had set an example of unity and speed to the Spanish. Originally, the English expeditionary army was placed under the command of Sir Arthur Wellesley, later duke of Wellington. Subsequently, for political rather than military reasons, the War Office placed two other generals —Sir Hew Dalrymple and Sir Harry Burrard—over Wellesley. It was Wellesley who defeated Junot; it was Dalrymple who signed a convention with him. The news of the convention was ill received in England, and all three senior British generals were recalled to London to testify before a court of inquiry. In their absence the command devolved upon Sir John Moore, who received orders to march into Spain. To avoid some difficult mountainous terrain, Moore took the long way, and it was only on November 23 that his sixteen thousand men reached Salamanca. Another British force—only thirteen thousand men—had in the meantime been landed to the north, at Corunna, under General Sir David Baird, and was on the march to join Moore. The junction took place on December 20.

By this time, however, Napoleon had become aware of the presence of a British army at his rear and set out with all available forces to capture it. Nothing could save Moore from disaster except a speedy retreat. Moore lost no time; yet although the race began with a considerable handicap in his favor, Napoleon's army, which crossed the Guadarrama Pass in a driving snowstorm, very nearly caught up with him. On New Year's Day, 1809, at Astorga, Napoleon suddenly decided to return to Paris—probably because of the intelligence he had received concerning Talleyrand's and Fouché's suspicious activities—and left the pursuit in the hands of Marshal Soult. Ten days later, Moore's forces —which had been joined at Astorga by the remnants of the Spanish Army of Galicia, under General de la Romana— reached Corunna at last, in a state of total exhaustion and demoralization. Six thousand men had fallen by the wayside between Astorga and Corunna. The transport fleet arrived only two days later; so did Marshal Soult's corps. The British repulsed the French heroically, but Moore was killed.

The next day the British embarked. Their bold foray, their agonizing retreat, and Moore's glorious death gave the British public some patriotic cheer; indeed, up to that point in the war, English arms had not particularly distinguished themselves on the land. Still, Moore's campaign was not exactly a victory. The best that can be said of it is that it created a diversion at a critical moment. If it had not been for that diversion, Napoleon would have used his time to subject the south and to reconquer Portugal. As it was, he never returned to Spain, and his successors, though able men, lacked his irresistible energy.

Moore's campaign would be less celebrated if Britain's participation in land warfare had been less sporadic. It would have been a mere episode. The defense of Saragossa by the Spanish was more than an episode, and though its only practical result was to tie up a considerable body of French troops for two months, its symbolic importance remains immense. Saragossa had suffered its first siege from June 13 to August 15, 1808. At that time, José de Palafox, who had led the rising in Aragon and been proclaimed its captain general, held the city with a motley improvised force of peasants and burghers. When General Verdier, whose troops had breached the outer wall, summoned Pala-

fox to surrender, the Spanish commander made the famous declaration that he would fight to the last wall in the last house. Soon afterward the French lifted the siege, but on December 20 the second siege began, and Palafox made good his word. This time he had forty thousand men to defend the city—the remnants of his army after its rout at Tudela—not counting the civilian population. Marshal Jean Lannes, the victor of Tudela, was given two army corps to invest the strategic city on the Ebro.

It took the French thirty-eight days to penetrate the outer defenses and three more weeks of street fighting before Saragossa was in their hands. Every house was a fortress and had to be blown up; every street was a battlefield. Twenty thousand of Palafox's soldiers and thirty thousand civilians had died in combat, of disease, and of hunger before the surrender was signed. The defense of Saragossa was one of the rare moments in history when a collective popular will asserted itself in spontaneous heroism. No supreme command had ordered the city to hold out; there was no supreme command. There was only the instinctive knowledge that a nation cannot keep its identity unless it is prepared to fight for it against all hope. At Saragossa the nation fought —women and children as well as men. The young woman who manned a gun after her lover was killed while loading it symbolized not only the heroic spirit of Spain but also that of the common people. Soon the example would be taken up in the Tyrol, in Russia, in Germany. The change was revolutionary: no longer could the rulers claim that they were the guardians of their peoples; the rulers had compromised, abdicated, or run away, and if they kept or recovered their thrones, this was due partly to the heroism and partly to the trusting good nature of their subjects.

The defense of Saragossa was duplicated in Catalonia, where the fortress of Gerona withstood the French siege for seven months. When Gerona surrendered on December 10, 1809, the entire surviving garrison, including the governor, General Mariano Alvarez, was literally prostrate from exhaustion and illness; but the siege had cost the French twenty thousand casualties. The defense of Gerona, remarks Sir Charles Oman, "was undoubtedly the most brilliant piece of service performed by the Spaniards during the whole Peninsular War." The "service," it must be understood, was to the commander of a new British expeditionary force, Arthur Wellesley, lately created Viscount Wellington. As the Spanish saw it, Wellington had come to Spain to help them; but Wellington saw it the other way round, and so, apparently, have British military historians ever since. By taking this view, it is easy to credit Wellington with every success in his campaign of 1809 and to blame its total collapse on the Spaniards. A different interpretation is possible, however.

Wellington landed at Lisbon on April 22 with about twenty-five thousand British troops. The size of his expeditionary force was scarcely impressive, considering that the French had two hundred thousand men in Spain, but Castlereagh, the minister of war, counted on the remaining Portuguese and Spanish forces to serve as supplementary cannon fodder, and there was a prevalent notion that every Englishman was worth two Frenchmen. When the English landed, a French army under Marshal Soult had begun the invasion of Portugal. There was nothing to stop Soult's advance except a few Portuguese battalions and the armed peasantry, which had taken its cue from Spain and resisted the invaders stubbornly.

Oporto was defended by some thirty thousand insurgents, led by the bishop; it fell after two days, several thousand Portuguese having been butchered or drowned in the Douro. Soult, however, dared not go farther, as his communications with the rest of the French army had been cut off by the insurgents in his rear. Thus Wellington was able to land his troops at Lisbon three weeks later and to attack Soult with twenty-five thousand Englishmen and sixteen thousand Portuguese. Soult was taken by surprise, and by the end of May the French had been driven out of Portugal. Leaving Soult to the care of the insurgents in Galicia, Wellington now turned against the corps of Marshal Claude Victor in Estremadura. Victor did not wait to be caught by Wellington and withdrew in the direction of Madrid, thus renewing contact with the French forces in central Spain. Since Wellington with his small force could not attack Victor in this strong position, he agreed to co-operate with the Spanish armies under Generals La Cuesta and Venegas.

The co-operation did not work out very well. On July 27 and 28 the British faced a concentration of nearly fifty thousand French troops at Talavera on the Tagus and were outnumbered almost two to one. However, their "thin red line" held out against the massed French columns in the two-day battle and eventually forced the French to withdraw. It was a Pyrrhic victory: the English suffered fifty-three hundred casualties—more than a quarter of their effective strength. Meanwhile, Marshals Soult and Ney had withdrawn their corps from Galicia and entered the Douro valley. Their movement ruined Wellington's plans for an attack on Madrid and threatened to cut him off completely. Wellington fell back to the Guadiana in the south and announced that in the future he would not co-operate with the Spanish armies unless he was given full operational command. Undoubtedly he was right in refusing to risk what forces he had left and in placing the blame for his failure on his Spanish colleagues. Yet ultimately the responsibility rested neither on him nor even on La Cuesta and Venegas, but on the British government, which at the height of a struggle for national survival was unable or unwilling to muster a land army of a size that even a country like Switzerland could have raised in a few weeks.

With Wellington sulking and licking his wounds on the Guadiana, the French experienced no difficulty in routing the Spanish armies and overrunning the entire south of Spain. Organized Spanish resistance collapsed after the disastrous battles of Alba de Tormes and Ocaña in November.

Seville fell on January 31, 1810, and only Cadiz, defended by the duke of Albuquerque, continued to hold out. (It was never taken.) By this time, Napoleon had won another campaign against Austria and was able to dispatch huge reinforcements to Spain. The situation seemed well in hand at last. Summing up the campaign of 1809–10, it may be said, without unfairness to Wellington, that his successes would have been unthinkable without the heroic stand of the Portuguese and Spanish guerrillas, which kept the French forces engaged in every corner of the Peninsula. Even though he had accomplished his primary mission— the expulsion of the French from Portugal—his forces would eventually have been annihilated had not the Spanish guerrillas continued their struggle, which indeed they did. In these circumstances, it seems a trifle ungrateful to put the blame for the failure of his extremely hazardous campaign in central Spain on Spanish shoulders.

When Marshal Masséna, the new French commander in the Peninsula, began his offensive against Portugal in late August, 1810, there were three hundred seventy thousand French troops in Spain. Five-sixths of this enormous army were, at all times, required to garrison the key cities, to contain the remaining pockets of resistance, particularly in Catalonia, to protect communications and supplies, to police the countryside and mountain passes, to besiege Cadiz, to hunt guerrilla bands; only the remaining sixth could be put in the field against Wellington. Against Masséna's sixty-three thousand the English commander could muster thirty thousand British troops and close to seventy thousand Portuguese and Spanish regulars and militia. Even so, Wellington did not attempt to hold the Portuguese border. Instead, he ordered the entire countryside between the border and Lisbon to be laid waste and the inhabitants to take refuge in the mountains or in the seaports.

Meanwhile, he had completed the construction of two formidable lines of fortification, the Lines of Torres Vedras, across the neck of the Lisbon peninsula. Behind these defenses, whose outer perimeter was about thirty miles long, he planned to withdraw with all his forces except for the Portuguese militia men, who were to remain concealed in the mountains. Unsuspecting and unopposed, Masséna advanced deep into Portugal. At Busaco he came upon the retreating Anglo-Portuguese army, attacked it, and was repulsed with heavy losses. Nevertheless, Wellington continued to retreat, abandoned Coimbra to the French, and on October 11 slipped through the Lines of Torres Vedras, accompanied by most of the population of the Portuguese province of Northern Estremadura. Masséna reached the Line the following day and soon found out that it was impregnable. For four months, until the beginning of March, 1811, the two armies remained in that position, facing each other without fighting. Yet whereas Lisbon was well supplied, the French were starving. Their marauding columns either found no food or were ambushed. On March 5 Masséna ordered a retreat; one month later, his army reached its starting point, Ciudad Rodrigo, reduced by one-third of its strength. Hunger, disease, and the guerrillas had taken at least twenty thousand French lives. As for the victors, their army had suffered no losses, but their victory had been won at the price of whole provinces destroyed and thousands of civilians starved, tortured, killed, or destitute. No phase of the Peninsular War was waged with more ferocity, and yet not a single major battle was fought. Wellington's triumph over Masséna is regarded as one of Britain's finest victories, but it is remembered with mixed feelings by the Portuguese.

Masséna's retreat marked the beginning of the end for the French in Spain. The allied armies passed to the offensive: on May 3 Wellington routed Masséna at Fuentes de Oñoro in the northwest, and on May 16 another Allied corps, under General William Carr Beresford, repulsed Soult at Albuera, in the south, and forced him to retreat toward Seville. Albuera was the bloodiest battle in the entire war—of the sixty-five hundred British infantry taking part in it, more than two-thirds were killed or wounded. Soult could not understand what had happened. "They could not be persuaded they were beaten," he wrote of the English. "They were completely beaten, the day was mine, and they didn't know it and wouldn't run." As a matter of fact, seeing the number of his casualties, Beresford *did* think that he had been beaten and said as much in his report to Wellington. "This won't do," Wellington replied. "It will drive the people in England mad. Write me down a victory." Beresford wrote down a victory, and a victory it has been ever since. Thus, sometimes, are battles won.

Dissatisfied with Masséna's performance, Napoleon recalled him and replaced him with Marshal Marmont. Against an entire country risen in arms and against a growing regular army commanded by an exceptionally able and determined general, Marmont could do no more than his predecessors. The French obtained some partial successes, but the tide of the war was against them. Ciudad Rodrigo fell to the Allies in January, 1812; Badajoz fell in May; on July 22 Wellington routed Marmont, who was seriously wounded in the battle at Salamanca; and on August 12 he entered Madrid, which King Joseph with his court and his remaining forces had been obliged to abandon. Wellington's failure to take Burgos, it is true, gave Joseph a chance to reorganize his army; as a result, Wellington had to fall back again in October, but Joseph was not to keep Madrid or his throne for long. While Wellington's army grew, Joseph's was reduced not only by casualties but by the steady withdrawal of troops needed for Napoleon's Russian campaign and, in 1813, for his campaign in Germany. It is clear that by 1812 Napoleon had given up all hope of bringing the Spanish war to a speedy conclusion. All he expected Joseph and his generals to do was to hold out until his Grand Army had defeated Russia; after that, he would deal with Spain at leisure. After the collapse of the Russian campaign, the French in Iberia no longer fought to keep Spain but to protect the French border.

Francisco Goya's Allegory of the City of Madrid: *the central female figure in the painting below personifies the capital city of Spain. On the shield at her right is the city's coat of arms. The oval frame to which she points originally contained a portrait of Joseph Bonaparte, who was king of Spain at the time the painting was executed. He had retained Goya as first court painter but he apparently refused to sit for him and Goya was obliged to work from a print when creating the likeness. After Joseph lost the throne, his portrait was replaced by the word* Constitución *and it in turn was covered with a portrait of Ferdinand VII. Later a representation of the Book of the Constitution was inserted and finally, the present inscription,* Dos de Mayo, *was painted on the canvas.*

Goya did the portrait of Ferdinand VII in general's garb (above) after the king's restoration.

The final blow was delivered to Joseph on June 21, 1813, when Wellington inflicted a decisive defeat on him and Marshal Jourdan at Vitoria. Even before the battle Joseph was in full flight toward the French border, with an endless train of carriages and vehicles of every description, carrying art treasures and other loot, munitions, supplies, and refugees. All this, as well as his entire artillery and about five million dollars' worth of currency, was abandoned to the victors on the battlefield. The remaining French forces and strongholds in Spain were defeated and captured by the Allies one by one in the months following the flight of King Joseph, and in October Wellington crossed the Bidassoa into France. At about the same time Napoleon was retreating across the Rhine from Germany; the German and Spanish campaigns were at an end: the campaign of France had begun.

Four years before the French defeat, when the war was still undecided and Spain was a blood-drenched, smoking ruin, a central Cortes, or parliament, began to hold its sessions at Cadiz. Since the larger part of the country was under French occupation, only a small number of the deputies were elected by popular suffrage. The rest were appointed by the regional juntas and by the colonies in America. Thus, in its composition, the Cortes of Cadiz represented mainly the middle-class liberal intellectuals— or, at any rate, those among them who were not supporting King Joseph. Few among them favored royal absolutism; even fewer may be said to have held radical or republican convictions. Theirs was a moderate compromise between traditionalism and the ideals of the early phase of the French Revolution. What they wanted was a constitutional monarchy. This, of course, was precisely what King Joseph wanted also. However, the mass of the Spanish people (except the middle class and the American colonists) was indifferent if not hostile to political reform. When the Cortes of Cadiz began its work by swearing to uphold the Catholic faith, the national integrity of Spain, and King Ferdinand VII, it gave voice to the cause for which the people were fighting; but when it went on from there to draw up a constitution, the document lacked all sense of reality, since neither the king nor the people were sympathetic to its content.

The Constitution of Cadiz, promulgated by the Cortes in 1812, has been unanimously praised by liberal historians. Like the American Constitution of 1789 and the French Constitution of 1791, it not only defined the functions of the various branches of government but also guaranteed certain basic civil rights—equality before the law, abolition of all feudal rights and dues, abolition of flogging in schools, abolition of corporal punishment and imprisonment for Indians who refused baptism, gradual abolition of slavery. Provision for the development of public education, though it hardly belonged in a constitution, was another admirable feature. Yet many of the main articles were curiously timorous or self-contradictory. Thus, according to the constitution sovereignty was vested jointly in the people and in the king; freedom of the press was guaranteed in political matters but censorship was retained in religious matters; the Inquisition was abolished, but the concept of religious offenses was maintained, and Bishops' Courts were given jurisdiction to deal with them.

These were minor weaknesses that could have been gradually eliminated if the constitution were applied in a liberal spirit. The relationship of the metropolis to the American colonies, on the other hand, was a problem that demanded an immediate rather than a gradual solution, and in this respect the Constitution of 1812 was most unsatisfactory. Peninsular Spaniards and American Spaniards were proclaimed to be equal; yet in the Cortes, Peninsular Spaniards were to be represented on the basis of one deputy for every fifty thousand inhabitants and the colonies on the basis of one deputy for every hundred thousand white inhabitants, with no representation whatever for Indians, Negroes, and persons of mixed blood. These inequalities were protested by the American leaders and contributed considerably to the secession of Spanish America from the metropolis.

Joseph Bonaparte, painted by Gérard

What matters in a constitution is not so much its provisions as the application that is made of it in practice. The Constitution of Cadiz never had a chance to prove itself, and it would be churlish to criticize it. However, its contradictions, its mixing of incompatible principles, are symptomatic of the Spanish predicament. The war of 1808–14 proved dramatically that the Spanish people were ready to fight and to die for their ideals and convictions; subsequent proof to the same effect was furnished only too often; but the ideals and convictions for which the people fought—first against the French and later against one another—were always a complex of contradictions, of rationality, and of passion. The motives for which any given region or segment of the population will take up arms for one side rather than the other, and fight to the death, will always remain incomprehensible to the outsider and—judging from the explanations given by Spaniards— to the Spaniards as well. The fate of the Constitution of Cadiz serves to illustrate this point. It was framed by men who had sworn uncompromising resistance to a ruler— Joseph Bonaparte—who had every intention of carrying out a program of reform similar to theirs, and it proclaimed the sovereignty of a ruler—Ferdinand VII—who was utterly indifferent to them, who had betrayed them, and who was far more subservient to Napoleon than Joseph Bonaparte would ever have been.

In March, 1814, King Ferdinand returned to Spain after promising to uphold the constitution. His first action, once in control, was to tear up the constitution, to reassert absolutism, to nullify all the reforms accomplished not only during his exile but even in the reign of his grandfather, to restore the Inquisition, to increase the number of monasteries, to forbid all newspapers except one, to close the theatres and universities, and to throw into prison the very liberals who had supported him. In 1820 the army, supported by the middle class, rebelled against his absolutism, restored the Constitution of 1812, and kept the king a virtual prisoner. Two years later the European powers, assembled in congress at Verona and gave France a mandate to intervene in Spain and to restore Ferdinand to power. French troops entered Spain, and the same masses that had defended their cities to the last party-wall fifteen years earlier now cheered the invaders. Thanks to the French army, King Ferdinand the Desired was restored to his full absolutist glory.

So lamentable a conclusion to so glorious an effort leaves one bemused and perplexed. What was the purpose of all this heroism? To keep a mean, craven, and treacherous king? To perpetuate intolerance and bigotry? This seems scarcely credible. It sounds more plausible to say that the Spanish people fought for national independence, for the right to solve their problems their own way; yet they did not fight in 1823, when a foreign army invaded Spain to impose the policies of foreign powers. Did Spain fight for the cause of Europe against Napoleon? Hardly: Napoleon was welcome to take the whole world so long as he left Spain and her possessions alone. Reluctantly one comes to the conclusion that the motives of the Spanish stand were almost wholly negative. The mass of the population rose in arms because their pride had been wounded and because they preferred all the evils they knew—famine, tyranny, torture, and death—to any foreign intrusion on their ways. In this respect, the Spanish uprising was the exact equivalent of the Cairo rebellion and of the guerrilla war waged upon the French in Egypt; the only difference was that the Spaniards were better fighters and had more endurance. Neither the reforms of Charles III nor the Constitution of 1812 had the support of the masses, and both were essentially alien in inspiration. Consequently the restoration of Ferdinand VII, though brought about by French arms, was not resented as an alien intrusion.

Granted that the Spanish rebellion was reactionary in nature; that, far from gaining anything by it, Spain was set a century backward and lost her empire as a result of it; that she would have fared much better had she accepted King Joseph; and that her whole performance was a magnificent example of quixotism. Yet the consistent liberal must concede that a nation has a duty to defend the values it believes in, even if they happen to be impractical or different from his values. The Spanish resistance to Napoleon was a completely democratic movement for a reactionary cause. This paradox explains the fact that in Spain it led to the victory of absolutism while elsewhere in Europe its example gave heart to the liberal forces.

Although guerrilla tactics have been used since time immemorial, the word *guerrilla* gained currency only in the age of Napoleon. Spain was the first civilized country to fight a guerrilla war on a large scale and to prove its effectiveness. That partisan warfare remains effective even against modern armies was amply demonstrated in the Second World War. Whether the Spanish war contributed appreciably to Napoleon's downfall is doubtful, however. It did tie down hundreds of thousands of French troops, but it did not prevent Napoleon from defeating Austria in the war of 1809, and his failure in the Russian campaign of 1812 cannot be ascribed to lack of troops. It was only in the German campaign of 1813 that the necessity to defend two fronts became fatal to Napoleon; but then he was paying the price for his attack on Russia rather than for his attack on Spain. It is entirely probable that the Spanish war did Napoleon more moral than military damage; but moral damage, decisive though it may be, cannot be assessed with any degree of certainty.

What is strange is Napoleon's failure to understand the nature of the war the Spanish people was waging on him. For the first twenty years of his life he had exalted the memory of the Corsicans who had fought for freedom against the Genoese and the French much as the Spaniards were fighting against him. If there was anyone who should have felt by instinct what kind of adversaries he was facing, it was he. Yet so far had he moved from his origins, and such are the effects of power and of continued luck, that he had lost his instincts. The men whom he would have exalted as heroes in his youth had become a mere rabble in his eyes; except during a few weeks late in 1808, he would not even demean himself by taking personal command of the operations in Spain. "The Spanish people is vile and cowardly, about the same as I found the Arabs to be," he wrote in 1808. Four years later, as he raced back from Russia with Caulaincourt, he still refused to accept the central truth. "It is because of his laziness, not from heroism," he declared, "that the Spanish peasant prefers the dangers of smuggling and highway robbery to the toil of farming. The Spanish peasants have taken advantage of the situation to lead the nomadic life of smugglers. . . . There is nothing patriotic in this." In all likelihood there is a grain of truth in what he said, but it hardly accounts for the *Dos de Mayo* or for the defense of Saragossa and Gerona. It was not so much Spain that caused Napoleon's downfall as Napoleon's blindness to what was happening in Spain. Had he been less blind, he would have realized that while it was safe to despise sovereigns and ministers and even armies, it was fatal to despise the people. This realization might have saved him from many a mistake.

THE DISASTERS OF WAR

Francisco Goya was one of Spain's greatest artists and the most mordant critic ever of man's inhumanity to man. The self-portrait shown above was done about 1795, shortly after he had suffered a long and severe illness during which he lost his hearing. With the penetrating eyes of a deaf man, Goya observed the corruption and abuse of power in royal circles to which he had access as first painter to the king. When Napoleon's armies invaded his country in 1808, Goya, despite his distaste for the Spanish monarchy, was strongly affected by the patriotic fervor that compelled his countrymen to carry on their desperate resistance to the foreign invaders. In a series of etchings known as *The Disasters of War,* Goya recorded the unspeakable horror and chaos of those years of incessant guerilla warfare. This collection constitutes his timeless indictment of the barbarism and futility of war.

Lo mismo *The same*

Y son fieras *And they are like wild beasts*

El buitre carnivoro   *The carnivorous vulture*

Although Goya retained his position as court painter under Joseph Bonaparte, he was deeply preoccupied with the Spanish uprisings. After the first siege of Saragossa, General Palafox, who had commanded the city's heroic resistance, asked the artist to come and see the ruins of the city where he had spent his childhood. Goya was strongly moved by the evidence of violence and havoc that he witnessed on his journey across the countryside. In 1810, at the height of Napoleon's power, when it seemed impossible that Spain could˙ expel the invader, Goya began the hazardous task of recording his bitter views of the war and its cruelties, with little thought that his work might ever be seen by the public.

The fighting that flared up in the provinces was savage and merciless. Hatred drove the partisans to acts of monstrous brutality, and scenes such as the one at top left, of peasants butchering French soldiers with improvised weapons, were common. (Goya's title, *Lo mismo,* refers to the preceding drawing in the series, which is captioned "With reason or without.") A number of the etchings, one of which appears at bottom left, pay tribute to the courage of the Spanish women whose patriotism drew them into battle. The "carnivorous vulture" shown above represents the French imperial eagle being driven off by a crowd of angry peasants.

Populacho *Rabble*

Para eso habeis nacido *Was it for this that you were born?*

Grande hazaña! Con muertos!   *Great deeds—against the dead!*

In Spain during the Peninsular War a virtually unarmed and leaderless populace rose in a frenzy of anger to expel a foreign ruler and the army on which he depended. The Spanish people struck out at the French soldiers with desperate ferocity, and the invading soldiers retaliated with matching savagery. There seemed no limit to the atrocities committed by both sides. Not even the dead were respected. The French mutilated the corpses of their enemies and strung them up to serve as a warning to other partisans. Goya's portrayal of one such scene (above) conveys with stark realism his horror at a crime committed against once robust young bodies, now hanging maimed and dismembered from a gnarled remnant of a tree. Other artists of the time celebrated the glory and pageantry of war; Goya saw only the tragedy, suffering, and needless death. In another etching (above left) he depicted a lonely figure, spewing out his blood, as he collapses upon a pile of corpses that lie like so much refuse on a barren hill. In the picture opposite a mob of enraged Spaniards is shown falling on a French sympathizer. To this subject Goya affixed a derisive comment, for the vengeance the Spaniards wreaked on their own countrymen suspected of collaborating with the enemy was as appalling as any French atrocity. When asked why he depicted these crimes, Goya replied, "To tell men forever that they should not be barbarians."

Las resultas *The consequences*

No saben el camino *They don't know the way*

Fiero monstruo   *Fierce monster*

Exhausted by her struggle against foreign domination, Spain looked forward in 1814 to an era of peace and justice. With the return of Ferdinand VII, many hoped for a new social order governed by a constitutional monarchy. Their expectations were of short duration. Abolishing the Constitution of 1812, Ferdinand launched a vicious campaign of persecution against those who had in any way collaborated with the French government and those suspected of holding liberal ideas. Goya himself came under suspicion, since he had served Joseph Bonaparte and had painted several portraits of French generals. Although he escaped imprisonment, many of his liberal friends did not. Disgusted with the despotic regime, Goya withdrew from public life to compose an epilogue to *The Disasters,* in which his indictment falls equally on the monstrosity of the war and the tyranny of its aftermath. That final group of fifteen engravings contains Goya's depictions of war as a satiated beast vomiting its victims (above) and a terrible vampire sucking the strength of the Spanish people (above left). In another print (opposite) Spaniards with ropes around their necks stagger into a dark chasm, symbolizing the prisons into which were thrown thousands of liberals who had fought to free their country.

RESOLUTE BRITAIN

Europe watches;
France arms;
History writes;
Rome destroyed Carthage!

Reflecting upon the rise and fall of ancient empires, Lieutenant Bonaparte during his garrison days at Auxonne reached a strange but significant conclusion: when a nation whose power rests on naval strength, shipping, and commerce (Carthage, for instance) is in conflict with a military, agricultural state (such as Rome), "experience nearly always proves" that the maritime state will be defeated, "because war destroys [its] commerce and gradually exhausts [it], whereas its opponents are toughened and strengthened." If the American naval historian Admiral A. T. Mahan reached an opposite conclusion a century later, this was because the outcome of Napoleon's struggle with England supplied him with the most forceful argument conceivable in favor of the supremacy of sea power. Napoleon himself, reflecting upon his own rise and fall at St. Helena, came close to admitting this thesis when he blamed his failure on the inferiority of the French navy; however, he never conceded that the outcome of the struggle was inevitable, and one may imagine him arguing the point with Admiral Mahan in the Elysian Fields.

Whether the outcome of the war was inevitable or whether it was due to chance or error is a question that can be debated ad infinitum. That the war itself was inevitable can scarcely be doubted. It might have been avoided if the peace negotiations between France and England held at Lille in 1797 had not broken down; in that case, Napoleon would probably never have risen to power. Once

he was in power, there could have been a truce (as in 1802–3) but never peace without a complete defeat of either England or France. Not that Napoleon was irrevocably opposed to peace with England: he held out the olive branch several times every year. But England could not accept a peace without a balance of power in Europe, and this kind of peace was unacceptable to Napoleon. The consequences of this deadlock were inevitable. Unable to deal England a direct blow, Napoleon had to attack her indirectly, thus upsetting the balance of power more and more, a development that made England increasingly irreconcilable. Nothing could have broken the vicious circle except Napoleon's voluntary withdrawal to the frontiers of 1792. This was the course advocated by Talleyrand, but Napoleon would not have been Napoleon had he followed such a conciliatory policy.

If Britain would not make peace, Britain had to be destroyed; the conclusion was self-evident. But how to destroy her? All Napoleon's triumphs were poisoned by this frustrating problem. Even before he came to power, he had sought to strike at Britain through Egypt. The purpose of that move was to force England to make peace by threatening to ruin her trade. Nelson's victory in the Battle of

From his flagship, the Victory, *Lord Nelson directed the defeat of the French and Spanish fleets at the Battle of Trafalgar. The ship is still berthed at Portsmouth, England's chief naval base.*

208

the Nile and the Anglo-Turkish stand at Acre foiled the project; yet even if Napoleon had gained control of Egypt and had marched into India, it is unlikely that England would have made peace. The contrary is more probable: England would have fought on with even greater vigor. Napoleon thought that the French occupation of Egypt was an asset in his negotiations for a general peace in 1801; actually, it was an obstacle, and the preliminary Peace of London was signed only after the French had evacuated Egypt. After nine years of war with France, England emerged with a more powerful navy, a larger merchant fleet, a more favorable balance of trade than before. France, on the other hand, had lost half her navy and virtually all her overseas trade during the same period of time.

Disagreements over Malta, Switzerland, and Piedmont resulted in the resumption of warfare in May, 1803. Napoleon ordered his troops to occupy the Electorate of Hanover and had all male British subjects in France placed under arrest; apart from these futile measures, there was nothing he could do to hurt England. The British declaration of war had come much earlier than he had expected, and it caught him with virtually the entire French fleet scattered in the Caribbean, the Atlantic, and the Indian Ocean. Even if united and combined with the Dutch navy, the French fleet was numerically inferior to the British; its crews were incomplete and inexperienced, and its command was demoralized. To deal an effective blow to England, Napoleon had to launch a gigantic program of naval construction; in addition—and this was more difficult for him to accomplish—he had to overcome the probably quite justified defeatism of his admirals.

Considerable doubt has been cast on the seriousness of Napoleon's intention to invade Great Britain. Indeed, the successive plans of invasion were so unrealistic and hazardous, and their secret was so ill-kept, that there is reason to suspect that the purpose of Napoleon's preparations was not as simple and direct as appearances indicated. There is no question that he abandoned the project at least temporarily on several occasions before its collapse in 1805, and that he nevertheless continued rather ostentatiously to push the preparations as if there had been no change of plan. There are several reasons why he may have resorted to so phenomenally expensive a bluff: first, the very hugeness of his preparations was likely to terrify the English and to bring about a change of policy toward France; second, he was building up a large army, ready to strike in any direction, without giving alarm to the next victim of his aggression, since he could always explain that his armaments were directed at England only; lastly, he was immobilizing the major part of the English land forces, obliging the English government to spend millions of pounds on the defense of the island itself, and keeping the British navy diverted from whatever offensive projects he may have had in other parts of the world.

It is true that he himself had to lavish millions on the construction of an invasion fleet and of invasion bases, at a time when he was short of funds, and it has been argued that no one would spend so much money on a mere feint. Moreover, in all his utterances after Waterloo, some of which were quite frank, he never gave the least hint that he had not earnestly intended to invade England; utterances to the contrary effect are innumerable. While there can never be any certainty on this question, it may be stated with reasonable confidence that the truth lies somewhere in the middle. Napoleon almost never made a decision with one single purpose in mind; in case his principal objective proved to be unattainable, one or several alternative courses of action remained open to him, so that no effort was entirely wasted. It was this pliability of his that explains in large part what seemed to be his luck.

That he would have liked to invade England can hardly be doubted; that he made vast preparations for that purpose, set several successive dates for his "immense project," as he called it, and was ready to carry it out as soon as an opportunity presented itself seems equally certain. But the opportunity never came, the plans were changed again and again, their execution was postponed from season to season, and nothing indicates that Napoleon ever counted firmly on their realization. If he hoped that England would be intimidated, his hopes were deceived. It is astonishing how well-informed the British government was of the progress of his armaments and even of his strategic plans through its spies, through French royalist agents, and through American and other neutral travelers; such carelessness would be inexplicable unless one assumes that it was intentional and part of a war of nerves. This assumption is supported by the tone of the French press, which dwelt lovingly on the appalling plight of the English lower classes and assured the public that the French army of invasion would be welcomed as liberators by the majority of Englishmen. As it turned out, the response of the English people to the threats of invasion was touchingly patriotic, but it was not unreasonable of Napoleon to expect that the governing classes could be frightened into a compromise with him.

Seen in this light, Napoleon's preparations for his "immense project" were neither a mere bluff nor a mad gamble. Even if there was only one chance in a hundred that the necessary favorable conditions for an invasion would materialize, he had to be prepared to take advantage of it. If the chance did not materialize, the threat nevertheless might intimidate the British and would, at any rate, drain their already strained resources, and if even that should produce no effect, he would at least have a huge, well-trained, and homogeneous army ready to pounce in another direction—Austria, Turkey, Egypt, or India.

Before the end of 1803, an army of workingmen had built several thousand transports and invasion craft of all sizes and constructed vast basins and artificial ports along the Channel coast, particularly at Boulogne and Etaples, while ships of the line were building at Brest, Rochefort,

Lorient, and Toulon. Aboard the transports, according to the original plans, an army of more than one hundred thousand men, including artillery and cavalry, would be rowed across the Channel on some calm and foggy day. Several difficulties, which Napoleon appears to have blinked at first, soon became painfully evident. While it was theoretically possible to complete the operation in twenty-four hours once the craft had left their basins, getting them out of the basins would require several days. Furthermore, as was demonstrated in several catastrophic practice sorties, the weather in the Channel was unpredictable, and the least squall raised havoc with the transports. Not only was it unlikely that there would be several successive calm days on the Channel, but it was also plain that the armed transports, no matter how numerous, could never defend themselves against British warships. Thus it was essential to gain temporary control of the Channel either by bringing a massive French squadron into it or by diverting the English ships away from it to other parts of the world.

Yet although ships of the line were building in several ports, Napoleon lacked experienced crews to man them, since a large number of seamen had been diverted to the transports, and there was a shortage of stores which made it difficult to equip them. Moreover, the ports were blocked by the English, and although the blockade was partially lifted here and there whenever the British ships had to water and victual, it was impossible to synchronize French sorties from the various ports either with one another or with the requirements of the Channel flotilla. The problems were well-nigh insuperable.

A number of plans had already been adopted and abandoned when, in December, 1804, the over-all picture was changed by Spain's declaration of war on England. (Charles IV's decision to abandon neutrality was partly the result of Napoleon's pressure, partly in protest against the seizure by the English of four Spanish treasure ships from America, carrying about $5,000,000 in bullion.) With the Spanish ships added to his own, Napoleon could expect to establish a temporary naval superiority, since the English navy was scattered over the world. In its main features, Napoleon's plan was to have the French squadrons of Toulon, Rochefort, and Brest rendezvous in the West Indies, join with the Spanish fleet, and then return to cover the invasion of England. A number of mishaps prevented this project from being carried out as originally planned, and for these Napoleon himself was largely responsible because he countermanded his own orders several times. As a result, the Rochefort squadron, after raiding the British Antilles, returned to its base without waiting for the Toulon squadron under Admiral Villeneuve, and the Brest squadron under Admiral Ganteaume missed its unique opportunity to fight its way out of the blockade which the British had formed. Thus, in the end, only Villeneuve's squadron and part of the Spanish fleet were able to take part in the operation.

Lord Nelson, who was in charge of the squadron block-ing Toulon, had already proved on a previous occasion that while there was none like him for winning a battle, the interception of fleets was not his forte. Villeneuve slipped out of Toulon with eleven ships of the line on January 18, 1805, while Nelson was not looking, but had to return to his home port a few days later, a storm having damaged several of his ships. Nelson had searched for him all the way to Alexandria before finding out that he was back in Toulon. On March 20 Villeneuve gave him the slip a second time, passed the Straits of Gibraltar, picked up an additional French ship and six Spanish ships at Cadiz, and on May 14 reached Martinique. Meanwhile, Nelson, who believed Egypt to be the French objective, had combed the Mediterranean once again, trying to find Villeneuve, who was half-way across the Atlantic by the time Nelson learned that he had passed Gibraltar.

Now the chase began. On June 4 Nelson reached the Barbados, where he added two more ships to his squadron of ten. Although Villeneuve had twenty ships to Nelson's twelve, intelligence of Nelson's arrival filled him with terror. In agreement with his Spanish colleague, Admiral Carlos Gravina, he decided to return to Spain forthwith, without awaiting the Brest squadron (which in fact never got out of Brest). On July 22, off Finisterre, he ran into Admiral Robert Calder, who was blocking El Ferrol with fifteen ships. Despite his decisive superiority, Villeneuve managed to let himself be badly mauled by Calder in an otherwise inconclusive engagement. Meanwhile the Rochefort squadron under Admiral Zacharie Allemand had received orders to cruise in the Bay of Biscay and establish contact with Villeneuve. On August 14 the two squadrons came within sight of each other, mistook each other for British ships, and withdrew; but for this farcical error, Villeneuve could have united thirty-four ships of the line under his command, sailed up to Brest, unblocked it, and gained that temporary superiority which Napoleon was so anxious to establish. Instead, he collected whatever French and Spanish ships he could unblock at El Ferrol and Corunna and set sail for the south, entering Cadiz on August 20. He now had a fleet of thirty-three sail. Admiral Collingwood, with only three sail, had the nerve to block him there, and Villeneuve made no attempt to drive the English admiral off.

Even before Napoleon had certain news of Villeneuve's withdrawal to Cadiz, he decided to postpone or abandon the invasion scheme and to move his troops into Germany. This, as has been seen in an earlier chapter, was the beginning of the Austerlitz campaign. In his dispatches to Villeneuve, the emperor did not hide his discontent with the admiral's timorous conduct and blamed him for the failure of the invasion. At the same time, he ordered Villeneuve to take his fleet out of Cadiz and to attack the enemy if he found him of inferior strength. These orders reached Villeneuve at about the time when Lord Nelson, aboard his flagship *Victory,* arrived off Cadiz. By mid-October Nelson had assembled twenty-seven ships of the line. Although Villeneuve had six more ships than Nelson, he was aware of the inferiority of his crews and officers, and he had an almost superstitious dread of Nelson. It was only on October 19, when he heard that another admiral had been designated to supersede him, that he decided to obey Napoleon's order. His honor was at stake. Still, he hoped to take his fleet into the Mediterranean without having to give battle. Nelson fell back to the south, to block the Straits of Gibraltar; on October 20, off Cape Trafalgar, he turned about and issued his last instructions for the battle that was to take place on the morrow.

Admiral Villeneuve accepted the battle with the full conviction that he was doomed. Aboard the British ships, morale was high to the point of exaltation. At 11 A.M. on October 21—a gray and squally morning—the *Victory* signaled Nelson's message to his ships: "England expects that every man will do his duty." With their bands playing and the crews cheering, the ships bore down on the French. Nelson's plan was to cut the French line in three, then concentrate on the French rear and center. The

Nelson's portrait, painted after his arm had been amputated

Royal Sovereign, Admiral Collingwood's flagship, was the first to penetrate the French line; the *Victory,* with equal impetuousness, broke through behind the tenth French ship shortly afterward. With the success of this bold maneuver, the battle was as good as won. Nelson's intention, however, was not only to win a battle but to annihilate the Franco-Spanish fleet. Perhaps he could have accomplished this had he lived through the battle, but this was not to be. At about one o'clock he was struck down by a bullet from the French ship *Le Redoutable,* fired, so it is said, by a Swiss sharpshooter. His weakness for wearing all his decorations even in battle had made him an easy target. While he lay in agony for more than two hours, the French van had turned and attacked the British ships engaged with the center; it was repulsed about three o'clock, a few minutes before Admiral Nelson died.

By five o'clock the battle was over, but a violent storm set in and caused the English the loss of thirteen of their prizes. Thus, in the end, of the thirty-three ships constituting the Franco-Spanish fleet, eleven were destroyed or wrecked, three were captured, and nineteen escaped. Both

Frenchmen and Spaniards, despite their low morale, had fought with more than ordinary courage, and their losses were staggering—almost six thousand men killed or wounded. The *Redoutable* alone, with a crew of 645, had 522 casualties. English casualties ran close to 1,700. The victory of Trafalgar, though undoubtedly the most glorious in the history of the English navy, was by no means as complete as the victory of the Nile, since more than half the enemy ships were allowed to escape, and the death of Nelson himself cast considerable gloom on it. There was little jubilation when the news reached London, especially since it was followed closely by the news of Napoleon's victories at Ulm and Austerlitz. For four years—from Nelson's death to Wellington's intervention in Spain— English arms, both on land and on sea, seemed condemned to fight in nothing but diversionary and usually ineffectual actions.

It is only in retrospect that Trafalgar appears decisive; at the time, neither the English nor Napoleon regarded it as such. On his return from Tilsit, in 1807, the emperor once again seems to have contemplated the possibility of reviving the invasion project. The transport fleet was still kept in readiness. The British seizure of the Danish fleet at Copenhagen and the escape of the Portuguese fleet from Lisbon, both in 1807, were perhaps even heavier blows to Napoleon than Villeneuve's defeat at Trafalgar. These actions, however, were scarcely heroic, and Trafalgar remained the symbol of victory. As events turned out, it was also the turning point of the war, for it marked the end of any serious attempt on the part of Napoleon to challenge British naval supremacy.

As has already been suggested, Napoleon in all likelihood never counted firmly on the realization of his invasion plans. Yet as early as 1788, when he was far from even dreaming that one day he would lead and coerce Europe into a titanic struggle with the British Empire, he could express the opinion that a continental power could defeat a maritime power by strangling its commerce and exhausting its resources. This idea was always present in his mind, but to carry it out he had to control the coasts and ports of Europe. In the autumn of 1806, with Spain his ally, Austria defeated, all Germany and Italy under his control, Belgium incorporated into France, and Holland a French puppet, the time seemed ripe for the execution of his project. To view the inauguration of the Continental System as a desperate device, adopted only because the invasion scheme had failed, is probably a distortion of the facts. Invasion, in Napoleon's eyes, was always the more risky form of waging war, whereas economic warfare if waged on a large enough scale seemed to him an absolutely safe way to bring England to her knees. Now, it is the risky course, not the safe one, to which one resorts in desperation.

The idea of ruining Britain by closing the markets for her products had already occurred to the leaders of the French Revolution; it was the seizure by French privateers of American ships carrying British goods that led to the undeclared naval war between France and the United States in 1797–1800. Napoleon's famous Berlin Decree of November, 1806, was merely a restatement, in ringing terms and on a vaster scale, of the decrees issued by the French Republic in 1793 and 1796. In the decree Napoleon accused England of violating international law by attacking ships engaged in commerce as well as by declaring coasts of other nations to be under blockade even though England had no ships there with which to enforce it; in retaliation he declared the British Isles under blockade and forbade all trade with them. No ship coming from a British port would henceforth be admitted to the ports of France and her allies. To this the British government retorted with the Orders in Council of January 7 and November 11, 1807, which imposed similar restrictions on ships coming from French ports or complying with the Berlin Decree. Certain exceptions were made, however, in favor of neutral ships in order to attract them to British ports. Napoleon replied with the Milan Decree of December 17, 1807, in which he misrepresented the British rulings as violating the rights of neutrals and announced that all neutral ships complying with them would be regarded as enemy ships. Since neither side was in a position to enforce its rules completely, the mutual blockade was, to some extent at least, a paper war. It is true that both sides, moreover, broke their own rules.

Thus the British government made it a practice to issue licenses to neutral ships and even to ships belonging to Napoleon's inactive allies—such as Russia and Prussia—for the purpose of exporting British manufactured goods. The number of licenses thus issued rose from twenty-six hundred in 1807 to eighteen thousand in 1810. This practice afforded some relief to British manufacturers but was highly unpopular with British shipping interests, which saw the carrying trade gradually transferred to neutral and enemy nations.

Napoleon inaugurated a somewhat similar system in 1809 to stimulate French exports. In the following year, he even permitted the import of certain British colonial goods, such as sugar and coffee, provided French manufactured goods of equivalent value were exported by the same carriers. Even stranger, Napoleon made no effort to prevent the export of wheat from France and allied countries to England, and in 1810 he saved England from the famine that was threatening after two successive harvest failures. His motives were not philanthropic but mercantilistic: the English had to pay in specie for the Continental grain, and the ships that carried the grain to England had to return empty. Thus, by supplying England with food, he produced an adverse effect on her balance of trade and reduced her already dwindling reserves of bullion. This, he figured (perhaps not incorrectly), would work greater hardship on the British ruling classes than the spectacle of a few hundred thousand peasants and proletarians suffering and dying of hunger.

While it is impossible to estimate to what extent the Continental System was vitiated by smuggling, there can be no doubt that smuggling was practiced on a heroic scale and became the most lucrative form of business in Europe. Smugglers plied their trade back and forth across the Channel almost every night and on foggy days. From the coast of northwest Germany long wagon trains of contraband goods clogged the roads into the interior, with the connivance of Napoleon's own brother, King Jerome of Westphalia. Holland carried on trade with Britain all but openly, and its king, Louis Bonaparte, another of the emperor's brothers, was the first sovereign to defy France by ignoring the Continental System.

King Louis' character was extremely complex, and he was probably the most neurotic member of the family. His neurosis may be partly explained by the fact that, at the age of twelve, he spent a year with his brother Napoleon, who undertook his education. Napoleon, then an impecunious lieutenant, sacrificed much of his time and money to Louis' upbringing, and Louis looked to him as to a father. But it was an exacting and imperious father; even after he had placed Louis on the throne of Holland, Napoleon still expected filial gratitude and submission from him. As it happened, Louis, who had been forced to marry Josephine's daughter Hortense, was Napoleon's step-son-in-law as well as brother. As a husband, he was far from ideal; not only was he homosexual and syphilitic, but he treated Queen Hortense with a tyrannical jealousy that betokened hatred rather than love.

Yet while his actions in private life were hardly those of a sane man, as a sovereign he was beyond reproach and soon gained the affection of his people. It was clear to him that strict adherence to the Berlin and Milan Decrees would mean the ruin of Holland. His lax interpretation of the blockade infuriated his imperial brother. "I advise you," Napoleon wrote to him in 1807, "to cultivate in private life that paternal and pliant character you display in government and to apply to public business the severity you show in your household." Louis did not heed the advice, and Napoleon's tone became more threatening. In December, 1809, fresh from another victory over Austria, the emperor put it to Louis: either Louis closed all Dutch ports to British goods, or Holland would be annexed to France. A few days later, French troops occupied the island of Walcheren and two Dutch fortress towns. Louis gave in, perhaps because he felt too ill to put up a struggle, but when Napoleon increased his demands still further in May, Louis had had enough. His advisers having pointed out to him the futility of armed resistance, he abdicated in his son's favor and, on the night of July 1, slipped out secretly from his palace; he did not halt in his flight until he had reached the baths of Teplitz in Bohemia.

On July 9 Napoleon annexed Holland to the French Empire. For good measure, in the latter half of 1810 and early in 1811, he annexed to France the entire northwest coast of Germany as far east as Lübeck, including parts of Jerome's territories and the Duchy of Oldenburg. This action did not endear him to the dispossessed duke's brother-in-law, Alexander I of Russia. About the same time, by the Fontainebleau Decrees of October, 1810, Napoleon ordered all British manufactured goods found in the French Empire to be publicly burned and established rewards for information leading to the discovery of contraband goods. In the German provinces of the Empire, where the effects of the blockade were felt very severely, the execution of the decrees brought public exasperation to a new pitch. Hamburg was totally ruined by the new measures: hundreds of ships lay rotting in the harbor and some of the principal industries—including sugar refining and cotton printing—were completely closed down.

To be effective, Napoleon's economic warfare against Britain had to be enforced with ruthless vigor. There was, however, an inherent flaw in it, and this flaw became increasingly apparent as Napoleon intensified his efforts: the main sufferers in the struggle were neither England nor France but France's allies and the neutrals, whose economies were being ruined at a much faster pace than England's. If applied severely enough and long enough, the Continental System might conceivably have brought England to acknowledge French supremacy; but before this goal could be achieved, a system completely contrary to their most vital interests had to be imposed by threats and force on such nominal allies as Sweden and Russia and on neutrals such as the United States. The reasons that brought the United States to the French side when the showdown began in 1812 will be examined in a later chapter, as will the circumstances that led Napoleon to make war on Russia and brought Sweden and Prussia into the war against him. As will be seen, they were the direct outgrowth of the tyrannical Continental System.

It was Napoleon's belief that so long as the French people were reasonably satisfied with his regime, he could hold the rest of the Continent by sheer terror. In France, in spite of the Continental System, the period 1806–10 was one of rising prosperity even though she lost all her West Indian colonies to the British and although her merchant

A fanciful representation of French invasion plans shows England attacked from sea and air, and underground.

fleet was destroyed or paralyzed. The most obvious reason for this paradox is that French manufactures found a large outlet on the French-dominated Continent. Another reason was that the agrarian reform and the abolition of internal trade barriers—which were the work of the French Revolution and not of Napoleon—were beginning to prove their beneficent effects.

New manufactures and manufacturing processes sprang into existence and were encouraged by the government. Applied chemistry, thanks to such pioneers as Berthollet and Chaptal, made it possible to find adequate substitutes for such colonial products as cane sugar and indigo. The manufacture of beet sugar had progressed to a sufficient point in 1812 for Napoleon to forbid all imports of cane sugar after January 1, 1813. While France reverted to cane sugar after recovering her West Indian colonies, Germany (where the original process of making beet sugar had been invented) and Central Europe in general have relied on beet sugar ever since. On the other hand, Napoleon's attempt to substitute Flemish cambric and lawn for fine cottons ran into the determined opposition of French womanhood, led by Empress Josephine, who, according to Napoleon, "rebelled and made loud outcries; the project had to be abandoned." In general, the ban on imports was carried out more leniently in France than elsewhere, and there was none of the drab austerity that its stricter execution imposed on Germany.

In the end, as everybody knows, Napoleon's Continental System succeeded no better against Britain than had his scheme for invasion. British historians, especially of the last century, have tended to credit this double failure to the resolute and heroic stand of the British people, who continued to face the Continental colossus alone when all

others had submitted. This patriotic fiction proved immensely beneficial in 1940–41, when Britain did indeed fight alone, against tremendous odds, defying death and destruction with collective heroism and determination. Now that it has been established that the British people are indeed as resolute as they always thought they were, there is no longer a need to perpetuate the old legend. During her struggle of twenty-two years against the French Republic and Napoleon, Britain stood alone from 1797 to 1799, from 1803 to 1805, and from 1807 to 1808—six years in all. During those solitary periods, not a single French shell exploded on English soil, nor did a single British soldier fight on the European Continent. Action was confined to the naval forces and to land operations in distant parts of the world. Even during the periods when Britain had allies, the British land forces engaged in combat never exceeded forty thousand men at a time; at Waterloo only twenty-four thousand troops under Wellington were English, the other forty-three thousand being German and Dutch.

There is no reason to doubt that the people of England would have defended themselves as valiantly as the people of Spain against a French invasion; but thanks to the English Channel, the British navy, and the Austrian emperor, they were never given a chance to prove it. They stood up bravely under the rigors of the Continental System, but the only people seriously affected by these rigors were the working class, and the only notable British military action in the first half of 1808 was the charge delivered by a regiment of dragoons against a crowd of unemployed factory workers at Manchester on May 24, three weeks after the *Dos de Mayo* in Madrid. That the resolute refusal of the British government, backed by the vast majority of the nation, to compromise with Napoleon kept European

resistance against him alive and eventually caused his defeat is a truth which it would be difficult to challenge. Yet while "Fight to the death!" was the slogan, "Comfort as usual" characterized the daily lives of the more respectable elements of the population. Impassioned patriotism filled the halls of Parliament and the columns of the press; if verse could kill, Wordsworth alone would have been the Corsican Usurper's undoing; but if Miss Jane Austen's novels, which give a more faithful picture of English county life than do patriotic histories, contain one single reference to the fact that a war was going on, this writer has not found it.

That this was so, let it be said without irony, was a blessing not only for England but for the world; for England was the only European country that had a parliamentary government, and she also was the only one that escaped becoming a battlefield or a garrison state. If England had participated more actively in the Napoleonic wars, the direction in which English institutions were moving might easily have been changed; that this would have been a pity is a point that hardly needs to be elaborated.

When England entered the war in 1793 to crush Jacobinism, William Pitt was at the helm and George III was relatively sane. Apart from naval engagements, history records no major clashes between French and English arms during the first phase of the conflict. Toulon was temporarily occupied, then abandoned; Corsica was ruled by a British viceroy for two years. In 1795 Spain and Holland made peace with France and became her allies; this development gave greater scope to British warfare, which Sheridan later defined as a "policy of filching sugar islands." Ceylon and the Cape Colony were filched from the Dutch, Trinidad from Spain, Martinique from France; though England restored some of these conquests to their former owners at the Peace of Amiens, the process was resumed along with the war in 1803. England's allies and part of the English public expected something more than the filching of sugar islands, but it was a long time before they got it. On the other hand, it is difficult to see how England's allies could have continued to oppose Napoleon without English subsidies, and with these Pitt was generous.

To put England on a military footing also required large expenditures, to which the English people subscribed no less generously. If a rising national debt be an index to patriotic feeling, the record of England during the Napoleonic wars is impressive: between 1793 and 1815, it rose from £230,000,000 to £830,000,000 and the budget from £27,000,000 to almost £200,000,000. In addition income taxes were introduced and indirect taxes increased, adding greatly to the hardships of the lower-income groups.

The expenditure was justified by Nelson's victory at the Nile in 1798 which restored Britain's confidence in her navy, which for several months had been racked by mutinies. On land in 1799 Sir Sidney Smith, single-handed except for the assistance of some twenty thousand Turks, stemmed Bonaparte's advance at Acre, and two years later

Lawrence's portrait of the duke of Wellington was painted the year before Waterloo.

an expeditionary force, under Generals Hutchinson and Moore, forced the French army in Egypt to capitulate. However, the Egyptian expedition of 1801 was hardly a fair test of strength between French and British land forces; the British forces (about seventeen thousand men) were assisted by two Turkish armies; even among the British contingent, not all men were British (there were some Germans and the Corsican Legion of Volunteers); the fighting strength of the French Army of the Orient had been reduced to eighteen thousand at the most; virtually all the French, except their commander, had only one wish—to go home; their commander, General Menou, was an incompetent madman. Even with all these advantages, the best the English could obtain was a capitulation by which the French were repatriated, with all their weapons, aboard British ships and at England's expense.

All the same, the victory restored John Bull's conviction that while the French had defeated the armies of Prussia, Spain, Austria, and Turkey, they had not come up against real soldiers, and that a handful of true Britons could halt them. This sort of irresponsible jingoism reached its height during the invasion hysteria of 1803, when a reputedly sane man like William Pitt brought a toast to "a speedy meeting with our enemies on our *own* shores."

No one could say what would have happened had Pitt's wish been fulfilled. In Napoleon's opinion, once the French army had landed, "four days were enough to reach London." Judging from the nature of Britain's defensive preparations, he may well have been right. The regular army was small, and a substantial part of it was stationed in Ireland, in India, and in the colonies. Its ranks were recruited from the dregs of society; however, what they lacked in intelligence and initiative they made up for with their phenomenal staying power. As Wellington was to demonstrate in Spain and at Waterloo, there was nothing that could break the famous British "thin red line"—this phenomenon Napoleon attributed to the beneficial effect of flogging, which was practiced quite liberally in the British army. The English soldier was probably the worst-treated soldier in Europe, and judging from the English casualty rates during the Napoleonic wars, English generals were more lavish with their soldiers' lives than were their French and German colleagues.

Thus, despite its smallness, the well-disciplined regular army might well have beaten back the French, had they landed, provided it was concentrated in the landing area. However, it was not so concentrated, although there could be little doubt concerning the area where the landing was bound to take place if it took place at all. Instead of strengthening the regular army and putting it where it was most needed, Prime Minister Addington's government called the entire nation to arms. The result was ludicrous.

In the first place, the government defeated its own purpose by exempting all volunteers from the *levée en masse.* Before the end of 1803, 342,000 volunteers had enrolled.

Now to be a volunteer, all a man had to do was to put on a uniform, join his local volunteer association, and do a bit of drilling; in every other way his life continued as usual. There were not enough arms to go around for the volunteers, but apparently it was the government's notion that a nation in arms meant a nation in uniform. "You never saw so military a country," wrote Lord Auckland. "Nothing but fighting is talked of." Even the prime minister came to Parliament in uniform; solicitors turned into volunteer colonels; shop clerks turned into dashing lieutenants; the duke of Bedford served as a private; martial music filled the air; each man was determined to give his life and all. If boasts and clothes were all that were needed to win a war, Napoleon was doomed.

Men fit for service who did not volunteer were subject to universal conscription, which operated by lot; however, if they drew the lot, they were entitled to buy substitutes. Since the price of a substitute soon rose to £30, the recruiting sergeants of the regular army, who could offer a bounty of only £7 12s. 6d. per head, were put out of business. Thus, while the more prosperous classes either volunteered for home defense or bought substitutes, the rabble was dragooned into service by the press gangs of the army and the navy. As for the peasantry, the government could think of nothing better than to issue them pikes to halt Napoleon's Grand Army. Knowing the unpredictability of Englishmen, it is not entirely impossible to visualize an army of Sunday soldiers and peasants armed with pikes thrashing the Frogs; nevertheless William Windham, a former secretary for war, was probably right when he estimated that if Napoleon could land only fifty thousand men, he had as good as won the war of England.

Although a French descent on Westmorland was improbable, William Wordsworth did his share in Britain's defense by donning a uniform and cheering the somewhat more exposed Kentish population:

We are all with you now from shore to shore:
Ye men of Kent, 'tis victory or death!

Indeed, all over England, in speeches, song, and doggerel, Nappy was being thrashed and the Frenchies whipped. Cruikshank's and, even more so, Gillray's caricatures of "Buonaparte" set a record for crudeness surpassed only by the anti-Semitic caricatures of Hitler's Germany, while booksellers contributed to the patriotic spirit by promoting libels in which Napoleon was represented as a murderer, the incestuous lover of his sisters, an epileptic, a chewer of rugs, the great-grandson of a galley slave, the grandson of a butcher, and the son of a whore. When Betsy Balcombe, a girl in her teens, met Napoleon at her parents' house in St. Helena, she expected to see an ogre, and this is hardly surprising if one considers that English nannies of that period sometimes threatened their young wards that Napoleon would come and eat them if they were naughty:

Baby, baby, he's a giant,
Tall and black as Rouen steeple,
And he dines and sups, rely on't,
Every day on naughty people.

Rumor credited the Bogeyman with the most fantastic schemes of invasion. He was building a bridge over the Channel; he was digging a tunnel under the Channel; he was preparing a fleet of balloons that would transport men, horses, and artillery in an airborne invasion.

Some say in wooden house he'll glide,
Some say in air balloon,

announced a broadsheet entitled *The Bellman and Little Boney.* Whatever the means he chose—under ground, over sea, or through the air—Britain was ready to meet him. "United and Hearty, have at Bonapartee," was the title of one of many lyrical inspirations produced in the year 1803.

By 1804, Boney having failed to show up, Britain simmered down. Still, apart from subsidizing Austria, Russia, and Sweden to renew war on France in 1805, Britain's contribution to the new alliance was not impressive. While Napoleon was beating the Austro-Russian armies at Austerlitz, a British expeditionary force was sailing to South Africa to recapture the Cape Colony from the Dutch; while Napoleon was annihilating Prussia, the same expeditionary force proceeded to South America to snatch Argentina and Chile from Spain. (It managed to hold Buenos Aires for a while, but eventually was expelled by the Spanish.) The arrival of eight thousand Hanoverian troops under Lord Cathcart on the Baltic island of Rügen in July, 1807, brought little comfort to Russia and Prussia, who had just made peace with Napoleon at Tilsit. The savage bombardment of Copenhagen, also in 1807, made neutral Denmark doubt that Britain was truly a "bulwark to the cause of Man," as Wordsworth said. Nor was the Allied cause much advanced by the dispatch in the same year of seven thousand British troops to Egypt, where they were soundly thrashed by the Turks under Mohammed Ali. Britain's allies were beginning to gain the impression that while they were fighting for England in Europe, England was fighting for herself in Africa and America, a sentiment that Napoleon was not slow in exploiting for his own ends. The only valuable service performed in the Allied cause by British land troops during the years 1805 to 1808 was the defense of Sicily, which prevented Napoleon from gaining mastery over the Mediterranean.

Undoubtedly it served England's interests best to let her Allies do the fighting on land while she exploited her naval supremacy to enlarge her colonial empire, find new markets for her manufactured goods, and wear out Napoleon. Since Trafalgar and Napoleon's tacit abandonment of the invasion scheme, the English navy was invulnerable. By 1808, however, England's allies had ceased to fight, and she

herself was beginning to feel the pinch of the Continental System. Prospects were gloomy, but the London season was as gay as ever. Unsold manufactured goods were piling up at the docks; more than five hundred British ships had been seized by French privateers over the past twelve months; tens of thousands of unemployed were starving; and every night until dawn the vigorous cream of resolute Britain danced at masquerades and routs. Such dogged defiance of adversity deserved a reward, and indeed the reward arrived on June 6, 1808, in the shape of a deputation sent by the Asturian *junta* to seek the aid of the British.

Apprised of the heroic resistance put up by the Spanish people against Napoleon, England forgot past grudges. The Spanish people had asked for help; swept away by enthusiasm, the British began by occupying Portugal. As has been shown in the preceding chapter, military operations in the Peninsula, though marked by heroic exploits, remained ineffectual on the whole until Wellington's great offensive of 1811. Still, Britain's contribution was decisive, for without Wellington's generalship and his small but first-rate army, Spanish resistance would have been crushed by the French. At the same time, the Spanish war was a godsend to England, for it opened up the Spanish-American market to British goods and greatly reduced the pressure of the Continental System.

England's attempt to create a diversion in Holland during Napoleon's Austrian campaign of 1809 was even a worse disaster than General Sir John Moore's retreat to Corunna in the same year. Forty thousand British troops—the largest British force used in any single operation throughout the Napoleonic wars—landed on the island of Walcheren at the end of July. They took Flushing and South Beveland, but there their advance was stopped by the French and Dutch. For five months they remained entrenched in the swamps, until malaria had killed or incapacitated more than half their number. What was left of them was repatriated in the last week of December. The mismanagement of the expedition provoked indignant attacks in Parliament and led to a duel between the foreign secretary, Mr. Canning, and the minister for war, Viscount Castlereagh. Neither was hurt and both resigned.

It was unfortunate that this unpleasantness should have followed so soon after another, involving the younger son of His Majesty. Early in February, 1809, Frederick Augustus, duke of York and Albany, bishop of Osnaburgh, and commander in chief of the British forces, was accused in the House of Commons of having connived with his mistress, a Mrs. Clarke, in the sale of army commissions at cut-rate prices. Mrs. Clarke, a "Babylonish person" according to a contemporary diarist, was called to testify before Parliament, and she testified without reticence. Only two things are clear from the testimony: that Mrs. Clarke had slept with His Royal Highness and that she had sold commissions. His Royal Highness admitted to having co-operated with her in the former activity but not in the latter, and nothing was proved against him; all the same he had to resign as commander in chief. His defeat was a decided loss to the British army, for he had been a capable commander, but it was a marked triumph for the left wing of the Whigs.

Except for Wellington's campaign in Spain and southern France, fought with a predominantly Spanish and Portuguese army, the Walcheren expedition was the last English intervention on the European Continent until Waterloo. Indeed, Napoleon's attack on Russia in 1812 not only made further interventions unnecessary but also weakened his forces in Spain and so opened the road to Wellington's victories. If England saved Spain, so did Spain save England.

Although Napoleon may have been quite justified in boasting that, with a bit of luck, he could have landed his army in England and reached London in four days, he evinced a basic misunderstanding of the English when he declared, as he did at St. Helena, that the French "would have appeared to the English not as victors but as brothers." His optimism was based, no doubt, on two considerations: the first consideration having been that of the rivalries between the English political parties; the second, the severe social stress caused by rapid industrialization and by the appalling callousness with which the upper classes habitually treated the lower classes.

To speak of political parties is perhaps misleading. The old division into Whigs and Tories had been blurred by the split of the Whigs; and the new division into Conservatives and Liberals, which gave the English party system its present form, was yet to come. Instead of parties, there were cliques and coteries—Mr. Pitt's friends, Mr. Fox's friends, Mr. Addington's friends (a circle eventually reduced solely to George III), the prince of Wales' friends, and so forth. Mr. Pitt stood uncompromisingly for war with France; yet, after waging it for nine years with unflagging energy, he defended the Peace of Amiens before Parliament in 1802. True, he had resigned as prime minister at the beginning of the peace negotiations; this, however, was not over the peace but, as will be seen shortly, over an entirely different matter. His successor as prime minister was Mr. Addington, who was a friend of Mr. Pitt, just as Mr. Pitt was a friend of Mr. Addington; but their respective friends were each other's enemies. Mr. Fox, who was Mr. Pitt's enemy (although many of his friends were Mr. Pitt's friends), had always stood uncompromisingly for peace with France and held dangerously liberal opinions; nevertheless, in 1804, Mr. Fox and Mr. Pitt got together to overthrow Mr. Pitt's friend Mr. Addington, who was pushing the war effort with insufficient vigor.

Once more, Mr. Pitt was prime minister, but he died at the beginning of 1806. He was succeeded by Lord Grenville, whose friend, Mr. Fox, was made foreign secretary and became the dominant member of the new cabinet. Grenville's "Ministry of All the Talents" included everybody's friends except those of the late Mr. Pitt and of Mr. Sheridan, who, being the prince of Wales' friend, was habit-

ually too drunk to keep awake at cabinet meetings. (Sheridan was judged sober enough to be appointed treasurer of the navy.) Mr. Fox, who in his youth had led a riotous life with his friends, died of dropsy in 1806, and in the following year Lord Grenville and his Talents had to resign over the same issue that had led to Mr. Pitt's resignation in 1801. For the twenty-three years following, the Whigs were out and the Tories were in, under the successive premierships of the duke of Portland (1807–9), Mr. Perceval (1809–12), the earl of Liverpool (1812–27), Mr. Canning (1827), Lord Goderich (1827–28), and the duke of Wellington (1828–30).

Confusing in itself, the political picture was further complicated by the king's intermittent insanity, which in turn was usually set off by the Irish Question. It was on this issue that Pitt foundered in 1801 and Grenville in 1807. The intolerable conditions under which Ireland, and particularly its Catholic population, was governed in the eighteenth century had led in 1791 to the formation of the movement of the United Irishmen, a group of Catholics and liberal Protestants whose ultimate aim was the separation of Ireland from the British Crown. Pitt's concessions to the Irish Catholics, embodied in the Relief Bills of 1792 and 1793, were deemed insufficient by the more radical Irish patriots, and in May, 1798, several of the southern counties rose in rebellion. The aid promised the Irish leaders by the French Directory came too late and was, at any rate, inadequate, and the insurrection was put down rather harshly. Wolfe Tone, the founder of the United Irishmen, escaped the gallows only by suicide.

Pitt now turned to a scheme advocated by a number of statesmen before him—the merging of Great Britain and Ireland into a single United Kingdom, which became effective on January 1, 1801. The measure was generally welcomed by the Irish Catholic leaders, who felt that any change was bound to be for the better. Indeed, it was Mr. Pitt's intention to follow up the Act of Union with the emancipation of the Irish Catholics. This meant, above all, the eligibility of Irish Catholics to the House of Commons, in which Ireland was represented by a hundred members, and some sort of establishment for the Roman Church in Ireland. When he heard of the scheme, George III denounced it as "the most Jacobinical thing I ever heard of" and as contrary to his coronation oath; he promptly went mad, and Pitt had to resign. When Pitt resumed office in 1804, he expressly promised never to mention the Catholic question again as long as His Majesty was alive. He kept his promise. However, when Grenville in 1807 suggested that English Catholics be allowed to hold commissions in the army on the same basis as Irish Catholics, the king threatened to become mad again, and Grenville resigned. In 1810, George III became mad for good—this time, it seems, because of the scandal over his favored son, the duke of York—and his Falstaffian heir, the prince of Wales, was made regent in 1811. By this time, however, the right-

OVERLEAF: *Addressing the House of Commons in 1793, the young prime minister Pitt stands beside the speaker's desk. The Whigs sit opposite, with their leader, Charles James Fox (wearing a hat), in the center of the front row. On his left is the playwright Sheridan.*

wing Tories were firmly entrenched as the majority party, and Catholic emancipation had to wait until 1829, when the duke of Wellington pushed the bill through Parliament over the opposition of his own party.

That England should fight Napoleon in the name of liberty while denying on religious grounds the most elementary civil and political rights to a substantial part of her own population struck not only Napoleon but also many Englishmen as an anomaly. The contradiction appeared even stranger when Catholic Sicily and Catholic Spain became England's staunchest allies—though in fact it was no stranger than that Catholic Irishmen should have looked to the anti-Christian government of revolutionary France for aid. Napoleon's conviction that religious passion invariably took precedence over political passion blinded him to the glaring fact that nationalism, in his age, took precedence over both. *Irish* Catholics undoubtedly looked to France, but only because they wanted to be rid of the English; if he expected *English* Catholics to side with him, he was mistaken.

He was equally mistaken in interpreting the impassioned oratory that the disciples of Mr. Pitt and the disciples of Mr. Fox lavished against each other as signifying a deep division of principles as far as he was concerned. To begin with, Parliament was still in many ways a gentlemen's debating society, and brilliant oratory an end in itself. More important, however, the opposition between Pitt and Fox concerning the war with France involved issues that ceased to exist when Napoleon overthrew the last vestiges of republican government. From the outbreak of war in 1793 to the Peace of Amiens in 1802, Fox had consistently advocated peace with revolutionary France. He sympathized with the principles of the French Revolution, and he saw in Pitt's wartime measures a decided threat to English liberties. The Habeas Corpus Act had been suspended in 1794 to guard against more or less imaginary Jacobin subversion, and the Treason and Sedition Bills of 1795 virtually abrogated freedom of speech and of convention. It may be said that the war against France was prosecuted far less energetically than the war against English liberalism. Yet when Fox visited Paris in 1802, had a look at the new France, and met the First Consul, it became clear to him that Bonaparte's regime was as reactionary as Mr. Pitt's had been.

Bonaparte's actions in the two years following could leave no doubt that he was an incomparably greater menace to freedom than Mr. Pitt, who despite all his hysterical anti-Jacobinism had remained a liberal at heart. The same alliance between royalists and republicans that Madame de Staël and others were bringing about in France to oppose "the Man," as they called Napoleon, also came into existence in England, with the added factor that England was fighting for national survival. The right-wing Tories and the conservative Whigs fought Napoleon as the Usurper and the Enemy of the Established Order; the liberal Tories and the radical Whigs fought him as the Betrayer of the Revolution and the Enslaver of Europe; they were all agreed in fighting him, and his notion that their disagreement signified national disunion was mere wishful thinking. All dictators since his time have fallen into the same trap: themselves blind to the values of liberty, they cannot conceive that people who disagree on its meaning can nevertheless unite in upholding their freedoms against patent despotism.

Napoleon deceived himself in thinking that the Opposition, merely because it was not as hysterically anti-French as the government, was actually in his favor. He was perhaps on safer ground in assuming that the English populace had no interest in the cause of its masters. "There is not a populace in the world, not even the Prussian, worse treated," he told his Irish physician, Dr. O'Meara, in 1818. The English ruling class was treating the rabble like "so many helots," he continued. "Oh, one day the people will avenge themselves, and terrible scenes will take place." Though mistaken in his prophecy, Napoleon was completely right in principle: compared to the English industrial proletariat, even the Russian serfs were enjoying an enviable lot. The only reason, it is true, why the proletariat was worse off in England than in other countries was that industrialization had made faster progress in England; soon the condition of the French working class would become equally as intolerable as that of their English compeers.

The causes that led to the so-called Industrial Revolution in eighteenth-century England have been often stated and debated by economic historians, and the term Revolution has been questioned with some justification. Technology had little to do with it, for it was just as advanced in other countries as in England; besides, the inventions that made the great industrial expansion of England possible were of a very primitive nature. Whatever the causes, the effects are beyond dispute: England at the end of the eighteenth century was well on its way to becoming a manufacturing country; increasing masses of the population were diverted from agricultural labor and small-scale rural industries to vast and hideous industrial centers; machines were replacing manpower; labor was cheaper and more abundant, agricultural products scarcer and dearer, and unemployment and vagrancy more widespread than they had been before. At the same time a new class was developing— the prosperous manufacturer, whose interests were equally incompatible with those of the laboring or unemployed masses and those of the land-owning aristocracy, which was in complete control of the legislative process until the parliamentary reform of 1832.

Unfortunately for the working class, the fact that the industrialists and the landowners were at odds did not mean that the landowners were its friends; on the contrary, the industrialists could maintain with some justification that the proletarians' lot was tied to their prosperity, and that the artificially high prices of agricultural products, kept up by protective tariffs, worked to the disadvantage of both industrialists and workers. The issue came into clear focus only at the end of the Napoleonic wars, but it was during the Napoleonic period that the living conditions of the lower classes reached their nadir. Napoleon's Continental System was only partially responsible for this situation; the main reason was the almost universal indifference of the ruling classes to the plight of the proletariat, which they either ignored or attributed to sin and sloth.

Napoleon's remark on the British ruling classes treating the rabble like helots was prompted foremost by the inhuman methods by which sailors and soldiers were pressed into service and by the appalling conditions under which they had to serve. Press gangs could round up anybody not steadily employed in some trade; corporal punishment and generally subhuman treatment were even more frequent in the navy than in the army, since it was harder to desert from a ship than from a barracks. It is scarcely surprising therefore that the first signs of rebellion should appear in the navy, with the mutinies at Spithead and the Nore in 1797. They were suppressed, although some of their demands were granted; but the great reservoir from which the armed forces were recruited, the working class, was also beginning to clamor for its rights.

The formation of labor unions in the textile industry led to the passage of the Combination Act of 1799, which forbade associations of workers as well as of employers. While many who voted for the bill did so in the conviction that they were promoting freedom of labor, the result was naturally favorable to employers. It was about that time, as has been mentioned in an earlier chapter, that Malthus and Ricardo began to prove the futility of trying to help the poor. On the other hand, Arthur Young, the agricultural expert, proved the necessity of helping the rich to keep the poor from starving. The General Enclosures Act of 1801, intended to increase England's agricultural production, resulted in the absorption of millions of acres of common lands by the large estates, wiped out the small farmers, and further increased the labor reservoir by driving hundreds of thousands into the cities. The Factory Act of 1802, though a gesture in favor of reform, did less to reduce the workers' plight than to point up its extremity; it forbade parents to hire out their children for factory labor if they were less than nine years old and limited child labor to twelve hours per day.

In 1808 a member of Parliament, George Rose, pointed out to the House of Commons that a skilled textile worker in Lancashire, working fifteen hours a day for six days a week, earned exactly eight shillings for his labor; but the argument did not impress the House sufficiently to pass a minimum wage law. Parliament was more responsive to the appeal of the Nottinghamshire manufacturers in 1811; their workers, emulators of one Ned Ludd, a half-witted workman who about 1779 had destroyed some stocking frames, systematically wrecked new machinery that threatened to put a large number of them out of work. Parliament

consequently made the destruction of machinery a capital offense. Fearless of capital punishment, the Luddites continued their activities for some time through the Midlands —misguided, no doubt, but even more desperate. Indeed, the number of capital offenses under the penal law then prevailing in England was so vast (there were about two hundred of them) that it is difficult to see how a pauper could avoid hanging, except for the virtual absence of a police system. Some reform was introduced, but it was Australia that proved to be the indigent felon's salvation.

The contrast between the prosperity of the British upper crust and the misery of the masses was shocking indeed, and it made good material for anti-British propaganda. All the same, it is most unlikely that the French would have been received like brothers by the English populace if they had landed. Whatever pro-Gallic feeling there was in England was confined to a small educated elite; the average Englishman always was and still is hostile and distrustful toward everything French; he is, moreover, loyal in a peculiarly insular way which becomes strikingly manifest in moments of crisis. Undoubtedly the country was crying for reform, but the temper was not revolutionary. What small groups of radicals there were, would have been the first to be suppressed by Napoleon's police. The popular image of Bonaparte as a blood-stained tyrant and bandit was admittedly exaggerated, but instinct told even the most radical among the English that if liberty, equality, and justice were ever to come to their shores, it certainly was not Napoleon who would bring them there.

At the end of his reign, George III was deaf, blind, and insane.

The insouciance with which the upper classes pursued their pleasures and indulged their vigorous appetites while governing the nation in a casual, gentlemanly, amateurish way was equally deceptive. True, the great ruling families, convinced of their innate superiority, held any intellectual or moralistic approach to questions of government in lordly contempt. Their healthy animal vitality was admirable; nevertheless their days were numbered. The middle class, with its tiresome morality and conscience, was on the way up and soon would impose its standards on English society. The same was true, of course, in France and other countries; yet whereas the French bourgeoisie, complacently entrenched behind the Code Napoléon and the benefits it had gained by the Revolution, remained self-righteously impervious to working-class conditions, the English middle class was handicapped by having a conscience.

Their conscience had its main roots in religious sentiment, and particularly in the religious revival of the eighteenth century. The majority, it is true, took refuge in the thought that virtue breeds wealth and sin breeds poverty, but there were some—and they were more articulate and insistent—who pointed out that poverty breeds sin. The same emotional tendencies that led to what has been called English prudery also led to social reform, and probably the latter result was more important in the long run. While passion for justice and equality stirred revolutions in other countries, British concern over public morality produced a climate favorable to humanitarian legislation. Moral sentiment penetrated even into the aristocracy; its ranks were not entirely closed to the moralizing middle class.

It is true that apart from the prohibition of the slave trade, by an Act of Parliament passed in 1807 due largely to the efforts of Fox and Wilberforce, no important reforms were passed during the Napoleonic period. Yet it was precisely this period that saw the awakening of the public conscience that led to the great political and social reforms of the second third of the nineteenth century. These reforms cannot be said to have come from either above or below; they were the result of a give-and-take characteristic of British public life, and they would have been unthinkable if there had not been an enlightened proletariat as well as an enlightened elite. Perhaps the most significant social development in England during the Napoleonic wars was the self-education of the English laboring class. The system had been developed by a Dr. Andrew Bell in Madras, who hit upon the idea that in the absence of schools and teachers, children could be made to teach one another. Joseph Lancaster, a Quaker, applied the system to a group of poor children in south London. It worked with astonishing success, and in 1810, with the support of such men as the philosopher James Mill and the liberal Whig leader Lord Brougham, the Royal Lancastrian Association was founded to spread it over the whole of Great Britain. Lancastrian curriculum included bible reading but without interpretation. Representatives of England's High Church were outraged by this gesture, and one of their spokesmen, Samuel Taylor Coleridge, dramatized their disapproval by hurling down Lancaster's book in a public meeting. A rival organization was set up in 1811 by the Church of England, lest the mass of the population should be brought up as Nonconformists. Thus, without any system of public education, a relatively literate working class came into being, capable of stating its demands rationally and moderately. The "terrible scenes" predicted by Napoleon did not take place, and by the end of the century the British working class had advanced farther, without violence, than had its brothers across the Channel after four revolutions.

If England emerged from her twelve-year struggle with Napoleon stronger than ever, the foremost commercial, industrial, and naval power in the world, with a vastly expanded colonial empire, with her political institutions intact and her national pride at its peak, she owed this not so much to patriotic self-sacrifice as to her geographical location and to her refusal to sacrifice her identity. Even the Channel could not have protected her from defeat if it had not been for her one hundred fifty battleships, which bore the brunt of the war effort. Thanks to the superhuman activity of their navy, the English people were able to continue their pursuits, sheltered from the storms of revolution and war. Their scientists and inventors, their poets and painters, their philosophers and economists, their scholars, their political leaders, their industrialists, their bankers, and even their rebels and eccentrics were able to carry on virtually unhindered. The only European nation thus favored, England modulated from the eighteenth into the nineteenth century without a break in her traditions and yet with a more modern outlook than had the rest of Europe. The war against Napoleon was won not by England but by Russia, Austria, and Prussia; but England won the last battle and she won the peace.

And yet, though England's share in the fighting was small compared to that of the other powers, it was against England that Napoleon's power broke. It is true that England brought about his downfall in a perverse way, for it is unlikely that Napoleon would have risen as high as he did if he had not had to contend with her. It was England's stubborn refusal to compromise with him that forced him to undertake the conquest of the world. Every failure against England obliged him to extend his power farther in other directions, until he overreached himself and fell. If, instead of sitting back, protected by her navy, and letting him run his fatal course of conquest, England had exerted herself more strenuously in the war, Napoleon might well have beaten her. Whether her Fabian strategy was deliberate or merely the result of "muddling through" is an arguable point; certain it is that the first and only chance Napoleon ever had to face an English general in battle was at Waterloo, when his case would have been hopeless even if he had won. Whether intentional or accidental, the denouement was well managed.

THE ENGLISH SCENE

In 1814, as Castlereagh began to shape his contribution to the making of peace, he warned of the "great moral change coming on in Europe," where "the principles of freedom are in full operation. The danger is that the transition may be too sudden to ripen into anything likely to make the world better or happier. . . . I am sure that it is better to retard than accelerate the operation of this most hazardous principle that is abroad." He echoed the cautious attitude that had prevailed in England throughout the war years, where behind a carefully tended façade of Georgian balance, forces were stirring which would burst forth only after the battle against revolutionary and imperial France was won. For the duration portents of the nineteenth-century reform spirit only flashed here and there, in the perennial bickering between factions in Parliament and in the limited response evoked by scattered outbreaks of unrest; on the whole England spent twenty-five years resisting change and carrying on business as usual. The subscription room of Lloyd's of London as it appeared in 1809 is shown above.

Above, Louis XVIII, strolling near London

LAND OF REFUGE

For the many thousand Frenchmen who fled from the excesses of the Revolution and the tyranny that followed, life in England held some degree of deprivation, if not unendurable hardship. Louis XVIII, uncrowned king of France, gardened and grew ever fatter, but lived quite unpretentiously at Hartwell, his provisional English residence; far humbler lodgings in London's St. George's Field gave comfortless shelter to a group of French émigrés whose survival depended largely upon charitable London ladies.

From artisan to Bourbon prince, the French were in general received with cautious courtesy; few Englishmen could forget that France not long before had supported the American Revolution. And even though royalist émigrés far outnumbered those of republican principles, England feared any presence on her shores of the radical sentiment that had touched off the conflagration in France.

Parliament nonetheless granted stipends to the émigrés, ranging from one shilling a day to hundreds of pounds a year; yet, barring the royal family and some celebrated personalities like those who gathered around Madame de Staël and Talleyrand at Juniper Hall, virtually all the French were forced to find employment. "Instead of breaking their hearts as Englishmen would do," wrote Joseph Farington, the English diarist, "from counts they turn cobblers or anything for a livelihood." Those with skills used them; those without, developed them. Comtesse de Guéry learned to make ices which brought British royalty, including the prince of Wales, to her cafe.

French émigrés from Toulon (left) land at Southampton in 1794.

227

During the war years, the face of England changed; on open land (above) where gypsies had roamed iron works were built (below).

THE NATION'S POOR

The plight of the urban and rural poor was far from a popular subject in England between 1793 and 1815. The nation's caricaturists—outspoken chroniclers of British politics, royalty, and the war effort in this period—barely touched upon the social ills that were becoming blatantly apparent to those who would see them; for example, although legislation had long before been introduced in Parliament to aid the "climbing boys"—children sent up to repair the chimneys and steeples of London—it was not until 1819 that these abused youngsters were treated as pitiable figures in satirical drawings rather than as spots of traditional local color in prints showing London life.

Certainly England's poor were not entirely neglected during the war years; but many of the early humanitarian gestures were calculated in part to keep the lower class in its place and to prevent uprisings which would hinder conduct of the war, even though they were often prompted by what their authors considered genuinely philanthropic motives. Hannah More, a bluestocking turned evangelical who held that the inequities of society could and should be repaired within the existing framework, left the London drawing-room circle to teach the poor to read; but as historian Steven Watson points out, she was unwilling to teach them to write, for she believed that such a tool in their hands might lead to rebellion, engulfing rich and poor alike in chaos such as had recently been visited on France.

In general what sympathy existed for the ever growing group of unfortunates was extended only where it did not encroach upon the traditional rights of the old order. In 1808 one observer defended the gleaners, whose privilege—gathering what remained in the fields after the harvest—was being curtailed. "In most parts," he apologized, "it must be confessed that the repulsive selfishness of our luxurious and expensive times is now as visible in this as in other cases." He sympathized with the "black, sooty figures" working the ovens of the iron foundries: "Such is the dreadful influence of despair, that we were told a person leapt into one of the largest of the fires." But he applauded what the "Government has done . . . by the game laws: Diversions of hunting and shooting are too agreeable not to have a dangerous influence, in making the lower ranks neglect their serious business and their families." He concluded that gun sports should be "confined to the few, whose serious business and fortune will not be injured by them."

Urban slums, like the one at right, multiplied during the war.

The east façade of Brighton Pavilion (at right) was designed under the careful eye of the prince regent by John Nash, who executed the aquatint shown here. The true focus of royal life, after George III ceased to influence it, shifted from London and the palace of St. James, where gentlefolk still gathered in the drawing-room (below), to Brighton, where the future George IV and his friends played pranks—like leaving a coffin before someone's door and running away—and changed their clothes incessantly. The style of their dress was set largely by the regent's intimate companion George Bryan ("Beau") Brummell, who personified the outlandish dandyism of the age. In building and décor, the regent set the mode, characterized at Brighton by the superimposition of oriental surface detail on a symmetrical, essentially Georgian ground plan. The prince also built Carlton House in London, restored Windsor Castle and added to it the Royal Lodge, rebuilt Buckingham Palace, and gave London Regent's Park. Left, a silhouette of George IV and his younger brother, the duke of York

THE STATE OF THE BRITISH MONARCHY

When King George III learned that the Allies had marched into France in 1814, he asked who commanded the British forces. "Lord Wellington, Sir," was the reply, to which the king is reputed to have said: "That's a damned lie. He was shot two years ago." Pronounced insane in 1810, George III became a relatively popular figure even in his confinement, for his eldest son was fast becoming the most scorned prince ever destined for the English throne.

As prince of Wales, the future George IV first scandalized the royal family and the nation with his reckless and lavish living habits, adding to them his *sub rosa* marriage to the Catholic widow Mrs. Fitzherbert. In 1795 to convince his outraged but still sane father to pay his enormous debts he had agreed to marry a proper princess, Caroline of Brunswick. He produced an heir, the princess Charlotte, and promptly separated from his wife to return to his irresponsible ways, reunited with his aging first love in the pleasure dome they had leisurely designed at Brighton.

For the extravagant style in which he lived, drank, ate, and attached himself to older women—while many in England struggled for a living wage—he was bitterly criticized by the brilliant caricaturists of the day. In 1816 the regent was denounced in Parliament as a man "who in utter disregard of the feelings of an oppressed and insulted nation, proceeded from one wasteful expenditure to another." In 1817 the regent's carriage was mobbed on the way to Parliament. Still, he entertained his friends, serving over a hundred different dishes at one dinner party, and continued to spend hundreds of thousands of pounds on his favorite pastimes—redesigning and rebuilding palaces, parks, and most notably, Brighton Pavilion.

According to the duke of Wellington, George IV feared nothing except ridicule; ironically, during his lifetime the nation accorded him little else. Half-mad the year before he died, he may have sought to comfort himself with deceitful recollections; he told Wellington that his father, the late king, had once said to him: "You are the one [man] on whom I have the greatest dependence, and you are the most perfect gentleman." His appalling behavior, however, was commonly held a partial cause of his father's insanity.

ENGLISH SPORTS IN THE GEORGIAN AGE

Lord Chesterfield was no doubt one of the few men of the Georgian age who would have urged a member of his class to rise above "these rustick, illiberal sports of guns, dogs, and horses, which characterize our English Bumkin Country Gentlemen." Urban or rural, war or no war, the upper class was hunt-crazy; to protect their ancient and exclusive right to the catch of the fields from poachers they set mantraps about the countryside and by 1816 a convicted poacher could · be sentenced to seven years in a penal colony.

All classes were privileged to enjoy the so-called blood sports, which included cockfighting, bull-running, bear-baiting, and any contest between two animals that concluded with one creature's bloody death. These contests, which were immensely popular until well into the nineteenth century, gratified another of the great English passions—gambling. Great sums of money were waged on these brutal matches as on virtually any competition.

By the end of the Georgian era cricket had acquired its status as England's national game. In an 1811 match between two women's teams, the players ranged from "fourteen years to upwards of fifty" and "dressed in loose trowsers, with short fringed petticoats descending to the knees and light flannel waistcoats." Less energetic ladies at this time indulged in a sudden fad for riding asses.

For several centuries horse races had been held in England but when George III ascended the throne the newly established Jockey Club—grand arbiter of proper conduct in the sport—began to exercise its authority; in 1780 the first Derby race was run, and in 1790 the innovation called steeplechasing was introduced. About the same time, savage fighting with bare fists had become so popular a spectacle that, according to a survey by the social historian Christina Hole, officials were afraid to interfere in illegal matches since the crowd might readily riot at the interruption.

Bathing for pleasure was the most significant addition to sporting life at the end of the eighteenth century in England. In the Elizabethan age swimming was deemed so dangerous that Cambridge students could be flogged or expelled for participating in the sport. During the next several centuries, however, people began "to take the waters" for their curative effect and flocked to inland spas like Buxton, Tunbridge Wells, Harrogate, and, the most elegant of all, Bath. When George III began to summer at the seashore town of Weymouth, swimming became a full-fledged sport.

Sea bathing was conducted with something less than abandon; swimmers dressed in bathhouses that were frequently mounted on wheels and harnessed to horses which backed the huts into the water. At Weymouth, according to Miss Hole, the crowds watched King George "bathing to the strains of the National Anthem," while at Brighton the prince regent and his playmates amused themselves by watching lady bathers through their telescopes.

The conduct of the war had little effect on England's pursuit of the sporting life. Contemporary engravings illustrate the three kinds of competitions in which the nation took the greatest delight during the Napoleonic era: at left, a group of spectators watch a horse race; above, a cricket match is in progress; below, a pack of hounds plays excitedly around horsemen before a hunt.

THE ARTS
IN WARTIME

In the insecure world of war and changing values, England was a fickle patroness of the brilliant men who made the beginning of the Romantic era one of the greatest periods in English letters. Byron's first published works were suppressed in 1806. In 1811 the early cantos of *Childe Harold* were widely acclaimed and polite society eagerly sought the poet's company, but by 1816 scandal raged over his separation from Lady Byron, who believed that her husband had consummated an "unnatural" affection for his half-sister. In April of that year Byron left England for good.

Of the many immortalized poets at work during this time, only Wordsworth lived to realize a full measure of fame; in 1843, long after his creative abilities had flagged, he became the country's poet laureate. Shelley, who had been expelled from Oxford for his outspoken atheism, left England in 1811; Keats, whose first sonnet, published in 1816, hailed Leigh Hunt's release from prison (where he had served a term for libel against the regent), was viciously attacked by the literary journals of the day. The young poet died in Italy in 1821. In the visual arts the work of J. M. W. Turner, who taught perspective at the Royal Academy, pleased the contemporary public only until 1815, when the artist began to suffuse his paintings with impressionistically rendered light.

The revolutionary spirit that had flared up across the Channel burned in each of these men, to a greater or lesser degree, and both inspired and reinforced their rebellion against the artistic conventions of the immediate past. Personally free of restraint, they gave themselves to whatever manner of excess their temperaments led them; Coleridge had become so severely addicted to drugs that after 1816 he lived permanently under a doctor's care; William Blake chose to live his mystical ecstasies in relative obscurity in London,

At the left, above, Kean as Richard III; below, Turner's self-portrait

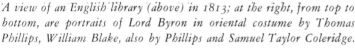

A view of an English library (above) in 1813; at the right, from top to bottom, are portraits of Lord Byron in oriental costume by Thomas Phillips, William Blake, also by Phillips and Samuel Taylor Coleridge.

attended only by his wife and a small group of his faithful friends.

The general interest in art and science steadily rose in England during the war years. Literary and philosophical societies proliferated from 1800 to 1815; circulating and subscription libraries opened in and out of London. Women attended lectures at the Royal Institution, and in rural areas, according to one observer, farmers' daughters, "instead of being taught their duty and the business of a dairy at home, receive their education at a Boarding School, are taught to dance, to speak French and to play upon the harpsichord." The *Encyclopaedia Britannica* was immensely popular. Journals of science came into being which reported the achievements of the day.

In London one of the most absorbing interests during the war was the theatre. When a boy actor named William Betty appeared on the English stage, he was labeled "Young Roscius" after a famous actor who rose from slavery to fame in Cicero's Rome; he so captivated London that William Pitt called for the adjournment of Parliament so its members might see the youngster play Hamlet. In 1803 Lady Bessborough wrote: "Expect no politics or news of any kind for nothing but the boy is talked of." In 1809 riots raged for days in London over an increase in the price of tickets to Covent Garden. Called the O.P. Riots (for old prices), they were taken quite as seriously as the "Bread! No War! No Famine!" uprising that surged around George III's carriage in 1795 and the 1816 outburst against the prince regent, although they offered far easier solution. John Kemble, the actor and manager of Covent Garden, was forced to reinstate the former price. Before the war ended, still another all-engrossing theatrical event occurred; in 1814 Edmund Kean made his historic debut in London as Shylock.

LONDON

A mighty mass of brick and smoke and shipping,
Dirty and dusky but as wide as eye
Could reach, with here and there a sail just skipping
In sight, then lost amidst the forestry
Of masts; a wilderness of steeples peeping
On tiptoe through their sea-coal canopy;
A huge, dun cupola, like foolscap crown
On a fool's head—and that is London Town!

Lord Byron, August, 1823

London from Blackfriars Bridge, 1802

Earth has not anything to show more fair;
Dull would he be of soul who could pass by
A sight so touching in its majesty:
The City now doth like a garment wear
The beauty of the morning; silent, bare,
Ships, towers, domes, theatres and temples lie
Open unto the fields and to the sky,
All bright and glittering in the smokeless air.
William Wordsworth, September, 1802

THE NEW PROSPERITY

Although England acquired her rich overseas empire almost unintentionally during the Napoleonic wars, she watched with care and pride as the means to operate her world-wide commerce developed at home. Despite the enormous sums Britain spent in support of the allied armies and in keeping her navy at sea, the nation was able to finance the construction of the vast London dock complex while the war raged. The city became the world's most active entrepôt of trade, importing raw materials for manufacture in England, exporting finished items and more raw materials to lands beyond Napoleon's blockade. During the same period canal building more than kept pace with the expanding enonomy and provided an efficient method of moving materials and manufactures in and out of the new Midland industrial centers.

Despite critical periods and crises in certain industries, England experienced boom years during the war. For those able to invest in the burgeoning economy it was a period of rewarding excitements. One industrialist was so enthusiastic about the varied uses of iron that he had his coffin made of the metal. A new stock-and-bond-holding class grew up during the war years, and by 1823 Brighton had become a paradise for commuting "stock-jobbers"; the town was "so situated," complained William Cobbett, who deplored the spread of suburbs, "that a coach which leaves it not very early in the morning, reaches London . . . and Change Alley . . . by noon."

British ships remained a common sight at Calcutta (above) during the Napoleonic era. Below, the Bank of England in 1808

[THIRD EDITION]
BOB ROUSEM'S
EPISTLE TO
BONYPART.

THIS comes hoping you are well, as I am at this present; but I say, Bony, what a damn'd Lubber you must be to think of getting *soundings* among us English. I tell ye as how your Anchor will never hold; it isn't made of good Stuff; so luff up, Bony, or you'll be *fast aground* before you know where you are. We don't mind your Palaver and Nonsense; for though 'tis all Wind, it would hardly fill the Stun'sails of an English Man of War. You'll never catch a Breeze to bring ye here as long as you live, depend upon it. I'll give ye a bit of Advice now; do *try* to Lie as near the *Truth* as possible, and don't give us any more of your *Clinchers.* I say, do you remember how Lord Nelson came *round* ye at the Nile? I tell ye what, if you don't take Care what you are about, you'll soon be afloat in a way you won't like; in a high Sea, upon a Grating, my Boy, without a bit of soft Tommy to put into your Lanthorn Jaws. I'll tell you now how we shall fill up the Log-Book, if you come; I'll give ye the Journal, my Boy, with an Allowance for *Lee-way* and *Variation* that you don't expect. Now then, at Five, A. M. Bonypart's Cock-Boats sent out to amuse our ENGLISH MEN OF WAR with *fighting*, (that we like). Six, A. M. Bonypart lands (that is, if he can), then we begin to blow the Grampus; Seven, A. M. Bonypart in a Pucker; Eight, A. M. Bonypart *running away;* Nine, A. M. Bonypart on board; Ten, A. M. Bonypart *sinking;* Eleven, A. M. *Bonypart* in *Davy's Locker;* MERIDIAN, Bonypart in the North Corner of ———, where it burns and freezes at the same time; but, you know, any Port in a Storm, Bony: so there I'll leave ye. Now you know what you have to expect; so you see as how you can't say I didn't tell ye. Come, I'll give ye a Toast: Here's Hard Breezes and Foul Weather to ye, my Boy, in your Passage; Here's may *you be Sea Sick;* We'll soon make ye *Sick of the Sea;* Here's May you never have a Friend here, or a Bottle to give him. And to conclude--- Here's the FRENCH FLAG where it ought to be, under the English.

HIS
BOB ✗ ROUSEM,
MARK.

P. S. You see as I coudn't write, our Captain's Clerk put the Lingo into black and white for me, and says *he'll charge it to you.*

Downes, Printer, Yarmouth.

An English broadsheet, dealing with the threat of French invasion, dares Napoleon to carry out his plan.

THE BRITISH NAVY

Recalling his Egyptian campaign, Napoleon commented upon the difficulties he had encountered quitting Africa after his fleet had been destroyed in the Battle of the Nile: "If it had not been for the English I should have been emperor of the East, but wherever there is water to float a ship, we are sure to find [them] in our way." Throughout the struggle against Napoleonic expansion, England's participation was felt most profoundly upon the seas. The result was two-fold, for the British navy consolidated England's world empire while bottling up the global schemes of her continental enemy.

Aboard the great ships of the line (the windowed stern of one appears above), newly confident naval officers had successfully defended their nation; when war resumed in 1803, Admiral Sir John Jervis declared: "I don't say the French can't come. I say they can't come by sea." Of the crucial period before Trafalgar, the American naval officer and historian Admiral A. T. Mahan wrote: "They were dull, weary, eventless months, those months of watching and waiting . . . before the French arsenals. Purposeless they surely seemed to many, but they saved England. The world has never seen a more impressive demonstration of the influence of sea power upon its history. Those far distant, storm-beaten ships, upon which the Grand Army never looked, stood between Napoleon and the dominion of the world."

In full sail, British ships of the line—vessels with two or three firing decks—break out of line formation to attack the French fleet from both sides in the Battle of the Nile (above).

THE ART
OF WAR
AT SEA

Nelson's sextant is shown at left.

Naval historians refer to Henry VIII as the father of the British navy. He believed England's best defense lay in a fleet which could attack an enemy's sea-borne invasion troops before they reached the island nation; this original conception led to the construction of a new navy and the emergence of sailing ships as instruments of war.

Earlier naval battles had been fought by oar-powered galleys, which were swift and maneuverable but not sturdy enough to withstand heavy duty at sea. Henry based the design of his new warships on the seaworthy, round-hulled sailing vessels that served as cargo boats and troop transports of the day—even though they were clumsy and carried only small firearms. Fortunately, while the fleet was being built, a gun designer named Hans Poppenruyter introduced the king to an invention he claimed could destroy an entire village. Tried and proved on land, the several-ton, cast-metal cannons were installed on the huge

ships' cargo decks—placed behind gunports the king's shipbuilders unwillingly pierced in the vessels' wooden sides. Although the new fleet never got into position to fire its guns in its first encounter with the French off Portsmouth in 1545, a tactical revolution was underway, for the "broadside" now armed the British navy and the embryonic "ship of the line" was at sea.

Formerly, in galley warfare, ships attacked the enemy fleet head-on, in line-abreast formation, ramming the foe with their deadly prows; as the ships engaged, seamen boarded the besieged ship and fought hand to hand. In order to fire their broadside guns, however, the new sail-powered warships formed a follow-the-leader line on a course parallel, if possible, to the enemy, firing from over three hundred yards away. Range and line-ahead formation thus became basic elements of naval tactics; but battles as a consequence were often nothing more than distant, polite exercises, the proper execution of which took precedence over sinking or capturing the enemy.

Eventually, a limited system of maneuvers called the Permanent Fighting Instructions controlled every commander's action; the most sacrosanct order, Number Three, required each ship to "keep in line with the chief" once the battle was on. When Nelson, without orders, wheeled out of the line at the Battle of Cape St. Vincent to engage an escaping Spanish squadron, there were few precedents to protect him against a charge of insubordination—at least one officer had been shot for disregarding instruction signals. But the mystique of the sacred line was finally giving way to a fight-to-the-finish psychology. Nelson accomplished the transition. Admiral Sir John Jervis, replying to an officer's query about Nelson's disobedient action said: "It certainly was so, and if you ever commit such a breach of your orders, I will forgive you also."

The most hated man aboard, the purser (below), rationed out the ship's stores and to fatten his share made "dead men chew tobacco." Midshipmen were often less debonair than the officer shown left; Henry Foularton of the Edgar "drank very hard and died regretting that a keg of gin should see him out."

THE SAILOR'S LOT

The life of England's "jolly tar" bore slight resemblance to the ballads his countrymen sang about him. Rarely written or sung by the seamen themselves, these songs celebrated the sailor's heroism, his fondness for drink, and his sadness in leaving home; but although they sympathized with him for the often brutal manner in which he was conscripted, the verses contained virtually nothing about the torments the crewman suffered at sea.

Shipboard days were long and difficult. Severe flogging might follow the smallest misdemeanor; Admiral Collingwood commented that "officers in certain ships beat the men into a state of insubordination." Naval doctors, many of whom had been failures on land, sometimes performed surgery with carpenters' tools or dumped overboard men critically wounded in battle. Daily rations included pork commonly so rotten the men threw it out the portholes rather than eat it. Their bread was alive with weevils and maggots and both beer and water became undrinkable soon after the ships put to sea. An eighteenth century chronicler, persecuted by naval authorities for his publications, wrote: "Seamen in the King's Ships have made buttons for their Jackets and Trowsers with the Cheese they were served with, having preferred it, by reason of its tough and durable quality, to buttons made of common metal."

One incentive to duty at sea was the prize money distributed when an enemy ship capitulated, but the seamen's share was minuscule compared to the fortunes officers could acquire. Other than their heroic reputation, their ration of rum, and the practice of allowing women on board in port and at sea, the sailors' rewards were few. Navy life meant adventure to the men on the foredeck, but from below came the sentiment: "Those who go to sea for pleasure would go to hell for pastime."

In the drawing above left, women aboard a ship in port carouse with men on the middle deck; the ship's cook, shown above, was frequently celebrated for his lack of skill. Below is a common sailor.

Admiral Sir John Jervis, earl of St. Vincent (above), served as first lord of the Admiralty; the august board's paneled office in London appears in the contemporary print (right).

WAR AND TRADE

A large part of the British fleet was drydocked at Portsmouth in 1789; a visitor there, recording her reaction to the sight, said it was "noble and tremendous . . . a sort of sighing satisfaction to see such numerous stores of war's alarms!" When hostilities broke out between England and France in 1793, the British navy was, in fact, ill-prepared for the conflict to come, and its strength was further taxed by an obligation to the nation's shipping industry; in addition to conducting a war at sea, the Admiralty, supreme administrative body of naval affairs, had to provide protection for England's commerce.

Trade support diluted the efficiency of the British fleet in several ways: merchant seamen, Britain's best sailors, could be exempted from the press; fast-sailing sloops and frigates, "the eyes of the fleet," were sometimes removed from military duty to accompany trading ships in the Channel and to convoy them far out into the ocean beyond the reach of raiders. More critically, an entire fleet action might be held up by the demands of commerce. Admiral Howe was not allowed to take the Channel Fleet to sea in 1794 until the merchant ships under his escort were ready to sail. In detaching a squadron to conduct them a safe distance from the enemy, Howe was left with a fleet too small to deliver a crushing defeat when he finally engaged the French.

MUTINY

One maker of artificial flowers, an optician, and a chimney sweep, as well as farmers, hatters, printers, and peddlers numbered among the crew of the *Victory* in 1805. England had no standing navy and the need for manpower during the long war years of the revolutionary and Napoleonic era grew so desperate that the press gangs—expediters of a traditional royal right to conscript experienced seamen into the navy in time of peril—frequently dragged off any able-bodied man who risked a stroll through town. Even an occasional gentleman, by class exempt, succumbed to the press officer's cudgel.

Impressed service had always amounted to imprisonment, and conditions on board, although unquestionably deplorable, were no worse during this period than in the past; yet with isolated exceptions, the men put up with the inequities of life at sea until 1797, the year of the historic mutinies at Spithead and the Nore.

An indirect cause of the uprisings was the Quota Act of 1795, which called up naval recruits from every town and county across the nation; when necessary, local officials met the demand with inmates of their prisons. These cell sweepings included men of some education, jailed for such crimes as debt or professional malpractice; under their galvanizing leadership, the long suffering seamen expressed their grievances to their superiors. Most rankling was their meager wage, unchanged since the reign of Charles II, and sometimes uncollectable.

Before the Channel Fleet at Spithead sailed in March, 1797, its crews sent a humbly phrased appeal to their commander, the aging Lord Howe, then attending to his gout at Bath. He turned the request for redress over to the Admiralty which, knowing Parliament would not grant the increase, could not afford to acknowledge the justness of the claim. Howe's replacement, Lord Bridport, pleaded the men's case before the naval board when the fleet was once again in port, but he was immediately ordered to put to sea. In open mutiny, the men refused to sail. England was astonished and shattered by the news; her beloved navy had deserted the nation when fear of invasion was at its peak. More astounding, however, was the patriotic discipline of the mutineers, who made it clear they would weigh anchor the moment the French were known to be at sea.

After another outburst, tense negotiations and the personal appearance of Lord Howe round the fleet at Portsmouth finally quelled the Spithead revolts. Although the more dangerous mutiny at the Nore was still to come—led by the unstable Richard Parker, a Quota conscript from debtor's prison—the settlement at Spithead set in motion long overdue naval reforms.

Contemporary prints show the press gang rounding up recruits (left); two naval pensioners at Greenwich (lower left), where the stipend was half the amount that army pensioners at Chelsea received; and a meeting of mutineers at the Nore (below). Some segments of public sentiment held Fox, a pacifist sympathetic to the Revolution, responsible for the mutinies; he is pictured under the table among the men behind the inscription, "Aye . . . we are at the bottom of it"; the black-hatted man at the right represents Richard Parker. Above, Parker confronts Admiral Buckner with a list of the mutineers' grievances.

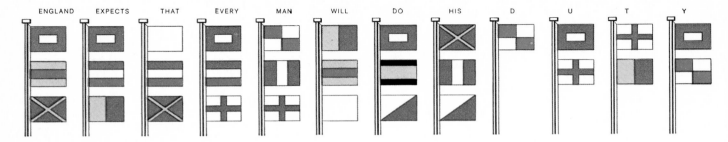

ENGLAND EXPECTS THAT EVERY MAN WILL DO HIS D U T Y

The signaled message above, flown from the Victory's *mast before the battle off Cape Trafalgar began, "was received with three cheers in every ship," according to a witness.*

ADMIRAL NELSON, LORD OF THE FLEET

In an age of heroes, few men were as reverently honored as Admiral Sir Horatio Nelson. England gave him her uncritical devotion, for with the brilliance of his victories he buoyed the spirit of a nation plunged in prolonged war. He fired the men who fought under him with his passionate will to win; a Captain Hall, who served in the Royal Navy in the early years of the nineteenth century, wrote: "It has been well observed that the simple fact of Lord Nelson's joining the fleet off Trafalgar double manned every ship of the line."

Long years of naval service equipped Nelson and the officers who equaled him in dedication—if not daring—for the task of making hardworking sailors out of their heterogeneous and largely unskilled wartime crews. Although British ships of the period were somewhat inferior to their French and Spanish counterparts the willingness of well-trained English seamen overcame this disadvantage.

Nelson began his own training as "captain's servant" on his uncle's ship when he was twelve years old, a common age for English youths to go to sea. Determined to succeed in the service, Nelson mastered a number of problems—not the least of which was his constantly recurring seasickness—and emerged when his country most needed him, a commander in whom judgment and skill combined with an almost obsessive greed for victory. He was unsatisfied, for example, with his triumph in the Battle of the Nile; he afterward said: "Had it pleased God that I had not been wounded stone blind [only temporarily], there cannot be a doubt but that every ship would have

been in our possession." Only two French ships of the line escaped and according to one French naval historian, "the consequences of this battle were incalculable. Our navy never recovered from this terrible blow to its power."

Fearless in combat, Nelson was frequently wounded, and despite the severity of his injuries, he always insisted on waiting his turn with his men for the surgeon's attention. Such actions won him his men's affection as well as their eagerness to serve with him. He had achieved his reputation early in the war; when only the press gang could supply crews to man most of the other ships of the British navy, Nelson's first flagship, the *Agamemnon*, carried scores of volunteers.

Nelson's last signaled message from the *Victory*— "Engage the enemy more closely"—described his concept of naval warfare as well as his notion of personal duty; to win, no risk was too great to take. As he left Portsmouth on his last mission, with a presentiment that he would not return, Nelson knew that in return for his courageous service he had won the devotion of his country. He correctly interpreted the crowd's cheers: "Before I had their huzzas—now I have their hearts." After Trafalgar, Britain was stunned to learn of Lord Nelson's death; her muted response to the great naval victory was more that of a nation in mourning than that of a nation triumphant.

While the Battle of Trafalgar raged, Nelson fell mortally wounded upon the quarterdeck of his flagship, the Victory; *the moment is recorded in a painting (detail right) by Turner.*

The painting above is a composite view of five ships on which Nelson served as captain, commodore, and admiral; from left to rig

*...*mnon, *the* Captain, *the* Vanguard, *the* Elephant, *and the* Victory *appear anchored at Spithead, with their sails rigged loosely to dry.*

THE ROAD
TO TYRANNY

*The present epoch
takes us back
to the age of Charlemagne.*

When Napoleon returned from Spain to Paris early in 1809, only four powers remained at war with him: Great Britain, Portugal, Sicily, and Sweden. The king of Sardinia wisely remained neutral. The Ottoman Empire, though it was neutral with regard to France, was at war with Russia. All the rest of Europe was either under Napoleon's rule or allied to him. The only place where his armies were still fighting was the Iberian Peninsula. It seems strange, on the surface, that one of his reluctant allies—Austria, which he had thrice defeated—should choose this inauspicious moment to prepare for war against him. The reason for this decision was threefold: Napoleon's high-handed treatment of the Spanish Bourbons caused fear in Vienna lest the Hapsburgs' turn come next; the Spanish insurrection had sparked anti-French sentiment in several parts of the Germanies; and the Austrian army, thoroughly reorganized since the disaster at Austerlitz in 1805, seemed capable of delivering a severe blow to Napoleon. Though technically at war with England, Austria had entered into secret negotiations with London and was promised (though only after hostilities had begun) that a large British expeditionary force would be landed in the north to create a second front. In these circumstances, Austria's decision to make war was less foolhardy than it appears in retrospect, and in fact it caused Napoleon a great deal of uneasiness.

The arguments in favor of war that the Austrian ambassador to Paris, Metternich, presented to his government were quite rational, though vitiated by miscalculations. Half of Napoleon's army, Metternich wrote, was tied up in Spain; the mass of Frenchmen were tired of war; the civil and military chiefs, among them Talleyrand and Fouché, would welcome a check to Napoleon's adventurous ambitions. (Some of these arguments may have been supplied to him by Talleyrand himself.)

It was not on the strength of rational arguments that the war party won out, however, but on the crest of an emotional patriotic wave. Humbled three times in twelve years, the Austrians saw in the Spanish uprising a challenge to their national self-respect. The call to all able-bodied men, between the ages of eighteen and twenty-five years and not serving in the regular forces, to enlist in the militia, or *Landwehr,* met with jubilant response. While Emperor Francis hesitated and his brother Archduke Charles counseled caution, Empress Maria Ludovica (Francis' third wife) and Archduke John (a younger brother) led the war cries. Mobilization began in January, 1809. The empress herself presented the *Landwehr* units with their standards; every theatre, coffee house, and public dance hall in Vienna resounded with patriotic song and declamation. On April 12 Archduke Charles began operations by invading Bavaria. Instead of a declaration of war, a ringing proclamation was issued over Charles' name, calling on the entire German people to rise in arms and throw off the French yoke. None of the German states responded to the appeal; only in

Both times he occupied Vienna, Napoleon stayed at Schönbrunn Palace. He used this room as his study, and the adjoining one (in which his son was to die in 1832) as his bedroom.

254

the Tyrol did the peasantry rise to throw out the Bavarians.

It was in the name of the German people that Emperor Francis made war on Napoleon, yet the larger part of the population of his empire was not German but Czech, Polish, Croatian, and Hungarian. His wife was Italian. It was not out of patriotism but out of loyalty to their monarch that his non-German soldiers fought in his cause. On the other hand, a large part of Napoleon's army consisted of German units, and they fought bravely. The German peoples were still far from united; it took Napoleon four more years to unite them against himself.

It is not amiss at this point to survey the German scene as it was at the opening of the campaign of 1809. Leaving out Austria, the Germanies were divided into three parts: the German territories west of the Rhine, including Cologne and Mainz, which were an integral part of the French Empire; the Confederation of the Rhine; and Prussia. The German *départements* of the French Empire had been under French rule since the revolutionary wars and were, on the whole, content with their lot. There was no reason for their inhabitants to regret their former secular and ecclesiastic feudal lords; the populations shared in the prosperity of France and were fully conscious of the rights they had gained through the Revolution and the institution of the Civil Code.

The same was true, if to a lesser extent, of the two member states of the Confederation of the Rhine that were most directly subject to French influence—the Kingdom of Westphalia, under Jerome Bonaparte, and the Grand Duchy of Berg, ruled by Napoleon's brother-in-law Marshal Murat from 1806 to 1808; in 1808 he became king of Naples and was succeeded in Berg by Napoleon's four-year-old nephew Napoleon Louis, prince royal of Holland. Both these states—Westphalia with its capital at Cassel, Berg with its capital at Düsseldorf—had been patched together with former territories of Prussia and other German states, ecclesiastic fiefs, imperial baronies, and petty principalities. Their unification, and the introduction of the Code Napoléon, the abolition of feudal rights and civil inequalities, and the removal of their former petty tyrants, were welcomed by the overwhelming majority of the population. "Your people must enjoy a degree of freedom, equality, and prosperity unknown to the people of the Germanies . . ." Napoleon wrote to Jerome in 1807. "Be a constitutional king."

Despite his extravagant habits, which consumed a large part of his kingdom's revenues, Jerome attempted sincerely (if sporadically) to follow his brother's advice and was ably assisted by his administration. Many of the highest posts were held by Frenchmen, it is true, but their German colleagues, who belonged to the intellectual and aristocratic elite of the kingdom, co-operated with them in a spirit of sincere dedication. The people might make fun of their youthful, pleasure-loving, spendthrift king and his comic-opera uniforms, but they did not really hate the French until Napoleon's heavy hand undid all the accomplishments that he had exhorted his brother to make.

Westphalia was an almost exclusively agricultural state, with very limited financial resources, and Napoleon's exactions in the forms of war contributions, charges for military occupation, requisitions, levies of troops, and even demands for the payment of debts incurred by the country's former rulers, soon brought the government face to face with bankruptcy. In vain did Jerome remonstrate with his brother, who in reply admonished him to lead a more frugal life and threatened him with annexing his kingdom to France. Much the same happened in the Grand Duchy of Berg, where the French commissioner Jacques Claude Beugnot governed in the grand duke's name. Beugnot's administration was exemplary, but its benefits were canceled by Napoleon's increasing exactions of contributions and manpower and by the adverse effect of the Continental System on the Grand Duchy's industries and trade.

It was only during the 1809 campaign, however, that Napoleon's demands began to be intolerable. When the campaign opened, German public opinion throughout the Confederation of the Rhine was either favorable or resigned to French hegemony. The sovereigns of the most important member states of the Confederation—Saxony, Bavaria, Württemberg, Baden, Hesse-Darmstadt, and, of course, Westphalia and Berg—held their titles and territories by the grace of Napoleon, and the population, except for a few exalted intellectuals, was obedient and peaceful to a fault. The public temper was to change considerably during the war of 1809; yet as late as 1811 Napoleon could still write to Marshal Davout: "Judge for yourself if we have anything to fear from a nation as sensible, as reasonable, as dispassionate, as tolerant as the Germans, a nation so far removed from any form of excess that not one of our men has been murdered in Germany during the war." If the statement had been made in 1809, it would still have been largely true; in 1811 it betrayed utter blindness to the explosive forces at work in Germany.

It was in Prussia that German nationalism found most fertile soil. This was due not to any peculiarity in the Prussian mentality but to the fact that no country was treated by Napoleon with such utter disregard for the limits of human patience—even German patience—as was Prussia. Some one hundred thousand French troops had remained in occupation of Prussia at Prussia's expense for a year after the Treaty of Tilsit; they were to be withdrawn upon Prussia's payment of a contribution eventually set by Napoleon at one hundred forty million francs. This amount exceeded by 40 per cent the total yearly revenues of Prussia *before* half of her territories had been taken away by the Treaty of Tilsit. After futile protests, the Prussian government agreed in September, 1808, to pay that sum, and Napoleon pulled his troops out of Prussia, except from the chief fortresses on the Oder, where they were to remain until the money was paid in full. All in all, Napoleon extracted between six hundred million and one billion francs from Prussia. Not only was the country bled white, but the agreement of 1808 contained the further humiliating condition that the size of the Prussian army was not to exceed forty-two thousand men.

Only fifty years earlier Prussia under Frederick the Great had withstood the simultaneous onslaught of France, Russia, and Austria and emerged victorious from the Seven Years War. Never had a nation sunk so low from so high in so short a period. Humiliation on such a scale was unacceptable to national pride, yet for the time being Prussia swallowed her pride and searched her conscience instead. Jena and Auerstädt had demonstrated with shattering clarity that arrogant self-confidence based on past performance is the surest way to disaster. If the French, whom the Prussians had beaten in battle after battle only two generations earlier, had managed to conquer Europe in less than two decades, the reason was that "The French Revolution . . . has brought the French people a wholly new vigor, despite all their turmoil and bloodshed. All their sleeping energies have awakened; their miseries and languors, their obsolete prejudices and infirmities, have been extinguished . . ." These words were written in 1807 by Karl August von Hardenberg, the Prussian foreign minister, in a memorandum to King Frederick William III. A nation that ignored the truth, he continued, was doomed. The objective of Prussia's policies henceforth must be a revolution from above which would accomplish what the French had done by a revolution from below.

The king, whatever his limitations, had for some time been convinced of the need for thorough-going reform and was easily persuaded by Hardenberg. He even consented to appoint as his minister for home affairs, in October, 1807, a man whom but several months earlier he had dismissed as "a refractory, insolent, obstinate, and disobedient official"—Baron vom Stein, who is universally though not quite justifiably acknowledged as the founder of modern Prussia. Stein's rugged features and crabbed character help to explain his appeal to posterity, as does the fact that the principal edicts of reform were carried out during his administration. Equal credit, however, belongs to the king himself, who initiated many of the measures, and to Hardenberg, who completed the work after Stein's dismissal at the end of 1808. The Edict of Emancipation of October, 1807, issued by the king at Memel, was probably the greatest social revolution ever accomplished by a stroke of the pen: serfdom, feudal privileges, restrictions on the sale of land, and all caste distinctions were abolished. No longer was the nobleman obliged to live on lard and potatoes extorted from his peasants; he could take up any trade and sell his land to whomever he pleased, for the distinction between "noble" land and other land had been abolished. No longer was the burgher barred from the privileges formerly reserved to the nobles—he could hold commissions in the army and buy land; nor was any legal distinction left between burghers and peasants. Jews, until then under a special regime, were also given full civic rights.

The Edict was put into execution with remarkable efficiency, over the protests of the great noble landowners. Unlike the Russian and American emancipations of serfs and slaves, it was followed in 1811 by a simple and workable land reform: two-thirds of the land held by peasants as tenants was given to them in full ownership as freeholders; the last third was awarded to the former lords in compensation for the rights and services to which they had been formerly entitled. Though the initiative for this agrarian reform was largely the king's, ultimate credit for it belongs to the French Revolution and to Napoleon, for it is safe to wager that without them the reform would have come only later and not quite so peacefully.

The reorganization and reform of the Prussian army was the work of Generals Scharnhorst and Gneisenau; yet here again Napoleon was the unwitting prime mover.

Austria's general, Archduke Charles

By crushing the Prussian army in 1806, he had demonstrated the need for reform; by limiting its size, he greatly facilitated its reorganization. A great deal of dead wood was eliminated; promotion became a matter of merit rather than birth; recruiting among foreigners was abolished; and quality and efficiency took precedence over numbers and blind discipline. Even the restriction to forty-two thousand men that Napoleon imposed on the Prussian army in 1808 was evaded to some extent—but not nearly as much as Prussian historians have asserted—by the so-called *Krümpersystem:* the army was constituted into cadres, or skeleton units, which were filled at regular periods with recruits; these were discharged after training and placed in the inactive reserve. (The system was imitated with apparently greater success by the German chief of staff, General Hans von Seeckt, after the First World War, when the Treaty of Versailles limited the Reichswehr to one hundred thousand men.)

Apart from the creation of a more efficient cabinet system, no political reforms on a national scale were instituted in Prussia. The king remained king by the grace of God, and all authority emanated from him. No form of parliament was created, and the budget continued to be controlled entirely by the executive, as indeed it continued to be even after the Bismarckian reforms later in the century. The revolution clearly came from above. In France the people by rising against the old regime had asserted their rights and sovereignty; in England the interplay of all the classes—which allowed for a continual mutual adjustment to maintain an equilibrium—resulted in the parliamentary and social reforms of the nineteenth century; in Prussia it was always axiomatic that the people had no rights except those graciously handed them by a wise and all-provident government. Since it so chanced that twice in a century—under Frederick William III and under Bismarck—the government generously granted reforms far exceeding those for which many other nations had to fight, the idea that the government knows best became deeply ingrained in the Prussian people, along with the notion that politics is not a subject for the inexpert. The only respect in which Frederick William III made a gesture toward popular self-government was on the local level, where municipal offices, hitherto appointive, were made elective.

No less important or significant than the social, economic, legal, and military reforms of the Prussian state was the educational reform. Ever since the reign of Frederick William I, Prussia had been ahead of most of Europe in the matter of public education, and if a need for reform was felt in this field, the reasons were more ideological than pedagogical. The impetus for the educational reform came from the philosopher Johann Gottlieb Fichte, who toward the end of 1807 began to deliver a series of public lectures in Berlin entitled *Addresses to the German Nation.* Though they received scant attention at the time, they exerted an incalculable influence on later German nationalist thought.

A disciple of Kant, Fichte had developed an idealistic philosophical system of his own that probably set a new record in unintelligibility and transcendental abstraction. With this, however, Fichte was not content; in his opinion, his philosophy was capable of finding expression in another mode—that of practical life. Prussia's humiliation and Germany's subservience to a foreign conqueror were, he claimed, the result of a moral failure. The German nation, forgetting its past greatness and achievements, had lost its soul. Each group pursued only its particular interests and comforts; all sentiment of national solidarity and mutual sacrifice had been lost; people were not German citizens but obedient subjects of their respective sovereigns. Fichte's indictment was essentially just. The world might come crashing down about the German burgher's ears; protected by his nightcap, he would sleep through the commotion and go about business as usual the next day. When, after Jena, the French army entered Berlin, the civil authorities reminded the population, in proclamations posted throughout the city, that "Calm is the citizen's first duty."

If there was a great deal of truth in what Fichte said, the remedy he proposed was strange. Like almost all German political thought, Fichte's was an eclectic mixture of ideas borrowed from the thinkers of other nations; the only peculiarly German element in it was its attempt to reconcile conditions as they were with conditions as they ought to be by linking them with a metaphysical bridge or—to use a less respectful term—verbiage. From Edmund Burke he borrowed the idea that the nation, the organic chain connecting past, present, and future, was the only enduring thing on earth and, consequently, the living expression of divine immortality. The same, of course, could be said of trees, ants, and rats, but only humans have a conscious memory that can be transmitted from generation to generation, and so their case is different. However, when Burke spoke of the nation as the living fabric that endures through the ages and must not be rent, what he had in mind was a nation such as the English or French, which really had a common tradition and institutions binding its components together.

Germany had nothing of the sort, and so something had to be substituted for it. Thus, the virtues and patriotic deeds of the ancient Germanic tribes were resurrected, or perhaps invented. The Cheruscan chieftain Arminius, who had destroyed the legions of the Roman commander Varus in A.D. 9, suddenly became a national hero. (The circumstance that Varus was caught by surprise, since he was under the impression, until the last minute, that Arminius was on his side, caused no uneasiness to Arminius' modern champions. When, in 1813, Napoleon's Saxon allies changed sides in mid-battle and turned their guns on the French, they could find moral solace in the fact that this was precisely what Arminius had done to save Germany from Emperor Augustus.) After Arminius, there was the German medieval empire, Roman in name, to be sure, but somehow embodying the unifying mission of the German race. French and Spanish guile kept the Germans divided in fratricidal strife; yet while the German princes fought one another and became Frenchified, the people through its centuries-long slumber retained in latent form its distinctive national characteristics, whatever those were.

The means by which these virtues would be reactivated and by which a new patriotic zeal for the common good of the nation would be instilled into the people was, according to Fichte, education. In his advocacy of education for patriotic citizenship he harked back to Rousseau and, more immediately, was influenced by the experiments of Pestalozzi. Also, in making education the chief tool of national regeneration, he conveniently side-stepped political issues and assigned a leading role to the academic class, to which he belonged. By temperament, Fichte undoubtedly inclined toward an idealistic liberalism; his idea that the German people had been singled out as bearers of some unique cultural mission to mankind was naive, perhaps, but not chauvinistic. Yet his novel notion that philosophy must be translated into action, that its role was not to question but to affirm, that skepticism must be replaced by absolute conviction lest the native hue of resolution be sicklied o'er with the pale cast of thought—all this had dangerous echoes in later German political theory. A philosophy that, after passing through the most rarefied realms of abstraction, comes back to earth to teach that people must not think is a dangerous thing when applied to political action.

Hardenberg's conviction that the nation could be regenerated only by bringing it up to date with the more progressive institutions of France and England was far more realistic and less productive of evil.

Fichte's doctrine, borrowed from Pestalozzi, that the purpose of schools was not primarily to impart abstract learning but to form citizens was put into practice to a very limited extent by Wilhelm von Humboldt, who as minister of instruction undertook to reform the Prussian school system along lines that have remained essentially unchanged to the present day and that were imitated in many other countries. Fortunately, the curricula of German schools continued to stress the value of studies for their own sake. It has become a textbook cliché that Fichte's *Addresses to the German Nation* sparked the outburst of German patriotism in the years 1808–14. Such a notion is no less ludicrous than the assertion that outbreaks of juvenile delinquency are caused by thousands of youths poring nightly over the collected works of the marquis de Sade. Very few people attend academic lectures or read philosophy. The mass of the German people took up arms against Napoleon in 1813 not because they had read Fichte, but because they hated the French, because the French had given them ample cause for hating them, and because it seemed safe to do so after Napoleon's Russian disaster. Still, it is probably true that Fichte's patriotic eloquence inspired the intellectual class, which was weary of being intellectual and welcomed the opportunity of submerging itself in the orgiastic joys of collective "belonging."

While Fichte was delivering his *Addresses* in Berlin, a group of Königsberg professors formed a society known as the *Tugendbund,* or League of Virtue, which hoped to regenerate Germany by fostering "morality, religion, serious taste, and public spirit," and whose anti-French ravings Stein qualified as "the rage of dreaming sheep." Another peculiar manifestation of the patriotic upsurge was the gymnastic association founded in Berlin by a school teacher, Friedrich Ludwig Jahn, known as *Turnvater*—a term that can be rendered only approximately as "Father of Calisthenics." *Turnvater* Jahn believed in patriotism through physical fitness and made his lads disport themselves athletically to be ready for the hour of revenge. The idea was unquestionably sound, but Jahn's importance has been overrated by chauvinistic historians. The folklore known as classroom history has attributed a greater role to the Königsberg moralists and the Berlin gymnasts in the overthrow of Napoleon than they deserve; but for the reform of the Prussian army and Napoleon's debacle in Russia they might still be there, practicing virtue and kneebends, without ever having slain a single Frenchman.

The public temper in Prussia on the eve of the Austrian war of 1809 was already patriotic enough for Napoleon to take heed and to demand the dismissal and expulsion of Baron vom Stein. The king had no choice but to comply; Stein fled, found asylum in Austria, and in 1812 became one of Czar Alexander's advisers. In not responding to Austria's appeal, the Prussian government probably acted wisely. Prussian participation in the war would not have affected the outcome as far as Austria was concerned, but it would have meant the complete ruin of Prussia and made it impossible to carry out the social and military reforms to which Prussia eventually owed its return to the status of a great power. In the unlikely event of a French defeat, Austria and not Prussia would have emerged as the leading German power, a possibility that the Prussian government contemplated with dread. Thus, when Austria opened hostilities in April, 1809, she stood completely alone. The troops promised by England landed at Walcheren only several weeks after the Austrians signed an armistice; Sweden was about to make peace; Portugal and Sicily could hardly be counted upon to save the Austrian Empire.

Both Napoleon and Archduke Charles blundered in the first phase of the war; but while Napoleon's marshals, especially Davout, made good for their master's mistakes, Archduke Charles failed to correct his own errors. On May 13, 1809—one month after hostilities had opened—Napoleon entered Vienna. This time, there had been a show of resistance and the city had been bombarded. Among the terrified citizens who took refuge in their cellars was Joseph Haydn, who in the seventy-seven years of his life had often delighted in making his tympani imitate the thunder of cannon. The shock and fright were too much for him, and he died three weeks later, undoubtedly the most illustrious casualty of the War of 1809.

On May 21, after ordering part of his forces to cross the Danube on a single bridge, Napoleon attacked the far superior army of Archduke Charles, which had reformed on the left bank. The Battle of Aspern and Essling raged for two days, with hardly a pause during the night. Both sides fought with desperate determination—the French because their retreat across the Danube was threatened, the Austrians because they saw a chance to annihilate Napoleon's army. Napoleon managed to extricate himself after losing nineteen thousand men in casualties, among them Marshal Lannes; the Austrian army, however, had suffered even heavier casualties—more than twenty-four thousand—and was unable to pursue its advantage. For practical purposes, the battle was a stalemate; Napoleon had been repulsed but not defeated. On the other hand, he had never come so close to being completely routed. To restore his reputation of invincibility, a "thunder clap" like that of Austerlitz was necessary.

Both Napoleon and Charles spent the next six weeks reinforcing their armies. On the night of July 4–5 the French army, which had been regrouped on the island of Lobau in the Danube, once again crossed to the left bank, during a heavy thunderstorm and torrential rain. The Austrian position was centered in the village of Wagram, eleven miles northeast of Vienna. The main attack on that position began shortly after sunrise on July 6 and reached its climax when Napoleon ordered a battery of one hundred guns to concentrate its fire on the Austrian columns. Then, while Davout battered the Austrian left wing and Masséna the Austrian right, Napoleon sent a compact column of thirty thousand infantry and six thousand horse against the enemy center. About two in the afternoon, after a heroic defense that cost the Austrians more than forty thousand casualties, Charles was obliged to order a retreat. French losses were almost as high—about thirty-four thousand

The Tyrolean leader, Andreas Hofer

men. Thus in two battles, within six weeks, well over a hundred thousand men had been killed or wounded. Having set this new record in carnage, the two commanders made an armistice on July 12, and peace negotiations began. There was no reason for Napoleon to feel triumphant: at Aspern he had narrowly escaped disaster at the hands of an army he had thrice beaten before, and Wagram, which concluded his last victorious campaign, had none of the brilliance of Austerlitz.

Perhaps Austria might have won the war of 1809 if she had not been obliged to split her forces. While Archduke Charles fought in Bavaria and in the plains northeast of Vienna, thirty thousand Austrian troops under Archduke Ferdinand advanced into the Grand Duchy of Warsaw. In June they were checked by the Poles under Prince Poniatowski and by the advance of a Russian army—which, however, was in no haste to come to actual grips with the Austrians. Another, somewhat larger army, under Archduke John, had crossed into Italy in April and defeated the inferior French-Italian forces under Viceroy Eugene of Italy. However, the news of Archduke Charles' reverses forced John to retreat east into Carinthia and thence into Hungary, pursued by Eugene. He arrived at Wagram just too late to be of any help to his brother. It is unlikely that his forces, which at that time were thoroughly exhausted and disorganized, could have affected the issue of the battle.

A different kind of warfare was fought in the Tyrol, where the mountaineers had risen in arms against the Bavarians. With the help of a regular Austrian army corps, they took Innsbruck but had to abandon it on May 22 when the Bavarian general Karl Philipp von Wrede advanced against them. One week later twenty thousand Tyrolean peasants took Innsbruck back from the Bavarians, after a furious struggle. The Tyrolean leader, an innkeeper named Andreas Hofer, refused to recognize the armistice signed after the Battle of Wagram and continued the struggle,

taking charge not only of the military command but also of the government of his rugged country. French forces now joined the Bavarians to quell the insurrection, which threatened to make the Alps into another Spain. Hofer ignored the peace treaty signed on October 14 and fought on against desperate odds. Guerrilla warfare lasted into December, with Hofer slipping past the enemy from valley to valley and keeping resistance alive. At last he fell into French hands—through treachery, it seems—and was executed by a firing squad in Mantua on February 21, 1810.

The exploits of two officers, the Prussian Major Friedrich von Schill and the duke of Brunswick, while they stirred the patriotic imagination as much as Andreas Hofer's stand, were as quixotic as they were dashing. Chafing under Prussia's inactivity while Austria was fighting, these men recruited volunteers and created two free corps. Schill's hussars attacked Stralsund and took it on May 28; but the hoped-for English ships did not appear, and a few days later Dutch and Danish troops recaptured the city. Schill was killed in the fighting; several of the captured officers were court-martialed and shot by Napoleon's orders, and the men were sentenced to the galleys. The duke of Brunswick, whose black-uniformed hussars wore picturesque skulls and crossbones on their shakos, was luckier than Schill. He invaded Saxony, managed to occupy Dresden in June, and—to Napoleon's indignation—forced the Westphalian army under Jerome to withdraw. After Austria signed the armistice in July, the duke and his "Black Troop" fought their way across Germany to the North Sea, where British ships rescued them; after a stay in England, they served under Wellington in Spain. Militarily, Schill's and Brunswick's glamorous exploits had only nuisance value; however, they soon passed into folk legend and contributed much to the awakening of the national spirit.

Peace was signed between Austria and France on October 14, at the palace of Schönbrunn. To Bavaria, Austria ceded Salzburg and several other districts; to the Grand Duchy of Warsaw, western Galicia; to Russia, eastern Galicia; to France, parts of Carniola, Carinthia, and Croatia as well as Friuli and Trieste, all of which were incorporated into the Illyrian Provinces of the French Empire. All in all, Emperor Francis lost more than three million subjects. In addition, Austria agreed to reduce her army to one hundred fifty thousand men and to pay a large indemnity in cash— a harsh condition for a country that for years had had to struggle along with an inflated paper currency.

Two days before the Treaty of Schönbrunn was signed, a young German named Friedrich Staps, the son of a clergyman, was caught in an attempt to kill Napoleon with a knife. This, and his near-defeat at Aspern, gave rise to sobering reflections in the emperor's mind. He was almost equally disturbed by the news of Fouché's energetic measures at the time of the English landing in Holland; the minister of police had called up the National Guard in the northeastern *départements* to help stem the invasion, and was acting for all the world as if he were governing France. It was clear that Fouché would make an attempt to take over, and had a good chance of success.

Napoleon had no heir that would be recognized, and it became apparent that if he were killed, the Empire would collapse. The thought of consolidating his power and ensuring the continued existence of his Empire after his death by marrying into a legitimate dynasty and producing an heir had occupied his mind for several years. This, of course, would necessitate his divorce from Josephine, a step from which he shrank, for he was genuinely attached to her. He had adopted her son Eugene early in 1806, yet it was doubtful whether Napoleon's brothers would acknowledge Eugene as his heir. However, the birth of a son to one of his mistresses late in 1806 and the pregnancy of another, Marie Walewska, in 1809 removed Napoleon's doubts as to whether he was capable of paternity. Divorce, marriage with a Russian or Austrian princess, and the production of a male heir now appeared to him a political necessity.

Having finally made up his mind to divorce Josephine, Napoleon proceeded with characteristic firmness. He arrived at the chateau of Fontainebleau from Vienna on October 20, 1809. In the evening Empress Josephine arrived to join her husband and found that the door connecting her room with his had been walled up; thus was the sentence of divorce served on her. The matter was kept secret until the conclusion of the victory celebrations, at which the presence of the empress was required. On December 15 a family council was called to approve the divorce; the next day a *senatus consultum* compliantly pronounced the civil divorce of the couple. The pope's consent was not sought or needed—for reasons that will be seen presently—but the primate of the Gallican Church obligingly approved.

Meanwhile, negotiations with the Austrian court were approaching a happy conclusion. The House of Hapsburg was never short of nubile archduchesses. One of them, Emperor Francis' daughter, Marie Louise—blonde, blue-eyed, sensual and bovine of expression, in her nineteenth year—found the approval of the negotiators and the emperor. She was pretty, came from a fertile family, and was more or less descended from Charlemagne. A bid had also been made for a Russian grand duchess, the czar's sister Anne, but the empress dowager had made difficulties, pronouncing her too young for the marriage bed. Thus Marie Louise was chosen as the sacrificial virgin to placate the ogre. The transaction was promoted by the new Austrian foreign minister, Metternich, who expected that an alliance with France would give Austria time to recuperate from her defeat. A marriage ceremony by proxy was performed in Vienna, where Archduke Charles acted in the place of the enemy who had but recently defeated him. On April Fool's Day, 1810, Napoleon, who had come to meet his bride at St. Cloud, married her in a civil ceremony; the religious wedding took place at the chapel of the Tuileries on April 2. Napoleon did not wait for

Tyrolean guerrillas escort a pair of captured French soldiers.

either ceremony to assert his marital rights, and he pronounced his bride a satisfactory bedmate. Less than three months later the new empress was with child. Meanwhile the former empress, Josephine, had retired to her château at Malmaison, where Napoleon visited her occasionally. Josephine was popular in France; Austrian archduchesses had been unpopular since Marie Antoinette; the divorce and the marriage were much criticized; but in Napoleon's eyes Marie Louise's pregnancy made up for all this.

The reason Napoleon did not seek the pope's consent to his divorce was that on June 11, 1809, he had been excommunicated by Pius VII. The events that led to this dramatic climax may be stated briefly. Pius VII, it may be recalled, had consented only reluctantly to the Concordat of 1801. The publication of the Organic Articles, which made the Gallican Church virtually independent of the Holy See, made the pope realize that he had been tricked. Yet there was nothing he could do without renewing the schism in the French Church and losing his territories to boot. He did, however, refuse in 1805 to annul Jerome Bonaparte's marriage with Elizabeth Patterson of Baltimore. Napoleon insisted that the marriage was void according to the decrees of the Council of Trent, because it had been contracted secretly. Pius replied that the decrees of Trent did not apply in Baltimore, because they had never been published there. Napoleon found the pope's stand peevish and annulled Jerome's mariage by an imperial edict.

At the same time the pope resented the introduction of the Code Napoléon into Italy, since it permitted divorce. He resented even more the occupation in 1805 of his port of Ancona by French troops. Napoleon explained that it

OVERLEAF: *The government built an arch of triumph (visible in the background of the painting) to celebrate Napoleon's marriage to Marie Louise. The emperor and his bride make their state entry into the Tuileries in a gilded carriage with a crown on its roof.*

was in order to protect the pope that he had snatched Ancona from him, and if the pope should be so unreasonable as not to see that point, he would reduce him to a simple bishop. "I am Charlemagne," he wrote in January, 1806, to his uncle, Cardinal Fesch, his ambassador in Rome; and again, a month later: "I am Charlemagne, the sword of the Church and their [the clergy's] emperor." Cardinal Fesch was a somewhat blustering diplomat; he relayed the message, and soon he and Pope Pius ceased to be on speaking terms. Fesch was recalled on the pope's request and replaced by a layman.

Relations, however, continued to grow worse. The pope absolutely refused to obey Napoleon-Charlemagne's preposterous demand that he expel the British minister to the Holy See and close all his ports to British ships. The British minister left of his own accord; the papal ports—Civitavecchia and Ostia—were seized by the troops of Joseph Bonaparte, then king of Naples. Early in 1808, the pope having refused to negotiate on Napoleon's terms, Napoleon ordered the March of Ancona annexed to the French Empire. At the same time, the emperor ordered General S. A. F. Miollis to occupy Rome lest it become a "refuge of brigands." The order was carried out on February 2, 1808: French troops seized the Castel Sant' Angelo and occupied the parts of the Papal States that had not yet been annexed. Two months later the papal army was incorporated into the French and the papal guard was dissolved; several cardinals were expelled; and the pope was obliged to appoint and dismiss several secretaries of state, since none was acceptable to Napoleon.

Finally, on May 17, 1809, at Schönbrunn, Napoleon issued a decree revoking the "donation of Charlemagne, our august predecessor" and thus abolished the pope's temporal power. On June 10 the papal standard was hauled down from the Castel Sant' Angelo, and the tricolor went up. On the following day the text of a papal bull was nailed to the doors of Rome's three main basilicas. Its language was surprising, coming from as mild and liberal a man as Pius VII. The pope, it asserted, was above all temporal rulers; Napoleon was cut off from the Church he had despoiled. To this excommunication, which echoed the language of Pope Boniface VIII to Philip IV of France, Napoleon replied exactly as Philip had done. On July 6 the pope was arrested; he was conveyed first to Grenoble, then to Avignon, and finally to Savona, between Nice and Genoa, where he remained confined. In only one respect did Napoleon's agents show more consideration for the pope than King Philip's had: they did not slap his face.

Napoleon's police did everything in their power to keep the bull of excommunication secret from the world. Nevertheless, thousands of copies of its text were circulated throughout France and Europe. To what extent it turned French public opinion against him it is difficult to say; it certainly produced a considerable effect in the Belgian *départements* and in the Vendée, where Catholicism was particularly strong. The excommunication probably produced less of a shock than the news of the pope's imprisonment. Even anticlericalists could not fail to see that it symbolized the approach of absolute tyranny on a scale Europe had never seen.

A few years later at St. Helena the emperor explained his intentions toward the pope. His objective, he asserted, had been to effect a total separation between Church and state. This separation he had envisioned in a rather peculiar manner. "I was in a position," he said, "to exalt the pope beyond all bounds and to surround him with such pomp and ceremony that he would have ceased to regret the loss of his temporal power. I would have made an idol of him. . . . Paris would have become the capital of Christendom, and I would have become the master of the religious as well as the political world. . . . my Church councils would have been representative of all Christendom, and the popes would have been mere chairmen. I would have opened and closed these assemblies, approved and made public their decisions, as did Constantine and Charlemagne." One's credulity is put to test by such words; yet there is no reason to doubt that he spoke them. What is perhaps even more surprising than Napoleon's boundless arrogance is his blindness to the fact that it was much more than the pope's temporal power that Pius VII regretted having lost, and his notion that making an idol of the pope would have consoled Pius for the total surrender of the Church's spiritual independence.

With the pope his prisoner, the emperor tried to regulate Church matters through an Ecclesiastic Commission, which, however, he dissolved in January, 1810, as it had not proved subservient enough. On February 17, by a *senatus consultum,* Rome was annexed to the French Empire as a free imperial city. The decree guaranteed the pope an annual income of two million francs (less than half of King Jerome's civil list!) and stipulated that all future

The French arrest the pope at his summer palace, the Quirinal.

popes, at their enthronement, must take an oath to respect the four Gallican Articles of 1682, which established the virtual independence of the French Church. Perversely, the Gallican Articles were to apply not only to France proper but to the whole French Empire—all of Belgium, large parts of Germany and Italy, and the Illyrian Provinces.

Pius rejected these monstrous conditions and refused to negotiate as long as he was kept a prisoner. With his valet substituting for his secretary, of whose services he had been deprived, the Supreme Pontiff issued letters to the diocesan chapters forbidding them to accept the bishops nominated by Napoleon. The letters were smuggled out; in reprisal, Napoleon deprived the pope of writing materials and even of his signet ring. The clergy that remained loyal to the pope was treated no less harshly. Thirteen of the cardinals brought to Paris on the emperor's orders refused to attend his religious wedding ceremony but, rendering unto Caesar what was Caesar's, appeared at the wedding reception. They were thrown out, exiled to provincial towns, deprived of their property, and forbidden to wear the robes and emblems of their dignity—whence their nickname, the Black Cardinals. In Italy, hundreds of bishops and priests refused to accept the Gallican Articles and were forcibly removed to Corsica.

Such resistance surprised the emperor as much as it angered him. He summoned a National Council of the Church, which met at Paris in the summer of 1811; the Council declared that it could do nothing unless it had assurance that the pope had agreed to its convocation; the emperor dissolved the Council and had several of its leaders imprisoned at Vincennes. He now tried to browbeat Pius into accepting the decree of February 17, 1810, without reservations. Pius replied by demanding his freedom; Napoleon invited him to resign; Pius refused to resign; and Napoleon reimposed the severe restrictions on the pope's liberty that had been relaxed during the negotiations. It was only after Napoleon's return to France following his failure in Russia that talks were resumed.

Napoleon's clash with the pope, his divorce, and his marriage with Marie Louise were symptomatic of a change in his policies as well as in his personality. Up to the year 1809 he could assert with some plausibility—as he did later, at St. Helena—that he "was always ruled by circumstances." He never had the least idea, he claimed, where he was heading. "I was not so insane as to attempt to bend events to conform to my policies. On the contrary, I bent my policies to accord with the unforeseen shape of events, and this is what often gave me the appearance of fickleness and inconsistency . . . " Even his order to arrest the pope and his second marriage may be explained, to some extent, by motives of political necessity; the pope's territories had to be seized to strengthen the Continental System, and if the pope had not excommunicated Napoleon, Napoleon would not have arrested him; Napoleon's remarriage was necessary to legalize his dynasty and to

On horseback, Napoleon inspects the remodeling of the Louvre.

ensure its survival. Yet while each of these actions may be interpreted as responses to circumstances over which Napoleon had no control, considered as a whole they reveal a different pattern. A definite aim did begin to take shape in Napoleon's mind; undoubtedly he was led to conceiving that aim by the gradual course of events, which appeared to be bringing him closer and closer to its attainment. The aim was nothing less than the unification of the world, or at least of the Old World, under French leadership.

Geographically the Napoleonic Empire of 1809–12 coincided approximately with the West Roman Empire of old and with the later Empire of Charlemagne. Geographically, politically, and economically it may be compared, despite all its Roman and Carolingian trappings, with the Common Market bloc of the mid-twentieth century. The many and profound differences, of course, leap to the eye, not the least among them being the maintenance of tariff barriers between the several states constituting the Napoleonic bloc; and yet the ultimate aim that Napoleon asserted he had in mind came very close to the ideals of the present-day planners for a united Europe. "Except for Turkey," he told Bourrienne as early as about 1802, "Europe is but one province of the world. When we make war, we make civil war." Apparently he said the same to Charles Fox at about the same time.

At St. Helena, in flat contradiction of his denial of ever having had any aims, he outlined his dream of an "association of European states" to his companion-in-exile the comte de Las Cases. It was easy, of course, in retrospect to justify with high-minded aims what in essence was the ruthless opportunism of an inordinately ambitious man; but to deny that he ever had any ideals would be foolish. With all his cynical realism, Napoleon was the product of the eighteenth century and of the humanitarian aspirations that led to the French Revolution. "One of my great conceptions," he told Las Cases, "was the agglomeration, the concentration, of those geographic-national entities that revolutions and politics have dissolved or broken up. Thus there are in Europe—though scattered—more than thirty million Frenchmen, fifteen million Spaniards, fifteen million Italians, thirty million Germans. I should have liked to make out of each of these peoples one single and uniform national body. . . . in this new order of things there was an improved chance of creating everywhere uniform codes, principles, opinions, feelings, outlooks, and interests. Then, perhaps, with the help of the universal spread of education, it would have been permissible to dream of applying the American Constitution to the great European family."

It is difficult to see how Napoleon expected to accomplish this project by annexing large parts of those "geographic-national entities," Germany and Italy, to the French Empire. Improvisation and opportunism marked all his policies, and from the evidence of his deeds little confidence can be gained in the sincerity of his words. Nor did he confide any such projects to anyone while he was in power. Yet from his conduct during the last years of his rule it may be inferred that he had some grand scheme, known only to himself, to whose accomplishment he subordinated all other considerations.

His adversaries maintained that his aim was very simple and obvious—world conquest. This was not entirely true. He had not always gone out of his way to provoke war—his enemies had repeatedly saved him that trouble; but he happened to win every war, and every time he won he took what he could. This process lasted until the war of 1809. After that, with Austria bound to him by a dynastic tie, only two powers stood between him and world hegemony—England and Russia. The universal enforcement of the Continental System became an obsession with him. The System was no longer a method of warfare: the strictness of its enforcement was the measure of his power. In a manner of speaking, the Continental System was the constitution of the "association of European states" that he was dreaming of. In evading the System his brother Louis, Pope Pius, and Czar Alexander did more than give comfort to the enemy; they challenged Napoleon's supremacy and weakened the sole bond that gave his complex of alliances any meaning and cohesion. And so he threatened his own brother with war, imprisoned the Vicar of God, and launched the largest army the world had ever seen against what he called the Russian Colossus.

A combination of favorable circumstances and his genius for exploiting them had made him one of the great conquerors in history. Being a conqueror, he could not conceive that the political union of Europe, or of mankind, could come about by a slow process of evolution and voluntary association. As he told Bourrienne as early as 1805: "I have a few ideas that aren't ripe yet, but they are far-reaching. . . . There must be a superior power that dominates all the other powers, with enough authority to force them to live in harmony with one another—and France is best placed for that purpose."

By 1810 at least some of these ideas had matured, and they came close to madness. "The French Empire shall become the metropolis of all other sovereignties," Madame de Rémusat quoted him as saying. "I want to force every king in Europe to build a large palace for his use in Paris. When an emperor of the French is crowned, these kings shall come to Paris, and they shall adorn that imposing ceremony with their presence and salute it with their homage." It was a part of his "ceaseless dreams," he said at St. Helena, "to make Paris the true capital of Europe. I wanted it to become . . . something fabulous, something colossal and unprecedented, with public establishments commensurate with its population." That the creation of a harmonious association of states was incompatible with the tyranny of one state over all the others is a thought that either did not occur to him or else struck him as being meaningless, since he probably regarded the association as possible only if it was imposed by force.

His scheme for the adornment of Paris remained largely in the planning stage, except for the Louvre, or *Musée Napoléon,* as it was then called. With virtually all the great art treasures of Europe then concentrated there, it not only was the most fabulous collection ever united under one roof but also symbolized the kind of international association Napoleon had in mind. "Paris would have been the capital of the world," he told Las Cases, "and Frenchmen the cynosure of nations." Uniform justice, equality of opportunity, the benefits of peace, trade, and industry—all these things, no doubt, were to be the reward of the nations enjoying the *Pax Napoleonica*; but all the greatness, all the glory, all the splendor, all the power were to be the prerogative of France, embodied in her emperor.

It seemed to him by 1811—when his son the king of Rome was born—that very little stood between his dream and its fulfillment. One more effort, and it would be accomplished. And so he broke his own rule: instead of following events, as he had done in the past, he now wanted to shape them. He began to ignore all warnings and advice, with the colossal self-assurance of a man who had never lost. It did not matter what his ministers, his marshals, his allies thought. "At home as abroad," he told Chaptal, "I reign only through the fear I inspire. If I renounced this system, I would be dethroned before long. That is my position, and these are the motives that guide me." He became increasingly impatient of any objections, any opposition in his councils. An almost constant irritability and ill humor was noticed by all those close to him. Though, for most of the time, he retained a sense of proportion that is rare in men who hold such tremendous power, his sense of reality occasionally seemed impaired.

With this, there was a decided physical deterioration. He became bloated; his marble complexion took on an unhealthy pallor and softness; his capacity for mental concentration weakened at times. Soon he would become subject to prolonged fits of drowsiness, sometimes on critical occasions when all his energy was required. These symptoms have been ascribed by some to the effects of a venereal infection at an advanced stage and by others as a glandular disorder; whatever their cause, they account in part for his often strange and unrealistic behavior during the Russian campaign and the campaigns of 1813–14.

His intolerance of contradiction and independence of judgment manifested itself in the dismissal of Fouché on June 3, 1810. The news struck France like a bombshell. Few men have had as much power as Fouché and used it as sparingly. Through his police and his spies, Fouché held virtually every Frenchman at his mercy; yet it was his policy to win friends in all quarters through his moderation and discretion rather than to make himself feared. Such power concentrated in the hands of a man of independent judgment frightened Napoleon. The man whom he appointed to succeed Fouché, General Savary, duke of Rovigo, retained all Fouché's former powers and in fact was given additional ones, but he was completely subservient to the emperor. "If I ordered Savary to do away with his wife and children," Napoleon once remarked, "I am sure he would not hesitate. . . . He is a man who wants to be continually corrupted."

Under Savary, censorship became tyrannical. State prisons were set up in which political suspects could be detained without trial for as long as a year. (Napoleon later admitted that it was a mistake to call them state prisons; they should have been styled "executive prisons for persons under general surveillance.") Prominent men and women known for their opposition to the regime were notified to take up residence in various provincial towns. (Among them were Madame de Staël and her friends Juliette Récamier and Mathieu de Montmorency.) The persecution of the clergy loyal to the pope has already been noted. Compared to the measures used in modern police states, those used by Napoleon and Savary seem remarkably mild; yet the direction in which they were moving was apparent and filled even many of the emperor's supporters with apprehension.

The masses were terrified by ever-increasing levies of conscripts. A severe crop failure led to famine in the winter of 1811–12, and while the emperor rocked the king of Rome in his imperial cradle, contemplating a new war and dreaming dynastic dreams, long lines of hungry subjects formed at street corners to be doled out ladles full of a nourishing and economical soup invented by Count Rumford. Supposedly, there was peace on the Continent, yet the Grand Army, far from being reduced in strength, continued to grow larger, devouring class after class of recruits, and from Spain the wounded and crippled streamed back to their homes, along with notifications of heroes' deaths on the field of honor. With the masses close to despair, his marshals and generals tired of war, his allies eager to shake off their yoke, and Wellington advancing victoriously in Spain, Napoleon could think of nothing

better to do than to make preparations for a war that hardly anybody except him seemed to want.

He was Charlemagne, he was Constantine the Great, he would be the temporal head of Christendom, and at his capital the kings of the world would pay him humble obeisance. He was not merely Napoleon; he was France—or France was he. He was all these things, and more: "You who know history so well," he asked the comte de Narbonne, his ambassador to Russia in 1812, "are you not struck by the similarities of my government with that of Diocletian—that tight-knit web of government that I am spreading over such distances, those all-seeing eyes of the emperor, that civil authority that I have been obliged to keep all-powerful in the midst of an entirely military empire?" Who were the pygmies that dared put obstacles in his path and obstruct his grandiose schemes?

Napoleon's Russian campaign of 1812 resulted in almost a million casualties. Rarely, if ever, has so murderous a war been fought over such flimsy issues. Napoleon's marriage with Marie Louise, by orienting French policy away from Russia and toward Austria, had given Czar Alexander some alarm. Since the Franco-Russian friendship had cooled almost to the freezing point, and since the continued enforcement of the Continental System would have spelled the ruin of Russian commerce, Alexander at the end of 1810 issued the first of a series of edicts that virtually ended the prohibition of British imports. About the same time Napoleon annexed the northwest coast of Germany, including the Grand Duchy of Oldenburg, thus dispossessing Alexander's brother-in-law. Alexander was as incensed at this insult as he was at the fact that the French Foreign Office did everything it could to prevent Turkey from making peace with Russia. Another point of friction was the Polish policy adopted by Alexander in 1811, when, in order to weaken the French-controlled Grand Duchy of Warsaw, he sent out feelers to the Polish leaders, suggesting the reconstitution of a Kingdom of Poland, with himself its king.

All these issues, however, did not add up to a compelling cause for the two mighty empires to make war on each other. Yet Alexander, who in his mystical moods felt a strong sense of mission, was beginning to spoil for a gigantic duel in which he would crush the Corsican Antichrist. At any rate, he refused to satisfy Napoleon's demands that Russian ports be closed to neutral vessels carrying British goods, and Napoleon refused to withdraw these demands, convinced as he was that if Alexander wanted war, he was bound

Napoleon, before invading Russia

to have it, and that if he did not want war, he would back down at the last minute. "Thus," wrote Napoleon to the king of Württemberg, "war will come despite me, despite him, despite the interests of France and of Russia. I have seen this happen so often that my experience of the past reveals these future events to me." Alas! very true—and yet, how frivolous! Returning to Paris in the summer of 1811, the French ambassador to St. Petersburg, Caulaincourt, was appalled to find how thoroughly the emperor was convinced of the inevitability of war. His attempts to point out the probable disasters that would result were utterly futile. "Once an idea which he considered expedient lodged itself in his head, the emperor became his own dupe," Caulaincourt noted. ". . . When he sought to seduce you he had already seduced himself."

It is true that Napoleon's formidable preparations for war could be justified to some degree by the vast preparations made by Alexander at the same time. But there is no indication that Alexander intended a direct attack on France. With all his sense of mission, he was a cautious and undecided man. His objective probably did not extend beyond the Oder River. He wanted Poland, and he demanded the withdrawal of all French garrisons in Prussia. To accept the demand would have been tantamount to defeat, and Napoleon could not afford a defeat. Besides, he had seduced himself into the belief that from Russia he could march on to India.

On March 5, 1812, Napoleon had a rather remarkable interview with Narbonne—whom he was about to send to Russia as special ambassador—in a last-hour effort to make Alexander yield. "What I fear in Russia," said Narbonne, "is her barbarity and her hugeness. I even fear, for the sake of your glory, a gigantic effort on her part." "I can't understand you, my dear Narbonne," retorted the emperor. "You, ordinarily so confident and cheerful! . . . A single blow delivered at the heart of the Russian Empire, at Moscow the Great, Moscow the Holy, will in a single instant put that whole blind and apathetic mass at my mercy. I know Alexander. I once had influence over him; it will come back. . . . Perhaps he will yield at the sole sight of the unprecedented armaments I am building up. . . . If not, well, let destiny be accomplished and let Russia be crushed under my hatred of England!" He continued in this vein for several minutes longer. Then, with a sudden flash in his eyes, he raised his voice in a trancelike exaltation: "After all, that long road is the road to India. Alexander the Great, to reach the Ganges, started from just as distant a point as Moscow. I have said this to myself ever since Acre."

The total of the forces about to be put in the field against Russia was staggering—over six hundred thousand, including about one hundred thousand cavalry. These, it is true, included Italian, Austrian, Polish, and German contingents. It was not as the emperor of the French but as the war lord of Europe, the leader of a host of nations, the king of kings that Napoleon threw his challenge to Russia.

Leaving Paris on May 9, 1812, he halted at Dresden to await Narbonne's return and to hold court amidst the sovereigns of Europe. The emperor of Austria, the kings of Prussia, Saxony, Bavaria, Württemberg, Westphalia, and Naples; grand dukes, and dukes, and princes; field marshals and marshals of the Empire—all bowed before him and watched with terror and fascination as the stocky little man, pacing amidst the royal throng with a peculiar springy, soft, and pantherlike step, held forth like a bandit chief giving his final instructions before a robbery. Awe, admiration, hatred, and above all fear held them gripped. It is safe to wager that more than half those present, including his own marshals and ministers, wished him dead.

Meanwhile, at Vilna, Narbonne had been conferring with Alexander. Before them a map of Russia was spread out. Alexander pointed at its vastness. He would withdraw to Kamchatka, if necessary, rather than consent to dishonorable peace. "I am not attacking," he concluded, "but I shall not put down my arms as long as a single foreign soldier remains on Russian soil." When Narbonne brought back the remark, Napoleon was unimpressed. It remained to be seen, he replied, whether Alexander's resolution would bear up under the test. Marching orders were issued on May 29. On June 23 half a million men began to cross the Niemen. "Russia is swept along by her fate! Let her destiny be accomplished," Napoleon proclaimed to the Grand Army. ". . . Are we no longer the soldiers of Austerlitz? Russia gives us the choice between dishonor and war. Our choice cannot be in doubt. Let us march forward, then! . . . The second Polish war shall bring glory to the armies of France, as did the first. But the peace we shall make will contain its own guarantee and put an end to that fatal influence which Russia has exerted for fifty years on the affairs of Europe."

Only four years later, on his little rock in the middle of the Atlantic, the emperor was brooding on the subjects of Russia and world conquest. Russia, he observed, was admirably situated. "Seated beneath the North Pole, resting its back against masses of eternal ice," the Russian Empire was safe from invasion three-quarters of the year. On the other hand, nothing would be easier for it than to conquer India and China, and Europe as well. If he were Emperor Alexander, he would "reach Calais according to a fixed timetable." And what would be the good of all these conquests, he asked himself—and instantly he supplied the answer: "To found a new society . . . Europe is waiting and praying for such a good deed. The old order is finished, the new order is not yet firmly established . . ." He then fell silent and, alone with his dreams on his speck of an island in the middle of nowhere, he began to measure distances on a map, with his calipers. He reached the conclusion that "Constantinople was by its situation the seat of universal domination."

World conquerors, it would seem, are incorrigible and unteachable.

THE IMPERIAL FAMILY

In the weeks before Napoleon's coronation his brothers and sisters spent hours squabbling over precedence. Those who were not given princely rank were furious at those who had it, and they all were resentful of Napoleon for favoring Josephine and her children. "One would think," the emperor angrily commented, "that I had deprived them of their rightful inheritance from our father the emperor." Much of the savage quarreling can be traced to the Bonapartes' formidable vanity, but another cause was the fact that Napoleon was heirless, and his life was constantly in peril. If he were to die, there was an empire for anyone with power to seize it. In later years the rivalry diminished, when Napoleon gave his brothers kingdoms of their own and fathered an heir. The child's ornate gilded cradle (above) appeared to betoken a splendid future for the family. The children of Letizia and Carlo Bonaparte ruled in Italy, Holland, Spain, Germany, and, of course, France itself, and for a few years it seemed as though their grandchildren would dominate the continent of Europe for centuries to come.

In 1812, when this view of Malmaison was painted, Josephine was living there in retirement after her divorce from the emperor.

SWEET AND MATCHLESS JOSEPHINE

"Sweet and matchless Josephine," Napoleon wrote to his future wife on the morning after he had become her lover. "How strangely you work upon my heart!" Despite her early infidelities, despite the animosity of his family, despite even her barrenness, which jeopardized the stability of his empire, Napoleon remained infatuated with her. Even before the coronation, and for years after it, the specter of divorce hovered over their marriage, but time after time Bonaparte forgot his resolution to divorce Josephine once he had embraced her. On one occasion, after Napoleon thought he had decided on a divorce, he kept the court waiting for an hour while he held his wife in his arms weeping, "My poor Josephine, I cannot leave you." With tears and lies and smiles, and cunningly timed swoons, she prolonged their marriage for years. Her efforts to control Napoleon were as impermanent as his to control Europe, but while they succeeded, they succeeded splendidly.

It is not difficult to understand why. Most of those who met Josephine agreed in crediting her with a great deal of kindness and charm. Much of her time was employed in spending money on furniture and clothes (she had hundreds of gorgeous dresses in her wardrobe, hundreds of hats, hundreds of expensive cashmere shawls), but she also devoted great efforts to interceding with Napoleon for clemency for those who had drawn his anger. Without her presence the imperial court would have been intolerable, for Napoleon was sadly lacking in the social graces and treated his courtiers like so many conscripts. For the emperor not the least of Josephine's charms was the fact that she was considered Napoleon's good genius and the guarantee of his success by the superstitious in France. (In fact his luck did change after his marriage with Marie Louise.) In spite of his military and amatory wanderings, then, Bonaparte was surprisingly uxorious. Indeed his affection for Josephine extended to her children as well. He adopted Eugene as a son and considered Hortense as his own daughter, and they in turn remained more loyal to him than many members of his own family did.

Isabey's drawing of Josephine (above) was done in 1798, the year of Napoleon's Egyptian campaign. While her husband was in Egypt Josephine openly carried on a love affair at Malmaison with Hippolyte Charles, a young officer who had been discharged from the army by Napoleon. The small marble-topped table shown below is presumed to have been part of the original furniture at Malmaison. Josephine's harp (at left), with the imperial eagle displayed at its top, was made at a later date, after its owner had been crowned empress.

PUPPET
KINGS

A nation arrayed in arms against him gave Napoleon less trouble than his own family did. Even though his brother was emperor, Joseph, the oldest of the Bonapartes, considered himself the head of the family, and the logical heir to France if Napoleon remained childless; he fought any move that seemed to detract from his imagined rights. When Napoleon wanted to adopt his brother Louis' son as heir, both Joseph and Louis opposed him. Louis, in particular, resented having his own son outrank him.

The emperor was disgusted by their pretentions. "My brothers are nothing except through me," he ranted. Giving them kingdoms made them less manageable than ever. Louis had hesitated to become king of Holland. The dampness of that country might imperil his delicate health, but once he went to The Hague, he ruled so conscientiously that he failed to place Napoleon's interests above those of the Dutch. Eventually he lost his throne and went into exile; he devoted himself to his illness and to his literary pursuits, among them writing querulous letters to other kings bemoaning the theft of his kingdom.

Joseph ruled two countries, first Naples and then Spain. His reforms in Naples were just bearing fruit when he succumbed to Napoleon's offer to rule over Spain and the Indies instead. He soon regretted his choice. When he arrived in Madrid and scattered largesse to the crowd, no one touched it; the Spaniards hated the French so much that they left their money lying in the street. Although Joseph tried to return to Naples, it was too late; Caroline Bonaparte's husband, Murat, had already been proclaimed king there. For years Joseph had to continue an unequal struggle against both the Spaniards and his own fears about his hopeless situation. "I blush with shame," he wrote to Napoleon, "in the presence of my so-called subjects."

When Joseph was finally expelled from Spain in 1813, Napoleon's own throne was tottering. The crisis brought about a family reunion of a sort. Joseph, Louis, and Jerome (who had been forced to flee Westphalia) returned to France, but even at this critical time each displayed the family's twin failings, egomania and an astonishing capacity for self-delusion. While Napoleon was battling the Allies in France, his brothers were dickering with him, urging him to insist on the restoration of their thrones as part of the general peace settlement. They failed to realize how fortunate they would be if Napoleon alone retained his throne.

Wicar's portrait of Joseph Bonaparte (opposite) shows the oldest of Napoleon's brothers when he was the ruler of Spain.

Louis Bonaparte (above) bore a close physical resemblance to Napoleon. The dashing king of Naples, Joachim Murat, whose portrait by Gérard is shown below, was more regal in appearance.

LUCIEN
AND
JEROME

Not all of Napoleon's brothers were swayed solely by self-interest. Lucien gave up a crown for love. For a time Jerome seemed to be following a similar course, but eventually he renounced his bourgeois wife to wed the princess Napoleon chose for him. His reward was the newly created kingdom of Westphalia. Jerome was a spendthrift and philanderer, a bad match for any woman, plebeian or patrician.

Lucien, however, was almost as heroic a figure as the emperor himself. As Napoleon challenged the universe, Lucien, single-handedly, took on an adversary almost as formidable—Napoleon. "You should not try to negotiate with the master of the world on equal terms," Elisa Bonaparte wrote to him in an attempt to get him to forswear his wife and reconcile himself to Napoleon. "Nature made us children of the same father, but his achievements have made us his subjects. Mamma and all of us would be so happy to be reunited . . . Dear Lucien, [give up your wife] for us who love you and for the sake of the people my brother will give you to govern . . ." Lucien had been offered a kingdom, the prospect of a royal marriage, and the opportunity to retain his bourgeois wife as a mistress, but he refused any compromise. For much of the time Napoleon was emperor, he remained an exile in Rome, where he purchased the title of prince of Canino. When the French conquered Rome, he fled for America, but the English captured his ship. They sent him to England where he lived the life of a country squire until Napoleon's downfall. There he consoled himself with the composition of an epic poem on the life of Charlemagne, which celebrated that emperor's support of the Church and inferentially condemned Napoleon's policy toward the pope. Napoleon might not have liked the epic, but Lord Byron, who read the manuscript, praised it.

When Napoleon returned from Elba, Lucien came back to France—in honor, for the emperor no longer demanded the surrender of his children's rights of succession to the throne. During the Hundred Days he rallied to Napoleon's cause many who, like him, had been identified with the liberalism of the Revolution. After Waterloo he even offered to join his brother on St. Helena, although he alone of all the Bonapartes had a secure position that he had earned for himself, as a prince in the papal dominions.

Lucien Bonaparte is shown at left. Opposite is Gros' resplendent portrait of young Jerome Bonaparte as Westphalia's king.

THE EMPEROR'S SISTERS

Of Napoleon's three sisters, only one, Caroline Murat, became a queen. Elisa, the oldest, had to content herself with the title of grand duchess of Tuscany. Pauline, the youngest, was merely a princess, but she at least had acquired her title in a normal manner, through her second marriage to the Roman prince Camillo Borghese. The other Bonapartes were eager to rule, but Pauline was satisfied with her title alone. In fact when Napoleon sent her and her husband off to govern Piedmont, she was desperately unhappy there and begged to return to Paris. "I am a French citizen," she angrily wrote to her brother, "and no one has the right to keep me out of my country against my will. . . . This damned climate and the ennui that oozes out of this palace will soon [kill me] . . ." To make her plea more convincing, she swallowed drugs to give herself convulsions until her doctors prevailed on Napoleon to permit her return to Paris. Thereafter she freely indulged in her chief interest, the pursuits of the flesh, which she found so compelling that it often seemed as though she was intent on conquering as many men as her brother did, albeit in a more intimate fashion.

Pauline was, if not ladylike, at least extremely feminine. Elisa, on the other hand, was remarkably mannish; she loved to review troops on horseback, imitating her brother's commanding manner. She tyrannized over her court at Florence and over her nondescript husband, a Corsican gentleman named Felix Bacciocchi. In Paris she had kept a salon for literati, who were attracted to it by neither her intelligence nor her charm, but by her name and influence. She transplanted her patronage of the arts to Florence, and there in the city of the Medici surrounded herself with painters and sculptors. Tuscany, which she governed, was actually controlled from Paris and Elisa had little real power. She consoled herself for that with the severity with which she executed Napoleon's orders.

When Caroline and her husband were sent to northwestern Germany to rule the Grand Duchy of Berg, they found it humiliating to be merely a grand duchess and duke, while other members of the family were monarchs. Eventually they were awarded the Kingdom of Naples instead. They relished the change so much, that when Napoleon's downfall was imminent, they were extremely reluctant to surrender their kingdom and, in the hope of retaining it, joined the coalition against their benefactor.

Caroline Murat (left), queen of Naples, betrayed the emperor in order to retain her kingdom after his fall. Elisa Bonaparte, grand duchess of Tuscany, was even more strong-willed. She is surrounded by a crowd of courtiers and artists (above) who divide their admiration between her portrait and her person.

When she was asked how she could bear to pose in the nude for the statue (below) which Canova made of her, Pauline Bonaparte blandly replied, "There was a fire in the studio." If the story is apocryphal, it nevertheless contains a germ of truth. Pauline was always very scrupulous about her comfort.

THE MARRIAGE
TO MARIE LOUISE

On their way to the chapel in the Louvre for their religious marriage, Napoleon and Marie Louise passed through the Grande Galerie (above), which was hung with art Napoleon had taken. The civil marriage, which is shown in Fontaine's watercolor below, had taken place the day before at the palace of St. Cloud.

"The welfare of France," Eugene de Beauharnais proclaimed to the Council of State in 1809, "demands that the founder of the fourth dynasty should attain old age, surrounded by direct issue as a protection and guarantee for all the French and as a pledge for French glory!" With the reluctant support of Josephine's children, and the triumphant approval of his family, Napoleon divorced his wife to marry into one of Europe's oldest royal houses and give France's fourth dynasty, the Bonapartes, an heir with a legitimate claim to royalty. Some of the French grumbled about the advent of another Austrian archduchess on their throne; they had, after all, decapitated the last one who had come to Paris to wed their king, but many welcomed the marriage as a symbol of the stabilization of Bonaparte's rule and as a promise of peace.

Marie Louise herself was not as enthusiastic. She spent the months before her betrothal praying that the emperor's choice might light on someone else. "I am only sorry for the unfortunate princess whom he will choose," she wrote. ". . . I myself," she added, "shall certainly not become the victim of policy!" But policy was far more potent than Marie Louise's desires, and when her father told her that she was to be empress of the French, the archduchess docilely promised to obey. Napoleon hoped for more than obedience from his bride. "Dare we flatter ourselves that you are not deciding on this step solely from a sense of duty and filial obedience?" he wrote to her once the betrothal had been determined. "If Your Imperial Highness has but a spark of inclination toward us, we shall carefully cherish this sentiment, and shall make it our supreme task to be always and in everything agreeable to you, so that some day we may hope to be happy enough to have won all your love." Napoleon tried to win it with more than words. Before his bride arrived from Vienna, he took waltz lessons in order to make her feel at home and removed from his palace walls any pictures that showed the French defeating the Austrians. His efforts succeeded. Marie Louise was more than twenty years younger than her husband, and her devotion often seemed more like that of a child than that of a wife, but Napoleon was satisfied with her. Until the birth of his son, he neglected a great many of his other concerns and devoted an extraordinary amount of attention to her. After that happy event, his interest in his young bride waned, but it never totally disappeared.

After their religious wedding, Napoleon and his bride appeared on a Tuileries balcony (right) to be cheered by their subjects.

In 1809 Napoleon gathered some puppet monarchs together. From left to right: Murat, Frederick Augustus of Saxony, Jerome, Frederic

of Württemberg, Louis, Napoleon, Josephine, Madame Mère, the queens of Spain, Holland, Naples, and Westphalia, and Pauline Borghese.

After the baptism of the king of Rome, Napoleon kissed the child and held him up for the acclamation of the crowd. In the painting of the scene (above) a sunbeam providentially shines down on the emperor and his heir. Marie Louise is shown (opposite) with her son.

NAPOLEON'S HEIR–THE KING OF ROME

"I envy him," Napoleon said of his newborn son. "Glory awaits him, while I had to run after it! . . . To seize the world, he only will have to stretch out his arms." To celebrate the birth of the child in 1810, wine flowed in the fountains of Paris, and illuminations took place throughout the Empire. The infant was named king of Rome; in that ancient city, from which the pope had been expelled, hundreds of cannons sounded welcome. But despite the celebrations and Napoleon's optimism no glory awaited the child. Indeed, as he himself later remarked, his birth and his death were to be the only significant events of his life.

After Napoleon's abdication Marie Louise returned to her father's protection and brought her son to the imperial court at Vienna. (His toy soldiers could not accompany him; they wore French uniforms. Instead, he got soldiers in Austrian dress.) The boy, called Franz by his Austrian relatives, who could not tolerate the name Napoleon, lived a placid and uneventful life, protected throughout his adolescence from any reading or conversation that might

make him think of returning to rule over his native land.

When the youth was finally permitted to read about his father, he naturally enough began to dream of emulating him. His opportunities to do so were meager. Although he was mentioned as a candidate for the thrones of Belgium, Poland, and Greece, Metternich refused to uncage him; the Bonaparte name was still too dangerous. His French supporters were unable to maintain contact with him. All he could contribute to the Bonapartist cause was the affecting, if passive image of a captive prince languishing in a gilded prison and suffering from that most romantic of maladies, tuberculosis. The prince's death in 1832 made little difference to the Bonapartists, for he had, in effect, been entombed anyway; they merely transferred their affections to the new pretender. But it gave the poets a noble opportunity to reunite Napoleon with his child. "O my son, my dear son," one of them wrote, "come console your father . . . We were too great to be happy on earth; we will have the reward of our virtues in heaven."

Napoleon conquered the singer Grassini and the actress Mlle. Mars (above). Desirée Clary (below) rejected his marriage proposal.

NAPOLEON'S LOVES

Weeping over the sacrifice of her virtue, the young Polish beauty Marie Walewska went to her rendezvous with Napoleon, in 1807, to offer herself to the emperor and plead in return for the re-establishment of Poland's independence. Marie's motives were high-minded, and her reluctance was real, but most of the other ladies whom the emperor conquered were considerably less shy when they visited him, and less disinterested. They were often motivated primarily by vanity, curiosity, or cupidity. These unworthy passions usually failed to disturb the emperor, however, for he himself came to these rendezvous unencumbered by sentimentality.

To him, women were "mere machines to make children," and his extramarital love affairs "pastimes that do not in the least engage my feelings." The emperor commandeered ladies for his bedchamber almost as dispassionately as he requisitioned horses for his army, and almost as often. When he saw one on the stage or at his court who captured his fancy, he delegated to one of his intermediaries the task of procuring her for him, a task which was usually accomplished with a good deal of discretion and success. On campaigns his aides were on the watch for likely candidates to provide him with recreation; at home his sisters often brought one of their ladies in waiting to his attention, in the hope of·weaning his affections away from Josephine. When Napoleon's interest lighted on Madame Récamier, he ordered his police commissioner Fouché to approach her, suggesting that she become a lady in waiting to the empress.

Mlle. George (left) was Napoleon's favorite for several years. The Polish patriot Marie Walewska (right) bore the emperor a son.

But it was apparent from Fouché's conversation ("The emperor has not yet met a woman worthy of him") that her services would actually be required by Napoleon himself. Madame Récamier had never even rendered services such as this to her own husband, and she politely declined the offer, preferring to remain a virgin. Virtue, alas, was not its own reward. She had to suffer the emperor's marked displeasure, which took concrete form when he refused to take steps to avert her husband's bankruptcy. Usually Bonaparte was as generous to his mistresses as kings customarily are. If he failed to lavish affection on them, he at least proffered them something that solaced most of them—money.

Napoleon's diversions were unseemly for a ruler who sought to promote the domestic virtues among his subjects. In general he preferred to keep his adventures quiet. In the early years, however, he was not quite so discreet. While he was in Egypt his mistress regularly drove out in his carriage through the streets of Cairo, in a sort of royal progress that earned her the nickname Cleopatra. Even when Napoleon was First Consul, the public was aware of his love affairs. Shortly after he had succeeded in the rather easy task of seducing the actress Mlle. George, she had occasion to declaim on stage the line: "If I have been able to seduce Cinna, I can seduce many more." The audience turned to Napoleon, who was sitting in his box watching the performance, and applauded him heartily. He was in no way disturbed by their tribute; in fact, he seemed to enjoy it. Mlle. George was a great beauty.

The public may have been kept ignorant of most of Bonaparte's love affairs, but his wife was not. Indeed, he often seemed to take a sadistic pleasure in informing her about them. When Josephine objected angrily to one affair, he had her break it off for him, a task that must have brought her meager satisfaction, for it was obvious that another mistress would soon succeed the one who had been discharged. Several of the women who held the post of reader to the empress were Napoleon's mistresses, and another paramour, Giuseppina Grassini (who had been imported from Milan where she performed at La Scala), was called on to sing at Malmaison regularly. With Marie Louise, the emperor was more considerate. It seems that he remained faithful to her until she left him.

Many of Napoleon's mistresses equaled him in the generosity with which they shared their favors. Grassini tried to seduce Czar Alexander, and after Waterloo was supported by the duke of Wellington. Before she met Napoleon, Mlle. George had been the mistress of Lucien Bonaparte. It was not until his carefully supervised mistress Eleonore Denuelle became pregnant in 1806 that Napoleon knew he was capable of fathering a child. Before then, even if one of his mistresses had become pregnant, there was no assurance that he was the father. Eleonore's son was one of three fathered by Napoleon; he became a gambler and lived on his wife's earnings. Napoleon's second son, borne by Marie Walewska, had a more honorable career, serving as a diplomat under the Second Empire.

THE
COLONIAL
WORLD

Our land armies have been . . . able to win
over all European armies. But as far as the sea
is concerned . . . we and all the other nations
of the Continent must lower our flags.
America, perhaps, someday—I don't say it's impossible. . . .

In several respects, Napoleon's attack on Russia in 1812 was the repetition, on a gigantic scale, of his Syrian campaign of 1799. On neither occasion had he any clear maximum objective. The minimum objective was the same in both campaigns—to forestall an enemy attack. He attained it very incompletely in Syria and not at all in Russia. The maximum aim was indefinite, or perhaps unlimited: for once he had beaten down the gates to the East, what was there to stop him? He would force Russia into an alliance; India would be his, and the Ottoman Empire as well; he would fulfill his old dream of colonizing the African continent from Alexandria to the Cape. England might build a thousand ships, and yet she could not prevent him from conquering continents. The Western Hemisphere was a different matter. Here Napoleon had abandoned all schemes of conquest. Still he would drive Britain from the Americas, too, and he had just made an excellent beginning: on June 18, 1812, four days before his army began to cross the Niemen, the Congress of the United States declared war on England. This, as will be explained later, was perhaps Napoleon's greatest diplomatic triumph. Unfortunately for his purposes, it came too late to be of use to him.

Napoleon's dream of world conquest came to nought in the catastrophic years 1812–14, yet his impact on the world that he failed to conquer was immeasurably great. It was particularly decisive in the Western Hemisphere, but

to some degree it was felt everywhere except in China, Japan, and Australia. To be sure the changes he brought about through the world by disrupting the structure of Europe were for the most part unintended; in fact they were not truly brought about by him but were eased or hastened by his impact. He was the unwitting midwife of the modern world. By 1812 he had accomplished his historic task: nothing more stood between the potentialities he had created and their fulfillment except he himself. Two years later he was driven from the stage.

In surveying the non-European world of the Napoleonic era it is convenient to start with the northern half of the Western Hemisphere. The United States of America would probably not have won its independence—or at any rate not have won it in so short a time—without the financial and military aid of France. The French Revolution, on the other hand, received much of its impetus from the American Revolution. In turn, the salient developments in American history from 1794 to 1815 can be told in terms of Franco-American relations.

The American administration under its first President was frankly hostile to the French Revolution, particularly after the deposition of Louis XVI. The Franco-

The bronze equestrian statue shown at right, which is located in Lima, Peru, represents Simon Bolivar, the revolutionary statesman and soldier who liberated northern South America.

American treaty of alliance of 1778 was still in force, but it was nullified in effect by Jay's treaty of 1794 with Great Britain, which gave English commercial interests equal rights in America with the French. America's disengagement from "entangling alliances" was viewed in France as an unfriendly if not hostile act. The representations made at Philadelphia by the French minister led to the appointment to Paris in 1797 of three negotiators—John Marshall, Charles Pinckney, and Elbridge Gerry—for the purpose of making a last attempt at a peaceful solution. In fact an undeclared war was already in progress on the high seas, where French war ships and privateers were capturing American merchantmen suspected of carrying British goods.

To Talleyrand, who had just become French foreign minister, it seemed that the American position was singularly weak. Though America owned one of the world's largest merchant fleets, she was in every other respect a negligible power, possessing neither an army nor a navy and vulnerable along her ill-defined border to the pressure of France's ally, Spain. Even morally, her position was dubious, since she was trying to renege on a treaty of alliance to which, in French opinion, she owed her existence. In Talleyrand's opinion, the least the American negotiators should do before he began to talk business with them in earnest was to remit the sum of fifty thousand pounds sterling into his hands as a token of good will. (Talleyrand's practice of demanding money as a prerequisite for talks earned him several millions in the course of years; it must be added in fairness to him that he rarely allowed the bribes to influence his decisions.) In this particular instance, he conveyed his demand through three agents—one American and two Swiss bankers, whom the Americans in their reports to Philadelphia designated as Messrs. X, Y, and Z.

Now, Americans in those days still were fairly tight about money (a characteristic Talleyrand should have known about, since he had spent several years in their midst), and throwing away dollars had not yet become an accepted part of national policy. Fifty thousand pounds struck the negotiators as an astronomical sum; they absolutely refused to pay it without instructions from their government. Talleyrand's insistence on the point was the one great blunder in his life. Apprised of the matter, President John Adams seized upon it with a glee barely disguised as indignation; indeed the XYZ Affair, as it came to be known, offered him an ideal opportunity to crush the Francophile Republican party. There was hardly anything the Republicans could say to excuse Talleyrand's sinful conduct, while Adams and the Federalists proclaimed that America's national dignity had been insulted. "Millions for defense, but not one cent for tribute" became the slogan of the day.

No war was declared, but the unedifying XYZ Affair was made public in the American and English press,

General Washington was named commander in chief of the minuscule American army, a Navy Department was created, and the United States navy—at first only a few frigates—was launched. To protect the country from subversive aliens and seditious Americans, Congress passed the Naturalization, Alien, and Sedition Acts of 1798, which made criticism of the government risky and unprofitable. The arming of American merchantmen led to a marked drop in the number of ships captured by the French—336 in 1797, 153 in 1798. Early in 1799 the Directory decided to abandon its vexatious laws on neutral shipping and approached the American government with a view toward negotiating a new agreement. As a result President Adams sent new emissaries to France; when they reached Paris, they found that General Bonaparte had seized power and become First Consul. Both in France and in the United States the climate was favorable to a reconciliation, and a general settlement was reached on September 30, 1800, when the Convention of Mortefontaine was signed. Though hardly a stirring event, the undeclared war thus concluded was of fundamental importance in the history of America: the United States because of this conflict was able to assert itself as a military power and had firmly established its neutrality.

Although it put an end to hostilities, the Convention of Mortefontaine did not revive the Franco-American honeymoon of 1778–83. It had been a one-sided love affair even then, since the majority of Americans shared in the general Anglo-Saxon prejudice against France; only the marquis de Lafayette, for some reason, appealed to the popular imagination. French enthusiasm for America cooled down when, in the late 1790's and the early 1800's, a number of disenchanted French émigrés—among them Talleyrand—returned from the United States to France and spread the news that not everything in the New World was better than in the Old. Americans were grossly materialistic, guided only by the profit motive; they were intolerant and hypocritical; they had no use for the higher things in life such as the arts; the upper class was arrogant, the lower class ignorant and uncouth: all the clichés, true, half-true, or false, concerning the American scene that are still widely accepted in Europe were already current in that early period.

Meanwhile, the excesses of the French Revolution had alienated a large segment of American opinion from France. What Francophile opinion there was derived not so much from friendship for France as from sympathy with the principles of the French Revolution. It was quite natural for the aristocratic Federalists to look toward England and for the democratic Republicans to look toward France, but it should be borne in mind that this split on foreign policy was merely a symptom of the split on internal policy. In their attitudes toward France, John Adams and his successor Thomas Jefferson were the American parallels of William Pitt and Charles Fox in England.

American public opinion on Bonaparte was divided throughout his career. Although no detailed study of the subject has ever been made, one may hazard the guess that he had few enthusiastic admirers, although many followed his progress with passionate interest. Most of those who wished him victorious did so largely because they hated England more than they did France. Both countries were feared, not without cause, and there was a general desire not to be dragged into their quarrels. The principal motive of the American Revolution had been a wish to be left alone; George Washington's warning against binding European alliances in his Farewell Address of 1796 expressed the wishes of the overwhelming majority of the American people and continued to do so until the end of the Second World War. No responsible leaders, whether Federalist or Republican, had the least desire to involve America in war for the sake of either England or France. What happened in Europe was a matter of indifference to the average American, so long as it did not affect him. His newspapers would inform him of terrible battles and momentous events that had taken place weeks or months before, and no matter which side he happened to favor, he found comfort in the knowledge that there was an ocean between him and Europe. Unfortunately, as so many times since then, what happened in Europe was bound to affect him eventually.

On October 1, 1800—the day after the signing of the Franco-American treaty—another treaty was signed, at San Ildefonso, between France and Spain. Under its terms, Louisiana, which France had ceded to Spain in 1763, was to be retroceded to France as soon as a general peace was concluded. The retrocession of Louisiana became effective with the signing of the Peace of Amiens in 1802. The definition of the term Louisiana was somewhat vague. Roughly speaking the territory included, besides the present state of Louisiana, all of Missouri, Kansas, Arkansas, Oklahoma, Nebraska, North and South Dakota, Iowa, and Minnesota, and parts of Montana, Wyoming, and Colorado; conceivably it also included the Floridas, whose status remained hazy until the United States took them by force—plus $5,000,000. Most of this tremendous western territory was a wilderness; the only Europeans who had penetrated it were a few trappers and missionaries. What Napoleon originally intended to do with it is not clear. As early as 1796 the French government had sent a mission to explore the then Spanish Louisiana Territory, possibly with the intention of taking it over in order to prevent a westward expansion of the United States. In acquiring Louisiana from Spain, Napoleon merely carried out a policy set before he had seized the power. To the American government the possibility of his establishing a vast French empire at its western borders was a disturbing thought. "The cession of Louisiana and the Floridas . . . to France works most sorely upon the United States," Jefferson wrote to Livingston, the American min-

ister in Paris; if France were actually to occupy them, "we must marry ourselves to the British fleet and nation." There was additional reason for apprehension in Washington: the First Consul had just dispatched an expeditionary force to the Caribbean.

Napoleon's colonial policy wavered from beginning to end, as indeed did all his foreign policy. His Egyptian campaign was undertaken largely on Talleyrand's initiative, to compensate for the probable loss of the French West Indies. When the Egyptian scheme collapsed in 1801, Napoleon and Talleyrand turned their eyes to America once again. By an agreement signed in 1795 Spain had promised to cede her half of the island of Santo Domingo (the present Dominican Republic) to France at the conclusion of a general peace; in 1800, as has just been seen, she promised the same for the Louisiana Territory; the general peace was in the making. England seemed ready to return the island of Martinique to France. With Santo Domingo, Martinique, Guadeloupe, and New Orleans in French hands, the prospect of French penetration of the uncharted wilderness of the West was not at all unlikely. However, there is no evidence that Napoleon gave more than a fleeting thought to that grandiose scheme; before he could think of occupying the American West he had to gain control over his main base in the Caribbean—Santo Domingo, which was his on paper only. In fact it was ruled by a former slave, the negro general Toussaint L'Ouverture.

The French half of the island of Santo Domingo (that is, the present Republic of Haiti) had been in a state of turmoil and civil war since the fall of the monarchy in 1792. From the struggle among Negroes, mulattoes, and whites, General Toussaint had emerged as the dominant figure. That extraordinary man, gifted with high military and statesmanlike abilities, deeply religious and ascetic, is one of the most baffling figures in the history of the Americas. Tradition has consecrated him as the martyred champion of liberty and of the Negro race; this he may well have been.

On the other hand, it is difficult to determine whether his shifty politics were the result of personal ambition, moderation, or opportunism. He governed his country in the name of the French Republic, yet actually in connivance with American and British interests; he had led the Negroes in support of the French Revolution, yet he opposed the distribution of land to the former slaves, encouraged the French planters to return to their properties, and even exerted pressure on the Negroes to go back to their former occupation as agricultural laborers. He may have done so because he realized that the economy of his country could not be developed without white capital and enterprise; on the other hand, it appears that he was ready to compromise a good deal for the sake of remaining in power. By 1800 he had defeated his main rival, the mulatto general Rigaud, and was in full control of Haiti. When

news reached him of the Treaty of San Ildefonso, he decided to anticipate events and to take possession of the Spanish half of Santo Domingo before French troops had a chance to do so. By February, 1801, after a lightning one-month campaign, he was master of the entire island; in July Toussaint convoked a junta which nominated him governor for life. In the same month he restored the Catholic Church and the Gregorian calendar and all but proclaimed the complete independence of Haiti.

These developments irked the First Consul. In the interests of civilization, he told the Council of State, the "new Algiers" that was forming in the Caribbean must be stamped out. In this decision, as he confessed later at St. Helena, he was influenced by the exiled French planters who spoke through the voice of Josephine. A number of historians have asserted that he could have come to terms with Toussaint without a military expedition and without prejudice to the French colonists; this, however, is by no means certain, and it is difficult to see why Bonaparte should have placed any trust in Toussaint's promises. Moreover, a show of weakness in the Caribbean would have compromised all the recent acquisitions made by France in America through the Treaty of San Ildefonso. Thus despite its unhappy issue Bonaparte's decision to send an army to Santo Domingo was not nearly so foolish as he himself later asserted it to have been.

No sooner had the Army of the Orient returned from Egypt than a new colonial expeditionary force of about thirty thousand men left France to take control of Santo Domingo. It was convenient to send those units whose insubordinate spirit made their presence in France undesirable to the First Consul. Their commander was General Leclerc, Pauline Bonaparte's husband, who was named captain general of the island. Early in February, 1802, the French ships arrived before the ports of Cap Haitien and Port au Prince. The negro commander, Henri Christophe (later king of Haiti), refused to let the fleet enter the ports, set fire to the two cities, and allowed the population to massacre whatever Europeans they could lay their hands on; the French troops landed amidst smoking ruins and mutilated corpses. Despite the Negroes' determined resistance most of the island quickly was brought under French control. Christophe and General Dessalines surrendered; Toussaint himself was tricked into a conference with the French, who arrested him and sent him to France in chains. He died a few months later in the grim fortress of Joux, on the border of Switzerland and France, killed no doubt by the icy climate of the Jura Mountains.

Even before Toussaint's arrest, yellow fever had begun to decimate the French army. Leclerc himself succumbed to the epidemic in November. In all, almost twenty-five thousand men were killed by disease, and only two thousand in action. Seeing that the French were doomed, the Negroes rose once more under General Dessalines. After thirteen nightmarish months of resistance, Leclerc's suc-

cessor, General Rochambeau, surrendered himself and the wretched remains of his army into the hands of the British, who evacuated them to Cuba. The Spanish half of the island, however, resisted the rule of General Dessalines, who took on the somewhat grandiloquent title of emperor; the last French garrison in Santo Domingo surrendered to British ships only as late as 1809, the Spanish residents having turned against the French.

At the beginning of 1803, long before the final collapse of the expedition to Santo Domingo, it became clear to Bonaparte that the resumption of war between France and England was imminent. In the circumstances there was little hope of sending substantial reinforcements to Santo Domingo, and it would have been sheer folly to drive the United States into an alliance with England by asserting French rights to Louisiana. On Easter Monday of 1803 Bonaparte, who could abandon vast projects as easily as he conceived of them, brusquely informed Talleyrand that he had decided to sell the entire territory of Louisiana to the United States. Negotiations began immediately between the American minister, Livingston, and the French plenipotentiary, Barbé-Marbois. Meanwhile, Jefferson had dispatched James Monroe to Paris as a special envoy; Monroe's mission was to secure, as a minimum, freedom of navigation on the Mississippi and the continued right of "deposit"—that is, free-port privileges—at New Orleans. If possible he and Livingston also were to purchase New Orleans and West Florida from France, for which purpose they were authorized to spend the not too generous sum of $10,000,000. When Monroe arrived in Paris in mid-April, he was dazed with astonishment when told by Livingston that a much bigger bargain was in the making—the acquisition of a territory that would double the size of the United States for 80,000,000 francs, or a sum that amounted to somewhat more than $15,000,000.

The idea of "Manifest Destiny" had not yet taken hold of American minds. Essentially the United States still was the eastern seaboard from Maine to the border of Florida; the rest was a wilderness. Its population was only about six million; its trade and industries were oriented toward Europe and the West Indies: to visualize a United States stretching to the Rocky Mountains required a great deal of imagination. Still, Livingston succeeded in persuading Monroe. Only the price remained to be settled. The American negotiators proposed the sum of 60,000,000 francs for the purchase of the Louisiana Territory; the difference between this and the 80,000,000 demanded by the French government would be used to indemnify the American citizens who had claims against France. (The total of their claims was estimated at about 20,000,000 francs.) The treaty was signed on April 30, a little over two weeks after Monroe's arrival in Paris. Rarely was so momentous a transaction agreed upon with such speed. "By this increase in territory," declared Bonaparte, "the power of the United States will be consolidated forever, and I have just given

England a seafaring rival which, sooner or later, will humble her pride."

Bonaparte, who regarded himself as the founder of American greatness, proved a better prophet in this respect at least than did those members of the Senate who voted against ratification of the treaty and denounced it as Jefferson's folly. Yet the apprehension of the New England Federalists was fully as justified as the optimism of Bonaparte and the Jeffersonians. Not only did the Louisiana Purchase bring about the decline of New England influence over American affairs, but it also doomed the European traditions whose disappearance Henry Adams spent his life in regretting. For better or worse, it created the United States that we know.

Whether or not this incalculably fateful turn in the world's history would have taken place even if the First Consul of the French Republic had not had a sudden change of mind on Easter night in 1803, is a question that cannot be answered with full assurance. In all probability the westward expansion would have taken place no matter who owned the Louisiana Territory. If so, Napoleon in doubling the size of the United States merely accepted the inevitable, gave England a powerful rival, and received 60,000,000 francs for selling a territory he had no right to sell under the terms by which he had acquired it *gratis* from Spain. If, however, the Louisiana Territory had remained nominally French, its settlement and acquisition by Americans would have been considerably delayed; with a power such as France backing and arming the Indian nations, the history of the West would have been quite different from what it was. To belittle the importance of Bonaparte's decision in shaping the destiny of America is to ignore the fact that even without any organized resistance the penetration of the West was far from an easy accomplishment.

While it may be idle to speculate on what might have happened if Napoleon had not sold Louisiana, there can be no doubt that the sale had an immediate impact on America. One year after the signing of the treaty, Meriwether Lewis and William Clark started out on the historic expedition across the continent to survey the real estate so recently acquired at four cents per acre. In the south, New Orleans, never a dull city, entered the most flamboyant period of its history. French Creoles, Spanish Creoles; octoroons, quadroons, mulattoes, Negroes; Yankee traders; French royalist émigrés; French and Spanish planters in flight from Santo Domingo, with their white wives, black-and coffee-colored concubines, and innumerable multi-hued offspring; officials, speculators, conspirators—all these went through their evolutions side by side, not exactly harmoniously but in lively if occasionally homicidal dissonance, caused by the clash of disparate traditions that were gradually hammered into a common destiny. A city of a little more than eight thousand inhabitants when it was sold to the United States by the First Consul, New Orleans doubled its population within a few years. Despite the efforts of the

French patriciate, the French language gave way in the early 1820's. Of the old traditions only the less edifying aspects were left; nor did the newcomers represent the most solid traditions of Anglo-Saxon America; and yet this picaresque den of vice was in all likelihood a wholesome corrective to the staid and austere virtues of Boston and Philadelphia.

Napoleon's Berlin Decree of 1806 and the British Orders in Council of January, 1807, placed the United States in a delicate position; indeed, its prosperity, and particularly that of the New England states, depended largely on its shipping. Hoping to avert American involvement in the European war, Jefferson had Congress pass the Embargo Act of 1807, which forbade all American ships to sail outside the territorial waters of the United States. Since both England and France were dependent to a large degree on American shipping for the importation of colonial products, the measure was expected to persuade either or both of the belligerents to reconsider their position at least with regard to American merchantmen.

The French outposts in the Antilles were struck particularly hard by the Embargo Act, since they were cut off from the homeland and depended almost entirely on the United States for their supplies. Contrary to Jefferson's hopes, however, both Napoleon and the British government intensified their mutual blockade, while American shipping interests were faced with ruin. On March 15, 1809, a few days after James Madison took office as President, the Embargo Act was repealed, and on May 20 Congress passed the Non-Intercourse Act, which permitted American ships to trade with all countries save France and England. Napoleon, after hesitating for several months, replied with the Rambouillet Decree of March 23, 1810, which forbade all ships under American flag and carrying merchandise to enter French ports. The next move was up to the United States. On May 1 Congress passed a bill repealing all restrictions on trade with the two belligerent powers, but took the precaution of providing that if either France or England revoked its restrictions on American trade, the Non-Intercourse Act would be revived against the other.

It was at this point that Napoleon began the tricky diplomatic game by which he hoped to embroil America in war with England. In a letter dated August 5, 1810, the French foreign minister, Champagny, wrote on the emperor's behest to the American minister in Paris, General Armstrong, that France would revoke the Berlin and Milan Decrees as far as the United States was concerned on November 1, provided that England revoked the Orders in Council; if England had not revoked the Orders by February 1, 1811, the United States must revive the Non-Intercourse Act against her. General Armstrong and the American government took it for granted that an actual decree to that effect would be issued by Napoleon; if Napoleon issued such a decree, he kept it secret from his own authorities. The English government with considerable justification doubted the existence of the decree and refused to revoke

The star-spangled banner is still there with bombs bursting in air, during the British bombardment of Fort McHenry in 1814.

the Orders in Council. As a result the United States put the Non-Intercourse Act into effect once again.

Napoleon's game would probably have been impossible in an age of more rapid communications. Although he had allegedly revoked the Berlin and Milan Decrees, French privateers continued to seize American ships. In the long run, his duplicity could not have remained concealed from the American government; but since every exchange of communications required several months, he succeeded in intensifying anti-British feeling in America. The announcement of his revocation of the Berlin and Milan Decrees had caused rejoicing in America; England's refusal to follow suit played into the hands of the war faction.

That faction—the War Hawks as it was called—had little if any interest either in Napoleon's struggle with England or in American shipping. Its spokesmen in Congress represented the younger generation whose eyes were fixed on the Western Frontier. They accused England, with justice, of arming the Indian tribes to halt America's western expansion, and their hero was General Harrison, who in November, 1811, defeated Chief Tecumseh in the Battle of Tippecanoe. Only a resolute attitude toward England, in their opinion, would stop the Indians from receiving continued aid from Canada; the more vociferous among the War Hawks were not averse to annexing Canada to the United States. Britain's refusal to revoke the Orders in Council offered a convenient pretext for war, and the War Hawks made the best of it, as did Napoleon.

The British government, on the other hand, was not at all anxious to go to war with America. On April 21, 1812,

it announced that it would revoke the Orders in Council with regard to America, provided it had satisfactory proof that Napoleon had revoked the Berlin and Milan Decrees. Apprised of this, the new American minister in Paris, Joel Barlow, an amiable and unwarlike poet from Connecticut, dashed to the French Foreign Office. To his surprise, the foreign minister calmly handed him a decree dated April 28, 1811—one year earlier—and expressed his astonishment that it had not been received in Washington, where a copy had been sent on May 2, 1811. According to Henry Adams and other American historians, the document had been drawn up only in 1812 and antedated to deceive President Madison; yet there is evidence in the Archives of the French Foreign Office that make this contention extremely dubious. In any case, it seems incredible that the document should have been received in Washington and then been ignored, and the matter remains a mystery. Whatever the truth, the belief that Napoleon tricked America into war by means of a forgery has undoubtedly contributed to the rise of the myth of honest and trusting America being taken in by European wile.

The English government accepted Napoleon's decree of April, 1811, at its face value and on June 16, 1812, at last revoked the Orders in Council. News of this reached Washington only some time after June 18, when Congress, impatient with British obstinacy, had declared war on England. Thus simultaneously Napoleon and the United States began their great onslaughts on the East and on the West. Compared to the Russian campaign of 1812 and its consequences, the American War of 1812 loses some

When a servant turned a crank in the side of Tippoo Sahib's six-foot toy (above), it emitted frantic cries and fierce growls.

of the drama with which it has been so patriotically endowed. The Battle of Lake Erie seems less world-shaking than the Battles of Borodino and Leipzig; the burning of Washington by the British was a sorry display compared to the burning of Moscow; and General Jackson's victory at New Orleans, the most important action fought in the war, was remarkable chiefly because it was fought two weeks after England and America had made peace at Ghent.

Nevertheless, though the War of 1812 was a poor provincial sideshow that could not compete with the great drama enacted in Europe, and although the peace treaty left matters pretty much as they had been before, its impact on the American nation gave it an importance out of all proportion to the issues involved or the battles fought. With it began America's consciousness of being a nation with a destiny, and with that consciousness came the rise of the hero of the war, General Andrew Jackson. It was an unnecessary war; if there had been a trans-Atlantic cable, it could never have been declared. Yet like all the other foreign wars into which America would stumble in the course of her history, it made her greater and stronger. It seems ungrateful for Americans to reproach Napoleon for his trickery, especially since it merely pushed them in a direction in which they wanted to go at any rate, and since it did him no good whatever.

It would be difficult to say whether it was England or the United States that won the War of 1812. In retrospect the whole affair seems a friendly scuffle between brothers who eventually made up their differences and remained on the best of terms. Yet if one examines the map of the world at the conclusion of the Napoleonic wars, one salient fact leaps to the eye; in terms of territorial gains the United States emerged with a major share, having doubled its size and acquired a claim to the Oregon country. As for England

it had been her claim throughout the wars that she sought no gains, territorial or other; she was fighting for the maintenance of a European balance of power, for her own survival, and for the preservation of her commercial and maritime interests. Few Englishmen of 1815 were aware of the fact that in the course of the past two decades, England had absent-mindedly collected the world's greatest colonial empire. In truth the British Empire grew in the same haphazard way as did its metropolis, London.

England's greatest acquisition was, of course, India. At the time of the outbreak of the French Revolution, England's dominant position in the Indian subcontinent seemed beyond challenge, but only a relatively small part of the territory—Bengal, Bombay, Madras, and several lesser establishments—was directly under British control. The Mogul Empire, though nominally in existence until 1858, had been disrupted by invasions, by internal strife, and by the struggle between France and England for supremacy. The local rulers governed independently for all practical purposes, waged continual war against each other in ever-shifting combinations, and were used as pawns by both France and Great Britain.

In British India a governor general appointed by the British Parliament ruled for the benefit of a private corporation, the East India Company, which held a monopoly on trade. Under the energetic administration of Warren Hastings, the chaotic fiscal and judiciary systems were reformed to some extent, and the military power of the Mahrattas in central India was checked. The vagaries of English internal politics led to Warren Hastings' recall, to his impeachment in 1785, and to the passage of Pitt's India Act of 1784, which sought to limit the authority of the East India Company by placing it under the control of the Crown. The Act furthermore forbade British officials to interfere in the affairs of the Indian states for any save defensive purposes. Hastings' successor, Earl Cornwallis, who governed from 1786 to 1793, reduced the corrupt and extortionary practices of the company's officials by increasing their salaries and by the creation of the bases of English legal and fiscal administration in India.

The outbreak of war between Britain and France in 1793 led to a renewal of French attempts to drive out the English from India with the help of native rulers. Pondichéry, the principal possession of France in India, was taken by British troops in 1793, but despite this loss French influence in Indian affairs became greater than it had been ever since Clive's victory at Plassey in 1757. Two of the most powerful independent rulers, the nizam of Hyderabad and Sultan Tippoo of Mysore, allied themselves with revolutionary France. The nizam hoped to retain control of his territories with the help of an armed force commanded by a French general and largely staffed by French officers; Sultan Tippoo—or Tippoo Sahib, as he was generally called—also had at his disposal some French military personnel but he was an aggressive warrior in his own right and by far the greater threat to the English of the two.

Tippoo's father, Hyder Ali, had expelled the Hindu dynasty of Mysore in 1761, usurped its throne, conquered neighboring territories, and made himself into the most powerful ruler in central India. He was defeated by Warren Hastings in 1781 and died in the following year. Tippoo, who succeeded him, swore eternal vengeance against the British. While waiting for the proper occasion to make good his oath, he delighted in watching the performance of a life-sized musical tiger, constructed by a French mechanic, in the act of devouring a British officer to the accompaniment of appropriate groans and snarls.

Although Tippoo pushed despotism to the point of having thirty thousand native Christians forcibly circumcised for the greater glory of Islam, he professed unbounded enthusiasm for the French Revolution, presided over the founding session of the French Jacobin club at his capital, Seringapatam, and applauded as the Frenchmen swore death to all tyrants. Through the intermediary of the French governor of Ile de France (i.e., the island of Mauritius in the Indian Ocean), Tippoo was in somewhat tenuous contact with the Directory in Paris, which expected great things from him in connection with Bonaparte's expedition to Egypt. After conquering Egypt Bonaparte was to communicate with Tippoo and if possible dispatch part of his forces, by land or by sea, to India; there he—or the general whom he would put in charge of the expedition—was to join with Tippoo, the Mahrattas, and the nizam and drive out the English. Nelson's victory at the Nile made the execution of this plan extremely difficult, if not impossible; nevertheless, at the end of 1798 Bonaparte was still trying to get in touch with Tippoo.

At this juncture a new governor-general arrived in Calcutta, replacing the rather inactive Sir John Shore. He was Richard Colley Wellesley, earl of Mornington (later marquess of Wellesley), older brother of Arthur Wellesley, the future duke of Wellington. A man of energy and determination, Wellesley resolved to crush Tippoo without waiting for further developments. Before attacking Tippoo he persuaded the nizam of Hyderabad to abandon the French alliance and to dismiss his French soldiers, who capitulated to the British without firing a shot. Then, in March, 1799, while Bonaparte was campaigning in Syria, Wellesley invaded the Sultanate of Mysore. The British defeated Tippoo's army and stormed Seringapatam on April 4. Tippoo was discovered under a heap of corpses; his states were divided between the East India Company, Hyderabad, and the rightful Hindu dynasty of Mysore.

Having concluded an alliance with the nizam in 1800, Wellesley addressed himself next to the task of reducing the rest of India to a state of vassalage. The Carnatic, Surat, Tanjore, and Oudh accepted settlements which brought them, in one form or another, under British control. The Mahratta confederacy resisted, and one of its leaders, Holkar, invaded Hindustan and laid siege to Delhi, but late in 1804 General Frazer defeated him decisively, thus breaking Mahratta power forever. With only Rajputana, Sind, and Punjab retaining independence, the conquest of India was virtually complete.

Wellesley's reward for this accomplishment was his recall. The East India Company was highly displeased with him: he had fought a costly war; he had made the blasphemous suggestion that free trade with England should be permitted and the company's monopoly abolished; he had installed the Mogul Shah Allam II as nominal emperor in Delhi; above all he had increased the holdings and dependencies of the East India Company to an extent that made the company feel apprehensive. Indeed, the continued administration of a subcontinent by a private corporation of shareholders was an unlikely prospect, and the company would have to surrender its privileges to Parliament. British India may be said to have been the creation of the marquess of Wellesley, but he created it against the wishes of the

Tippoo's sons surrender to the British during the Mysore wars.

An early view of Sydney, Australia, shows its government buildings and convicts' quarters. Some aborigines are in the foreground.

British government and of the East India Company. The company, it is true, was dissolved only in 1858, but its trade monopoly was abolished in 1813.

India was not the only country acquired by England with her left hand while she was fighting France with her right. Providentially for Britain, France concluded alliances with Holland and Spain, thus giving England an excuse for occupying a number of colonies. These seizures were intended as temporary military measures, but when peace was made after Napoleon's downfall, not all of the conquered territories were returned to their former owners. The Dutch colonies of Ceylon and the Cape Colony were not returned; nor was Trinidad restored to Spain, nor Mauritius to France. Malacca, though handed back to Holland in 1818, was retroceded to Great Britain a few years later. Strategic considerations rather than acquisitiveness determined the British government to keep these conquests.

The colonization of Australia was probably of greater importance to Britain in the long run than was the subjection of India. Captain Cook, who anchored off Botany Bay in 1770, claimed the coast for England by right of discovery, although Dutch and possibly also Spanish and Portuguese navigators had sighted the continent long before him. Claiming unknown lands was a mere ritual; for fourteen years the British government showed no interest whatever in Australia. Its sudden interest in 1784 was due to the loss of the American colonies. Contrary to what might be expected, the proponents of schemes for the colonization of

New South Wales had no intention of creating a new America in the South Seas; the American experiment had been a bitter disappointment and there was no wish to repeat it. The earliest plan submitted to the government proposed that New South Wales be settled with American loyalists and Chinese immigrants—a piquant combination. This plan did not commend itself to the government, but it gave the home secretary another idea. The loss of the American colonies meant among other things that there was no more a place to which England could conveniently transport her convicts. English prisons were bulging with evil-doers of both sexes, and Botany Bay seemed an ideal place for transportation. Enabled by an Act of Parliament passed in 1784, the government designated New South Wales as a penal colony; the first shipment of convicts arrived in Botany Bay in 1788. Captain Phillip, the first governor, found the Bay an inconvenient location and moved the colony to the present site of Sydney. There was a shortage of food, supplies, and women but an overabundance of rum, which was used both for solace and as a substitute for currency. Conditions were wild and rough. Admiral Bligh, who took over the governorship in 1806, attempted to restore discipline by the same methods he had used when he commanded H.M.S. *Bounty* and the results were no more successful than they had been then. The so-called Rum Rebellion broke out in 1808, and Major Johnston, the military commander of Sydney, put Governor Bligh under arrest.

Bligh's recall in 1809 and his replacement by Colonel

Macquarie ended the tyrannical rule of the colony by naval commanders. Macquarie's methods, however, were somewhat high-handed too. He particularly resented the free settlers, who had begun to arrive in 1793 and whom he regarded as intruders. While he insisted with some justice that "emancipists"—that is, convicts who had served their time or been pardoned—should enjoy equal rights with the free settlers, he made the bizarre contention that free settlers were subject to the same discipline as convicts and put it on record that he had a right to flog "profligate men," even though free, without a trial.

Such were the beginnings of a Commonwealth which, a century and a half later, was to number almost eight million inhabitants and to enjoy one of the world's most enlightened and democratic systems of social legislation. The basis of Australia's wealth—wool—was laid as early as 1796, when merino sheep were imported from the Cape Colony. The interior of the continent began to be explored in 1817, bringing in its wake the virtual extermination of the aborigines. The development of the country was slow, however, and it was due to the initiative of the settlers and the governors, rather than to any planning in London, that it developed at all. The only effect of the Napoleonic wars on Australia was the British occupation in 1803 of Tasmania on the rather far-fetched ground that the French would otherwise seize that inconsequential island.

It might be supposed that Napoleon should have had a greater impact on Canada, whose population still was predominantly French, or that he should have taken an interest in that former colony of France. As it happened, Napoleon had almost no impact on Canada and took no interest in it whatever. Severed from their French metropolis in 1763, the Canadians readily submitted to their fate. They remained loyal to the British Crown while France assisted the United States in its struggle for independence. Monarchist and intensely Catholic, they were indignant rather than enthusiastic as news of the French Revolution trickled through to them. The British Crown allowed them to retain their language, their laws, their traditions, their religion. The predominantly rural character of Canada, the numbing effect of its sudden severance from the mother country, the absence of intellectual centers such as Boston and Philadelphia, the lack of any tradition of self-government—all these factors combined to create a sense of isolation that may explain the submission, the intellectual lethargy, and the economic stagnation which was characteristic of most of French Canada.

French Canada felt abandoned. Voltaire had called it "a few acres of snow"; Louis XV had ceded it with little regret; Bonaparte did not even trouble to claim it back when negotiating the Peace of Amiens. Not that Canadians seriously believed that Bonaparte could have obtained Canada if he had demanded it—but they would have felt better if at least he had tried. Moreover, the more thoughtful among them were well aware that the only reason why England would not consider giving up Canada was to keep either France or the United States from obtaining it. England, indeed, was not very much interested in Canada. As an anonymous English writer put it: "The possession of this dreary corner of the world is productive of nothing but expense. . . . Nevertheless, it pleases the people of England to keep it, much for the same reason that it pleases a mastiff or bulldog to keep possession of a bare and marrowless bone, towards which he sees the eyes of another dog directed. And a fruitful bone of contention has it proved and will it prove betwixt Great Britain and the United States before Canada is merged into one of the divisions of that Empire." When the United States tried to conquer Canada in the War of 1812, the French population was staunchly aligned with its British defenders: since there was no hope of a reunion with France, British domination was a lesser evil than absorption by the United States, which would have destroyed Canada's national identity. Despite the vast changes that have transformed Canada since then, the dilemma remains largely the same in the mid-twentieth century—not only for French Canada but for all of it.

Napoleon, who could give perspicacious advice to others that he would not take himself, made some acute and prophetic remarks on colonial imperialism while exiled in St. Helena. "The colonial system such as we have known it is finished for everybody," he declared somewhat prematurely but in the long run correctly. "England's mastery of the sea is no longer questioned. Then why, in these new circumstances, should she continue in her old routine, instead of creating a more advantageous political combination? England ought to anticipate a kind of emancipation of her colonies, for she is bound to lose a large number of them in time, and it is up to her to take advantage of the present in order to make sure of securing new ties and more favorable relationships with them." It was some time before Great Britain adopted this view and gave her colonies dominion status. This development too was the result, not of a preconceived policy, but of a gradual and almost unconscious adaptation to changing circumstances.

Nineteenth-century colonial imperialism, whatever its causes, did not originate in Great Britain but rather in Napoleonic France. Its champions tended to put the cart before the horse: there was a widely accepted belief that England owed the prosperity of her trade and shipping to her colonial empire, whereas in fact the colonial empire grew almost as a by-product of her trade and shipping. The Egyptian campaign of 1798 was undertaken to build a colonial empire and failed because of French naval inferiority; for the same reason Napoleon failed in his colonial schemes for the Caribbean and America. In the year he sold Louisiana, his thoughts turned to Africa again: a French force occupied Tamatave in Madagascar; it was expelled by the British seven years later. In 1808 he planned another expedition to Egypt, but Admiral Collingwood's squadron in the Mediterranean made the adventure impossible by sea, and Czar Alexander's lack of co-operation prevented an invasion by land.

From that point on, he abandoned all colonial ambitions, or at least he postponed their realization indefinitely. As will be seen, he made no attempt to control the Spanish colonies. Yet all his ideas concerning the colonization of North Africa, of increasing French influence in the Levant, of building the Suez Canal, of creating a colonial empire in Black Africa were taken up again by his successors. They were not so much his own ideas as they were adaptations of the theories of the French mercantilists of the seventeenth and eighteenth centuries, notably Colbert and Choiseul. Great Britain, and later Germany, merely followed France's lead in the mad scramble for colonies that characterized much of nineteenth-century history. With the wisdom of hindsight, Napoleon remarked at St. Helena that his expedition to Santo Domingo had been a great folly: even if it had succeeded, it would have done no one any good except a few wealthy plantation owners. Now that colonialism seems to be rapidly approaching its end, his remark takes on a new validity.

While parts of the world were being subjected to colonial rule, other parts were emancipating themselves from it. Two great empires were breaking up—the Ottoman Empire and Spanish America. While Ottoman Turkey cannot be regarded as a colonial state in the ordinary sense, it had some of its characteristics. The nationalities that made it up were ruled by a haughty minority whose sole purpose was to extract revenue from them. What the treasure ships from Mexico and Peru were to Spain, the yearly tribute levied from the subject nations was to Constantinople. However great the virtues and energy of the original conquerors, a system of government devised for the sole purpose of exploitation is bound to lead to decay.

The Ottoman Empire at the end of the eighteenth century seemed on the point of falling apart. Its African dependencies—Egypt, Tripoli, Tunis, Algiers—paid only nominal allegiance; the Crimea had been lost to Russia, which obtained the right to interfere in Turkish affairs as protector of the Christian minorities; and many of the pashas who governed their provinces in the sultan's name defied his commands and acted like independent rulers. Ali Pasha of Yannina, once a brigand chief, lorded it over Albania and Epirus; Djezzar Pasha of Acre, the Butcher, a Bosnian adventurer with an unusually gory criminal record, was virtual king in Syria and did not scruple to have the sultan's messengers put to death if their messages displeased him. The sultan himself was at the mercy of his elite corps, the Janissaries. Meanwhile Russia, Austria, and France were preparing to carve up the disintegrating Empire, which in all likelihood was saved only by the circumstance that they could not agree on the distribution of the spoils.

Toward the end of his Italian campaign of 1796–97 and at the beginning of his expedition to Egypt, Bonaparte exchanged some mysterious communications with Ali Pasha of Yannina, who professed to be a great admirer of France. He also addressed messages to the people of Greece suggesting that their liberation was close at hand. What was his purpose is not clear. Conceivably he merely wished to secure the pasha's good will in case either Turkey or Russia should attack the French-held Ionian Islands off the shore of Epirus; conceivably he thought of making the Ionian Islands the nucleus of a Greek state under French protection; conceivably he aimed at detaching the Greek leaders from Russian influence; conceivably he merely wanted to stir up trouble to discourage the sultan from opposing him in Egypt. At any rate, shortly before Turkey declared war on France, Prince Constantine Ypsilanti, then serving in the Turkish court as dragoman, lectured the French *chargé d'affaires* on the frivolity of Bonaparte's interference in Greece. Its only result, warned Ypsilanti—himself a Greek —would be the massacre of several thousand of his countrymen by the Turks. Ali Pasha was no more seduced by Bonaparte's blandishments than were the Greeks, who continued to rely on Russia. When a Russian fleet laid siege to the Ionian Islands, Ali Pasha cooperated with it and drove the French from their outpost on the mainland as well.

Early in 1801 Bonaparte reached an agreement with his new ally, Paul I of Russia, on partitioning the Ottoman Empire. Unhappily for Bonaparte and luckily for the sultan, Paul was strangled a few weeks later. The capitulation of the French in Egypt in the same year allowed the grand vizier to place that province under Turkish control; this he accomplished by the simple device of ordering the massacre of the leading Mameluke beys, whose safety he had guaranteed to the English commander, General Hutchinson. Syria also reverted to effective Turkish rule thanks to the death of Djezzar in 1804. Having made peace with France in 1802, Sultan Selim III, an energetic and enlightened man, sought to profit from his unexpected victory to reform the administration and the army of his Empire. His decrees of 1804–5, which reorganized the French-trained artillery and the regular infantry, threatened the hereditary privileges of the Janissaries, who employed every conceivable means to prevent their being carried out. Brawls and even pitched battles between the Janissaries and the regulars became common occurrences.

The conservatives' resistance to Selim's reforms drew strength from two setbacks which were blamed on Selim's lack of piety. In Arabia the Wahabis, a puritan Moslem sect, had declared a Holy War on the sultan; led by the powerful Saudi tribe, they conquered Mecca and Medina in 1804, and by 1811 they controlled all Arabia. At the other end of the Empire, in Serbia, the Christian population rose in revolt against their oppressors in 1804. It was as spontaneous an uprising as that in Spain four years later. Its leaders were a peasant, Karageorge ("Black George"), and a swineherd, Milosh Obrenovich, both illiterates, and the founders of the rival dynasties whose bloody feuds were to fill the annals of Serbian history. The Serbs defeated the

A battle scene during the Greek wars of independence, from a series of paintings commissioned to illustrate a Greek general's memoirs

pasha of Nish and repulsed the forces sent to suppress their rebellion. In 1806 they took Belgrade, massacred the Turkish population, and established their own government. The supreme authority was vested in the Skupshtina, which resembled a military junta more than a parliament. The suddenness with which the Serbian peasants, downtrodden for centuries, succeeded in winning liberty and in governing themselves was an amazing phenomenon and perhaps just as significant as the Spanish uprising. Unfortunately the Serbs soon became the pawns of powers greater than they.

In the summer of 1806, when these events were taking place in Serbia, Napoleon was at war with Russia. To divert some of the pressure on him, he sent a special ambassador, General Sébastiani, to Constantinople with the mission of embroiling Turkey in war with Russia. This mission Sébastiani accomplished brilliantly, using Russian interference in the provinces of Moldavia and Walachia as a lever. By the Treaty of Kuchuk Kainarji, in 1774, Turkey had yielded to Russia the right to intervene in the two Danubian principalities in the role of protector of the Christian population. The bulk of the population of Moldavia and Walachia was Rumanian, but the ruling class was Greek, and the principalities were governed in the sultan's name by Greek *hospodars*. The *hospodars* sent their yearly tribute to Constantinople, but in every other respect they acted as if they were the czar's agents rather than the sultan's.

General Sébastiani, warning the Turkish government of Russian intrigues in the principalities, urged firm action and promised French support. An alliance was signed, and on August 24 the sultan deposed the *hospodars*. This amounted to a declaration of war, and Russian forces promptly invaded the principalities. In his operations against the Russians, Sultan Selim was hampered by the Janissaries, who fought the regular Turkish infantry more often and with greater success than they fought the enemy. On May 29, 1807, the Janissaries invaded the seraglio, deposed and imprisoned the sultan, and put his cousin Mustafa IV on the throne.

One month later, on June 25, Napoleon and Czar Alexander had their first interview on a raft off Tilsit; the enemy against whom Napoleon had incited the sultan to fight was now Napoleon's friend and partner. News of the sultan's deposition was greeted with relief at Tilsit, since it afforded Napoleon a convenient excuse for abandoning his Turkish ally. Mustafa's reign was short. An army loyal to the deposed sultan took Constantinople in 1808 with the intention of restoring him. They found that Selim had been strangled by Mustafa's eunuchs; they put Mustafa to death and raised Mustafa's brother Mahmud to the throne. Mahmud II, a disciple of his cousin Selim, came a century too late. Strong-willed, capable, ruthless if necessary, he was determined to transform Turkey into

In the Mohammedan ceremony depicted above, Sultan Selim III receives greetings from high Ottoman officials. He attempted to re-

...nize the corrupt administration of his vast Empire but was imprisoned and later strangled by the Janissaries, who resented his reforms.

a modern state, and he might have succeeded if the process of disintegration and the awakening of national consciousness had not gone so far. That he could accomplish anything at all was due to luck: Napoleon's difficulties in Spain and Alexander's designs on Constantinople (which Napoleon refused to grant him) led to the abandonment of their scheme for partitioning the Ottoman Empire in the very year that Mahmud came to power.

The Russo-Turkish war continued without any significant changes in the enemies' military positions, Alexander being too busy taking Finland from Sweden to order a large-scale offensive against Turkey. Moreover, Alexander's alliance with Napoleon was slowly turning into enmity, and he had no desire to antagonize England, his nominal enemy, by weakening the Ottoman Empire too much. He held on to Moldavia and Walachia, and he gave support to Serbia; apart from that he did very little. Nevertheless such was the disorganization of the Turkish armed forces that the Russians could not help advancing. By 1811 they had crossed the Danube into Bulgaria, and they might have taken Constantinople if Napoleon's warlike preparations had not made peace with Turkey advisable. The Treaty of Bucharest, signed on May 28, 1812—three weeks before the Grand Army began operations against Russia—was a severe blow to Napoleon, who had counted on Turkey to divert part of Alexander's forces to the south. The Turks had learned from experience to dread a French alliance, and they were glad to conclude a relatively favorable peace at a time when their military position in the Balkan peninsula had become almost desperate. For the third time in eleven years the Ottoman Empire escaped destruction by sheer luck.

Apart from the cession of Bessarabia to Russia, the Treaty of Bucharest restored the Turkish borders of 1806. The main loser in the war was Serbia, which Alexander coolly abandoned to the Turks. Karageorge fled to Austria. In 1815 his lieutenant, Milosh Obrenovich, led another insurrection against the Turks, and in 1817 he ordered the murder of Karageorge, who had returned from exile. Sultan Mahmud II recognized Milosh as prince of Serbia in the same year and granted the country a measure of self-government. Though she obtained complete independence only in 1878, Serbia thus led in the movement which, in the course of the nineteenth and twentieth centuries, resulted in the creation of numerous independent national states out of the ruins of the once-powerful Ottoman and Austro-Hungarian Empires.

The Greek independence movement, which elicited more enthusiasm in Western Europe than did that of the Serbs, was a part of that process. Like all independence movements in the Balkan peninsula, it sprang from three main sources: the intolerable political and economic oppression exercised by the ruling nationality (in this instance the Turks, in other instances the Hungarians and Austrians); the revival of national traditions harking back to a more glorious and heroic past; and the encouragement given by Russia, whose steady policy it was to whittle down the power of her Turkish and Austrian neighbors. That Russia, the most autocratic state in Europe, was the most consistent supporter of liberty for the peoples of Eastern Europe (except Poland, to be sure) is one of the ironies of power politics. The secret patriotic society *Hetairia Philike,* which sparked the Greek War of Independence in 1821, was founded in Russia, at Odessa, in 1814, and was headed by a Greek émigré who was also a general in the Russian service, Alexander Ypsilanti; another Greek émigré, Capodistria, became Russian foreign minister in 1820. It was with Russian support that Ypsilanti organized the rebellion of Walachia in 1821, which gave the signal for the Greek insurrection; and it was Russian military intervention which led to the recognition of Greece as an autonomous principality in 1829. Complete independence followed three years later. If England and France joined Russia in intervening for the heroic Greeks against the unspeakable Turk, this was not because they were infected with the enthusiasm of Lord Byron and of liberal opinion in general but because they wished to offset Russian influence in Greece, an aim which they accomplished by giving reborn Hellas a ruler of their own choosing, a Bavarian prince who ascended the throne in 1832 as Otto I.

Among the few democratic features of the Ottoman regime was the opportunity, given to every Turkish soldier, to rise to the highest power. In this respect the career of Mohammed Ali, an Albanian of humble birth, resembled that of Napoleon, whom he admired and took for his model. He was even born in the same year as Napoleon. By 1799 he had risen from the ranks to a subaltern command; he was one of the few who escaped destruction when Napoleon drove the Turkish army into the sea at Abukir. In 1805 he was appointed pasha of Cairo; in 1811 he annihilated the last remnants of Mameluke power by inviting the Mamelukes to a feast at the citadel of Cairo, where he had them ambushed and massacred by his regulars.

This gave him a free hand to extend Turkish rule in the Sudan all the way to the Ethiopian border, to drive the Wahabis into the desert, to amass fabulous riches, and to establish himself as the uncontested ruler of an African empire which he ruled from Cairo. Cruel and despotic, he undertook the Westernization of Egypt with a ruthless energy reminiscent of Czar Peter the Great, a task in which he was assisted by foreign advisers, mostly French. He created an Egyptian army—the first since pharaonic times—built the Delta Barrage, introduced the cultivation of cotton (which became Egypt's main export crop), and in 1841 forced the sultan to recognize him as hereditary governor of a virtually independent Egypt. His descendants reigned—after 1866 as khedives, or viceroys, and later as kings—until the deposition of King Ahmed Fuad II in 1953. Unlike the secession of Greece and of Serbia, which were the work of national movements, the secession of Egypt was the work of a single man, whose main motivation was lust for power and money. Nevertheless it was under Mohammed Ali that the people of Egypt, enslaved by foreign rulers since the time of Cambyses, regained its consciousness as a nation. Indirectly the rebirth of Egypt must be credited to Napoleon, because he cleared the path for Mohammed Ali by breaking the power of the Mamelukes, and his grandiose African projects served his disciple as an inspiration.

It is no exaggeration to say that the Ottoman Empire owed its survival for another hundred years to the uprising of the Spanish people in 1808. The same uprising precipitated the disintegration of the Spanish Empire in America. Conditions in the Ottoman Empire were extremely different from those in Spanish America, yet the same urge for self-government and national independence eventually led to the same process of "Balkanization," the same fragmentation into smaller political units, the same prominence of the military class in affairs of government, the same chronic state of unrest and revolution, the same unceasing struggle between democratic aspirations and dictatorial fulfillment.

The history of the secession of Spanish America from Spain is bewildering in its complexity and in its paradoxes. This in itself is a seeming paradox, since Spanish America—which extended at the end of the eighteenth century from Minnesota to Cape Horn—was characterized by a number of features that should have worked for uniformity and cohesion. Its government, at the highest level, was centralized in the person of the king of Spain and in the Council of the Indies in Madrid. Though it was divided into several viceroyalties and captaincies general, headed by men who held almost royal powers, its institutions were controlled in every detail by a jealous and ever-vigilant central authority. The ruling class was uniformly Spanish and Catholic. Even the grievances held against Spain by the secessionists were the same throughout the colonies: all the important posts were held by European-born Spaniards; creoles (American-born Spaniards) were treated as second-class subjects; Spain used the colonies only to exploit them: she drained their natural resources, excluded all non-Spanish ships

A patriot warrior from a regiment of Argentinian gauchos

from their ports, and forbade the development of industries that would compete with Spanish exports (even wine-growing was prohibited); and the Spanish authorities—civil, military, and ecclesiastic alike—were tyrannical, corrupt, and bigoted. Yet the centralization of authority and the uniformity of institutions and grievances were balanced by a number of complicating factors.

One of the main causes of division was simply the immensity of the territory and the formidable geographic obstacles separating its component parts. Communications between Madrid and Buenos Aires, between Madrid and Mexico were easier than between Mexico and Buenos Aires. Distances and natural obstacles, however, do not explain why adjacent countries such as Argentina and Uruguay failed to unite.

Another dividing factor was racial. Apart from the Spanish population, there were almost eight million Indians, part of whom were "civilized"—that is, Catholic and under direct Spanish rule —while those favored by geography retained their independence; there were the mestizos—part Spanish, part Indian; there were the mulattoes—part Spanish, part Negro; there were the sambos —part Negro, part Indian; there were the Negroes, for the most part slaves; and there was an infinite variety of sub-groups. If the distribution of the underprivileged races had been fairly uniform through Spanish America, it might have exerted a unifying effect on their Spanish masters; but their distribution was very uneven, and so was the level of civilization of the various Indian nations. In some parts of the continent, the leaders of the independence movement had to reckon with the mestizos and Indians; in other parts, they could safely ignore them. The diversity of racial composition, and consequently social status, also prevented the merging of the oppressed races into a single revolutionary movement. The social and economic inequalities inherent in the race structure created problems that inevitably divided the revolutionists. To what degree should social and economic reform accompany political changes? This was a question bound to come up as soon as a revolution was successful. There were innumerable other divisive factors: personal rivalries and ambitions, ideological differences among the

José de San Martín was commander of Argentina's rebel army.

leaders, and a tendency toward regionalism equally characteristic of Peninsular and of American Spaniards.

There had been signs of unrest in Spanish America for some time before Napoleon's seizure of Spain gave the signal for a general uprising. In 1780 Tupac Amaru, claiming descent from the Incas and styling himself king of South America, led a widespread rebellion that was cruelly suppressed by the Spaniards. In 1781 a number of towns in New Granada rebelled against the Spanish officials and demanded economic and fiscal reforms; the government promised to grant their demands, broke its promise, and had the leaders of the rebellion executed. The expulsion of the Jesuits during the reign of Charles III had few repercussions in Spain, but in America, where it was carried out with great severity, it had very serious results. The Jesuit missions in America had been outposts of humane liberalism and enlightenment. Deported to Italy, with their missionary work destroyed and their property confiscated, the former Jesuits were among the first to propagandize openly for the complete separation of the Spanish colonies from the motherland. Strangely enough their arguments were identical with those advanced by the educated creole elite, which was inspired by the writings of the French *philosophes* and by the examples of the American and the French Revolutions. Spanish rule in America, wrote an exiled Jesuit Father in 1790,

could be epitomized in four words—"ingratitude, injustice, slavery, and desolation." "Spain," he continued, "has attempted to persuade the common people that it is a crime to reason upon matters of the greatest importance to every individual . . . Our distance from Spain . . . is less significant than the difference in interests. We imperatively need a government in our midst for the distribution of benefits, the object of the social union." To hear a Spanish Jesuit speak the language of Thomas Jefferson is, perhaps, surprising; it is not surprising that the priest's pamphlet, written in 1790, was first published in Philadelphia in 1799.

Francisco de Miranda, born in Caracas in 1750 and regarded by some as the father of the Spanish American Revolution, held essentially the same views as the Jesuit Father quoted above. However, although he was a disciple of the French Enlightenment, he was a born conspirator rather than an intellectual or a statesman. A soldier of fortune, he had fought with the Spanish during the American Revolution and taken part in the attack on Pensacola. He later fought under Dumouriez in the French army, was imprisoned as a suspect during the Reign of Terror, and, having failed to obtain French support for his revolutionary schemes in America, slipped across the Channel in 1798. In London he posed as the agent of the Spanish American colonies and bombarded both the British and the American government with schemes that would liberate his homeland and at the same time strike a hard blow against Spain, then France's ally. In 1806 he sailed with a handful of adventurers from New York to Venezuela, expecting to rouse his countrymen to a general uprising. The fact that his force landed with British naval support roused the Venezuelans' suspicions; they did not co-operate, and Miranda's expedition ended in fiasco. He returned to England, which in the meantime had sent a force under Admiral Popham to seize South Africa. On his own initiative, it would seem, but inspired no doubt by Miranda's optimistic projects, Popham proceeded from the Cape to South America, where he briefly occupied Buenos Aires but was eventually expelled. Apparently, no matter how desperately the Spanish Americans wanted to be liberated, they did not want to be liberated by the English. Miranda, however, thought otherwise. Representing himself as the authorized spokesman of a vast Spanish American revolutionary organization (which it seems existed in his mind only), he succeeded in persuading Sir Arthur Wellesley that an army of ten thousand men if landed on the Venezuelan coast would sweep all Spanish America in an uprising. Wellesley in turn persuaded the British cabinet; an army was being got ready in Ireland; Wellesley was given its command.

Just at that point Napoleon forced Charles IV and Ferdinand VII to abdicate and placed his brother Joseph on the Spanish throne. The general uprising that followed changed England from an enemy into an ally of Spain

At the head of his army, the victorious Iturbide passes through the arch of triumph as he enters Mexico City in September, 1821.

and completely upset Miranda's plans. Rarely had a single man come so close to precipitating such huge events, and Miranda was understandably disappointed. "I think," Wellington recalled many years later, "I never had a more difficult business than when the Government bade me tell Miranda that we would have nothing to do with his plan."

What actually precipitated the Spanish American Revolution was Joseph Bonaparte's accession to the Spanish throne. Since the Spanish colonies were not subject to Spain but to the king personally, they had some legal justification in refusing to acknowledge Joseph as their sovereign. In this refusal all Spanish Americans were agreed. European-born Spaniards and creoles alike, from Mexico to Buenos Aires, as soon as news of Joseph's accession became known, announced that they recognized no other king than Ferdinand VII. However, though all said the same thing, not all thought alike. The Spanish viceroys and captains general and the upper clergy, backed by the king's troops, declared themselves loyal to Ferdinand VII, partly because they were reluctant to accept French rule, partly because they feared that otherwise the creoles would proclaim complete independence and expel them. The creoles were equally hostile to French rule, but the majority among them favored complete independence and merely paid lip service to King Ferdinand, waiting only for the opportunity to overthrow the colonial regime.

The leadership apparently was there, or else the opportunity created it. In 1809 news reached Spanish America

that Napoleon had completely defeated the Spanish insurgents. The news, it turned out, was premature, but it was believed with alacrity by all those who desired independence, for it meant that henceforth the Spanish colonies were on their own. From 1809 to 1811 one colony after another rose in rebellion against the Spanish governors and proclaimed its independence, though some of them continued to protest their loyalty to Ferdinand.

The revolutionists were not equally successful everywhere. In the viceroyalty of Rio de la Plata they were victorious under the leadership of Mariano Moreno and later of José de San Martín, but Uruguay and Paraguay seceded from the new republic and went their own ways. In the present republics of Chile, Peru, Ecuador, and Bolivia the royalists crushed the insurrection and remained in control until San Martín defeated them in his astounding Andean campaign of 1817–21. In Venezuela Miranda, who had returned and was proclaimed dictator, capitulated to the Spaniards in 1812; the struggle, however, was continued in the rest of New Granada by Simon Bolívar, one of the most colorful, romantic, and impressive figures of his time, and ended triumphantly in 1824. Bolívar's dream of a federated Latin America unfortunately came to nought, and even his creation of Greater Colombia eventually split into the present republics of Colombia, Venezuela, Panama, and Ecuador. In Central America the independence movement failed in 1811–14, revived in 1821 as part of the Mexican independence movement, and resulted in 1823 in the recognition by Mexico of the United Provinces of Central America; the new state subsequently broke up into Guatemala, El Salvador, Honduras, Nicaragua, and Costa Rica—a rather extreme example of Latin American Balkanization.

Perhaps the most tragic failure was that of the Mexican Revolution, which began in 1810 under the leadership of a creole priest, Miguel Hidalgo y Castillo. Hidalgo was by no means a conventional priest: he was accused by the Inquisition of almost every conceivable heresy; he was an ardent disciple of the French *philosophes* and economists; his parish house at Dolores was the meeting place of the local intelligentsia and at the same time a headquarters for the local industries which he developed to improve the living standards of the Indians. That he kept a concubine by whom he had two daughters is a fact that may be mentioned but that does not distinguish him from the majority of Mexican parish priests at the time. Unlike the armies of the South American secessionists, Hidalgo's host, which swelled to eighty thousand, was joined in large numbers by Indians and mestizos and made demands for social reforms that terrified the property-owning creoles.

In 1811 a much smaller royalist army under Felix Calleja defeated Hidalgo at the Bridge of Calderón. Hidalgo was captured and shot, and his leadership passed to a mestizo priest, José María Morelos, who brought a large part of Mexico under his control and convened a congress that promulgated a constitution in 1814. Morelos was routed in the following year by Agustín Iturbide, a creole in Spanish service, and was executed like his fellow priest Hidalgo. The revolution—a genuine social revolution—was crushed. When Mexico proclaimed its independence in 1812, the conservative landowners were in control; their tool, Iturbide, had himself crowned as Emperor Agustín I in 1822.

Although the American colonies had proclaimed their independence, they sent delegates to the Spanish Cortes that met at Cadiz until it was dissolved by Ferdinand VII in 1814. Their aim was not in every case complete separation from Spain; some of the leaders believed that independence in personal union with Spain, through the monarch, was a preferable solution. If their ideas had prevailed, a Spanish Commonwealth of Nations might have been created, or else Spanish America would have followed a course similar to that of Brazil, which continued as an independent empire under the royal house of Portugal until 1889. But the Cortes of Cadiz, despite its liberalism, drew up a constitution that placed the colonies in a subordinate position. The American delegates argued and protested to no avail, yet there was a hope that the Constitution of 1812 might be revised. It was only in 1814, when Ferdinand dissolved the Cortes and abrogated the Constitution, that the break between the colonies and the homeland became final. By a stroke of the pen Ferdinand destroyed the last hope of keeping together an empire which, if it had retained at least economic union and allegiance to a single sovereign, might have been able to develop its immense resources. This was not to be, nor was Bolívar's plan for federation. Instead, as is the general rule in states founded by military force, innumerable dictators and *caudillos* began their unceasing struggle for power, compounding the disunity among the sister republics with disunity within them, and the wealth, the energy, the intelligence, the idealism of an entire continent were squandered.

The leadership in the Americas, which eventually passed to the United States, could have been kept by Spain but for King Ferdinand's arrogant stupidity. It is curious to note that North American leadership in Latin America was precisely what Napoleon hoped to accomplish. In a set of instructions sent to his minister in Washington in 1811 he urged him "to encourage the independence of all the Americas," to explain the French stand not only to President Madison but to all the representatives of the rebellious colonies, and even to send arms to the rebels. In 1812, while racing back to Paris in a sleigh across the frozen plains of Poland, he explained his Latin American policy to Caulaincourt. "The emperor held that the secession of these colonies was a major event that would change global politics, strengthen the policies of the · United States, and within ten years threaten the power of England," Caulaincourt recalled later. All this, Napoleon continued, was ample compensation for the loss of America to Spain. "He had no doubt that Mexico and all the other large overseas colonies of Spain were about to proclaim their independence and form one or several states under a constitution that would make them incline to act as auxiliaries of the United States, as their best interests demanded. 'It is the beginning of a new era,' he said. 'It will bring about the independence of all colonies.' "

In the long run, Napoleon's prophecy seems surprisingly accurate. Yet he was strangely mistaken if he thought that North American influence in Spanish America would threaten the power of England. Even during the Napoleonic wars, when she fought as an ally of the king of Spain, England tended to encourage rather than discourage the Spanish American independence movement, since it opened up markets for British goods that would have remained closed as long as South America was under Spanish rule. And the enunciation of the Monroe Doctrine in 1823 was the direct result of an agreement between Britain and the United States, both of whom saw their Latin American markets threatened by Spain's effort to regain her lost colonies. The "independence of all colonies" was indeed to come, but it was not brought about by the emancipation of Spanish America. The dependency of the Latin American nations on the great powers that patronized them remained unchanged and in some cases was even increased by fragmentation and Balkanization. The "new era" predicted by Napoleon began only in the mid-twentieth century.

"ISOLATED" AMERICA

America's aim, Thomas Jefferson reminded his countrymen in 1801, was to pursue "peace, commerce, and honest friendship with all nations, entangling alliances with none." In time to come that last warning phrase was misattributed to Washington and, as an utterance claimed for the Father of His Country, became dogma for isolationists. Washington had indeed issued similar warnings, but he was no uncompromising isolationist. He knew that as a practical measure America must grow stronger before tangling again with European powers.

News of Washington's death in 1799 reverberated throughout Europe. No patriot in modern history so remarkably personified the ancient and heroic virtues revered at the time, a reverence reflected in the toga'd bust by Giuseppe Ceracchi above. Eager to identify his new regime with American republicanism Napoleon decreed ten days of official mourning and ordered a sculpture of the American hero placed beside those of Caesar, Mirabeau, and other ancient and modern worthies in the Tuileries. Three years later the First Consul sent Ceracchi to the guillotine for plotting in the cause of republicanism. On the overleaf is shown the Tontine Coffee House, which stood at the corner of Wall and Water Streets, in New York City, about 1798.

THE SEA: A BARRIER AND A HIGHWAY

In his Farewell Address Washington fondly remarked on the "detached and distant situation" of America, comments amplified by Jefferson a few years later when he spoke of America as "kindly separated by nature and a wide ocean from the exterminating havoc" Napoleon was wreaking on Europe. But America did not actually enjoy such splendid immunity from the turmoil abroad. At first Americans had regarded the French Revolution with more than sympathetic interest; to many it seemed almost like an extension of their own revolution. Reports of Dumouriez's rout of the duke of Brunswick's forces were hailed with almost hysterical excitement; bells were tolled, cannons boomed, and tipsy celebrants filled the cities' taverns.

But as time passed there were more sober reckonings. By the treaty signed in 1778, during the troubled days of the War of Independence, America had guaranteed France's possession of West Indian islands. Yet any resistance to British attacks there would involve another war with England, and for this the young nation was not prepared. In the spring of 1793 Washington proclaimed that America must remain neutral, despite formal obligations to its old ally. Public and political opinions were split between those who saw England as a continuing threat to America's economic independence and those who felt that trade with England was a mainstay of American economy, between

those who favored the Jacobins and those who saw in them the threat of anarchy and godlessness. The blundering arrogance of Citizen Genêt, who on orders from the French revolutionary government tried to make the United States a base for his country's privateers against English commerce, merely exacerbated matters.

Meanwhile American merchantmen were trafficking about the globe, profiting everywhere as neutral traders along the world's seaways. The little town of Salem, Massachusetts, became for a while one of the most celebrated ports in the world; in some remote parts that swarmed with its gaily decorated ships, it was believed that the town *was* the United States—a rich and important country. As Europe struggled, business boomed in the trading centers of the new republic. Shipping in and out of New York advanced by giant strides. For a decade Philadelphia remained the capital of the nation as well as its handsomest city; but New York was on its way to becoming the "commercial emporium of America." In its new exchange at the Tontine Coffee House on Wall Street merchants and brokers gathered to do their business and to talk about it. In a world at war American commerce ran increasing hazards of crossfire between the contending nations; but there were fortunes to be made wherever ships could ply, and the game was worth the risks.

During the European wars America was often the only neutral trading nation. Fortunes were made supplying British troops in the Peninsular War; as Napoleon closed other ports, Americans developed a thriving commerce with Russia via the Baltic. Crowninshield's Wharf, Salem, is shown above, lined with ships, in 1801. Below, a view of Second and High Streets, Philadelphia, the same year

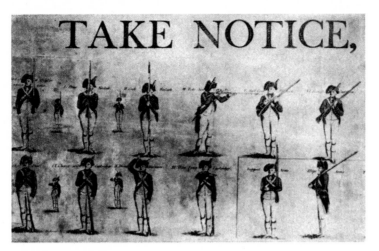

A COLD
WAR
AT
SEA

A recruiting poster of 1798, part of which is reproduced above, calls
upon "all brave, healthy, able bodied, and well disposed young men"
to join the troops forming under General Washington "for the defense
of the liberties and Independence of the United States." The cold war
with France brought about a general state of preparedness, most of
which was directed to sea. Below, a scene in a Philadelphia shipyard
shows the building of the 36-gun frigate Philadelphia "in preparation
for the defense of American commerce." The fate of this handsome
vessel is described on the following pages. The conclusion of the
action between the Constellation and L'Insurgente is depicted at right.

Genêt capped his follies by plotting the overthrow of Washington's government, by which insolence he further reduced American enthusiasm for the French cause and for which stupidity he was recalled to France by Robespierre. Rather than return to the guillotine that surely awaited him in his homeland, Genêt understandably preferred to remain in the United States. He married the daughter of Governor George Clinton and settled down to a quiet life in New York State.

American relations with England were no better than with France. In open violation of the Treaty of 1783 that had ended the Revolutionary War, England still held fortified trading posts in the Northwest Territory—strategic points (that were not being neglected) for fomenting trouble along the frontier. Even more galling, by a British Order in Council American ships suspected on any or no evidence of bearing cargoes from French colonies or provisions for those colonies were subject to seizure and detention. Whether this was England's monopolistic mercantilism at its worst or a stern and necessary measure to strangle Napoleon did not matter to Americans. It involved indignities and losses they could not tolerate.

In 1794, pursuing his peaceful policies, Washington sent John Jay to London to negotiate these and other Anglo-American differences. The concessions made by Jay to secure a treaty seemed to many Americans humiliating. But to France the apparent reconciliation represented a realignment of hostile forces and a gratuitous affront from the ally she had so recently helped to free from British rule. Now French decrees against American shipping were issued by the Directory. The XYZ fiasco did less than nothing to cool national tempers, and an undeclared but real war broke out on the high seas. By June, 1797, some three hundred American merchantmen had been seized by French warships, a record that made England's earlier spoliations of commerce seem mild. Aroused by French insults and depredations, America united in a patriotic fervor the country had not known since the Battle of Lexington. An army of ten thousand men was authorized, although it did not materialize; the marine corps was revived; and haste was made to outfit the navy with the finest frigates that could be brought into service, among other vessels. When the Baltimore-built frigate *Constellation,* Commodore Truxtun, overtook, subdued, and captured *L'Insurgente*—swiftest and one of the most redoubtable of the French frigates—in a fierce action off the coast of Nevis Island in the West Indies, American pride in its newly invigorated navy was unbounded.

NEW WORLD EMPIRE

Meriwether Lewis as portrayed in his frontiersman's garb in 1806

The likelihood of a declared war between France and the United States was sharply reduced in 1800 when President John Adams sent a commission to negotiate with Napoleon, who was by then decidedly in power. Vice-President Jefferson had let it be known to Talleyrand that a policy of appeasement might bring about a pro-French government in the next American elections. Napoleon was cordially inclined, hoping to discourage any possibility of a naval alliance between England and America. The Directory was blamed for past transgressions and the French press began suggesting that the "good sense of the American people" would avoid the threatened war. A resolution of the differences between the two nations was delayed while the First Consul waged the battles of his second Italian campaign, but in the early autumn of 1800 a pact was signed pledging "firm, inviolable, and universal peace, and a true and sincere friendship" between the two peoples. French spoliations were to be suspended and the United States was finally freed from the entangling alliance of 1778. The next day, Napoleon made an agreement of even greater consequence—the Treaty of San Ildefonso, in which Spain promised to retrocede the Louisiana Territory to France.

That vast "world of unexplored deserts and thickets," as Constantin Volney described Louisiana, had been a pawn in European diplomacy for more than a generation. France, Spain, and England would each have liked to expand their colonial interests in the American West, as well as to dam the rising flood of America's western migration. A sizable French expedition, bound for Louisiana, was actually assembled in Holland in the

The painting of New Orleans (left) at the time of the Louisiana Purchase foretells its bright future under the wings of freedom.

The above drawing by a member of the ship Columbia's *crew shows Captain Gray directing the construction of a new sloop at Clayoquot Sound, Vancouver Island, in 1792. The* Columbia *(on an earlier voyage) was the first American vessel to circumnavigate the globe. Below, the Spanish mission of San Carlos in California, after a sketch by one of Captain Vancouver's crew, also drawn in 1792*

winter of 1802–3, but it was icebound before it could sail. When spring came, Napoleon's designs in the Western Hemisphere had been thoroughly confounded. Later that year America peacefully took over the title to Louisiana in what was probably the most audacious and important real-estate deal in history. The fact that Napoleon did not have the proper authority or the moral right to sell and that Jefferson did not clearly have the constitutional right to buy were details that had to be ignored for the sake of the bargain. The next year Jefferson dispatched Lewis and Clark on their epic journey to learn what they could of the new territory and to chart a practical route to the Pacific coast.

Along that coast during the closing decades of the eighteenth century the United States had become involved in international rivalries that again bore heavily on its own future destiny. Moving up from Mexico, Spain had effectively occupied what is now the State of California. In 1778, on his last, tragic voyage, Captain Cook had landed at Nootka Sound, on what was to become known as Vancouver Island, and here a decade later Spain and England met in open conflict. The ships of four other nations, Russia included, were cruising those far western waters when, in 1792, the little ship *Columbia* from Boston, Captain Gray, paid its second visit to the profitable fur-rookeries of the northwest. Ignoring advice from Captain Vancouver, who was sent by England to discipline the Spanish and to survey the coast, Gray sailed through a bleak fog to discover the Columbia River and to lay grounds for America's later claim to sovereignty in those parts.

THE TRIPOLI WAR

Jefferson's political opponents cast him as a confirmed Francophile and a man of Jacobin principles. They feared that his election to the presidency in 1800 would result in a reign of terror. "The Democrats are divided into speculative theorists & absolute terrorists," wrote John Marshall at the time of the inauguration. "With the latter I am disposed to class Mr. Jefferson." As it happened the four years of Jefferson's first term in office were among the most tranquil in the history of the nation. Among other reassuring measures, Jefferson reduced the army to a mere twenty-five hundred men. In one respect, however, he displayed a more militant spirit than either Washington or Adams. From time immemorial the pirates of the Barbary Coast had preyed on commerce in the Mediterranean, demanding tribute, enslaving their captives, and extorting ransoms. The maritime nations of Europe commonly purchased immunity of sorts from these predatory barbarians, as did the United States during Washington's and Adams' presidencies. On the theory that any damage done to a competitor's trade would benefit their own, various European powers even encouraged the corsairs to assault ships of rival nations. But Jefferson, although he was dedicated to peace and economy, calculated that in the end it would be cheaper to fight than to pay blackmail and dispatched a naval squadron to suppress this menace to American trade, to assuage this hurt to American pride. In a chase off the Tripolitan coast the frigate *Philadelphia* foundered on a reef and was captured by the pirates and its entire crew imprisoned. In a heroic foray by other American seamen, the ship was destroyed before it could be put to use by the Tripolitanians. In May, 1805, the pasha of Tripoli was brought to terms. The jubilant pope, whose coasts were particularly exposed to piratical raids, publicly proclaimed that Americans had done more to suppress the barbarians than all the rest of Christendom combined.

Nelson called the destruction of the Philadelphia *"the most bold and daring act of the age." Within twenty minutes eighty American seamen under Stephen Decatur, in direct line of shore batteries, boarded the captured vessel, subdued the Tripolitanian guard, and escaped as the ship burst into flames.*

THE FRENCH SOJOURN IN AMERICA

Every serious change in French internal affairs—the fall of the Bastille, the counter-revolution of Thermidor, the coup d'état of 18 Brumaire—shook groups of Frenchmen loose from their native land. Some left in quest of tranquility, to move to a more compatible political environment, away from the disturbances and violence introduced by the Revolution. Others fled for their very lives, to escape the guillotines, prisons, or the armies. This intermittent emigration continued for more than a score of years and, like that later set in motion by Hitler's pogroms, enriched the lives of various lands. A large proportion of the émigrés remained in Europe, but many thousands crossed the Atlantic to America, some merely to await a more favorable turn of events at home, others to settle permanently in the New World.

The vanguard of this emigration met with a disgraceful piece of land-jobbery and broke up in bitter disillusionment. A group of American speculators acting as the Scioto Company and including "many of the principal characters of America" (the celebrated Yankee poet and ardent Francophile Joel Barlow was its Paris representative) organized a French agency just one month after the fall of the Bastille and by extravagant advertising persuaded large contingents of Frenchmen to buy lands for new homes in the Ohio wilderness. A mania swept Paris as eager purchasers succumbed to dreams of a Rousseauan Eden in the backwoods of America. "We hope soon to arrive at our new territory," wrote one of the hopeful escapees while en route, "where we shall find things in their original state, as God made them and not perverted by the ungrateful hand of man." Unfortunately, the company had failed to secure title to the land it had so successfully promoted. Congress tried to make amends, and some of the disenchanted travelers settled the town of Gallipolis, Ohio, in 1790; but the affair had ugly repercussions both at home and abroad.

This fiasco was not enough to halt the flow of emigration to the United States. A settlement named Asylum was undertaken along the banks of the Susquehanna to provide a safe retreat for Louis XVI, but it was never finished. As the Revolution took its gory course and flared into the Terror, a horde of other Frenchmen set sail for a haven overseas. In 1793 came Talleyrand. He loathed his exile, but he had been expelled from his temporary roost in England and he had no place else to go but America. Along with a distinguished company of his countrymen he took up residence in a Philadelphia boarding house to wait for the storm to blow over. Philadelphia swarmed with such émigrés. Most of them were cut off from their properties,

and Penn's "green country town" was treated to the curious spectacle of French counts teaching fencing to Quaker lads and dancing to Quaker lasses to make a living. The melancholy young Chateaubriand, who was there (and who was bored by Philadelphia and Philadelphians), reported that even an Iroquois tribe had a French dancing master. And after the d'Enghien affair came General Moreau, the victor of Hohenlinden; he later moved to Morristown where he lived for eight years before returning to Europe to join the Allies' resistance to Napoleon.

Moreau de Saint-Méry, who had been *de facto* president of the Paris Commune in better days, ran a book store in Philadelphia which was a rendezvous for the vicomte de Noailles, the duc de Rochefoucauld-Liancourt, Comte Rochambeau, the duc d'Orléans—who, as Louis Philippe, a generation later became the "citizen king" of France—and for still other displaced persons of rank. Moreau de Saint-Méry was a reciprocating cultural agent; as a side line to his book business he introduced contraceptives into America and, when he returned to Paris, he took with him the American idea of street numbering, with even addresses for one side, odd ones for the other. During his sojourn on the banks of the Schuylkill, Talleyrand continued his international intrigues. The gastronomist Brillat-Savarin, between fiddling in a theatre and teaching French to make ends meet, made notes on the American cuisine which he later incorporated into his *Physiologie du Goût*.

There were those who came to stay permanently. The English scholar Joseph Priestley, "an eighteenth-century Bertrand Russell," found refuge in Pennsylvania after a Birmingham mob, incensed by his "Jacobin" notions, burned his home and books. On New Year's Day, 1800, Eleuthère Irénée du Pont arrived in America to found on Brandywine Creek in Delaware the firm of DuPont de Nemours Père, Fils et Compagnie, at first devoted to powdermaking—and subsequently to other things. And three years later, to avoid possible conscription in the First Consul's armies, came young John James Audubon (the bastard boy whom rumor later claimed to be the Lost Dauphin), the famed ornithologist who was to become celebrated in Europe as the "American woodsman."

Another young man, Jerome Bonaparte, came to America by chance, fell in love with and married a Baltimore belle, Elizabeth Patterson (*"une grande fille, bien fraiche"*); but his older brother refused to recognize the marriage when Jerome brought his bride to Europe in 1805. Years later Joseph Bonaparte, sometime king of Naples and of Spain, settled in Bordentown, New Jersey, adopting the title of comte de Survilliers.

In the drawing above, the Baroness Hyde de Neuville pictured her ship cabin en route to America in 1816. Earlier she and her husband had spent seven years of exile in America to escape Napoleon's absolutism. The baron was now returning as minister from France. Left, top to bottom: Joseph Priestley, General Moreau, and Eleuthère Irénée du Pont. Below, John Syme's portrait of John James Audubon

WAR AND PEACE

While he was still president Jefferson had tried to avoid open conflict with France and England by keeping American ships in port, among other measures, but his efforts had pleased virtually no one except the British, who were happy enough to see the ships of their commercial rivals bottled up. For Americans confiscation and impressment on the high seas were objectionable and costly. But profits rose with the risks, and in any case, to many, Napoleon seemed a worse ogre than John Bull. When the restrictions were removed, American merchantmen winged out to sea to take their chances.

However, in February, 1812, Jefferson wrote to Charles Pinckney that although his "hobby" was peace he was forced to believe that war with England was the necessary alternative to abject submission to British arrogance. A year earlier the London *Courier,* stating the case with simple candor, had declared: "The sea is ours, and we must maintain the doctrine—that no nation, no fleet, no cock-boat shall sail upon it without our permission." Yet when President Madison finally launched "his" war, as the political opposition termed it, he had only divided support. The greatest enthusiasm was displayed by Western congressmen, far removed from salt water and the problems of "free trade and sailors' rights," but who saw their chance to undertake an expansionist crusade against Canada and the Indians of the West.

In almost every sense the War of 1812 was an anticlimax. It was an unnecessary and futile conflict. The most irritating measures were being unconditionally repealed by the British as Congress declared the war; the final peace treaty never mentioned the chief causes of the war; and the last bloody battle at New Orleans—America's only substantial victory on land —was fought after the treaty was signed. Even for Napoleon—who hoped it would divide and distract the forces against which he was contending, but who during its course rapidly lost his crown and empire— the War of 1812 might as well never have happened.

Two weeks after the Treaty of Ghent formally ended the War of 1812, 7,500 British veterans of the Napoleonic wars, transported in a fleet of 50 ships, landed at New Orleans and attempted a suicidal frontal assault on a force of Americans, most of them Western riflemen, who were entrenched behind a barricade of cotton bales. The British suffered over 2,000 casualties, the Americans 71.

America viewed the War of 1812 as a glorious assertion of national dignity and prowess. In the above allegory America triumphan

...vances toward the temple of peace; at the left Hercules, representing American strength, dictates the final terms to Britannia.

THE
RUSSIAN
NEMESIS

I was wrong in staying at the Kremlin for thirty-five days;
I should have stayed for two weeks only.

When Napoleon invaded Russia, he did not anticipate that in addition to the Russian army, of whose command he had a low opinion, he would have to fight the Russian people—that "blind and apathetic mass" of superstitious barbarians and slaves. It was more convenient to regard war as a personal contest for power among sovereigns, a concept he had inherited from the eighteenth century. While their armies butchered one another on the battlefields, the sovereigns themselves never forgot that they all belonged to the same club; that despite their differences, they had a certain community of interests; and that the game was played according to certain rules. As the son-in-law of the Hapsburg emperor, Napoleon regarded himself as a member of the club, entitled to the benefits of the club rules. Thus, in the midst of the Russian campaign, he continued to convey to Alexander assurances of his undying personal friendship.

Napoleon undertook the Russian campaign to conquer not Russia, but Alexander. His official aim was the liberation of Russian Poland and Lithuania, yet he was ready to sacrifice these countries if he could regain Alexander's alliance. He would win one or two great victories, then treat with Alexander as sovereign to sovereign. As at Tilsit, he would persuade the impressionable emperor to conclude an alliance, coax him back into the Continental System, and dazzle his imagination with brilliant projects of conquest in India and the Near East. The

essential difference—that this time he was fighting Russia on her own soil—he brushed aside, even when Alexander himself pointed it out to Napoleon's ambassador, Narbonne.

In regarding his opponent as irresolute and impressionable, Napoleon was undoubtedly right. Like all Russian sovereigns, Alexander sat uneasily on his throne. Even his legitimacy could be doubted. His grandmother, Catherine the Great, had usurped the power and tacitly consented to the murder of her husband, Peter III. To her son and successor, Paul, whom she detested, she gave to understand that he was the son not of Peter, but of one of her lovers. Toward the end of Paul's reign, it became apparent (at least to his enemies) that his mind was unhinged. In 1801 a group of officers, all friends of Alexander, conspired to arrest and depose the eccentric czar; complications arose, and to save the plot from complete failure, the conspirators were unfortunately obliged not only to arrest Paul but to kill him too.

It was over the body of his strangled father that Alexander ascended the throne. The grandson of a usurper and murderess, the son of a madman, the emperor, czar, and autocrat of all the Russias by the grace of God and the help of assassins, Alexander was haunted by a sense of

The camp bed that Napoleon used on the Russian campaign is preserved in the Invalides. On the table beside it are the emperor's dispatch case and spyglass and his characteristic hat.

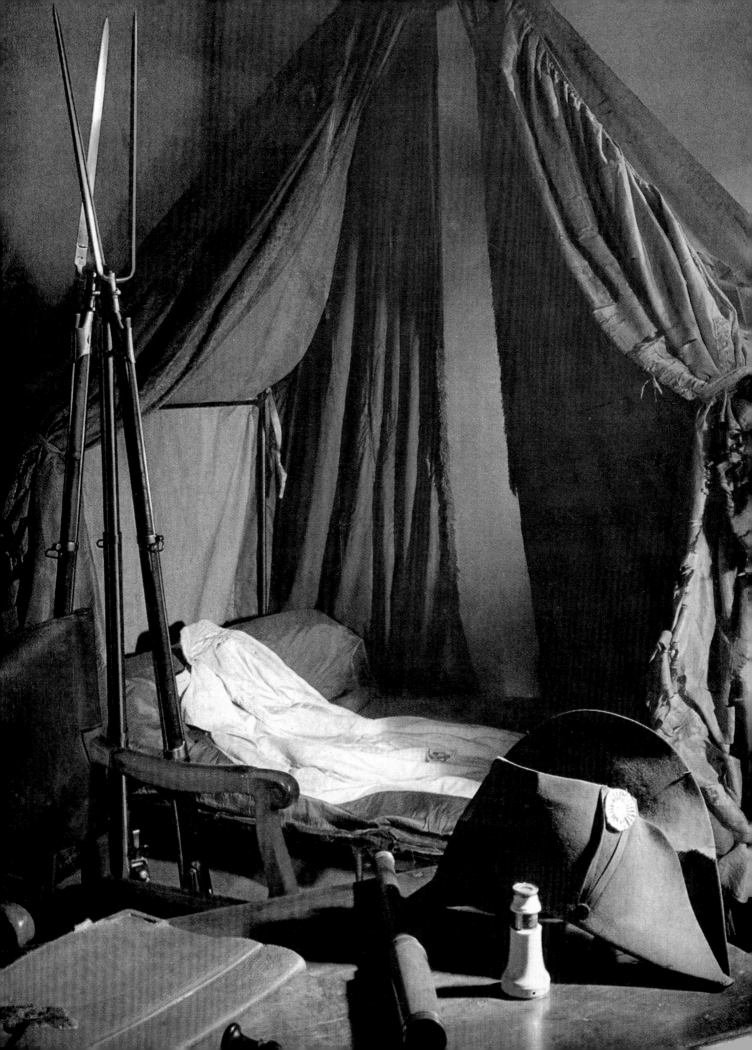

mission and of guilt. He had been educated by a Swiss tutor, Frédéric César de La Harpe, in the liberal principles of the Western Enlightenment; the discrepancy between his ideals and the realities he had to face as the ruler of a country such as Russia was enough to throw anybody's mind off balance. Had he had any clear idea of what his mission was, he might have expiated his guilt by exerting his near-absolute power in its accomplishment. But he did not know. "To be very able, he lacks only decision," Napoleon said of him, and indeed Alexander was endowed with every quality required in a great ruler save independence of judgment. He was never wholly himself, but always under the influence of somebody or something.

Among the chief influences on Alexander during the first years of his reign was Prince Adam Jerzy Czartoryski, whom he had befriended in his youth and made his foreign minister in 1803. Czartoryski managed the seemingly impossible feat of being both a Polish patriot and a loyal Russian minister. His plan to reconstitute an independent Polish kingdom in personal union with Russia—in which the Russian czar would also be the king of Poland—had to be abandoned after Napoleon's victory at Friedland. At Tilsit Napoleon gained a temporary ascendancy over Alexander's mind; among the Russian nobility, however, Alexander's sudden reconciliation and alliance with his former enemy was generally condemned, and spokesmen of the anti-French party continued to have the emperor's ear. In 1808, at Erfurt, Talleyrand convinced Alexander (who for some time had suspected as much) that his mission was in Europe and that its salvation depended on him.

Yet Alexander wavered for two or three more years. His two principal advisers during the period following the Congress of Erfurt, Speranski and Arakcheyev, incarnated, as it were, the two halves of his torn soul. Mikhail M. Speranski, the son of a village priest, had succeeded in rising to the highest administrative posts by sheer merit and intelligence. His far-reaching plans for reforms appealed to the disciple of La Harpe, and indeed, if they had been fully carried out, the history of Russia might have taken a quite different course from that which it did. Some of Speranski's projects were realized by Alexander: a Council of State was created on the Napoleonic model, the administrative machinery was reorganized at its highest level, and minimum requirements were introduced in the selection of the upper echelons of the bureaucracy. But Speranski's plan for a limited form of representative government was shelved for another century.

To carry out even the modest reforms Speranski initiated, Russia needed a period of peace. While relations between Alexander and Napoleon deteriorated steadily, Speranski continued to defend a policy of friendship with France. But his counsel was nullified by a number of factors, among them the ruinous effects of the Continental System on the Russian economy, the provocative actions of Napoleon in Germany, and the revival of Czartoryski's

project for a Polish kingdom. Moreover, Alexander came under the increasing influence of advisers who played on his conflicting ambitions to be the champion of European freedom at the same time as the defender of Russian tradition. Baron vom Stein, exiled from Prussia on Napoleon's request, had a considerable part in turning Alexander to active hostility against Napoleon; yet even more powerful was the rather sinister influence of Aleksei A. Arakcheyev, who was to dominate the latter part of Alexander's reign.

Arakcheyev, who described himself proudly as an unlettered country squire, had risen to favor under Czar Paul, whose bodyguard he had organized and who had made him a count. In 1808 Alexander made him his minister of war, and Arakcheyev reorganized the Russian army along the harsh disciplinarian lines that had endeared him to Czar Paul. The most energetic spokesman for the landowning class, which saw its continued dominance threatened by any liberalization of the autocratic system, Arakcheyev represented that extreme spirit of nationalist, anti-Western reaction that delayed the reform of Russian institutions until it was too late. Speranski's dismissal early in 1812 marked Arakcheyev's victory over the emperor's divided mind and removed the only outspoken opponent that there had been to war with France.

If Napoleon was right in regarding Alexander as an unstable character capable of reversing his decisions under the influence of others, he nevertheless saw him in a false light—an error he shared with most of his contemporaries. Baffled by Alexander's inconsistencies—his alternating fits of liberalism and reaction, of mystic piety and amatory frivolity, of high idealism and shrewd bargaining—they regarded him as deep, devious, and treacherous. Wily he was, no doubt, but treacherous he was not; and he was primarily dominated by his emotions. At the time Napoleon invaded Russia, Alexander had come under the sway of the mystical exaltation that was sweeping both the Russian Orthodox Church and the Evangelical sects. As readers of Tolstoi's *War and Peace* may recall, people otherwise sound in mind had taken to interpreting the Apocalypse of Saint John and found positive proof in it that Napoleon was the Antichrist. Alexander, without going to such extremes, nevertheless had convinced himself that the Corsican represented the antithesis of the Christian ideals that in his opinion must form the basis of government and of the European community; these ideals he, Alexander, felt himself called upon to restore. Though unstable, he was stubborn, and it would have required some extraordinary turn of events to make him reverse himself. Moreover, he still felt the sting of the accusations of weakness and cowardice that had been heaped upon him after Tilsit; this time he would prove his mettle.

Napoleon had not counted on Alexander's firmness, and even less on the Russian people's resistance. Indeed, it was difficult to see why an enslaved peasantry should rise in arms to defend its oppressors, and the glaring characteristic of Russian society in 1812 was that in Russia proper, over nine-tenths of the population were serfs. Russia was by no means the only country where serfdom persisted, but the condition of her serfs came closer to slavery than that of the serfs in central Europe.

Moreover, whereas serfdom in other countries had tended to diminish, it had increased tremendously in Russia over the past two centuries. Peter the Great and his successors, especially Catherine II, while transforming Russia into a European power and concentrating all authority in their own hands, set their empire back as much as they modernized it. To win the support of the upper classes, they systematically reduced the rights of the peasants and increased those of the landowners. In the sixteenth century, when serfdom was instituted in Russia on a large scale, the peasants were bound to the land but not to their masters; in the eighteenth century they became the outright property of their masters. They could be sold separately from the land, individually or by family. They were advertised for sale in newspapers along with dogs, horses, and used carriages. Young noblemen short of cash would gamble them away in card games or transfer them in payment for a courtesan's embrace. A person's fortune was measured not in cash, not even in land, but by the number of "souls" he owned. The expression "soul" was not entirely without meaning: though treated as chattels, the serfs nevertheless were regarded as Christians and as Russians. Their owners could punish them corporally, imprison them, or even exile them to Siberia, but they had not—in theory at least—a power of life and death over them. On the other hand, the peasant serfs were bound to furnish recruits for the czar's army, and they made up the bulk of it.

The serf's condition varied considerably according to his status. House serfs—that is, domestic servants—on the whole enjoyed better living conditions but less freedom than did peasant serfs. Among the peasants those belonging to the state were generally better off than privately owned ones, who had to give as many as three days' labor each week to their masters. There were, moreover, local variations, and, as might be expected, a serf's treatment depended to a large degree on the more or less humane disposition of his master or mistress.

All in all, the educated elite of Russia was agreed that serfdom was a national disgrace. Inhuman in itself, the institution debased not only its victims but also its beneficiaries. In the two capital cities—Moscow and St. Petersburg—the brilliance of social life, the presence of large foreign colonies, of intellectual stimulus, of cosmopolitan ferment hid the national sore under a glittering veil. True, all this magnificence and luxury fed on the sweat of the peasants, but in this the Russian elite was in no way different from any other in Europe, and many of its members were foremost among the advocates of reform. It was

the provincial gentry, the owners of small or medium-sized estates, on whom serfdom exerted its most corrupting effect and who opposed its reform or abolition most vehemently. Living barely above the level of the peasants whom they exploited, isolated on their estates and in their dreary small towns, they had sunk into a state of mental and physical laziness from which nothing could stir them except greed and the fear of having to exchange their parasitical mode of existence for a more active one. They were the living corpses whom Nikolai Gogol described so well in his *Dead Souls*.

The yoke of serfdom paralyzed the peasants less than it did their owners. Though capable of bearing more suffering than most men, the Russian peasantry was by no means reconciled to the condition to which it had been reduced. A series of rebellions had shaken Russia in the eighteenth century, culminating in the war that Emelyan Pugachev, an illiterate Cossack, waged against Catherine the Great in 1773–75. Claiming that he was the dethroned Peter III, Pugachev gathered an army of peasants, Cossacks, runaway serfs, and Tatar bands; at one time his forces held most of the Volga region, conquered Kazan, and threatened to spread the rebellion to all Russia. In his proclamations Pugachev granted all serfs full freedom, "without recruiting levies, poll tax or other money taxes, with possession of the woods, the hay meadows, the fishing grounds, the salt lakes, without payment and without rent," and invited his followers to wreak vengeance on the landowners, to "seize them, punish them, hang them, treat them in the same way as they, having no Christian feeling in them, oppressed you, the peasants." At least fifteen hundred of the gentry class were massacred by Pugachev's bands before Catherine's soldiers suppressed the uprising with equal brutality. The result of the rebellion was the still further enslavement of the peasants. At the time of Napoleon's invasion they seemed more submissive, but they had not lost their aspirations for freedom.

The peasants' hatred of their oppressors did not extend to the czar. No matter how much misery and injustice they had to bear, they escaped the despair of total abandonment by making excuses for their ruler, their father: the czar was deceived by evil advisers, he was kept in ignorance of what was being done to his children. Pugachev could never have won his massive following if he had not claimed that he was the deposed Peter III. This loyalty to their sovereign, who represented to them the only hope of finding justice on earth, was paralleled on another plane by their deep religious faith, which promised justice in Heaven. If God was their father in Heaven and the czar their father on earth, their country was to them "Holy Mother Russia," something sacred to be defended with their lives against defilement by foreigners and unbelievers. Kept in ignorance and superstition by an ignorant, superstitious clergy, they endured patiently the most intolerable hardships, yet avoided the apathetic fatalism of slaves:

they had kept intact the two qualities that enable even the most brutalized people to rise to dignity and heroism—belief in justice and love of country.

Alexander's proclamation to his people, issued at the time of the French invasion, appealed to these deep-seated feelings: Napoleon had come to destroy Russia; the entire nation must rise against "this Moloch" and his "legions of slaves. Let us drive this plague of locusts out! Let us carry the Cross in our hearts, and steel in our hands!" The proclamation was read in all the churches, and the priests supplemented it with embellishments of their own. "They convinced these peasants that we were a legion of devils commanded by the Antichrist, infernal spirits, horrible to look upon, and whose very touch defiled," wrote the comte de Ségur, at the time an aide-de-camp to Napoleon.

Alexander's appeal and the priests' exhortations produced the desired effect. The entire nation was seized by patriotic fervor. The nobles contributed their sons, their wealth, and their serfs; the merchants gave their money and destroyed their stores to keep them from falling into the hands of the French; the gentry and the peasants laid waste their land as they fled from the approaching enemy. According to Ségur—an acute observer, though given to tall tales and exaggeration—the scorched-earth policy was not motivated exclusively by patriotism and military necessity. The ruling class, he says, "were distrustful of their slaves." The possibility that Napoleon might promise them freedom if they rose against their masters terrified the upper class. "We were advancing," says Ségur, "and we thought that these crude fabrications [of the priests against the French] would disappear with our coming. But the nobles retreated into the interior with their serfs, as if at the approach of a deadly plague, sacrificing riches, homes, everything that might detain them or be of use to us. They put hunger, fire, and the desert between themselves and us; for it was as much in fear of their serfs as of Napoleon that this high resolution was carried out. It was no longer a war of kings that we were fighting, but a class war, a party war, a religious war, a national war—all sorts of wars rolled into one." In truth, the scorched-earth policy was not as general as Ségur asserts, being largely limited to the path taken by Napoleon's main army. Moreover, it was not so much the result of a set policy as of circumstances: both the retreating Russian army and the villagers for the most part carried with them only what they needed to sustain themselves. Nevertheless, Ségur's point—that the spirit of sacrifice was due as much to the landlords' fear of their peasantry as to their patriotism—is probably well taken.

This kind of war was a definite breach of the club rules. It is true that Napoleon himself, when he crossed the Niemen, had called (with middling success) upon the Polish and Lithuanian population to rise against their Russian oppressors; however, he resisted the advice that was urged upon him to proclaim the emancipation of the serfs and to invite a general uprising in Russia. "I felt

that to arm a population of slaves would have condemned the country to frightful sufferings. I would not even think of it," he explained to the German sovereigns early in 1813. Apart from his fundamental conservatism, he was motivated by another consideration: by emancipating the serfs he would create chaos in his rear, endanger his supplies, and transform a power contest into a revolutionary war, thus destroying his last hope of reaching a settlement with Alexander.

It dawned only gradually upon Napoleon what kind of war was being waged against him. He expected that the enemy would give him battle in the first few days of the campaign. There were skirmishes and minor engagements, but the Russians withdrew and refused battle. He was annoyed when Vilna fell to him without a blow. He had not yet even entered Russia proper, and already he had lost ten thousand horses while trying to overtake the Russians in forced marches, in a torrid heat that alternated with unusually severe thunderstorms. At Vitebsk the Grand Army halted. According to Ségur's account of the campaign, Napoleon intended to stop there, organize the conquered Lithuanian, Polish, and Byelorussian territories, and resume the offensive only in the following spring. Although Ségur's testimony cannot be neglected, since he was present at General Headquarters, the available evidence does not support it. The possibility of halting the advance was considered, it would seem, and Napoleon showed signs of hesitation. The main reason for his staying two weeks at Vitebsk, however, was in all likelihood that he expected to receive peace overtures from Alexander. As no such offers arrived, he grew daily more restless and impatient to march on to Smolensk.

Napoleon's Russian campaign is usually described as if it had been the march of a single huge column from Vilna to Moscow and back. Actually, the theatre of operations and the front of the French and their allies were unusually extensive. The theatre of operations reached from the Baltic Sea—where the left wing, under Marshal Macdonald (also in command of the Prussian forces), advanced as far as Riga—to about three hundred miles south, where the Austrian corps under Prince Schwarzenberg were operating. Marshal Davout had but recently superseded King Jerome in the command of the right wing of the main army; the slowness of its advance under Jerome was undoubtedly responsible in part for the miscarriage of Napoleon's original plan, which was to defeat the main Russian army under Barclay de Tolly, before it could be joined by a smaller army under Prince Bagration. This junction took place at Smolensk on August 2. In these changed circumstances, Napoleon had every reason to call off his pursuit of Barclay and to spend two weeks in Vitebsk before launching the lightning advance that he hoped would crush the combined Russian armies at Smolensk with a single blow.

He was to be disappointed once again. The main forces

of the Grand Army gathered before Smolensk on August 16, having approached the city along the southern bank of the Dnieper. Both Barclay and Bagration hastened to the relief of the city, but the expected battle did not materialize. During the night of August 16–17, Bagration's army slipped away, undetected by Napoleon, leaving only a strong garrison—about twenty thousand men—in the city. The following morning, Napoleon waited in vain for the enemy to show up: Barclay remained inactive on the northern bank, and Bagration was gone. In the afternoon the emperor ordered a general attack on Smolensk, which until then he had only bombarded. The fighting was extremely severe: the French lost almost nine thousand men, the Russians more than ten thousand.

As night fell, the inner walled city—or kremlin—of Smolensk was still in Russian hands. Seated on a campaign chair in front of his tent, the emperor observed the progress of the attack. Several large conflagrations had started in the city. The French believed them to be the result of their shells. "It's like Vesuvius erupting," Napoleon cried out to Caulaincourt. "Don't you think this is a beautiful sight?" "Horrible, Sire," said Caulaincourt. "Bah!" shrugged the emperor. "Remember, gentlemen, what a Roman emperor said: 'The corpse of an enemy always smells sweet.' " What remained of the Russian garrison evacuated the city during the night, and the next morning the Grand Army entered Smolensk. "We passed through the smoking ruins in military formation," reminisces Ségur, "with our martial music and customary pomp, triumphant over this desolation, but with no other witness to our glory than ourselves."

Barclay's army had vanished during the night of August 17–18, except for a few troops in the suburbs of Smolensk on the right bank of the Dnieper, whence the French expelled them in the morning. The larger part of Smolensk —though by no means all—had been destroyed by fire. It is doubtful whether, as Napoleon claimed, the Russians set the fire deliberately. Certain it is that between Smolensk and Moscow the Russians left a wake of devastation. Nevertheless, the scorched-earth policy—if policy it was— was not carried out on nearly as large a scale in Russia as it had been by Wellington in Portugal. Napoleon had praised Wellington for devastating Portugal. "There's a man for you!" he had remarked. "Only Wellington and I are capable of carrying out such measures." In Russia he took a different view of the same measures: "Armies of Tatars," he complained, were destroying the fields and the cities, and the Russians were plainly uncivilized. What proved the Russians to be barbarians in Napoleon's eyes proved them to be patriots in their own history books. The difference is not necessarily very great.

The Russians' strategy of retreat had no more been planned in advance than had their scorched-earth strategy. It was due to divided counsels in the high command, to the numerical inferiority of the Russian forces, and to a

healthy respect for Napoleon's habit of winning battles. On several occasions—particularly at Smolensk—the Russian command had actually intended to give battle and lost its nerve at the last moment. What the French took to be a preconceived plan to draw them farther and farther into Russia, to lengthen their supply lines, to wear down their troops by sheer attrition, and to deprive them of resources by the systematic devastation of the countryside and the cities—all this was a strategy that took shape spontaneously, almost by accident, and was rationalized only later. Its effectiveness cannot be denied, but its costliness is sometimes overlooked.

After his failure to give battle at Smolensk, the Russian commander in chief, Barclay de Tolly, came under violent criticism. His foreign origin—he was of Scottish and Baltic descent—earned him the hatred of the chauvinists; his apparent timorousness, which in fact was wisdom, offended national pride; moreover, the nobility was beginning to wonder how much more of its property it would have to sacrifice before the invaders were expelled. The prospect of withdrawing to Siberia—a notion that Alexander apparently entertained on and off—was not appealing. Pressed from all sides—even by his sister, who accused him of cowardice—Alexander reluctantly agreed to sacrifice Barclay and to replace him with a man whom he detested, Field Marshal Kutuzov, the one-eyed veteran of the Polish and Turkish wars, the idol of the army, and a four-square Russian if ever there was one. In his heart, Kutuzov was convinced that Barclay's strategy was the only safe one, and he adopted it eventually; but the circumstances under which he accepted the command committed him to risk at least one battle to save Moscow. Drawing together all

An Asiatic warrior in the Russian army, painted by Carle Vernet

the forces that were available to him, he decided to make his stand on the Moskva River, at the village of Borodino.

With the wisdom of hindsight, almost everybody—including Napoleon—has criticized Napoleon for not stopping his pursuit at Smolensk. If he had wintered there, so the argument runs, he could have reorganized his forces and resumed the offensive in the spring. According to Ségur, all his marshals begged him not to let himself be drawn deeper into Russia, and Murat even went so far as to throw himself on his knees before him—a gesture not in keeping with Murat's character. The truth of this will probably never be known, but there is no question that Napoleon insisted on resuming the pursuit immediately and pushing on to Moscow. He still wanted a decisive battle; Moscow offered richer resources than did devastated Smolensk; and if he captured the capital, he believed, Alexander would sue for peace.

On August 19, at Valutina, a large part of Barclay's army stumbled into the French advance guard that had set off in its pursuit. It was the first major encounter of the campaign, and a bloody one. Napoleon, who had mistaken it for a mere rear guard action, arrived on the battlefield only the following day. It was a worse shambles than usual. To lift the morale of the smoke-blackened survivors, he generously handed out promotions and decorations on the spot. The troops cheered him, but as he returned to his headquarters at Smolensk the progress of his carriage along a road choked with limping cripples, stretchers, and ambulances sent him into a somber mood. In Smolensk he passed carts loaded with amputated limbs. In the hospitals the surgeons ran out of dressings and used paper and birchbark fibers as substitutes; many of those who survived surgery died of starvation, for the supply service had virtually broken down. In addition to the battle casualties, hundreds of men fell victim to the Russian secret weapon, vodka, dying by the roadside from a combination of raw spirits and exposure. Such, it must be emphasized, was the condition of the Grand Army not during its tragic retreat but during its victorious advance. Yet it must also be admitted that it would probably have been just as disastrous to stay through the winter in Smolensk as to stay in Moscow; the only real alternative, retreat without a decisive battle, amounted to defeat in Napoleon's eyes, and he could not accept defeat. It was thus that he preferred to gamble all on Moscow.

On September 5 Napoleon's forces came face to face with Kutuzov's army at Borodino. The next day, from his observation post, the emperor witnessed an extraordinary spectacle in the Russian camp. "In the midst of the troops," says Ségur, "Kutuzov was seen advancing, surrounded by all religious and military pomp. The commander in chief had had the popes and archimandrites put on their richest, their most majestic vestments . . . They preceded him, bearing their precious religious symbols, in particular the beloved icon from Smolensk, which, they claimed, had

been miraculously saved from the profanation of the sacrilegious French." Kutuzov's address was then read, not only to his troops, but also to the thousands of peasant militiamen who had joined his army, carrying crosses and shouting "God wills it!" just as the first crusaders had done seven centuries earlier. Kutuzov's speech, which must have been as extraordinary as the spectacle, roused his army to a high pitch of religious and patriotic fervor. There were no ceremonies in the French camp. The only icon there was a portrait of Napoleon's one-year-old son, the king of Rome, which had just arrived from Paris. Napoleon had it exposed in his tent, expecting his officers to feel inspired by it for the next day's battle.

On the following morning Napoleon could barely speak. A severe grippe made him shake with fever, and an inflammation in the prostate gland racked him with pain. The battle raged in utter confusion from dawn until late afternoon, and it ceased only after some thirty thousand Frenchmen and forty-five thousand Russians had been killed or wounded. The Russians lost 40 per cent of their total strength, yet only some eight hundred were taken prisoner. "Those Russians," Napoleon observed to Caulaincourt, "let themselves be killed like machines. . . . They are citadels that have to be demolished with cannon."

On more than one occasion during the battle Napoleon seems to have had the opportunity to annihilate the Russian forces, but the separate actions of the several corps on both sides were so confused or ill-synchronized that each time the opportunity was missed. Slumped on his camp chair, looking sick and miserable, his eyes dulled by fever, almost indifferent to what was going on, Napoleon stub-

bornly refused to listen to his generals and aides, who implored him to commit his sacred reserve, the Old and the Young Guard, who might have turned the blind and brutal slugging match into a decisive victory. The right moment had not come, he said; he would have to see the chessboard more clearly. When his generals kept pressing him, he exclaimed at last: "And if there is a second battle tomorrow, what shall I fight it with?"

Technically Borodino was a French victory. Napoleon kept the battlefield, and the road to Moscow had been opened. Yet none of his entourage dared congratulate him on it. The mood at French headquarters was one of horror, consternation, and sorrow. The casualties had been staggering even in the highest ranks: forty-three French generals had been killed or wounded. The next morning the emperor roused himself to inspect the battlefield and to see what he had wrought. Among the twisted debris and some fifty thousand corpses of men and horses there were about twenty thousand wounded, who were screaming and moaning. The ambulance service, despite the exertions of the chief surgeon, Dr. Larrey, was virtually inoperative. The wounded dragged themselves to shelter if they could; others begged their comrades to finish them off. A desolate, dark sky hung low over the field, and an icy rain soaked the dead and the dying.

Napoleon was visibly shaken. What disturbed him even more than the spectacle of pain and death was that the French had taken only eight hundred Russian prisoners. His victory was hollow indeed. Yet when he returned to his headquarters and learned that the Russian army was in full retreat, his hopes revived. Interrupting Marshal

Bessières, who was reading the list of casualties among generals, he regained his voice to exclaim: "One week of Moscow, and this will not matter any more!"

On September 14, early in the afternoon, a party of scouts was sent to reconnoiter a hill above the Moscow road. The first man to reach the top stopped short and shouted excitedly, "Moscow! Moscow!" Soon the whole group of scouts clambered up the hill at a run, clapping their hands in a sudden fit of hysterical joy. Napoleon himself, infected by their curiosity, rode up to gaze at the prize spread out before him. Illuminated by an oblique shaft of sunlight, the domes and cupolas of Moscow's innumerable churches glittered in a riot of gold and color; above them shone the huge gold-plated cross of Ivan the Great in the Kremlin. With its hundreds of palaces and gardens, its bazaars, its endless rows of wooden houses, Moscow seemed a vision from the Arabian Nights' tales. "So here at last is that famous city!" said Napoleon. "It is high time," he added soberly. He then settled down to wait for a deputation to surrender the keys of Moscow. No deputation appeared, however—only a Russian officer who requested an armistice to allow the Russian troops time to evacuate the city. The request was granted. At sunset still no deputation had appeared, but some French officers who had slipped into Moscow returned with the incredible news that Moscow was empty: it had been deserted by its entire population.

Napoleon refused to credit the news and continued to wait for a formal surrender—in vain. He entered Moscow after nightfall. The news was only too true: of the city's quarter million population, a mere handful had stayed behind—mostly French residents, several thousand wounded and sick, stragglers, and some of the rougher inhabitants. As the French columns marched through the empty streets, says Ségur, "filled with wonder at the sight of such complete solitude, they responded to the awe-inspiring silence of this modern Thebes by a silence equally solemn. These warriors shivered inwardly at the lonely echo of their horses' hoofs among the deserted palaces . . ."

How the fire started that night no one really knows. According to Ségur, it was set deliberately and systematically on the orders of the governor of Moscow, Count Rostopchin. Rostopchin never admitted to the charge; however, since his daughter later married one of Ségur's nephews, Ségur may have obtained information from him not shared by others. Yet even if Rostopchin did not give the fateful order, and if the fire started by accident, there can be no doubt that once it had started it was deliberately spread, partly by bands of patriots, partly by looters, both French and Russian. On the morning of September 15, when Napoleon took up residence in the Kremlin, there was still hope that the conflagration would be brought under control; the following morning, nearly the entire city except the Kremlin was aflame.

From a window in the Kremlin, Napoleon watched the spectacle in consternation, while fire-fighters on the roofs extinguished the flaming debris that kept raining on them. "An extreme agitation took hold of him," says Ségur, "so that one would have thought he was being consumed by the fires around him." Yet even though told that the Kremlin had been mined, he refused to evacuate the palace until a fire broke out in the arsenal. As it turned out, the Kremlin was saved, and Napoleon and his troops ran a greater risk making their way to the suburbs through the flaming streets than they would have had they remained where they were. The emperor himself led the way "through a narrow winding street already afire from one end to the other" (here, perhaps, Ségur exaggerates) and past a convoy of powder wagons that miraculously did not blow up. When he reached Petrovski Palace, outside the city, the fire was at its height, and it subsided only on September 18, leaving nearly the whole great capital a smoking ruin.

The ruins were still smoking when Napoleon was faced with a fourfold choice: Should he pursue Kutuzov's army in its southward retreat to Kaluga? Should he re-enter Moscow? Should he march north against St. Petersburg? Should he retreat to Smolensk, Vitebsk, or even Vilna, and resume the campaign in the spring? With the Grand Army reduced by one-third, winter approaching, and a large part of the resources of Moscow destroyed or dilapidated in the looting, the latter course seemed the most prudent, but Napoleon rejected it, since it would have been tantamount to admitting defeat. He decided to return to Moscow in the hope that Alexander would make peace or at least would agree to an armistice.

The sight that greeted him as he rode back to the ruined city was decidedly surrealistic. It has been unforgettably recorded by Ségur: "Enormous fires had been lit in the middle of the fields, in thick, cold mud, and were being fed with mahogany furniture and gilded windows and doors. Around these fires, on litters of damp straw, ill protected by a few boards, soldiers and their officers, mud-stained and smoke-blackened, were seated in splendid armchairs or lying on silk sofas. At their feet were heaped or spread out cashmere shawls, the rarest of Siberian furs, cloth of gold from Persia, and silver dishes in which they were eating coarse black bread baked in the ashes and half-cooked, bloody horseflesh . . ." Mingled with the French were some ten thousand Russian soldiers, stragglers who were allowed to wander about unhindered, although some still bore arms, and with whom the French good-naturedly shared their fires after tolerating them as looting companions. When orders came to arrest the Russians, most of them had vanished.

The disorder and license in the city were past belief. All the loot of Moscow was spread out in the smoldering squares and traded among the soldiers. "Gold, being easier

to carry, was bought at a great loss for silver, which the knapsacks would not hold," Ségur reports. "Soldiers were seated everywhere on bundles of merchandise, on heaps of coffee and sugar, in the midst of the finest wines and liquors that they were trying to trade for bread." In the circumstances there were no severe measures Napoleon could take to stop the looting. To prevent the resources from being wasted completely he put the pillage on an organized basis, ordering each corps to take its turn at collecting whatever stores were still salvable.

On September 20 Napoleon wrote a letter of protest to Alexander: "How is it possible to destroy one of the most beautiful cities in the world and the labors of centuries for so small an aim? But this is the conduct which has been followed since Smolensk and which has reduced six hundred thousand families to beggary. . . . Since the Russian army had left Moscow unprotected, common humanity and Your Majesty's own interests required that this city be entrusted to my safekeeping. The administration, the magistrates, and the militia should have been left here. It was thus that things were done in Vienna, on two occasions, in Berlin, and in Madrid. . . . Fire authorizes looting, which the soldier permits himself to save the remnants from the flames. . . . I do not believe it possible that Your Majesty, with your principles, your kindheartedness, your rectitude of mind, could have authorized these excesses, which are unworthy of a sovereign and of a great nation." Alexander did not respond to these overtures, nor to a letter brought to Kutuzov's headquarters by one of Napoleon's marshals. He would rather let his beard grow and eat potatoes with the serfs, he declared in one of his fits of mystical exaltation, than make peace as long as a single foreign soldier remained on Russian soil.

While Napoleon waited for a reply that never came, five precious weeks passed by in inactivity and indecision. Foraging expeditions in the vicinity of Moscow brought ever more meager results, autumn weather was setting in, and the men began to suffer from the cold, for they had worn out their boots and had not been issued winter clothing. In the countryside the activities of peasant guerrillas and of the Cossacks became bolder and bolder. Still, Napoleon could not bring himself to abandon his conquest and to retreat to safer territory, where he might spend the winter and unite his dwindling forces with the auxiliary corps he had left in the rear. To while away the time, he would prolong his meals, read novels, or sit for hours in his armchair in a dull stupor. By mid-October he had apparently made up his mind to retreat to Smolensk, but still delayed issuing final orders. On October 18 he received intelligence that Murat, whose troops were testing the Russian positions to the south on the road to Kaluga, had been repulsed by Kutuzov, with heavy losses. Napoleon instantly regained his energy and ordered his army to advance to Kaluga, leaving only a small body of troops in Moscow under Marshal Mortier, who was to blow up the

Along the banks of the Moskva River the towers of the Kremlin can be seen surrounded by the fire that raged through Moscow for four days. The Kremlin itself escaped destruction, but most of the rest of the city was laid waste by the conflagration.

Kremlin before evacuating the city. (Mortier carried out the order very negligently: only the arsenal was blown up.)

Napoleon had entered Moscow with about ninety thousand men fit for combat; reinforcements had brought his strength to over one hundred thousand when he began to retreat. Kutuzov's army (not counting Cossacks, untrained recruits, and peasant militia) was slightly inferior to Napoleon's, but its morale was as high as the morale of the French and the French allies was low. The main body of the French army was still orderly as it marched out of Moscow, but behind it there followed what seemed a Tatar horde. Carriages, wagons, even pushcarts loaded with loot formed a chaotic jumble several miles long. Bearded peasants, forcibly recruited to drive or carry the plunder; "crowds of men of all nations, without weapons or uniforms, and lackeys swearing in a Babel of tongues and urging on with threats and blows tiny ponies that were harnessed with rope to elegant carriages"; hundreds of Frenchwomen and their children, former residents of Moscow; and the usual contingent of prostitutes and camp followers—all this confused mass of humanity and vehicles choked the road in what must have been one of the great traffic jams in history. Napoleon made his way through it with great difficulty and without uttering a word.

The slowness of his army's progress enabled the Russians to head off the French and Italian advance elements under Viceroy Eugene at Maloyaroslavets on October 24. The town changed hands several times in the course of the savage fighting, which lasted until late at night; at the cost of very heavy losses the French succeeded in driving out the Russians, who then took up what seemed to be an impregnable position just to the south, blocking the Kaluga road. Napoleon arrived only after the battle. In a filthy hut belonging to a weaver, he held a council of war: Should he attack Kutuzov the next day, force his way to Kaluga, and retreat to Smolensk along a route where he still might find provisions? Or should he turn north toward Mozhaisk and follow the trail of desolation along which he had come?

Marshal Bessières, who had inspected Kutuzov's position, declared it to be unassailable. "O Heavens!" the emperor cried out, clasping his hands. "Are you sure? Is it really true?" Bessières emphatically repeated his assertion. The emperor hung his head in dejection and remained silent, while his marshals argued about the best road of retreat. Murat and Davout, who had been quarreling all through the campaign, nearly came to blows. At last, pulling himself out of his torpor, Napoleon ended the argument by deciding to take the Mozhaisk road. This decision, which doomed the remnants of the Grand Army to annihilation, turned out to be unnecessary. On the very day that Napoleon took the road to Mozhaisk, Kutuzov decided to avoid a battle with him and ordered his army to retreat in the opposite direction, toward Kaluga. If Napoleon had held his decision for only one day, the agony of the following weeks might have been avoided.

Kutuzov's decision that day and his conduct during the rest of the campaign have puzzled many historians. On

333

Kutuzov commanded the Russians during most of the campaign.

several occasions it was in his power to annihilate Napoleon's army and to capture the emperor himself; instead of seizing them, he was content to harass the French. The suggestion has been made that Napoleon's prestige was still so great that Kutuzov feared a contest; it does not carry much conviction. A more plausible explanation is, perhaps, that Kutuzov was not eager to annihilate Napoleon; all he wanted was to drive the invaders out of the country, and this as he knew, he could accomplish without a battle, since hunger, disease, the cold, and the Cossack raiders would take care of it. The man who most insistently urged Kutuzov to give battle was Sir Robert Wilson, the English commissioner at Russian headquarters, and Kutuzov, who distrusted all foreigners, suspected that if he followed Wilson's advice he would merely sacrifice Russian lives to the interests of British policy. Even though Kutuzov wisely avoided battle, the pursuit of the retreating French cost the Russians almost as heavy casualties as the French—about two hundred thousand men.

The Grand Army reached Mozhaisk on October 28, having burned and destroyed everything they could not take with them. A few miles beyond Mozhaisk they came upon a ghastly sight—the battlefield of Borodino, seven weeks after the battle. "We all stared around us," Ségur reminisces, "and saw a field, trampled, devastated, with every tree shorn off a few feet above the earth. . . . Everywhere the earth was littered with battered helmets and breastplates, broken drums, fragments of weapons, shreds of uniforms, and blood-stained flags. Lying amid this desolation were thirty thousand half-devoured corpses. The scene was dominated by a number of skeletons lying on the crumbled slope of one of the hills; death seemed to have established its throne up there. . . . The emperor hurried by [the battlefield], and no one else stopped, hunger, cold, and the enemy urging us on."

Even more horrible than the site of the battle was the military hospital that had been set up in a monastery nearby and whose inmates were dying of hunger, exposure, and sheer neglect, surrounded by pestilential filth. Napoleon ordered them to be placed on every available vehicle, but many were dumped by the roadside: the drivers preferred to sacrifice them rather than their plunder. Just before Gzhatsk, the French found several hundred Russian prisoners of war whose heads had been shattered by their Polish, Spanish, and Portuguese escorts. Napoleon immediately ordered that these executions be stopped. "After that," says Ségur, "we simply let our unfortunate prisoners die of hunger in the enclosures [in which] we penned them up for the night, like cattle."

While Napoleon with the Guard and the Westphalian troops made his way to Smolensk, the other corps of the Grand Army had to battle the Russian forces that had caught up with them. They reached Vyazma after heavy fighting on November 3, with Marshal Davout's corps bringing up the rear. Three days later, as the retreat continued, the first heavy snow fell. "Everything in sight became vague, unrecognizable," says Ségur. "Objects changed their shape; we walked without knowing where we were or what lay ahead, and anything became an obstacle. . . . Yet the poor wretches [the soldiers] dragged themselves along, shivering, with chattering teeth, until the snow packed under the soles of their boots, a bit of debris, a branch, or the body of a fallen comrade tripped them and threw them down. Then their moans for help went unheeded. The snow soon covered them up and only low white mounds showed where they lay. Our road was strewn with these hummocks, like a cemetery." The temperature was $5°$ F., and it was to sink even lower. Numbed by the cold, the men dropped their muskets, broke rank, fell behind in small groups of stragglers, whom the Cossacks and the peasants slaughtered mercilessly. The hardy ones who continued the march, sustained by visions of rest, food, and warmth at Smolensk, lived almost exclusively on horseflesh, only half-cooked on bivouac fires that would barely burn. In the morning, around the extinct fires, rings of frozen bodies could be seen, marking the spots of the soldiers' last sleep. Discipline disintegrated with the army: regiments shrank to battalion strength, battalions to platoons.

Napoleon reached Smolensk on November 9 and stayed for five days to reorganize what troops remained to him—fifty thousand at the most. Smolensk proved a disappointment. There were barely enough supplies to dole out to the units; stragglers were left to starve, the quartermasters insisting on army regulations that forbade the distribution of rations to individual soldiers. Thus hundreds who had survived the cold and the Russian attacks died victims of red tape. Others, determined to live, turned to banditry.

To stay in Smolensk—the original plan—had become inconceivable, what with Kutuzov's army pressing from the rear, another army, under General Wittgenstein, approaching from the north, and the Russian Army of the Danube, under Admiral Chichagov, from the south. Thus Vilna became the next goal and Lithuania the promised land. On November 17 Napoleon decided to attack Kutuzov in order to draw him off the corps of Davout and Ney. The maneuver succeeded as far as Davout was concerned, thanks to the determination of the Imperial Guard and to Kutuzov's refusal to engage all his forces. It was hazardous to wait for Ney, however, and Napoleon decided to continue the march and to sacrifice the rear. Ney, the "bravest of the brave," was already being mourned as dead when, several days later, he made contact with Viceroy Eugene. He had lost seven-eighths of his troops, who had been reduced to a thousand during almost a week's continuous marching and fighting.

Minsk, with its ample stores, having fallen to Admiral Chichagov, Napoleon had no choice but to fight his way through to Vilna by whatever way he could, holding off in the meantime three Russian armies that were pressing on him from all sides. At Borisov, on the Berezina River, the remants of his army were reinforced by the corps of Marshal Victor, which he had left in the rear during his advance on Moscow. These men were still fresh, and they were utterly ignorant of the disaster that had befallen the main army. Their astonishment, says Ségur, was extreme: "When . . . they saw in Napoleon's wake a mob of tattered ghosts draped in women's cloaks, odd pieces of carpet, or greatcoats burned full of holes, their feet wrapped in all sorts of rags, they were struck with consternation. They stared in horror as those skeletons of soldiers went by, their gaunt, gray faces covered with disfiguring beards, without weapons, shameless, marching out of step, with lowered heads, eyes on the ground, in absolute silence, like a gang of convicts." All the same, those skeletons of soldiers managed, during the following three days, to fight one of the most astounding holding actions in history.

With Victor's troops and with the corps of Marshal Oudinot, which had reached Borisov ahead of the main army, Napoleon's forces swelled to between thirty and forty thousand men (in addition to as many stragglers). The Russian forces arrayed against him numbered three times as many—sixty-five thousand under Kutuzov, thirty thousand under Wittgenstein, and thirty thousand under Chichagov. To break out of their ring, he had to force a passage across the Berezina. The undertaking seemed impossible, yet he undertook it. The bridge at Borisov had been partially destroyed and could not be rebuilt under enemy fire. A more promising spot for the crossing was to the north, at the village of Studzianka. Fortunately for Napoleon, Chichagov, who was out of touch with the other Russian armies, was convinced that Napoleon would try to cross at Borisov. Thus, when the French van arrived at Studzianka on November 25, only a small Cossack detachment was there to guard the opposite shore. At sunrise the next morning, while some cavalry detachments forded the river to clear

A contemporary Russian engraving shows the "exemplary courage of twenty Russian peasants . . . sentenced to death for their devotion to their religion, their czar, and their native land."

the far bank, the pontoniers began the construction of two trestle bridges. Up to their chins in water and battling the ice floes, they succeeded in completing the smaller bridge by 1 P.M. The larger bridge was finished three hours later; although it broke several times in the following seventy-two hours, the pontoniers—men of inexhaustible stamina —repaired it each time.

Oudinot's corps and the artillery crossed on the first day, November 26. Ney followed the next day, as did the Guard and the emperor himself. The western bridgehead thus was made secure; on the east bank, however, General Partouneaux's division, which had been left at Borisov to stem off Wittgenstein's army, was virtually annihilated and forced to surrender. This success, and the fact that the French army was now divided by the river into two approximately equal parts, encouraged Wittgenstein and Chichagov to launch simultaneous attacks on both banks the following day, November 28. Despite their decisive superiority, they were repulsed in an all-day battle by Victor on the eastern bank and by Ney and Oudinot on the western one. While the fighting raged, the stragglers, the baggage trains, and the civilians kept on crossing; when Russian shells began to explode in their midst, their confusion turned into panic. Some cut their passage through the inextricable jumble of vehicles, horses, and humans with their swords and bayonets; women and children were trampled to death; hundreds fell into the water and were pushed back as they tried to climb onto the bridge. Then the larger bridge suddenly parted in the middle. Unaware of the accident, those in the rear kept pushing the ones in front, forced them over the edge, and fell in themselves. Yet even in this panic horror, some retained their humanity. Amidst the screaming, cursing mob, Ségur reports, an

A German lieutenant, C. W. Faber du Faur, filled a sketchbook with impressions of the Russian campaign. Above, a soldier stealing geese; below, scenes of the great retreat from Moscow

artilleryman could be seen leaping into the river to rescue a small child and, as he carried it to the far shore, trying to console it for the loss of its mother.

The bridge was repaired, and about nine in the evening Victor began to march his corps across it and the foot bridge, cutting his way through the mob. The next morning, the pontoniers, seeing the Russians approaching, set fire to the bridges. Several thousands, including some women and children, were stranded on the bank. Some tried to swim, some leaped on ice floes, some sought to make a dash over the burning bridge, others stayed and resignedly waited for the Russians. All in all, Napoleon lost at least twenty-five thousand men in the crossing. Most of these, however, were stragglers. That he managed to cross at all and to salvage the bulk of his remaining forces was a miracle of tenacity and heroism.

After the crossing of the Berezina, the army disintegrated entirely. On December 3 only about nine thousand men remained in formation; a week later even half of these had fallen by the wayside. The temperature sank to −13° F. To warm themselves for a few minutes, the soldiers would set whole houses on fire. Some of the details given by Ségur seem scarcely credible: "The light of these conflagrations," he writes, "attracted some poor wretches whom the intensity of the cold and suffering had made delirious. They dashed forward in a fury, and with gnashing teeth and demoniacal laughter threw themselves into those raging furnaces, where they perished in dreadful convulsions. Their starving companions watched them die without apparent horror. There were even some who laid hold of the bodies disfigured and roasted by the flames, and—incredible as it may seem—ventured to carry this loathsome food to their mouths." (One hopes that here Ségur's sense of drama carried him somewhat beyond the literal truth.)

Such was the end of the Grand Army, which half a year earlier had been more than six hundred thousand strong. At Kovno, on December 14, Ney held off the pursuing Russians with a few artillerymen and a handful of German infantry while the last remnants of the Grand Army crossed the Niemen into East Prussia; he was the last man to cross the bridge.

On December 3 at Molodechno Napoleon dictated his famous Twenty-ninth Bulletin, announcing the annihilation of the Grand Army. It concludes with the famous words, "His Majesty's health has never been better." On the evening of the 5th, accompanied by Caulaincourt and by his Mameluke Roustam, he entered a carriage and began his headlong dash to Paris, leaving Murat in command. By carriage and by sleigh he crossed Lithuania, Poland, East Prussia, Germany, and France in two weeks, unrecognized, stopping overnight only at Dresden, for a conference with the king of Saxony, and indulging in a continuous soliloquy which Caulaincourt recorded almost verbatim. When he arrived at the Tuileries, without warning, during the night of December 18–19, wrapped in his great fur coat, the palace guards thought they saw a ghost.

It is to Napoleon's credit that he delayed his return until after there was nothing further he could do for his army. His thoughts had been fixed upon Paris ever since his retreat from Smolensk: he must dash back and raise a new army before the news of his debacle had produced its impact on Europe, particularly on Germany, which seemed ready for an uprising, and on France, where a strange and farcical coup d'état had just demonstrated the weakness of his regime. The latter affair, of which Napoleon received news on November 6 through a courier, was particularly disquieting. A General Claude François de Malet, arrested in 1808 for complicity in a republican plot to overthrow the emperor, had recently been released from prison into the care of a Dr. Dubuisson, in Paris, who kept a clinic for mentally disturbed patients. Several other political prisoners, most of them royalists, also had been released into the doctor's care, and together with Malet they hatched a conspiracy against Napoleon that was insane enough to have very nearly succeeded.

On the night of October 23 Malet slipped from Dr. Dubuisson's home, put on his uniform, and, accompanied by two young men, presented himself at a barracks of security troops. He awakened its commandant, told him that Napoleon had died in Russia, and produced a forged order requesting that the commandant put his men under Malet's control. The commandant complied. At the head of his troops, Malet proceeded to the prison of La Force, where he gained admission, set free two other generals, La Horie and Guidal, convinced them that Napoleon was dead, and invited them to help him carry out a bloodless revolution that would allow an electoral assembly to choose between a republican and a Bourbon restoration. They believed his story. La Horie and Guidal went to the Ministry of Police, where they arrested Savary and locked him up; to the Prefecture of Police, where they arrested the prefect; and to the War Office, where they arrested the minister of war, Marshal Clarke. Meanwhile, at the Hôtel de Ville, Malet persuaded the prefect of the Seine, Frochot, to swallow the same story and to get ready a hall for the reception of the provisional government.

All went well until Malet went to arrest the commandant of the Paris garrison troops, General Hulin, who resisted and whom Malet shot with his pistol. In the ensuing confusion, Malet was recognized by two officers and arrested. He was court-martialed and shot along with twelve accomplices. Even more remarkable than the credulity of Malet's dupes was the submissiveness with which they accepted a change of regime, without even giving a thought to the existence of the empress or the king of Rome. Thus, even as the Grand Army was vanishing before Napoleon's eyes, the dream of dynastic security vanished as well. Before he left France in the spring of 1813 to campaign in Germany, Napoleon took care to provide for a regency council, headed by the empress, that would govern the empire in the event of his absence or his death.

In his bulletin of December 3, 1812, and in his explanations to his German allies, Napoleon had placed the blame for his rout on the barbarity of the Russian winter and of the Russian nation. Actually, he could have avoided the catastrophe if he had not obstinately piled mistake upon mistake and allowed wishful thinking to take the place of calculation. Nevertheless, he was justified in his belief that if he could keep the loyalty of his allies, his situation was by no means desperate. The loyalty of his allies, however, was very shaky, and Prussia was the first to defect. On December 30 General Yorck, in command of the Prussian auxiliary corps (a unit which, having had a relatively small share in the fighting, was still intact), signed an agreement with the Russian general opposing him. By the terms of the Convention of Tauroggen, so-called after the small Lithuanian town where it was signed, the Prussian corps was declared to be neutral until Yorck had received further instructions from his king, and the Russians were able to march unopposed through Prussian territory in pursuit of the French.

In making this agreement, Yorck had acted entirely on his own initiative, and he was at first disavowed by King Frederick William. Vacillating by nature, at the mercy of the large French garrisons stationed in Berlin and elsewhere in Prussia, as terrified of Napoleon as he was eager to shake off his yoke, the king played a two-faced game in the first three months of 1813. While assuring the French ambassador in Berlin of his continued loyalty to Napoleon, he also entered into negotiations with Alexander. During the last days of February, at Kalisch, the representatives of the two sovereigns concluded a treaty of alliance; this was kept secret until March 13, when, at Breslau, Frederick William openly declared war on France. The response to his call to arms was enthusiastic; indeed, in their patriotic exaltation the Prussian people were far ahead of their king, who had long hesitated to unchain a popular movement. Most of this enthusiasm, however, was purely vocal, and it was largely limited to the urban middle class and to intellectuals: the number of volunteers who joined the colors fell below what had been expected, and it was necessary to resort to conscription. In fact, although the campaign of 1813 came to be known in German history as the War of Liberation, it was the Russians rather than the Prussians who drove the French out of Prussia in the early months of that year, and it took Prussia several more months to regain her military strength.

Prussia's patriotic fervor was disquieting to the other German sovereigns. They distrusted the all-German nationalist sentiments of its intellectual leadership; they also distrusted the territorial ambitions of the House of Prussia. The Germans' "War of Liberation" from France might easily turn into a war of liberation from their own sovereigns or into a Prussian bid for hegemony over all the Germanies. For the time being, the sovereigns of the Con-

OVERLEAF: *The remnants of the Grand Army crossed the Berezina on two hastily constructed bridges. A watercolor by an unknown artist shows some of the men swimming the icy river.*

federation of the Rhine turned a deaf ear to the exalted appeals of the patriots. As for Austria, she had withdrawn her forces from the struggle by a secret convention with Russia, but she hesitated to break with Napoleon before she could form an army equal in strength to that of Russia, which she feared almost as much as she feared France.

When Napoleon took the field in the spring of 1813 to stem the Russian advance at the Elbe, the states of the Confederation of the Rhine were still his allies, and his new Grand Army was German, Italian, and Polish as well as French. In appealing to his troops, he sought to counteract German nationalism and hatred of France with a European nationalism directed against Russia. The propaganda line was set by his proclamation of May 3: "In the past campaign, the Russians found no defense against our armies except in the ferocious methods practiced by their barbaric ancestors: armies of Tatars burned the fields and cities and Holy Moscow herself! Today they come into our homes . . . to preach revolt, anarchy, civil war, and murder. . . . They want to set off a moral conflagration from the Vistula to the Rhine so that they may, according to the custom of despotic governments, put a desert between themselves and us. The madmen! Little do they know the Germans and their loyalty to their sovereigns, their prudence, their love of order, their good sense! How little they know the power and the courage of the French! . . . We shall throw these Tatars back into the atrocious climes which they must never leave. . . . European civilization owes you a debt. Soldiers! Italy, France, and Germany offer you their gratitude."

Thus the propaganda pattern was set for ages to come: on the one hand, the intoxicated German nationalism with its exaltation of war, reveling in fantasies of revenge against France; on the other hand, the Russian bogeyman, the myth of barbarian Asiatic hordes raping, looting, setting cities on fire, come to destroy European civilization—a myth that can be conveniently buried or unearthed according to the requirements of the occasion. A year later Napoleon instructed his minister of police to publish in the press details about "Sixty-year-old women and young girls of twelve raped by groups of thirty to forty soldiers" and to convince the public that the Russians intended "to march on Paris and to burn down the city after carrying away whatever they could find." The conduct of the Russians in France during the campaign of 1814 was no worse than that of the Grand Army in Russia two years earlier and probably better than that of the Prussians. Far from burning Paris, Czar Alexander saved it from Prussian vindictiveness; nevertheless, it became an article of faith that Russian soldiers loot more thoroughly and rape more and older women than do any other soldiers.

While Napoleon, having just led half a million men to destruction, was raising another army of several hundred thousands, many of them barely out of childhood, and while Prussia was preparing to change sides and to make war,

yet another and quite unexpected adversary joined the anti-Napoleonic coalition. Since the eighteenth century, the Kingdom of Sweden had been oscillating between a pro-French and a pro-Russian foreign policy. Gustavus III had been decidedly pro-French, but when in 1792 he was about to champion a European coalition in defense of the French monarchy against the revolutionists, an assassin's bullet put an end to his plans. In 1805 his son, Gustavus IV, who seemed to have borrowed his principles of policy from Don Quixote, joined the coalition of England, Russia, and Austria against Napoleon. At Tilsit, it may be recalled, Czar Alexander sacrificed his Swedish ally to his new friendship with Napoleon, who generously encouraged him to seize Finland from Sweden. In the unequal struggle the Russians had emerged victorious, overrunning Finland and marching over the frozen Baltic to seize the Åland Islands.

When Gustavus persisted in continuing the struggle, risking the occupation of all Sweden by Russia, the nobles and the army rebelled and in March, 1809, forced him to abdicate. Gustavus went into exile and was succeeded by his uncle, the duke of Södermanland, who became king as Charles XIII. Peace with Russia, Denmark, and France was signed at last by the beginning of 1810. Charles XIII having no heir, a Danish prince was at first adopted as crown prince. The successor-designate, however, died quite suddenly in May, 1810. A rumor accused Count Axel von Fersen—once the friend of Queen Marie Antoinette and later the adviser of Gustavus IV—of being responsible for the prince's death, and Fersen was beaten to death by a furious mob outside the Senate House in Stockholm.

The question of the Swedish succession having taken on a rather explosive character, the aging king, who was eager to delegate his authority to a younger man, cast about for another heir to the crown. His choice landed on Marshal Bernadotte, prince of Ponte Corvo and brother-in-law of Joseph Bonaparte, king of Spain. Bernadotte had commanded the French troops in northern Germany during the hostilities with Sweden, and the Swedes had been impressed not only by his imposing appearance and bearing but also by his chivalrous conduct toward the vanquished. Once a confirmed republican, convinced of his superior abilities, inclined to make a great show of idealism in his speeches, but prudent in action, Bernadotte had always resented Napoleon Bonaparte's rise, had plotted against him on occasion, and was thoroughly distrusted by him. Since they were more or less related, Napoleon was unable to withhold his consent (which he granted somewhat grudgingly) to Bernadotte's accepting the Swedish offer. Although Charles XIII lived on until 1818, he soon delegated matters of government to the new prince royal, who ruled Sweden long before he became king as Charles XIV.

Even before Bernadotte's arrival in Stockholm, Napoleon had forced Sweden to join the Continental System and to declare war on England, but since the actual execution of the Berlin and Milan Decrees would have meant the destruction of Swedish commerce, Bernadotte paid mere lip service to them, while the English government, aware of his delicate position, made no serious effort to interfere with Swedish shipping. As a result relations between Sweden and France became increasingly tense; nevertheless, when Napoleon invaded Russia, he apparently hoped that Bernadotte would either join him or, at the very least, assume a threatening enough stance to force the Russians to keep a large military force immobilized in Finland. In these hopes he was disappointed. In the late summer of 1812 Alexander and Bernadotte met at Åbo (now Turku) in Finland and reached an agreement of friendly neutrality that released the Russian troops in the north for combat against the Grand Army.

Negotiations for a closer alliance continued, largely through the unofficial intermediary of Bernadotte's old friend Madame de Staël, who had just crossed Russia in her flight from Napoleon and had held several conversations with Alexander before proceeding to Stockholm. About the same time her companion, literary adviser, and the tutor of her children, August Wilhelm Schlegel, published a widely read pamphlet that helped to prepare the Swedes for their country's joining the anti-French coalition. Bernadotte had designs on Norway, which indeed he was to wrest from the Danish crown in 1814; he was also tempted by the prospect—suggested to him by Madame de Staël and by Schlegel, who became his secretary—of ascending the French throne after Napoleon's downfall. On March 3, 1813, he concluded an alliance with England; two months later part of the thirty thousand Swedish troops promised landed in Pomerania. Their presence was to contribute considerably to Napoleon's defeat in Germany; the emperor never forgave his former marshal for tipping the scales against him. "A Frenchman held the destiny of the world in his hands," he remarked of Bernadotte at St. Helena. "He was one of the principal direct causes of our misfortunes."

With a new coalition forming against him, Napoleon sought to conciliate those who were still on his side, notably Austria and his own nation. His brutal treatment of the pope had turned a large part of the population against him, and the devout Emperor Francis had interceded on Pius' behalf. Napoleon had barely returned to Paris when, amidst the preparations for a new campaign, he began to devote a large part of his precious time to an attempt at reconciliation with his prisoner. Pius had been transported in the preceding year, on Napoleon's orders, from Savona to the château of Fontainebleau. The journey had taken place under the most gruelling circumstances; the pope, who was shaking with fever and on the point of death, was allowed only once throughout the eleven days of the voyage to stop and rest for more than an hour. "May God pardon him," Pius murmured as his carriage went at a gallop through the cobbled streets of Lyons, "since, for my part, I have already pardoned him."

It took Pius a month to recover at Fontainebleau; during that time Napoleon's army in Russia began to disintegrate. Now the emperor needed the pope's help. He wrote to him, suggesting a meeting, and had the empress in person take the message to the prisoner. On January 18, 1813, Napoleon arrived at Fontainebleau; on the 25th he and Pius signed a preliminary agreement for a new Concordat. Exactly what was said and done during that week no one knows, since the emperor and the pope conferred in strict privacy. That the pope had to suffer several violent outbursts on the emperor's part seems certain. Pius himself afterward confirmed that he had been treated extremely rudely, but denied that the emperor had actually taken hold of his robe and shaken him, as had been rumored. Although he stood firm against Napoleon's threats and won virtually every point in dispute, he signed the agreement with considerable reluctance, since it dealt exclusively with matters of Church government and failed to restore the Papal States to him. It was only a year later, when France was being invaded by the Allies, that Napoleon offered Pius the restoration of his territories; and when Pius rejected the offer on the ground that no special treaty was required to return stolen property, Napoleon had him packed off to Savona once again. (Pius' captivity ended only when the Allies reached the outskirts of Paris; on March 19, 1814, the emperor was obliged to order him released, and he was able to return to Rome.)

During the months that Napoleon spent at Paris, the Russians and Prussians had forced the viceroy Eugene—who had replaced Murat as the emperor's lieutenant on the eastern front—to fall back to a line roughly following the Elbe and Weser Rivers. A holding action was the most he could accomplish, since his troops, consisting of the French garrisons stationed in Prussia, the remnants of the Grand Army, and the German auxiliaries, were an extremely weak force. Nevertheless, Napoleon's

Outside the Austrian city of Graz, a troop of volunteers prepares to set off to join the War of Liberation against Napoleon.

situation appeared by no means desperate when, on April 25, he joined his new Grand Army at Erfurt to open his offensive. The two hundred thousand troops that he had virtually stamped out of the ground were a larger force than the combined Russian and Prussian armies then in Germany, and the coalition he was facing was weaker than the Austro-Russian coalition he had defeated in the Austerlitz campaign. But Napoleon was no longer the man he had been at Austerlitz, and his army lacked the training, the cohesion, and the spirit of the first Grand Army. Of the Polish, German, and Italian contingents, only the first was reliable; many of the units consisted of raw recruits; and the cavalry was decidedly inadequate. After a few initial successes, these weaknesses became only too apparent.

Napoleon set out from Erfurt on May 1 with the main part of his forces, to march on Leipzig, which he occupied two days later after inflicting a severe defeat on the Allies at Grossgörschen. As the Allies fell back, he recovered Dresden and on May 19–21 defeated them again in the bloody Battle of Bautzen. These victories, however, were both costly and indecisive, and Napoleon's resources were giving out. On May 18 he had sent Caulaincourt to Czar Alexander's headquarters to open peace negotiations, and on June 4 he agreed to an armistice that was to last until July 20. The truce had been mediated by the Austrian government, whose stand had become increasingly equivocal. In consenting to the truce, Napoleon was probably motivated by a desire to make peace before Austria changed sides; in case peace should not materialize, he would reorganize his army and attempt to split the Russo-Prussian alliance at the conference table. In this calculation he made several mistakes: the Allied armies were in even worse shape and more demoralized than his, and the armistice was to them an unhoped-for boon; moreover, the armistice gave Austria a chance to prepare her about-face, allowed Bernadotte's troops time to reach the zone of combat, and offered the Allies an opportunity to work on the feelings of the Saxons, Bavarians, and Württembergers. Yet if the armistice was a grave mistake, once he had accepted it, Napoleon made an even worse error in not making peace at the price proposed by the Allies.

With Metternich acting as mediator, the French, Russian, and Prussian representatives conferred at Prague in desultory fashion for several weeks. It soon became apparent that both the Allies and Austria were merely stalling for time. On June 24 the Russian, Austrian, and Prussian representatives signed a secret treaty laying down their minimum demands for peace with France: the Grand Duchy of Warsaw was to be dissolved and partitioned; Prussia to be restored to her 1806 boundaries; Illyria to be returned to Austria; the Confederation of the Rhine dissolved; the Hanseatic cities restored to independence. If Napoleon refused these conditions, Austria

was to join the coalition against him on July 20. The conditions of this Treaty of Reichenbach were by no means impossible to accept, but the Allies were fully aware that Napoleon was not the man who would accept them as long as he kept any hope of winning a victory; nor were they eager that he should accept them.

Even the most hardened realists have blind spots of naïveté, and Napoleon was no exception. There can be little doubt that he had seriously held on to the belief that Emperor Francis of Austria would never make war on the husband of his daughter, notwithstanding abundant historical examples of such base behavior. The sudden realization of Austria's duplicity cured him of his dynastic delusions and filled him with anguish. He summoned Metternich to his headquarters at Dresden. The interview, according to Metternich, lasted for nine hours, most of them stormy. It was, says the minister, "a most curious mixture of the most heterogeneous subjects, of intermittent friendliness with the most passionate outbreaks." Napoleon started by asking Metternich how much England had paid him for his treachery—hardly a diplomatic beginning. The minister remaining cool and haughty, the emperor worked himself into the kind of threatening tirade of which he was a master, until Metternich interrupted his boasts by pointing out that most of his soldiers were mere boys. Flinging his hat to the ground, the emperor shouted in a rage: "You don't know what passes in a soldier's mind . . . a man like me troubles himself little about a million men." When Metternich failed to pick up his hat for him, both men began to pace up and down the room in silence, with the imperial hat remaining on the ground between them, a symbol of Metternich's defiance and of Napoleon's stubborn refusal to humble himself.

Calming down at last, Napoleon took on a cajoling tone and led Metternich to the map room. But Metternich refused to bargain, and at the end of the exhausting interview the break was complete. The only concession made by Austria was to extend until August 10 the time limit for Napoleon's acceptance of the Allies' terms. On August 12 Emperor Francis declared war on his son-in-law, bringing the total of Allied troops in central Europe to more than half a million. Within a few weeks Bavaria also announced her defection from the French alliance and joined the Coalition. In Spain Wellington had just routed King Joseph at Vitoria. From one end of Europe to the other the nations were arrayed against their weakening conqueror; against them, he pitted the last crop of French youth, his own stubborn will, and the gambler's trust in the possibility of one lucky and decisive blow. In a long "Note on the general state of my affairs," which he addressed to himself in Dresden on August 30, he ended his considerations with this characteristic remark: "Great events, a great battle, would end both the campaign and the war." Apparently Russia had taught him nothing.

THE CZAR'S PEOPLE

When Czar Alexander I visited Moscow just before the French invasion, he found his way to the Kremlin blocked by crowds of excited citizens. "Keep back, my children! Let me pass!" he called to them, but they pressed forward nevertheless, eager to touch his carriage. "No, no, you are our father," they answered. "Ride over us, trample on us . . . !" Russia had joined Europe in the eighteenth century, but to Westerners the nation was still unfathomable. Visitors might find the aristocracy familiar, but the rest of the people, and the cities, except for St. Petersburg, were indescribably exotic. (Above, St. Basil's Cathedral in Moscow.) Europeans could never understand that what the Muscovites proclaimed was true. They were the czar's, and he could, if he liked, trample on them. That submissive state of mind had long vanished from the West, if indeed it had ever existed there. Everyone in Russia had been bound to the czar in service, the lower orders as serfs, the gentry as soldiers and government administrators. The gentry gradually shook off their service obligations, but the peasants could not, and by 1800 most of the population were little better than slaves.

REFORM AND REACTION

In some ways the difference between Russia and the rest of Europe was even more marked in 1889 than it had been in 1789. In 1789 most European nations were ruled by autocrats, as Russia was; the common people were impoverished and powerless and the aristocrats continually tried to increase their own privileges. But during the following century the rest of Europe advanced at a much faster rate than Russia did. In her writings and in her actions, Catherine the Great showed herself to be an enlightened monarch; she wrote a treatise on politics that was censored in prerevolutionary France because it was too liberal. Alexander came to the throne with a strong determination to reform his country. He even toyed with the idea of abolishing the autocracy and setting up a republic. But when it actually came to surrendering any of their imperial power, both Alexander and his grandmother reined their generous impulses. Their subjects, the gentry, were equally jealous of their prerogatives and refused to give up any of their rights over the serfs. Both rulers failed to approach a solution for Russia's major problems, serfdom and despotism. Both rulers ended their reigns with a reaction against liberalism, a reaction that their successors carried to an irrational extreme.

The brief reign of Catherine's son Paul (1796–1801) was a nightmare. The czar terrorized his subjects, inflicting on them cruel and arbitrary punishments for the most trivial misdemeanors. Before he was assassinated Paul had outlawed Western books and French clothing and closed down most of Russia's printing presses. His efforts to limit the amount of time that a serf owed to his master did inaugurate a change in the official attitude toward serfdom, but, unfortunately, the reform was unenforceable. In any case, it was motivated by the czar's insane hatred of the gentry, rather than by liberalism.

When they did attempt reform, both Catherine and Alexander were more effective. During Catherine's reign the length of military service was decreased to twenty-five years; before then conscription had meant a life sentence. The use of torture in judicial investigations was abolished, although the knout was not outlawed until 1845. Under Catherine and Alexander the corrupt and clumsy system of government administration was made slightly less corrupt and slightly less clumsy. The privilege of purchasing real estate was no longer limited to members of the aristocracy. For the first time the Russian government began to spend substantial sums of money on education. New universities were founded, schools were set up for young ladies, and promising youths were sent abroad to study. An educational reformer who had organized schools throughout the Hapsburg empire was imported from Austria to supervise education in Russia. Religious tolerance was granted to most Christians, including the heretical Old Believers, who had been persecuted before and would be persecuted again. Even the Jews who became Russian subjects after the partition of Poland were treated in a manner that was almost tolerable, comparable to that accorded them in much of Europe before the French Revolution; certainly their life was better then than it was to be later in the nineteenth century, when anti-Semitic pogroms were encouraged by the government.

Alexander I (opposite) came to the throne after his father's assassination.

Above, Catherine the Great; below, her son, Paul I, in his robes as grand master of the Knights of Malta

The Bolshoi (or court) Theatre (above) was one of the many St. Petersburg structures built by Western architects in the neoclassical style. More indigenous to Russia were the "snow mountains" like the one shown below. The Russians delighted in the chilly but exhilarating exercise of sliding down them. In summer they rode down more sedately in carts.

While awaiting a fare, a St. Petersburg coachman rests on his sledge.

ST. PETERSBURG–A CITY FACING WEST

Enforcing his reforms at sword's point, Peter the Great had begun the Westernization of Russia. To turn his nation's face toward the West, he had built a new capital for it on the Gulf of Finland, at the point where the Baltic coast reaches closest to the Russian heartland. St. Petersburg grew quickly; the city was a natural outlet for Russian trade with Europe and by 1800 had become a splendid metropolis. Moscow was still a holy city, the seat of the metropolitan of the Russian Church and the social and intellectual capital of the minor gentry. St. Petersburg, dominated by the imperial court, was crowded with government officials and foreign emissaries, higher nobles and merchants with international connections. Moscow's architecture, with its wooden houses and onion-domed churches, was traditionally Russian. St. Petersburg became one of the masterpieces of baroque art; its monuments, most of them built by Western architects imported by the czars, would not seem out of place anywhere in Europe.

St. Petersburg took more than the court away from Moscow. Through the construction of an extensive network of canals, it was linked to all the rivers of northern Russia and became the hub of the nation's commercial system. Because land transport was so bad before the coming of the railways, river towns only a hundred miles from Moscow became economic satellites of St. Petersburg and were opened to Western influences as Peter the Great had planned. The northern region of the empire produced Russia's major exports—flax and hemp, timber, iron, and tallow—much of which was sent to England for the use of the British navy. During the enforcement of the Continental System, when no ship headed for England or carrying English goods could enter the port, the city suffered badly. That unfortunate episode came to an end when Alexander finally realized that the system designed to destroy England had brought Russia close to ruin, while England, Russia's best customer, still flourished. St. Petersburg remained Russia's major trading outlet until well into the nineteenth century, when the southern port of Odessa became a busy rival, exporting the enormous surplus of grain that was grown on the steppe-lands north of the Black Sea.

Much of St. Petersburg's export trade was in the hands of English merchants, but it was the French who had the most profound influence on the city and the court, and eventually on Russian society as a whole. At the time of the Napoleonic invasion, one English visitor tartly complained that the Russians "can't eat their dinner without a French cook to dress it . . . can't educate their children without unprincipled adventurers from Paris to act as tutors and governesses . . ." "In a word," she concluded, ". . . every association of fashion, luxury, elegance, and fascination is drawn from France." The influence of the French in Russia had begun at the imperial court and was given great impetus by Catherine the Great's admiration for the *philosophes*. Soon it radiated far beyond St. Petersburg. By the end of Catherine's reign the aristocracy had covered its native manners with a veneer of French style, and the intelligentsia had greeted French liberalism with such enthusiasm that the empress herself became frightened.

OVERLEAF: *In 1803 Czar Alexander I ordered a festival to celebrate the hundredth anniversary of the foundation of St. Petersburg. In this view, citizens cross the Neva on a wooden bridge to crowd around an equestrian statue of the founder, Peter the Great.*

A contemporary engraving shows Moscow as it was before the destruction of the city in 1812. The placid Moskva River divides the city

two. At left stand the buildings of the Kremlin, surrounded by towered walls. The city's merchants lived on the opposite side of the river.

A GREAT NATION BOUND IN SERVITUDE

"For the largest part the peasants of Russia are slaves," Czar Alexander I once wrote; "I do not need to dilate on the degradation and the misfortunes of such a position." In 1811, just before Napoleon's invasion of Russia, 58 per cent of all the men in the country (and their families) were bound serfs, slaves of an individual lord. The rest of the peasants—and peasants made up about 95 per cent of Russia's population—were owned by the state, which tied them to the land they worked and might dispose of them at any time by granting them to a court favorite or factory owner. State peasants were far freer than ordinary serfs, but they had no guarantee that they would stay that way. In the four years of his reign Paul I gave away six hundred thousand serfs, a thousand of them on one occasion as a reward to a wit who had impressed the czar with his talent for repartee.

There was virtually no restraint on the control that masters exercised over their serfs. Aside from the more predictable outrages—whippings, rape, and the like—there were other practices of a unique cruelty. Serfs could be sold without their land, or given away in settlement of a debt. Families could be broken up through the sale of individual members to separate masters. (Although this practice was frowned upon, it was legal in most areas.) It was also possible to exile an incompetent serf to Siberia and then be recompensed for it by the government through the exemption of another serf from conscription. Indeed, many masters exiled one serf in order to retain another.

By the time of Alexander the classic pattern of serfdom had been established. The serf customarily worked three days a week for his master and the rest of the time for himself. However, some owners demanded much more than three days' work from their peasants. Those serfs who were allowed to pay burdensome dues to their owners for the privilege of working only their own land or engaging in trade were far better off than those who were forced to work on their master's land as well.

Whatever in the peasant's life was not controlled by the lord was regulated by the elected officers of the *mir,* or village commune. The system of communes has roots in ancient Russian practice; by the eighteenth century most villages had organized one. The commune decided who was to be conscripted and who was to remain at home. It cared for the aged, the sick, and the poor and assigned villagers to their labor. Its main function was the redistribution of village land at regular intervals, to ensure that no individual or family came to control, by purchase or inheritance, too much land while others had too little. Of course, the serfs'

owner could veto any decision that the commune made.

There were ways of escaping serfdom, but they were not very enticing. The classic method had been flight abroad or to border territories, where serfs could find new land or join nomadic hordes. Some of these refugees formed a distinct group, the Cossacks, who were tolerated because they acted as a buffer against the Tatars. When the Tatar threat disappeared, the Cossack lands were incorporated into Russia, and one avenue of escape was closed. Another escape route was the army, which gave freedom to the conscript's family, but required him and his sons to serve for life, until reforms in 1793 reduced the term of service to twenty-five years. Another possibility was exile to Siberia, the usual punishment for village troublemakers. Exiles were provided with land, livestock, and a plow and were given a subsidy by the government until they were self-sufficient. Peasants who maneuvered themselves into a sentence of exile to reach freedom were often sorry; it was a long walk to Siberia, and many perished along the way.

Not all serfs were engaged in agriculture. A special class of state serfs ran the post between St. Petersburg and Moscow. Others were required to bring produce to market along the rivers and canals. These unhappy men were obliged to harness themselves to barges and haul them upstream, unbelievably difficult labor that took a great toll of the workers. In 1815 there were four hundred thousand boatmen engaged in this work on the Volga alone. Other serfs were assigned to work in factories. A merchant or aristocrat who started an iron factory was rewarded for his contribution to Russia's industrialization with the use of a hundred or more peasant families for each blast furnace he built. Usually these peasants were obliged to devote a few months each year to factory work. Their farms were often quite far from the factories, and they had to spend a month or more traveling to and fro to fulfill their obligations.

A few talented serfs became rich through trade or manufacturing and managed to acquire great holdings, despite the interdiction against a serf owning real property or other serfs. They were required to register everything in their master's name, but usually masked some of their assets, for if their owner knew how rich they actually were, he would exact as large a share of their earnings as he could. Ironically, these serfs found it most difficult to purchase their freedom. By a lifetime of hoarding, the ordinary serf might save a few rubles to buy his freedom; but the serf who could be milked of a large sum each year by his master was not released quite so easily.

Below, a village. Above, the interior of a peasant hut. The inmates slept on top of the oven and shared their home with chickens.

Westernized aristocrats adopted European fashions, but most Russians in both the city and the countryside still wore beards and flowing robes. In the market place of a Russian town, both the market porters and the traders wear traditional Muscovite costumes. A barrow of frozen poultry, and frozen carcasses of lambs, cattle, and pigs, are displayed for sale; at left, a butcher splits the head of a swine in half with his axe.

THE
LAST
GAMBLE

Everything failed me just when everything had succeeded!

When, after the breakdown of the Prague conference, hostilities were resumed in mid-August, 1813, Napoleon still had several advantages over his opponents. To begin with, unlike the Allies, he had a clear purpose: to win a decisive battle and to compel the Allies to make peace on his terms. Any alternative was unacceptable to him. The Allies, on the other hand, though they too quite naturally desired a victory, had no settled program in common; in fact, until the beginning of March, 1814, it looked as if their alliance might fall apart at any moment. Furthermore, their command was divided and there was no single head to direct their military or diplomatic operations.

Their main army—some two hundred fifty thousand Austrians and Russians—had its operational base in Bohemia and was commanded by the Austrian field marshal Prince Karl von Schwarzenberg. A capable man, albeit inclined toward excessive caution and slowness, Schwarzenberg was hampered at every moment by the presence of the three Allied sovereigns at his headquarters. Emperor Francis, to be sure, had no pretensions to military ability, but Czar Alexander, who fancied himself the Agamemnon of the Coalition, interfered constantly, and King Frederick William, though scarcely a great strategist, also was argumentative on frequent occasions. Schwarzenberg's headquarters, with the three sovereigns on hand, had the character of a supreme command, certainly, but it was not always

able to maintain its authority over the other two armies that the alliance had mustered against the French.

The larger of these two armies, based in the north, consisted of some one hundred twenty thousand Russians, Prussians, and Swedes and was commanded by Bernadotte. Whether for political motives of his own, or because he feared Napoleon, his former master, or because he lacked decision—whatever the reason—the Swedish crown prince displayed remarkably little energy and co-operation, and if his army contributed to the final victory, this was due less to him than to the most distinguished of his subordinate commanders, the Prussian general von Bülow. The third army, composed of Prussian and Russian units, had its base in Silesia. Its commander, Field Marshal Gebhard Lebrecht von Blücher, who soon was to earn for himself the nickname Marschall Vorwärts!, was alone among the Allied army chiefs in displaying the kind of speed and daring to which Napoleon owed his victories. Unlike his colleagues, who were more courtiers and politicians than military men, Blücher was a crude, blusterous, hard-drinking soldier whose only politics was his violent hatred of Napoleon and of France. His strategy might be summed up by his favorite

Even Waterloo failed to destroy Napoleon's confidence. "All is not lost . . . there is still time to retrieve the situation," he wrote his brother after the battle. Opposite, the battlefield

In his flight from Leipzig, Prince Poniatowski was drowned. He had been made a marshal by Napoleon the day before the battle.

command, "Forward!", but he did possess the essential qualities of a great general: doggedness and the ability to turn up unexpectedly at the most opportune moment.

It is remarkable that Napoleon, who possessed the advantage of his reputation and of his undivided military and political authority, should have failed to exploit them until it was too late. There was a marked decline in his mental energy and in his ability to make quick decisions; although these qualities occasionally returned to him in brief flashes, he was often strangely lethargic and hesitant. His aim, no doubt, was to defeat the Allied armies one by one, but he seemed unable to make up his mind which to attack first. His victory (August 27, 1813) over Schwarzenberg's army at Dresden put fear into the Allied command, but it was not decisive, and it was nullified by the capture of General Vandamme's corps at Kulm three days later and by the failure of Marshal Oudinot, whom he had detached with a large force, to take Berlin. While the Allies raised new troops and received reinforcements from Russia, Napoleon's army dwindled steadily. Its continuous marches and countermarches exhausted and reduced the troops as much as did the inconclusive engagements they fought in, and desertions—especially among the German and Italian troops—rose alarmingly. Thus, when Napoleon concentrated his main forces in the neighborhood of Leipzig in mid-October, their number was less than two hundred thousand. Yet even though the three Allied armies, which were within striking distance, outnumbered the French by more than three to two, Schwarzenberg was reluctant to agree to Blücher's plan for a simultaneous attack by the combined armies, and it was only under Alexander's pressure that he agreed at last to give a decisive battle.

Though conventionally dated October 16–18, the Battle of Leipzig (or Battle of the Nations, as it is called in Germany) opened on October 14 with a sharp engagement between Murat's infantry and cavalry and Schwarzenberg's advance forces. Murat succeeded in holding on to favorable terrain for the impending battle. Napoleon himself arrived at Leipzig on the 14th; the next day was spent in preparations on both sides. Only Schwarzenberg's army had reached the battlefield, and since it was but slightly larger than Napoleon's the emperor hoped to rout it before Bernadotte and Blücher had time to arrive. He very nearly succeeded in doing just that on the 16th, when shortly after noon the noise of a distant cannonade (at first mistaken for thunder) announced the approach of Blücher's army. While the main battle continued undecided, Marshal Marmont with his corps tried to stem Blücher's advance at the village of Möckern. Here the fighting was fierce. The Prussians had to take the village house by house, in hand-to-hand combat, and it was only after resisting six assaults that the French gave way and fell back toward Leipzig. Meanwhile, on the main battlefield, the French advance had been checked. Neither side was victorious, and both sides spent the following day readying themselves for the final clash.

The Allies' inactivity on October 17 is understandable. They were waiting for the arrival on the following day of Bernadotte's army and of seventy thousand reinforcements under the Russian field marshal Bennigsen to give them a decisive superiority. Napoleon's inactivity, on the other hand, is more difficult to explain. He could have retreated and thus avoided an almost certain rout, or he could have attacked Schwarzenberg, whose army was in fairly sorry shape. Possibly he had insufficient intelligence of Bernadotte's and Bennigsen's movements. In any event, instead of resorting to either course, he sent an emissary to his father-in-law to propose an armistice. Emperor Francis did not answer, and on the morrow Napoleon's much reduced army faced an enemy twice its strength. Until 4 P.M. on October 18 Napoleon could still hope for a draw. Indeed, Bennigsen reached the battle only at 2 P.M., and Bernadotte at 4:00. Shortly before the onslaught of Bülow's corps (part of Bernadotte's army) began to turn the battle against him, another serious blow was delivered to Napoleon: in mid-battle the Saxon troops, who up to that point had remained loyal to the emperor, faced about and turned their guns on the French. They were received like long-lost brothers by the Prussian ranks, but not by the king. "These Saxon gentlemen are a little late," Frederick William remarked. King Frederick Augustus of Saxony himself did not take part in the betrayal but remained loyal to Napoleon until the end. There was between the two men something close to friendship; moreover, as grand duke of Warsaw, the king of Saxony had a greater stake in the Napoleonic order than had the other German sovereigns.

It was close to nightfall, but some fifteen hundred guns were still blazing and the French still held on to their main positions, when Napoleon rose from his campstool, on which he had been brooding for some time, and ordered a retreat across the Pleisse River. Indeed, it was the only alternative to annihilation, for although the Allied casualties ran higher than the French, Napoleon's forces had been reduced to about one hundred twenty-five thousand. The retreat from the battlefield took place during the night. Since in order to reach the only available bridge the troops had to cross Leipzig, a spectacular traffic jam soon developed. A French and Polish rear guard under Marshal Poniatowski was left in Leipzig, which the Allies attacked soon after daybreak on October 19; its desperate stand continued for several hours, even after the bridge was blown up prematurely by someone's blunder. When no further resistance was possible, many threw themselves into the water, among them Poniatowski, who drowned. The list of prisoners taken was headed by the king of Saxony and by several generals. The number of killed or wounded during the four days of battle that lasted from October 16 to 19 has been estimated at one hundred twenty thousand, more than half of whom belonged to the victorious side.

Napoleon's retreat across Germany was too swift for the Allies, whose pursuit was ineffective. By this time all Germany had risen against the French. Bavaria had joined the Allies even before the Battle of Leipzig; soon afterward King Jerome fled from Cassel, and the Kingdom of Westphalia collapsed. On November 2, after three days of fighting near Hanau with a Bavarian army under von Wrede, the remnants of the Grand Army crossed the Rhine at Mainz. Only about eighty thousand men were left (not counting stragglers), and a large fraction of these were wiped out by a typhus epidemic after re-entering France.

In fifteen months Napoleon had lost two armies, totaling close to a million men. Except for a few fortresses, whose French garrisons still held out, Germany was liberated, and its dispossessed princes had recovered their lands. In southwest France Wellington was advancing from the Spanish border. In Holland the people were rising against the French officials, whom they expelled. In Italy Murat, to save his throne, made an alliance with the Austrians, who were pressing the French under Eugene. Within the space of two months the Napoleonic Empire had crashed to the ground like a great city in an earthquake. Yet if Napoleon regretted not having accepted the peace terms offered him at Prague only four months earlier, he did not show it.

Nor did the victorious Allies regard him as beaten; they halted their pursuit on the Rhine, undecided whether or not to invade France. Emperor Francis, who distrusted Russia and Prussia, and Bernadotte, whose acquisition of Norway from Denmark was assured, were content to leave Napoleon on the French throne and to make peace. In the Prussian camp Blücher's request for an all-out offensive was overruled by his prudent sovereign. In the Russian headquarters the situation was the reverse: here the gen-

On his retreat through Germany after the disastrous Battle of the Nations, a pensive Napoleon bivouacked among his troops.

erals advised caution and the czar himself was determined to march his armies all the way to the French capital.

Despite the pressure of the British government, which backed Alexander's and Blücher's call for war to the finish, moderate counsels prevailed at first. Early in November, at Frankfort, Metternich in the Allies' name offered Napoleon's representative a generous peace settlement which would have restored France to roughly the borders of 1797, leaving her in possession of the entire left bank of the Rhine, including Belgium. Whether Austria had actually obtained the consent of her allies, and particularly of England, when Metternich made the offer is not certain, yet there can be little doubt that if Napoleon had unhesitatingly and unconditionally accepted the proposals, he might have forced the Allies to abide by their terms or, better still, split their alliance. Instead, he let three weeks go by in shifty diplomatic maneuvers, and by the time he seemed ready to accept the terms the Allies had withdrawn them. On December 22 the Allied armies began to cross the Rhine into France. With the Austrian forces advancing through Switzerland and with Wellington's army in the southwest they had more than half a million troops and fifteen hundred guns. Napoleon could muster an army of less than a hundred thousand soldiers to meet the massive Allied offensive.

Napoleon's only chance to keep his throne and escape utter destruction was to rally the nation behind him in defense of French soil. Militarily, a successful defense was not impossible, since the Allied armies were strung out from the North Sea to the Alps; by defeating them piecemeal he might force them to renew the offer they had made at Frankfort. As will be seen, his strategy nearly succeeded. Politically, Napoleon's hold on the throne would be firmer

Instead of pursuing Napoleon's army, the Allies determined to conquer Paris. Above, Marshal Moncey directs the defense of the city.

than ever if he succeeded in repulsing the invaders at the head of a nation in arms. It is true that France was exhausted. To stir the people to yet another effort some dramatic gesture was needed. Napoleon expected to achieve this effect by addressing a joint session of the Legislative Body, the Senate, and the Council of State. The imposing meeting took place on December 19. In his speech, the emperor, while asking the nation for fresh sacrifices, assured it that he would place no obstacle in the way of an honorable peace. The decision whether to continue the war or to make peace would not be the emperor's alone; all the records pertaining to the recent negotiations with the Allies would be submitted to two commissions of five men each, appointed by the Senate and the Legislative Body. The commissioners' recommendations would, in turn, be presented to each of these two bodies for its approval.

In taking this course, Napoleon anticipated a unanimous endorsement of his policies by both chambers, which would transform what many regarded as his war into a national war. His position at home and with regard to the Allies would be greatly strengthened. To his surprise the endorsement was not vouchsafed him. The Senate, it is true, proved docile and submissive, but the Legislative Body adopted a report that echoed not the emperor's wishes but the state of French public opinion. It politely invited the emperor to issue a declaration to the effect that his sole purpose in continuing the war was to preserve French national independence and territorial integrity. If the Allies refused to guarantee these, France would defend herself. Yet Frenchmen needed something more than patriotic enthusiasm: they wanted a guarantee from the emperor that their liberty, their personal security, their property, and their political rights would in the future be protected from arbitrary interference. The report had been adopted by a vote of 223 to 31. While it did not challenge Napoleon's authority, it gave unmistakable warning that he could not count on the continued loyalty and sacrifices of his nation unless he changed his ways—France had had enough of glory.

The report enraged Napoleon, for it questioned his identity with the nation. In reply he adjourned the Legislative Body on December 31, and on the following day hurled a passionate tirade at the deputies who had come to present their wishes for the New Year. Instead of helping him, they were making things more difficult. They did not represent the people; only he did, having been confirmed in his authority by four plebiscites. Only he had the right to speak for France; they represented only the *départements,* whither he invited them to return. He was France; he was the throne. "Supposing even that I am at fault," he concluded, "you should not have reproached me in public. Dirty linen should be washed in private. Besides, France needs me more than I need France."

Having taken measures to speed the conscription, to mobilize the National Guard, and to establish a regency during his absence at the front, Napoleon left Paris on January 25. The regent was Empress Marie Louise, assisted by Cambacérès and by King Joseph; her name was popularly given as a nickname to the new recruits, most of whom were only beardless boys.

As Napoleon took the field toward the end of January, 1814, his genius and energy flared up once more in a final and astounding blaze. He seemed to be not one Napoleon but several, boldly taking the offensive against a vastly superior enemy and, at the same time, spurring his subordinates, both military and civilian, to new heights of activity. Concentrating his offensive against the most active of his adversaries, he defeated Blücher's army on January 29 at Brienne, where he had been a schoolboy once; recovered from a defeat inflicted on him, on February 1, by Blücher and Wrede at La Rothière; and in the following two weeks broke up Blücher's army in four successive battles. He then turned on Schwarzenberg's army and forced it to fall back. During the same period peace negotiations were started at Châtillon, where the Allies had their headquarters. Lord Castlereagh, the British foreign minister, had arrived there some time earlier; Caulaincourt, Napoleon's new foreign minister, arrived on February 5. Relations between Austria on the one hand and Russia and Prussia on the other were approaching the breaking point, and only the intervention of Lord Castlereagh managed to mend the rift in the alliance before negotiations got under way.

Caulaincourt's instructions were to accept the terms offered two months earlier at Frankfort, but the Allies had stiffened their demands: France was to revert to her borders of 1791—that is, surrender the left bank of the Rhine, Belgium, Savoy, and Nice. To Napoleon the thought that France, after conquering Europe at the cost of a million lives, should revert to exactly what she had been at the start of two decades of glory was unbearable. No true gambler quits when he breaks even. Interrupted during Napoleon's offensive against Blücher, the negotiations were resumed on February 18. Caulaincourt urged the emperor to accept the Allies' terms, but Napoleon insisted on keeping France's "natural frontiers," which in his opinion included Belgium

and the left bank of the Rhine. His stand resulted in the collapse of the negotiations and cost him his last chance of retaining his throne. Demoralized by their recent defeats, the Allies decided on a withdrawal beyond the Marne and the Oise; before taking this decision, however, they had drawn closer together, and embodied their resolve to fight the war to the finish in the Treaty of Chaumont, signed on March 9. The treaty bound England, Austria, Russia, and Prussia not to negotiate separately with Napoleon, to prosecute the war until France accepted her pre-revolutionary boundaries, and to maintain their alliance for twenty years.

On the day the treaty was signed, Blücher, who in the meantime had regrouped his army and received reinforcements, defeated Napoleon at Laon; three days later Wellington captured Bordeaux. The circle was closing in. Yet even at this point Napoleon refused to admit defeat. He recaptured Rheims from the Russians and on March 17 sent new peace proposals to the Allies—a compromise between the Frankfort and the Châtillon terms. It was too late. There could be no more doubt in the Allies' minds that the opportunity for a complete victory had come. Napoleon continued to maneuver for two more weeks and gave his opponents considerable uneasiness, but his movements were those of a hunted animal rather than those of a commander of armies. The empress fled Paris on March 29 to the south, taking the king of Rome with her; Napoleon, who arrived at Fontainebleau on the following day in the hope of leading the defense of Paris, was never to see either his wife or his son again.

The last battle was fought on March 30, at the outskirts of Paris, below the heights of Montmartre, where Marshals Marmont and Mortier sought to repulse Blücher's and Schwarzenberg's forces. They were defeated, and Kings Joseph and Jerome, who watched the battle from the heights, sped away in flight, authorizing the marshals to conclude an armistice. This the marshals did, agreeing to evacuate Paris. On March 31 Czar Alexander and the king of Prussia rode down the Champs Elysées at the head of their victorious troops. It was the first time since the Hundred Years' War that a foreign army had entered the French capital. Emperor Francis, who was at Dijon, avoided the embarrassment of having to take part in the triumphal entry into a city from which his daughter had been forced to flee but two days earlier.

March 31, 1814, was Talleyrand's day. Alexander had barely entered Paris when Talleyrand offered him his house as residence. Alexander accepted. The two men settled the fate of the emperor in their first discussion since the Congress of Erfurt. Up to the moment of Talleyrand's call on the Russian emperor, the Allies had been uncertain of what to do with Napoleon. Should he be allowed to retain his throne if he consented to the Allies' terms, or should he be compelled to abdicate? If he were compelled to abdicate, who should assume his succession? The British government was committed to the restoration of Louis XVIII, who was already packing his trunks at Hartwell. Emperor Francis was not averse to having his grandson, the king of Rome, succeed to the throne. The Prussians were talking about partitioning France. But the fate of France lay in the hands of Alexander, the ranking sovereign present in Paris that day, for whatever immediate step he took was bound to determine the future.

Being undecided, he professed to be keeping an open mind and asked for Talleyrand's opinion. Talleyrand showed no hesitation whatever. What the Allies lacked, he told Alexander, was a principle. He, Talleyrand, would supply it—the principle of legitimacy. The House of Bourbon must be restored to the throne. Alexander voiced his doubts. Would the French nation, would the administrative and legislative bodies of France accept and support a Bourbon king? Talleyrand had his answer ready: if the Allies made plain their resolve not to make peace or to negotiate with Napoleon or any member of his family, France would welcome the Bourbons, for the overriding desire of the French was for peace and stability. Impressed with this argument, Alexander turned to King Frederick William and to Schwarzenberg. Would they consent to issuing a joint Allied declaration in the sense indicated by Talleyrand? They did, and a few hours later the proclamation was posted. A provisional government was appointed on April 1 (it consisted mainly of Talleyrand's whist partners), and the following day the Senate, on Talleyrand's urging, declared Napoleon deposed.

While on March 31 Alexander and Talleyrand were settling his fate at Paris, Napoleon held a council of war at the château of Fontainebleau, about forty miles to the southeast. He still had troops; to these he could add Marmont's and Mortier's corps, which had just evacuated the capital. With these forces he decided to march on Paris and force the enemy to give battle. The scheme was bold, and it might have succeeded and sparked an uprising inside Paris; yet even if successful, it would merely have prolonged the war without changing its ultimate issue. Fortunately Napoleon could not even begin to put it into execution. In the early afternoon of April 4, as he was about to give his army its marching orders, several of his marshals walked into his room and implored him to reconsider his decision, which would plunge France into civil war; it was his duty to abdicate. To their surprise the emperor agreed without demur and drafted an instrument by which he abdicated the throne in favor of his son. He had not yet signed it, however, when he changed his mind. "Nonsense, gentlemen," he cried, throwing himself on a sofa and slapping his thigh, "let's forget all this and march tomorrow!" But the marshals were adamant, and at length the emperor resignedly put his signature to the document. Ney, Macdonald, and Caulaincourt were appointed to take it to Alexander in Paris. On their way they were joined by Marmont, who on Napoleon's orders had moved his corps to Essonnes, between Paris and Fontainebleau.

At Alexander's headquarters there followed another and no less extraordinary scene. Caulaincourt was a persuasive man whose opinions and character inspired respect and confidence; moreover, having been ambassador to St. Petersburg, he knew Alexander well. Backed by the three marshals, he persuaded the czar to reverse the position he had taken five days earlier under Talleyrand's influence. When Napoleon's emissaries left his room, the czar invited the French provisional government, who had been waiting in an antechamber, to join him. A regency governing for the king of Rome, he explained to them, might be the best solution after all. It would enjoy the support of the French army and of Austria and it would avoid the factional strife that must inevitably attend the return of a Bourbon king. In reply Talleyrand and his colleagues pointed out that the Allies were now thoroughly committed to Louis XVIII and could not sacrifice him without dishonor; moreover, if the king of Rome were recognized as Napoleon's successor, Napoleon would be back within a year. Alexander pondered this, recalled Napoleon's emissaries, dismissed them again, and again recalled Talleyrand and his colleagues. The debaters did not adjourn until two in the morning.

It was an accident that made up Alexander's mind for him. Shortly before Napoleon signed his abdication the provisional government had invited Marmont, whose loyalty to the emperor was wavering, to put his corps at its disposition and to march to Normandy. This Marmont had agreed to do after receiving guarantees of Napoleon's personal safety and liberty. The emperor's abdication and Alexander's wavering changed the picture; however, while Marmont and his fellow emissaries argued through the night with Alexander, Marmont's second-in-command at Essonnes took matters into his own hands and marched his forces to Versailles. Early in the morning of April 5 Alexander was apprised of the move, which signified that at least part of the French army had deserted Napoleon: there was nothing more to fear from that quarter. "You see," he said to one of his advisers, "it is Providence that wills it; it manifests and declares itself. No more doubt, no more hesitation." Thus the question whether France was to be governed by the heirs of Saint Louis or the heirs of the French Revolution was determined by the premature order of an obscure general and by Alexander's tendency to see the hand of Providence in chance events. Napoleon's emissaries were instructed that the emperor's abdication must include the abdication of the rights of his entire family.

The settlement offered by the Allies was humiliating to a man who had ruled Europe from Spain to Poland, but after much inner struggle Napoleon accepted it. He and the empress were to receive an annual revenue of two million francs; the other members of his family, two and a half million francs. The empress was to be given sovereign possession of the duchies of Parma, Piacenza, and Guastalla. Napoleon himself was offered Elba as a sovereign principality. The negotiations took a week and at the last moment, on April 12, he refused to ratify the treaty. During the night he swallowed a dose of poison which he had carried on his person for years. He became violently ill but recovered, and in his recovery saw the hand of destiny: what was Providence to Alexander was Fate to him. He signed the Act of Abdication on April 13 but lingered another week at Fontainebleau, abandoned by almost everybody, including his Mameluke Roustam.

On April 20, as the carriage that was to take him into exile was waiting, he took leave of his Old Guard, which stood drawn up in the court of the château. The scene was charged with emotion, and when he embraced the flag and the eagle in a farewell to glory, his mustachioed veterans gave free course to their tears. Then, escorted by four Allied commissioners, the fallen emperor began his journey across France. Everything went well as far as Valence; in a few places the populace even shouted *"Vive l'Empereur!"* as the procession of carriages passed by. Napoleon's mood was cheerful and philosophical. "After all," he remarked to his travel companions after surveying his career, "I've lost nothing, for I began the game with a six-franc piece in my pocket and I've come out of it very rich." As he got deeper into Provence, however, the atmosphere changed. At Orgon he saw himself being hanged in effigy by a mob. Screaming women converged threateningly on his carriage, calling him the butcher of their husbands and sons and making ready to tear him to pieces while he cowered in terror behind his grand marshal of the palace, General Bertrand. Count Shuvalov, the Russian commissioner, put an end to the scene by haranguing the crowd. "Look at him!" he shouted. "You can see that contempt is the only weapon you ought to use on this man." While the crowd cheered Shuvalov, Napoleon nodded his approval; once out of Orgon he thanked the Russian for saving his life.

In his terror, he disguised himself as a postilion and rode in front of his own carriage; later he posed as Colonel Campbell, the British commissioner. At Aix, where popular demonstrations were particularly violent, he put on yet another disguise—the Austrian commissioner's uniform, the Prussian commissioner's cap, and the Russian commissioner's cloak. It was only when he boarded a British battleship, the *Undaunted,* at Fréjus, that he recovered his composure. It must be said in justice to Napoleon that the journey through Provence was the only occasion on which he displayed physical cowardice and that many a man capable of facing the greatest dangers with serenity would experience the same terror in presence of an infuriated mob. Yet Napoleon did not forgive himself for his display of weakness: the memory of it tortured him until ten months later when he wiped it out by his return.

On May 3, one day before Napoleon's landing at Elba, Louis XVIII made his entry into Paris, after a quarter century of exile—in Germany, in England, in Poland, in Courland, and finally again in England, at Hartwell. Unlike most of his fellow émigrés—particularly his younger brother, the comte d'Artois—he had been mellowed rather than embittered by the experience. In his sixtieth year, inordinately corpulent, apoplectic, and gout-ridden, he was a man of studious tastes, exquisitely polite and tactful, cured of all illusions, religious yet tolerant, moderate and conciliating in his views, and endowed with more wit and wisdom than was common among royalty of the time. Long before his recall to the throne he had resigned himself to the necessity of accepting constitutional government more or less on the English model if ever he wanted to be king. Thus, when Talleyrand and the Napoleonic Senate stipulated early in April, 1814, that Louis's recall was contingent on his acceptance of a constitutional charter, Louis made no difficulties on that score.

Being immobilized by gout, he was forced to delay his return by several weeks and delegated his authority to his brother, the comte d'Artois, who entered Paris on April 12 and was received with a jubilant enthusiasm that astonished even him. It was the first and last occasion in the life of the future Charles X on which he professed liberal sentiments. For two or three weeks Paris seemed an urban Garden of Eden in which victors and vanquished, Napoleonic marshals and royalist courtiers, former revolutionists who had voted for the death of Louis XVI and die-hard émigrés who had sworn to avenge his death, all rejoiced together at their deliverance from war and tyranny and maneuvered separately to snatch for themselves the juiciest fruits in the new Paradise. The idyll was of short duration. Even before his return to Paris, Louis XVIII, prodded by his émigré advisers and encouraged by the reception given his brother, declared that the Constitution drawn up by the Senate was defective and would have to be modified. The welcome given him when he arrived in the city was not nearly as enthusiastic as the one that had been given to his brother.

The Charter which Louis XVIII "granted" to the nation on June 14 dissatisfied both the liberals and the extreme royalists. It provided for a Chamber of Peers, appointed by the king, and for an elective Chamber of Deputies— thus following the English model—but it reserved the right of legislative initiative exclusively for the crown. It left the Napoleonic legal and administrative system intact. It declared the Catholic faith to be the state religion but guaranteed complete freedom of worship. None of these features was particularly objectionable to either faction; what the returned émigrés resented was, in the first place, that there should be a constitution at all, in the second place that the high officials of the Napoleonic regime retained the posts and dignities which the émigrés coveted for themselves, and lastly that the Charter confirmed the validity of the sale of national property to its new owners. This last provision meant that the lands and buildings confiscated during the Revolution from émigrés and from the Church would not be restored to their former owners but retained by those who had purchased them from the state. Since several million Frenchmen had purchased national property, any other solution to the problem would, beyond any doubt, have immediately precipitated another revolution; but as Talleyrand put it, the émigrés had forgotten nothing and learned nothing, and they continued to clamor for the restoration of their property. As for the liberals, their main objection to the Charter was that the king had "granted" rather than accepted it, thus making it an act of royal favor instead of a contract entered into by the king with the sovereign people: it seemed to them that, by a stroke of the pen, Louis XVIII had swept aside the principles that had been established by the French Revolution.

The mass of a nation rarely evinces much interest in constitutions so long as they work and guarantee a minimum of justice and liberty, which the Charter of 1814 unquestionably did. If unrest and discontent mounted steadily despite the unaccustomed blessings of peace and freedom, the reasons must be sought in a number of petty vexations affecting people's everyday lives. One of these was the retention of the unpopular Napoleonic fiscal system; another, the pinch-penny policies of the minister of finance, Baron Louis, who set about the liquidation of the national debt with an admirable but perhaps excessive zeal. The main victims of Baron Louis' parsimony were the thousands of officers of the Napoleonic army who were discharged at half-pay. The replacement of the tricolor by the white flag of the Bourbons was an insult to the entire nation; tired as the French were of war, the tricolor symbolized to them their glory, their honor, and the liberty for which they had fought under it. The Bourbon restoration was only a few months old when it became plain that the abyss created by the Revolution between the old and the new France was about to open up again and that the hatreds, far from having subsided after two decades, had only grown in intensity. Headed by the comte d'Artois, the Ultraroyalists plotted the abrogation of the Charter and the restoration of royal absolutism. Bonapartist generals and officers on half-pay plotted the overthrow of the Bourbons and the recall of Napoleon. Fouché plotted for the transfer of the crown to the duc d'Orléans and as an alternative for a regency under Empress Marie Louise; to allay the objections of the European powers to the latter scheme, he went so far as to suggest that having Napoleon assassinated might ease his wife's way to the regency. To Napoleon, who kept a close watch on France from Elba, it seemed that the moment was not far when France would be ripe for him.

The disappointment and discontent that followed Napoleon's downfall in 1814 was not limited to France. In Spain the people welcomed King Ferdinand as their noble liberator and discovered him to be a witless bully. In northern Italy a stupid and brutal Austrian bureaucracy replaced Viceroy Eugene's intelligent administration and exasperated all but the most obstinate reactionaries. In Germany the peoples of the various states, who had led rather than followed their sovereigns in the liberation of their fatherland, were cheated of their hopes for unity and constitutional government. Both France and her victors had had their time of hope and glory and greatness; now the intoxication had evaporated; and nothing was left but petty haggling and a piecemeal reneging on all promises. These developments, too, did not escape the watchful eyes of Napoleon in his island retreat.

Peace between France and the Allies had been signed at Paris on April 30, and the treaty was made public on June 14, 1814. The terms were not vindictive: France was reduced to her 1792 borders; most of her colonies were restored to her; no indemnities were exacted from her; and the Allied troops were withdrawn from France. The victors' generosity was motivated, no doubt, by their desire to give Louis XVIII the best possible start. The twenty-two-year-long war had been fought by the nations, but the peace was made by the sovereigns.

There remained the far more difficult task of settling the fate of the rest of Europe. To that end the Allies agreed to convene a general peace conference at Vienna, to which France was also invited to send representatives. Paradoxically enough the famous Congress of Vienna, which lasted from September, 1814, to June, 1815, never met in a formal sense. There was no official opening, no plenary session; no speeches were made, and the entire work was accomplished by small committees or behind the scenes. As early as August, Vienna began to fill up with sovereigns, statesmen, deputations, and agents representing various interests. The Russian delegation was headed by Czar Alexander; the English delegation by Castlereagh, later replaced by Wellington; the Prussian delegation by Chancellor von Hardenberg and Wilhelm von Humboldt. Emperor Francis played host to the Congress but took little part in its work and was represented by Metternich, who had originally proposed the Congress and who was to play the leading part in it. Metternich's most notable assistant was the publicist Friedrich von Gentz, a disciple of Edmund Burke and perhaps the most articulate and forceful exponent of the conservative philosophy of politics.

Talleyrand, who arrived only late in September to represent Louis XVIII, was at first not admitted into the inner circle of the four great Allied powers. Apart from the representatives of the Big Five, there were thousands of plenipotentiaries and agents representing the interests of the lesser powers, of the diminutive powers, and sometimes of nonexistent powers, as well as spokesmen for various groups and associations. All the German states and free cities, all the princes who had been mediatized in 1806, all the Italian states, most of the Swiss cantons, the German

After almost twenty-five years of exile, Louis XVIII returned to Paris. He is shown above in Napoleon's study at the Tuileries.

Catholic Church, the German Jewish communities, and even a publisher, Cotta of Augsburg, were represented.

Liberal public opinion expected a great deal more from the Congress of Vienna than a mere territorial settlement—a system of collective security, some step toward disarmament and permanent peace, an international tribunal to arbitrate disputes, a convention outlawing the slave trade, and some recognition of the principle of national self-determination and representative government. What made the liberals hope for all this, it is difficult to see, for no promises had been made or even hinted at; but hopes for a better order will inevitably arise after every cataclysm, though their fulfillment may be slow.

The Congress of Vienna during its first weeks appeared to be reluctant to address itself to even the most immediate problems facing it. The superficial observer could see nothing but a succession of balls, receptions, parades, concerts, and gala performances. It was at this time that Beethoven first came to the attention of the international

public, after having composed the larger part of his life's work, by conducting a performance of his worst composition, "Wellington's Victory," complete with artillery. "The Congress dances, but it isn't going anywhere," remarked the witty prince de Ligne a little unjustly and a little too often. All this glamorous glitter, however, merely diverted attention from the serious business that was being carried on behind the scenes.

The main problem facing the statesmen at Vienna was the creation of a stable Europe on the ruins of the Napoleonic system. The complexity of the problem was as immense as was the conflict of interests; still, it is possible, without doing too much violence to the facts, to reduce the number of conflicting principles involved to three outstanding ones. The first of these was the principle of legitimacy, which required that as far as was practicable the legitimate sovereigns of Europe were to be restored to the possessions they had held in 1792. The second was the principle of nationality, a new concept, which demanded that national entities be allowed to determine their own fate. The third was the principle of equilibrium, which ruled out any solution to territorial problems that would unduly strengthen one of the great powers at the expense or to the disadvantage of one or several others.

That the principle of nationality was sacrificed cannot be denied, although a slight and hypocritical bow in its direction was made by the creation of the Kingdom of Poland, united with the Russian crown, and of the Lombardo-Venetian Kingdom, united with the Austrian crown. That legitimacy was the guiding principle of the Congress, as has so often been asserted, is but partly true. Wherever that principle was in conflict with the principle of equilibrium, it was compromised. It was advocated principally by Talleyrand who used it, with brilliant success, as an instrument for securing for France equality with the other great powers. With the restoration of Louis XVIII, he argued, France was no longer a defeated enemy, and the continued existence of an alliance against a legitimate monarch whose cause the victors had championed was an absurdity. Although Talleyrand's thesis was not fully accepted by the Allies at first, a split among the great powers soon allowed him to demonstrate triumphantly that even a defeated France had to be reckoned with.

Two closely connected questions occasioned the rift among the Allies—the future of Saxony and the future of the Grand Duchy of Warsaw. The ruler of these two states, King Frederick Augustus, was still detained as a prisoner of war; the fact that he had not abandoned his alliance with Napoleon served as a convenient pretext for Prussia to press for the annexation of the entire Kingdom of Saxony. As for the Grand Duchy of Warsaw, Russia, Prussia, and Austria had agreed on its partition but not on their respective shares. Russia laid claim to about three-fourths of its territory, and Prussia was willing to let her have it, provided the Congress approved her annexation of Saxony; Austria, on the other hand, objected to such an increase of Russian power along her borders and was particularly disturbed by Alexander's scheme for creating a Kingdom of Poland with himself at its head.

Despite these difficulties, the Allies were about to reach an agreement when the matter was complicated by an outbreak of anti-Prussian feeling in Saxony and by French opposition to the annexation scheme. Bavaria and some other German states joined France in backing the king of Saxony, and Castlereagh's attempt to mediate the dispute ended in failure. On December 11, at Warsaw, Grand Duke Constantine, the czar's brother, issued a proclamation to the Polish people calling on them to unite as an independent nation under Alexander. This manifesto made the rift complete, lining up Russia and Prussia on the one side and Austria, England, and France on the other. Austrian troops marched to the Polish frontier, and France ordered a partial mobilization. At this point, Talleyrand intervened openly with a series of memoranda in which he stressed that the spoliation of the king of Saxony would violate the principle of legitimacy; he also succeeded in uniting the lesser German states against Prussia. Thus only eight months after Napoleon's abdication Europe was again on the verge of war. On January 3, 1815, England, Austria, and France drew up a secret military alliance against Russia and Prussia; the conversations among the adversaries continued, however, despite the mounting tension.

Since none of the powers really wanted war, they began to display a willingness to compromise as soon as it became clear that continued persistence in their respective stands must lead to armed conflict. By admitting Talleyrand to their inner councils on a permanent basis—thereby transforming the Committee of Four into a Committee of Five—they conceded to him the main objective he had sought to attain by his divisive tactics, and the main obstacle to agreement was removed. The Saxon question was settled among the Five by mid-February: Frederick Augustus was restored to his throne but had to cede more than a third of his kingdom to Prussia. (It took three months, however, to make the luckless king accept the settlement.)

Before the end of February, 1815, the Congress had settled, though incompletely and in principle only, the Saxon question, the partition of the Grand Duchy of Warsaw, a number of territorial re-adjustments in Italy (but not the vexed question of the future of Naples, contested between Murat and the House of Bourbon-Naples), the frontiers and organization of the Swiss Confederation, and the creation of the Kingdom of Holland. Agreement on the abolition of the slave trade foundered on Spanish opposition, and the best that could be done was to draft a joint resolution condemning that inhuman practice and inviting each government concerned to pass appropriate legislation against it at the earliest convenient date.

Other questions of equal importance were still unsettled when, early in March, Vienna was stunned by the news that Napoleon had landed in France and was marching on Paris. His peace offers were rejected; indeed, they were never even considered. On March 13 the four great Allied powers issued a declaration of war not against France but against Napoleon in person and outlawed him for breaking the Treaty of Fontainebleau and for disturbing the public peace. On March 25 a new formal alliance was signed, which all European powers, including the king of France, were invited to join. (Only Spain and Sweden failed to do so.) While Europe was preparing for the new and final showdown, the Congress of Vienna sped its work through the last stages. Even so, it was only on June 9—nine days before Waterloo—that the European Committee adopted the Final Act of the Congress, which embodied all the separate agreements and settlements reached up to that point. The main changes the Final Act brought about in the structure of Europe were the aforementioned creation of a

Polish kingdom united with the Russian crown and of a Lombardo-Venetian kingdom under the Austrian crown; the creation of the Kingdom of Holland (including Belgium as well as the Netherlands) under the House of Orange; the virtual doubling of the size of Prussia, which was awarded part of Saxony and territories on both banks of the Rhine; and the creation of a Germanic Confederation consisting of thirty-eight sovereign states and free cities, with a federal diet with its seat at Frankfort. Thus, despite all their efforts to restore the *status quo* of 1792, the victorious powers had been unable to undo the profound changes brought about by the Napoleonic age.

Broadly speaking, the Final Act of the Congress, though it fell far short of an ideal settlement, was an important step toward the creation of a stable European system and toward the realization of a European community. But it failed to find lasting solutions in those areas where it went contrary to national aspirations either toward independence (as in Belgium and Poland) or toward unification (as in Germany) or toward both (as in Italy). Moreover, its stress upon legitimacy, though it was perhaps necessary to create a common area of agreement, and to restore the basis of monarchic government, was fundamentally opposed to the trend of the time: the French Revolution and the Napoleonic wars had definitely established the fact that it was nations rather than monarchs that were the fundamental units of the international community.

When in February, 1815, Napoleon decided to attempt his last gamble for victory, he undoubtedly hoped that his landing in France would complete the split in the uneasy alliance of the great powers. In this he was doubly mistaken: the crisis of the alliance reached its climax in early January, and when Napoleon landed two months later the rift was virtually healed; furthermore, even if he had landed in January, the effect would have been to pull the alliance together rather than to split it. His hope that the Allies would not make war on him if he assured them of his acceptance of the Treaty of Paris was also based on wishful thinking. His estimate of the state of French public opinion, however, was as accurate as it was bold.

During the ten months of his exile on Elba, the emperor had ample time to reflect on his mistakes and to meditate on some stroke of genius by which he could undo them. The administration of his tiny principality and household, to which he addressed himself with the same solemn thoroughness as if he were still ruling an empire, was insufficient to occupy his time; his rides and excursions, his minuscule army, his monotonous evenings spent in the company of his sisters and his mother, with whom he quarreled almost nightly over cards, and his numerous mistresses (various

Isabey depicted the introduction of the duke of Wellington to the statesmen gathered at Vienna. The duke is seen in profile at far left. At right, Talleyrand is seated with his arm resting on the table. Metternich stands in the foreground before an empty chair.

ladies in waiting and Marie Walewska, who came for a brief and torrid visit) were hardly sufficient to satisfy his insatiable urge for activity. He kept a watchful eye on the Continent, interviewing travelers and entertaining secret correspondences. The Congress of Vienna was making no progress; the Allies were falling apart; the regime of Louis XVIII was becoming increasingly unpopular; the larger part of the French people and of the army would welcome his return; Italy was seething with discontent; in England the Whig opposition, led by Lord Holland, would restrain the government from making war on him. He had not yet fulfilled his destiny, and to fulfill it, all that was required was boldness.

Then and later Napoleon admitted to few mistakes. One of the mistakes he admitted, however, was his marriage to Marie Louise. Her refusal to follow him to Elba (she had in the meantime found a lover) was not the least of his disappointments; yet what he regretted more was having put too much trust in dynastic connections. The bland treachery of his father-in-law, of his brother-in-law Murat, of the king of Bavaria, and of his own ministers and marshals opened his eyes to the fact that his power rested not on the support of the kings and of the great, but on the common people of France. It was not at St. Helena that Napoleon began to fabricate the legendary image of himself as the son of the French Revolution and as the embodiment of the revolutionary mission; the realization that he could never be legitimated by his fellow sovereigns but only by the will of his people was forced on him by the very sovereigns into whose club he had sought admission. His actions following his return to France suggest that while the liberalism he suddenly professed was insincere, he had decided to base his power more firmly on the support of the middle and the lower classes.

On February 26 with an "army" of about a thousand men (including some six hundred Guards who had been authorized to follow him into exile), Napoleon embarked aboard his ship *L'Inconstant* and several smaller craft. A few simple ruses and a great deal of luck enabled his flotilla to elude the British cruisers that were keeping a watch over the island, and on March 1 the invading army landed in the Gulf of Juan, between Fréjus and Antibes. They spent the night unmolested on the beach and the following morning began to march north. A madder adventure had never been attempted or, at any rate, once attempted, had never succeeded.

Napoleon could justify his invasion of France with a number of pretexts, notably Louis XVIII's failure to pay the yearly indemnity stipulated by the Treaty of Fontainebleau and the well-founded rumors that the Allies at Vienna were plotting to deport the emperor to some distant place. (St. Helena had been mentioned among others.) More important in Napoleon's decision was his inability to let an opportunity slip past him and the equally well-founded

rumor that Fouché was plotting to overthrow the Bourbons and set up a government without him. His proclamation to the army was a masterpiece of rhetoric and propaganda: "Soldiers! In my exile I heard your voice. I have come back in spite of all obstacles and all dangers. Your general, called to the throne by the choice of the people and raised on your shields, is restored to you: come and join him. . . . Come and range yourselves under the flags of your leader! He has no existence except in your existence; he has no rights except your rights and those of the people; his interests, his honor, his glory are none other than your interests, your honor, your glory. Victory will march at a quickstep. The eagle and tricolor shall fly from steeple to steeple to the towers of Notre Dame! Then you can show your scars without dishonor, then you can pride yourselves on what you have accomplished: you will be the liberators of the fatherland! In your old age, surrounded and admired by your fellow citizens . . . you will be able to say with pride: 'I too was part of that Grand Army that entered twice within the walls of Vienna, within those of Rome,

of Berlin, of Madrid, of Moscow, and which cleansed Paris of the pollution that treason and the presence of the enemy had left in it.' "

Although it was sent by semaphore telegraph, the news of Napoleon's landing reached Paris only on March 5 and Vienna on March 7. At first it caused no particular concern in either place; indeed, it seemed inconceivable that with his handful of men Napoleon should be able to overcome the army of Louis XVIII. However, the inconceivable happened: Napoleon reached Grenoble without interference. Surprise, a nostalgic loyalty to the emperor, and the local commanders' and officials' reluctance to act without specific orders combined in Napoleon's favor. At the outskirts of Grenoble, Napoleon walked up in person to face the garrison troops come to stop him; he addressed them, and they broke into cheers and went over to him. From then on his progress became a triumphal procession. At Lyons he issued a proclamation dissolving the two houses of Louis XVIII's parliament and promising to convene a constitutional assembly in order "to improve and change our con-

stitutions according to the interests and will of the nation." At Châlons Marshal Ney, who had left Paris after assuring the king that he would bring Bonaparte back in a cage, experienced a dramatic change of heart: he fell into his former master's arms and brought his troops over to him.

Meanwhile, at Paris, the government and court of Louis XVIII folded up like a house of cards. Except for the king's niece, the eccentric duchesse de Berri, nobody thought of offering resistance. Princes, courtiers, ministers, and their wives took off in panic flight; such was their haste to save their persons and belongings that they forgot to remove or destroy Talleyrand's dispatches from Vienna, including a copy of the secret treaty of alliance against Russia and Prussia signed on January 3. (Napoleon, upon finding it, promptly sent it on to Alexander.) On March 19, furtively and at night, the king himself slipped out of the Tuileries; his flight did not end until he and his court reached Ghent. The following day Napoleon entered the Tuileries.

Paris received him with a mixture of enthusiasm and apprehension. The aristocratic Faubourg St. Germain was deserted; in the popular quarters he was cheered. His strongest support came from the army, and particularly from the officers on half-pay who flocked back to the colors. Morale was less high among the generals: Berthier, who had accompanied Louis to Ghent, went on to Germany, although invited to return and to resume his post as chief of staff; Marshals Macdonald, Gouvion Saint-Cyr, and Victor had remained loyal to Louis XVIII or stayed neutral; those who, like Marshal Ney, had gone over to the cause of the emperor soon began to feel that in their intoxication they might well have made a mistake.

As it became increasingly plain that the Allies were determined to open hostilities at the earliest possible moment, Napoleon's immediate concerns were to raise an army and to rally the nation behind him. Conscription was extremely unpopular, and he resorted to it only on the eve of the Waterloo campaign. What he sought to bring about was a revival of the spirit of 1793 that had produced a nation under arms. For that purpose it was necessary to refurbish his imperial and dictatorial regime with some of the liberal and Jacobin trappings of the French Revolution. He appointed a commission of the Council of State to amend the Constitution; the guiding spirit of the commission was Madame de Staël's friend Benjamin Constant, who until the day before Napoleon's return had proclaimed in the press that he would rather risk death than pass into the camp of the Usurper. Joseph Bonaparte persuaded him to call on the emperor; a single conversation with the Usurper sufficed to make Constant change camps; he accepted his nomination to the Council of State. There was no time to waste; the Additional Act, as the new Constitution was called, was drafted in a week. Far from being the democratic constitution that had been promised, it was undistinguishable from the charter that had been granted to France by Louis XVIII less than a year before.

Both the plebiscite that ratified the Additional Act and the composition of the newly elected Chamber of Representatives were disappointing to the emperor. Only a fraction of the electorate (about 1,500,000) took part in the plebiscite; of the 629 representatives elected, 40 were republicans, more than 500 were liberals, and only 80 were Bonapartists. (The royalists took no part in the elections.) France, after a quarter century of revolution, wars, and changes of regime, had become apathetic. The theatrical ceremony of June 1, in which the representatives and the army swore fidelity to the emperor and the emperor swore fidelity to the Constitution, deceived hardly anybody and filled most of the spectators with dismay. What possessed Napoleon to appear, on such an occasion, garbed in the costume of a Caesar? "Never," remarked an eyewitness, "has an orator shown more adroitness in substituting thrilling phrases for positive concessions, and referring everything to a future in which he still expected to be lord of all. Never was an actor at more pains to depict imperial majesty in all its splendor, but never did Napoleon choose a worse time to exchange his war costume, his gray overcoat, his old sword, his little hat and his boots, for white silk stockings, embroidered shoes with rosettes, a stage sword, a coat, a sash, a cloak dazzling with embroidery."

The apathy that marked the plebiscite also characterized the response to the call to arms. The standing army Napoleon had inherited from Louis XVIII was barely more than two hundred thousand strong, and of these only about fifty thousand were available for immediate service. With the addition of the veterans, it still was below three hundred thousand in June. To make up for the deficiency the National Guard was called up, naval units and part of the constabulary were assigned to army service, and several thousand workingmen from the Lyons and Paris regions were put under arms. Only half of the National Guardsmen answered the call; several provinces ignored it altogether. And, although Napoleon told a delegation of workers that "It is men born in the upper classes of society who have dishonored the name of France: patriotism and regard for national honor survive unimpaired in the townspeople, the men of the countryside, and the ranks of the army," he hesitated to arm the populace and assured the apprehensive Chamber of Representatives that he would do so only as a last resort.

The Additional Act was not nearly revolutionary enough to stir popular enthusiasm. As for the townspeople and the men of the countryside, they were by no means solidly aligned behind the emperor. In the Vendée a general insurrection broke out in mid-May, and Provence was in a state of near-rebellion; there was not a single segment of the population on whose loyalty the emperor could firmly

count except the army. Though small, it was the best army he had had since Austerlitz, composed almost exclusively of seasoned soldiers, devoted to him, and unalloyed by foreign elements. Yet how could it defeat the combined armies of all Europe? Could even a great victory save Napoleon from eventual defeat? Without the resolute support of his nation and hopelessly outnumbered in the field, how could he possibly hope to extricate himself from the trap into which he had walked?

Napoleon's fate had been sealed at Vienna on March 13, when the Allied powers declared him to be outside the law. Only peace or victory could maintain him on the throne: there was no possibility of either. Throughout the hundred days from his arrival in Paris to his final abdication, his every action was an automatic gesture performed in a surrounding of make-believe. He was not gambling his last trump: he held no more trump. Yet the game had to be played to the end, inexorably, for destiny had to be fulfilled and after all there was always a chance that a bluff might succeed. He *might* gain a victory; a victory *might* split the Allies; nothing, he felt, could be counted for certain until it had happened.

When Napoleon took the field France was without allies. King Joachim Murat of Naples, repenting his defection after Leipzig, had attacked the Austrians in Italy and taken Rome, Florence, and Bologna but was disastrously defeated at Tolentino on May 3 and had to flee to France. His gesture was premature and foolish and did Napoleon more harm than good. (Murat's insane attempt, some time later, to regain Naples with a handful of men ended with his execution by a firing squad; there had always been a suicidal streak in his character.) If Murat had held his fire until Napoleon gave him the signal, he might at least have created a diversion that would have tied up part of the Austrian army. Yet even then his assistance would have been of little value, the Neapolitan army being about the worst in Europe. Napoleon hoped that his speed would gain him a victory. He must strike before the Prussian army and the Anglo-Dutch army which Wellington was forming in Belgium could take the offensive; then, if he was victorious against Wellington and Blücher, he could turn against the Austrians and Russians, whose approach was slow. Farther than this he did not allow himself to think.

Wellington had left Vienna for Brussels late in March. All he found was some ten thousand British troops and a few Hanoverian units. If Napoleon had attacked him then, he could have wiped Wellington out; but Napoleon was still hoping that England would accept his offer of peace, and French public opinion was not prepared to back an aggressive war. Ten weeks after Wellington's arrival at Brussels, the British forces had swelled to about 35,000. Together with additional Hanoverian forces and the Dutch-Belgian levies, most of them untrained troops, he disposed of about 107,000 combat troops. These were spread along a front extending from Ghent to Mons. In southern Belgium a Prussian army of 116,000 under Blücher held the Meuse valley from Charleroi to Liége. On June 12 Napoleon left Paris to join his army—about 125,000 against the more than 220,000 of Wellington and Blücher—with the intention of placing it in the gap between Mons and Charleroi and thus separating the two Allied armies. Speed and surprise were essential to prevent either enemy army from concentrating. And, indeed, both Wellington and Blücher were taken completely unawares.

On June 15 the French crossed the Belgian frontier, drove back a Prussian corps, and occupied Charleroi. Wellington received intelligence of these events too late in the day to do anything about them and spent the evening at the duchess of Richmond's celebrated ball in Brussels. The next morning the duke rode to Ligny to confer with Blücher, who had managed to concentrate the larger part of his forces near that town. He promised to come to Blücher's aid in case he was not himself attacked, then rode off to Quatre Bras, where he was in the process of concentrating his forces. About 2 P.M. that day—June 16—Napoleon fell upon the Prussians at Ligny while Ney attacked the Anglo-Dutch at Quatre Bras. In both battles the French were successful. About dark, Napoleon drove Blücher off the field with heavy losses on both sides; Ney in the meantime had held Wellington at Quatre Bras. The next morning, upon hearing of Blücher's defeat, Wellington withdrew northward toward Brussels while the scattered Prussians slowly rallied at Wavre.

After so brilliant a start the emperor might have been expected to follow up his advantage with the same lightning speed that he had displayed since the beginning of the campaign. However, the difficulty of determining the direction in which Blücher's main forces had withdrawn and the necessity of reorganizing his own exhausted troops prevented Napoleon from deciding on the next move until the early afternoon of June 17. His only action during the morning had been to detach Marshal Grouchy with some thirty thousand troops (including part of his cavalry) with the specific orders to follow Blücher's retreating army, to prevent it from joining Wellington's forces, and to keep Napoleon informed of its movements. Napoleon himself, after joining with Ney, set out in pursuit of Wellington. Late that evening, after a march made difficult by incessant thunderstorms, the French army reached the outposts of Wellington's position at Mont St. Jean, near the village of Waterloo. Meanwhile Grouchy had been looking for Blücher's army and discovered it at last on the road to Wavre. At Wavre the main Prussian army was joined by the corps of Generals Bülow and Thielmann, until then separate from it. Grouchy sent this intelligence to Napoleon along with some misleading details: part of the Prussian army, he wrote, was falling back toward Liége; he would prevent the rest from joining Wellington on the morrow. Actually,

almost the entire Prussian army began its march toward Brussels at dawn on June 18. Grouchy, conforming to Napoleon's orders, followed on its heels, but Prussian rearguard action slowed down his advance and gave Blücher's main army a chance to reach the battlefield before the end of that fateful day.

As it happened, half of Blücher's forces arrived at Waterloo only about 7 P.M., six hours later than Wellington had expected and just in the nick of time. The same factor that caused their slowness—the preceding day's rains, which had put the roads into very poor shape—also saved them from coming too late. For Napoleon had begun his attack on Wellington's positions only at 11 A.M., having waited to allow the soggy terrain to dry. Then, for six hours, Napoleon hurled all his available forces save the Guard against the Anglo-Dutch positions. "Never did I see such a pounding match," Wellington observed later. Yet while the Dutch and Belgian forces wavered, the British stood fast; it was about 6:30 P.M. that Ney's divisions dislodged the battered English and Hanoverian defenders from the farm of La Haie Sainte, thus breaching Wellington's line atop the heights of Mont St. Jean. The assailants themselves were too exhausted to exploit their advantage, and Napoleon refused Ney's request that he commit the Guard. By this time Bülow's corps, which had arrived in advance of the rest of Blücher's army, had joined in the battle; although reinforced by part of yet another Prussian corps, under General Pirch, it had been held off successfully since 4 P.M. by a far inferior French force. About 7 P.M., however, another Prussian corps—under General Ziethen—arrived and made contact with Wellington's left. The duke was thus enabled to repair the damage done his line half an hour earlier and to present once again a solid front.

At last Napoleon threw his Guard into the battle in a final and desperate assault; it was thrown back with murderous fire, and its retreat gave the signal for the rest of the French army to break ranks in a headlong flight. It was not a defeat but a rout as complete as any that Napoleon had ever inflicted on his opponents. Within a matter of minutes the army virtually ceased to exist. Only a part of the Old Guard fought on stubbornly to protect Napoleon's retreat. According to an apocryphal version, its commander, General Cambronne, when summoned to surrender, replied: "The Guard dies but does not surrender;" but his more often quoted answer, *"Merde!"* is what he probably said. With everything lost save Grouchy's corps, which never showed up on the battlefield, the emperor rode off in the direction of Paris, making his way through the disorganized remnants of his fleeing army; at Philippeville he changed to a carriage.

Napoleon, and many other writers following his version of the battle, blamed the disaster on Grouchy's failure to stop Blücher's march or to join the main French army in time. In truth Grouchy had followed his orders to his best

OVERLEAF: *An English eye-witness painted the duke of Wellington and his staff at the battle of Waterloo. The duke, his hat in his hand, is at left on his favorite horse, Copenhagen.*

ability, though perhaps not very intelligently, and Napoleon's new orders, to join in the battle and attack Bülow, reached him much too late to be carried out. Another widely accepted contention—that the arrival of Blücher's army saved the day for Wellington—is equally questionable: Blücher's arrival was not a providential accident but had been counted on by Wellington throughout the battle; rather it was his lateness which almost lost the battle. It is true, however, that the arrival of the Prussians turned an undecided battle into one of the most decisive routs in history. In the last analysis the outcome of Waterloo was due neither to Wellington's generalship nor to Napoleon's or Grouchy's mistakes but to the phenomenal staying power of the British infantry, which kept the issue in suspense until Blücher's belated intervention. Wellington's forces had suffered far too heavy losses to take up the pursuit, which was left to the Prussians.

Napoleon arrived in Paris early on June 21 and took up residence in the Elysée Palace. "He speaks of his situation with astonishing calm and complete detachment," Benjamin Constant noted in his diary. It was the third great army he had lost in three years, and he serenely expressed his intention to continue the war with what troops he had left, the National Guard, and a *levée en masse*. When it was pointed out to him that the Chambers would not stand for this, he contemplated dissolving the Chambers. Matters were no longer in his hands, however; they had been taken over by Fouché, just as Talleyrand had taken them over a year earlier.

Although Fouché had consented to serve Napoleon as minister of police, he had remained in touch with the Bourbons and the Allies. It was for Louis XVIII's restoration that he was now working, without appearing to do so. His instruments were the liberal leaders, Lafayette at their head, whom he convinced that Napoleon was about to dissolve the Chambers and set up a military dictatorship. On Lafayette's initiative both Chambers carried a resolution declaring the fatherland to be in danger; both Chambers would remain in permanent session as long as the emergency existed, and anyone who would attempt to dissolve them was guilty of high treason. Napoleon made no attempt to fight the Chambers. On June 22 he abdicated in favor of the king of Rome and a provisional government, headed by Fouché and Carnot, was formed. The emperor lingered at the Elysée Palace for three more days, then withdrew to Malmaison—a melancholy choice for a residence, since Josephine, its owner, had died there but a few months earlier.

Meanwhile Blücher was advancing, followed by Wellington. The Prussian field marshal had vowed that he would seize the emperor, dead or alive, and have him shot like an ordinary outlaw. To the emissaries of the French provisional government he refused the armistice they requested unless they surrendered Napoleon to him. At the same time

Louis XVIII, upon Wellington's urging, had entered France in the wake of the Allied armies and was making his way to Paris. Wellington's advice may have saved France from dismemberment; only the king's early return and his recognition by the other Allies as the rightful sovereign of France effectively deprived Prussia of any success in pressing her vindictive scheme.

On June 29 Napoleon was still at Malmaison, with the Prussian van but a few miles away. He had offered, in vain, to put himself at the head of the forces of the provisional government and to defend Paris. He had also made use of his time to collect as much liquid cash as he could, including three millions in gold from the Treasury. His mood alternated between despair, sudden flashes of optimism, indecision, and apathy. At last, on the 29th, he yielded to the pressing request of Fouché, who gave him to understand that he would have to arrest him if he did not take to instant flight. For eleven days Napoleon completely disappeared from view.

Fouché, who had made up his mind that only the restoration of Louis XVIII could save France from the Allies' vengeance and from civil war, persuaded the provisional government that further resistance was futile. It was with some difficulty, however, that Wellington overcame Blücher's insistence on an unconditional surrender. The terms of the capitulation, which allowed the French forces to retire beyond the Loire, were agreed upon on July 3. On July 7 the Allies entered Paris; the next day Louis XVIII returned to the Tuileries. The Chambers, after recognizing him as king, obediently dissolved themselves. Fouché had won his game. On the eve of the king's entry into Paris, he had come to the Abbey of St. Denis, the burial place of the French kings, to make his submission to Louis, who had halted there. The scene has been immortalized by Chateaubriand, who happened to be present: "Suddenly a door opened, and Vice entered silently, leaning on the arm of Crime: Fouché was leading Talleyrand by the arm. This infernal vision went slowly past me, entered the king's study, and disappeared. Fouché had come to swear fealty and homage to his master. The faithful regicide, kneeling before him, laid his hand, which had caused the head of Louis XVI to fall, in the hand of the royal martyr's brother; the recreant bishop stood surety for the oath." "What do you think of it?" Louis asked Chateaubriand the next day. Chateaubriand felt that the monarchy was going to the dogs, and said so. "Well, dear vicomte," said the king after a pause, "I'm entirely of your opinion."

Whatever one may think of Fouché's character, it must be said in justice to him that the course he took was the only wise one: it saved France. Nor was he eager, if he could help it, to let Napoleon fall into the Allies' hands. When the emperor left Malmaison in the company of a few faithful, it had been agreed that Fouché would put a frigate at his disposition which would take him from

During the Hundred Days, Prudhon painted Napoleon's portrait.

Rochefort to the United States. He arrived at Rochefort on July 3 only to discover that the port was under British blockade. If he had left Paris immediately after his abdication, he might have made his way to America, for on June 30 the coast had still been clear. For four days Napoleon waited at Rochefort, hoping either for favorable winds that might enable him to elude the blockade or for the arrival of a safe-conduct to the United States, which had been requested from the British Admiralty.

Neither arrived, but on July 7 General Becker, whom Fouché had entrusted with the mission of seeing the emperor out of the country, received an order to transfer Napoleon to a frigate in order to insure his safety. On the following day Napoleon went aboard the *Saale*. On July 10 he sent two of his companions, his former minister of police, Savary, and Las Cases, aboard H. M. S. *Bellerophon,* commanded by Captain Maitland, to discover whether the safe-conduct had arrived, whether the English government would object to his sailing to America, and whether Maitland would allow him to sail aboard a neutral ship. Maitland, in the meantime, had received strict orders not to let "General Bonaparte" escape. Nevertheless he answered that he would seek specific instructions from his commanding admiral, Sir Henry Hotham. When Las Cases returned to the *Bellerophon* on July 14, Maitland declared that he had not yet heard from Hotham but that, if Napoleon chose to take the chance, he would take it

on himself to convey him safely to England. "If however he adopts that plan," Maitland added, "I cannot enter into any promise as to the reception he may meet with." Though Maitland, in making this suggestion, was somewhat less than candid, his qualifying phrase must absolve him from the accusation of outright trickery. Las Cases brought Maitland's reply to Napoleon, who sent him back to Maitland that same evening with the message that he would come on board the *Bellerophon* the next day.

To say that Napoleon voluntarily surrendered himself to Maitland after being promised asylum in England is very far from the truth. He was trapped, he had no other choices save those of being captured at sea or falling into the hands of the Bourbons, and he had received no specific promise except that his life would be safe. The letter dated July 13 that Napoleon addressed to the prince regent proves that he had decided to throw himself at the mercy of England even before Maitland could have made any promises. Nothing could show more dramatically how low the emperor had fallen than that letter, a mixture of ruse, self-pity, and histrionics (although it invariably moves Napoleon's worshipers to tears): "Your Royal Highness: The victim of the factions that divide my country and of the hostility of the great European powers, I have ended my political career, and I come, as Themistocles did, to claim a seat by the hearth of the British people. I put myself under the protection of British law, which I claim from Your Royal Highness as the most powerful, most constant, and most generous of my enemies." The parallel of Napoleon and Themistocles seems as far-fetched as that of the prince regent and Artaxerxes, and the implied assumption that English law confers immunity and the right of asylum to Britain's defeated enemies surely is untenable.

Aboard the *Bellerophon,* where he occupied Maitland's cabin, Napoleon continued to act very much the emperor, presiding over the captain's table, conversing a great deal, and showing not the least sign of apprehension or depression. The *Bellerophon* anchored at Torbay on July 24, and for two days she was surrounded by boats filled with curiosity seekers who gaped at the prisoner as at a strange animal. Napoleon, mistaking their interest for sympathy, made no attempt to hide from them. The newspapers that were brought on board and translated for him boded no good, but he discounted as idle rumors their reports that he was to be transported to St. Helena. From Torbay the *Bellerophon* proceeded to Plymouth, where on July 31 Admiral Keith came on board to notify General Bonaparte that he was to be taken to St. Helena. Napoleon protested, made a violent scene, all to no avail. He was removed to the *Northumberland* on August 7. After ten weeks of sailing, on October 17 the rocky outline of the island of St. Helena came into view. Napoleon had finished making history; he would now devote himself exclusively to making his legend.

The Bellerophon, *with Napoleon aboard, spent two days at Torbay in Devon. The English rowed out to view the man who had involved them in more than a decade of war. A few days later the emperor was transferred to the* Northumberland *for the trip to St. Helena.*

HISTORY'S JUDGMENT

Napoleon rose to power by being all things to all men. His fall did not diminish the universal interest he commanded. To romantics he was the epitome of heroism; to Nietzsche, the exemplar of power. To the critic and historian Taine, his career was that of an artist; to the leaders of the New World he symbolized the tyranny and cupidity of the Old. The following pages present a selection of judgments that have been made about Napoleon by his contemporaries and posterity.

I have just finished reading O'Meara's Bonaparte. It places him on a higher scale of understanding than I had allotted him. I had thought him the greatest of all military captains, but an indifferent statesman and misled by unworthy passions. The flashes however which escape from him in these conversations with O'Meara prove a mind of great expansion, altho' not of distinct developement and reasoning. He siezes results with rapidity and penetration, but never explains logically the process of reasoning by which he arrives at them. This book too makes us forget his atrocities for a moment in commiseration of his sufferings. I will not say that the authorities of the world, charged with the care of their country and people had not a right to confine him for life, as a Lyon or Tyger, on the principle of self-preservation. There was no safety to nations while he was permitted to roam at large. But the putting him to death in cold blood by lingering tortures of mind, by vexations, insults, and deprivations, was a degree of inhumanity to which the poisonings, and assassinations of the school of Borgia and the den of Marat never attained. The book proves also that nature had denied him the moral sense, the first excellence of well organised man. If he could seriously and repeatedly affirm that he had raised himself to power without ever having committed a crime, it proves that he wanted totally the sense of right and wrong. If he could consider the millions of human lives which he had destroyed or caused to be destroyed, the desolations of countries . . . the destitutions of lawful rulers of the world without the consent of their constituents, to place his brothers and sisters on their thrones, the cutting up of established societies of men . . . and all the numberless train of his other enormities; the man, I say, who could consider all these as no crimes must have been a moral monster, against whom every hand should have been lifted to slay him.

Thomas Jefferson

Now Napoleon—there was a fellow! Always enlightened by reason, always clear and decisive, and gifted at every moment with enough energy to translate into action whatever he recognized as being advantageous or necessary. His life was the stride of a demigod from battle to battle and from victory to victory. . . . it could . . . be said that he was in a permanent state of enlightenment, which is why his fate was more brilliant than the world has ever seen or is likely to see after him.

J. W. von Goethe

What a mighty bubble! What a tremendous Waterspout has Napolion been according to his Life, written by himself? He says he was the Creature of the Principles and manners of the Age. By which no doubt he means the Age of Reason; the progress of Manilius's Ratio; of Plato's Logos etc. I believe him. A Whirlwind raised him and a Whirlwind blowed him a Way to St. Helena. He is very confident that the Age of Reason is not past; and so am I; but I hope that Reason will never again rashly and hastily create such Creatures as him. Liberty, Equality, Fraternity, and Humanity will never again, I hope blindly surrender themselves to an unbounded Ambition for national Conquests, nor implicitly commit themselves to the custody and Guardianship of Arms and Heroes. If they do, they will again end in St. Helena . . . and Sacre Ligues.   *John Adams*

Bolívar

The fate of the world has been decided at Waterloo. Europe has been freed by this immortal battle, the consequences of which may be greater than any ever known in the history of the world, especially with respect to America, for she will see that vast theatre of war, that has for more than twenty years ravaged Europe, transferred to her shores. If it is true that Bonaparte has escaped from France and seeks, as it is reported, asylum in America, then, whatever the country of his choice, that country will be destroyed by his presence. With him will come the English hatred of his tyranny and Europe's jealousy of America. The armies of all nations will follow in his tracks, and all America, if necessary, will be blockaded by the British fleet.

If Napoleon is welcomed by North America, she will be attacked by all Europe; consequently, Bonaparte will attempt to gain the support of the Independents of Mexico, the neighbors of the United States. If South America is struck by the thunderbolt of Bonaparte's arrival, misfortune will ever be ours if our country accords him a friendly reception. His thirst for conquest is insatiable; he has mowed down the flower of European youth . . . in order to carry out his ambitious projects. The same designs will bring him to the New World . . .   *Simon de Bolívar*

Mme. de Staël

It has often been said that if Bonaparte had kept measure, he would have maintained himself in power. But what is meant by "keeping measure"? If, sincerely and dignifiedly, he had established the English form of government in France, no doubt he would still be emperor. His victories created him a prince; it took his love of etiquette, his need of flattery, his titles, his decorations, his courtiers to make the upstart reappear in him. Yet no matter how senseless his policy of conquest may have been, it may be that once his soul had sunk so low as to see no more greatness except in despotism, he became incapable of managing without perpetual war: for what would a despot be without military glory in a country such as France? Was it possible to oppress the nation . . . without at least giving it the fatal compensation of oppressing other nations in turn? The greatest evil plaguing mankind is absolute power.   *Mme. de Staël*

The life of Europe was centered in one man; all were trying to fill their lungs with the air he had breathed. Every year France presented that man with three hundred thousand of her youth; it was the tax paid to Caesar, and, without that troop behind him, he could not follow his fortune. It was the escort he needed that he might traverse the world, and then perish in a little valley in a deserted island, under the weeping willow.

Never had there been so many sleepless nights as in the time of that man; never had there been seen . . . such a nation of desolate mothers; never was there such a silence about those who spoke of death. And yet there was never such joy, such life, such fanfares of war, in all hearts. Never was there such pure sunlight as that which dried all this blood. God made the sun for this man, they said, and they called it the Sun of Austerlitz. But he made this sunlight himself with his ever-thundering cannons which dispelled all clouds but those which succeed the day of battle.

It was this air of the spotless sky, where shone so much glory, where glistened so many swords, that the youth of the time breathed. They well knew that they were destined to the hecatomb; but they regarded Murat as invulnerable, and the emperor had been seen to cross a bridge where so many bullets whistled that they wondered if he could die. And even if one must die, what did it matter? Death itself was so beautiful, so noble, so illustrious, in his battle-scarred purple! It borrowed the color of hope, it reaped so many ripening harvests that it became young, and there was no more old age. All the cradles of France, as all its tombs, were armed with shield and buckler; there were no more old men, there were corpses or demigods.

Alfred de Musset

Musset

What I should like to describe is . . . not so much the actions of Napoleon's life as Napoleon himself—that singular, incomplete, but truly *marvelous* being, whom one cannot contemplate attentively without treating oneself to one of the most curious, one of the strangest spectacles that can be found in the universe.

I should like to show how much, in his prodigious enterprise, he actually owed to his genius, and with what opportunities the condition of the country and the temper of the times presented him; how and why that indocile nation [France] was then speeding, quite spontaneously, toward servitude; with what incomparable art he discovered in the most demagogic achievements of the Revolution precisely everything that was suited to despotism, and how he made despotism their natural outcome. Starting with his interior administration, I want to contemplate the spectacle of his almost divine intelligence grossly laboring at the compression of human freedom; that perfect and scientific organization of force, such as only the greatest genius living in the most enlightened and civilized age could conceive of; and, under the weight of that admirable machine, society flattened, stifled, and increasingly sterile, intellectual activity slowing down, human mind languishing, souls shrinking, great men ceasing to appear, and a limitless, flat horizon against which nothing can be seen, no matter in which direction one's eyes may turn, save the colossal figure of the emperor himself.

Alexis de Tocqueville

Tolstoi

A man of no convictions, no habits, no traditions, no name, not even a Frenchman, by the strangest freaks of chance, as it seems, rises above the seething parties of France, and without attaching himself to any one of them, advances to a prominent position.

The incompetence of his colleagues, the weakness and insignificance of his opponents, the frankness of the deception, and the dazzling and self-confident limitation of the man raise him to the head of the army. The brilliant personal qualities of the soldiers of the Italian army, the disinclination to fight of his opponents, and his childish insolence and conceit gain him military glory. Innumerable so-called *chance* circumstances attend him everywhere. The disfavour into which he falls with the French Directorate turns to his advantage. His efforts to avoid the path ordained for him are unsuccessful; he is not received into the Russian army, and his projects in Turkey come to nothing. . . .

On his return from Italy, he finds the government in Paris in that process of dissolution in which all men who are in the government are inevitably effaced and nullified. And an escape for him from that perilous position offers itself in the shape of an aimless, groundless expedition to Africa. Again the same so-called *chance* circumstances accompany him. Malta, the impregnable, surrenders without a shot being fired; the most ill-considered measures are crowned with success. The enemy's fleet, which later on does not let one boat escape it, now lets a whole army elude it. In Africa a whole series of outrages is perpetrated on the almost unarmed inhabitants. And the men perpetrating these atrocities, and their leader most of all, persuade themselves that it is noble, it is glory, that it is like Caesar and Alexander of Macedon, and that it is fine.

That ideal of *glory* and of *greatness,* consisting in esteeming nothing one does wrong, and glorying in every crime, and ascribing to it an incomprehensible, supernatural value—that ideal, destined to guide this man and those connected with him, is elaborated on a grand scale in Africa. Whatever he does succeeds. The plague does not touch him. The cruelty of murdering his prisoners is not remembered against him. His childishly imprudent, groundless, and ignoble departure from Africa, abandoning his comrades in misfortune, does him good service; and again the enemy's fleet lets him twice slip through their hands. At the moment when, completely intoxicated by the success of his crimes and ready for the part he has to play, he arrives in Paris without any plan, the disintegration of the Republican government, which might have involved him in its ruin a year before, has now reached its utmost limit, and his presence, a man independent of parties, can now only aid his elevation. . . .

Chance, millions of *chances,* give him power; and all men, as though in league together, combine to confirm that power. *Chance* circumstances create the characters of the rulers of France, who cringe before him; *chance* creates the character of Paul I, who acknowledges his authority; *chance* causes the plot against him to strengthen his power instead of shaking it. *Chance* throws the Duc d'Enghien into his hands and accidentally impels him to kill him, thereby convincing the crowd by the strongest of all arguments that he has the right on his side since he has the might. *Chance* brings it to pass that though he strains every nerve to fit out an expedition against England, which would unmistakably have led to his ruin, he never puts this project into execution, and happens to fall upon Mack with the Austrians, who surrender without a battle. *Chance* and *genius* give him the victory at Austerlitz; and by *chance* it comes to pass that all men, not only the French, but all the countries of Europe except England . . . forget their old horror and aversion for his crimes, and now recognise the power he has gained, acknowledge the title he has bestowed upon himself, and accept his ideal of greatness and glory, which seems to every one something fine and rational.   *Leo Tolstoi*

Marx

Camille Desmoulins, Danton, Robespierre, Saint-Just, Napoleon—these were the heroes . . . who, with Roman trappings and phrases, accomplished the mission of their own epoch: they unleashed and established modern bourgeois society. The first four of these smashed feudalism. . . . The fifth, Napoleon, created inside France the conditions that made it possible for free competition to develop, for the redistributed land to be exploited, and for the newly liberated productive energy of the nation to be put to use; beyond the borders of France, he swept away the feudal institutions. . . . Once the new form of society had been established, those antediluvian giants disappeared from the earth, and with them vanished the resurrected Romanism—the Brutuses, Gracchuses, and Publicolas, the tribunes and senators, and Caesar himself.   *Karl Marx*

The first form of government of which men can conceive when they emerge from a state of savagery is either democracy or despotism; they are the first phase of civilization. Aristocracy . . . has everywhere replaced both those primitive governments; it is the second phase of civilization. Representative government . . . is a new, a very recent innovation, and it constitutes . . . the third phase of civilization . . . Napoleon was the supreme product of that second phase of civilization. . . . He never understood the third. Where could he have studied it? . . . he had no time to read after he finished his schooling. All he had time for was to study men.

Napoleon, then, is a nineteenth-century tyrant. Who says tyrant says superior mind; and it is inconceivable that a superior mind can fail to absorb, . . . the common-sense ideas that are in the air. . . . It is very curious to follow in Napoleon's soul the struggle between the genius of tyranny with the deep rationality that made a great man of him.   *Stendhal*

Nietzsche

Napoleon: We see the necessary relationship between the higher and the terrible man. "Man" reinstalled, and her due of contempt and fear restored to woman. Highest activity and health are the signs of the great man; the straight line and grand style rediscovered in action; the mightiest of all instincts, that of life itself,—the lust of dominion,—heartily welcomed.   *Friedrich Nietzsche*

Suddenly the master faculty reveals itself: the *artist,* which was latent in the politician, comes forth from his scabbard; he creates in the ideal and the impossible. He is once more recognized as that which he is: the posthumous brother of Dante and of Michelangelo; and verily, in view of the definite contours of his vision, the intensity, the coherence, and inner consistency of his dream, the depth of his meditations, the superhuman greatness of his conception, he is their equal: his genius has the same size and the same structure; he is one of the three sovereign spirits of the Italian Renaissance.

Hippolyte Taine

Through his brilliant Italian Campaigns, onwards to the Peace of Leoben, one would say, his inspiration is: 'Triumph to the French Revolution'; ... Withal, however, he feels, and has a right to feel, how necessary a strong Authority is; how the Revolution cannot prosper or last without such. To bridle-in that great devouring, self-devouring French Revolution; to *tame* it, so that its intrinsic purpose can be made good, that it may become *organic,* and be able to live among other organisms and *formed* things, not as a wasting destruction alone: is not this still what he partly aimed at, as the true purport of his life; nay what he actually managed to do? Through Wagrams, Austerlitzes; triumph after triumph,—he triumphed so far. There was an eye to see in this man, a soul to dare and do. He rose naturally to be the King. ...

And accordingly was there not what we can call a *faith* in him, genuine so far as it went? That this new enormous Democracy asserting itself here in the French Revolution is an insuppressible Fact, which the whole world, with its old forces and institutions, cannot put down; this was a true insight of his, and took his conscience and enthusiasm along with it,—a *faith.* And did he not interpret the dim purport of it well? *"La carrière ouverte aux talents,* The implements to him who can handle them": this actually is the truth, and even the whole truth; it includes whatever the French Revolution, or any Revolution, could mean. Napoleon, in his first period, was a true Democrat. And yet by the nature of him, fostered too by his military trade, he knew that Democracy, if it were a true thing at all, could not be an anarchy: the man had a heart-hatred for anarchy. ...

But at this point, I think, the fatal charlatan-element got the upper hand. He ... took to believing in Semblances; strove to connect himself with Austrian Dynasties, Popedoms, with the old false Feudalities, which he once saw clearly to be false;—considered that *he* would found "his Dynasty" and so forth; that the enormous French Revolution meant only that! ... He did not know true from false now when he looked at them, —the fearfulest penalty a man pays for yielding to untruth of heart. *Self* and false ambition had now become his god ... What a paltry patch-work of theatrical paper-mantles, tinsel and mummery, had this man wrapt his own great reality in, thinking to make it more real thereby! ...

But this poor Napoleon mistook: he believed too much in the *Dupeability* of men; saw no fact deeper in man than Hunger and this! He was mistaken. Like a man that should build upon cloud; his house and he fall down in confused wreck, and depart out of the world. *Thomas Carlyle*

CARICATURES

For a man so sensitive to criticism, Napoleon was singularly unfortunate to have lived during the great age of political caricature. The prints made by his enemies were witty and malicious, often vulgar, and even more often, unerringly to the point. They were enormously popular, especially in England, where there were numerous printsellers who had varied political opinions but who were united in disdain for the French emperor. This war against Napoleon was dominated by the English caricaturists, most notably Gillray and Cruikshank; they were joined by continental artists, including a few daring Frenchmen, one of whom portrayed a mincing emperor (above) taking a lesson in proper deportment from his friend, the famous tragedian, Talma.

One of Napoleon's schoolfellows at the Ecole Militaire sketched the future emperor racing off to aid the Corsican patriot, Paoli, while a teacher holds on to his queue in an attempt to restrain him. Cruikshank's engraving of the siege of Toulon (above) shows a toy Captain Buonaparte, under a ragged tricolor, setting off a toy cannon to liberate the town from the English.

Another Cruikshank cartoon (left) shows Napoleon fleeing from Egypt, under the enigmatic gaze of an oversized sphinx. The caricature is part of a series published in 1815, while Napoleon was exiled in Elba, to illustrate a mock epic in fifteen cantos which described the emperor's career. An idea of its style can be derived from one of the verses that this caricature accompanies: "The cunning he display'd in fight,/ He manifested in his flight." For so stirring a tale, the moral is rather a modest one: "Whoe'er attempts t'improve his lot/ May lose the whole that he has got;/ For speculation and ambition/ Oft leave a man in low condition." The money for Napoleon's Egyptian campaign had been plundered by the French from the treasury of Berne. In the Swiss cartoon reproduced above, the Directors are shown squeezing the canton of Berne in a vise. "Push hard," the caption reads, "Swiss gold will buy us Egypt."

As can be seen in the caricature above, an English interpretation of the opinions held about the emperor by citizens of various nations, the French were enthralled by Napoleon. Abroad, however, according to the caricature, he was hated by many and feared by most. His influence extended far beyond Europe; a grudging respect for its scope is evident in the number of nations represented here. Even in 1808, when this caricature was published, Europeans apparently felt that sanctimoniousness was one of the major elements of American foreign policy. (Here, as in many other caricatures of the period, the United States is represented as a Quaker.) A French propaganda print (at lower left) shows the ladies of England stirring up an adverse wind with their fans to keep the French invaders from crossing the Channel. "Quick! Hide yourself. They are here," whispers one of them to a British soldier who is trying to find shelter behind her skirt. Cruikshank's depiction of Napoleon's coronation (right), with its cocky emperor, apprehensive pope, and plump Josephine, is considerably less reverent than David's famous painting of the scene. Above, at left, a cartoon entitled "The Arch Dutchess Maria Louisa going to take her Nap" shows another ceremony of a more delicate nature, in which Napoleon is confronted by his disappointed bride on their wedding night.

The labels and speech for the figures read:

GERMANY. ...a great deal / ...shake my head.
PRUSSIA. Mum.
FRANCE. Long live the Emperor.. / Vive La Liberté!!
TURKEY. I quake whenever his / name is mentioned.

PORTUGAL. I'm Off.
AMERICA. Verily the Spirit doth / move me to shake hands.
ASSIA. I beg he may be kept / at a distance.
ENGLAND I laugh at him, and defy him / but still I dont much like him

A pretty piece of Business / we have made of it Brother Joe.

I always told you Nap, what / would come of making too free / with the Spanish.

A dejected pair, Napoleon and King Joseph commiserate with each other over their difficulties in Spain. OVERLEAF: *A Gillray cartoon of 1808 shows "Spanish patriots attacking the French Banditti—Loyal Britons lending a lift." In the foreground of the battlefield are a sturdy British soldier and an even sturdier nun.*

In Russia the cartoonist Ivan Terebenev satirized Bonaparte savagely. In one of his cartoons (below) a French escort drives a troop of Cossack prisoners through Germany. Since the French have failed to capture any Russians, they have had to be content with displaying puppets. In caricatures, at least, the Russians had better luck in seizing prisoners. At left, a Russian shepherd displays his prize, Bonaparte in wolf's clothing, his tail between his legs. Above, two peasants force the emperor to dance to their tune.

Fleeing astride a disenchanted imperial eagle, after Waterloo, Napoleon loses his sword and crown. The cartoon is by Cruikshank.

LEGACY
AND
LEGEND

*The future will tell whether it would not have been better
if neither I nor Rousseau had ever lived.*

"Greatness has its beauties, but only in retrospect and in the imagination": thus wrote General Bonaparte to General Moreau in 1800. His observation helps to explain why the world, only a few years after sighing with relief at its delivery from the ogre, began to worship him as the greatest man of modern times. Napoleon had barely left the scene when the fifteen years that he had carved out of world history to create his glory seemed scarcely believable. Only the scars of the war veterans and the empty places in the widows' beds seemed to attest to the reality of those years, and time soon eliminated even these silent witnesses. What remained, in retrospect and in the imagination, was legend and symbol.

History experienced and history remembered are two very different things. Sitting by his fireside, surrounded by his grandchildren, the veteran of the retreat from Moscow will find more happiness in telling for the hundredth time the sufferings that he remembers but no longer feels than in the sum total of all the good moments in his life, which he cannot even remember. His grandchildren's notions of the years of glory will be even further removed from reality. The circumstance that all this glory ended in defeat carries little weight: better to have been great and defeated than never to have been great at all. Just what that greatness consists of is not clear. "But Glory's glory," says Byron; "and if you would find/What *that* is— ask the pig who sees the wind!"

At first glance the balance sheet of Napoleon's adventure seemed to indicate a great deal of waste. After two decades of war, after the loss of far more than a million lives and of millions in property, France emerged reduced to her borders of 1790, saddled with a bill for almost a billion francs in reparations, and with several of her provinces under Allied occupation. These, indeed, were the terms imposed on her by the Second Treaty of Paris, signed after Waterloo. Yet in fairness to Napoleon it must be pointed out that the human and material losses should not be debited exclusively to him. The wars that Waterloo concluded had started when he was still a mere lieutenant, and it is more than probable that even if he had died or retired from public life in 1802, there would have been wars all the same. Nor was it he who began the course of conquest that made these wars inevitable; that process began when the French revolutionary government announced that it would liberate the peoples of Europe and gained momentum when its armies occupied Belgium, Holland, the left bank of the Rhine, and northern Italy.

Napoleon's fault was not that he embarked on a career of conquest, but that he was unable or unwilling to stop it while still victorious, or to cut his losses while there

In the Army Museum at the Invalides, where Napoleon lies buried, a statue of one of the emperor's warriors stands surrounded by imperial eagles and rows of regimental battle flags.

was still a chance. His return from Elba was an irresponsible adventure that only a blind admirer would seek to justify; without it France would have escaped foreign occupation, the payment of indemnities, and the humiliation of having to restore, under the terms of the peace treaty, the invaluable art treasures taken from the capitals of Europe. Even so, France was not nearly as exhausted as she seemed: she succeeded in paying the indemnities within the surprisingly short space of three years. By 1818 the last occupation forces evacuated France, which also was allowed to join the alliance of the four great powers.

The Quadruple Alliance—which became the Quintuple Alliance with the adhesion of France in 1818—was signed on the same day as the Second Treaty of Paris, November 20, 1815. In effect a renewal of the Treaty of Chaumont, it pledged the four signatory powers (England, Austria, Russia, and Prussia) to come to each other's assistance if the Treaty of Paris were violated. Its most interesting feature was the provision that the members of the Alliance would meet in conference from time to time to take measures to safeguard the peace or stability of Europe whenever these were threatened.

As it turned out, there was no threat to peace as long as the system of the Alliance remained effective: the five great powers, and the other powers subordinate to them, were much too concerned with internal threats to their stability to entertain any projects of external aggression. The theory generally held by the statesmen of the period —Metternich at their head, and Gentz at his right hand— was that the wars of the preceding quarter century had resulted not from a contest for power among sovereigns but from the subversive spirit of the French Revolution. Revolution was dynamic and expansive; it could not stop at the national boundaries, and it could not be contained: it had to be squashed. Thus it was the sacred duty of every sovereign to repress any movement or tendency endangering the established order, and it was the duty of all other sovereigns to assist him in that task if necessary.

The theory still has its champions, and indeed it is not altogether indefensible. It *was* the French Revolution that precipitated a series of wars of conquest, and revolutionary situations are always dangerous to the general peace. Yet the statesmen of the post-Napoleonic period were deluding themselves if they believed that revolutions were caused simply by a perverse spirit of insubordination that can be stamped out by police action and censorship, and they were decidedly unrealistic in their assumption that they could prevent several scores of volcanoes from erupting simply by sitting on them. This, however, was precisely what they tried to do: as a result, their blind spirit of reaction against all aspirations for liberal government and social justice became popularly confused with the idealistic if vague compact known as the Holy Alliance.

The Holy Alliance was, in fact, not an alliance but a manifesto, drafted by Alexander of Russia and signed, with some reluctance, by the emperor of Austria and the king of Prussia on September 26, 1815; subsequently all sovereigns of Europe save the king of England, the pope, and the Ottoman sultan endorsed it. The salient feature of that extraordinary document was that the sovereigns who signed it pledged themselves to regulate their conduct toward their subjects and toward one another according to the principles of Christianity. Hardly anybody could object to the adoption of Christian principles as the basis of government and of international relations, even if the definition of these principles was left somewhat vague.

Alexander had not yet quite been emancipated from his liberal ideals, and he undoubtedly hoped to promote an enlightened policy of government—which would reconcile the aspirations of the subjects with the authority of the sovereigns—and a system of European collective security, possibly even some form of international organization. (Since his territorial ambitions were directed toward Turkey, and since he had acquired most of Poland, he could safely forswear war against his Christian neighbors.) On the other hand, the role of moral arbiter which he had assumed was distasteful to his colleagues, and the basic assumption of the Holy Alliance—that Europe was an association of sovereigns rather than of governments and of nations—was hateful to all liberals. In fact, the Holy Alliance was forgotten in all but name as soon as it was signed, and its place was taken by the Quadruple (later Quintuple) Alliance, in which Austria was the dominant power. The suppression of all liberal tendencies rather than the promotion of Christian principles was the chief purpose of Metternich's system, which came to be called the "Holy Alliance" in derision as much as in error. The jibe that it was an alliance of the sovereigns against their peoples lay too near at hand not to become universal; and although no such alliance really existed, the actions of the Allied governments at that time seemed to many to indicate that it did.

The Allies had made war on Napoleon as a tyrant and an oppressor of nations; yet once they had got him out of the way, they did him the favor of representing him as the torchbearer of the French Revolution. They did him the further favor of repeating his mistakes and besting him at them. In Spain the obscurantist and despotic regime of Ferdinand VII led to revolution in 1820. In Italy the obscene brutality of such rulers as Ferdinand I of the Two Sicilies produced the same result in the same year. In Germany the Carlsbad Decrees of 1819 established an inquisitorial tribunal to investigate secret societies and instituted a reign of terror in the universities, which were regarded as hotbeds of liberal and nationalist ideas. Austria became a police state. In Poland the autonomous institutions were gradually restricted and eventually abolished by the Russian authorities. In England civil liberties were partially curtailed. At the Congresses of Troppau, Laibach, and Verona (1820–22) the Allied powers resolved to intervene militarily in Naples and in Spain to put down the revolutions. In France Louis XVIII and his moderate ministers Richelieu and Decazes fought a losing battle with the Ultraroyalist majority in the Chambers; with the accession of Louis' brother Charles X in 1824, the forces of reaction triumphed there too. If the struggle against Napoleon was a struggle for liberty, it now seemed that the terrible war in Spain and the Battles of Leipzig and Waterloo had been fought in vain.

Although Napoleon had been no less conservative than Metternich, Alexander, and Castlereagh, he no longer appeared in retrospect as the oppressor he had been. Had he not consolidated the gains of the French Revolution, opened all careers to talent, introduced the Civil Code to Germany and Italy, restored independence to Poland, and ultimately fallen victim to the forces of bigotry and reaction that now were holding him a prisoner on a tiny rock and "cobbling at manacles for all mankind"? In the popular mind he began to be transformed into the image of Béranger's songs—the "Little Corporal," the friend of the soldiers and of the little people, to whom he had shown the road to greatness, the man in the shabby uniform and the little hat, the martyred enemy of kings and priests and nobles. "Tell us of him, grandmother,/Tell us of him," say the children in Béranger's "Memories of the People," and millions of Frenchmen knew its touching if somewhat sentimental lines by heart. The feeling was not limited to France; in England, admiration for Napoleon became quite fashionable, and Heine's "Two Grenadiers" became one of the most popular poems in the German language.

At St. Helena Napoleon used the five and a half years left him to perfect his legend and his myth. Nothing could be more ironic than the contrast between the atmosphere of pettiness that pervaded his little court and the lofty image that was manufactured there. Apart from a staff of domestic servants whom he had been permitted to take with him, his entourage consisted of the comte Bertrand, a general of engineers, and his wife and children; the comte de Montholon and his wife and son; General Gourgaud, who had been the emperor's chief orderly officer; and the comte de Las Cases, who also brought a son. None of these was particularly distinguished, and two of them—Montholon and Las Cases—Napoleon had barely known before going into exile. None of them, with the possible exception of Gourgaud, accompanied him out of mere loyalty. Bertrand feared that he might be court-martialed and shot by the Bourbons (as was to be the fate of Marshal Ney); Madame Bertrand, upon hearing that her destination was St. Helena instead of England, had tried to throw herself out of a cabin window; Montholon and Las Cases hoped to capitalize on their relationship with Napoleon, as indeed they eventually did. Las Cases left for Europe in 1816, Gourgaud in 1818. Only Montholon (whose wife left) and Bertrand and his wife remained to the end. Apart from this handful of companions and

his servants—notably his valet Marchand, who also served him as secretary—Napoleon's only regular company consisted of Dr. Barry O'Meara, an Irishman who had been a British naval surgeon and who was assigned to Napoleon as a personal physician, and of Dr. Francesco Antommarchi, who replaced O'Meara after the latter was sent back to Europe in 1818 by the British authorities.

Once established at Longwood, his sprawling residence, Napoleon held court with the same formal etiquette as if he were still at the Tuileries. He insisted on being addressed as "Your Majesty." Bertrand continued to fulfill the functions of grand marshal of the palace and acted as foreign minister; Montholon combined the offices of aide-de-camp, minister of finance, minister of the interior, and prefect of the palace; Gourgaud doubled as chief orderly officer and grand master of the horse; Las Cases, as chamberlain and secretary. Perhaps this pretense was necessary for the emperor's dignity and morale; certainly it did little to dispel the tedium that hung over Longwood like a permanent fog. Squabbles and intrigues among Napoleon's companions and a running petty feud with the British governor, Sir Hudson Lowe, helped to relieve the boredom of the daily routine.

During the first few months of his stay, Napoleon was affable enough and entertained relatively cordial relations with the British authorities, although they denied him the imperial title. The arrival of Sir Hudson Lowe in early 1816 changed all this. The antipathy between the two men was apparent from their first meeting, and after August, 1816, Napoleon refused to receive the governor, who was not to see him again except on his deathbed. Undoubtedly Sir Hudson lacked the tact and the intelligence to handle as difficult a prisoner as Napoleon, but even if he had possessed these qualities in abundance, his prisoner would have made it a matter of policy to make him appear a monster of cruelty.

The object of Napoleon's grievances, which he knew were bound to trickle through to the outside world, was to create the impression that the English government had sent him to St. Helena to hasten his death, and that Sir Hudson Lowe was not only his jailer but also his executioner. St. Helena has a salubrious climate; Napoleon represented it as a kind of Devil's Island. He was free to ride about anywhere on the island so long as he kept within view of a British military escort; he soon refused to ride out, on the ground that the presence of the escort was offensive to him, and then claimed that Sir Hudson was determined to ruin his health by preventing him from taking exercise. A saucepan in need of resilvering became the object of a long and embittered exchange of notes: the emperor suggested that Whitehall was trying to poison him with verdigris. According to Gourgaud's diary, the court of Longwood consumed seventeen bottles of wine, eighty-eight pounds of meat, and nine chickens a day, not counting champagne and liqueurs, at the expense of the British government; this did not prevent the emperor and his suite from acting as if they had been left destitute, nor stop them from complaining that Sir Hudson Lowe was determined to poison them with rotten meat.

The sorest point at issue, however, was the Englishman's insistence on referring to the emperor as "General Bonaparte." The issue might have been avoided if Napoleon had taken on an assumed name, as was the custom among fallen royalty; this he refused to do as a matter of principle. He had been anointed by the pope, the sovereigns of Europe had recognized him and paid him homage, the French nation had elected him; nobody could take this away from him, just as no one could undo Austerlitz, Jena, and Friedland. He owed it to himself, he owed it to his son to maintain his imperial dignity at all costs in the eyes of the world, for the day might come when he or his heir would be recalled to the French throne. As a result Napoleon withdrew in proud isolation. He received fewer and fewer visitors; he gave up even his carriage rides; he turned down all invitations to local activities such as the ball of the Cricket Society; he barricaded himself in his house whenever the governor called; he lived behind closed shutters; he arranged his garden in such a manner as to conceal himself when he took his constitutionals. He never received any of the four Allied commissioners stationed at St. Helena to make sure of his presence, which they could ascertain for the first time only when he was dead. Meanwhile the officers of his court, who remained in contact with the outside world, kept alive the dreary campaign of insinuations and pinpricks against Sir Hudson Lowe.

Thus the legend of Napoleon's martyrdom was built up. As early as October, 1817, Pope Pius VII, whom Napoleon had treated far worse at Savona and Fontainebleau than Sir Hudson treated Napoleon at St. Helena, informed his secretary of state that "Napoleon's family have made it known to Us . . . that the craggy island of St. Helena is mortally injurious to health, and that the poor exile is dying by inches. . . . We instruct you to write on Our behalf to the allied sovereigns, and in particular to the prince regent. He is your dear and good friend, and We wish you to ask him to lighten the sufferings of so hard an exile. Nothing would give Us greater joy than to have contributed to the lessening of Napoleon's hardships. He can no longer be a danger to anybody. We would not wish him to become a cause for remorse." Thus spoke a man who might well have claimed to be a martyr, in charity about a man who had very nearly killed him. In actual fact Napoleon's health was excellent at the time. Nevertheless, only a few weeks before the Vicar of Christ intervened in his behalf, Napoleon had the following message delivered to Sir Hudson Lowe: "You have miscalculated the heights to which misfortune, the injustice and persecution of your government, and your own conduct have raised the emperor. His head wears more than an imperial crown—it wears a crown of thorns. It is not in your power, or in that of the like of you, to obscure the radiance of that crown."

For a man of Napoleon's activity to be confined on a tiny island must, indeed, have been torture; one wishes he had borne it with more dignity and fewer histrionics. His comparison of himself with Christ seems exceptionally inappropriate; and yet, as will be shown, it was accepted without shock within a few years of his death. The myth of his martyrdom was only part of the mythology manufactured at St. Helena, thanks to which he became the deified son of the common people. And (let the question be asked without any blasphemous intent) what is Christ if not just that? To be sure, Napoleon laid no claim to divinity, but he did, in his writings and in his endless monologues, create an imaginary Napoleon whose sole aim it had been to lead humanity into the light of reason; who had been defeated by the forces of darkness, crucified by the English at the hands of Sir Hudson Lowe, and buried in a nameless grave; and who would rise again, when the time was ripe, in the person of his successor—his son, as he hoped.

The first of the gospels brought back from St. Helena was that according to Dr. O'Meara, *A Voice from St. Helena,* published in London a year after the emperor's death. It is concerned more with the emperor's crown of thorns than with his imperial crown. The second, and most influential, of the canonical books was the Gospel according to the comte de Las Cases, *Le Mémorial de Ste-Hélène,* first published in 1823. Like O'Meara, though with far superior literary skill, Las Cases gives an account of Napoleon's martyrdom and intersperses it with generous quotations and paraphrases of the emperor's conversations; he also inserts tantalizing fragments from Napoleon's dictations relating the main events of his career, and he allows the reader glimpses of daily life at Longwood, stressing all those aspects that might rouse human sympathy and deliberately ignoring all those that would have shown the hero in a less than heroic light.

It was Las Cases who recorded Napoleon's remark that "A legislator must know how to take advantage of even the defects of those he wants to govern." Las Cases himself was living proof of the truth of Napoleon's dictum. By birth and by education he was a royalist and should have rallied to Louis XVIII. By temperament he was a frustrated intellectual whose only chance of gaining recognition was sycophantic hero-worship. It was a sure instinct that made him attach himself to Napoleon—for just a year, it is true, but that was enough to serve his purpose, and Napoleon's as well. It was intentionally, in all likelihood, that Napoleon embroiled Las Cases in difficulties with the British authorities, thus making sure of his prompt and forcible return to Europe, where he would be able to spread word of the emperor's martyrdom and greatness.

Las Cases did not neglect to do this, and few passages in the *Mémorial* sum up Napoleon's reappraisal of his role in history as succinctly as does the following: "I have closed the gaping abyss of anarchy, and I have unscrambled chaos," Las Cases quotes Napoleon as saying. "I have cleansed the Revolution, ennobled the common people, and restored the authority of kings. I have stirred all men to competition, I have rewarded merit wherever I found it, I have pushed back the boundaries of greatness. All this, you must admit, is something. Is there any point on which I could be attacked and on which a historian could not take up my defense? My intentions, perhaps? He has evidence enough to clear me. My despotism? He can prove that dictatorship was absolutely necessary. Will it be said that I restricted freedom? He will be able to prove that license, anarchy, and general disorder were still on our doorstep. Shall I be accused of having loved war too much? He will show that I was always on the defensive. That I wanted to set up a universal monarchy? He will explain that it was merely the fortuitous result of circumstances and that I was led to it step by step by our very enemies. My ambition? Ah, no doubt he will find that I had ambition, a great deal of it—but the grandest and noblest, perhaps, that ever was: the ambition of establishing and consecrating at last the kingdom of reason and the full exercise, the complete enjoyment, of all human capabilities! And in this respect the historian will perhaps find himself forced to regret that such an ambition has not been fulfilled . . ." And indeed, such was the magnetism of his personality that few historians have not been mesmerized into accepting at least some of these lines. As for his detractors, Napoleon made an equally prophetic statement: "I am destined to be their prey," he said, "but I have no fear of becoming their victim. They will be biting into granite . . . The memory I leave behind consists of facts that mere words cannot destroy. . . . I shall survive—and whenever they want to strike a lofty attitude, they will praise me."

In 1846 the comte de Montholon published his version of the martyrdom of Napoleon. It contains a statement which, according to Montholon, Napoleon had dictated to him eighteen days before his death as a political testament intended for his son. Although it sounds authentic enough in parts, the document bears a curious resemblance to the

A print published during the Hundred Days shows the profiles of Napoleon, Marie Louise, and the king of Rome outlined by a bouquet. The violet was a Bonapartist emblem.

views of Napoleon's nephew, who a few years later was to make himself emperor of the French as Napoleon III. "My son must have no thought of avenging my death," Napoleon allegedly dictated to Montholon; "he must take advantage of it. Let him never forget my accomplishments; let him forever remain, as I have been, French to the finger tips. All his efforts must tend to a reign of peace. . . . I have been obliged to subdue Europe by force; today, Europe must be persuaded. I have saved the Revolution, which was on the point of death; I have washed off its crimes, I have held it up to the eyes of Europe resplendent with glory. I have implanted new ideas in the soil of France and Europe: their march cannot be reversed. Let my son reap the fruit of my seed."

Napoleon continued by predicting, correctly, the downfall of the Bourbons and, equally correctly, the support that England would give his successor. "But," he went on with the wisdom of hindsight, "in order to live on good terms with England, it is necessary at all costs to favor her commercial interests." As for France: "I did not govern for or through the nobles, the priests, the bourgeoisie, or the workers. I governed for the entire community, for the whole great French family. To keep a nation's interests divided is a disservice to all classes and gives rise to civil war." Equality of opportunity, Napoleon continues, must be a cardinal principle of his successor's government. Concessions must be made to liberalism: "My son will have to reign with a free press. In our day this is a necessity. . . . The inevitable must be accepted and turned to advantage." Yet even on his deathbed Napoleon had a curious notion of what constituted a free press: "In the hands of the government, a free press may become a powerful ally . . . To leave it to its own devices is to sleep next to a powder keg."

After trampling the nations of Europe underfoot, Napoleon suddenly made himself the champion of their aspirations: "Our enemies are the enemies of mankind. They want to put chains around the people, whom they regard as a herd. . . . Europe is marching toward an inevitable change. To retard her march is to waste strength in a futile struggle. . . . There are national aspirations that must be satisfied sooner or later, and toward this aim we must march." And how can these conflicting aspirations be reconciled? Why, by carving up the world into colonies, to be sure: "With the shreds of the uncivilized countries, the happiness of civilized nations can be bought." While appealing to colonial greed, Napoleon—or rather, perhaps, Montholon—also played on the European twin fears of social revolution and Russian imperialism: "If the people break their chains, Europe will be flooded with blood; civilization will disappear amid civil and foreign wars." The transition from monarchy to democracy must be slow and gradual. As for Russia, if she "should march against civilization, the struggle will be less long but the blows will be more fatal."

It matters little whether Napoleon actually dictated this political testament or whether Montholon concocted it: the document sums up, in a few pages, the whole of Napoleonic propaganda in the years after Waterloo. It appeals to the opinions and emotions of the most diverse groups—to the Jacobin proletariat, to the moderate liberals and conservatives, to French nationalists, to internationalists and pacifists, to German and Italian advocates of national union, to colonial imperialists, to anti-Russian prejudice, to the champions of a stable social order and to the champions of democracy. There is, of course, nothing wrong in a program that aims to please everybody, except that as a rule it is a prelude to dictatorship.

The memoirs of St. Helena published before the accession of Napoleon III—Las Cases', O'Meara's, Montholon's, and the largely apocryphal ones of the impossible Dr. Antommarchi—stand in marked contrast to those published after the collapse of the Second Empire. Gourgaud's diaries were published only in 1899, Bertrand's were deciphered and published in the 1950's. They were not written for publication and serve no propagandistic purpose. As may be expected, the Napoleon who emerges from their pages is quite different from that of Las Cases and company. Of Napoleon the liberal and humanitarian, dreaming of noble projects, imbued with deep religious feelings, courteous and considerate to his companions in exile—such as he appears in Las Cases and in Montholon—there is scarcely a trace. Instead we find a tyrannical egotist and cynic. In his conversations with Gourgaud, he seems to have taken a positive pleasure in shocking and corrupting the somewhat naive young man, a good Catholic, who was pining away for his aged mother and his sister. "Bah!" he said, "the main thing is one's self. . . . Isn't it true, Gourgaud, that it's a lucky thing to be selfish, unfeeling? If you were, you wouldn't worry about the fate of your mother or your sister, would you?" From his companions he demanded undivided loyalty and love; yet he never ceased to wound Gourgaud's feelings with brutal remarks: "What do I care how people feel about me, so long as they show me a friendly face! . . . You ought to realize that you shouldn't bore me with your frankness. Keep it to yourself. I tell you once more, I pay attention only to what people say, not to

what they think. . . . All being said, I like only those people who are useful to me, and only so long as they are useful."

The same brutal cynicism pervades nearly all the more significant statements quoted by Gourgaud. According to Las Cases, Napoleon believed in God. To Gourgaud he observed: "Everything is matter. Besides, if I had believed in a God who rewards and punishes, I would have been timid in war. . . ." "But, Sire," objected Gourgaud, "without religion, who prevents secret crimes?" "Bah!" said Napoleon. "The law, that's what makes men stay honest. Morality for the upper classes, the gallows for the rabble. Who keeps me from marrying my sister? Morality. And what if it's on a desert island? . . . Bah! Monsieur Gourgaud!" As for Christianity, it triumphed because Jesus came at the right time, when circumstances were ripe for him. "It's like myself," he added. "If I rose from the bottom to be emperor, this was possible because of the circumstances and a favorable public opinion."

According to Las Cases, Napoleon had aimed at liberalizing his regime. To Gourgaud the emperor confided, on the subject of the Additional Act of 1815: "I intended to send the Chambers packing once I was victorious and safe." His political philosophy as revealed by Gourgaud contrasts sharply with the humane sentiments ascribed to him by Las Cases and would have done little, if published, to make him popular in France: "There is nothing like summary courts-martial to keep the lower classes and the rabble in line. Only by terror can the Bourbons maintain themselves in France. If they weaken, they are lost. . . . Hang, exile, persecute—that's what they must do. . . . The French nation has no character. . . . The Bourbons ought to send one hundred thousand veterans to Santo Domingo and let the climate and the blacks take care of them, thus getting rid of both the soldiers and the blacks."

Some of the most touching sayings attributed to Napoleon by Las Cases and Montholon relate to his love for Josephine, his affection for Marie Louise, his devotion to his son. His conversations with Gourgaud and Bertrand on the subject of the fair sex were less than delicate. Women, he told Gourgaud, are "mere machines to make children." He found it ridiculous, he said, "that a man should not be able to have more than one legitimate wife. When she is pregnant, it's as if he had no wife." As for Josephine: "I really did love her," he admitted to Bertrand, "but I had no respect for her. . . . She had the prettiest little —— imaginable. . . . Actually, I married Josephine only because I thought she had a large fortune."

Among the imperial habits Napoleon refused to renounce at St. Helena was that of commanding women into his bed. Madame de Montholon, twice divorced for adultery, seems to have obeyed the emperor's summons with her third husband's knowledge, and the paternity of her daughter Napoléone, born at St. Helena, is generally credited to Napoleon. · After Albine de Montholon's departure for France, Napoleon contracted a sudden passion for Madame

Text continued on page 407

THE
EPILOGUE

At St. Helena Napoleon labored to build a legend out of the story of his exile, posing as the hero of the French Revolution who had been imprisoned and tortured by the forces of reaction. Actually, his captivity could have been pleasant. His estate, Longwood, was comfortable, if not luxurious; high on a hillside in the interior of the island, it was surrounded by extensive gardens, as the water color below shows. The emperor rarely gave the St. Helenans an opportunity to observe him at home (above); he remained in isolation and carefully tried to control the news of himself that was disseminated in Europe.

Although he is not found in the religious calendar, St. Napoleon became popular in France as the patron of warriors. One image (opposite) shows him with the emperor's features. Many crude and brightly colored prints made in the town of Epinal record incidents in Napoleon's career that seized the popular imagination. Below, he is shown saluting the bravery of wounded Austrian troops who had fought against him in Italy. Above, in a print entitled Chacun son Métier, he genially reproves a market woman, who had offered him political advice, with the suggestion that she tend to those concerns she knows best.

OVERLEAF: *In the roadstead at St. Helena, Napoleon's coffin is brought aboard ship for the trip back to France.*

Fighting against great odds, Napoleon leads his troops along a muddy road during the campaign of 1814. This canvas, by the noted

...orical painter Meissonier, is one of the many romanticized paintings recalling the Napoleonic era that were popular later in the century.

Bertrand, who lived with her husband in a cottage at some distance from Longwood. The tragicomedy of the emperor's futile attempts to make her his mistress has been faithfully recorded in Bertrand's diaries. Napoleon tried to induce his personal physician, Dr. Antommarchi, who was also Madame Bertrand's physician, to act as go-between. Antommarchi refused. Annoyed and suspicious, Napoleon ordered Antommarchi to cease treating Madame Bertrand. This, too, Antommarchi refused. Napoleon flew into a rage. In the presence of a valet, he accused Antommarchi of being "a blockhead, an ignoramus, a fop, a sneak" (all this was probably true), and Madame Bertrand's lover to boot. Bertrand should make him chief valet to his wife, since the doctor was endowed with a valet's sexual equipment; Madame Bertrand was a slut who went into ditches with all the English officers. Comte Bertrand found this entire scene "irresistibly droll."

Human, all too human, no doubt; yet it is difficult to conceive that at the close of the century a devout Catholic writer, Leon Bloy, could write in all earnestness: "Napoleon is the Face of God in the darkness." It is true that Bloy could not have read Bertrand's diaries, but there is reason to believe that even if he had, he would not have changed his mind. The mythological image of Napoleon that came into existence in the late nineteenth century was quite distinct not only from factual truth but even from the legend created by Napoleon and his evangelists. The legend attributed human traits to Napoleon that he actually lacked and modestly ignored those that he possessed in abundance. The myth brushed aside the sentimental inventions of the legend and, by raising Napoleon above good and evil, made him into a god. It would be foolish to judge the prisoner of St. Helena solely by the weaknesses he displayed during his years of decay; yet these weaknesses can be neither condoned nor denied without raising him above humanity. "He forgot that a man cannot be God," Marshal Foch remarked of Napoleon. If this was so, his final illness and agony must have reminded him that he was a man.

General Bertrand's diary contains a terrifyingly detailed account of the emperor's agony; the hiccups, the vomiting, the stools, the expectorations—everything is recorded with the most painstaking accuracy. Napoleon's illness had been diagnosed as an inflammation of the liver. Actually, according to the majority of medical authorities who have studied the several accounts of his illness and the reports of the physicians who were present at his autopsy, Napoleon appears to have suffered from stomach ulcers for some time. The treatment prescribed for his supposed liver ailment aggravated that condition, and the ulcer became malignant. The liver, at the autopsy, was found to be somewhat larger than normal; the stomach was a mass of cancerous growths. Shortly before his death, Bertrand recorded this moving impression of the dying man:

"In the morning, he had asked twenty times if he might have some coffee. 'No, sire.' 'Will the doctors let me have a spoonful?' 'No, sire, not just yet. The stomach is too much inflamed. You might vomit a little sooner.' He has vomited perhaps eight or nine times during the day.

"How many thoughts on so great a change! Tears came into my eyes as I watched this man, who was so terrible, who gave his commands so proudly, so absolutely, pleading for a spoonful of coffee, begging leave and obeying like a child, asking again and being refused, harking back and never succeeding, never resenting it. At other times in his illness he used to scout his doctors and their advice and do as he pleased. Now he had the docility of a child. This was the great Napoleon: pitiful, humble."

Napoleon died in the presence of sixteen persons—his companions, their families, several physicians, and a couple of servants—on May 5, 1821, at 5:49 P.M. He pronounced his last intelligible words some time after four o'clock in the morning. Their authenticity, as quoted by Montholon, has long been doubted but has been confirmed by Bertrand. They were something like *tête de l'armée*—"at the head of the army." After that there were only moans and groans. During the last twelve hours of his agony he lay motionless, with only an occasional tear rolling down his cheeks from his unseeing eyes.

While still lucid, Napoleon had spoken repeatedly of his son. Throughout his stay at St. Helena he had never referred to his heir except as the "king of Rome." On his deathbed he asked several times: "What is my son's name?" Agonies make humans out of demi-gods, and death is democratic: the emperor and the king become father and son. But when the last breath is spent, pose and myth take over again. According to the baron de Norvins, whose *History of Napoleon* contributed much to the legend, the following prose poem, in the emperor's own hand, was found among his papers after his death: "A new Prometheus, I am nailed to a rock to be gnawed by a vulture. Yes, I have stolen the fire of Heaven and made a gift of it to France. The fire has returned to its source, and I am here! The love of glory is like the bridge that Satan built across Chaos to pass from Hell to Paradise: glory links the past with the future across a bottomless abyss. Nothing to my son, except my name!" It does not much matter whether these somewhat incoherent words are apocryphal or not. They bear a close enough resemblance to some of the things that Napoleon unquestionably did say.

"Men of genius are meteors destined to be consumed in lighting up their century": these words Napoleon wrote at the age of twenty-two. While negotiating the Concordat of 1801, he remarked to Bourrienne: "As far as I am concerned, there is no immortality but the memory that is left in the minds of men." And in 1802 he wrote to his brother-in-law General Leclerc, who was about to die of yellow fever on the island of Santo Domingo, with little glory: "Everything on earth is soon forgotten, except the opinion that we leave imprinted on history."

Meteor or flash in the pan—which was Napoleon? His-

The glorification of his wars was begun by Napoleon, who commissioned this painting of the bard Ossian greeting French generals who had been conducted to Valhalla by the Valkyries.

torians continue to argue. If meteor, just how did he light up his century? Was he Prometheus or a lucky opportunist? To what degree did he himself fabricate the memory he left in the minds of men? Does the opinion he left imprinted on history reflect what he actually did and was? Or is it true, as he himself said, that historical truth is no more than "an agreed-upon fiction"?

The last of these questions is the easiest to answer, at least as far as he himself is concerned: there is no agreed-upon fiction about Napoleon, and disagreement will probably go on forever. In his case at least, Schiller's famous dictum, *"Die Weltgeschichte ist das Weltgericht"* ("World history is the world tribunal"), must be qualified with the addition that sometimes the jury remains hung.

It was not only to while away his time but also to prepare his brief for the world tribunal that Napoleon spent a large part of his six years of banishment writing, or rather dictating, the history of his career. His chief sources were the bulletins published in the official *Moniteur* and his memory. "These *Moniteurs,*" he remarked with disarming ingenuousness to Las Cases, "which are so devastating to so many reputations, are invariably useful and favorable to me alone. Really talented and careful historians will write history with official documents. Now, these documents are full of me; it is their testimony that I solicit and invoke." Small wonder, since he wrote or edited them himself. "To lie like a bulletin" was a proverbial expression in Napoleon's army, and "really careful historians," even professional admirers of Napoleon, can no longer afford to rely on his bulletins and official correspondence as their sole source.

Yet the bulletins, and the histories of his campaigns that Napoleon based on them, remain the unshakable foundation of the Napoleonic epic such as it survives in the minds of men. Scholars may spend years and volumes in proving that the facts and figures are false or distorted, but they cannot prove that Napoleon did not win the victories he won, that he did not make himself emperor and lord of kings, that he did not change the face of the world, that he did not leave a more profound impression on the imagination of posterity than did any other man of modern times. Falsified narratives and figures cannot by themselves account for these facts or explain his success, even though they may upon occasion turn a near defeat into a victory or a mistake into a decree of destiny. More helpful to an understanding of Napoleon's appeal to the imagination are the electrifying quality of his style, the lucidity of his mind, the nervous energy that emanates from nearly every page of his writings. To quibble about truth makes the critic look petty and spiteful; indeed, as Napoleon said, to strike a lofty attitude one must praise him.

What Mark Antony says of Caesar—"The evil that men do lives after them, the good is oft interred with their bones"—was assuredly not true of Napoleon. In death the defeated emperor rose to even greater heights than those he had achieved at the moments of his triumphs; how mean,

how small the victors looked in the shadow of the giant whom they had chained to his rock! That his genius was based on a pedestal of a million corpses seemed of little importance to a generation bored with peace. Some of his apologists followed his own line—that the wars had been forced on him—and their argument was not entirely baseless. Others only regretted that he had not won the final battle, which would have justified the sacrifice he had exacted. Would it not have been better for Europe if he had been victorious? (The strong probability that such a final victory was impossible for him does not seem to have affected that school of thought.) Others yet seemed to miss the intoxication of war and glory, which was so conspicuously absent in France in the long era of peace following Napoleon's downfall. Greece and Poland were fighting for freedom, while the rest of Europe ran only after money. More and more the Napoleonic wars of conquest appeared as the continuation of the wars of the French Revolution, a struggle between the forces of freedom and progress against the forces of tyranny and reaction. Peace, so it seemed, offered no outlet for noble and idealistic impulses.

When the reactionary regime of Charles X was overthrown in July, 1830, and replaced by the bourgeois regime of King Louis Philippe of Bourbon-Orléans, Bonapartism as a political force was still virtually nonexistent; it was a mere spiritual climate. Napoleon's heir, the duke of Reichstadt (formerly the king of Rome), known to Bonapartists as Napoleon II and as *l'Aiglon* (the Eaglet), was a virtual prisoner in Austria, a pathetic youth, abandoned by his mother and dying of tuberculosis. After his death in 1832 the heir apparent became Prince Louis Napoleon, a young man of twenty-four, son of Louis, king of Holland, and of Hortense de Beauharnais. (Lucien and his line were ruled out from the succession; Joseph, who lived the life of a gentleman-farmer in New Jersey, had given up his political ambitions and had no male heir.)

The chances of Prince Louis Napoleon's being called to succeed to his uncle's imperial throne seemed slim. Indeed, while the majority of Frenchmen looked back with pride and nostalgia on the Napoleonic age of glory, it is doubtful that many of them would have seriously desired a repetition of the performance. Moreover, Louis Philippe very shrewdly took most of the wind out of the Bonapartists' sails. His liberal program seemed to be a fulfillment of the aims credited to Napoleon in Las Cases' *Mémorial.* His adoption of the tricolor flag symbolized the acceptance of the Revolution and of the Napoleonic Empire as part of the French tradition. He failed, it is true, to lift a finger to help the Polish patriots, whose uprising was brutally suppressed by Russia, or to encourage the liberal revolutionary movements in Italy and Germany, which had looked to the French Revolution of 1830 as the dawn of a new age of freedom. On the other hand, he completed the conquest of Algeria, thus furthering the fulfillment of Napoleon's colonial projects for Africa and reviving the military tradition of France. His appearance and personality were prosaic, to be sure; his umbrella was a poor substitute for the imperial eagle. Perhaps it was to compensate for the drabness of his regime that he took the imprudent step, in 1840, of having Napoleon's body brought back from St. Helena and laid to rest in the chapel of the Invalides in Paris, thus honoring the emperor's last wish—to be buried "on the banks of the Seine, amidst the French people whom I loved so well."

The leader of the expedition sent to bring back Napoleon's body was one of the king's sons, the prince de Joinville. Among his suite were Bertrand, Gourgaud, and Napoleon's former valet Marchand. On October 15, 1840, these men gazed for the last time at the features of the man whom they had followed to Egypt, to Moscow, to St. Helena, as he lay in his opened coffin. His beard and fingernails had grown a little; his boots were mildewed, the luster of the goldbraid and the medals tarnished, yet his flesh seemed perfectly preserved. The ravages of cancer had restored to his once full features the lean and youthful look of the First Consul. Gourgaud was then fifty-seven years old; Bertrand, sixty-seven. Napoleon had died at fifty-one, but his traits were those of a man in his thirties; the bloated tyrant had been transmuted by death into the immortal hero of his youth.

Exactly two months later, on a chilly December day, Napoleon's coffin, drawn by sixteen horses, passed under the Arc de Triomphe, built to commemorate his victories, and down the Champs Elysées. At that moment the gray mist lifted and the "sun of Austerlitz" appeared. An immense mass of people lined the avenue in silence. But, as the coffin passed, preceded by the veterans of the Imperial Guard, the old shout could be heard again for the first time in a quarter century: *"Vive l'Empereur!"* And thus, by the voice of national memory, rising ghostlike in the chill winter air, the dead emperor was raised to immortality.

Vive l'Empereur! Did the shout fill Louis Philippe with misgivings? He had hoped, by the emperor's return, to symbolize the unity of France—not only the unity of living Frenchmen but also that of the past, present, and future. But symbols have no value unless they stand for realities, and the reality was that France was by no means united. The Revolution had not become part of the past; its "principles" had no more been consolidated by Louis Philippe's bourgeois and increasingly authoritarian regime than by Napoleon's imperial dictatorship. Its forces were still at work. The people had overthrown Charles X only to have a Louis Philippe imposed on them, a man whose sole advice to the poor was to get rich and who seemed a sinister embodiment of all the callousness of the industrial age.

The "July Monarchy," which lasted from 1830 to 1848, may have seemed a drab and inglorious age to the romantic poets; to the rising industrial bourgeoisie it was an exciting age of adventure; to the proletariat, an age of despair. The pace of industrialization was perhaps even more spectacular in France than in England, where the process had started much earlier, and the resulting evils were correspondingly more shocking. The workingmen's insurrections in Lyons in 1831 and in Lyons and Paris in 1834, which were suppressed with incredible brutality, served as warning signals of the coming explosion; yet instead of passing legislation that would have alleviated the hardships of the workers and the unemployed, Louis Philippe's government suggested that they work harder to improve their lot, jailed the radical leaders, and censored the press. The moderate liberal opposition, while protesting the curtailment of political rights and advocating electoral reforms, showed no more sympathy for the revolutionary social and economic theories of the radicals than did the government. The radicals themselves, forced underground and divided into several ideological groups, possessed neither a clear and practical program nor the political organization needed to stage a successful revolution, as the year 1848 was to prove.

If during the first years of his regime Louis Philippe appropriated most of the Bonapartists' program, his failure later on to mitigate the evils of industrial capitalism presented a new opportunity to the Bonapartists. The man most clearly aware of this was the Bonapartist heir himself, Prince Louis Napoleon. Exiled with his mother Hortense after Waterloo, he had been educated in Germany and Switzerland. When the July Revolution of 1830 placed Louis Philippe on the French throne, Louis Napoleon was a young man of twenty-two, full of ambition and idealism, fiercely loyal to his great uncle's memory, attracted to the utopian theories of the Saint-Simonians, and in correspondence with the *Carbonari,* the secret revolutionary society whose network extended over all the Italian states. He thought for a while of joining the Polish insurrection; he did take part in 1831 in the insurrection of the *Carbonari* against papal rule. The adventure came to nothing, and the prince's elder brother, the former grand duke of Berg, died in the course of it.

Since neither his father nor his uncles were interested in claiming the Napoleonic succession, and since the duke

Among the memorabilia of Napoleon's last days is the silver night lamp that was kept burning during his final illness.

of Reichstadt died in the following year, Louis Napoleon, much to his family's embarrassment, set himself up as Pretender. In 1836 he judged that Bonapartist sentiment in France had grown sufficiently strong for him to stage a coup d'état. With a handful of supporters, he attempted to instigate an uprising of the garrison of Strasbourg, whence he expected to march triumphantly to Paris, as his uncle had done after his return from Elba. The conspiracy collapsed utterly. Louis Philippe chose to treat the affair as a mere escapade and was content merely to deport the youthful prince across the seas to New York.

Louis Napoleon did not linger in America but went to London, where he divided his time between the pleasures of society and of study and writing. In 1839 he published a strange concoction, *Des Idées Napoléoniennes,* in which he amplified Las Cases' legend of a liberal Napoleon—son of the Revolution, liberator of Europe's nationalities, and apostle of peace—by crediting his uncle with a number of socialistic ideas. Sincere though it may have been, Louis Napoleon's socialism was calculated to appeal to the growing radical movement in France. The fact that he also wrote a biography of Julius Caesar, who came to power at the head of the popular party, is suggestive. And, as has been pointed out, it does not seem purely accidental that the alleged political testament of Napoleon, which the prince's friend Montholon published several years later, should bear such remarkable similarity to the prince's ideas.

In 1840 Louis Napoleon with some sixty men attempted another uprising, this time at Boulogne. The enterprise was no less ill-advised than the Strasbourg conspiracy had been. Louis Philippe took a dim view of it, and the prince was sentenced to detention for life at the fortress of Ham. His imprisonment was not very rigorous. He wrote, he studied, he received visitors, and he was allowed to correspond with his supporters, with several radical journalists, and with Louis Blanc, the most articulate of the socialist leaders, who advocated the replacement of capitalism by state-financed producers' associations. With his book *The Extinction of Pauperism* (1844) the future emperor contributed to pre-Marxist socialist literature, while Karl Marx himself, who at that time was living in Paris, was in the process of demolishing all such utopian dreams: the *Communist Manifesto* was to appear but four years later.

In 1846 Louis Napoleon managed to escape from his fortress and returned to England. The February Revolution of 1848, which overthrew Louis Philippe and set off revolutionary outbreaks all over Europe, did not seem to favor the Bonapartist cause at first. Indeed, to say that Louis Napoleon sailed to power on the Napoleonic legend is an untenable contention, no matter how often it has been repeated. The most that the legend did for him was to remove the chief obstacle in his path and create an emotional climate that made the idea of a Bonaparte becoming head of the French state less fantastic and undesirable than it would have been without the legend. Still, there is no evidence that

a strong Bonapartist movement existed in 1848; certainly the comte de Chambord, legitimate heir to Charles X, had at least as large a following as did Prince Louis Napoleon. The struggle that followed the establishment of the Second Republic in February, 1848, was essentially between the moderate liberals, whose foremost spokesman was the poet Alphonse de Lamartine, and the radicals, represented in the provisional government by Louis Blanc. The systematic sabotage by his colleagues of Blanc's program for public works and labor legislation led to several mass demonstrations and, in June, to a full-scale insurrection of the Parisian workers, which was put down with considerable bloodshed after several days' fighting by the troops under General Louis Eugene Cavaignac. The "specter of communism" (the phrase had just been coined) united liberals and conservatives in common fear. Cavaignac was given dictatorial powers and chosen by the right-wing republicans as their candidate in the coming presidential election.

Louis Napoleon, meanwhile, had watched events from England with, for him, unusual caution. Several *départements* had elected him deputy to the National Assembly; he declined to serve as deputy, but returned to France to run for president against Cavaignac and won by an overwhelming majority. The moderate republicans voted for him because they regarded him as a strong man who would save the Republic from extremists of both the right and the left; the radicals did not so much vote for him as they voted against Cavaignac. There is nothing to indicate that a large segment of the electorate voted him into office as a successor to Napoleon I.

It was in his mind, not in the electorate's, that Louis Napoleon was called upon to complete his uncle's work. It was not on the wave of the Napoleonic legend that he was carried to dictatorship in December, 1851, but by a carefully prepared coup d'état and over the corpses of the insurgent workers. The plebiscite that a year later made him emperor in name as well as in fact was a foregone conclusion. It was not so much a vote of confidence in the "Napoleonic idea" or in the Bonaparte dynasty as an act of resignation. The French people have been called fickle because they seem to oscillate between rebellion and submission; in fact, their behavior is generally predictable: a period of successive convulsions and uprisings is almost invariably followed by a tired acceptance of a strong authoritarian figure that guarantees stability.

The events of the reign of Napoleon III fall outside the scope of this book. It is not irrelevant, however, to make certain fundamental comparisons between the First and the Second Empires and to examine to what extent Napoleon III realized the aims that he and the Napoleonic legend attributed to Napoleon I.

In everything pertaining to the acquisition, consecration, and expansion of dictatorial power, the similarities between the uncle's and the nephew's methods are striking: in fact, they set a classic pattern. The well-prepared coup d'état by which the head of the state overthrows the institutions he has sworn to uphold; the use of plebiscites to legitimize the coup d'état; the recourse to censorship to silence opposition in the name of unity; the maintenance of hollow constitutional trappings; the military and imperial pageantry; the appeals to the nation to forget all factional strife, ideological differences, and class interests and to unite behind the dictator, who embodies the interests, the honor, and the glory of the nation—all these devices were put to use by Napoleon I and borrowed by Napoleon III. They have become commonplace in the twentieth century, but they were new when the first Napoleon applied them.

Here, however, the resemblance ends. Whatever Napoleon I's remote aims may have been, he was a soldier, and above all a sublime opportunist, uncommitted to ideologies, theories, or parties. He rose to power on the tide of the French Revolution, and by the logic of circumstances his wars grew out of and extended the revolutionary wars. Thus, in spite of all his conservatism, conservative Europe remained his implacable foe. This cannot be said of Napoleon III. Although he had been trained in the Swiss artillery and liked to play at soldier, he was no soldier, and what wars he made were not forced on him as, to some extent, they had been on his uncle. It was not the French Revolution of February, 1848, that bore him to power: that revolution had ceased to be revolutionary in June, when Cavaignac's troops massacred the Parisian workers. It is true that, though halted early in France, the revolution spread all across Europe—but far from identifying himself with it, Napoleon III welcomed its suppression and even lent Pope Pius IX an army to suppress it. Unlike his uncle, Napoleon III had entered politics with a vague ideological program, a compound of the Napoleonic legend and of nineteenth-century social, economic, and political theories. Of this, he put very little into execution; instead, he based his dictatorship on an alliance with the Catholic party, thus disregarding his uncle's fundamental principle that the ruler of France must remain uncommitted to any faction.

When Napoleon III became emperor, France was not at war, nor was she threatened with war, nor did she embody any principles that clashed with those of the other European powers. The France of the Second Empire was just one great power among others, differing from them in no essential. This could hardly be said of the France of Napoleon I. The First Empire had been dynamic, a soaring rocket propelled by the combined energies of the French Revolution and of Bonaparte's boundless ambition. The Second Empire never got off the ground; the revolutionary energy had been doused even before Prince Louis Napoleon came to power, and whatever dynamism there was in the prince's ambitions was nullified by his earnest idealism and his desire for Victorian respectability.

To what extent did Napoleon III carry out, or attempt to carry out, the Napoleonic program that Las Cases, Montholon, and he himself had publicized and in part invented?

His participation in the Crimean War, if intended to check Russia's "march against civilization," did little to accomplish that purpose. His war of 1859 against Austria paved the way for the creation of a united Kingdom of Italy under Victor Emmanuel II, but the protectorate he exercised over the last remnant of the Papal States, Rome, delayed the completion of Italy's unification until his downfall. In his policy toward Prussia and Austria he was the dupe of Bismarck and honored neither his own doctrine, favoring the creation of large national states, nor the time-honored French policy of keeping Germany divided. His Mexican adventure in favor of Emperor Maximilian showed little understanding of political realities and was directly contrary to the policies that Napoleon I had followed in selling Louisiana to the United States. His ignominious defeat and surrender to the Prussians at Sedan in 1870, which marked the end of the Second Empire, exposed the hollowness of the entire Napoleonic revival.

In his ambition to be the arbiter of Europe, Napoleon III failed more completely than had Napoleon I in his ambition to be her conqueror. What of his internal and colonial policies? His reluctant return, beginning in 1860, to a more liberal regime was in harmony with the ideas he had professed before his accession to power; yet his ambition to unite all parties and classes failed utterly, and his downfall left France more divided than ever, with the Commune of Paris and the forces of Thiers' provisional government locked in a deadly struggle. His program of social reform remained unfulfilled. While industry and commerce, thanks partly to the encouragement he gave them, were making tremendous strides, the lot of the working class remained unchanged. Colonial expansion, which was part of the Napoleonic program, continued and new spheres of influence were acquired in both Asia and Africa; however, the French colonial empire reached its height only after Napoleon III's downfall. Of all the grandiose schemes that he had inherited from his uncle, the emperor accomplished only two; these, however, were of enduring importance. The construction of the Suez Canal, which was inaugurated in 1869 in the presence of Empress Eugénie, was due primarily to Napoleon III's initiative and to French capital. His other great accomplishment was the transformation of Paris into a city worthy of being the capital of the world.

Among the many projects that Las Cases' *Mémorial* ascribed to Napoleon I, there was at least one that he undoubtedly cherished in complete sincerity: to make Paris the greatest and most beautiful city in Europe. The turbulence of the times and the brevity of his reign prevented him from carrying it out, but he did make a beginning. He transformed the Louvre into a museum; he built the Rue de Rivoli from the Place de la Concorde almost to the Palais Royal, clearing the slums that covered that area; he opened the Rue de la Paix and the Rue de Castiglione, rebuilt and extended the quays along

The emperor's death mask: a bronze cast made from the original

Monument to Napoleon though it may be, Paris has not a single thoroughfare or public square named after the emperor. (There is only a Rue Bonaparte, named for the general.) The only statue of him to be found outdoors in Paris, gazing over the city from atop a column cast from the bronze of captured cannon, stands in a square named after the duc de Vendôme; it depicts Napoleon not in his imperial robes and laurel wreath but in his gray coat and his famous hat. The only monument to his imperial splendor is his tomb. The symbolism, undoubtedly, is deliberate—part tribute, part rejection.

The collapse of the Second Empire, which left France overrun by a victorious army, torn by civil war, and deprived of two provinces—Alsace and part of Lorraine—marked also the collapse of Bonapartism. Despite its undeniable accomplishments and the material progress it had fostered, the Second Empire had done nothing that could not have been done without a Napoleonic revival. In two ways only did it enhance the memory of the First Empire—by comparison and by giving permanent shape to the Napoleonic legend. The comparison was made most stingingly (and a little unfairly) by Victor Hugo, who from the Channel island where he had exiled himself taunted *"Napoléon le Petit"* and extolled *"Napoléon le Grand."* As for the legend, it was consecrated by official historiography and especially by the publication of Napoleon I's correspondence, supervised by an editorial committee that exercised considerable discretion as to what should and what should not be included. The tendency to glorify Napoleon by no means ended with the fall of the Second Empire; on the contrary, it reached its climax during the strife-torn first three or four decades of the Third Republic. This seeming paradox—that Bonapartism was dead while the worship of Napoleon flourished—deserves some further elucidation.

To begin with, the assertion that Bonapartism was dead must be qualified. What is meant here by Bonapartism is a political program predicated on the restoration of an imperial regime under the Bonaparte dynasty. That dream had vanished at Sedan. No doubt, the House of Bonaparte still has some adherents, but certainly not as many as has the House of Bourbon-Orléans, and it can hardly be said that that dynasty has a mass following. Indeed, it was not only Bonapartism that collapsed in France in 1870 but the monarchic idea in general. On the other hand, and in a different sense, Bonapartism remained very much alive on the French political scene. This transmuted version of Bonapartism is characterized by its distrust of parliamentary procedure, its hatred of liberalism in any form, its contempt for democratic notions, its exaltation of glory, honor, and patriotism for their own sakes. Drawing its strength from the various groups of the extreme right, it repeatedly threatened to take over France during the first half of the present century, beginning with the Dreyfus Affair.

Yet the mass of the French people rejected it, and the

the Seine, added four bridges, and erected numerous public buildings and monuments. He also constructed the Ourq Canal, which for several decades was the chief (if highly inadequate) source of the city's water supply. Although there was a great deal of building under Louis Philippe, it was left for Napoleon III to transform the city into what it is now. Several of his uncle's projects were incorporated in his plans—for instance, the erection of the Halles Centrales, or Central Markets, the finest and most impressive in the world, albeit inconveniently located.

However, the general conception which gave Paris its present character was that of Baron Georges Eugene Haussmann, prefect of the Seine, a man of extraordinary energy, tenacity, and vision. It is to Napoleon III's credit that he supported Haussmann, despite the bitter opposition he encountered in many quarters, until his work was virtually completed. Modern Paris is the permanent monument erected by Napoleon III to Napoleon I. Enough of the old was left to stand to make it also a monument to the genius of France; yet stamped on the whole are the salient qualities of the first Napoleon's genius. Everything is conceived on a grand scale; order, logic, and harmony inform the general conception, yet there is no attempt to force pre-existing features into a rigid plan.

fact that some of its exponents came into positions of power only under the protection of Hitler (whose present to the French people, the body of the duke of Reichstadt, was accepted with indifference) discredited it completely. To view the Fifth Republic as a Bonapartist revival is as untenable as it is facile. Certain lessons, to be sure, have been adopted by its first president from the Napoleonic experience— notably the use of plebiscites to sidestep parliament or to sanction such inevitable measures as the restoration of independence to Algeria; the insistence on the necessity of a strong presidency (borrowed from the American system at least as much as from Napoleon's precedent); and a tendency to appeal to the nation's historic consciousness (a tendency to which no taint of Bonapartism is attached when it manifests itself in English-speaking countries). But if in the France of the Fifth Republic there are any survivals of Bonapartism, they are to be found among the opponents rather than among the supporters of its first president, whose respect for political liberties and legality will probably be recognized by future historians as characteristic of his regime. Bonapartism as such has become engulfed in the rightist political ideologies of the twentieth century, to which it admittedly contributed a great deal.

The very event that put a final and sobering stop to the Napoleonic adventure—the defeat and humiliation of France in 1870-71—was also conducive to an intensification of the Napoleonic cult. No nation in modern times had achieved such military glory as had France during the brief span from 1796 to 1812. Whatever the atrocities and sufferings Napoleon's wars had inflicted on mankind, they could easily be glossed over as inevitable though regrettable concomitants—and indeed, if compared with those perpetrated by Hitler's Third Reich, or even with the record of Louis XIV, they seem almost negligible. No man ever held as much power as Napoleon and surrendered less to its temptations: the only respect in which he did not keep measure was in the accumulation of power; in its exercise he was moderate. To a proud nation humbled by defeat, the memory of past greatness and glory is a necessity. However much harm it might have done them, however little they might wish to repeat it, Frenchmen can look without shame and with some pride on their epic adventure. A defeated or humbled France can no more forget Lodi, the Pyramids, Austerlitz, or Moscow than the Israelites by the waters of Babylon could forget Jerusalem.

It is thus scarcely surprising that the historians who wrote on Napoleon between 1870 and the First World War should have emphasized the greatness of the adventure and the genius, the vision, the luminously ideal qualities of Napoleon himself. Their scholarship was monumental, though their judgment was occasionally partial. Some were of a liberal or republican orientation; others were rightist to varying degrees. Characteristically enough, none belonged to the socialist left. The somewhat vainglorious rhetoric in which the words *la gloire* and *l'honneur* recur with irritating frequency is more characteristic of the French bourgeoisie and military class than of the working class, which on the whole has rejected the memory of Napoleon.

A Frenchman's estimation of Napoleon still remains to a large degree a question of his politics. It is unsafe, of course, to disparage the emperor, for any attack on him is likely to be interpreted as a slur on the glory of *la grande nation*. To strike a lofty pose (and, incidentally, to be elected to the French Academy) a historian is still well advised to praise him. Nevertheless, Napoleon is not, and never has been, the national hero of France. The national hero is Saint Joan of Arc, and this, perhaps, is a matter for meditation.

Although there is a cult of Napoleon in France, that cult probably has far more adherents in other countries, especially Germany. The fact that Napoleon was Corsican may have made it easier for people who have no love for France to make him into their hero, but it is not sufficient to explain the phenomenon. Whatever one thinks of Napoleon, one must admit that he transcended time and place, that he was universal, and that his fascination has affected the most diverse minds and temperaments.

However, Napoleon has never bewitched French liberal intellectuals to the extent that he bewitched their counterparts in Germany, England, and other countries. The main intellectual tradition of France, from Madame de Staël and Chateaubriand to Tocqueville and Taine and to modern French scholars, has been anti-Napoleonic. And indeed, the more the growing body of scholarship contributes to the knowledge of Napoleon's character, the more it seems to confirm the original judgment of the liberal Madame de Staël and the conservative Chateaubriand. To Madame de Staël Napoleon was the embodiment of egoism, a cynical opportunist whose sole principle was self-aggrandizement, a foreigner who raised himself to power by trampling on French liberty and who maintained himself in power by gambling, from day to day, with the lives of Frenchmen, a Satanic figure to whom men, ideas, virtues, religions, and even God were mere tools to be manipulated.

Chateaubriand, more of a poet and less of a politician than Madame de Staël, took a more balanced view of Napoleon but concurred in the essentials. He recognized that "Napoleon was a poet in action," and thus he understood the powerful hold that his epic and dramatic career must have over the minds and emotions of men. Yet if he appreciated Napoleon as an artist who surpassed even him, Chateaubriand, as a self-dramatizer, he did not forget the realities behind the stage trappings. "It is the fashion of the day," he wrote, "to glorify Bonaparte's victories. Gone are the sufferers, and the victims' curses, their cries of pain, their howls of anguish are heard no more. Exhausted France no longer offers the spectacle of women plowing the soil. No more are parents imprisoned as hostages for their sons, nor a whole village punished for the desertion of a conscript. . . . It is forgotten that everyone used to lament those victories, forgotten that the people, the court, the generals, the intimates of Napoleon were all weary of his oppression and his conquests, that they had had enough of a game which, when won, had to be played all over again, enough of that existence which, because there was nowhere to stop, was put to the hazard each morning."

Forgotten it was—or, if not forgotten, shrugged off as the price of greatness. The human realities of Napoleon's epic—untidy, ugly, sometimes sickening—were soon washed off by the rain of time, and only the work of art remained, perfect, classical, unique. One man, born on a remote island, with no advantage but his intelligence, his genius, his will power, his magnetism, his indomitable energy, his supreme ability to command and be obeyed, had raised himself above kings, emperors, and popes, had swept away the edifice of centuries, had inspired millions to help him accomplish the impossible, and had, in his own words, "pushed back the boundaries of greatness." He had shown modern man what he could do: for this, like Prometheus, he had been chained to a rock.

Yet to Stendhal's Julien Sorel, and to countless youths since him, the gift he had made to mankind, the gift of his example, could no more be suppressed than could Prometheus' gift of fire: no goal was impossible of attainment. To the poet Heinrich Heine, a German-Jewish liberal, Napoleon's calm and classical features seemed to say: "Thou shalt have no other god but me." To the pagan Maurice Barrès, Napoleon was the great "professor of energy." To Dostoevski's Raskolnikov, Napoleon symbolized the individual's right to raise himself above the laws of men and to take a human life. Napoleon is the mythological figure of the self-made man—one of the few mythological figures the modern age has been able to produce—and the incarnation of power. His will was irresistible. No figure since that of Christ lent itself so readily to self-identification, secretly among sane people and overtly among madmen.

Napoleon's impact on the modern imagination has been incalculably great. Who would have dreamed of being a Napoleon before Napoleon? After him, the dream lacked originality. Undoubtedly Hitler, one of the most mediocre figures in world history, dreamed of being Napoleon. One might think that such a disciple would bring his master into disrepute. On the contrary, a comparison between Napoleon and Hitler can only increase one's admiration for Napoleon's sanity, moderation, and economy of cruelty. Napoleon loved only himself, but, unlike Hitler, he hated nobody. In good as in evil, he was without emotion, and he did only so much of either as he believed necessary for his purposes. Moreover, he was the only great dictator of modern times who was not the slave of a political doctrine.

As a self-made man and demigod, Napoleon is unique in history and therefore, as it were, timeless. But what of his impact on the modern world—not as a symbol or a mythological figure but as a historical force? How did he find the world, and how did he leave it? Was he, as Paoli had predicted, something out of Plutarch, an anachronistic intrusion upon the modern world, or was he a modern, a pathbreaker for a new age? Did his adventure merely interrupt the historic process for two decades, or did it further that process? These are complex questions, and only tentative answers to them are possible.

When he began his career, he found the world in chaos and convulsion. The old order was collapsing; the new order had failed to materialize. Like the hero of some myth or fairy tale, he picked up the pieces of the old order, took advantage of others' quarrels to make himself their master, won kingdoms and vast fortunes, gave wealth and honor to his brothers, sisters, and in-laws, reached for ever more since it was so easy and finally overreached himself. When his career ended, he left the world still subject to the same explosive tensions that had eased his way to power but so exhausted from his exploits that it postponed its search for a new order by half a century. Perhaps, had he not appeared on the stage, the old order would have been restored fifteen years earlier than it was; on the other hand it is doubtful that the forces that were then shaping today's world—industrial and technological progress, the resulting prosperity of the middle class and the grievances of the laboring class, the general trend toward political equality and national unification—would have been appreciably slower to make themselves felt.

In many ways (though by no means in all), Napoleon was insensitive to the forces that were shaping the future. Except in some scattered remarks he made at St. Helena, when he had time to reflect on the age, he was blind to the potentialities of steam power and of other inventions that were changing the world. A conservative by temperament, he distrusted innovations of any sort. He sought to establish a dynasty when monarchy was beginning to go out of fashion—and the dynasty he wished to establish was based on the Carolingian model, at that; he created a nobility after a revolution had been fought to abolish it; and in restoring the Church he gave it a position which, as subsequent history has shown, was out of keeping with modern trends.

He disparaged all theories of progress. He paid no attention to the masses—the *canaille,* as he called them—and he willfully ignored the national pride and aspirations of Italians, Germans, Spaniards, Poles, and Russians. He was equally conservative in warfare; his innovations in that art, including his use of unprecedented masses of troops and artillery and his masterly logistics, which made the employment of such masses possible, were important innovations, to be sure, but they grew out of circumstances rather than a wish to revolutionize warfare. In general, he never looked farther ahead than the next day and regarded all experiment as dangerous nonsense. In all these respects—except, perhaps, the military—he cannot be said to have been a modern or to have made a significant contribution to the modern age.

Yet to see in him an anachronistic reincarnation of a hero of antiquity is equally incorrect. His vision of a universal empire may recall Augustus and Diocletian rather than modern times, but who would say that Augustus and Diocletian were not more modern than Talleyrand or Metternich? His passion for uniformity and standardization was decidedly modern. But his main achievement, if it may be called that, was the revolution he brought about in the techniques of power and of manipulating men. His use of the press and of propaganda, his mastery of applied psychology to make people do what he wanted them to do, his rhetoric, his bulletins, his genius at self-dramatization, his flair for pageantry, his superb exploitation of human vanity, ambition, and gullibility, his genius at fanning fear and greed by turns, and, finally, his artful creation of his own legend—all this places him squarely in our own times. Nor has any successful dictator since Napoleon neglected the techniques that he was the first to apply in a systematic way.

In the science of manipulating men, Napoleon was undoubtedly ahead of his times—a dubious merit. But what was his influence on the historic process of his own times and the decades following? It is generally contended that while he set back the Revolution in France, he promoted the spread of its principles elsewhere, notably in Germany, Italy, and Spain. This he assuredly did, though not always wittingly or deliberately. The importance of the Civil Code in extending the concept of legal equality has been somewhat exaggerated by Napoleon's apologists. If he helped to sweep away the remnants of feudalism and to arouse the political consciousness of the peoples of Europe, he accomplished this in a negative way. His victories and conquests demonstrated the decrepitude of old institutions and the need for reform; his oppression, his insensitiveness to the national pride of nations other than the French, eventually roused them to action and gave them a sense of dignity and importance that no Holy Alliance could suppress. The Spanish uprising of 1808, the Russian resistance of 1812, the German War of Liberation of 1813 can hardly be said to have been intended by Napoleon; yet they were direct results of his actions, and they changed the world.

Napoleon was not eager to liberate Latin America; yet his aggression in Spain did just that. He was not anxious to make a world power of the United States; yet his sale of the Louisiana Territory did just that. He had no desire to create German unity; yet by reducing the number of sovereignties from more than three hundred to thirty-six (in order to create useful puppet states rather than to benefit Germany) and by fanning German nationalism, which was directed against him, he did more for German unity than any man except Bismarck. There is no evidence that he wished to unite Italy, but he gave the Italians

just enough taste of national independence to set the Risorgimento in motion. He had no desire to strengthen the spiritual power of the pope and sought to foster Gallicanism instead; the result he achieved was to discredit Gallicanism forever and to give the papacy a moral authority it had not had for centuries. The last thing he desired to do was to undermine the institution of monarchy, on which he based his entire edifice; yet by treating kings as if they were postmasters, by demonstrating the utter moral decay of European monarchy, and by his own anachronistic imperial mummery Napoleon dealt monarchy as destructive a blow as did the executioner who beheaded Louis XVI.

Napoleon's clock was stopped at the moment of his death, 5:49 P.M.

One feels at a loss, trying to fit the brief era of Napoleon's domination into the scheme of history. Somehow he does not seem to belong there. His positive achievements merely continued the centralizing trends set by Richelieu and Louis XIV. In nearly all other respects, his historical role was that of an unconscious tool of destruction, clearing the way for a modern age that little resembled the age he thought he was creating. The first of the modern dictators, he was less the creature of his times than were his successors and imitators, and he remains unique. Some have found it convenient, therefore, to discount the entire Napoleonic era as an adventure, brilliant but hopeless, made possible by the chaos of the times, paid for by millions of lives, unnecessary and senseless—a pageant of classical glory interrupting the prosaic evolution of modern industrial society. What the historical temperament discounts as a freakish intrusion, the poetic temperament extols as a creation of the will and a manifestation of energy, complete in itself, like a work of art, in which the terrible is transmuted into the sublime, and which has no other purpose than itself.

And yet, unnecessary as the adventure may have been except for the glorification of one man, it is impossible to enter that man's tomb without experiencing a poignant emotion. His fatal attraction remains alive; even to those who would defend themselves against it. The conquered flags, worn thin as cobwebs, mere ghosts of flags, conjure up the ghosts of glory. "What a romance my life has been!" Napoleon exclaimed once. What an epic he gave mankind to remember! Who else could give the world such a spectacle? What poet could imagine what he did in action? What an artist! What deception!

In Ingres' Apotheosis of Napoleon, *the emperor, crowned with laurel, ascends to heaven.*

ACKNOWLEDGMENTS

The editors particularly wish to acknowledge their indebtedness to Colonel John Elting of the United States Military Academy for his valuable advice. We are very grateful to the following individuals and institutions for their generous assistance and for their co-operation in making available pictorial material in their collections.

A La Vieille Russie
  Paul Schaffer
Jean Adhémar, Head Curator, Cabinet des
  Estampes de la Bibliothèque Nationale, Paris
Morel d' Arleux family, Paris
Sidney Berry-Hill
Bibliothèque des Beaux Arts, Paris
  Mademoiselle Bouleau
Bibliothèque de la Comédie Française, Paris
  Madame Chevalley
Bibliothèque du Ministère des Armées, Paris
  Mademoiselle Lenoir
Bibliothèque Nationale, Paris
  Edmond Pognon
  Mademoiselle Villa
British Museum, London
  Department of Prints and Drawings
Anne S. K. Brown Military Collection,
  Providence, Rhode Island
  Richard B. Harrington, Librarian
Miss Doris Bryen
Docteur Bureau, Pont l'Evèque, France
Lieutenant General Garrison H. Davidson
Docteur Albert Duruy, Paris
Vicomte Fleuriot de Langle, Curator, Bibliothèque
  Marmottan, Paris
Dean Franklin L. Ford, Harvard University
Joseph Hefter
Mademoiselle Lejeune, Paris
Manufacture Nationale de Sèvres
  Mademoiselle Brunet
Alfred Marie, Curator of the Prince Napoleon
  Collection, Paris
Metropolitan Museum of Art, New York
  Randolph Bullock
  Miss Janet Byrne
  Miss Lillian Green
Musée de l'Armée, Paris
  General Henry Blanc
Musée Bertrand, Chateauroux
  Raymond Naudin
Musée de Besançon
  Madame Cornillot
Musée Carnavalet, Paris
  Jacques Wilholm
Musée de la Coopération Franco-
  Américaine, Blérancourt
  Max Terrier
Musée Denon, Châlon-sur-Saône
  Armand Cailliat
Musée Historique des Tissus, Lyons
  Robert de Micheaux
Musée du Louvre, Paris
  Curators and personnel
Musée National de Malmaison, Paris
  Pierre Schommer
Musée National de Versailles, Paris
  Gerald van der Kemp
  Jean Coural
H. I. H. Prince Napoléon
National Maritime Museum, Greenwich, England
  Department of Prints and Drawings
New York Public Library, New York
  Karl Kup
  Miss Elizabeth Roth
  Wilson G. Duprey

Palais des Beaux Arts, Lille
  Albert Chatelet
Father Hernan Cortés Pastor, Dean of the
  Metropolitan Chapter, Saragossa, Spain
Hofrat Dr. Hans Pauer, Director, National
  Library, Vienna
"La Prensa," Lima
  Mrs. Pédro Beltran
M. I. Artamonov, Director, State Hermitage
  Museum, Leningrad
M. M. Uspenski, State Historical Museum, Moscow
Mrs. Eugenia Tolmachoff
Mrs. Audrey R. Topping
Victoria and Albert Museum, London
Oliver Warner
His Grace the Duke of Wellington
Wellington Museum, Apsley House, London
Captain Wade de Wiese, U.S. Naval Academy
Charles Otto Zieseniss, Chargé de Mission,
  Musée National de Versailles, Paris

GRATEFUL ACKNOWLEDGMENT IS MADE FOR PERMISSION TO QUOTE FROM THE FOLLOWING WORKS: J. Christopher Herold, *The Mind of Napoleon*, Columbia University Press, New York; *Mistress to an Age*, copyright © 1958 by J. Christopher Herold, reprinted by permission of the publishers, The Bobbs-Merrill Company, Inc., Indianapolis. Count Philippe-Paul de Ségur, *Napoleon's Russian Campaign*, translated by J. David Townsend, Houghton Mifflin Company, Boston. Lester J. Cappon, editor, *The Adams-Jefferson Letters*, Vol. II, The University of North Carolina Press, Chapel Hill. Vicente Lecuna, translator, *Selected Writings of Bolívar*, Colonial Press, New York. Leo Tolstoy, *War and Peace*, translated by Constance Garnett, Random House, Inc., New York. Oscar Levy, editor, *Complete Works of Nietzsche*, Vol. XV, George Allen & Unwin, Ltd., London. E. E. Y. Hales, *The Emperor and the Pope*, copyright © 1961 by E. E. Y. Hales, reprinted by permission of Doubleday & Company, Inc., New York. Jean Savant, *Napoleon in His Time*, translated by Katherine John, Thomas Nelson & Sons, New York.

THE PORTFOLIO "HISTORY'S JUDGMENT" CONTAINS SELECTIONS FROM THE FOLLOWING WORKS: Thomas Jefferson: *The Adams-Jefferson Letters*. J. W. von Goethe: J. P. Eckermann, *Gespräche mit Goethe*. John Adams: *The Adams-Jefferson Letters*. Simon de Bolívar: *Selected Writings of Bolívar*. Madame de Staël: *Considérations sur la Révolution Française*. Alfred de Musset: *The Confession of a Child of the Century*. Alexis de Tocqueville: *L'Ancien Régime et la Révolution*. Leo Tolstoi: *War and Peace*. Karl Marx: *Der achzehnte Brumaire des Louis Bonaparte*. Stendhal (Marie Henri Beyle): *Napoleon I*. Friedrich Nietzsche: *The Will to Power*. Hippolyte Taine: quoted in Nietzsche, *The Will to Power*. Thomas Carlyle: *On Heroes and Hero Worship*.

THE SOURCES FOR THE QUOTATIONS AT THE BEGINNING OF EACH CHAPTER ARE THE FOLLOWING: 26 Paoli to young Bonaparte. 42 Attributed to Napoleon by Las Cases. 72 Attributed to Napoleon by Fontanes. 104 Attributed to Napoleon by Joseph Bonaparte. 140 Napoleon to Josephine—Napoleon to Frederick William III of Prussia. 182 Attributed to Napoleon by Las Cases. 208 Final sentence of Napoleon's unsigned editorial in the *Moniteur*, May, 1803. 254 Napoleon to the Committee on Church Affairs, 1811. 286 Attributed to Napoleon by Lucien Bonaparte. 324 Attributed to Napoleon by General Gourgaud. 356 Napoleon on the Battle of Waterloo, according to Las Cases. 392 Napoleon at Rousseau's tomb, according to Stanislas Girardin.

PICTURE CREDITS

The source of each picture is listed below. Its title or description appears after the page number, which is in boldface type, followed by the artist's name (where appropriate) and the location of the work. Photographic credits appear in parentheses. Where two or more pictures appear on one page, the references are separated by dashes.

The following abbreviations are used:

BN—Bibliothèque Nationale, Paris

Brown—Anne S. K. Brown Military Collection, Providence, Rhode Island

Car—Musée Carnavalet, Paris

CDL—Cabinet des Dessins du Louvre, Paris

Mal—Musée National de Malmaison, Paris

MMA—Metropolitan Museum of Art, New York

NMM—National Maritime Museum, Greenwich, England

NPG—National Portrait Gallery, London

NYPL—New York Public Library, New York

Ver—Musée National de Versailles, Paris

THE FRENCH REVOLUTION

11 Mob attacking the Tuileries, detail, by Bertaux. Ver 12 Louis XVI by Duplessis. Ver 13 "Fête de nuit au Petit Trianon" by Chatelet. Ver 14-15 Storming the Bastille, engraving. BN 16 Mirabeau, color drawing by Bonnien. Ver—Mme. Roland by Prud'hon. Ver 17 Danton, drawing by David. Private collection, Paris—Marat, painting by J. Boze. Car (Giraudon) 18-19 Scene of August 10, 1792, drawing by Gérard. CDL (Giraudon) 20 Simon beating Louis XVII, drawing by Prieur. BN—Marie Antoinette, drawing by David. Louvre (Bulloz) 20-21 Execution of Louis XVI, engraving. BN 22-23 Feast of the Supreme Being, drawing. BN 24 Loiserolles, engraving by Duplessi-Berteaux. BN 25 Robespierre, engraving. BN

HERO FOR AN AGE

27 View of Corsica (Pierre Tetrel) 28 Destruction of the French fleet at Toulon from J. Jenkins, *The Naval Achievements of Great Britain from the Year 1793 to 1817,* London, 1817. NYPL Prints Division 30 "Oath of the Horatii" by David. Louvre (Giraudon) 31 Paoli by Richard Cosway. Galleria Uffizi, Florence (Alinari) 35 Letizia Ramolino, painting by Bourgeois from a box lid. Car—Carlo Bonaparte, miniature by Isabey. Prince Napoleon Collection, Paris—Napoleon's home in Ajaccio. Mal 36 Bonaparte, drawing by Pontornini (Giraudon) 37 Brienne, drawing by Regnier. BN 38 Louis XVI, water color. BN 41 Bonaparte at Toulon, drawing by Paul Grégoire. BN—Napoleon's note to Carteaux. Musée de l'Armée, Paris (Bulloz)

THE RISE TO POWER

43 St. Mark's horses (Fritz Henle-Photo Researchers) 44 Planting a "liberty tree," Austrian cartoon. BN 45 Billeting soldiers, drawing by Lafitte. BN 46 Fighting in the Rue St. Honoré, engraving. BN 47 Josephine by Gros. Mal 50 Josephine at Lake Garda by Lecomte. Mal 53 Medal by Duvivier. BN—French troops in Bassano, drawing by Taunay. CDL 54-55 Battle of Arcole by Bacler d'Albe. Ver 56 "The Triumphs of the French Armies," engraving. BN 58-59 Battle of the Pyramids by Gros. Ver 60 Kléber, drawing by Dutertre. Ver—Preliminary drawing for the painting "Napoleon visiting the Pesthouse at Jaffa" by Gros. CDL 62 Sèvres porcelains with Egyptian scenes after Denon. The collection of the Duke of Wellington 63 18 Brumaire, engraving from drawing by Descourtis. BN 65 Denon at Cassel, drawing. BN 66 The duke of Modena fleeing, drawing by Taunay. CDL 66-67 Removing St. Mark's horses, engraving from drawing by Carle Vernet. BN 67 Looting at Parma, drawing by Meynier. CDL 68-69 Drawing by Valois. Manufacture de Sèvres 70 Arc de Triomphe du Carrousel, drawing. BN 71 Denon, drawing by Zix. CDL

IDEAS IN CONFLICT

73 Beethoven relics (Lessing-Magnum) 75 Mme. de Staël, drawing by Debucourt. BN 76 Rousseau, water color. Car 78 New Harmony as planned by Owen, engraving from a drawing by an English architect. Library of Congress 79 New Harmony, drawing by Lesueur. Museum of Natural History, Le Havre 81 Freemasons' ceremony, engraving. BN 82 "Cloister Graveyard in the Snow" by Friedrich, painting now lost (MMA) 85 Chateaubriand by Girodet. Ver 86 Condorcet, engraving after A. de Saint-Aubin. BN—Bentham by Pickersgill. NPG—Schlegel, engraving by Zumpe. BN—Goethe by Tischbein. Frankfort Museum (Bruckmann-Giraudon)—Jefferson by Gilbert Stuart. Colonial Williamsburg—Humboldt by Rembrandt Peale. Collection of Mrs. Ralph L. Colton, Bryn Mawr—Burke, painting from Reynold's studio. NPG—Herder, engraving by Graff. Johann Gottfried Herder-Institut, Marburg, Germany—Schiller, engraving by Müller after Graff. BN—Fulton by West. New York State Historical Association—Schopenhauer by Angilbert Gobel. Royal Collection at Cassel (Hanfstaengl-Giraudon) 89 Mme. Récamier by Gérard. Car 90 Dress, 1786, from *Le Bon Genre.* MMA, Dick Fund—Dress, 1790, engraving. BN—Dress, 1797, engraving. Car—Dress, 1797, engraving. Car—Dress, 1798, engraving. Car—Dress, 1810, from *Costumes Parisiens.* MMA, Dick Fund 91 "Incroyable," aquarelle by Carle Vernet. CDL 92-93 "Le Café Frascati,"

FROM CONSUL TO CAESAR

THE CONQUEST OF EUROPE

THE AGONY OF SPAIN

RESOLUTE BRITAIN

THE ROAD TO TYRANNY

collection, Paris—Table. Mal 272 Joseph Bonaparte by Wicar. Ver (Giraudon) 273 Louis Bonaparte by Wicar. Ver (Giraudon)—Murat, detail, by Gérard. Ver (Giraudon) 274 Lucien Bonaparte by Lefevre. Ver (Giraudon) 275 Jerome Bonaparte by Gros. Ver 276-77 Elisa Bacciochi and court. Ver 276 Caroline Murat by Gérard. Prince Napoleon Collection, Paris 277 Pauline Borghese by Canova. Museo Borghese, Rome (Anderson) 278-79 Three water colors by Fontaine. Private collection, Paris 280-81 Napoleon and family, engraving. BN 282 Marie Louise and the king of Rome by Joseph Franque. Ver (Giraudon) 283 Baptism by Goubaud. Ver (Giraudon) 284 La Grassini by Vigée-Lebrun. Musée des Beaux-Arts et de Céramique, Rouen (Bulloz)—Mlle. Mars, engraving after Gérard. Mansell Collection, London—Désirée Clary by Gérard. Musée Marmottan (Bulloz) 285 Mlle. Georges by Gérard. Private collection (Bulloz)—Marie Walewska, engraving after Lefèvre. BN

THE COLONIAL WORLD

287 Statue of Bolívar in Lima, Peru 290 Belley by Girodet. Ver 293 Fort McHenry by Alfred J. Miller. Maryland Historical Society 294 Tippoo's Tiger. Victoria and Albert Museum 295 Surrender of Tippoo's sons, engraving after Singleton. British Museum 296 Sydney Cove, engraving. British Museum 299 Battle of Vassilika from the memoirs of a Greek general illustrated by a Turk, painting on wood. Historical and Ethnological Museum, Athens 300-1 Selim III. Topkapu Palace Museum, Istanbul (Ara Güler) 303 Argentine trooper, water color. Casa Pardo, Buenos Aires 304 San Martín by Joseph Gil. National History Museum, Buenos Aires 305 Iturbide. Museum of History, Mexico 307 Marble bust of Washington by Ceracchi. MMA, Bequest of John L. Cadwalder 308-9 Tontine Coffee House by Francis Guy. New-York Historical Society 310-11 Crowninshield's Wharf by George Ropes. Peabody Museum, Salem 311 View of Philadelphia, engraving by W. Birch. Pennsylvania Historical Society 312 Recruiting poster. Pennsylvania Historical Society—"Preparation for War to defend Commerce" from W. Birch, Views of Philadelphia, Philadelphia, 1800. Free Library of Philadelphia 313 Constellation and Insurgente, engraving. Collection of the late Irving S. Olds, New York 314 Meriwether Lewis by Saint-Mémin. McCullough Collection, New York 314-15 A view of New Orleans by Boqueta de Woiseri. Chicago Historical Society 315 Captain Gray building a ship, drawing by George Davidson. Dr. G. H. Twombley, New York—Mission of San Carlo, water color by William Alexander. E.E. Ayer Collection, the Newberry Library, Chicago 316-17 Burning the Philadelphia. Mariners Museum, Newport News, Virginia 319 Priestley, chalk by Ellen Sharples. NPG—Ship's cabin, water color and pencil by Baroness Hyde de Neuville. New-York Historical Society—Moreau, engraving after Dumontier. Car (Bulloz)—Audubon by John Syme. Fine Arts Commission, White House—Eleuthère Irénée du Pont by Rembrandt Peale. E. I. du Pont de Nemours & Company, Wilmington, Delaware 320-21 Battle of New Orleans by Hyacinthe de Laclotte. Collection of Edgar William and Bernice Chrysler Garbisch, New York 322-23 Allegory on the Treaty of Ghent, engraving. Collection of the late Irving S. Olds, New York

THE RUSSIAN NEMESIS

325 Napoleon's camp bed. Musée de l' Armée, Paris (Lessing-Magnum) 329 Asiatic warrior, water color by Carle Vernet. CDL 330-31 Smolensk, engraving after A. Adam. State Historical Museum, Moscow 333 Moscow burning, engraving by Schmidt. Bibliothèque Marmottan, Paris 334 Kutuzov, engraving after A. Orlovsky. State Historical Museum, Moscow 335 Executing Russians, engraving by I. Terebenev. State Historical Museum, Moscow 336 Soldier stealing geese, and soldiers retreating, from the sketchbook of Faber du Faur. Brown 338-39 Crossing the Berezina, water color. Musée de l'Armée, Paris 341 Departure of volunteers, engraving. Bildarchiv. d. Ost. Nationalbibliotek, Vienna 343 St. Basil's Cathedral, Moscow, engraving. 344 Czar Alexander I. A la Vielle Russie, New York 345 Catherine the Great by Michael Chibanov. State Russian Museum, Leningrad—Czar Paul I. Knights of Malta, Rome 346 St. Petersburg scene, engraving. A la Vielle Russie, New York—Snow mountains, engraving. The Old Print Shop, New York 347 Coachmen's stand from E. Orme, A Picture of St. Petersburg, London, 1815. Brown 348-49 View of St. Petersburg, Swiss engraving. Courtesy Gottfried Keller Foundation, Berne 350-51 View of Moscow from Robert Bowyer, An Illustrated Record of Important events in the Annals of Europe during the last four years, London, 1816. NYPL Prints Division 353 Peasant's living room from Friedrich Hempel, Tableaux Pittoresques de l'Empire Russe, Leipzig and Paris, n.d. Brown—A Russian village from Atkinson and Walker, Picturesque Representation of the Manners, Customs, and Amusements of the Russians, London, 1803-4. MMA, Whittelsey Fund 354-55 Russian market from Friedrich Hempel, Tableaux Pittoresques de l'Empire Russe, Leipzig and Paris, n.d. Brown

THE LAST GAMBLE

357 Waterloo (Lessing-Magnum) 358 Death of Poniatowski, German engraving. BN 359 Napoleon's bivouac, water color by J. A. Atkinson. Brown 360 Defending Paris by Horace Vernet. Louvre 365 Louis XVIII, copy after Gérard by Marigny. Ver 367 Congress of Vienna, water color by Isabey. Royal Collection, Buckingham Palace. Copyright reserved 368-69 Crowd at Lyons, drawing by Jacomin. BN 372-73 Battle of Waterloo, water color by J. A. Atkinson. BN 375 Napoleon by Prud'hon. Collection of the Princesse de la Tour d'Auvergne (Flammarion) 376 Napoleon on the Bellerophon, Austrian engraving. BN

HISTORY'S JUDGMENT

376 Bolívar. Dr. Alfaro, Panama (Pan American Union)—Madame de Staël by Gérard. Ver (Giraudon) 377 De Musset by Charles Landelle. Louvre (Giraudon) 380 Tolstoi. BN (Giraudon) 381 Marx. (Bettman Archives)—Nietzsche, engraving. (Giraudon)

CARICATURES

383 Talma and Napoleon, engraving. BN 384 Teacher restraining Bonaparte, drawing. Archives Nationales, Paris—Toulon, and Flight from Egypt, both by Cruikshank from Life of Napoleon by Dr. Syntax, London, 1815. BN 385 Swiss caricature, engraving. BN 386 Marie Louise's Nap, engraving. BN—English ladies, engraving. BN 386-87 National opinions of Napoleon, engraving. New-York Historical Society 387 Napoleon and Joseph, engraving. BN—Coronation by Cruikshank from Life of Napoleon by Dr. Syntax, London, 1815. BN 388-89 Spanish patriots, engraving by Gillray. NYPL Prints Division 390 Napoleon dancing, engraving by I. Terebenev. State Historical Museum, Moscow—Napoleon captured, and Russian prisoners, both engravings by Terebenev. NYPL Slavonic Division 391 Napoleon fleeing Waterloo, engraving by Cruikshank. British Museum

LEGACY AND LEGEND

393 Old soldier. Musée de l'Armée, Paris (Lessing-Magnum) 397 "Le Bouquet Imperial," engraving. BN 399 Napoleon at St. Helena, water color by G. G. Gross. Bildarchiv National Bibliotek, Vienna—Longwood, water color by Marchand. Mal 400 Two Epinal engravings by Georgin. BN 401 Saint Napoleon, engraving. BN 402-3 Napoleon's coffin by Eugene Isabey. Ver 404-5 French campaign by Meissonier. Louvre (Giraudon) 406 Ossian receiving Napoleon's generals by Girodet. Mal (Bulloz) 409 Night light. Prince Napoleon Collection, Paris 412 Death mask, bronze. MMA, gift of Mrs. Robert W. DeForest 415 Clock. Prince Napoleon Collection, Paris 416 Apotheosis of Napoleon by Ingres. Louvre (Giraudon)

PHOTOGRAPHY: New York, Geoffrey Clements, Frank Lerner; Providence, Brown University Photographic Laboratory; Paris, Claude Michaelides, Luc Joubert, Mme. Guiley-Lagache, Josse-Lalance, Robert Descharnes; Vienna, Alpenland; London, Zoltan Wegner, John Freeman, Derek Bayes; Madrid, Scala. Maps on pages 8-9 and 178-79 prepared by Charles Goslin.